THE NATURE AND SCOPE OF RESTITUTION

THE UNIVERSITY OF
WINCHESTEF

The Nature and Scope of Restitution

Vitiated Transfers, Imputed Contracts and Disgorgement

by

PETER JAFFEY

·HART·
PUBLISHING

OXFORD – PORTLAND OREGON
2000

Hart Publishing
Oxford and Portland, Oregon

Published in North America (US and Canada) by
Hart Publishing c/o
International Specialized Book Services
5804 NE Hassalo Street
Portland, Oregon
97213-3644
USA

Distributed in the Netherlands, Belgium and Luxembourg by
Intersentia, Churchillaan 108
B2900 Schoten
Antwerpen
Belgium

Hart Publishing Ltd is a specialist legal publisher based in Oxford, England.
To order further copies of this book or to request a list of other
publications please write to:

Hart Publishing Ltd, Salter's Boatyard, Oxford OX1 4LB
Telephone: +44 (0)1865 245533 or Fax: +44 (0)1865 794882
e-mail: mail@hartpub.co.uk
www.hartpub.co.uk

British Library Cataloguing in Publication Data
Data Available
ISBN 1 901362–48–5

Typeset by Hope Services (Abingdon) Ltd.
Printed in Great Britain on acid-free paper
by Biddles Ltd, Guildford and King's Lynn.

Preface

At least in terms of the volume of literature generated in recent years, the law of restitution is fully a match for longer-established areas of study like contract and tort. The enormous recent literature does not seem to have quelled the controversy surrounding the area, however, and I hope it has not quelled the appetite for further contributions. This book examines the principles underlying the law of restitution, and offers a framework for the analysis of the leading cases and for the development of the law. I hope it will be of interest not only to academic and practising specialists in restitution but to specialists in other areas, including contract, property and trusts, whose interest or suspicion has been aroused by the looming presence of the law of restitution. Although the approach is more theoretical and discursive than is customary for a textbook, I think it will also be suitable for the more inquiring student taking a course in restitution or investigating issues in contract or trusts.

I am very grateful to my father, Tony Jaffey, and to James Penner, previously a colleague at Brunel University, who provided very helpful comments on the whole manuscript, and also to Steve Smith, who did the same for Chapter 2. I am also very grateful to Seeromanie for her encouragement and support.

Peter Jaffey
June 2000

Outline Contents

Contents

Part III: Reversing vitiated transfers: restitution and property

Table of Cases

Table of Statutes

Part I

Introduction

1

Vitiated Transfers, Imputed Contracts, and Disgorgement

INTRODUCTION

IN RECENT YEARS, various claims have been brought together by academic commentators under the rubric of the law of restitution, on the basis that they are governed by a single unifying principle, according to which the plaintiff's claim serves to reverse the unjust enrichment of the defendant at the plaintiff's expense. The area of law as so defined is now widely recognised as an independent subject in research and teaching, and increasingly as an area of expertise in practice. In this book an alternative theory is offered of the various claims that are now regarded as making up this field of law. It is argued that this alternative analysis is based on a stronger theoretical foundation and is also, on the whole, more faithful to the well-established rules of the common law.

This chapter will begin with a brief sketch of the core of the law that is understood to make up the law of restitution.[1] For ease of exposition, law and equity have been treated separately, and the causes of action have been referred to by their traditional names. This is the core of the raw material that the theory of unjust enrichment and also the alternative analysis proposed here seek to explain. This chapter will then proceed to set out the analysis that will be developed through the rest of the book, and to point out the main shortcomings of the theory of unjust enrichment.

A BRIEF SURVEY OF THE SUBJECT MATTER

At common law

What is now described as the law of restitution is largely composed of claims that were previously described, for reasons that will be discussed below, as claims in "quasi-contract". Most quasi-contractual claims were made in the form of a claim for "money had and received" or a claim for a "quantum meruit". It is unnecessary to consider the origins of these expressions.

---

[1] This provides the core of the subject matter for the various textbooks and casebooks on restitution.

The claim for money had and received

The most common form of the claim for money had and received is where the plaintiff made a payment to the defendant and claims to recover the sum paid on the ground that the payment was made by mistake, or under duress, or because of other circumstances affecting the decision to make the transfer by virtue of which he should not be held to it.[2] A claim for money had and received also arises in various cases where the defendant received a sum from a third party that for some reason he ought to have made over to the plaintiff, or at least ought not to be allowed to retain himself. This is the case where the defendant received a sum from the third party to be passed on to the plaintiff, and he subsequently acknowledged to the plaintiff that this was so; where the defendant received a bribe in his capacity as the plaintiff's agent; and where the defendant received a payment by virtue of his occupation of an office that was rightfully the plaintiff's. Another type of case is where the plaintiff is compelled by law to satisfy a liability of the defendant's and is entitled to recover the sum paid from the defendant.[3]

The quantum meruit

The quantum meruit is a claim for reasonable payment for goods supplied or services rendered.[4] It arises, for example, where the defendant agreed to pay for the goods or services without first agreeing a specific price. This might be the case where the defendant simply requested the goods or services in circumstances where it was clear that they were to be supplied for payment. Such a claim appears to be contractual. However, a quantum meruit can also be non-contractual. An example appears to be where a quantum meruit is awarded for work done under a purported contract that turns out to be void or unenforceable. Such a claim is now said to be restitutionary. Another example is where the plaintiff salvaged the defendant's ship without any prior agreement and is entitled to recover reasonable payment from the defendant.[5] Furthermore, some commentators consider that even where there is a valid agreement between the parties, a claim for payment for work done in connection with the contract can be a non-contractual, restitutionary claim.

Damages

Generally in law the measure of damages is the plaintiff's loss. But this is not always the case. For example, where the defendant trespassed on the plaintiff's

---

[2] See generally Part 3.

[3] This was actually a claim for money paid to the defendant's use, not money had and received.

[4] See generally Part 2. Quantum meruit will be used to include quantum valebat, relating to a good or chattel supplied.

[5] See below, Chap. 3. This type of claim is equivalent to a quantum meruit but, because it originated in the admiralty jurisdiction rather than at common law, was not generally so described.

land, or used his goods without permission, the plaintiff can recover damages measured by what would be a reasonable licence fee for the use, which may not represent any loss to the plaintiff, who may have suffered no loss at all. The same is true for damages for the infringement of a patent or copyright.[6] Also, where the defendant has committed a tort with a view to profit, the court will sometimes award "exemplary" or "punitive" damages that serve to strip the defendant of his profit, or even go further than this in order to punish him.[7] Damages that give the plaintiff a measure of payment for the unauthorised use of his property, or strip the defendant of his gain, instead of compensating the plaintiff for his loss, are now widely described as restitutionary.

Rescission

Where the plaintiff made a payment or transfer of goods under a voidable contract, and then avoids or rescinds the contract, he is entitled to recover back the money paid over or the goods or their value. He or the other party may also have a claim for payment for work done in connection with the contract.[8]

In equity

Liability to account

In equity, a fiduciary or trustee is held liable to account to his beneficiary or principal for any profit made through a breach of duty or from a position in which there was a possibility of a conflict of interest.[9] The liability to account is also imposed where the defendant is not a fiduciary but has committed a wrong that was originally enforceable in equity, for example breach of confidence, passing off or the infringement of a patent, copyright or trade mark.[10]

Liability of a recipient of property transferred in breach of trust or fiduciary duty

If the plaintiff's trustee or fiduciary transfers property belonging to the plaintiff to the defendant in breach of trust or fiduciary duty, the defendant is said to take the property on constructive trust and incurs a liability to return the property or its value, unless he was a bona fide purchaser or "equity's darling". The doctrine of tracing allows the plaintiff to pursue such a claim in respect of the traceable proceeds of the original property, which means property acquired in exchange

---

[6] See below, Chap. 4.
[7] See below, Chap. 11.
[8] See below, Chaps. 3 and 6.
[9] See below, Chaps. 11 and 13.
[10] See below, Chap. 11.

for the original property or some part of a mixture of the original property and other property.[11]

These various claims are generally understood to form the heart of the modern law of restitution. In each case, according to the theory of unjust enrichment, the claim operates to reverse the unjust enrichment of the defendant at the plaintiff's expense. It is certainly true that in all such cases the claim is "benefit-based", or at least "benefit-related", in the sense that the receipt of a benefit by the defendant is an essential element of the plaintiff's claim.[12] The theory of unjust enrichment is considered below; but, first, the next section sets out the approach adopted in this book, according to which these various claims should be understood as instances of three distinct claims that are not reducible to a single underlying principle.[13] These are the claim for restitution for a vitiated transfer, the non-contractual or restitutionary claim for reasonable payment under an "imputed contract", and the claim for disgorgement. As will appear, each of the three types of claim has a natural affinity for, and a disputed boundary with, a related area of law: for restitution for a vitiated transfer, this is the law of property; for the claim for reasonable payment it is the law of contract; and for disgorgement it is what might be called the law of legal responses, and in particular punishment. It follows that what is now regarded as the law of restitution is not a single body of law equivalent to, say, contract or tort.

THREE CLAIMS

Restitution for vitiated transfers

The nature of the claim

A claim for restitution for a vitiated transfer is a claim for the value of a transfer to the defendant. Its effect is to reverse a transfer of value from the plaintiff to the defendant. The transfer may be a transfer of money, including cash and transferable contractual rights to payment, like money in the bank or investments, or other choses in action like shares or intellectual property, or transferable rights in tangible things, whether goods or land; in short it can be any sort of transfer of transferable value or wealth. Generally "transfer" will be used to refer to a transfer of value or wealth in whatever form, and "wealth" or "value" to refer to transferable value.

The claim to reverse a transfer is based on the fact that the transfer was vitiated. A transfer is vitiated where it is not justified to hold the plaintiff to it,

---

[11]   See below, Chaps. 9 and 10.

[12]   But see Chap. 2 at n 47 and Chap. 3 at n 83–84.

[13]   A brief analysis along these lines, although different in certain respects, was presented in Jaffey (1998a).

which means, broadly speaking, that the transfer was not the result of a true decision properly attributable to the plaintiff. It is an important part of the law of restitution to determine what counts as a "vitiating factor", and the issue is the subject of Chapter 5. The two most important vitiating factors are mistake, where the plaintiff's decision to make the transfer is impaired by a mistake, and absence of authority, where the transfer is made by someone other than the plaintiff and without his authority, as where an agent of the plaintiff acts without authority or someone simply takes the plaintiff's property without authority from him.[14] At common law, the claim for restitution for a vitiated transfer traditionally takes the form of a claim for money had and received.[15]

The rationale of the claim

The claim for restitution of a vitiated transfer protects the plaintiff's right to determine the disposition of his own wealth by reversing transfers of his wealth that were not properly attributable to a decision by him, so restoring the loss of wealth. The plaintiff's wealth is also protected by the law of tort, where the plaintiff suffers loss to his estate through a breach of duty by the defendant, as for example where he negligently or deliberately takes or damages the plaintiff's property. In the case of tort, the justification for compensating the plaintiff for his loss is that the defendant committed a wrong, and should be responsible for loss caused by it. In the case of the restitutionary claim, the claim does not depend on the commission of a wrong by the defendant; the defendant is held liable because the plaintiff's loss through the transfer was causally linked to a gain by the defendant of value to which he had no entitlement (causally linked in the sense that the transfer caused both the loss and the gain). As between the plaintiff, who suffered a loss of his wealth that he did not genuinely choose to incur, and the defendant, who received a windfall, it is just to reverse the transfer and restore the plaintiff's loss. It would be strictly correct to say that the rationale and effect of the restitutionary claim are to compensate the plaintiff, although generally the word compensation is avoided in this context, because it usually refers to the case where the plaintiff's loss results from a wrong committed by the defendant. The receipt of a benefit by the defendant, which is taken to be the hallmark of the claim, is indeed crucial, but stripping him of the benefit is not its objective or rationale. Unless it was obtained through a breach of duty, the receipt of a benefit can hardly be regarded as intrinsically objectionable; instead the windfall receipt is a condition that justifies a liability to restore the plaintiff's loss.

---

[14] For reasons that will be considered in Chap. 5, lack of authority has not been explicitly recognised as a vitiating factor.

[15] But it could take other forms, e.g., it could be an equitable claim, or a claim in conversion or detinue, as considered in Chap. 10.

The defendant's position

The rationale for the claim implies that it is the mere fact of receipt of a windfall that renders the defendant liable.[16] The liability is strict in the sense that it does not require that the defendant committed a wrong, or that he knew of or suspected the presence of a vitiating factor.[17] Sometimes the vitiation of the transfer was caused by a wrong committed by the defendant, as where the plaintiff's mistake was induced by the defendant's fraud. In such a case the plaintiff can equally make a claim in tort for compensation for loss caused by the wrong, for which the windfall receipt is irrelevant.[18] But, for the purposes of the restitutionary claim, it remains unnecessary for the plaintiff to rely on the defendant's wrong as such, or, in other words, on the wrongful character of the defendant's conduct, as opposed to its vitiating effect.

The rationale for the claim is based on the assumption that, because the defendant received a windfall, it would not be unfair to impose a liability that deprives him of it. But the claim may be unfair to the defendant if his position has changed in consequence of the receipt, as for example where, in ignorance of the fact that his increased wealth is due to a vitiated transfer, he has incurred expenditure that he would not have chosen to incur if he had known of the restitutionary liability. Thus the defendant is entitled to a "change of position" defence, as recognised in *Lipkin Gorman v Karpnale*.[19] One can say that the plaintiff's claim is for the value received less the measure of the defendant's change of position. It is helpful to call this measure—the value received less the measure of the defendant's change of position—the "surviving value", and to say that the plaintiff has a claim to the surviving value in the defendant's estate.[20] The change of position defence and the important concept of surviving value will be considered in Chapter 7.

Restitution and property

As noted above, the restitutionary claim to reverse a vitiated transfer can arise in respect of a transfer of any type of wealth. But generally a transfer of wealth is at the same time a transfer of property belonging to the plaintiff. Where there is a transfer of property belonging to the plaintiff, to which the plaintiff retains ownership, the plaintiff is understood to have a distinct claim in the law of property rather than the law of restitution, based on the assertion of his continuing ownership. There appears to be an important distinction between this claim in

[16] i.e., the claim arises from a right–liability primary relation in the sense of Appendix 1.

[17] See further Chap. 7. Whether the restitutionary claim is always a strict liability claim has been the matter of some controversy: see for example the discussion in Birks (1992a), chap. 2.

[18] Or possibly, as considered below, a claim for disgorgement in tort to strip the defendant of a gain made through a wrong, for which the plaintiff's loss is irrelevant.

[19] [1991] 2 AC 548.

[20] As discussed in Chaps. 7 and 9, "surviving value" has been used in more than one sense.

the law of property, and the restitutionary claim, which apparently arises not from ownership of the property transferred, but from the fact that the transfer of value embodied in the property was vitiated. The relationship between these two types of claim is notoriously controversial, and there is heated debate over whether particular causes of action are properly understood as arising in restitution or property. The difficulty is compounded by controversy over the circumstances in which a claim should be "in rem" rather than "in personam". These difficulties will be considered in Chapters 9 and 10.

The transfer of value and the performance of work

Doing work that confers a benefit on the defendant (including providing goods or services and incurring expenditure to that end) must be distinguished from making a transfer of value or wealth to the defendant. Doing work may involve a loss of wealth, as where expenditure is incurred in connection with the work, but it may also involve other types of loss or harm, as where the plaintiff suffers pain or discomfort in performing the work or is deprived of the enjoyment of his time for other purposes; and it may not involve any loss at all. It may also enhance the wealth of the defendant, but often the benefit conferred is not a form of wealth, but some other type of benefit, like information or an experience. Unlike a transfer of wealth, the performance of work cannot be reversed. The issue is not whether the plaintiff has a claim to reverse a vitiated transfer, but whether he is entitled to be paid for his work, which may include compensation for loss incurred or reimbursement of expenditure incurred in doing the work.

Non-contractual claims for payment: imputed contracts

Claims for work done in conferring a benefit

People have an interest in exchange for mutual benefit, typically payment by one party for work done for him by another. The usual rule is that such an exchange cannot be imposed, but must be made by agreement: if the plaintiff does work in conferring a benefit on the defendant without any prior agreement, the defendant does not generally incur any liability to pay for the work.[21] The rule against such liability is justified on the ground that it protects the defendant's freedom to determine how he applies his resources and what the value to him is of the various benefits that he might use his resources to acquire.[22] However, there are some cases where a liability to pay for a benefit imposed without prior

---

[21] The case usually cited in support of the proposition is *Falcke v Scottish Imperial Insurance* Co. (1886) 34 Ch D 234. See Chap. 3 below.

[22] See further Chap. 3.

agreement does arise. In general, as discussed in Chapter 3, there are two conditions for such a claim for payment to arise. First, the plaintiff must have acted without officiousness, which means that he did not seek to impose an exchange of benefit for payment on the defendant in circumstances where he might have made an agreement. This might be where he acted in an emergency or by mistake. Secondly, the defendant must have received a measurable benefit; then it is possible to fix a reasonable measure of payment for the benefit that will give effect to a mutually beneficial exchange. A standard case where the two conditions are satisfied is where the plaintiff has provided assistance in an emergency, where it was impossible or impracticable for the parties to make an agreement: this is "necessitous intervention". Where the conditions are satisfied, the court in effect "makes a contract" for the parties because they were unable to do so.

This claim is generally regarded as restitutionary, and assimilated with the claim for restitution for a vitiated transfer on the basis that both claims effect a "reversal of unjust enrichment". A claim for payment for work done and expenditure incurred in conferring a benefit is, however, as pointed out above, quite distinct from a claim to reverse a vitiated transfer of wealth. The claim for payment is not a claim to restore a loss of wealth transferred to the defendant. Doing work does not necessarily entail a loss (although it may do so in the form of expenditure or it may entail an opportunity cost), and if it does it is not by way of a transfer of wealth to the defendant, and so there is no necessary correspondence between the loss incurred and the measure of the benefit conferred.[23] Furthermore, the measure of payment generally corresponds to neither the plaintiff's loss, which may be nil, nor the defendant's gain. Typically it will lie somewhere in between, so that the exchange is mutually beneficial, just as for an agreed exchange. The claim for payment serves not to reverse a transfer, but to impose an exchange. It does not protect the plaintiff's wealth; instead, it protects the plaintiff's interest in being paid for the application of his resources, including his labour, knowledge and skill, as well as his wealth, in a way that is of benefit to others.

Historically, whilst the claim for restitution for a vitiated transfer took the form of a claim for money had and received, the claim for payment typically took the form of a claim for a quantum meruit. "Restitutionary" is an apt description of the claim to reverse a vitiated transfer; but it is not so apt for the claim for payment, which is not concerned with restoring anything to the plaintiff, or restoring him to a previous position. However, in deference to established usage, the claim will generally be referred to as the restitutionary or non-contractual claim for payment for work done or for a benefit conferred. Alternatively, and preferably, it can be described as a claim arising from an imputed contract or imposed or forced exchange. This is apt because the

---

[23]   Stoljar (1987), 612; Stoljar (1989), 197–9.

function of the claim is analogous to that of a contractual claim for payment in giving effect to a mutually beneficial exchange.

There is no necessary requirement of a vitiating factor for this claim, by contrast with the claim arising from a vitiated transfer. In a case of necessitous intervention, for example, the plaintiff fully intends to confer a benefit in return for payment, and the claim gives effect to the plaintiff's intention, rather than protecting him from an act that he did not freely decide to take. However, sometimes, as mentioned above, the presence of a vitiating factor like mistake may be the basis for saying that the plaintiff was not officious. The mistaken assumption that the restitutionary or non-contractual claim for payment is the same thing as the claim for reversal of a vitiated transfer has led commentators to identify supposed vitiating factors governing the non-contractual claim for payment, like "moral compulsion", which is sometimes thought to be the basis for the claim arising from necessitous intervention.[24]

The overlap between restitution and contract

The law of restitutionary or non-contractual claims for payment arising under an imputed contract and the law of contract have in common that they are both concerned with giving effect to exchanges. It follows directly that the restitutionary claim for payment under an imputed contract has no role to play with respect to a benefit that was actually conferred pursuant to a valid contract; it is surely clear that the exchange must be governed here exclusively by the agreement. This view will be defended in Chapter 2; but, amidst much confusion and controversy, many commentators take the view that what is described as a restitutionary claim can arise on the termination of a valid contract in respect of a benefit conferred under the contract. This claim is taken to be an alternative to any claim that arises under the law of contract. Part of the reason for this misconception appears to lie in the traditional "classical" theory of contract, which will accordingly have to be considered in Chapter 2.

The use claim

The discussion above has concerned the case where the plaintiff conferred a benefit by performing work. Another way for the defendant to receive a benefit from the plaintiff (other than through a transfer of wealth) is for the defendant to use the plaintiff's property without permission. Here it seems that the plaintiff should be entitled to payment for the use of the property. This is the use claim: the owner's claim for payment for the unauthorised use of his property. The justification for giving effect to an exchange of payment for benefit here is not that it was impossible for the parties to negotiate and that they would have done if they had been able to; generally they could have negotiated, but the

---

[24] See below, Chap. 5.

plaintiff would not have permitted the defendant to use his property, or not at a price that the defendant would have been willing to pay. In this type of case, because the benefit is taken unilaterally rather than conferred unilaterally, fairness to the plaintiff requires that he be paid. The use claim is generally recognised, for example with respect to the unauthorised use of land, chattels and intellectual property, but, as considered in Chapter 4, it is often confused with a claim for compensation for loss caused by a wrong or a claim for disgorgement of the profit made through a wrong. But payment for the use of property is distinct from both of these in terms of its justification and the measure of liability.

Disgorgement

A claim for disgorgement is a claim for the value of the benefit received by the defendant through a wrong committed by him against the plaintiff. As discussed in Chapter 11, disgorgement gives effect to the principle that a wrongdoer should not be permitted to profit from his wrong (whether this principle is understood to be based on the rationale of removing an incentive to wrongdoing, or preventing the intrinsic evil of profiting through a wrong, or publicly condemning the wrong). Thus disgorgement, like punishment, is designed to promote the public interest in compliance with legal duties rather than to satisfy the private interest of the plaintiff in the performance of the duty broken.[25] Disgorgement, in other words, is not remedial but quasi-punitive; in fact, it is best understood as being a component of punishment. By contrast, the claim for restitution for a vitiated transfer, and the claim for payment for a benefit conferred (including the use claim) are ordinary remedial claims, which serve to remedy a wrong or a state of affairs from the standpoint of the plaintiff.[26]

The basic principle that a wrongdoer should not profit from his wrong is hardly open to doubt. Nevertheless disgorgement is controversial, because the law customarily provides only for remedies, not punishment or disgorgement, in civil proceedings. Disgorgement or punishment in civil proceedings is open to the objections, first, that the proceedings are not the appropriate means for administering them, because they require a greater degree of evidential and procedural protection for the defendant than is normally provided through civil proceedings; and, secondly, that disgorgement or punishment by way of a pecuniary liability to the plaintiff gives the plaintiff a windfall, since the plaintiff receives a payment not to satisfy an interest of his, but merely to ensure that the defendant is deprived of the sum in question. The "procedural objection" to disgorgement is considered in Chapter 11.

Disgorgement is often confused with the use claim. They are undifferentiated in the category of "restitution for wrongs" or "restitutionary damages" now

---

[25] See further Chap. 11.
[26] Thus because "claim" refers to a remedial right it is strictly speaking inapt for disgorgement.

generally recognised by some academic commentators.[27] Thus the claim for payment for the unauthorised use of property is often equated with the claim for disgorgement for trespass. But the use claim does not strictly require the commission of a wrong, and the measure of liability for the two claims may be different.[28]

THE IMPLIED CONTRACT THEORY OF RESTITUTION

The present academic orthodoxy is the unjust enrichment theory of restitution, which is considered below. Much of the work in establishing the theory of unjust enrichment consisted in overturning the old "implied contract" or "quasi-contract" theory of restitution. Quasi-contract, which is the major source of what is now described as the law of restitution, consisted principally of the claim for money had and received arising from a vitiated payment, and certain forms of the quantum meruit claim for reasonable payment for work done.

These claims were described as quasi-contractual because they were understood as being based on an implied promise. The reasons for this lie in the history of the forms of action; they can be summarised briefly as follows.[29] One of the forms of action was assumpsit, the form for an action on a promise. Assumpsit covered a claim to payment of a sum arising from a promise to pay it, as where the defendant had promised to pay for goods supplied. But assumpsit came to be used for any claim to recover a sum owing, whether the liability arose from a promise or not. This form of the assumpsit was known as indebitatus assumpsit. Because of the origin of the assumpsit the plaintiff was required to recite a fictional promise to pay. It seems that it was originally recognised that an action on an actual but implied promise—as for example where goods are requested but there is no express promise to pay—could be brought in assumpsit,[30] and that this was then extended to fictional implied promises. One form of claim to recover a sum owing that was made through indebitatus assumpsit was the claim for money had and received,[31] to recover a sum paid by mistake or under some other vitiating factor. Thus the claim for money had and received had to recite an implied promise. This was a pure fiction, since clearly the basis for a restitutionary claim to reverse a vitiated payment is not a promise to repay the sum received, but the defendant's receipt of the payment.

Since the abolition of the forms of action, the plaintiff has been required only to allege the actual facts from which it is contended that the claim arises, and then to argue for the proposition of law that generates a claim in the light of

---

[27] Especially Birks (1989*a*), 313.
[28] See below, Chaps. 4 and 11.
[29] See Goff & Jones (1998), 5–11; Birks (1989*a*), 35.
[30] This is attributed to *Slade's case* (1602) 4 Coke Rep 91; Birks (1989*a*), 35.
[31] Like quantum meruit, one of the "common counts".

those facts.[32] This should have meant that the criteria for the existence of a legal relation, or in other words for a valid claim, would make no reference to any fictional fact. Unfortunately it did not in itself lead to any enlightenment about the true nature of the restitutionary claim. It became the received wisdom that the common law was divided into only the two divisions of contract and tort; and accordingly claims in indebitatus assumpsit that had previously been required to recite an implied promise continued to be treated as contractual, or at least "quasi-contractual" and based on an implied contract.

It is not clear to what extent the fiction of implied contract was really misunderstood as in some way actually involving a contract, or whether the fiction was recognised as such. The decision of the House of Lords in *Sinclair v Brougham*,[33] many years after the abolition of the forms of action, is cited as an example of a case where the implied contract fiction confused the House of Lords. The plaintiffs deposited money in an account at a building society. However, the contracts of deposit were held to be void because they were part of a banking business that was outside the power of the building society. The claim for money had and received based on the vitiated payment of money by the plaintiffs to the building society under the void contract was refused on the ground that it was based on an implied promise, and it was said that the implied promise could no more be enforced than could the actual agreement that was the basis for the void contract. But although an actual implied agreement cannot be enforceable where an actual express agreement is not, the non-enforceability of the agreement between the parties cannot, in itself, negate a liability that is not based on the agreement, but on the receipt of a transfer; and this cannot be affected by the fact that the liability is said, by way of a fiction, to be based on an implied promise or agreement.[34] As Lord Atkin subsequently pointed out in a much-quoted passage:

> These fantastic resemblances of contracts invented in order to meet requirements of the law as to forms of action which have now disappeared should not in these days be allowed to affect actual rights.[35]

The quantum meruit was also a form of indebitatus assumpsit. Here, however, the implied promise was liable to be an actual implied promise rather than a fictional promise, as where the defendant has requested the plaintiff to provide goods or services. It seems that the form of the claim in indebitatus assumpsit meant that the question whether the promise was fictional or not was suppressed, and the consequence even now is a continuing controversy over the circumstances in which a quantum meruit is contractual rather than non-

---

[32] *Letang v Cooper* [1965] 1 QB 232.
[33] [1914] AC 398. See further Chap. 6 at n 217.
[34] Birks (1989a), 38. For other examples of the implied contract fiction, see the discussion of *United Australia v Barclays Bank Ltd* [1941] AC 1 in Chap. 11 and the discussion of *Phillips v Homfray* (1983) 24 Ch D 429 in Chap. 4.
[35] *United Australia v Barclays Bank Ltd* [1941] AC 1, 28. See more recently *Westdeutsche Landesbank Girozentrale v Islington LBC* [1996] AC 669, 710, *per* Lord Browne-Wilkinson.

contractual or restitutionary. This has been one source of the controversy mentioned above over the relationship between the contractual claim for payment and the restitutionary or non-contractual claim for payment. Two opposite errors have emerged. First, there seems to be a continuing risk that the implied contract fallacy will be revived to deny a quantum meruit in circumstances where an actual contract is excluded, even though the claim is not actually contractual. Lord Templeman has been accused of this old heresy in the recent case of *Guinness v Saunders*,[36] which concerned a claim for payment by a director against his company in circumstances where no actual contract had come into existence because the putative contract was made without authority from the company.[37] On the other hand, in an over-zealous reaction to the implied contract fallacy, some commentators have tended to regard some cases where a claim has been allowed on the basis of an actual implied agreement as being examples of the implied contract fallacy, even though a genuine implied contract is in the circumstances a perfectly plausible basis for a claim, if not the only justifiable basis.[38] This is one of the reasons behind the over-extension of restitution and its intrusion into situations where a claim for payment actually arises from the agreement of the parties, and should be understood as a matter of contract law.

The scope and content of the law of quasi-contract or restitution under the implied contract theory are a matter of historical accident and are entirely arbitrary. The theory offers no basis for determining when a contract is to be implied, or for justifying or guiding the law. The implied contract is entirely epiphenomenal, serving no substantive purpose at all.

RESTITUTION AS "UNJUST ENRICHMENT AT THE EXPENSE OF THE PLAINTIFF"

According to the now widely accepted theory of unjust enrichment,[39] the law of restitution is the law concerned with the "reversal of unjust enrichment at the plaintiff's expense",[40] or "preventing a man from retaining [a] benefit derived from another which it is against conscience that he should keep",[41] or "the general principle of morality that you should not retain an enrichment which, according to the moral standards of the time, was unjustly received at your neighbour's expense".[42] More specifically, according to the now standard

---

[36] [1990] 2 AC 663.

[37] See e.g. Burrows (1993), 308.

[38] See generally Chap. 3.

[39] For a recent account of the historical development of the theory of unjust enrichment, beginning at the end of the last century, and the major contributors to it, see Ibbetson (1999), 287ff.

[40] Burrows (1993), 1.

[41] *Per* Lord Wright in *Fibrosa Spolka Akcyjna v Fairbairn Lawson Combe Barbour Ltd* [1942] 2 All ER 122, 135.

[42] Birks (1985), 68, alluding to the neighbour principle underlying the law of negligence; and see generally Birks (1989*a*), chap. 1.

formulation developed by Goff and Jones[43] and Birks,[44] the theory of unjust enrichment holds that a claim arises when three conditions are satisfied: (1) the defendant has received a benefit; (2) the receipt was "at the plaintiff's expense"; and (3) the circumstances are such that it would be unjust for the defendant to retain the benefit, or in other words that there is an "unjust factor".[45]

An important division is recognised between two categories of restitution, particularly emphasised by Birks,[46] corresponding to two meanings of "at the plaintiff's expense". In the first category, described as "unjust enrichment by subtraction", the gain is at the plaintiff's expense because it has arisen through a transfer from the plaintiff, leaving him with a loss corresponding to the defendant's gain. In the other category, described as "restitution for wrongs", the gain is at the plaintiff's expense in the sense that it was obtained through a wrong to him. "Unjust enrichment by subtraction" broadly encompasses (and conflates) the claim for restitution for a vitiated transfer and the non-contractual claim for payment; "restitution for wrongs" corresponds to disgorgement, but as it is conventionally expounded the category conflates disgorgement with the use claim.

"Unjust enrichment" is a vague expression; it might plausibly be adopted to describe a claim for restitution for a vitiated transfer, or a restitutionary or non-contractual claim for payment for a benefit conferred, for the purpose of distinguishing either claim from, say, a claim in contract or tort. Similarly it might reasonably be used to refer to a wrongfully obtained profit that is subject to disgorgement. But the theory of unjust enrichment as it has been presented in the textbooks is that the various traditional causes of action outlined in the survey at the start of the chapter, and therefore also the three claims under the analysis set out above, fall within a single field of law united by the single underlying principle of unjust enrichment. As defined in this way, the theory of unjust enrichment is inconsistent with the three claim analysis: although the three claims might be said to be benefit-related or enrichment-related in the sense that an element of the claim is benefit received, they are not reducible to a single underlying principle.

Although there has been some scepticism and much controversy, most commentators now take the view that the theory of unjust enrichment is established in English law. It is commonplace for it to be taken for granted not only by writers in the field but also by writers whose work only touches on the field in passing. The three-stage analysis mentioned above has been recited in judgments in the Court of Appeal and the House of Lords.[47] A recent history of the English law of obligations claims boldly that "the writings of Birks and others will prove to have been crucial in the moulding of the law of unjust enrichment in the

---

[43] Goff & Jones (1998), 15.

[44] Birks (1989a), 21.

[45] See, e.g., Goff and Jones, 675; Birks (1989a), 21; L.D. Smith (1992).

[46] Birks (1989a), 313.

[47] e.g., by Lord Steyn in *Banque Financière de la Cité v Parc (Battersea) Ltd* [1998] 2 WLR 475 at 479, and by Millet LJ in *Portman Building Society v Hamlyn Taylor Neck* [1998] 4 All ER 202, 206.

twentieth and twenty-first centuries" in just the way that the works of earlier writers led to the establishment of the law of tort and contract.[48] It has been suggested that the recent case of *Lipkin Gorman v Karpnale*[49] puts the recognition of the theory of unjust enrichment beyond doubt.[50] But although that case, which involved a claim for restitution for a vitiated transfer, no doubt extinguishes any lingering support for the implied contract theory, and may provide the basis for the future integration of the various manifestations of the claim arising from a vitiated transfer, especially claims in law and equity,[51] neither *Lipkin Gorman v Karpnale* nor any other case in which the theory of unjust enrichment has been mentioned provides support for it over the three claim analysis above, which also, of course, involves the rejection of the theory of implied contract and the integration of different forms of the claim for restitution for a vitiated transfer. Indeed, it is open to doubt whether a particular case, which is strictly authoritative only with respect to the rule necessary to dispose of the issue before the court, can successfully establish a theory governing the field in question in the face of continuing controversy.[52]

Objections to the theory of unjust enrichment

One objection to the theory of unjust enrichment is a broad objection based on a comparison between harm and benefit as the basis for a claim. A harm is intrinsically a bad thing; this is mere tautology. It is not of course the case that every harm generates a claim for compensation. The harm may not have been caused by anyone else, and, even if it was caused by someone else, the person responsible may nevertheless have been entitled to act in the way that caused the harm. But it is clearly understandable that legal relations should arise whose function is to protect against harm, as in tort or contract.[53] A benefit, by contrast, is not intrinsically a bad thing. A benefit received by "act of God" is, unlike a harm so caused, a matter for celebration, not regret. This suggests that responding to benefits should not be the systematic basis for a field of law. It does not mean that the receipt of a benefit cannot be relevant to a claim; merely that one would not expect the claim to be directed principally at removing the benefit. This is what we see with respect to the first claim, which is concerned

---

[48] Ibbetson (1999), 291–2.

[49] [1991] 3 WLR 10.

[50] Ibbetson (1999), 288; Birks (1991*a*).

[51] As noted in Burrows (1997), 96–7. In fact the implied contract theory was surely dead long before this; and in *Lipkin Gorman* no explicit step towards integration was taken. The case also leaves in serious doubt the relation of restitution and property, as considered in Chaps. 9 and 10.

[52] Otherwise, one would think that the development of the theory would be precluded by Lord Diplock's proposition that "there is no general doctrine of unjust enrichment recognised in English law": *Orakpo v Manson Investments* [1978] AC 95, 104.

[53] Some would object to this characterisation of contract; under the reliance theory discussed in Chap. 2, contract protects the "reliance interest" as defined there.

with restoring a loss of wealth; and similarly the second is concerned with satisfying the plaintiff's interest in payment for work done in expectation of payment.[54] The third claim is indeed concerned with removing benefits, and one might say here that the benefit, having been obtained wrongfully, is itself an evil that should be eliminated; alternatively one might say that the benefit is removed as a means of discouraging the breach of legal duties.[55] Benefit is relevant to these claims, but the relevance of benefit differs as between them; they are not different manifestations or forms of the same claim, and are based on distinct principles, not derived from a single overarching principle.

There are other, more specific problems. As mentioned above, an important division is currently recognised between restitution for unjust enrichment by subtraction, which is a combination of restitution for a vitiated transfer and restitutionary claims for payment, and restitution for wrongs, which is generally understood to be something in the nature of disgorgement.[56] Claims for restitution for unjust enrichment by subtraction are ordinary civil claims that serve to provide a remedy to the plaintiff, restoring or satisfying an interest of his. They are classified by reference to the nature of the interest and the principle according to which it is protected, as discussed above. Disgorgement, on the other hand, is not an ordinary civil remedy that restores or satisfies an interest of the plaintiff's, but a quasi-punitive response that serves the public interest.[57] It can in principle arise in respect of a breach of duty of any sort, and thus it cannot be classified by reference to the nature of the interest protected or the principle that justifies the protection given to it. The idea that disgorgement is based on the same underlying principle as restitution for unjust enrichment by subtraction has led some commentators to think of it as being some form of remedial right or claim, serving to satisfy an interest of the plaintiff's, and this has distorted the understanding of the proper role of disgorgement and its relation to punishment.[58] The same misunderstanding is encouraged by the conflation of disgorgement with the use claim, which *is* an ordinary remedial claim for payment, under the category of "restitution for wrongs".

As noted above, the principle of unjust enrichment fails to distinguish between the restitutionary claim to reverse a vitiated transfer and the restitutionary claim for payment, by assimilating them into a single category of restitution for unjust enrichment by subtraction. The important differences between the two were discussed above. The division between the two was traditionally reflected in the common law: a claim for restitution for the vitiated transfer generally took the form of a claim for money had and received, and the claim for payment the form of a quantum meruit. Unjust enrichment theorists have

---

[54] The payment satisfies the "reliance interest" as defined in Chap. 2.

[55] See further Chap. 11 at 375.

[56] e.g. L.D. Smith (1992), 694.

[57] See further Chap. 11.

[58] e.g. Birks (1989a), 316, referring to compensation and restitution for wrongs as alternative "remedial strings"; Barker (1995), 471. The approach is reflected in the entirely separate treatment of restitution for wrongs and punitive damages in LCR (1997); cf Jaffey (1998b).

argued that the separate treatment of these two claims is based on a failure to recognise that they are based on the same principle, but relate to different types of transfer, involving different types of benefit, in one case a transfer of money, and in the other a transfer of services or work. The difference between the two types of case is, it is thought (apart from historical accident), merely a matter of valuation—i.e. that work or services are more difficult to value than money—and not to any more fundamental distinction of principle.[59] But in fact the provision of work or services is not a transfer of a form of wealth and cannot be reversed as if it were.[60] Some commentators, in particular Stoljar, have pointed out that the principle of unjust enrichment does conceal a genuine distinction along these lines.[61]

The failure to distinguish between the three types of claim has led to difficulty in identifying principles and concepts applicable to what are actually three distinct claims. For example, there has been much discussion of possible techniques for measuring the defendant's benefit, which is also understood to be the measure of the plaintiff's claim. For the claim for restitution for a vitiated transfer the measure of liability corresponds to the value of the transfer, which is at the same time the measure of the plaintiff's loss and the measure of the defendant's benefit through the transfer.[62] The defendant's benefit is also the measure of disgorgement, although here the benefit does not correspond to the plaintiff's loss. But the position is quite different with respect to the claim for payment, and the attempt to assimilate the claims under a single principle of unjust enrichment has led to the fiction that the measure of payment for a benefit equals the value of the benefit to the recipient and also the cost of providing it, whereas in fact these are likely to be three different measures.[63]

The failure to distinguish between the claims has also caused confusion over the relation between each claim and the distinct field of law with which, as mentioned above, each is associated. Thus the proper relation between a restitutionary claim to reverse a vitiated transfer of wealth and a claim arising in property law in connection with the same or a similar transfer has been obscured by the assimilation of restitutionary claims to reverse transfers with claims for payment and claims for disgorgement. Similarly, the conflation of the restitutionary claim for payment with the claim to reverse a transfer has obscured the fundamental point noted above that, because the claim for payment serves the same function as contract (to effect an exchange), there is no

---

[59] Birks (1989a), 7,109ff; Birks (1992a), 91–3; Barker (1995), 458.

[60] The supply or transfer of goods can fall into either category. Restitution for a vitiated transfer of goods at common law is detinue or conversion, whereas the claim for payment for goods supplied is the quantum valebat.

[61] Stoljar (1989), 18; also Watts (1995); Hedley (1985) 61–2; Penner (1997); and see Simester (1997), 110. Goff & Jones (1998) asserts that there is a single underlying principle of unjust enrichment, but in fact generally deals with money, services and goods separately.

[62] This may not be the case where the transfer is not of pure wealth but of some form of property capable of having a special value to its owner: see Chap. 9.

[63] See further Chaps. 2 and 3.

plausible basis for any such claim in circumstances where the parties can contract, and still less where they actually have done. And, as mentioned above, the
treatment of disgorgement under the same principle as ordinary civil claims has
obscured its proper relation to punishment.

Unjust enrichment and uncertainty

One commonly stated objection to the theory of unjust enrichment is that it is
too vague to serve any purpose in legal argument. Thus it was once said:[64]

> [i]t would be a remedy far worse than the disease if the basis of the common law rule
> was scrapped, and for it substituted a rule which left the whole matter to the discre-
> tion of the judge.

And, in a similar vein, a reference to unjust enrichment once provoked the
response that:

> [w]hatever may have been the case 146 years ago, we are not now free in the 20th cen-
> tury to administer that vague jurisprudence which is sometimes attractively styled
> "justice as between man and man".[65]

The theory of unjust enrichment is a form of theoretical argument, in the
sense that, as discussed further below, it seeks to identify general principles that
underlie particular rules and decisions and so provide the basis for enhancing
the coherence of the law. Thus, as the proponents of the theory have argued, it
is not a sufficient criticism of the theory that it is too vague to be applied directly
to the facts, in place of the pre-existing rules, because this is not its function.[66]
There can be no objection to the theory merely on the basis that it is imprecise
or "open-textured", or that it is open to rival interpretations. But the vagueness
of unjust enrichment is due to the fact that it seeks to encompass quite distinct
claims. The consequence is that it is not clear what even the nature of the relevant injustice in "unjust enrichment" is, until, that is, the field is resolved into
the distinct claims identified above, for each of which the nature of the injustice
is clear, but distinct from that for other claims. The various claims within unjust
enrichment, in other words, are merely given a facade of uniformity by sub-
suming them under an indeterminate concept of "injustice" or the "unjust factor". One might make a comparison with what appears to be an analogous
definition of tort as the law of "unjust harm" or "unreasonably-caused harm".
Here, by contrast, the broad nature of the issue of injustice at stake is reasonably clear: it is the conflict between the defendant's interest in freedom of action
and the plaintiff's interest in freedom from harm, and this at least provides a

---

[64] Holdsworth (1939), 43.
[65] *Baylis v Bishop of London* [1913] 1 Ch 127, 140 *per* Hamilton LJ. The case was 146 years after
Moses v Macferlan (1760) 2 Burr. 1005.
[66] Birks (1989*a*), 18–19; Goff & Jones (1998), 15.

basis for classification and comparison and for deeper investigation. Thus one might say that the objection to the theory of unjust enrichment is not that it is vague, so much as that it is "inert and useless".

Birks specifically denies this charge.[67] Without the theory, he argues, the law will lack any "shared and stable pattern of reasoning" or "common framework"; it will be fragmented, and issues that are in substance the same will be treated differently, and with different terminologies; and it will be forced to use fictional concepts. These are indeed liable to be the consequences of a lack of proper theoretical underpinning for the law. But it is merely to beg the question of the validity of the theory of unjust enrichment to say that the theory avoids such difficulties.[68] If it is right, as argued above, that what the theory of unjust enrichment regards as a single body of law is better understood in terms of three distinct types of claim, the theory will tend to generate problems of this sort rather than to eliminate them, creating its own fictions (like the fiction of benefit mentioned above), and fragmenting other areas of law in order to form the law of restitution based on unjust enrichment.[69]

A SUBSTANTIVE AND A REMEDIAL SENSE OF RESTITUTION

The law is usually classified in terms of substantive categories. A substantive category is a category defined in terms of the nature of the grounds on which a claim arises; contract and tort are categories of this sort.[70] Similarly the law of restitution for vitiated transfers and the law of restitutionary or non-contractual claims arising from imputed contracts are substantive categories, defined in terms of the conditions that generate a claim. The advantage of substantive classification is to advance the analysis of the grounds on which claims arise. The law of a substantive category will include a remedial part dealing with the appropriate remedy when a claim arises. For contract and tort, this is normally compensation. The law of compensation is not itself a substantive category; it is a remedial category, which intersects with substantive categories like contract and tort.

It might appear that "restitution" is a remedial category like compensation. This is apparently Birks's view: he says that restitution "cannot stand in the same series as 'contract' and 'tort'. They denote events which trigger legal responses while 'restitution' denotes a response triggered."[71] Restitution, meaning the reversal of a transfer, appears to be the remedy that is appropriate for a

---

[67] Birks (1989a), 199ff, although not in response to this argument.

[68] As noted by Dietrich (1998), 46.

[69] This is the effect of the theory of unjust enrichment on the law of contract and the law of property, as discussed in Parts 2 and 3 respectively.

[70] The grounds on which a claim arises are specified by the primary relation in the sense of Appendix 1.

[71] Birks (1989), 16. Similarly, Virgo says: "The law of restitution is about the award of a generic group of remedies . . .": Virgo (1999), 3.

claim arising from a vitiated transfer (or a claim in unjust enrichment).[72] However, this is difficult to reconcile with the normal usage of "restitution". Books on restitution (including this book and Birks's)[73] are not concerned with remedial issues, as a book on compensation or damages is, but deal with the circumstances in which a claim arises, just like a book on contract or tort. And "restitution" is used to refer to a substantive category of claim where (as is common) it is said that a claim arises in restitution not in contract or tort.

The normal usage, which will be adopted here, is surely that, although restitution naturally refers to a remedy of reversing a transfer, it is used implicitly in a substantive sense, because it is used to refer to such a remedy only in relation to a particular substantive category of claim, for which such a remedy is the normal response. Thus, as a matter of conventional usage, the law of restitution is the substantive area of law concerned with claims arising from vitiated transfers. No doubt the convention developed out of a lack of understanding of the basis of the claim, which made an explicit substantive classification elusive.[74] One might say that "restitution" may also be used, again in a substantive sense, to refer to non-contractual claims for payment arising from an imputed contract, although, on the view taken here, this is a distinct body of law. This usage seems well established in modern times and is accordingly used in this book, but it is presumably based on confusion with the claim arising from a vitiated transfer, probably due to the implied contract theory as well as the theory of unjust enrichment. The sense of "restitution" must be understood as distinct, and it would be desirable if the usage disappeared, not only to avoid confusion with restitution for vitiated transfers but also because the remedy does not actually consist of the reversal of a transfer. The use of "restitution" to refer to disgorgement is still less apt, but again apparently quite well established, at least in the literature.

Birks at one time proposed the "quadration thesis", according to which every case of restitution is a case of unjust enrichment, and vice versa.[75] This would certainly account for the use of "restitution" in a substantive sense in relation to a substantive category of unjust enrichment. The quadration thesis is open to objection, first, on the ground that because unjust enrichment is understood to encompass claims for payment and for disgorgement the appropriate remedy is not always restitution in the natural sense of reversing a transfer. Secondly, if restitution means any reversal of a transfer, it seems that it can be available in circumstances that are not understood to fall within unjust enrichment at all. Say the defendant committed a tort against the plaintiff that caused a transfer of

---

[72] But it is not the appropriate description for payment for work done or for disgorgement.

[73] The very influential Birks (1989*a*).

[74] See Appendix 1.

[75] Birks (1989*a*), 17–18. It may be that "restitution for wrongs" was excluded from the thesis. Much discussion of the quadration thesis has related to the question whether restitution can be a remedy for a proprietary claim as opposed to an unjust enrichment claim. The controversy is based on a misconception of the nature of proprietary claims, as discussed in Chaps. 9 and 10.

property from the plaintiff to the defendant.[76] The plaintiff is entitled to compensation for the tort, and it may be that the appropriate means of effecting such compensation is to compel the defendant to return the property if it is still in his hands. (The advantage of effecting compensation in this way is to avoid the problem of measuring the value of the plaintiff's loss.) Then one might say that the remedy of restitution is available in respect of the tort.[77] Similarly, the plaintiff may have transferred money or property to the defendant under an agreement that provided for it to be returned in specified circumstances. If such circumstances arise, it seems again that one might say that the plaintiff has a remedy of restitution based on the contract.[78] In fact it is not customary to refer to cases in contract or tort as restitutionary, even if the remedy is the reversal of a transfer,[79] and this seems to be simply because, as a matter of convention, restitution is used in the substantive sense identified above to refer only to claims arising from a vitiated transfer, or an imputed contract.

There is a further problem concerning the relation of restitution and unjust enrichment. The problem of uncertainty with respect to the concept of unjust enrichment was mentioned above. Birks argues that, although in the abstract the concept may be vague and uncertain, a more precise meaning in particular contexts can be derived from the case law:[80]

> "Unjust" can never be made to draw on an unknowable justice in the sky . . . The essential point is that [the role of "unjust"] [is] only to identify in a general way those factors which, according to the cases themselves, [call] for an enrichment to be undone.

Unjust enrichment is defined in terms of the cases; and it seems that the cases in question are identified as those where restitution as a remedy was available; i.e. where the remedy was reversing a transfer (or, more broadly, "undoing an enrichment"). Thus Birks also says that instead of using "unjust" to describe the enrichment he could equally have used "reversible".[81] In other words, Birks requires a concept of restitution as a remedy in order to identify the cases that provide him with a definition of unjust enrichment as a substantive category. But it is not apparent why one should be able to define a substantive category in

---

[76] e.g. an assault or duress or misrepresentation etc.

[77] Quite apart from whether the plaintiff can show a vitiated transfer, which one imagines would generally, if not invariably, be the case.

[78] Another example might be where the plaintiff's property has been taken without his permission and has come into the defendant's possession (whether or not a wrong by the defendant was involved, as in the first example above). One might say that the plaintiff has a right to have his property returned to him—i.e. to a restitutionary remedy—by virtue of his continuing ownership of the property, so that the claim arises in property law rather than the law of vitiated transfers. See further Chap. 9.

[79] However, there seem to be some instances where restitution is said to be based on a wrong rather than on receipt: see e.g. with respect to undue influence Chap. 5 at 195; and the discussion of knowing receipt in Chap. 10. See also the discussion of restitution for complete failure of consideration, Chap. 2 at 53 ff.

[80] Birks (1989a), 19.

[81] Birks (1989a), 19.

terms of the availability of a type of remedy: there is no reason to suppose that a category so defined is a true substantive category, governed uniformly by a certain principle or set of criteria determing when a claim arises. As pointed out above, "restitution" in the sense of reversing a transfer is a possible remedy in cases of contract and tort, as well as vitiated transfers, and so it seems that unjust enrichment defined by reference to the availability of such a remedy would encompass some claims in contract and tort.[82] One might say that "restitution" must be understood in a sense that excludes such cases and is confined to unjust enrichment. But then it seems that whilst unjust enrichment is defined by reference to the availability of restitution, restitution is defined as the response to unjust enrichment.[83] The circularity arises from the absence of any meaningful definition of unjust enrichment in terms of the grounds for a claim.[84]

Lastly it should be reiterated that "restitution" is inapt for disgorgement, which does not consist of the reversal of a transfer, and, furthermore, is not a remedy at all, although often so described: as mentioned above, there is a distinction between a remedy on the one hand and disgorgement on the other as responses to a wrong.[85] Disgorgement can in principle arise in relation to any type of wrong and cannot have an implicit substantive sense.

"THEORETICAL ARGUMENT"

In a rough and ready way one might contrast two opposing approaches to legal argument, which might be described as theoretical and blackletter respectively.[86] A blackletter approach tends to confine the law to narrowly formulated rules based directly on particular decisions, often in the precise form in which they were stated by the judge. A theoretical approach seeks to identify broader principles, often not stated in the cases, that underlie these rules and decisions and provide a basis for the development of the law in such a way as to identify and eliminate anomalies and false distinctions and to make the law clearer and more coherent. The approach put forward here is theoretical in this sense, as is the theory of unjust enrichment. No attempt will be made here to offer any further characterisation or jurisprudential analysis of theoretical argument. But it

---

[82] If restitution refers to a remedy that does not include such cases, the narrower sense has not been elucidated, and so provides no help in defining unjust enrichment. In fact, as considered in Chap. 9, there is a more precise definition of the remedy of restitution for a vitiated transfer, which distinguishes it from what appears to be the same remedy of reversing a transfer in contract and tort, and with respect to this more precise understanding the quadration thesis does apply with respect to vitiated transfers and restitution: see Chap. 9 at n 18.

[83] Cf Dietrich (1998), 46.

[84] A similar circularity problem has arisen with respect to fiduciary relationships: see Chap. 13 at 402.

[85] Discussed further in Chap. 11. Disgorgement is a response to a wrong, but a remedy can arise in response to a wrong or to some other type of "causative event": see Appendix 1.

[86] No doubt "blackletter" is used in various senses. No hard and fast distinction between the two approaches is envisaged.

is surely the case that the exclusion of theoretical argument has pernicious effects on the law in the long term.[87] Where the law develops without regard to underlying principle or coherence it tends to become blighted by artificial distinctions and excessive detail, leading to obscurity, uncertainty and unfairness. There seems no doubt that in recent years there has been a shift away from a strict blackletter approach towards a more theoretical approach.[88]

Some of the criticism that has been directed at the theory of unjust enrichment really amounts to opposition to theoretical argument in general. This might be said of the argument that "*no* theory would do, that there was . . . no such thing as a 'basis' for Restitution";[89] and similarly of the statement that: "I am happy to have the law of Restitution studied as one unit, on the basis that we have to split up the law of Obligations on some basis or it will swamp us".[90] These appear to reflect the anti-theoretical assumption that the law is a set of arbitrary rules, arrived at by the common law by accident of history and divided into categories only for reasons of convenience, and not because there are any underlying principles that dictate such a classification.[91] A similar view might be that, although the law can be classified in the light of underlying principles, these principles are irrelevant to the process of determining what the law is. This seems to be the implication of the following statement of Lord Diplock:[92]

> There is no general doctrine of unjust enrichment recognised in English law. What it does is to provide specific remedies in particular cases of what might be classified as unjust enrichment in a legal system that is based upon the civil law.

Similarly, the criticism mentioned above of the theory of unjust enrichment as lacking in certainty, although legitimate for the reasons given, might be understood as a rejection of the role of theoretical argument altogether.[93] From an anti-theoretical standpoint it is inconsequential how a particular rule or claim is characterised in terms of underlying principles, and the long campaign to install the principle of unjust enrichment as the basis for a field of law appears to be not so much mistaken as futile and wrongheaded.

Unfortunately, anti-theoretical attacks on the theory of unjust enrichment seem sometimes to have been combined with, and diverted attention from, powerful substantive criticisms of the theory of unjust enrichment of the sort advanced here; this seems to be true, for example, of some of Hedley's criticisms.[94] Conversely, proponents of the theory of unjust enrichment sometimes seem to assume that, if they overcome the objections to the theory based on

---

[87] See the discussion in Atiyah (1979), 660–71; also Birks (1989*a*), 19.

[88] For a good recent example, see *Kleinwort Benson v Lincoln City Council* [1998] 3 WLR 1095, discussed in Chap. 5.

[89] Hedley (1985), 58; rejected by Birks (1985), 69; Burrows (1993), 6.

[90] Hedley (1985), 56. "Restitution" here must presumably be understood to refer to an arbitrary division of convenience.

[91] Cf Atiyah (1986), 48.

[92] *Orakpo v Manson Investments Ltd* [1978] AC 95, 104.

[93] Above at 20.

[94] e.g. Hedley (1985).

hostility to theoretical argument in general, they have succeeded in establishing the validity of their theory.[95] This is not true of course. The problem with the theory of unjust enrichment is not the ambition behind it but its defects as a theory.

[95] Burrows (1993), 6; Birks (1985), 70.

Part II
Claims for Payment: Restitution and Contract

2

Contract and Exchange

CONTRACT AND RESTITUTION

THIS CHAPTER IS concerned principally with whether claims arising from contracts that have terminated early through breach or frustration are ever in any sense restitutionary. One might have thought that such cases would by definition be exclusively a matter for the law of contract, and that there would be no question of any other type of claim. There is a valid contract between the parties, and the rights of the parties are surely a matter for the law of contract. This is indeed the position that will be defended here.[1] A contrary position has been forcefully advocated by academic commentators, to the extent that it seems almost to be regarded as orthodox.[2] On this view, whenever a contract terminates early by breach or frustration, a restitutionary claim can arise, whether or not there is also a contractual claim. It is argued below that this restitutionary approach has resulted partly from a faulty understanding of the law of contract, in the form of what will be referred to as the classical theory. Accordingly the first part of the chapter deals with the nature of agreements and the contractual rights that arise from them.

EXCHANGE AND AGREEMENT

People have an interest in exchanging benefits, i.e. goods or services or land in return for payment. Generally such an exchange takes effect in accordance with an agreement, by which the parties will settle the terms of the exchange. An agreement that is recognised as creating legal rights is a contract, and its legal enforceability gives the contracting parties the confidence to perform the agreement without the risk of losing out if the other party fails to reciprocate in accordance with the agreement. The law of contract is thus also, generally, the law governing the exchange of benefits.

---

[1] This chapter will not deal with disgorgement, which will be dealt with in Chap. 13.

[2] e.g. Birks (1989*a*), chap. VII; Goff & Jones (1998), Chap. 20; Burrows (1993), chap. 9; Skelton (1998). The approach is also adopted in some contract textbooks.

The classical theory

An agreement, if enforceable as a contract, is a means of creating a new legal relation between the parties to it, by the voluntary act of the parties.[3] Thus making an agreement involves the exercise of a normative power. This power is conventionally taken to be the power to promise, meaning the power to assume an obligation by the communication to the promisee of an intention so to do.[4] An agreement is taken to be an exchange of promises, each party to the agreement promising to perform as specified in the agreement. Thus, where an agreement is recognised in law as a contract, each party incurs a legal obligation to perform as specified. Generally one party has an obligation to provide goods or services, and the other has an obligation to pay for them. Each party can perform in the knowledge that the other has a legal obligation to provide the reciprocal performance.[5] This is the conventional understanding of a contract. It will be referred to as the classical theory of contract.[6]

The reliance theory

An agreement is open to a different interpretation, according to which it involves the exercise of a different type of normative power. This is the power to assume responsibility for reliance. On this interpretation, when two parties make an agreement that specifies a certain performance for each of them, the agreement should not be understood as involving promises to perform, or as thereby necessarily generating legal obligations to perform; instead each party accepts responsibility for the other's reliance on the assumption that the agreement will be performed. This interpretation is the basis for what will be referred to as the reliance theory of contract.[7] Under the reliance theory, a contracting party has protection for his "reliance interest". The reliance interest is the interest in payment for work done in reliance on the agreement; it encompasses compensation for expenditure or other loss in reliance, and also return on labour or capital applied. Thus a reliance claim, meaning a claim that satisfies the reliance interest, may differ from what is usually referred to as a claim for "reliance loss", because payment for work done is not necessarily reducible to compensation for loss (although it may sometimes be convenient to use "reliance loss" to refer to the measure of recovery necessary to satisfy the reliance interest).[8] It is

---

[3] This draws on Jaffey (1998c).

[4] e.g. Raz (1977), 211.

[5] The legal relation created between the parties is a right–duty relation in the sense of Appendix 1.

[6] The classical theory as so defined presupposes but is not defined in terms of freedom of contract, which is sometimes taken to be the hallmark of the classical theory.

[7] There are other forms of the reliance theory: see Jaffey (1998c).

[8] The expression "reliance interest" is associated with Fuller & Perdue (1936), 54. In this famous article the expression was used to refer only to a measure of loss, not in the wider sense proposed here to encompass payment for work done in reliance.

right that the reliance interest should encompass the interest in a return on labour or capital as well as compensation for loss, because it is the function of the agreement to enable a contracting party to secure this return in addition to covering his expenditure. Often, however, the plaintiff's loss in reliance will be his opportunity cost, which will be the profit he would have made on another contract; in such a case, this loss effectively displaces the measure of payment for actual expenses or actual work done as the measure of the reliance interest.[9]

From each party's point of view, the exchange is really the benefit of the other party's performance in return for, or in satisfaction of, his own reliance interest, and this is how the reliance interest is satisfied in the normal course. Where the defendant has not performed as agreed, some part of the plaintiff's reliance interest may be outstanding, and the defendant will be liable to satisfy it, generally by way of a pecuniary liability. It is possible that after the completion of the contract as agreed, the plaintiff may find himself worse off than if he had not made the contract; in other words, it may turn out that he has made a bad bargain. But of course it cannot be that a defendant who has completed performance in accordance with the contract remains liable to make up a shortfall in the satisfaction of the plaintiff's reliance interest: the plaintiff must be understood to have accepted, by agreeing to the terms of the contract, that his reliance interest is fully satisfied by performance of the contract in the terms specified. This will be referred to below as the "valuation" in the contract, or the "contractual valuation", viz., the equation of the measure necessary to satisfy the whole of the plaintiff's reliance interest[10] with the value to him of the reciprocal performance due. The valuation not only places a price on the plaintiff's work (including expenditure), but also involves an allocation of risk between the parties. The plaintiff accepts the risk that his own cost of performance will be greater than expected, or that the value to him of the counter-performance will be less than expected, either because of a misjudgment or because of changes in circumstances after contracting.

Under the classical theory, the parties have an obligation to perform in the manner specified in the agreement, whereas under the reliance theory there is generally no duty to perform. By virtue of the contract a contracting party incurs not an obligation of performance but responsibility for the other party's reliance interest, and generally this can be satisfied through a pecuniary liability as an alternative to performance.[11] However, the contracting party can become

---

[9] A distinction can be drawn between reliance through performance of the contract, and reliance by a contractor through expenditure or otherwise for his own purposes in anticipation of the receipt of the contractual benefit. This is Fuller & Perdue's distinction between essential and incidental reliance: Fuller & Perdue (1936), 78. See below at n 77.

[10] i.e. his reliance interest assuming he has relied to the fullest extent on the expected counter-performance. The value of the counter-performance is the "subjective value" and it caps the aggregate of the essential and incidental reliance: Fuller & Perdue (1936), 79.

[11] Thus the legal relation between the parties created by the agreement under the reliance theory is a right–liability relation, where a remedial liability arises on the occurrence of an event not constituting a breach of duty, viz., the non-performance of the contract: see Appendix 1.

subject to a duty of performance when performance by him is necessary in order to ensure that the reliance interest is satisfied: in other words, where "damages are inadequate".[12] For convenience, and consistently with established usage, "breach of contract" will be used to refer to any case where the defendant refuses or fails to perform in accordance with the contract, whether or not there was a duty to perform.

On a "blackletter" approach to the law,[13] one might consider the classical and the reliance theories to be remote from or even irrelevant to the day-to-day rules of contract law. But the two theories prescribe or support different rules in many respects, and they can be compared in terms of how well they account for the case law.[14] The argument below is that the reliance theory provides a more coherent basis for a number of aspects of the law, including, amongst the issues considered at various points in this book, economic duress,[15] disgorgement,[16] fiduciary relationships,[17] failure of consideration,[18] the quantum meruit,[19] "wrongdoers' claims",[20] frustration,[21] and bona fide purchase.[22] Nevertheless, there is no doubt that the language of the law often reflects the classical terminology of promising and obligation. The implication is that, although the courts tend to speak in terms of promising (although contracting parties themselves may not), they have tacitly understood and enforced agreements in terms of assumption of responsibility for reliance, and that this is a source of confusion and contradiction in the law.

Apart from accounting for the established rules of law, there is another reason to prefer the reliance theory. This is that usually an agreement is intended to regulate an exchange, and for this purpose the power to assume responsibility for reliance is the more apt normative power. For an agreement to serve its purpose of protecting a contracting party against the risk of non-performance by the other party, the agreement must have the effect of ensuring that the contracting party will not lose out through embarking on the contract, which means that he must know that (by enforcing the agreement if necessary) he will be left in no worse a position than he would have been in if he had not entered into the contract, and also that, if he is to do work under the contract, he will be paid for what he actually does. An agreement consisting of assumptions of responsibility for the reliance interest exactly achieves this. By contrast, under the classical theory each party has an obligation to perform and a right to performance from the other party. As a rule this goes further than necessary to satisfy the reliance

---

[12] Here the relation will be a right–duty relation: see Appendix 1.
[13] See the discussion in Appendix 1.
[14] See Jaffey (1998c).
[15] Chap. 5.
[16] Chap. 12.
[17] Chap. 13.
[18] See below at n 90 and Chaps. 3 and 6.
[19] See below at 35 ff.
[20] See below at 51–53.
[21] See below at 66 ff.
[22] Chap. 7.

interest, and therefore further than necessary to enable the exchange to proceed. This suggests that generally it is appropriate to interpret an agreement in accordance with the reliance theory.[23]

Two other points concerning the classical and reliance theories should be noted. First, the reliance theory as set out here is quite distinct from the theory that denies that the claims and liabilities traditionally described as contractual are based on agreement at all, which is also sometimes described as the reliance theory. This will be referred to as the "death of contract" theory, and it will be relevant to discuss it in Chapter 3. The reliance theory as advanced here takes such claims and liabilities to be based on agreement but denies the conventional interpretation of agreement. Secondly, even if an agreement is properly understood to consist of an exchange of promises generating obligations of performance in accordance with the classical theory, such promises surely *entail* assumptions of responsibility for reliance.[24] If the defendant made a promise to do X, he must be understood to have assumed responsibility for reliance by the plaintiff on the expectation that he will do X. It follows that the various claims that are argued below to arise from assumptions of responsibility under the reliance theory should also arise as alternative claims under the classical theory. For the purposes of the present chapter, this means that it is not actually necessary to demonstrate that the reliance theory is superior to the classical theory and should displace it. However, at other points in the book it will be seen that only the reliance theory as an alternative to the classical theory will provide an adequate foundation for the law;[25] and in any case contrasting the reliance theory with the classical theory provides a convenient form for exposition.

THE USUAL CONTRACT REMEDIES

Before considering claims that are supposed to be restitutionary, it is important to consider contract remedies in general. Partly this is designed to show the plausibility of the reliance theory, but also it is a necessary prerequisite to the discussion of restitution in this and later chapters.

---

[23] This does not of course imply that people do not sometimes make promises, or that an agreement may not sometimes involve promises rather than assumptions of responsibility. As a rule it seems that promising is more apt in the social or personal context, where remedies are very much beside the point and the promise—for example, a promise of fidelity—is given in the context of a personal relationship to which the giving and fulfilment of the promise contribute.

[24] Cf MacCormick (1992*b*), who seeks to justify promises in terms of assumptions of responsibility for reliance.

[25] e.g. with respect to disgorgement in Chap. 12, duress in Chap. 5, and fiduciary relationships in Chap. 13.

Specific performance

Under the classical theory, the parties to a contract have a duty to perform it. This implies that, at least as a general rule, the court should order specific performance.[26] However, as commonly formulated the rule is that specific performance is available only where "damages are inadequate".[27] One might argue that the law is quite consistent with the classical theory because the only circumstances in which specific performance is not awarded is where it is of no consequence because damages are adequate. But there is no reason under the classical theory why the court should have to make this judgment of adequacy. Since the defendant has a duty to perform and the plaintiff a correlative right to performance, it should be up to the plaintiff to decide whether to accept damages instead. After all, the plaintiff is in the best position to decide whether damages are a satisfactory equivalent to the performance to which he is entitled. On the other hand, as pointed out above, under the reliance theory a contracting party has a duty of performance only where actual performance is necessary in order to ensure that the other party's reliance interest is satisfied, because a pecuniary liability is inadequate. Where this is the case, the responsibility for the reliance interest will generate a duty of performance, and so a correlative right to performance, and to an order of specific performance. The question whether the defendant has become subject to a duty to perform is important in contexts other than simply whether the plaintiff can get specific performance: it is relevant to withdrawal and mitigation, which is considered next, and to various issues considered in other chapters, including disgorgement,[28] economic duress,[29] and fiduciary relationships.[30]

Generally a pecuniary liability is sufficient to satisfy the reliance interest where the plaintiff can pay to secure performance from someone else equivalent to that which he was expecting from the defendant, i.e. where the performance is not unique. It may not always be easy to say whether equivalent performance is available. The court will have to make a judgment of how scrupulous it should be in avoiding the slightest risk that the plaintiff's reliance interest is not fully satisfied, at the expense of the defendant's freedom not to perform. Generally, one can say that where no equivalent performance is available the plaintiff has become dependent on the defendant, and that the dependence generates a duty of performance.[31]

---

[26] Some commentators have accordingly argued in favour of the wider availability of specific performance: e.g. Friedmann (1995), 629–32; L.D. Smith (1994), 135–40.

[27] *Sky Petroleum v VIP Petroleum* [1974] 1 WLR 576; *Co-operative Insurance Society v Argyll Stores* [1997] 2 WLR 898, 902–3. In the latter it was crucial that "the interests of [both parties] were purely financial" (at 900, *per* Lord Hoffmann), which is to say that damages were adequate.

[28] Chap. 12.

[29] Chap. 5.

[30] Chap. 13.

[31] Cf Collins (1997), 397.

Commonly specific performance is available where the plaintiff has con-tracted to buy a unique product, for example land or a work of art.[32] In such a case, however, it is possible that the plaintiff has not actually relied on the agreement at all, so that no duty of performance should arise. As discussed below, because of the difficulty in proving reliance in some cases, in connection with the recovery of damages it is generally presumed that the plaintiff has relied on the agreement once it has been entered into; but, because of the additional burden for the defendant, it is arguable that a duty of performance should not arise unless there has been a significant, identifiable act of reliance. At any rate, there is a stronger argument for a duty of performance in such a case. There are many examples of this type of case:[33] where the plaintiff has made an agreement to take supplies from the defendant for his business and in reliance on the agreement has adapted his business to rely on these supplies, which are available only from the defendant;[34] or where the plaintiff has adapted his business to rely on software subject to an agreement with the defendant for continuous mainte-nance, which can only be supplied by him;[35] or where the plaintiff has con-tracted for supplies for an event, and it is now too close to the date of the event to get supplies from elsewhere;[36] or where the plaintiff has transferred property to the defendant subject to a negative covenant, which by its nature cannot be performed by anyone else;[37] or where the plaintiff has transferred a business to the defendant subject to a liability to make a regular payment out of the busi-ness to a third party;[38] or where the defendant's contractual performance is intended to protect against a risk of harm to the plaintiff.[39]

Withdrawal and mitigation

If a contracting party has a duty to perform, he cannot withdraw from the con-tract without the agreement of the other party; this would be inconsistent with

[32] *Lowther v Lowther* (1806) 13 Ves. 95. Nowadays it seems implausible to say that a house or piece of land is always unique. It has been suggested that in the case of the sale of land the plaintiff is liable to have made a significant adjustment to his position in reliance on the agreement, e.g. by giving up his house or job, or at least that this is the historical basis for the rule: Collins (1997), 391.

[33] The examples given involve either specific performance or other circumstances in which it is relevant that a duty to perform has arisen, in particular where specific performance is not possible and the issue is whether there should be disgorgement or punitive damages: see Chap. 12 below.

[34] *Sky Petroleum v VIP Petroleum* [1974] 1 WLR 576; *Freeman & Mills v Belcher* 900 P 2d 669 (Cal. 1995), a case on punitive damages: see Chap. 12.

[35] This is discussed as an example of oppression by Collins (1997), 391.

[36] Cf *B & S Contracts and Design v Victor Green Publications* [1984] ICR 419, a case of duress: see Chap. 5 at 188.

[37] e.g. *Wrotham Park Estates v Parkside Homes Ltd* [1974] 2 All ER 321, where an injunction was denied but "restitutionary damages" awarded. This was properly an issue of disgorgement but was disposed of as a use claim: see Chap. 4. See also *Greene v West Cheshire Railway* (1871) LR 13 Eq 44.

[38] *Beswick v Beswick* [1968] AC 58.

[39] *City of New Orleans v Firemen's Charitable Association* (1891) 9 So 486, a case on disgorge-ment: see below Chap. 12.

the nature of a duty. But if, as generally under the reliance theory, the contracting party is not subject to a duty to perform, but merely a responsibility for reliance, it follows that he can choose to withdraw from further performance, subject to a liability to satisfy the reliance interest of the party with respect to reliance incurred before withdrawal. In denying specific performance as a general rule, the law seems effectively to recognise a freedom to withdraw. But one might argue that even if the defendant will not be compelled to perform, it must be the case that he has a duty to perform and is not permitted to withdraw if, notwithstanding a purported withdrawal, the plaintiff is entitled to continue to act on the assumption that the defendant will perform and then recover damages in respect of such reliance. This is the issue of "mitigation of damages". Ostensibly the law is that the plaintiff does not have to mitigate his losses until the contract has terminated as a result of the plaintiff's agreeing to termination or "accepting a breach",[40] and this suggests that the defendant does have a duty to perform and cannot withdraw unilaterally. But in reality the plaintiff is treated as bound to accept that the contract has terminated once the defendant has made it clear that he will not perform, and so has to mitigate from this time,[41] and this is consistent with the assumption that the defendant has no duty to perform.[42]

Damages and the expectation measure

The usual measure of damages for breach of contract is the expectation measure, which is the sum necessary to put the plaintiff in the position he would have been in if the contract had been completed. The plaintiff receives the value of the outstanding performance due to him, less the cost he has saved from not having to complete his own performance. This is understood to be a direct application of the classical theory. If the defendant had a duty to perform, and the plaintiff does not receive actual performance, he should at least receive the value of the performance to which he was entitled.[43] The plaintiff may, if he wishes, claim instead in the measure of his ascertainable loss in reliance, for example his expenditure, as he will be inclined to do where it is difficult for him to prove the value of the benefit he would have received.[44] This is usually described as a claim for reliance loss. But the recovery of the loss incurred is consistent with the classical theory on the basis that it is assumed, in the plaintiff's favour, that he would not have made a loss on the completed contract, and it follows, as has been recognised, that recovery

---

[40] *Howard v Pickford Tool Co Ltd* [1951] 1 KB 417; *White & Carter v McGregor* [1962] AC 413.
[41] *British Westinghouse Electric v Underground Electric Railways* [1912] AC 73; *Lazenby Garages Ltd v Wright* [1976] 1 WLR 459.
[42] Atiyah (1986), 124.
[43] See e.g. Friedmann (1995); Fried (1981), 17–21.
[44] *Anglia Television v Reed* [1972] 1 QB 60.

should be capped to the expectation measure if the defendant can show that the reliance loss claimed exceeds it.[45]

But the expectation measure is also generally appropriate as a measure of liability under the reliance theory. Where there is a competitive market for what the plaintiff is buying or selling, the plaintiff would have been able to make an alternative contract on equivalent or almost equivalent terms with a third party, by which he would have obtained the same or almost the same benefit as he was due to receive through the contract with the defendant. In such a case, the expectation measure provides a good approximation of the plaintiff's loss in reliance on the contract in the form of his opportunity cost.[46] In other cases, where there was no equivalent contract available to the plaintiff, he may well nevertheless have had other options open to him, such that he would not have entered into the contract if its terms had been even slightly less favourable to him. This is liable to be difficult to prove, however, and if the plaintiff is to be protected from this difficulty, here again his opportunity cost should be equated with the expectation measure. One might argue that, if the contract comes to an end almost immediately after it was made, it is implausible that the plaintiff has already incurred any reliance loss, let alone reliance loss amounting to the expectation measure. But it may be very difficult for the plaintiff to prove that he has acted in reliance or to what extent, and again it is reasonable, at least where the defendant was responsible for the contractual breakdown, to apply a presumption in the plaintiff's favour that on making the contract he immediately lost the opportunity of an equivalent benefit. To the extent that he can still obtain an equivalent benefit after the contract ends, his recovery will be reduced under the doctrine of mitigation, but here the onus is on the defendant to show that this is the case.

Although the expectation measure is generally appropriate under both theories, this is so for quite different reasons. Under the classical theory the plaintiff has a contractual right to performance by the defendant corresponding to the defendant's duty to provide it, whereas under the reliance theory the plaintiff merely has a right to the satisfaction of his reliance interest, which performance by the defendant achieves. Accordingly under the classical theory the expectation measure is in itself necessarily the correct measure, because it is the measure of the value of the performance that the plaintiff is entitled to. Under the reliance theory, on the other hand, the expectation measure is appropriate as a proxy measure for the true, underlying reliance claim.

---

[45] *C & P Haulage v Middleton* [1983] 1 WLR 1461; *CCC Films (London) Ltd v Impact Quadrant Films* [1985] QB 16.

[46] Fuller & Perdue (1936), 62. This will include loss incurred before the contract was made but in anticipation of it, as in *Anglia TV v Reed* [1972] 1 QB 60.

Accrued liabilities and contractual payment provisions

Under the classical theory, there is a very clear distinction between a claim for damages for breach of contract and a claim for the contract price. Damages arise from the defendant's breach of duty and represent the value of the performance that the defendant was obliged but failed to provide, whereas the contract price is a liability that accrues when the condition for payment is satisfied, typically on completion by the plaintiff of his performance. It seems, ostensibly at least, that under the classical theory no contractual claim can arise unless either the defendant has committed a breach of his duty of performance, or a claim to the contract price has accrued under a payment provision. As will be considered further below, this has sometimes caused difficulty, for example in the case of an "entire contract", which is a contract that provides for payment only by lump sum on completion. If the plaintiff has carried out work under the contract, which is then frustrated, it seems that under the classical theory he has no claim at all, because there has been no breach by the defendant, and no liability has accrued under the payment clause.[47] The same problem arises where the plaintiff himself caused the termination by his failure to perform.[48]

Under the reliance theory, as the plaintiff performs the contract he incurs reliance for which the defendant become responsible, and accordingly his reliance claim accrues as he performs. Normally the claim is satisfied by the defendant's performance in due course, but if not the plaintiff has a pecuniary claim. The claim will normally, according to the presumption discussed above, be in the expectation measure, but, as discussed below, it may sometimes be in the actual underlying reliance measure. The plaintiff's right to payment increases in measure as he performs and simply tends towards and eventually culminates in the right to the contract price.[49] It follows that if for some reason the contract is not completed, the plaintiff can still in principle have a claim in respect of his reliance before termination of the contract, even if the contract provided for payment by a lump sum on completion. On this approach, the effect of a contractual provision concerning the time of payment is not actually to generate the liability for payment, which arises from performance itself. Instead the payment clause values the plaintiff's performance and provides for the practical matter of payment in the normal course; and also by providing for payment in advance or on completion it allocates the risk of non-recovery as a result of insolvency or of having to litigate when a party to the contract is unable or unwilling to satisfy a liability under it.[50]

[47] *Cutter v Powell* (1795) 6 Term Rep 320.
[48] *Bolton v Mahadeva* [1972] 2 All ER 1322. Stoljar has referred to this as the "debt fallacy", attributing it to the influence of the old form of action in debt: Stoljar (1956), 295–300. The argument seems to be equivalent to saying, as it is sometimes put, that the defendant has contracted for the whole benefit and not for some part of it.
[49] Under the contractual valuation the reliance measure in respect of complete performance equals the contract price.
[50] See further below at 51–53, 66–68.

The nature of the quantum meruit

A quantum meruit is a claim for reasonable payment for work or work and materials or for goods supplied.[51] "Work" or "work and expenditure" will generally be used to cover all of these. A claim for reasonable payment for work done in the absence of an agreement, for example in a case of necessitous intervention, is a claim for a restitutionary, non-contractual quantum meruit. This type of claim is considered in the next chapter. But a claim for reasonable payment in the form of a quantum meruit can also arise under a contract, where the contract did not contain an agreed price, as for example where the defendant hires the plaintiff to do work without specifying a precise price or rate, the assumption being that he is to be paid at a reasonable rate for the work that he does.[52] The claim is clearly contractual, just as if there were an agreed price, but for a reasonable sum in the absence of an agreed price.

The controversial type of case is where a contract, which may or may not provide for an agreed price on completion, is terminated early as a result of non-performance or frustration. Then it appears that a party may have a claim for reasonable payment for the work he has actually done under the contract. This claim arises either as an alternative to a claim for expectation damages, or on its own where no claim for expectation damages arises, as where the contract was frustrated or came to an end as a result of the plaintiff's own failure to perform. An example is provided by *De Bernady v Harding*.[53] Here the plaintiff contracted to sell tickets on behalf of the defendant for seats to view the funeral procession of the Duke of Wellington. The defendant then repudiated the contract by telling the plaintiff not to sell tickets for him, and the plaintiff claimed for his expenses and work done under the agreement. The court held that he could recover on a quantum meruit. Another much discussed example is *Planché v Colburn*.[54] Here the agreement was that the plaintiff would write a book to be published by the defendant, for which the defendant would pay a specified sum on submission of the manuscript. However, the defendant withdrew from the project before the manuscript was submitted. Again the plaintiff was allowed a claim for payment for the work he had done in the form of a quantum meruit. These are cases where the plaintiff seems to have a normal contractual claim for damages as an alternative to the quantum meruit claim, because the defendant was in breach. Some other cases are considered later, where the contract was frustrated or ended as a result of the plaintiff's own failure to perform, and so

---

[51] With respect to a good or chattel, the claim is strictly the quantum valebat rather than the quantum meruit.

[52] *Powell v Braun* [1954] 1 All ER 484.

[53] (1853) 8 Exch 822.

[54] (1831) 8 Bing. 14.

the defendant was not in breach, and the quantum meruit is the only possible claim.

There is great controversy over this type of claim. Under the classical theory, because a contractual claim is understood to arise either from an accrued liability under a payment clause or from the breach of an obligation by the defendant, it seems that the quantum meruit cannot be contractual at all. This seems particularly clear in a case where the contract was frustrated or ended as a result of the plaintiff's own breach.[55] There seem to be two alternative analyses in the cases and commentary of the quantum meruit in this type of case. One is that the quantum meruit claim arises under a new, secondary or supplementary contract between the parties that provides for payment at a reasonable rate for the work actually carried out.[56] Then the quantum meruit would be an example of the case mentioned above where there is a contractual claim for payment based on an agreement to pay an unspecified but reasonable sum. This may sometimes be a plausible analysis, but is surely a complete fiction in most cases, including the cases mentioned above. There is no suggestion in those cases that there was genuinely a second or supplementary contract between the parties under which the defendant could be liable to pay for work for which there was no liability under the original contract. The other approach is that the claim is a restitutionary claim, arising directly from the provision by the plaintiff of a benefit to the defendant rather than from the agreement. This is an increasingly popular view,[57] and also appears to have some judicial support.[58] On this approach, the implied secondary or supplementary contract is really a form of the implied contract fiction discussed in Chapter 1, by which a restitutionary liability was at one time described as arising from an implied contract.[59]

The restitutionary analysis; contractual performance as a conditional transfer

On the non-contractual, restitutionary analysis, the quantum meruit claim is understood to arise from the provision of a benefit to the defendant, rather than from the agreement. In Chapter 1, the important distinction was drawn between the claim for restitution for a vitiated transfer and the restitutionary or non-contractual claim for payment, a distinction that is concealed by the theory of unjust enrichment. The argument for a restitutionary claim on termination of a contract does not distinguish between the two.

---

[55] Birks (1983), 149.
[56] *Sumpter v Hedges* [1898] 1 QB 673; *De Bernady v Harding* (1853) 8 Exch 822; *Miles v Wakefield MDC* [1987] AC 539, 552, *per* Lord Bridge.
[57] It appears to be the standard view in restitution texts.
[58] e.g. *Miles v Wakefield MDC* [1987] AC 539, 553, *per* Lord Brightman.
[59] e.g. Virgo (1999), 356.

A non-contractual claim for payment

If the quantum meruit is not contractual, it appears much more plausible to say that it is a restitutionary or non-contractual claim for payment arising as an alternative to the contractual claim for payment, rather than a restitutionary claim to reverse contractual performance as if it were a vitiated transfer. Although it makes sense to speak of the reversal of a transfer of money or goods under a contract, it is misconceived to think of reversing contractual performance in general, including work done under a contract. As discussed in Chapter 1, work done (including expenditure incurred) in providing something to the defendant cannot, by its nature, be reversed; it can only be paid for.[60] This difficulty is disguised in the idea of the quantum meruit as the "value of services" or the value of work done,[61] as if this were the value of a transfer, but this is irredeemably ambiguous as between, on the one hand, the extent of work done and the appropriate measure of payment for it, and, on the other, the value of the benefit conferred.

Examples of the non-contractual claim for payment are considered in the next chapter, where they arise *in the absence* of a valid contract. Where there is no contract, the claim for payment arises as a substitute for a contractual claim, because of the failure or inability of the parties to contract: hence the apt description as a claim under an "imputed contract". By definition, there is no room for such a claim where the parties have actually made an agreement to govern payment for the work in question. Even if the agreement is determinative when the exchange is completed, one might argue that a different regime should operate if the contract breaks down before completion. Thus it has been argued that the restitutionary claim does not conflict with the agreement because it is available only once the contract has terminated early rather than going to completion.[62] But of course contract law provides for the remedies that arise on termination; this is when issues in contract law normally arise, and the contractual regime continues to apply after termination to determine the claim and measure of liability. A non-contractual claim would be liable to subvert these contract rules. One might argue that the contract law rules are inapt for some reason; one cannot argue, however, that contract law can continue to govern the issue, but that an inconsistent claim for payment can arise as an alternative.

Conversely, if there is to be a non-contractual claim for payment as an alternative to the contractual claim in respect of part performance of a contract, there seems no reason why the alternative claim should not be allowed when the contract has been completed.[63] If the contractual regime can be overridden in

[60] As noted, e.g., by Goff J in *BP v Hunt (No. 2)* [1979] 1 WLR 783, 799.
[61] See e.g. Birks (1991*b*), 121; see further, Chap. 3, 86 ff.
[62] Virgo (1999), 40; Birks (1989*a*), 47; Burrows (1993) 250–1.
[63] Smith notes that the termination of the contract does not make it invalid in any sense, but argues in consequence that the restitutionary claim should arise whether the contract has terminated or not: S.A. Smith (1999), 253.

one case, why not in the other? In fact, a quantum meruit does not appear ever to have been allowed for a sum in excess of the actual accrued liability for the contract price,[64] although it seems that some commentators are in favour of such a claim.[65] The only theoretical basis for such a claim would be the "death of contract" theory, which is discussed in the next chapter.

"Reversing contractual performance"

In fact, as the restitutionary analysis is usually formulated, the quantum meruit seems to be understood to represent the reversal of a transfer from the plaintiff to the defendant, the transfer being the plaintiff's contractual performance.[66] The quantum meruit is thought of as the value of the performance, as if it were a transfer.[67] Even accepting, for the sake of argument, the idea of contractual performance as a transfer of wealth, and the quantum meruit as a claim to reverse it, why should there be a claim to reverse a transfer under the contract? In other words, what basis is there for treating the transfer as vitiated? A plaintiff performing a valid contract does so by his own free choice,[68] and this is no less the case where the contract terminates early as a result of breach or frustration. The position is different where the contract is void or voidable and rescinded; here there is a vitiating factor, although its nature is controversial.[69] It was at one time thought that contractual termination operated to rescind the contract ab initio, as if the contract were void or voidable and had been rescinded. But termination cannot affect the intentions of the parties on contracting or the original validity of the contract, and this view has been rejected as heretical.[70]

The restitutionary conditional transfer theory

In fact, the usual restitutionary argument is not that there is a vitiating factor, but that there is a so-called "unjust factor" that operates in an analogous way to

---

[64] Burrows (1993), 270; Goff & Jones (1998), 530. The more usual case where the contract terminates before the contact price has accrued is considered below.

[65] Burrows (1993), 270–1; Skelton (1998), 77.

[66] The idea of reversing contractual performance to protect the "restitution interest" is found in Fuller & Perdue (1936), 54–5, 71–3, although they seem to have regarded it as a contractual claim to protect the restitution interest, rather than a non-contractual restitutionary claim. They treated the restitution interest as the plaintiff's interest in having the value received by the defendant through the plaintiff's performance restored to him, as if it were a transfer. Accordingly they equated the plaintiff's loss and the defendant's gain (except in the case, which they distinguished, where the plaintiff's performance had not yet accrued to the defendant). On this approach, the quantum meruit can equally be regarded as a reliance claim measured by the plaintiff's loss or a restitutionary claim measured by the defendant's gain. Cf below at 47–48.

[67] See, e.g., Birks (1989a), 226ff, 238ff; Burrows (1993), 267; Skelton (1998), chap. 1; Virgo (1999), 348.

[68] Unless there is a vitiating factor of the sort discussed in Chap. 5.

[69] See Chap. 6.

[70] *Johnson v Agnew* [1980] AC 367.

generate a restitutionary claim. The unjust factor is said to be the failure of the condition or basis on which the contractual performance was provided.[71] This sense of conditional performance can be understood from the case of a simple conditional payment. Here the plaintiff makes a payment to the defendant on the condition that a specified event will happen, so that if the event does not happen the defendant must repay the sum paid to him. For example, the plaintiff might have paid £100 to the defendant on the condition that the defendant does not receive an equivalent sum from his father. If the condition is not satisfied, because the defendant receives the sum from his father, the plaintiff is entitled to the repayment of the sum, but only, it seems, if the defendant was notified of the condition and accepted it.[72] The argument is that where the plaintiff performs under an agreement by which the defendant is to provide a specified counter-performance, the defendant's performance of the contract—or, more precisely, the plaintiff's receipt of the benefit of counter-performance—is a condition of the plaintiff's performance in just the same sense,[73] so that if the plaintiff does not receive the benefit of the expected counter-performance, the defendant becomes liable to return the value of the plaintiff's performance. This is understood to be the quantum meruit. It seems that the defendant is taken to have been notified and to have accepted the condition by way of his acceptance of the contract, although the condition is imposed and binds the defendant independently of it. This theory will be referred to as the "restitutionary conditional transfer theory",[74] although its proponents generally refer to it as the restitutionary theory of "failure of consideration", for reasons that will be explained below.

One would have thought that, where a payment is made subject to a condition, the basis for the claim for repayment on the failure of the condition must be contractual. This is surely the reason the law requires that the condition should be expressed and accepted by the defendant. The defendant agrees to the condition, and in reliance on this the plaintiff makes the payment to him. If the condition is not fulfilled, the defendant is liable under the contract to repay the sum paid. If this is so, and the contractual claim for the repayment of a simple conditional payment is merely a manifestation of the usual contractual claim, then of course characterising contractual performance as a conditional transfer cannot generate any distinct non-contractual claim. But let us accept for the sake of argument that the claim for repayment arising from a simple conditional payment on the failure of the condition is not contractual, but arises from the imposition of a condition by the plaintiff on his transfer, which binds the

---

[71] Birks (1989a), 224; Virgo (1999), 323; Burrows (1993), 252. The approach invokes a dictum of Lord Wright in *Fibrosa Spolka Akcyjna v Fairbairn Lawson Combe Barbour Ltd* [1943] AC 32, 64–5. The approach is assumed almost without argument in a recent article: S.A. Smith (1999).

[72] *Chillingworth v Esche* [1924] 1 Ch. 97; Birks (1983) 141–62; Birks (1991b), 114, 115–6.

[73] Condition is not used to mean a conditional term of the contract or a precondition to performance.

[74] The discussion here broadly corresponds to that in Jaffey (1998a).

defendant irrespective of any agreement between the parties.[75] Then it might appear to follow that in a contractual situation involving counter-performance by the defendant the plaintiff can on the same basis be treated as having made his performance subject to a non-contractual condition that the defendant provide the agreed counter-performance, so that non-performance by the defendant should generate a distinct non-contractual claim for the reversal of the plaintiff's performance. But even on this assumption the analysis is untenable. It implies that that the transaction is self-contradictory, in consisting at one and the same time of a contract between the parties and also the notification of a non-contractual condition binding on the other party that may have consequences inconsistent with the contract, by generating a claim that would not arise under the contract.

These various arguments show that the restitutionary explanation of the quantum meruit arising on the termination of a valid contract is quite unconvincing. The obvious alternative is that the claim is contractual. This might seem evidently correct, because the claim arises out of the non-performance of a contract. As suggested above, the reason the contractual analysis has seemed wrong is that in accordance with the classical theory it is thought that a contractual claim must be either a claim for damages in the expectation measure or a claim for payment under a payment clause. But the reliance theory provides the missing analysis, because it shows how the quantum meruit can be understood as a contractual claim.

The quantum meruit under the reliance theory

Under the reliance theory, a contract claim is simply a claim for payment for work done in reliance on the agreement. The claim satisfies the reliance interest, measured in accordance with the contractual valuation.[76] In the usual case, the plaintiff will rely on the expectation measure as a proxy for the true reliance claim. But sometimes it may be appropriate to claim the reliance measure as such, rather than the expectation measure. This is the quantum meruit.[77] Sometimes also the plaintiff claims in the measure of his expenditure because it

---

[75] It is not strictly necessary for present purposes to establish whether the claim arising from a conditional transfer is always contractual or whether there is a non-contractual "conditional gift" claim. In the latter case, the requirement in the law that the condition should be expressed must apparently be understood not as a contractual requirement concerned with the defendant's acceptance, but merely as an evidential matter, serving to avoid any doubt that the condition was indeed imposed: Birks (1991*b*), 115; see further Chap. 3 at 101.

[76] The contractual valuation is explained above, at 31.

[77] The quantum meruit measures reliance through performance, not reliance for other purposes, as e.g. where the plaintiff incurs expenditure for his own purposes in anticipation of payment. Thus it relates to "essential reliance" rather than "incidental reliance" in Fuller & Perdue's terminology: Fuller & Perdue (1936), 78. Whether incidental reliance ought to be covered depends on whether the defendant took responsibility for such reliance, which might depend on the nature of the contract. Possibly it should also depend on whether the defendant was in breach.

is difficult for him to prove the value of the benefit he would have received—i.e. a claim for damages for "reliance loss".[78] Both the quantum meruit and the claim for reliance loss are examples of a pure reliance claim, as opposed to an expectation claim as a proxy for the reliance claim.

The contract will generally state a price in money for the plaintiff's work. This values the plaintiff's performance, and provides a means for measuring the quantum meruit: the contractual valuation equates the plaintiff's reliance measure in respect of the whole performance with the contract price. Thus the reliance measure is that part of the contract price that is attributable to the work actually done, according to whatever factors were liability in setting the price for the whole; i.e. according to the extent of expenditure, and the degree of labour or expertise or risk involved in the work done relative to the whole envisaged performance, to the degree that those factors were relevant in determining the whole contractual price.[79] The measure of liability on this basis can be described as the pro rata measure. As performance approaches completion, the quantum meruit approaches the contract price.[80] The pro rata measure may fall below a market rate or what might be regarded as a "reasonable rate" for the plaintiff's work, but the plaintiff should nevertheless be bound by it. The pro rata measure reflects the basis on which the plaintiff's time, labour and skill were valued by the parties, and so should determine the measure of liability, even if it turns out to be inapt because it was badly judged or because of a change of circumstances. There is little authority in favour of the pro rata measure or against it, and some controversy amongst commentators.[81] The controversy arises principally because the claim is thought to be restitutionary, and the issue is discussed on that basis; if it is accepted as contractual, it is surely clear that the contractual valuation should apply.

Generally the expectation measure is available as a proxy for the reliance claim, to avoid the difficulty of proving the measure of the reliance claim, even though it may sometimes over-compensate. The expectation measure, which will normally be measured as the contract price less the plaintiff's saved costs from not having to complete his own performance,[82] will generally be preferable

---

[78] *Anglia Television v Reed* [1972] 1 QB 60; *Commonwealth of Australia v Amann Aviation Pty Ltd* (1991) 174 CLR 64.

[79] One might object that a crucial factor in agreeing the whole contract price was the value to be received by the defendant, and that the claim in respect of the work involved in part performance should also take account of the value of the benefit actually received from that part performance. But the purpose is not to determine the price that would have been agreed for the part performance, but the proportion of the price that is attributable to the work done. The justification is that the plaintiff's claim is for the protection of his reliance under the contract and this is a reasonable way to measure it.

[80] If the counter-performance is not the payment of money, but something more complex, the quantum meruit remains in principle the appropriate proportion of the value to the plaintiff of the defendant's counter-performance.

[81] See below at 50.

[82] Dividing the contract price notionally between the plaintiff's costs and his return in respect of his labour (which is his net profit, although net profit might in practice be defined to exclude a certain measure of payment for labour), the reliance measure will be that part of the contract price that

to the plaintiff: it will generally exceed the reliance measure, and it will generally be easier to measure than the appropriate proportion of the contract price. However there are circumstances in which the plaintiff may choose or should be required to claim in the pure reliance measure, i.e. a quantum meruit or claim for reliance loss, rather than in the expectation measure.

First, as mentioned above, the plaintiff should be denied the benefit of the expectation measure presumption in his favour at the expense of the defendant where there is no reason to favour the plaintiff over the defendant: i.e. where the termination of the contract was not due to the defendant's breach, as where the contract was frustrated, or where it was the plaintiff's own breach that brought the contract to an end. Secondly, the plaintiff might choose to make a pure reliance claim for actual expenditure and reasonable remuneration rather than a claim in the expectation measure where the expectation measure is difficult to prove. This might be the case where the plaintiff has incurred ascertainable expenses or carried out identifiable work, but his payment under the contract was to be, say, by way of a share of profits in some speculative venture.[83] However, if the defendant can bring evidence that the claim is excessive by reference to the contractual valuation it should be reduced accordingly; as the "reliance loss" cases show, there should be an "expectation measure cap".[84] Thirdly, the reliance measure will exceed the expectation measure where the contract is a losing contract for the plaintiff, in the sense that the contract price will fall short of the plaintiff's costs of performance. The expectation measure will be the costs so far incurred less the expected shortfall on the contract as a whole, whereas it seems that the pro rata reliance measure will be the costs so far incurred less only the relevant proportion of the shortfall. In such a case it seems that the plaintiff should be entitled to the reliance measure rather than the expectation measure. The plaintiff will still make a loss over his part performance, but will not have to bear the whole of the loss that he would have made over the whole contract.[85]

The reliance theory shows how the quantum meruit can be understood as a contractual claim. But it is worth reiterating that it would be possible to recognise a contractual quantum meruit of this sort under the classical theory. If a contract is understood as an exchange of promises generating enforceable obligations, the promises surely entail assumptions of responsibility for reliance on

relates to costs and return on labour in respect of work actually done, and the expectation measure will be the whole contract price less that part of the contract price that relates to the costs of the work not done. Thus the expectation measure will generally exceed the reliance measure by the return on labour or net profit in respect of the work not done. This could be a wide margin, if the plaintiff has incurred little reliance on the contract.

[83] See e.g. *Commonwealth of Australia v Amann Aviation Pty Ltd* (1991) 174 CLR 64.

[84] *C & P Haulage v Middleton* [1983] 1 WLR 1461; *CCC Films (London) Ltd v Impact Quadrant Films* [1985] QB 16.

[85] Although the quantum meruit or reliance claim may exceed the expectation measure in such a case, the claim is still based on the contractual valuation; the argument is not that the quantum meruit can exceed the expectation measure because it is not subject to the contractual valuation: cf at 50 below.

the promise. Thus liability for payment for work done could be understood to accrue to the plaintiff as an alternative to relying on non-performance as a breach of a duty of performance by the defendant.

Reliance, benefit, and the measure of liability

Leaving aside the problem of the basis of the restitutionary claim, the difference between the restitutionary approach and the reliance approach seems to be that the reliance theory is concerned with payment for the work done in part-performance, and the restitutionary theory with payment for what was received.[86] Thus in principle it seems that the measure of the restitutionary claim should depend on the extent of the benefit received through part performance, and the measure of the reliance claim on the extent of work done.[87]

Where the defendant has received no benefit

Thus a clear clash between the reliance approach and the restitutionary approach is where the plaintiff has done work that has not yet benefited the defendant at all. Here it is clear that a quantum meruit can be awarded. A much cited example is provided by *Planché v Colburn*,[88] the facts of which were given briefly above. There the work in question was to prepare a book, and the contract terminated before the book was submitted, so the defendant received nothing. The restitutionary analysis of the quantum meruit has struggled to deal with this type of case. If the claim is understood to be a non-contractual claim based on the receipt of benefit rather than on the agreement, it is difficult to see how a claim can arise, whereas if the claim is a contractual reliance claim no difficulty arises.

One response to this difficulty has been to argue for a concept of what amounts to deemed benefit, i.e. for a principle that work done pursuant to a contract should be deemed to benefit the defendant for the purposes of a restitutionary claim.[89] It is true that the parties to a contract can define for themselves what their exchange consists of, or in other words what they are willing to pay for, and one can say that the exchange is beneficial to a party even if the other party's performance does not enhance his wealth or otherwise provide him with something that other people might consider to be a benefit. The provision of a benefit to a third party under the contract is in this sense a benefit to the

---

[86] Or reversal of benefit: see above 40.

[87] One might expect the two measures to correspond if the proportion of work done corresponds to the proportion of the benefit received (i.e. if the contractual valuation applied to both), but this may not be the case before completion because the benefit will not necessarily accrue as the work is done and at the same rate, and sometimes contractual performance will be worthless to the defendant unless completed because it cannot be completed by anyone else.

[88] (1831) 8 Bing. 14.

[89] Birks (1989*a*), 126–7, 232; Birks (1991*b*), 141.

contractor who requested it. It might be inferred from this that the law of contract recognises deemed benefits,[90] and that the distinction between reliance by the plaintiff under the contract, or "requested reliance", and benefit to the defendant under the contract is entirely arbitrary and that they can be equated.[91] Thus it might be argued that the restitutionary approach is consistent with cases like *Planché v Colburn* where no benefit has been received, but requested work has been carried out.

But the argument is misconceived. For most purposes, the receipt of a benefit is not relevant to the contractual liability, which arises from the agreement, and reliance on the agreement, not from the receipt of a benefit.[92] But, in any case, the argument confuses two quite separate matters.[93] The first is whether a contractual performance benefits the party who requested it, and the second is whether, assuming that the contractual performance is beneficial, part performance is also beneficial. Just because one can say that contractual performance in the form of, say, a benefit to a third party is beneficial to the defendant who requested it, even though no wealth or service or other tangible benefit has accrued to the defendant himself, it does not follow that one can deem the defendant to have been benefited where the performance has been cut short after the plaintiff has made preparations but before any actual benefit has reached the defendant, as in a case like *Planché v Colburn*. The argument is really a contrivance for reconciling the restitutionary approach with a case like *Planché v Colburn*. It is surely more sensible to accept that the quantum meruit is a contractual reliance claim, not a restitutionary claim at all. Some commentators have actually accepted that the quantum meruit claim in *Planché v Colburn* was a contractual reliance claim, although apparently without inferring that this is generally true of the quantum meruit claim in respect of work under a valid contract.[94]

Problems of measurement if the claim is restitutionary

If a quantum meruit claim is a non-contractual, restitutionary claim, the issue arises of how the measure of liability should be determined. Curiously, the issue seems to have been addressed in relation to two issues that are apparently treated as distinct. The first is understood to be how to measure the benefit received by the defendant for the purposes of the restitutionary claim; this seems

---

[90] The exchange doctrine of consideration, which might originally have been understood to require an exchange of benefits, is satisfied by an act of "requested reliance" even if the act is not designed to provide something that would be recognised as a benefit independently of the contract: Furmsten (1996), 75.

[91] Fuller & Perdue (1936), 71; cf Birks (1991*b*), 137ff.

[92] Although, as considered below, measuring the benefit received can sometimes be relevant to determining the measure of a contractual claim. See below at 52, 59, 67.

[93] Cf Chap. 3 at 90.

[94] Burrows (1993), 267. Another view seems to be that it was a non-contractual reliance claim: Beatson (1991), 21–44. See further Chap. 3 below.

to include the issue of the relevance of the contractual valuation. The second issue is understood to be whether the restitutionary measure of liability should be subject to a "contractual ceiling", i.e. whether it should be curtailed to avoid subverting the contractual valuation.

(1) On a restitutionary approach, the problem of how to value the benefit received and how to determine the appropriate payment for it arises from the fact that people vary in their tastes and resources and therefore in the prices that they are prepared to pay for a particular benefit. Thus it is not easy to say what the benefit is worth to the defendant, or what he ought to pay for it.[95] This is why the general rule is that no claim for payment for a benefit conferred is allowed without a prior agreement to pay that settles the terms for a mutually beneficial exchange:[96] if a benefit is conferred by contract, one can be sure that, at least at the time of the contract, the defendant thought that the benefit would be worth it at the agreed price. If the plaintiff is allowed a non-contractual, restitutionary claim in respect of a benefit conferred, how is an appropriate measure for the claim to be determined? A number of tests have been suggested. These are described as tests of benefit, meaning tests of the value of benefit, conceived of as being the value of a transfer from the plaintiff to the defendant. They are better understood as determining a measure of payment for the benefit received, not a measure of the benefit itself. On the view advanced in this book—that the quantum meruit arising out of the performance of a valid contract is always contractual—these tests have no relevance in this context. However, they may be relevant in cases where a claim for payment arises in the absence of a valid contract, and will be considered in the next chapter in connection with such cases. Just one such test, the "bargained-for benefit" test,[97] will be referred to here to illustrate the weakness of the restitutionary approach in the present context.

According to the bargained-for benefit test, although the claim is non-contractual, the contract can be relied on as an indication of an appropriate price for the benefit, since it shows how the defendant valued the benefit. This means, in effect, that the claim should be measured by the contractual valuation, so that the appropriate payment is measured as a proportion of the payment for the whole contractual benefit, as argued above, mutatis mutandis,[98] with respect to the reliance claim.[99] However, the contract is not actually a conclusive indicator of the true value of the benefit at the time when it is received, nor of an appropriate price for it. There is no guarantee that an agreed exchange will turn out to be mutually beneficial; as events turn out, it may be that the defendant does not value what he receives in the degree that he envisaged, and would not in retrospect have paid what he agreed, because of a change in his tastes, or his

---

[95] To refer to what he has received as a "benefit" actually begs this question, but is a convenient usage.

[96] This is considered further in the next chapter.

[97] Burrows (1993), 14–15.

[98] With respect to the reliance claim, it is the proportion of the work done that is relevant.

[99] Above at 45.

resources, or in a change in circumstances that affect the value of the benefit to him, or because he made a misjudgement or miscalculation in making the contract. Of course it is in the nature of an agreement that he is bound to pay what he agreed to pay, even though he now considers that he is paying more than the benefit is worth to him. This gives effect to the contractual valuation in the sense explained above, which also holds the parties to an implicit allocation of risk. But it is difficult to see why a restitutionary claim in respect of a benefit actually conferred should give effect to the contractual valuation or allocation of risk; and if the bargained-for benefit test is applied, ostensibly for the purpose of a restitutionary claim, the effect is in reality to enforce the contract.[100]

(2) Secondly, apparently separately from the test of benefit, there has been a debate in the literature over whether the restitutionary measure (as determined by the bargained-for benefit test or some other test) should be subject to the "contractual ceiling", which amounts to the pro rata measure.[101] It is widely thought that the quantum meruit should be subject to a contractual ceiling in some sense,[102] although some commentators deny this.[103] There are one or two overseas authorities that suggest that the quantum meruit is assessed quite independently of the contract, and so can exceed the pro rata measure or even the expectation measure. A notorious example is provided by the American case of *Boomer v Muir*,[104] where, on the termination of a contract as a result of a breach by the defendant, the plaintiff was awarded a quantum meruit that gave him an overall return on the contract that vastly exceeded the contract price.

On the contractual approach the contractual ceiling is, as it were, an internal constraint arising from the nature of the claim, whereas on the restitutionary approach it is an extraneous constraint.[105] If there is a non-contractual claim at all, it is difficult to see why it should be subject to such an extraneous constraint.[106] The argument for it seems to be that the ceiling prevents subversion

---

[100] Save that presumably the contractual valuation is applied with respect to benefit rather than work done.

[101] It might refer instead to the expectation measure; cf Skelton (1998), 2. As argued above, the pro rata measure is the proper measure of the quantum meruit on a contractual analysis where the plaintiff is confined to the pure reliance claim; and where the plaintiff is entitled to the expectation measure but for evidential reasons claims a quantum meruit for his actual work and expenditure it should be subject to the expectation measure cap, except, as discussed above at n 85.

[102] Goff & Jones (1998), 30, 534; Birks (1989a), 288.

[103] Birks (1991b), 136; Burrows (1993), 269; Skelton (1998), 84; see also Law Commission (1981), paras. 2.52–53 and Burrows (1984), 81.

[104] (1933) 24 P 2d 570. See also *Lodder v Slowey* [1904] AC 442, where the issue was not fully discussed; *Renard Construction (MD) Pty Ltd v Minister for Public Works* (1992) 26 NSWLR 234, 276–8. The American and Australian positions are discussed in Skelton (1998), 53ff.

[105] Birks (1991b), 136. If the bargained-for benefit test applies, the measure prescribed appears to correspond to the contractual ceiling in the pro rata sense in any case.

[106] It has been argued that if there is no contractual ceiling, there may still be a "valuation ceiling", meaning that although the contract does not operate directly to limit the restitutionary claim, nevertheless it is relevant for evidential purposes in determining the restitutionary measure: Birks (1991b), 136.

of the contract; but this seems to preclude any non-contractual claim that does not merely replicate the contractual reliance claim.[107]

The quantum meruit on frustration or in favour of a party in breach

Where the plaintiff has done work under a contract that was frustrated, as argued above it seems that under the classical theory no claim can arise unless a liability accrued before termination under a payment clause. This is because under the classical theory a claim is understood to arise either from a breach of duty or from a debt arising from a payment clause. This may seem unjust, but was the position at common law until the law was amended by the Law Reform (Frustrated Contracts) Act 1943. For example, in *Cutter v Powell*[108] the plaintiff contracted for an agreed lump sum, payable at the end of the voyage, to be second mate on the defendant's ship, and then died half way through the voyage, frustrating the contract. His estate sued for a quantum meruit for the work actually done, but the claim was denied on the basis that under the contract the right to payment accrued only on completion.

The argument applies in the same way where the plaintiff's breach of contract led to termination. Here again the position is that no quantum meruit is available. The leading case is *Sumpter v Hedges*.[109] The plaintiff was contracted to carry out building work but failed to complete it. The contract provided for payment by a lump sum on completion of the work. It was held that, since he had not completed the work, he was not entitled to payment under the contract, and his claim for a quantum meruit failed. There are suggestions in some cases that the courts might depart from *Sumpter v Hedges* and allow a quantum meruit for work done by the plaintiff in this type of case, even though he has not completed performance,[110] and the Law Commission has proposed a statutory reform to allow such a claim.[111]

Under the reliance theory, a reliance claim is not based on a breach of duty to perform the agreement, but on work done under the agreement. Thus prima facie either or both parties to a contract may have a reliance claim when a contract terminates early as a result of frustration, although neither party should have the benefit of the expectation measure presumption to protect him from difficulties of proof. Frustration is considered further below. Where the plaintiff

---

[107] Subject to the proviso, as noted above, that on part performance a restitutionary quantum meruit on a pro rata measure would be based on the proportion of the total benefit received, and the contractual quantum meruit on the proportion of the work done. For an economic argument equivalent to the rejection of any claim inconsistent with the contractual valuation, see Kull (1994).

[108] (1795) 6 TR 320. This was an "entire contract": see above, at 38.

[109] [1898] 1 QB 673.

[110] *Hain Steamship v Tate & Lyle* [1936] 2 All ER 597; *Miles v Wakefield MDC* [1987] AC 539.

[111] Law Commission (1981). The position is slightly ameliorated by the doctrine of substantial performance, according to which payment becomes due to the plaintiff once he has performed substantially, even though not perfectly, subject to a counterclaim by the defendant for the cost of completing or correcting the work if the plaintiff is in breach, e.g. *Hoenig v Isaacs* [1952] 2 All ER 176.

was himself in breach, again both parties have made an assumption of responsibility for reliance, and both are entitled to protection for their reliance interest; but here priority must go to protecting the reliance interest of the defendant through the expectation measure presumption. The defendant will be responsible for satisfying the plaintiff's prima facie reliance claim, in the form of a quantum meruit or reliance loss claim, only in so far as the defendant has been left with, as it were, a surplus over his expectation interest; in other words, only to the extent that he has been left better off than he would have been if the contract had been completed. Thus one can say that the plaintiff has a prima facie reliance claim, capped by the defendant's surplus over his expectation interest.[112]

Under the classical theory, where it is assumed that no claim can arise out of the contract in such cases, it is thought that if a claim were available it would have to be restitutionary. Thus the Law Commission's argument in favour of a "wrongdoer's claim" was couched as an argument for the recognition of a restitutionary claim; and it is widely thought, as considered below, that the claims arising on frustration under the statutory regime are also restitutionary claims.[113] As argued above, there is no basis for any such restitutionary claim; and the treatment of what is in reality a contractual claim as a non-contractual, restitutionary claim tends to cause unnecessary complexity and confusion, because it means that there is a dual regime governing the claims available on termination.

Furthermore, under the classical theory it seems that a provision for lump sum payment on completion must be understood to be intended to impose the whole risk of non-completion on the plaintiff, in the sense that if the contract is not completed for any reason he has no right to any payment for what he has done. But, if this was the intention of the parties, then, even if there were some plausible basis for a non-contractual claim on termination in some circumstances, it should presumably be excluded by the contract as inconsistent with the intended allocation of risk; and this is consistent with the decisions mentioned above where a quantum meruit was denied. The possibility that a lump sum payment clause is not intended to have this effect is consistent only with the reliance theory, where (as mentioned earlier in this chapter) the clause can be understood to have the function of valuing the plaintiff's performance for the purpose of the contractual valuation, providing for the practical matter of payment in the normal course, and allocating the risk of non-recovery due to insolvency and the risk of having to litigate to recover a sum due under the con-

---

[112] This amounts to extrapolating from the approach that applies in a case of substantial performance: see e.g. the Scots case of *Thomson v Archibald* 1990 GWD 26–1438. For further explanation, see below with respect to frustration. The approach may correspond to what some commentators have described as restitution within contract, or restitution as a contractual claim: see e.g. Perillo (1973); Dieckmann & Evans-Jones (1995).

[113] e.g. Birks (1983), 152; Law Commission (1981).

tract.[114] In itself, and without anything more explicit, one would think that a provision for lump sum payment on completion should not be understood to go further than this and place a risk of non-payment on the plaintiff in the event of non-completion for any reason.[115] In any case, for present purposes the crucial point is that the issue is how to construe the contract under the contract law rules of construction, not whether a restitutionary claim should be available to make up for the supposed absence of a contractual claim, as is often assumed.[116]

PREPAYMENTS AND TOTAL FAILURE OF CONSIDERATION

Claims in respect of prepayments

This section concerns the claim in respect of a payment made under an agreement, when the plaintiff has paid without receiving the benefit due in return. Here the plaintiff is not the party who does the work, as in the section above, but the one who receives and pays for it.[117] The accepted position here seems to be as follows. If the defendant is in breach, the plaintiff will have an expectation claim. But he may, it seems, choose to claim in respect of his prepayment as a reliance loss, but subject to proof by the defendant of the expectation measure cap. In one case, however, the plaintiff can recover the full amount of the prepayment even if it exceeds the expectation cap: this is where there has been a "total failure of consideration". There is, broadly speaking, a total failure of consideration where the defendant has not performed any part of his contractual performance (i.e. no part at all). For example, if the plaintiff pays the defendant £100 in advance for goods that the defendant never delivers, the plaintiff's expectation claim is less than £100 if the price of the goods has fallen on the market, but the plaintiff is nevertheless entitled to recover the full amount of £100.[118] Where the defendant is not in breach, i.e. where the plaintiff is in

---

[114] Law Commission (1981), para. 2.32; Stoljar (1956). These risks can best be reduced by a scheme for payment by instalments, which seeks to give the plaintiff instalments that satisfy his reliance interest as he proceeds, instead of either payment in advance or payment on completion. This tends to minimise the extent to which the parties have outstanding reliance claims in the event of breakdown.

[115] Particularly with respect to frustration; possibly it is easier to infer an intention to place such a risk on the plaintiff where he is in breach. It seems that in *Cutter v Powell* it may have been difficult to find another second mate during the voyage, and so the plaintiff may have been paid at an especially high rate as a quid pro quo for committing himself to the whole voyage: see Stoljar (1956). This might justify denying him a reliance claim if he were in breach.

[116] This is how the issue has sometimes been expressed: see e.g. *Appleby v Myers* (1867) LR 2 CP 651. In Law Commission (1981) the difference between the majority and minority positions was expressed in terms of whether a restitutionary claim should be allowed, but the arguments were largely in terms of the allocation of risk under the contract.

[117] The analysis is not affected by the fact that in a more complex contract there may not be simple division of work and payment.

[118] *Hunt v Silk* (1804) 5 East 449; cf *Bush v Canfield* (1818) 2 Conn 485. The position is the same if the defendant delivers but the plaintiff is entitled to reject the goods because they are defective, and does so.

breach, or the contract is frustrated, the general rule appears to be that the plaintiff has no claim at all (subject to the statutory provisions on frustration, which are considered separately below); however, if the defendant did not perform at all, so that there was a total failure of consideration, the plaintiff does have a claim to recover a prepayment, certainly in the case of frustration,[119] and possibly in the case where the plaintiff was in breach.[120]

One issue here is the general absence, just as with respect to the quantum meruit, of any claim for the plaintiff where the defendant was not in breach, i.e. on frustration or where the plaintiff was in breach. As argued above, this is best understood as a mistake resulting from the classical theory. But here there is the complication that the plaintiff *does* have a claim when the defendant was not in breach in the exceptional case where there was a total failure of consideration. It is curious that a plaintiff who has made a payment in advance can recover the whole of the prepayment if there is a total failure of consideration, even if the defendant was not in breach, but, once the defendant has begun performance, if the defendant was not in breach the plaintiff has no claim at all, even if the prepayment vastly over-pays the defendant for what he has actually done under the agreement. Secondly, again the expectation measure cap is the general rule, which appears to reflect the contractual valuation; but again there is the complication that where there is a total failure of consideration the expectation measure cap does not apply.

Clearly there is an important issue concerning the nature and significance of the claim arising on a total failure of consideration. The meaning of "total failure of consideration" will be considered below; for the moment it is best treated simply as a verbal formula. The claim is generally understood to be a non-contractual, restitutionary claim, and this appears to explain why it is not subject to the expectation measure cap and why it is available where the defendant is not in breach (which under the classical theory is taken to mean that the claim cannot be contractual). The restitutionary analysis is also consistent with the traditional form of the claim as a claim for money had and received.

The restitutionary conditional transfer theory

One explanation of total failure of consideration is offered by the restitutionary conditional transfer theory. As discussed above, according to the restitutionary conditional transfer theory the quantum meruit is a claim to reverse performance under the contract (or more plausibly to be paid for it), on the basis that the performance was made conditionally and that on the termination of the contract the condition has failed and the performance should be reversed (or paid for). Similarly it is argued that the claim in respect of a prepayment is a restitutionary claim to reverse the payment that arises on the basis of the failure of the

---

[119] *Fibrosa Spolka Akcyjna v Fairbairn Lawson Combe Barbour Ltd* [1943] AC 32.
[120] *Dies v British & International Mining & Finance Corporation* [1939] 1 KB 724.

condition on which it was paid, viz., that the contract would be performed. In fact, the restitutionary conditional transfer theory seems to have originated in connection with the claim to recover a prepayment on total failure of consideration,[121] and was then developed to apply to the quantum meruit. "Failure of consideration" or "total failure of consideration" is understood to refer to the failure of the condition on which the claim is based, and this is why the theory is known to its adherents as the restitutionary theory of failure of consideration, or the theory of failure of consideration as an "unjust factor".

The claim in respect of a prepayment might appear more promising ground for the restitutionary conditional transfer theory, because, unlike the provision of work, a prepayment is at least a transfer capable of being reversed. However, the other objections to the restitutionary conditional transfer theory put forward above apply equally here. In particular, the theory is incompatible with the law of contract. It is true that one might make a prepayment conditional on a contract being agreed; then if no contract is agreed, the prepayment would be recoverable.[122] This looks like the restitutionary conditional transfer theory, but the claim is surely contractual.[123] In any case, this is not what happens when the plaintiff makes a prepayment pursuant to a binding contract; or at least, if any condition is attached to the prepayment, it is a part of the contract.

Moreover, the conditional transfer theory does not offer any obvious explanation of the "total failure" limitation. If failure of consideration means failure of a condition, the condition being the non-performance of the contract, it seems that the condition fails whenever the contract does not go to completion, not just when performance did not begin. Thus it is difficult to see what the significance or rationale of the "total failure" requirement could be; and accordingly proponents of the theory argue that the total failure requirement should be abandoned and that a restitutionary claim should arise from "partial failure of consideration" where the defendant has begun to perform but has not completed performance.[124] Certainly, it seems unfair, as suggested above, that the mere fact that the defendant has begun performance should preclude a claim from arising, even where the defendant has received full payment and done only a fraction of the work. Where there is "partial failure", it seems that the restitutionary conditional transfer theory would give a claim to the defendant arising from his part performance, in just the same way as for the plaintiff, i.e. a claim for "counter-restitution". The court would have to set the two claims off against each other (and against any contractual claim that would arise if one party were in breach).[125]

---

[121] This is the context in which the theory was expounded by Lord Wright in *Fibrosa Spolka Akcyjna v Fairbairn Lawson Combe Barbour Ltd* [1943] AC 32, 64–5.

[122] It is argued that *Chillingworth v Esche* [1924] 1 Ch. 97 is an example of such a claim: Birks (1983), 153.

[123] See above at 42.

[124] e.g. Birks (1993), 213; Burrows (1993), 255.

[125] As mentioned previously, it is a complex and cumbersome feature of the restitutionary conditional transfer theory that on termination of the contract one must apply two different regimes, one in contract and one in restitution, presumably to be set off against each other.

It is also argued that, although the total failure limitation may not be justified, it is at least explicable in terms of the problem of measurement, as illustrated, for example, by *Whincup v Hughes*.[126] This was a case of frustration (and would now be decided differently under statute, as considered below). The plaintiff paid the agreed price in advance for the whole six-year period of his apprenticeship with the defendant. The defendant died after only one year, and the plaintiff sought to recover back some part of the prepayment. If the defendant had been in breach, the plaintiff would have been able to claim expectation damages which would presumably have been easy to establish as the cost of an apprenticeship for the remaining period to be served; or alternatively he could in principle have claimed the prepayment as reliance loss subject to an expectation cap proved by the defendant. But here there was no expectation claim and the court rejected the possibility of any other claim. It is thought that to determine the measure of a restitutionary claim the court would have had to deduct from the prepayment the defendant's restitutionary claim for a quantum meruit for the work done by him under the contract (i.e. a claim for counter-restitution on the restitutionary approach). The main difficulty in allowing the plaintiff's claim was thought to be that it was impossible to determine what proportion of the prepayment was attributable to the supervision provided by the defendant before his death and what to the outstanding period, i.e. the pro rata price for the defendant's work before his death. Because the defendant's counter-restitutionary claim could not be measured, it would not be fair to allow the plaintiff's restitutionary claim. However, as considered above, the courts have certainly been willing to measure a quantum meruit in respect of part performance in some circumstances, and the measurement explanation of the total failure limitation is unconvincing.

Thus, as with respect to the quantum meruit, the analysis of the claim arising on a total failure of consideration in terms of the restitutionary conditional transfer theory is weak. And, again, the claim is better explained in terms of a contractual analysis under the reliance theory.

Prepayments and total failure of consideration under the reliance theory

A contractual analysis

Under the reliance theory, a contracting party has protection for his reliance interest. This means he can claim for a prepayment as a reliance loss under the contract.[127] If the defendant has not begun to rely on the contract, there is no reason in principle to allow him any claim under the contract, and so the plaintiff should be able to recover the whole of a prepayment, as a reliance loss, with-

---

[126]   (1871) LR 6 CP 104.

[127]   Atiyah has suggested that the claim arising from total failure of consideration is contractual: Atiyah (1979), 489; see also Perillo (1973).

out deduction.[128] In the sense discussed above, the prepayment received by the defendant puts him in surplus over his reliance interest.[129] It is only once the defendant incurs reliance on the agreement that he can be prejudiced by a liability to return the whole of the prepayment. This is why a claim for total failure of consideration is not subject to any cap.[130] Thus total failure of consideration should be understood to mean that the defendant has not begun to rely on the contract through contractual performance. It may be that he has begun to rely on the contract in the sense of using the prepayment for his own purposes, without beginning performance; but the prepayment is made to give the defendant security for payment so that he can begin performance, and there is no reason why the defendant should be able to invoke the contract if has relied on it without beginning performance.[131]

In accordance with the classical theory, it is normally thought that a contractual claim can arise only as against a party who has committed a breach of a duty of performance under the contract (unless a contractual liability has accrued under a payment clause), and thus that the claim arising on total failure of consideration, which can arise against a party who has not committed a breach, must be restitutionary. Under the reliance theory, in principle a contractual claim to recover a prepayment can arise where the defendant was not in breach. A case that shows that a prepayment can be recovered in contract, even by a party who was in breach, consistently with the reliance theory analysis, is *Dies v British and International Mining and Finance Co.*[132] The plaintiff contracted to buy a consignment of goods from the defendant and paid in advance, and then refused to take delivery and claimed the return of his prepayment. The plaintiff was himself in breach, but his claim was successful. The judge said that:

---

[128] It might seem by analogy with the quantum meruit that the reliance claim in respect of a prepayment should be measured in terms of the value of the counter-performance due to the plaintiff. This would mean that the reliance measure if the whole price is paid in advance would be the value to the plaintiff of complete performance by the defendant, which would normally exceed the value of the prepayment, but might not do so. But, because a payment is entirely reversible, unlike work or expenditure, there is no reason why the allocation of risk effected through the contractual valuation should be applied merely because a payment has been made in advance rather than on completion, either for the plaintiff's benefit or against him. It is not the normal function of a provision for a payment in advance to impose this risk on the plaintiff. Instead it should be imposed on the plaintiff only in so far as the defendant's contractual performance has been carried out, because this is irreversible and to the extent that it has been done the parties should bear the risk attached to contractual performance through the contractual valuation.

[129] See above at 52.

[130] The position here should be contrasted with that where the plaintiff makes a claim for a quantum meruit in respect of work done under the agreement. In that case, even where the defendant has done nothing under the agreement, there is no question of a claim arising free of the expectation measure or the contractual valuation on the basis of total failure of consideration. Whereas a payment can be reversed, leaving the defendant, where he did not begin to perform, as he was before the contract was made, and so with no prejudice to his reliance interest, work done and expenditure cannot be reversed, only paid for, and a claim for payment must invoke the contract and cannot exceed the pro rata measure under the contractual valuation.

[131] Under this analysis, one could say that the claim is restitutionary in a remedial rather than a substantive sense: see Chap. 1.

[132] [1939] 1 KB 724.

the real foundation of the right which I hold exists in the present case is . . . the right of the purchaser, derived from the terms of the contract and the principle of law applicable, to recover back his money.[133]

Thus the judge accepted that a claim to recover a prepayment could be contractual, even when the claim was made against a party who was not in breach. However, the judge took the view that the claim that he upheld was not itself a claim arising on total failure of consideration; and it is not entirely clear how he understood the doctrine of total failure of consideration.[134] But the decision demonstrates that a contractual claim can in fact do all the work of the claim arising on total failure of consideration in recovering a payment under a contract and in this sense supports the contractual analysis under the reliance theory.

The judge's contractual analysis in *Dies* has been criticised by some commentators as the application of the old implied contract fiction,[135] presumably on the supposition that, in the light of the classical theory, a genuine contractual claim cannot arise unless the defendant is in breach, or a liability has accrued under an express payment clause; but the implied contract fiction is the fiction that a claim is based on a contract where there is no contract between the parties (or where the contract is irrelevant to the issue), as in the case where a claim for restitution for a mistaken payment was said to be based on an implied contract. In *Dies* the prepayment was made pursuant to the contract and in reliance on it and no fiction is involved in saying that the claim was contractual. What really smacks of fiction is the argument that a claim arising from the breakdown of a valid contract is not contractual but restitutionary.[136]

"Partial failure of consideration"

Under this contractual analysis under the reliance theory, just as for the restitutionary analysis under the conditional transfer theory, there is no good reason to distinguish in principle between the case of total failure of consideration and cases where there has been some performance by the defendant; in other words, there is no basis for the "total failure" requirement. Under the reliance theory

---

[133] At 744, *per* Stable J.

[134] Possibly he thought, like the court in *Chandler v Webster*, as considered below at 61, that total failure of consideration referred to the case where the contract was void or rescinded: see at 744.

[135] Burrows (1993), 274.

[136] Further support for the contractual analysis of the recovery of prepayments comes from the recent case of *Pan Ocean Shipping v Creditcorp (The Trident Beauty)* [1994] 1 WLR 161. The House of Lords noted that where the plaintiff had paid an instalment in respect of the hire of a ship, and the ship was not made available for the part of the period to which the instalment related, there was a contractual claim to recover the part of the payment that related to the period for which the ship was unavailable. The court appeared to think that a separate non-contractual doctrine of failure of consideration could also sometimes arise, but it is difficult to see why any such non-contractual claim should be thought necessary once the contractual claim is recognised. The case is considered further in the next chapter, at 122.

approach, the case of total failure of consideration is merely the extreme situation where there has been no reliance by the defendant. Where there has been some degree of reliance by the defendant, the plaintiff should still have a claim in respect of the prepayment as a reliance loss, with an appropriate deduction in favour of the defendant in respect of his reliance interest, i.e. a quantum meruit. If the plaintiff was himself in breach of contract, the defendant will be entitled to the expectation measure as a proxy for the reliance interest, and the plaintiff's claim will be limited to the surplus over the defendant's expectation interest in the sense discussed above.[137]

The contractual analysis of partial failure is supported by the recent case of *Cargill International v Bungladesh Sugar & Food Industries*.[138] Here the contract contained a performance bond given by the plaintiff designed to give security for any liability that the plaintiff might incur under the contract. The defendant enforced the performance bond on the termination of the contract, and the issue was whether the plaintiff could recover any surplus of the sum paid over to the defendant under the performance bond beyond what was necessary to cover the plaintiff's liability for damages. It was held that the defendant had to return the surplus. The judge said that it was:

in the nature of a bond . . . that, in the absence of some clear words . . . there will . . . be an "accounting" between the parties . . .;[139]

and he added later:[140]

The basis upon which recovery may be made in respect of an overpayment is, I think, contractual . . . it is necessary to imply into the contract that moneys paid under the bond which exceeded the buyer's actual loss would be recoverable. . . [the term is implied] . . . as a matter of necessity or on the basis that the implication . . . was . . . obvious.

In exactly the same way, a claim to recover back a contractual prepayment is contractual, not restitutionary. In the light of the nature of the contract, and the mutual responsibility for reliance assumed by the two parties, the requirement for an "accounting" between them is to be inferred unless excluded by agreement. A claim arising on partial failure of consideration would be a matter of "accounting" in this sense.

There have been many calls for the total failure requirement to be abandoned, and a claim arising on "partial failure of consideration" to be recognised,[141] although the call is usually made from the standpoint that the claim is

---

[137] This means that the plaintiff's contractual reliance claim in respect of the prepayment may sometimes be in excess of his expectation measure, as is recognised in the case of total failure of consideration. Generally this will be the case where it was a bad contract for the plaintiff. The plaintiff then partially escapes from his bad bargain, but without denying the defendant the benefit of the contractual valuation; cf above at 46.

[138] [1996] 4 All ER 563.

[139] At 568.

[140] At 573.

[141] e.g. Goff & Jones (1998), 552; Burrows (1993), 255; Skelton, 33.

restitutionary not contractual. The academic argument has some judicial support, although as yet there is no authority.[142] The effect on the law envisaged under the restitutionary theory is roughly equivalent to the effect under the contractual analysis under the reliance theory—the two theories are clearly directed at broadly the same defects in the present law.[143] However, first, it is open to argument whether the restitutionary claim would be subject to the contractual valuation, and, secondly, the restitutionary regime would operate in parallel to a contractual regime separately providing damages for breach of contract in a case where one party was in breach. Under the reliance theory regime, the claims are necessarily in accordance with the contractual valuation, and there is only one regime, which would involve, in cases where one party was in breach, a presumption in favour of the other party to protect his expectation interest.

A restitutionary claim under the reliance theory?

On the argument above, the reliance theory shows that the claim arising on total failure of consideration can be explained as a contractual claim, and this, it is suggested, is the best explanation—indeed the only coherent explanation. Nevertheless, it seems likely that the claim arising on total failure of consideration has not traditionally been understood as a contractual claim, but as a restitutionary claim. This is the likely implication of the form of the claim as money had and received; and, also, as discussed above, the implication of the fact that the claim arose in circumstances that could not on any account be understood as involving a breach of duty by the defendant, and was not confined to the expectation measure.

But it is important to note that, if the claim was understood as a restitutionary claim, it need not necessarily have been understood, in the sense of the restitutionary conditional transfer theory, as a claim arising from the failure of a condition. There is a more plausible (although still unsustainable) sense in which the claim might have been thought to be restitutionary.[144] Under the reliance theory, the contract serves to protect the parties' reliance on it. If the defendant, who has received a prepayment, has not relied on the contract at all, one might think of the contract as being in a sense unenforceable by him, or void so far as he is concerned. Then one can say that the plaintiff has a restitutionary claim to recover the payment just as if the payment had been made under a void or unenforceable contract.[145] However, once the defendant begins to perform, the contract is enforceable by him and the restitutionary claim is precluded. This will be referred to as the restitutionary claim under the reliance theory.

---

[142] *Westdeutsche Landesbank Girozentrale v Islington LBC* [1996] AC 669, 682, *per* Lord Goff; *Goss v Chilcott* [1996] AC 788, 798, *per* Lord Goff. These cases concerned void or unenforceable contracts, and this is a crucial distinction on the analysis presented here, although not under the restitutionary conditional transfer theory, as considered in the next chapter.

[143] Above 53–54.

[144] This was the approach adopted in Jaffey (1998*a*).

[145] See further Chap. 6.

Like the conditional transfer theory, this analysis ultimately fails, because it discloses no vitiating factor. Whereas under a void contract the plaintiff makes a mistake if he makes a transfer under the void contract thinking that it is valid, the plaintiff makes no mistake when he makes a transfer under a contract that the defendant has not yet relied on. But this analysis of the claim as a restitutionary claim under the reliance theory rather than under the conditional transfer theory does provide an explanation for the traditional "total failure" condition, because the rationale for the claim clearly limits it to a case where the defendant has not performed the contract at all, whereas neither the contractual analysis nor the restitutionary conditional transfer analysis provides any rationale for the limitation.[146] Furthermore, as considered next, the explanation in terms of the restitutionary claim under the reliance theory makes more sense than the restitutionary conditional transfer theory of the expression "failure of consideration".

"Failure of consideration" and the contractual doctrine of consideration

Consideration is generally regarded as a contractual concept. According to the modern exchange doctrine of consideration, there is said to be consideration for a contract if the agreement involves an exchange or reciprocal benefit. In the absence of consideration in this sense there is no valid contract. But it is clear that "total failure of consideration", as the expression is used in relation to the recovery of a prepayment, does not mean that the exchange doctrine of consideration is not satisfied; it applies where a payment was made under a contract for which there was good consideration in this sense, but where no part of the reciprocal performance was ever actually carried out.

The point was in issue in *Fibrosa Spolka Akcyjna v Fairbairn Lawson Combe Barbour*,[147] and the treatment by the House of Lords in that case of the earlier case of *Chandler v Webster*.[148] In *Chandler v Webster* the plaintiff paid in advance for the use of a room with a view over a coronation procession. The contract was frustrated by the cancellation of the procession, and the plaintiff sued to recover the sum paid in advance. The court held that no claim to recover the prepayment for total failure of consideration was available because a valid contract for good consideration had been made. The court interpreted "total failure of consideration" in a contractual sense, to mean that the contract was voidable or had been "wiped out".[149] But *Chandler v Webster* was overruled in *Fibrosa*.[150] In *Fibrosa* the Polish plaintiff paid in advance for machinery to be

---

[146] The measurement argument mentioned above would apply in the same way for both, but is implausible, as suggested above.
[147] [1943] AC 32.
[148] [1904] 1 KB 493.
[149] At 499.
[150] [1943] AC 32.

supplied by the English defendant. Before delivery the contract was frustrated by the invasion of Poland in the Second World War. The plaintiff sued for repayment of the payment in advance on a total failure of consideration. The House of Lords held that there was a total failure because the defendant had performed no part of the contract; the claim was not based on showing that there was no consideration in the sense that there was not to be an exchange under the terms of the agreement, which was clearly not the case. Lord Simon VC said:

> [W]hen one is considering the law of failure of consideration and of the quasi-contractual right to recover money on that ground, it is, generally speaking, not the promise which is referred to as the consideration, but the performance of the promise.[151]

If "failure of consideration" does not mean that the agreement does not involve an exchange, in accordance with the exchange doctrine of consideration, it might seem that it does not refer to the contractual doctrine of consideration at all. Thus *Fibrosa* is understood (and was understood by the court) to mean that the doctrine of total failure of consideration is a restitutionary doctrine that applies where the contract has not been performed by the defendant, and more particularly that it should be understood in accordance with the conditional transfer theory.[152] But, as argued above, there is no plausible basis for saying that non-performance of a contract can constitute the failure of a condition for the purposes of a non-contractual claim; and there is a more plausible interpretation of "failure of consideration". In its original sense, on one view at least, to say that there was consideration for an agreement was simply to say that there was a ground for enforcing it in law as a legal contract.[153] In this sense, "failure of consideration" implies that the contract is void or unenforceable for some reason. It was by a later usage that "consideration" came to be used more specifically to refer to the exchange element itself,[154] as a particular requirement for enforceability. Furthermore, it is clear that there is a strand of authority, possibly quite ancient, which holds that the plaintiff's reliance on an agreement or promise constituted good consideration,[155] and this suggests that a total absence of reliance on a contract might have been understood to constitute a total failure of consideration.[156] This is consistent with the interpretation of the claim arising on the total failure of consideration as a restitutionary claim

---

[151] [1943] AC 32, 48.

[152] e.g. Lord Simon at 48, Lord Wright at 64–5.

[153] Atiyah (1986) 181; Birks (1989a), 223. In fact it remains true nowadays that an agreement is sometimes enforced even though there is no exchange involved. Conflict with the contractual doctrine of consideration is avoided because the agreement is not described as a contract or thought of as being enforced through the law of contract: e.g., Atiyah (1976). For example, this is arguably the case with respect to certain types of estoppel, fiduciary relationships, liability for mistatements and "equitable fraud".

[154] *Ibid.*

[155] Milson (1981), 357; Atiyah (1979), 184ff; Collins (1997), 68ff.

[156] It is true that on this interpretation "total" in "total failure of consideration" is redundant, failure of consideration meaning total non-performance.

under the reliance theory as explained above.[157] On this approach, the difficulty in *Chandler v Webster* and *Fibrosa* arose from confusion between the modern exchange doctrine of consideration and an older form of consideration doctrine, not between a contractual and a non-contractual sense of consideration.

This argument is not designed to support the interpretation of the claim arising on a total failure of consideration as a restitutionary claim under the reliance theory; as argued above, this interpretation is flawed because it does not disclose a vitiating factor, and the contractual analysis under the reliance theory is to be preferred. But the argument is useful in combating the idea that failure of consideration must refer to failure of condition if it does not refer to the exchange doctrine of consideration. Furthermore, this approach is consistent with the fact that "failure of consideration" has always been used to describe the ground for restitution where a payment has been made under a void contract, as well as where a valid contract was totally unperformed. The meaning of failure of consideration in relation to void contracts arose in the recent case of *Westdeutsche Landesbank Girozentrale v Islington LBC*,[158] which is considered in Chapter 6.

When is there total failure?

There has been some controversy over what amounts to "total failure" of consideration. On one view, there is a total failure where the defendant has done nothing under the contract (the no-reliance test), and on the other view there is a total failure of consideration where no benefit has been conferred on the plaintiff, even if the defendant has done some work under it (the no-benefit test). The no-benefit test appears to be the conventional understanding.

Often the no-benefit test and the no-reliance test will correspond, because the plaintiff is benefited just as the defendant incurs reliance. For example, this will be the case where the defendant's performance consists of delivering a standard product to the plaintiff.[159] But sometimes the defendant will do part of his contractual performance before any benefit is conferred. In two recent such cases, the House of Lords preferred the no-reliance test to the no-benefit test and declined to find a total failure of consideration. In both cases, *Hyundai Heavy*

---

[157] Cf Atiyah (1979), 181.

[158] [1994] 4 All ER 890 (Hobhouse J and CA), [1994] 2 All ER 961 (HL).

[159] Any work that the defendant has done in connection with obtaining or making and preparing the good is not work done in reliance on the contract because, since the good is a standard one, it is not referable to any particular contract; see e.g. *Giles v Edwards* (1797) 7 Term Rep 181. There has been controversy over cases, in particular *Rowland v Divall* [1923] 2 KB 500, where the plaintiff has been permitted to recover the contract price instead of damages after having had the goods for some considerable time. Here the plaintiff bought a car from the defendant that did not actually belong to him and was permitted to recover the contract price instead of damages after the car was restored to its true owner a number of months after he had acquired it from the defendant. But this should be understood as a case where the contract could be rescinded, not discharged for breach (the two are conflated in the case), so that the total failure requirement for valid contracts would not apply; indeed, this is explicit in the judgment of Scrutton LJ. See further Chapter 6

Shipping v Papadopoulos[160] and *Stocznia Gdanska v Latvian Shipping*,[161] a contract to construct and deliver a ship had terminated before delivery but after the ship had been partly constructed, and the issue was whether the buyer could claim that there had been a total failure of consideration because he had received no benefit from the contract. In both cases it was held that there was no total failure of consideration.[162] This caused some difficulty to the court, which in both cases attempted to distinguish between contracts for the sale of goods where the conventional no-benefit test would apply, and contracts for work and materials, where the no-reliance test would apply, but no basis for such a distinction was offered.[163]

Although this issue is important under the law as traditionally understood, both the contractual reliance theory approach and the restitutionary conditional transfer approach reject the total failure requirement. Consequently the question whether the no-benefit or the no-reliance test should apply is not a crucial issue as between the two. However, the analysis of the claim arising on total failure of consideration as a restitutionary claim under the reliance theory, which is the only analysis that provides a rationale for the total failure requirement, clearly supports the no-reliance test. Advocates of the restitutionary conditional transfer theory have preferred a no-benefit test.[164] This seems to be because, if the total failure limitation has arisen from the measurement problem,[165] it should relate to the case where the defendant has no quantum meruit in respect of his work, and this, according to a restitutionary approach, is taken to be where the plaintiff has not received any benefit.[166] Thus some commentators have argued that the approach in *Hyundai* and *Stocznia* is wrong because it is inconsistent with the no-benefit test.[167] Others have adopted a "deemed benefit" approach;[168] this fiction has been criticised above.

In practice, given the lack of any sound rationale for it, the courts are likely to interpret the total failure requirement in such a way as to cause least unfairness. Thus in a case like *Fibrosa* (before the statutory reform of remedies arising on frustration), where, if a claim had not been allowed, the defendant would have ended up with a large profit since it seems that the prepayment received

---

[160] [1980] 1 WLR 1129.

[161] [1998] 1 WLR 574.

[162] The same view is found in *Baltic Shipping Company v Dillon (The Mikhail Lermontov)* (1993) 176 CLR 344, 390–1 *per* McHugh J. On the other hand in the older case of *Fibrosa*, it was held that there was a total failure of consideration because no benefit had been received, even though expenditure had been incurred (although it was not entirely clear whether this expenditure was specifically referable to the contract).

[163] *Hyundai* is sometimes compared to *Dies*, above, because in both cases the party claiming total failure was in breach. In *Dies*, the contract was for the supply of goods, not for work and materials, and so on the repudiation of the contract one can say that there had been no reliance on it.

[164] Burrows (1993), 256; Skelton, 24–5.

[165] Birks (1989a), 228–9.

[166] In fact, as noted above, it is clear that a quantum meruit does sometimes arise in the absence of any such benefit, which has led to the idea of a deemed benefit.

[167] Burrows (1993), 256.

[168] Birks (1989a), 237.

greatly exceeded its small measure of reliance,[169] and the plaintiff a large loss in return for no benefit at all, the court might be inclined to hold that there was a total failure of consideration notwithstanding some degree of reliance. But in a case where the plaintiff has an alternative claim in damages, it is right to deny the claim for total failure unless the no-reliance test is satisfied, in order to protect the defendant's interest in receiving payment for the work it has actually done, as was held in *Hyundai* and *Stocznia*.

Forfeiture of a prepayment made by the party in breach

Where the plaintiff has made a payment in advance, and the contract comes to an early end, the plaintiff should have a prima facie contractual reliance claim to recover the prepayment, subject to an appropriate deduction to protect the defendant's interest, as discussed above. But sometimes it seems that the contractual provision for a prepayment by the plaintiff is actually intended to place the risk of non-completion on the plaintiff. This is when the prepayment is said to be an irrecoverable deposit or forfeit.[170] The effect is analogous to a provision denying the plaintiff a quantum meruit claim in respect of work done under the contract unless the contract is actually completed, as considered above in relation to *Sumpter v Hedges*.[171]

A provision for an irrecoverable deposit might be intended to overcome the difficulty for the defendant of proving the full measure of loss. Whether this is plausible will depend on the size of the deposit, but in principle there seems no objection to such a provision. Alternatively, the provision might be intended to create the threat of a penalty in order to coerce the plaintiff into performing, by denying him his reliance loss even if this leaves the defendant with a windfall surplus over his reliance interest. Such a provision would be expected to apply only where the plaintiff's breach was within his control, and certainly not on frustration. Forfeiture provisions of this sort are open to objection as penalty clauses, and the courts have exercised a discretion not to enforce them.[172] Generally, the objection to penalty and forfeiture clauses is that inflicting punishment is not the function of the civil courts. The difficulty with the objection is that no punishment is ever available for breach of contract even where it is appropriate, and so it is not surprising that contracting parties should have tried to create a deterrent to breach by express provision.[173]

---

[169] In fact it is not clear whether any work referrable to contract: see McKendrick (1991), 150.

[170] *Mayson v Clouet* [1924] AC 980.

[171] [1898] 1 QB 673; see above 51–53.

[172] *Stockloser v Johnson* [1954] 1 QB 476; see generally Beatson (1991), 45–77. The jurisdiction apparently does not apply to the analogous case of non-recovery of a quantum meruit by virtue of a lump sum payment clause as in *Sumpter v Hedges*.

[173] See further Chaps. 11 and 12.

The law on remedies arising on frustration, which is governed by the Law Reform (Frustrated Contracts) Act 1943, provides an opportunity for further discussion of the issues considered above. There are understood to have been two types of unfairness in the common law that the statute was intended to overcome. One is where the plaintiff carried out work for the defendant (which may have included incurring expenditure) under a contract that provided for a lump sum payment on completion only, and the contract was frustrated before completion. Then the plaintiff was not entitled to any payment for the work he had done before frustration. This is illustrated by *Cutter v Powell*.[174] The other type is where the plaintiff paid in advance and the contract was frustrated before he had received the full benefit due to him under the contract. Then, as *Whincup v Hughes*[175] illustrates, the plaintiff could recover nothing, unless he could show total failure of consideration, in which case he could recover his prepayment in full. It appears also that, if the defendant had done some work or incurred expenditure the plaintiff could still recover the prepayment in full if no benefit had actually been conferred on the plaintiff.[176] This caused unfairness of the first sort, the defendant having done work or incurred expenditure for which he had no right to payment.

Frustration and the reliance theory

The underlying problem in these cases, as has been argued above, is the classical theory, which appears to deny the possibility of any claim other than a claim arising from breach of duty or an accrued liability under a payment clause. As already discussed above, on the reliance theory approach a party should have a prima facie reliance claim in respect of his work done or loss incurred under the contract before frustration, including any prepayment made, to the extent that his reliance interest has not been satisfied before frustration by the receipt of payment or performance. Overall, a party should have a claim so far as necessary to equalise the extent to which the two parties fall short of the satisfaction of their respective reliance interests.[177] To determine the remedy, the court would have to ascertain the prima facie reliance claim, or surplus over the reliance interest, of each party, and then the equalising payment necessary to bring together the parties' respective shortfalls from the satisfaction of their

---

[174] (1795) 6 TR 320.

[175] (1871) LR 6 CP 78.

[176] *Fibrosa Spolka Akcyjna v Fairbairn Lawson Combe Barbour Ltd* [1943] AC 32; but see 63–5 above.

[177] It may be possible for there to be an aggregate surplus on frustration rather than aggregate shortfall but there is no obvious reason for it to be apportioned once the reliance interest has been satisfied: see below with respect to *BP v Hunt* n 201 .

reliance interests. A rule of equalisation in this sense follows naturally from the reliance theory interpretation of the contract as involving the assumption by each party of responsibility for the other's reliance interest.[178] It amounts to an "accounting" between the parties.[179]

Generally one can say that one party will do work and incur expenditure (i.e. supply goods or services) for which he is to receive payment, and the other is to make a payment for which he will receive a benefit. The former will be described as the Worker and the latter as the Payer. The Worker will have a prima facie claim for a proportion of the whole payment due to him, corresponding to the proportion of the work he has done,[180] i.e. in the pro rata measure, less any payment received. If the full payment has been received the Worker will have a surplus over his reliance interest (since ex hypothesi he has not completed his performance). The Payer's position can be more difficult. If the Payer has paid and the work can be completed, his prima facie reliance claim can be taken as the cost of completion. This will put the Payer in the position he would have been in if the contract had been completed, and this can be taken to satisfy the reliance interest. It is usually difficult to value the benefit received in any other way, because it is usually only of any value if the work is completed. If the Payer has not yet paid, he will have a surplus over his reliance interest in the measure of the contract price less the cost of completion. If the work cannot be completed, it may be best just to disregard the benefit—or the effect of the part performance, as it might then be better to describe it—so that the prima facie reliance claim is just for any money already paid under the contract. In other situations, different approaches may be called for.[181]

Thus, in a case like *Cutter v Powell*, the plaintiff Worker has provided a certain proportion of the whole work due from him. His prima facie reliance claim is the pro rata measure with respect to the price for complete performance. The defendant Payer's prima facie reliance claim is the cost of completion less the unpaid price. Say the plaintiff was due to be paid £100 and had completed half of the total work due from him, and the defendant was forced to pay £60 to someone else to take over from the plaintiff for the rest of the voyage. The plaintiff's prima facie claim is for £50, and the defendant has a surplus over his reliance interest, or negative claim, as it were, of £40 (the cost of completion less the unpaid price). The equalising payment is £45 from the defendant to the plaintiff, leaving each party to bear half of the overall net shortfall of £10. In a case like *Whincup v Hughes*, say the plaintiff Payer has paid £100 in advance for a five-year apprenticeship, and the defendant Worker has died after two years. Say the plaintiff can pay £70 to finish off his apprenticeship with someone else.

---

[178] One might argue that equalisation should be in terms of the proportionate shortfall, but this issue will not be pursued.

[179] See n 169 above.

[180] Here the possibility of opportunity cost, in the full expectation measure, is disregarded.

[181] e.g., if part performance cannot be completed, it may have to be dismantled, and this will introduce different considerations.

Then his prima facie reliance claim is £70. If the £100 received by the defendant can be attributed proportionately across the whole five-year period, the defendant has a negative reliance claim or surplus over his reliance interest of £60. The overall net shortfall is £10 and, if each party is to bear half of this, the equalising payment is £65 from the defendant to the plaintiff. In a case like *Fibrosa*, the plaintiff Payer has paid, say, £100 in advance for machinery. The defendant Worker has done work on the machinery, representing, say, 10 per cent of the total work involved, but the plaintiff has not received any part of the benefit. The plaintiff's prima facie reliance claim is for £100, and the defendant has a surplus of £90. The overall net shortfall is £10, and if this is to be shared the equalising payment is £95 to the plaintiff. These illustrations, which are all drawn from cases that preceded the Act, are obviously rather artificial, but they show how one would expect the reliance theory to be applied in principle. No doubt there can be practical difficulties in applying such principles in some circumstances, but this does not in itself cast any doubt on their validity as the principles that justify and guide the determination of the remedy.

The Law Reform (Frustrated Contracts) Act 1943 and the reliance theory

The Law Reform (Frustrated Contracts) Act 1943 leaves considerable room for argument over the principles that underlie the Act and should govern its interpretation. As one might expect from an English statute, it seems most likely to have been drafted with a view to particular defects in the common law, exposed by the facts of particular cases, rather than on the basis of any carefully thought-out theory. Naturally this means that it is likely to have anomalous effects in some other situations. There are two important provisions in the Act. Section 1(2) reads as follows:

> All sums paid or payable to any party in pursuance of the contract before . . . the time of discharge . . . shall, in the case of sums so paid, be recoverable from him . . . and, in the case of sums so payable, cease to be so payable: provided that, if the party to whom the sums were so paid or payable incurred expenses before the time of discharge in or for the purpose of the performance of the contract, the court may, if it considers it just to do so, having regard to all the circumstances of the case, allow him to retain or, as the case may be, recover the whole or any part of the sums so paid or payable, not being an amount in excess of the expenses so incurred.

Section 1(3) reads as follows:

> Where any party to the contract has, by reason of anything done by any other party thereto in, or for the purpose of, the performance of the contract, obtained a valuable benefit (other than a payment of money to which the last foregoing subsection applies) before the time of discharge, there shall be recoverable from him by the said other party such sum (if any), not exceeding the value of the said benefit to the party obtaining it, as the court considers just, having regard to all the circumstances of the case and, in particular—(a) the amount of any expenses incurred before the time of

discharge by the benefited party . . . including any sums paid or payable by him to any other party in pursuance of the contract and retained or recoverable by that party under the last foregoing subsection, and (b) the effect, in relation to the said benefit, of the circumstances giving rise to the frustration of the contract.

The principles underlying these two provisions have been the subject of some controversy.[182] They are not aptly drafted to give effect to the reliance theory analysis above, but can be so construed for most purposes. On this basis, subsection (2) allows the plaintiff Payer a claim where the equalising payment is due to him, and subsection (3) allows the plaintiff Worker a claim where the equalising payment is due to him. For example, subsection (2) would apply where the plaintiff Payer has made a payment and not received the full benefit due in return, as in *Fibrosa*. The plaintiff has a prima facie reliance claim in respect of his prepayment, to be weighed against the defendant's prima facie claim in respect of his work done and expenses. "Expenses" in the statute is effectively to be construed to include payment for work done.[183] Thus in the subsection the upper limit to the deduction from the plaintiff's claim to recover the prepayment should be equated with the defendant's prima facie reliance claim, and the actual amount of the award with the equalising payment.

However, the plaintiff Payer's prima facie reliance claim should also take account of the extent to which his reliance interest has been partially satisfied by the receipt of a benefit under the contract. For example in *Whincup v Hughes* the plaintiff had made a payment and the defendant had done part of the work required, as in *Fibrosa*, but in *Whincup* the plaintiff had also received part of the benefit of the contract, and this should reduce his prima facie reliance claim, as considered above. Under the Act, however, the effect of the benefit has to be considered separately in subsection (3), so that to deal with a case like *Whincup* the two subsections have to be applied together. The Payer has a claim under subsection (2), and then the Worker a counterclaim under subsection (3) to offset the Payer's excess under subsection (2). This procedure was anticipated (although no doubt not quite in these terms), because subsection (3) refers to the possibility of an antecedent claim under subsection (2). But it is not ideal because it is unhelpful to think that there is a claim based on the prepayment to the Worker and a distinct counterclaim based on the benefit received by the Payer, as opposed to a single exercise in balancing the parties' respective reliance interests overall.

Subsection (3) would apply to a case like *Cutter v Powell*, where the plaintiff Worker has a prima facie reliance claim based on his work done, and the defendant Payer has received a benefit through part performance of the contract. The measure of the claim under subsection (3) was described by Goff J in *BP v Hunt*[184] as the "just sum", which in accordance with the subsection is some

---

[182] See e.g. the discussion in McKendrick (1991).

[183] See s.1(4). Payment for work done is part of the reliance interest as considered above: see above 30.

[184] [1979] 1 WLR 783; upheld [1981] 1 WLR 232 (CA); [1983] 2 AC 352 (HL).

amount less than the "value of the said benefit" received by the Payer, which the judge referred to as the "maximum amount". In accordance with the reliance theory, the value of the benefit, or maximum amount, should be understood as the surplus over the reliance interest, which, measured in terms of the contractual valuation, will normally be the contract price less the cost of completion, assuming no payment has been made.[185] The just sum should be the equalising payment in the light of this surplus and the Worker's prima facie reliance claim.

There are certain difficulties in reconciling the reliance theory approach with subsection (3); or, in other words, one might say that the subsection is defective in certain respects in the light of the reliance theory analysis. First, the equalising payment under the reliance theory depends on the plaintiff Worker's prima facie reliance claim as well as the defendant Payer's surplus; but in providing for the payment of the "just sum", the subsection makes no reference to any interest of the plaintiff that the claim is understood to satisfy, merely the defendant's benefit. However, in assessing the just sum, the court will presumably examine the work done and expenses incurred by the plaintiff and consider what measure of payment would be appropriate for it in the light of the contract.

A more important problem is that the measure of the plaintiff's claim—the "just sum"—cannot exceed the "maximum amount" under the statute, whereas the appropriate equalising payment under the reliance theory may well exceed the defendant's surplus over his reliance interest, because the equalising payment may leave both parties with a shortfall. The difficulty will arise where the work done by the Worker has not yet given rise to a benefit to the Payer, or has given rise to only a small benefit to him relative to the extent of work carried out by the Worker. More precisely, if the Worker's prima facie reliance claim is at least twice the value of the benefit to the Payer, then the equalising payment will exceed the value of the benefit (i.e. the surplus). For example, consider a case like *Fibrosa*, where work is done[186] but no benefit has accrued from it to the Payer, but assume that (contrary to the actual position in *Fibrosa*) no payment has been made in advance. The Worker has a prima facie reliance claim in respect of his work and expenditure, and the value of the benefit to the Payer is nil. The equalising payment ought to be half of the prima facie reliance claim, but in fact no claim is permitted at all under subsection (3). On the other hand, as considered above, where there is a payment in advance, as in the case of *Fibrosa* itself, the Worker's prima facie reliance claim is taken into account by way of a deduction of the Payer's claim under subsection (2). There is no apparent justification for this asymmetry. Although an agreement for pre-payment or post-payment is designed to allocate certain risks, it is surely not designed to allocate the risk of frustration.[187] The point is illustrated by *Gamerco v*

---

[185] If a payment has been made it should be understood to reduce the surplus, as provided for under the subs.

[186] But see above n 169.

[187] McKendrick (1991), 158.

ICM/Fair Warning,[188] where the plaintiff pop promoter was allowed to recover the full amount of a prepayment to the defendant pop group under s 1(2) when the concert was cancelled as a result of a frustrating event, but had no claim in respect of expenses incurred in preparation, which had not conferred any benefit on the defendant.

In *BP v Hunt*, Goff J considered that ostensibly "benefit" for the purposes of subsection (3) could be taken to mean either the "end product" of the work done, or the work done itself. He thought that in principle the latter construction was preferable, but he accepted that (for most purposes) the true construction of the Act was that the benefit was the "end product".[189] One would have thought that it would be quite clear that the work done in conferring a benefit is distinct from the benefit it confers, and that sometimes work is done in advance of any benefit actually being received by the other party. Furthermore, not every benefit actually conferred is readily described as an "end product", because some benefits are in the form of an experience that has no lasting form, although in *BP v Hunt* the benefit was in fact an "end product". Presumably treating the work done as the benefit means deeming the Payer to have received a benefit in the value of the prima facie reliance measure of the Worker in respect of the work done, irrespective of the extent to which the benefit of the work has actually accrued to the Payer.[190] The fictional treatment of work done as a benefit under subsection (3) would sometimes alleviate the problem that in a particular case the just sum should exceed the maximum amount, but it would not generally solve it. For example, say work is done by the Worker such as to generate a prima facie reliance claim of £100, but the Payer has actually received no benefit from it. The equalising payment ought to be £50, but this is precluded by the statute, because the value of the benefit received—the maximum amount—is nil. If the Payer is deemed to have received a benefit in the measure of £100, then the equalising payment will be £100, which is incorrect also.[191] What is necessary is that the reliance incurred through work and the benefit conferred as a result should be recognised as distinct, and the equalising payment has to be allowed to exceed the value of the benefit. It seems likely that this difficulty was overlooked because the issue did not arise in the leading cases like *Cutter v Powell*, *Fibrosa* and *Whincup v Hughes*. Possibly instead it was due to restitutionary thinking, which, by ignoring the reliance interest, tends to promote the same confusion.

Subsection (3) explicitly deals with the case where the benefit received is destroyed by the frustrating event, by requiring the court, in subsection (3)(b), to take into account "the effect, in relation to the said benefit, of the circumstances giving rise to the frustration of the contract". This seems to have been

---

[188] [1995] 1 WLR 1226. See Clark (1996).
[189] [1979] 1 WLR 783, 801–3.
[190] Cf above at 47.
[191] The fiction might be closer to the correct result where some part of the benefit has actually been received.

drafted with an eye to the facts of *Appleby v Myers*.[192] Here the plaintiff Worker was to make and install machinery in the defendant Payer's factory. After the plaintiff had done most of the work, but before the time when payment was due under the contract, the factory was destroyed by fire so that the work could not be completed and the contract was frustrated. The plaintiff was not allowed any claim, in accordance with *Cutter v Powell* and the entire contract rule. Under subsection (3), one would think that the defendant in *Appleby v Myers* had received a benefit at the time of frustration, measured by the payment due less the cost of completion (this is the measure, even though the work could not, as it turned out, be completed). In *BP v Hunt* Goff J thought that the effect of subsection (3)(b) in a case where the frustrating effect was to destroy the benefit would be to reduce the "maximum amount" to nil and so eliminate the possibility of any claim. This appears to preclude any claim on the facts of *Appleby v Myers*.

Goff J's interpretation of the provision seems to be the natural construction of the Act, because the Act treats the value of the benefit received as the upper limit to the claim, and if the effect of the frustrating event on the value of the benefit is to be taken into account, it seems to reduce this upper limit. But it would be fairer, as Treitel has pointed out,[193] to interpret the proviso as reducing the just sum rather than the maximum amount, so allowing some measure of payment for the work; after all, it may be right to require the Worker to bear some of the consequences of the destruction by reducing the just sum,[194] but there is no reason why he should always bear the whole burden of it. It should be noted, however, that Treitel's argument amounts to recognising an interest in payment arising from reliance, irrespective of benefit, and so implies that the just sum should always be permitted to exceed the "maximum amount", in order to deal with the case where at the time of frustration the value of the benefit was disproportionately small compared to the amount of work so far done, whether or not this was due to the frustrating event.

The Act and restitutionary principles

In *BP v Hunt*, Goff J thought that the Act should be interpreted on the basis of restitutionary principles, and this view has also been adopted by some commentators (although not by the Court of Appeal in *BP v Hunt*).[195] It may be, as suggested above, that a restitutionary approach has seemed necessary or appropriate because the classical theory seems unable to explain claims that do not arise from a breach of contract. Goff J's view was that a single principle of

---

[192] (1867) LR 2 CP 651.

[193] Treitel (1999), 853.

[194] Although one might think that in a case like *Appleby v Myers* the defendant factory owner should bear the whole loss to his own factory.

[195] Goff & Jones (1998), 555ff; Birks (1989a), 249ff; Burrows (1993), 287.

restitution for unjust enrichment underlies both subsections, the difference between them being that subsection (2) deals with benefits in the form of money and subsection (3) with benefits of other kinds.[196] The single principle appears to combine the claim to reverse a vitiated transfer and the claim for payment for work done, subsection (2) bearing more similarity to the former and subsection (3) to the latter.

For the reasons discussed earlier in the chapter, it is unhelpful to think in terms of any non-contractual claim arising on frustration. There has been no vitiated transfer because the contract was valid. And generally payments or transfers under an agreement are not made conditionally, and if they are the condition takes effect under the contract and cannot be the basis for any non-contractual claim under the restitutionary conditional transfer theory. Also, if the claim arising on frustration is non-contractual, an acute difficulty arises with respect to the valuation of benefits received, as discussed earlier in this chapter (except where the benefit is in the form of money). For example, if a contract required a house to be decorated in a way that is attractive to the Payer but is liable to be unappealing to anyone else and so not to increase the value of the house,[197] the only feasible basis for saying that the Payer has received a benefit is likely to be to measure what he has received in terms of the extent to which it has satisfied the contractual reliance interest, i.e. in terms of the cost of completion.[198]

The unusual facts of *BP v Hunt*,[199] which concerned money benefits, do not provide much illumination. The defendant had an oil concession for a territory in Libya. He agreed with the plaintiff company that the plaintiff would develop the concession at its own expense; in return the two would share the oil produced equally, but the plaintiff would get in addition 3/8 of the proceeds of the defendant's share of oil until the plaintiff had recouped the costs of development. However, after a few years, the concession was expropriated by the Libyan government, frustrating the contract. The plaintiff had not yet recouped the expenses of development, but the defendant was left with quite a large profit from the venture, through the oil sold before the expropriation.[200] Under subsection (3) the plaintiff was allowed a claim in respect of the benefit received. The measure was the amount necessary to make up the plaintiff's loss on the contract, but no more, even though this still left the defendant with a large profit on the contract. It is difficult to see, on a restitutionary approach, why the defendant should be allowed to keep the whole of the overall profit on the venture, leaving the plaintiff merely with no net loss. One might argue that the decision

---

[196] The division is supposed to reflect the evidential differences between money and benefits: *BP v Hunt* [1979] 1 WLR 783, 799 *per* Goff J; Birks (1989*a*), 249ff; Burrows (1993) 283ff.

[197] An example used by Goff J in *BP v Hunt* [1979] 1 WLR 783, 803.

[198] As discussed above, it is difficult to see what the basis would be for using the contractual valuation for a non-contractual claim.

[199] The facts are simplified.

[200] This was taken to be the benefit received, because the increased value of the concession due to its development by the plaintiff was lost through the expropriation.

is consistent with the reliance theory, in operating only to eliminate the plaintiff's reliance loss, but arguably the reliance theory would also require some further return for the plaintiff.[201] The reason for denying any further return seems to have been that the profits on the contract were entirely speculative and the plaintiff was taking the risk of no return. But the plaintiff took the risk that no oil would be found, not the risk of expropriation, and the field had proved potentially lucrative.

The main problem with the Act, which was mentioned above, is also a defect of a restitutionary analysis: this is the lack of recognition of reliance as the basis for a claim irrespective of benefit. As discussed above, subsection (3) does not recognise reliance as an independent factor distinct from the benefit that it can generate, and so precludes a claim where no or no sufficient benefit has been conferred through the work. The presumption that a claim can arise only when a benefit is received is a characteristic defect of a restitutionary analysis in relation to contract, and here, as elsewhere, it has prompted the resort to a fiction that reliance or work done is itself a benefit.[202] As noted above, even apart from the invidiousness of fictions, it is unsuccessful, because what is required is a distinction between the reliance and the benefit resulting from it, the former being relevant to the Worker's prima facie reliance claim and the benefit to the Payer's surplus.

To some extent subsection (2) provides protection for reliance incurred through work done in conferring a benefit, even when no benefit has yet been conferred, in the form of the deduction in respect of the Worker's reliance from the Payer's claim to recover a prepayment. This creates an asymmetry, as mentioned above, between the case where the Worker is paid in advance and the case where the Worker is paid on completion. The fact that the Worker is confined to a "passive" reliance claim in response to the Payer's claim to recover a prepayment might seem explicable under a restitutionary analysis as an example of the change of position defence.[203] But the change of position defence does not explain the operation of the subsection.[204] The expenses do not have to be incurred in reliance on the payment, but in reliance on the agreement. Thus the proviso operates where the Worker incurred reliance before the payment was received.[205] Conversely, the subsection limits protection to reliance incurred through contractual performance, whereas a change of position defence would

---

[201] Arguably there is no need to have a transfer to equalise surpluses where there is an overall surplus, as opposed to equalising shortfalls; but the measure of the reliance interest—the prima facie reliance claim—should allow for payment over and above actual expenditure or other loss as a return on labour and capital.

[202] Cf above at 47.

[203] *BP v Hunt* [1979] 1 WLR 783, 800 *per* Goff J. The change of position defence is considered in Chap. 7.

[204] Burrows (1993), 284–5; McKendrick (1991), 156–9.

[205] Even if the payment was never received, provided that it was due. Furthermore the Worker is protected in respect of work done, not just loss as under change of position.

presumably apply to any expenditure in reliance on receipt.[206] Furthermore, the subsection envisages apportionment of the measure of the Worker's reliance as between the Worker and the Payer; the measure of his reliance is the maximum limit to the deduction from the Payer's claim, not the automatic measure of the deduction. But, if the rationale were change of position, the Worker should in principle be able to shift the whole of his reliance loss to the Payer; there would be no basis for apportionment.[207] Apportionment, or equalisation, or "accounting", is appropriate under a contract, as argued above, because it reflects the responsibility assumed by both parties for the reliance of the other; thus the subsection appears to recognise the Worker's reliance interest under the contract. If this is the case, however, there is no reason why the Worker should be confined to a passive claim in respect of it.

Many people have concluded that a restitutionary analysis of claims arising on frustration is inadequate. (It is worth noting in passing that if this is so the same conclusion must follow for any case of early termination of a contract, where the same issues in principle arise.) Burrows, although apparently noting flaws in the restitutionary analysis, suggests that "it is a sensible discipline to clarify where the firm land of restitution runs out and the shifting sands of loss apportionment begin".[208] Sadly Burrows's firm land is something of a mirage to most explorers in the area. Some other common law jurisdictions have adopted the rationale of "loss apportionment", involving, in broad terms, equalising the net loss and benefit of the two parties.[209] It would be too large an exercise here to consider to what extent loss apportionment as it has been applied in these jurisdictions is consistent with the reliance theory approach set out here, although it certainly appears similar. One possible point of difference is that strictly a claim for payment for work done is not a claim for loss and would not figure in a pure loss-benefit calculation to the extent that payment exceeds the costs incurred. Another concerns whether benefits are measured in terms of the contractual valuation, i.e. relative to the reliance interest, and measured where possible through the cost of completion.

---

[206] Cf above 57 If the protection arises from a prima facie contractual reliance claim it is reasonable that it should be confined to reliance incurred through performance, on the basis that the purpose of the prepayment under the contract was to enable the Worker to perform, and expenditure in reliance on it for other purposes is at the Worker's own risk under the contract.

[207] With respect to a restitutionary claim to reverse a vitiated transfer, the recipient of the transfer, as an innocent stranger, is entitled to complete protection; see further Chap. 7.

[208] Burrows (1993), 287.

[209] See McKendrick (1991); see also Haycroft & Waksman (1984).

3

Imputed Contracts and Restitutionary Claims for Payment

INTRODUCTION

T HE LAST CHAPTER was concerned with cases where a claim arises out of an agreement between the parties, governing an exchange of a benefit for payment. The main issue that arises in this chapter is whether, without having made an agreement, the plaintiff can do work or incur expenditure that benefits the defendant, or might be expected to benefit him, and then claim payment for it from him. The basic rule is that he cannot:

> The general principle is, beyond all question, that work and labour done or money expended by one man to preserve or benefit the property of another do not according to English law . . . create any obligation to repay the expenditure. Liabilities are not to be forced upon people behind their backs any more than you can confer a benefit upon a man against his will.[1]

It is sometimes said that a defendant can be liable in restitution to pay for a benefit that he has requested, even though there is no contractual liability because he did not make an agreement to pay. But, where the defendant requests the plaintiff to provide goods or services in the course of his work, it is surely implicit that he is agreeing to pay for the goods or services supplied.[2] Requested benefits are a standard example of contracted-for benefit, and do not represent an exception to the general rule above. It is argued that sometimes a request may generate a liability to pay where the conditions for contractual liability—for example certainty—are not satisfied. But, if this is ostensibly so, whatever a court may say, it is surely far more plausible to say that the court is actually relaxing the conditions for contractual liability; it is very difficult to see what the basis for liability is if it is not the agreement implicit in the request, or why otherwise the request should be determinative of liability.[3] It seems that by way of a reaction to the fiction of implied contract any reference to implied contract is nowadays regarded with suspicion. But the implied contract fiction was principally concerned with the claim for restitution for a vitiated transfer, where the claim was clearly not contractual; and the fact that the implied contract in such

---

[1] *Falcke v Scottish Imperial Insurance Co* (1886) 34 Ch D 234, 248 *per* Bowen LJ; also *China Pacific SA v Food Corporation of India* [1981] 2 All ER 688, 695 *per* Lord Diplock.

[2] Chap. 2 at n 52.

[3] See below at 87.

a case was a fiction does not provide any reason for thinking that an implied contract is fictional in a case where it is based on a request by the defendant.[4]

The rule that an exchange is not enforceable without agreement is justified in the generality of cases for two reasons. First, people differ in their tastes and resources and, accordingly, as a matter of evidence, it is often impossible to say how much, if anything, one person would be willing to pay for a benefit, and whether this would be sufficient to provide what the other person would regard as adequate payment for his work in providing it. Requiring an agreement is the most reliable way of ensuring that the exchange will be mutually beneficial. Even if an agreed exchange turns out not to benefit one party, it is not unfair on him, because he can reasonably be expected to bear this risk if he has agreed to the exchange. Secondly, even if the evidential problem could be overcome, the defendant's right of autonomy should generally preclude any liability for payment from arising from a benefit conferred on him without his agreement; i.e. it would deprive him of his right to determine the use of his resources.[5]

The two conditions

But insisting on a prior agreement in all cases is too strict. It is reasonable to dispense with the requirement, and allow a claim for payment for a benefit conferred without agreement, where two conditions are satisfied.[6] First, it must be certain, or reasonably certain, that the defendant benefited from the plaintiff's act, to an extent that will leave him with a net benefit after the payment that he is required to make, or, in other words, that there is scope for a mutually beneficial exchange of payment for benefit. This will be the case where the benefit to the defendant is such that any person in the defendant's position, whatever his particular tastes and resources, would be certain, or reasonably certain, to have contracted at an ascertainable price that would be acceptable to the plaintiff. This will be referred to as the "benefit condition". In addition, secondly, there should be no claim where the optimal method of securing a mutually beneficial exchange—agreement—was feasible, or, at least, where there was no good reason why the defendant did not secure an agreement before acting, i.e. where the defendant acted "officiously", to use the word commonly used in this context in the case law. This is the "officiousness condition".[7]

---

[4] See below at 118.

[5] There is room for argument over the relation between the two reasons, in the sense that ultimately the value of autonomy presumably arises from variability in taste.

[6] The two conditions stated correspond to the conditions given by Levmore (1985) as "wealth dependency", meaning the variability in the value of a benefit to the defendant according to his resources and his tastes, and "market encouragement", meaning the tendency of a rule permitting imputed contracts to encourage or discourage actual contracting.

[7] As it has recently been put, "it is difficult to see why it is unjust that a person who has not made an agreement (though he is quite capable of making one) and not been requested to act should not be left with the risk of not being paid": *Becerra & Page v Close* (1999) unrep, *per* Thomas J.

Where a claim is allowed on this basis, it serves the same purpose as contract in effecting a mutually beneficial exchange between the parties, and so in a sense the law simulates the operation of contract. Like a contractual claim, such a claim protects the plaintiff's "reliance interest", viz., his interest in obtaining payment or at least reimbursement of expenditure (in money or by some other benefit) through work done in reliance on the expectation of such benefit,[8] although here the reliance is not necessarily on the defendant's agreement, but more broadly on an expectation of payment for his work arising from the nature of the circumstances.[9] The claim is customarily referred to as a restitutionary claim, but, as discussed in Chapter 1, it must not be confused with the restitutionary claim to reverse a vitiated transfer. Indeed, as discussed in Chapter 1, it would be better if a different expression were in use for this claim for payment, not only to make the distinction, but also because "restitution" is inapt, since (by contrast with the position for restitution for a vitiated transfer) there is no question of restoring something to the plaintiff or restoring the plaintiff to a previous position. It might be appropriate to refer to the claim as a claim under an imputed contract. "Imputed contract" might be dismissed on the ground that it resurrects the fiction of implied contract; but there is no fiction here because the reference to an imputed contract does not purport to invoke an actual agreement as the basis for the claim, and the usage is justified because of the analogy with contract.

IMPUTED CONTRACTS

Necessitous intervention

One type of case where the two conditions above appear to be satisfied is "necessitous intervention", where the plaintiff lends assistance to the defendant in an emergency. The two conditions are satisfied where the emergency makes it impossible for the parties to contract; and where the assistance provided saves the defendant from an obvious harm, so that it is clear that any person in his position would certainly have accepted the assistance at the price decided upon by the court.

Maritime salvage and analogous cases

There are a number of lines of authority which appear to reflect a principle of necessitous intervention. The standard example is provided by the law of maritime salvage. A claim for payment is available to a salvor who, by intervening to save a vessel in distress, has saved the defendant shipowner from loss of or

---

[8] This is equivalent to saying that the plaintiff did not mean to make a gift of his services: see below at n 19.

[9] Cf Stoljar (1987), 613.

harm to his property, whether the vessel itself or its cargo.[10] Although nowadays the plaintiff salvor can no doubt usually contact the defendant by radio and reach agreement before acting,[11] at one time that was often impossible, but nevertheless a salvor was entitled to reasonable payment for his services in the light of the benefit conferred on the defendant through the loss avoided. There is some limited support for a similar claim in favour of a rescuer or someone who has provided medical help in an emergency.[12] There is a line of cases that demonstrate that, where the plaintiff has undertaken arrangements for burial in the absence of the defendant, who is the person legally responsible to do so, the plaintiff can recover his outlay in paying an undertaker, or reasonable payment if the plaintiff is the undertaker himself.[13] It is also clear that a claim can arise where the plaintiff incurred expenditure in providing for someone who was incapable of doing so for himself, for example someone who is mentally impaired, or a child, against that person or his estate.[14]

There are also a number of cases in the category of "agency of necessity". Here the plaintiff is generally the bailee of the defendant's goods. In unforeseen circumstances, for which no prior arrangement has been made, he is faced with the need to take action to safeguard the goods, and it is for some reason impossible to communicate with the defendant. Then the plaintiff has been held to have a duty as bailee to look after the goods and a corresponding claim for reimbursement.[15] In some such cases, there is room to argue that the plaintiff and defendant are in a contractual relationship, and that the right of reimbursement is an implicit term of the contract, but in other cases it seems that there is no contractual relationship.

However, these various lines of authority have not been explicitly recognised judicially as being based on a general principle of necessitous intervention, or on the satisfaction of the two conditions suggested; and there have also been cases that appear to deny a claim in cases where such a general principle would appear to justify one.[16] In particular, claims arising from the preservation of property on land have been denied, and the salvage doctrine held to operate only at sea.[17] This seems to represent an anti-theoretical, blackletter approach in the sense of denying the importance of developing the law with a view to underlying principle and coherence.[18]

---

[10] An example is *The Telemachus* [1957] P 47.

[11] Although the contract is liable to be affected by duress: see Chap. 5 at 192.

[12] For example the US case of *Cotnam v Wisdom* (1907) 104 SW 164. Stoljar (1989), 198–9; Muir (1991).

[13] e.g. *Jenkins v Tucker* (1788) 1 Hy. Bl. 90.

[14] *Re Rhodes* (1890) 44 Ch D 94.

[15] *Great Northern Railway Co v Swaffield* (1874) LR 9 Exch 132; *China Pacific SA v Food Corpn of India (The Winson)* [198] AC 939.

[16] See generally Rose (1989).

[17] *Nicholson v Chapman* (1793) 2 Hy. Bl. 254; *The Goring* [1988] AC 831.

[18] See Chap. 1. A comparison is often made with the civil law doctrine of negotiorum gestio, which does appear to reflect such a general principle: see e.g. Stoljar (1989), 219ff.

Certain widely accepted propositions concerning these types of cases are consistent with the simulation of contract or imputed contract approach. First, the plaintiff must not have acted with a view to making a gift of his services.[19] Secondly, the plaintiff must have intended to advance the interests of the defendant as well as the plaintiff;[20] or, in other words, he must have considered the appropriateness of the exchange from both points of view, rather in the manner of a fiduciary.[21] This implies that in the circumstances the plaintiff was an appropriate person to act,[22] and that there was no better person to act, who would have acted and to whom the plaintiff ought therefore to have deferred.

The measure of payment

It follows from the argument above that the measure of payment should be the price that the parties would have agreed to,[23] which will lie between a minimum, the amount necessary to cover the plaintiff's costs, and a maximum, the full value to the defendant of the benefit received by him. This will leave some scope for settling a fair price.[24] Where there is a market rate for the plaintiff's work, this would generally be the appropriate measure (assuming it falls within the range). It is said, at least in relation to maritime salvage, that the claim is not for reasonable remuneration for work done, but for an amount that is a sufficient incentive to encourage salvors to intervene where appropriate; as it has been put, the claim is for a reward rather than remuneration.[25] But it is doubtful whether the distinction is valid. Reasonable remuneration is clearly no less than is sufficient to make it worthwhile for salvors to act as such, just as, in agreed exchanges, the price agreed makes the contract worthwhile for both parties. It is true that because the salvor will not recover anything on the occasions on which he attempts an intervention and is unsuccessful, he will require a higher return on the occasions on which he is successful than he would if his time and resources were never wasted. This might suggest that the measure of his claim exceeds reasonable remuneration vis-à-vis the defendant. But where the plaintiff takes a risk that his work may not be successful, this is a factor that is

---

[19] Goff & Jones (1998), 472, 482; *Re Rhodes* (1890) 44 Ch D 94. One might say that the plaintiff must have acted as if he were contracting, and this is true of salvage cases where the practice is well established. In other cases, the plaintiff may not know of the practice of recovering payment, but one can still say that he did not mean to make a gift.

[20] Goff & Jones (1998), 471, 482; *The Winson* [1982] AC 939,965 *per* Lord Simon of Glaisdale. This amounts to saying that the defendant thought that there was a reasonable price that would reflect a mutually beneficial exchange.

[21] The court will determine whether the circumstances required intervention, but it is fair to say that the plaintiff should also have understood it to be in the defendant's interests.

[22] Goff & Jones (1998), 481.

[23] But in the light of the position as now known, i.e. in the light of the actual benefit conferred.

[24] The surplus of the value received over the price paid is sometimes referred to as the "consumer surplus".

[25] Rose (1989), 200; Goff & Jones (1998), 472.

relevant in determining what the parties would have agreed to, for salvors just as, say, for estate agents.[26]

Other rationales

Various other rationales for necessitous intervention have been offered. Proponents of the unjust enrichment theory of restitution argue that the claim is designed to reverse an unjust enrichment, conceived of as reversing a transfer from the plaintiff to the defendant on the ground that it was subject to an "unjust factor". The objections to treating the provision of a benefit through work and expenditure as a transfer have been set out already.[27] The unjust enrichment approach suggests that the measure of liability is necessarily the measure of the defendant's benefit; or, if the claim is conceived of as reversing a transfer, it might be thought that the appropriate measure is the plaintiff's loss. There has been some controversy on this issue.[28] As argued above, neither loss nor benefit provides the measure of liability, although both are relevant to it; the true measure will lie between the two. There has also been some controversy over the "unjust factor". One suggestion is that there is a vitiating factor of "moral compulsion"; in other words, the plaintiff was forced to act by his sense of moral obligation. But, leaving aside the case where someone acts out of the fear of divine punishment, or possibly as a result of some form of neurosis, the fact that a decision was made according to moral criteria—for example to help others at some risk to oneself—does not imply that it was vitiated in any way.[29] In fact, if the intervention was made as a form of charity it is doubtful whether a claim arises.[30]

Another approach is that the "unjust factor" is the policy of promoting necessitous intervention.[31] The idea here is that the law is designed to provide an incentive for intervention in order to maximise the welfare of society in general and seafarers in particular. Although it is misconceived to think in terms of the reversal of a transfer, and unhelpful to describe a policy as an unjust factor,[32] nevertheless the provision of an incentive for intervention might well be relevant as the basis for the "two conditions" rule for an imputed contract. However, one might argue instead that, rather than being designed to maximise welfare, the "two conditions" rule may be justified purely in terms of moral principle or fairness as between the two parties.[33] On this basis, the existence and scope of the

---

[26] Reimbursement is the least that the plaintiff would have agreed to, and if the plaintiff is not providing professional services, a claim limited to reimbursement might be appropriate.

[27] See Chap. 1 at 9–10.

[28] See below at n 40 and n 86.

[29] The only possibility of vitiation in such cases is that the plaintiff may act on the understanding that he will be able to claim payment, in circumstances where it turns out that the conditions for a claim were not satisfied, i.e. mistake.

[30] Above, n 19.

[31] Birks (1989*a*), 304.

[32] See further Chap. 5.

[33] "Principle" is used here in the Dworkinian sense in which it is distinguished from policy.

rule depend on balancing the plaintiff's interest in a return on his labour and resources, and the defendant's interest in receiving a benefit, and in deciding on the use of his resources. It is of course a very general and controversial issue whether a "policy" or efficiency argument should be preferred to an argument of principle or fairness; and the issue is controversial with respect to contract in particular. Judicial language with respect to maritime salvage suggests that the rationale for necessitous intervention is efficiency or creating incentives.[34] On the other hand one might think that the general approach would be the same as for contract, and here it is more common to hear that an agreement is enforced as a matter of justice between the parties, rather than in order to promote aggregate welfare.[35]

One might speculate about how the scope of the rule might differ under the two different approaches. One would think that on a fairness approach the defendant's liability should depend on his having actually received a benefit, i.e. on the success of the intervention; the defendant does not accept any part of the risk, as he might in the case of an actual agreement, that it may not be successful. On the other hand it may be that it would be efficient, in terms of promoting intervention, for the plaintiff to be rewarded whether or not he was successful, although this is no doubt a matter of speculation.[36] With respect to maritime salvage, it seems that no claim arises unless the plaintiff is successful. But it has been suggested that no benefit has been required in the American cases where a doctor attempts to provide treatment.[37] More generally, under the fairness approach one might expect a greater degree of scrupulousness in ensuring, in deference to the defendant's autonomy, that the plaintiff communicates with him before acting if conceivably possible, and in denying a claim if any uncertainty arises over whether the intervention benefited or was liable to benefit the defendant. The efficiency approach, concentrating on net benefit over the generality of cases, might call for a more rough and ready approach that encourages intervention over a broader range of cases with less scrupulous concern for whether the defendant would actually benefit in a particular case or whether communication might have been possible.[38]

---

[34] e.g. *Nicholson v Chapman* (1793) 2 Hy. Bl. 254, 257: "recompense for the encouragement of [salvors]", *per* Eyre CJ.

[35] See also Chap. 12 at 397–400.

[36] Maybe intervention would be less committed if payment did not depend on success. The economic approach prescribes the measure of payment that would have been agreed beforehand, in ignorance of subsequent success or failure, i.e. "ex ante".

[37] Stoljar (1989), 198–9. But where the patient dies, he may still have received a benefit in the form of an increased chance of surviving, and maybe a less unpleasant death.

[38] Whether this is so would depend on difficult empirical issues, concerning the relative competence of the court and the parties at judging the value of a benefit to the defendant. The argument of fairness does not deny that it might be in the public interest to create incentives for intervention in a wider range of cases; the argument is simply that the incentives should not come out of the defendant's purse except in cases where it is fair to make him pay.

Unjust sacrifice and the measure of liability

Necessitous intervention was considered by Stoljar to be based on a principle of "unjust sacrifice" rather than unjust enrichment.[39] He preferred an unjust sacrifice analysis because he thought that the measure of the claim was not the value of the benefit provided, as an unjust enrichment approach appears to imply, but the plaintiff's loss in providing the benefit conferred. The unjust sacrifice approach was confirmed, he thought, by the fact that, as he thought, a claim could arise where the defendant had not received a benefit at all, as in the case mentioned above where a doctor could recover for an unsuccessful medical intervention. It is true, as argued above, that the measure of liability is not the measure of benefit; but, on the other hand, neither is it the plaintiff's loss, as the unjust sacrifice approach implies. It is for the measure of appropriate payment for the work done in providing the benefit, in the light of the nature and extent of the plaintiff's work and expenditure and the value of the benefit conferred on the defendant.[40]

Benefits conferred by mistake

There are other situations (apart from necessitous intervention) where the plaintiff can recover payment for work done or expenditure incurred in conferring a benefit on the defendant even though there was no agreement between the parties. These can be understood in terms of the same two conditions mentioned above, the officiousness condition and the benefit condition. In these cases outside necessitous intervention, the usual reason for the plaintiff's failure to contract is a mistake by him; for example, he may have mistakenly thought that he had contracted with the defendant when this was not actually the case. This satisfies the officiousness condition. However, whereas for necessitous intervention the circumstances are such as to satisfy both conditions at once, the mistake does not provide any reason for thinking that the benefit condition is satisfied, and this has to be addressed separately. Although the issue has not been addressed in terms of the framework proposed here, various tests have been proposed that might be thought to serve this purpose. These include the tests of incontrovertible benefit, bargained-for benefit and free acceptance. Generally these tests are thought to be concerned with measuring the defendant's benefit for the purpose of transferring it to the plaintiff, in accordance with the theory

---

[39] Stoljar (1987).

[40] Stoljar, *ibid.*, equated the plaintiff's loss with the "value of the services" provided by the plaintiff. The expression is inapt to refer to the loss incurred by the plaintiff in providing the services, in accordance with the unjust sacrifice approach. It might be used to refer to the value of the benefit conferred on the defendant, or more plausibly the price determined for the plaintiff's services, which is by definition the true measure of recovery, but is neither the plaintiff's loss nor the defendant's benefit.

of unjust enrichment, whereas (on the approach here at least) they should strictly be understood to be concerned with determining that the benefit condition as defined above is satisfied.

Incontrovertible benefit

In some cases the benefit is clear, or "incontrovertible". One type of case is where the defendant has received a benefit that he would certainly have chosen to acquire if he had appreciated the circumstances or been in a position to act. This covers cases of necessitous intervention. An example arising from mistake is provided by *Craven-Ellis v Canons Ltd*.[41] Here the plaintiff was purportedly appointed managing director of the defendant company, but the contract of appointment was void because it was not entered into in accordance with the procedure laid down by the company's articles. The plaintiff was denied payment under the contract, but succeeded in a claim for a quantum meruit. The plaintiff was under the impression that he did have a contract, and this is why he proceeded to do work without a valid contract. Part of the ground for the decision was that the defendant "would have had to get some other agent to carry out" the services provided by the plaintiff if they had not been provided by him,[42] because it could not function without a managing director.

Another example is where the plaintiff's work discharged a legal obligation of the defendant, as in the Canadian case of *County of Carleton v City of Ottawa*.[43] Here the plaintiff authority, which was statutorily responsible for providing for homeless people within its boundaries, mistakenly took responsibility for a woman who was actually the responsibility of the defendant authority. The plaintiff was allowed reimbursement of its costs. Because the defendant was bound to provide for the woman, one can say that it would certainly have had to arrange for what the plaintiff had provided. A similar case is where the plaintiff mistakenly makes a payment to a third party, X, a creditor of the defendant, that discharges the defendant's debt to X, thereby conferring a benefit on the defendant.[44]

There is also an incontrovertible benefit where the benefit received by the defendant has been realised as a form of wealth i.e. a "wealth benefit". (In fact discharging a debt surely amounts to the conferral of wealth.)[45] For example, say the plaintiff has mistakenly carried out work on the defendant's car. If the defendant sells the car, and the work done has increased the sale price, there is an incontrovertible benefit in the form of the part of the proceeds of sale that are due to the work, and the plaintiff should be allowed a claim for reasonable

---

[41] [1936] 2 KB 403.
[42] At 412.
[43] (1966) 52 DLR (2d) 220.
[44] e.g. *Liggett (Liverpool) Ltd v Barclays Bank Ltd* [1928] 1 KB 48.
[45] This is relevant to the discussion of subrogation in Chaps. 8 and 9.

payment up to the amount of this realised value of the benefit.[46] Where the benefit is realised in money in this way, the difficulty of valuing the benefit to the plaintiff is obviated.[47]

The more controversial case is where the plaintiff's work has increased the market value of the defendant's property, but the defendant does not sell it; i.e. there is a realisable increase in market value, which remains unrealised.[48] If the defendant does not sell the property but is treated as benefited to the extent of the realisable increase in market value he will be prejudiced to the extent that he valued the work less than the market. He may even be forced to sell the property to raise the money to pay the plaintiff, and this may prejudice him significantly if he is unable to replace the property with something that he regards as equivalent to his original property with the proceeds of sale left after paying the plaintiff. Arguably, in cases where the defendant's product is more or less interchangeable with other equivalent products, and the defendant will be able to replace his original property after sale, he should be liable to pay, but not otherwise. This might be the case with a car, say, but not a house. One might say, in other words, that the defendant can be expected to bear a small degree of inconvenience and a small risk of prejudice in order to satisfy the plaintiff's interest.[49]

Where there is no incontrovertible benefit, the problem of variability in tastes and resources means that it is very difficult to say what value the defendant has received, if any, and what he would have been willing to pay. The problem is sometimes referred to in this context as the problem of "subjective devaluation".[50] The idea is that a benefit has a prima facie objective or uniform value, usually equated with the market value, which is "devalued" by the defendant when he denies that the benefit is worth the market value to him in the light of his own tastes and resources. But there is no sense in which the benefit is even prima facie worth the market value to the defendant. Its value to him is simply the value he attributes to it in the light of his own tastes and resources, to which the market value is irrelevant. (The market value, after all, is simply where supply and demand meet, and does not represent an objective value in any other sense.)[51]

---

[46] This happened in *Greewood v Bennett* [1973] 1 QB 195, although the point was not discussed.

[47] In principle, however, this argument applies only if the sale of the car was not prompted by the plaintiff's work: it may be that the defendant valued the car as it originally was more than the sale price, but did not want to keep the car after the plaintiff's work on it. A similar case is where the work creates a detachable benefit, which can be sold or given to the plaintiff. Sutton discusses detachable benefits in connection with free acceptance: Sutton (1990), 253; Verse (1998), 99.

[48] Burrows (1993), 10; Birks (1989a), 121–4; Goff & Jones (1998), 23.

[49] An analogy is drawn with mitigation, where the plaintiff tort victim is expected to take measures to limit the defendant's liability: Verse (1998), 96. Maybe more extensive work by the plaintiff will justify a greater imposition on the defendant.

[50] Birks (1989a), 109ff.

[51] Value in money "is not a property internal to a thing like its weight or size. It is the price which ... would have been paid ... in the market", per Nourse LJ in *Smith New Court Securities Ltd v Scrimgeour Vickers* [1994] 1 WLR 1271, 1281.

Various so-called "subjective" tests have been suggested that purport to take account of the defendant's actual tastes and resources. According to Birks, the function of the traditional requirement to plead a request in a claim for a quantum meruit was that the presence of a request by the defendant was evidence that the defendant had been subjectively benefited.[52] In fact, it is surely far more plausible that the justification for the requirement of a request was that the request carried the implication of an agreement to pay, and the requirement therefore reflected the basic rule that a claim for payment does not arise without an agreement.[53] The two main forms of subjective test of benefit in the modern literature are the tests of "bargained-for benefit", which seems to encompass "requested benefit", and "free acceptance". These tests are academic not judicial inventions,[54] not recognised as such in the case law, and, as with incontrovertible benefit, they have been put forward under a different framework from that adopted here.

"Bargained-for benefit"

Burrows advocates what he calls the "bargained-for" measure of benefit: the defendant "can be regarded as . . . benefited where the plaintiff performs what the defendant bargained for" (which includes what the defendant requested).[55] Presumably Burrows also means to say that where the defendant requested or bargained for the benefit, he can be taken to have benefited to the extent of the price he bargained to pay for it, or a reasonable or market price if he did not bargain for an actual price, or, more correctly, that he benefited to the extent that this price would be appropriate payment for the benefit received.

Normally, of course, when the defendant bargained for the benefit, the agreement itself generates a contractual claim for payment. But if the contract is void, one might argue that in the absence of a contractual claim the agreement nevertheless serves to indicate that the defendant will benefit from the work requested to an extent sufficient to justify payment as envisaged by the agreement. Consider the case of *Rover v Cannon*,[56] where it has been suggested that the bargained-for benefit test might apply (although this was not the approach of the court).[57] Rather simplified, the facts were as follows. The defendant film distributor had contracted with the plaintiff for the plaintiff to dub and distribute the defendant's films in Italy. The plaintiff had done some of the work specified

---

[52] Birks (1989*a*), 113.

[53] Above at n 77. Recently in *Becerra & Page v Close* (1999), unrep, Thomas J, it appears to have been accepted without argument that a restitutionary claim based on a request could arise as an alternative to a contractual claim arising from the request.

[54] The concept of bargained-for benefit is due to Burrows (1988); Burrows (1993), 14. The concept of free acceptance is due to Goff & Jones (1998), 18; and to Birks (1974); Birks (1989*a*), 265ff; Birks (1991*b*).

[55] Burrows, 14. Bargained-for benefit was also considered in Chap. 2.

[56] [1989] 1 WLR 912.

[57] Burrows, 15. Burrows suggests that the test is not a conclusive measure of benefit, but does not explain how it should be departed from.

before it emerged that the contract had been entered into before the plaintiff company had been incorporated. Consequently the court held the contract to be void; nevertheless the plaintiff succeeded in a claim for a quantum meruit for the work it had done.

The benefit was conferred by mistake, because it was assumed that the contract was valid, so the officiousness condition was satisfied; the issue is whether the benefit condition was satisfied. A contracting party will often find, after making the contract, that circumstances have changed so as to alter the value of the contract to him. Even if the circumstances turn out to be exactly as he envisaged, he may discover that he has misjudged the value of the contract to him, or changed his mind about it. None of this allows him to escape from a contractual liability, of course; he has accepted this type of risk by making the contract. But it is clear that, although the fact of the agreement shows that the defendant thought at the time when he contracted that an exchange in the agreed terms would be, or would probably be, beneficial to him, it does not show that it turned out actually to be beneficial to him.[58] Indeed, in *Rover v Cannon* after the contract was made the defendant became unhappy with it and began to look for some means of escaping from it, which clearly shows that it no longer considered the envisaged exchange to be beneficial. Thus treating the benefit condition as satisfied by virtue of the void contract in reality constitutes enforcing the agreement, not measuring the benefit; it is after all the function of the agreement to determine the terms of the exchange and to preclude any escape from the risk mentioned above.[59] It is far more plausible to say that the claim arose out of an agreement between the parties, whether on the terms agreed in the void contract or other terms, arising from the conduct of the two parties in carrying out the agreement.[60] In fact the grounds for awarding a quantum meruit were not considered, because the claim was conceded.[61]

Free acceptance

Another suggested test of benefit has been "free acceptance". If the defendant knows that a benefit is being offered to him non-gratuitously and fails to take an opportunity to reject it, he is said to have "freely accepted" it and cannot object that it is of no value to him.[62] It is inferred that the defendant must pay a reasonable or market price to the plaintiff, not exceeding the price that the defendant should have realised it was the intention of the plaintiff to charge. Consider for example *Boulton v Jones*.[63] Here the plaintiff sent goods to the defendant in

---

[58]   A similar point is made by Garner (1990), 55.

[59]   Furthermore, where, as here, a contract is void for lack of authority, it must be unjustifiable to use it as an authoritative measure of benefit as against the party whose assent was unauthorised. And the same objection will apply to some other grounds of invalidity, like incapacity.

[60]   Cf Stoljar (1989), 236ff.

[61]   The ground of restitution is usually taken to be failure of consideration, as considered below.

[62]   Birks (1989a), 104.

[63]   (1857) 2 H & N 564.

response to an order from the defendant that was actually directed to the plaintiff's predecessor in business. The defendant would not have made the order to the plaintiff himself because he wanted to take advantage of a right of set-off arising from a debt owed by the predecessor but not by the plaintiff. It was held that because of the mistake there was no contract of sale, and the plaintiff was denied any payment for the goods. The defendant did however consume the goods, although before he became aware of the mistake. It is argued that the plaintiff should have had a claim for payment for the goods in restitution based on free acceptance.[64]

But free acceptance does not show that the defendant values the benefit to the extent that he would be prepared to pay the market price for it; one could only infer this if the defendant believed that he would incur a liability to pay the market value if he did not reject the benefit. In *Boulton v Jones*, in fact, the defendant was only willing to buy the goods on the basis of the set-off, which implies that he might not have been willing to pay a market price—without the set-off, he might not have ordered the goods from anyone.[65] Free acceptance does show, however, that the defendant prefers having the benefit to not having it; or, in other words, it shows that the defendant would be willing to pay *some* price for it, if not the market price.[66] If the court could determine this price accurately, then it would be reasonable to allow a claim in this measure. Unfortunately, free acceptance provides no help in doing this.

It might be argued that the bargained-for benefit test gets around the objection to free acceptance as a measure of benefit because it shows that the defendant values the benefit sufficiently to justify the contractually agreed payment,[67] whereas free acceptance merely shows that the defendant wanted the benefit at some unknown price. But, as argued above, to require the defendant to pay the contractually agreed amount is not justified on the basis that it is a true measure of benefit, but only on the basis that it upholds the contract. Bargained-for benefit can only operate as a ground of liability, and in the case of bargained-for benefit the ground is actually the contract and the liability contractual.

Similarly, free acceptance is sometimes defended not as a test of benefit, but as a ground of liability. Thus it is said that its relevance is not that it shows that the benefit was worth the market value to the defendant, but that it justifies holding him liable to pay the market value even if it is actually worth less than that to him; in other words, it denies him the right of "subjective devaluation" of the benefit he has received.[68] The ground of liability is the defendant's unconscientiousness in failing to act to stop the plaintiff from wasting his time in

---

[64] Birks (1989*a*), 115.

[65] Goff & Jones (1998), 597.

[66] Burrows (1993), 12, says that free acceptance shows that the defendant is indifferent to the benefit, but this is not necessarily the case.

[67] Burrows, ibid., merely notes that bargained-for benefit test shows the "positive desire" of the defendant.

[68] Birks (1991*b*), 129.

providing a benefit. Free acceptance as a ground of liability is considered later in this chapter.

The dispute over "pure services" and free acceptance

Beatson has argued against free acceptance as a test of benefit on the ground that its effect can be to allow a restitutionary claim where the defendant has not actually received any benefit.[69] It seems that this can be the case because sometimes work is done that will in due course benefit the defendant, but has not yet done so at the time when the defendant freely accepts by refraining from stopping the plaintiff from continuing the work. There are certain cases of this sort, which have sometimes been thought to be restitutionary claims based on free acceptance;[70] in particular Beatson cites *Planché v Colburn*[71] and *Sabemo Pty Ltd v North Sydney Municipal Council*.[72] On Beatson's view these cases are better explained as contractual claims or non-contractual reliance claims. (In this book they are treated as contractual.)[73] Beatson's objection to free acceptance as a measure of benefit is surely legitimate,[74] because if nothing has yet been received there can clearly be no benefit.

Unfortunately Beatson formulates his argument against free acceptance in a way that unnecessarily invokes the concepts of "pure services" and "wealth", and this has led to some confusion. He uses the expression "pure services" to refer, broadly speaking, to work that does not generate a wealth-benefit in the hands of the defendant. "Wealth" is transferable value, i.e. money or property or other transferable assets, as discussed elsewhere.[75] Thus, for example, providing education or medical treatment or entertainment does not confer wealth on the defendant, because it does not leave him with money or an asset that he can exchange for money, whereas building or supplying or repairing a product or doing work on land might well do so.[76] Beatson argues that unjust enrichment, which he takes to be the subject of the law of restitution, is concerned only with wealth (or in other words that "enrichment" means wealth), and therefore that a pure service cannot, by definition, generate a restitutionary claim. Clearly free acceptance can apply to pure services, and he therefore rejects free acceptance as a test of benefit.[77]

---

[69] Beatson (1991), 21–44.

[70] In particular Birks (1991*b*), 137ff.

[71] (1831) 8 Bing. 14.

[72] [1977] 2 NSWLR 880.

[73] This is considered further below; and see Chap. 2.

[74] And if free acceptance is a ground of liability it suggests that it is not restitutionary, as considered further below.

[75] See Chaps. 7 and 9.

[76] Subject to the problem of realisability discussed above.

[77] By contrast, he considers that the test of incontrovertible benefit is a test of wealth: Beatson (1991), 33. But "incontrovertible benefit" is not confined to wealth benefits. The defendant has not necessarily received wealth when he receives a benefit that he would otherwise have used wealth to acquire. The benefit is what the defendant receives, not what he might have paid for it. Burrows

Some commentators seem to have interpreted Beatson as saying that pure services do not confer any benefit. This cannot be right; of course pure services can confer a benefit, although a non-wealth benefit; if they did not, they would not be sought after or paid for.[78] Presumably Beatson does not mean to deny this, although other commentators have been at pains to point it out to him. The more plausible interpretation of Beatson's argument is that there is no restitutionary claim notwithstanding that there is a benefit, because only wealth benefits count for the purposes of restitution. The problem is that Beatson does not say why this is so. It is true that restitution for a vitiated transfer only arises in respect of transfers of wealth, but there is no reason why this should be the case for a restitutionary claim for payment for work done in conferring a benefit.[79] By contract, people pay for non-wealth benefits, and in principle there is no reason why a restitutionary claim for payment in respect of a non-wealth benefit should not arise also, if the conditions for such a claim are satisfied. No doubt the benefit condition will present more of a difficulty for a non-wealth benefit; arguably a strict test for the benefit condition might confine the restitutionary claim to wealth-benefits,[80] whereas a more relaxed test would not. But there is nothing in the nature of the claim that precludes it from arising in relation to a non-wealth benefit if the benefit condition can be satisfied.[81]

In fact, as noted above, Beatson's real concern is not with pure services or wealth at all, but with services, whether pure or not, that have been cut short before any benefit was conferred. Indeed, the cases cited by Beatson do not actually seem to have involved pure services. For example in *Planché v Colburn* the plaintiff was commissioned to deliver a manuscript, which is not a pure service. The argument against free acceptance based on restricting restitutionary claims to payment to cases involving the receipt of wealth is misconceived and unnecessary to Beatson's principal argument against free acceptance as a test of benefit, which is that it would allow a restitutionary claim where there is no benefit of any sort, whether a wealth-benefit or not.

An "objective" test

Another approach to the benefit condition might be always to allow the plaintiff a market rate for his work. This is sometimes described as the objective

---

argues that where the defendant is the beneficiary of pure services he receives a "negative benefit" in the form of the sum of money that he is relieved of having to pay for the services: Burrows (1993), 8. This argument presumably serves to equate the benefit through a pure service with wealth in the form of the money saved. In its true sense, a negative benefit is the extinction of a debt or liability. But pure services do not confer a negative benefit in this or any other helpful sense. They confer a positive benefit in the form of, say, pleasure, or information, or education, rather than wealth. On Burrows's approach all benefits are negative, because it can be said of any benefit that it has saved the recipient the cost of paying for it. See also Chap. 4 at 145.

[78] Birks (1991*b*), 132.
[79] Along with other unjust enrichment theorists, Beatson does not distinguish between these two.
[80] See above at 86.
[81] Cf Penner (1997).

approach, on the basis that it assumes that the defendant would value the benefit sufficiently to be willing to pay the market rate, irrespective of his own personal tastes and resources; i.e. the objective test precludes subjective devaluation. This approach would protect the plaintiff at the defendant's expense. This seems unjustifiable, because one would think that the plaintiff rather than the defendant should bear the risk that the defendant does not value the work sufficiently to justify paying the market rate.

One case that might be thought to support the objective approach is *Greenwood v Bennett*.[82] Here a car was stolen from the plaintiff owner and sold to an innocent recipient who had repairs and improvements carried out. The owner recovered the value of the car, but the recipient was entitled to have the cost of the work deducted from the measure of liability, without any discussion of whether the improvements would actually have been desired by the owner.[83] This has been widely understood as a restitutionary claim by the recipient in respect of the work done on the car, in particular by Lord Denning in his judgment.[84] However, the majority in the Court of Appeal considered that only a "passive claim" could arise, i.e. the recipient could claim in respect of his work only by way of a defence to a claim by the owner. If the car had reached the owner's hands, the recipient would have had to make an "active claim" for payment, which would have failed. This is inconsistent with the interpretation of the claim as a restitutionary claim for payment, because with respect to such a claim there is no basis for any distinction between an active and a passive claim, i.e. between a claim and a counterclaim or defence. On the other hand, it is consistent with the interpretation of the recipient's discount as based on change of position, as a defence to the owner's claim for the value of the car.[85] The change of position defence would reduce the owner's claim by the amount that the recipient had spent in reliance on his understanding that he owned the car. This analysis is also consistent with the measure of the discount, which was in fact the amount spent by the recipient, rather than the value of the work to the owner or some figure in-between. The change of position analysis would not have been apparent at the time of the case, because the change of position defence had not been openly recognised, and also because the owner's claim in respect of the chattel is mischaracterised as tortious rather than restitutionary.[86]

Outside the case of incontrovertible benefit, there is very little authority for any right to payment for a benefit conferred by mistake. In particular, it seems

---

[82]   [1973] QB 195.

[83]   In fact as has been pointed out, there seems to have been incontrovertible benefit, because at least some of the work effected necessary repairs that the owner would have had to carry out, and in any case the appreciated value of the car was realised by sale: Birks (1989a), 124.

[84]   See Birks (1974), 19.

[85]   Change of position is considered in Chap. 7 below.

[86]   It is a mischaracterisation where the recipient is innocent; see Chap. 10 below, at 326. It is unfortunate that the statutory provision introduced after the case measures the allowance as the increased value of the goods due to the work, even though the claim is still a passive claim only: s.6(1) of the Torts (Interference with Goods) Act 1977.

that generally no claim arises in respect of mistaken improvements to prop-erty.[87] The general reluctance to allow a claim other than in cases of incontro-vertible benefit favours the defendant over the plaintiff, in the sense that the defendant is protected against even a small risk of a forced exchange that is not beneficial to him, at the expense of denying the plaintiff a claim for payment or even reimbursement of expenses. This approach of confining claims to cases of incontrovertible benefit means that there are bound to be cases where it is rea-sonably clear that an exchange would be mutually beneficial at some price, if not at a market price, as in the example of *Boulton v Jones*. A general freedom to make an appropriate award in the light of all the circumstances might enable the court to give some protection to the plaintiff, even if he does not get his full rate for the work or even reimbursement of all his costs, without unfairness to the defendant. On such an approach the terms of a void contract might be taken to give some indication of the value of the benefit, although without binding the defendant so as to impose on him the risks of change in value that he would have to accept for the purposes of a contractual claim. This approach would amount to a compromise between confining claims to incontrovertible benefit, which may be unduly favourable to the defendant, and allowing a claim based on objective benefit, which is unduly favourable to the plaintiff. However, it is a reasonable objection that such an approach would involve very difficult deci-sions not based on well defined criteria, and might create an excessive risk of prejudice to the defendant.[88]

Compulsory discharge of the defendant's liability

Sometimes the plaintiff confers a benefit on the defendant by way of the dis-charge of a legal liability of the defendant's.[89] A couple of cases of this sort have been mentioned already.[90] Many cases involve the discharge of the defendant's liability by the plaintiff acting under legal compulsion. Here the plaintiff has a legal obligation to a third party to make a payment or provide some other sort of benefit for which the primary responsibility lies with the defendant. There are various examples. In *Gebhardt v Saunders*,[91] the plaintiff incurred a legal oblig-ation to clear the drains of the house in which he was a tenant when a notice was served on him by the local authority. At the time, the precise cause of the prob-lem was unknown, and it turned out to be due to a structural defect, which meant that the ultimate responsibility was with the defendant, who was the owner of the premises, not the plaintiff as tenant. It was held that the defendant

[87] See generally Sutton (1990).
[88] Levmore (1985) discusses some other examples of successful non-contractual claims for pay-ment in US law, e.g. a plaintiff lawyer's claim against a third party "involuntary plaintiff", and a claim for contribution to the cost of land drainage benefiting land adjacent to the plaintiff's land.
[89] See also Chap. 8 in connection with subrogation.
[90] Above at 85.
[91] [1892] 2 QB 452.

was liable to reimburse the plaintiff for the expenses incurred in complying with the order, because the plaintiff had discharged what was principally the defendant's liability. Most cases involve the discharge by the plaintiff of a pecuniary liability of the defendant, i.e. a debt. The oldest example is where a third party seizes property on the defendant's land pursuant to a right to distrain for a debt due, and the property seized turns out to be the plaintiff's. If, in order to recover his property, the plaintiff pays the third party the amount owed by the defendant, the plaintiff is entitled to be reimbursed by him.[92] Another example is where the plaintiff warehouse owner is liable to pay the import tax due on imported goods stored in the warehouse, which he is then able to recover from the defendant, the importer.[93] The most common example is under the doctrine of contribution, where the plaintiff and the defendant are both liable to pay the same debt to the third party or to pay compensation for the same wrong. Ultimately, each is responsible for a part of the debt or compensation due to the third party; but as against the third party each is liable to pay the full amount. To the extent that the plaintiff discharges more than his own share of the liability, he can recover from the defendant.[94]

In these cases, the circumstances meet the two conditions for the restitutionary claim for payment arising from an imputed contract. First, since the plaintiff acted under legal compulsion he cannot be said to have acted officiously. Secondly, the discharge of the defendant's legal liability must be an incontrovertible benefit to him, because he would certainly have satisfied the liability; indeed, generally by relieving the defendant of a claim on his wealth the discharge amounts to a wealth-benefit.[95] (This presupposes that the defendant's liability to the third party is indeed discharged, and this must be an incident of the scheme of legal compulsion.) The claim will usually take the form of reimbursement of the plaintiff's outlay. But, in principle, in a case where the plaintiff does work himself in conferring a benefit, rather than employing someone else to do it or paying off a debt, there seems no reason why he should not be entitled to payment that exceeds his actual outlay.[96]

The orthodox unjust enrichment analysis of this type of case, in disregard of the distinction between the claim to payment arising from an imputed contract and the claim to reverse a vitiated transfer, treats the claim as a claim arising to

---

[92] e.g. *Exall v Partridge* (1799) 8 Term Rep 308.

[93] *Brook's Wharf and Bull Wharf Ltd v Goodman Brothers* [1937] 1 KB 534. Cf *Moule v Garrett* (1872) LR 7 Exch 101.

[94] *Deering v The Earl of Winchelsea* (1787) 2 Bos & Pul 270. The law governing contribution in respect of compensation for wrongs is largely governed by the Civil Liability Contribution Act 1978.

[95] As discussed in Chap. 8 and Chap. 9 in connection with subrogation, the claim arising from the discharge of a debt can be expressed as a subrogated claim, which ensures that the measure of reimbursement cannot exceed the measure of benefit conferred.

[96] It may be that the defendant could have done the work at lower cost. But the plaintiff should be entitled to full reimbursement provided that he took reasonable care in selecting someone to do the work. This is surely the fair arrangement given that the plaintiff was compelled to act on behalf of the defendant.

reverse a vitiated transfer. There is thought to be a transfer from the plaintiff to the defendant (via the third party), which is affected by a vitiating factor of "legal compulsion".[97] One might argue that legal compulsion is a form of duress:[98] after all, any legal obligation carries the threat of legal sanction. But it would be inconsistent to hold that a transfer compelled by law is also vitiated in law and should be reversed.[99] Any such doctrine would subvert the operation of the law entirely, because any payment made under a legal obligation would necessarily be recoverable, including payments made pursuant to a court order.[100] Furthermore, there may be no transfer of wealth from the plaintiff to the defendant, as where the plaintiff incurred expenditure or did work that provided a benefit to the defendant.[101]

At the heart of these cases is the question why the plaintiff should have been compelled to provide a benefit to the defendant. This is related to the fact that these are all three-party cases. None of them involves a duty to confer a benefit on the defendant directly, as opposed to conferring a benefit indirectly by way of the discharge of the defendant's liability to a third party.[102] Why is it that the plaintiff is forced to pay the third party, only to recover in turn from the defendant, instead of being free, as one might expect, to require the third party to direct his action against the defendant himself? The rationale for the legal compulsion is practical. In circumstances where there may be difficulties in establishing which of the plaintiff or defendant is liable to the third party, or the extent of their respective liabilities to him, or where there may be practical difficulties for the third party in taking proceedings and enforcing judgment against the defendant directly, it may be reasonable to relieve the third party of these difficulties by making the plaintiff responsible to the third party for the defendant's liability, in effect requiring the plaintiff to sort out the evidential and other practical difficulties with the defendant.[103] Because the rationale is

---

[97] e.g. Birks (1989*a*), 185ff; Burrows (1993), chap. 7.

[98] Birks (1989*a*), treats legal compulsion as being in the same category as duress.

[99] See Chap. 5 at 183.

[100] Burrows argues that the transfer can be vitiated as against a third party although not the transferee who exercised the legal compulsion: Burrows (1993), 205. But the vitiation of the transfer depends on the vitiation of the decision to make it, and here there is surely one decision that is either vitiated or not; it cannot be vitiated as against a third party whilst not vitiated as against the transferee.

[101] Cf Beatson (1991), above n 69. The discharge of a liability is a negative benefit in the true sense: cf Burrows (1993), 8; above n 77.

[102] Where the performance is carrying out an activity, like unblocking a drain, say, the liability must be de facto discharged, but with respect to a pecuniary liability there is a legal question whether the payment discharges the liability. Discharge is a necessary incident of the scheme involving the legal compulsion, which is to allow the third party to recover from the plaintiff instead of the defendant, not from both.

[103] There might be, broadly, two types of reasons for doing this. First, it may be that, as in the contribution cases, the plaintiff bears partial responsibility for the third party's loss, so that one might say that as against the third party he is responsible for the whole loss. Then there is no reason why the third party should have to be involved in the apportionment of liability as between the plaintiff and defendant. Secondly, it may be that the plaintiff has no such responsibility, but that making him liable and forcing him to recover from the defendant is an expedient means of ensuring

not to shift the ultimate liability but merely the risk and difficulty in taking proceedings against the defendant, there is also of necessity an imputed contract, by which the defendant has to pay or reimburse the plaintiff for the work or expenditure that he was compelled to undertake on behalf of the defendant. One might reasonably say that the plaintiff's claim is not so much a restitutionary claim to payment but a sui generis claim arising as part of the scheme of legal compulsion, in order to give effect to the object of shifting the risk of non-recovery from the third party to the plaintiff. But nothing much seems to turn on this distinction.[104]

An interesting case arising in this context is *Esso Petroleum Co Ltd v Hall Russell & Co*.[105] Here oil spilled from a ship belonging to the plaintiff oil company and caused damage to the third party. The plaintiff was party to an arrangement with other oil companies according to which each company undertook to compensate anyone who was damaged by oil from that company's ships, irrespective of whether legal liability could be established against it. In accordance with the agreement the plaintiff paid compensation to the third party. In fact the plaintiff was not legally liable, since the spillage was due to the negligence of the manufacturer of the ship, the defendant, from whom the plaintiff sought reimbursement. The voluntary arrangement with other oil companies was clearly intended (partly at least) to serve the same general function as the legal compulsion schemes above, i.e. to protect the third party from the practical difficulties of establishing a legal claim against the true wrongdoer. Thus one might argue that the scheme, although set up by voluntary arrangement rather than arising under the general law, should have been recognised by analogy as involving payment of compensation by the plaintiff on behalf of the defendant, thereby discharging the defendant's liability and generating a claim for reimbursement from the defendant. On the other hand, the defendant might reasonably object that such a scheme must arise under the general law rather than by private arrangement and that, vis-à-vis him, the private arrangement was merely officious. In fact the House of Lords denied that the plaintiff had any claim for reimbursement against the defendant.[106] The plaintiff could recover from the defendant in such a case only by negotiating with the third party for an assignment of the third party's right to compensation against the defendant before paying him.[107]

that the defendant can be made ultimately liable, because the plaintiff is in the best position to identify the defendant and take proceedings against him if necessary. This is the case with respect to import duties, or distress, or discharge of the owner's duty by the tenant.

[104] The two different approaches are contrasted in the judgment of Charles J in *Gebhardt v Saunders* [1892] 2 QB 452, 458.

[105] [1989] AC 643.

[106] The issue was not discussed in these terms in the judgments. The reason given by Lord Goff (at 663) was that the payment by the plaintiff did not discharge the defendant's liability; but this seems merely to beg the crucial question.

[107] In true legal compulsion cases, the plaintiff cannot of course negotiate the terms on which he pays the third party. Here, as noted by Lord Goff, it may have been inconsistent with the terms of the oil companies' voluntary agreement.

Suretyship

A supposed case of legal compulsion—indeed it is thought to be a standard example[108]—is where the plaintiff is the defendant's surety, i.e. the plaintiff has agreed with the defendant and the defendant's creditor to pay the defendant's debt in the event of his default. If the plaintiff has to pay the creditor, he has a claim against the defendant for reimbursement. As in the cases above, the plaintiff incurs an obligation to satisfy a liability that is principally the defendant's, and in consequence acquires a claim against the defendant for reimbursement. It is also true that the defendant's liability arises in order to protect the creditor from the difficulty of recovery or the risk of non-recovery from the defendant. But the case of the surety is quite distinct from the true cases of compulsory discharge considered above, because in the case of the surety the liability arises from a scheme agreed between the plaintiff, the defendant and the third party creditor, not under the general law. Thus here the defendant's liability to the plaintiff arises out of the contract of suretyship between the plaintiff and the defendant,[109] not by way of a restitutionary claim for payment under the general law;[110] and the liability is discharged not by operation of the general law as an incident of the scheme of legal compulsion, but because the plaintiff has the defendant's authority under the surety contract to pay off the debt in the event of the defendant's default.

The controversial case of *Owen v Tate*[111] demonstrates that the surety's claim to reimbursement is based on the contractual relationship with the defendant and not on the legal compulsion itself. The defendant had a debt to the creditor bank that was secured by way of a mortgage on the property of X. With a view to benefiting X, who had asked him for help, the plaintiff deposited a sum of money with the bank by way of a guarantee of the debt, in order to protect X against the risk of default by the defendant. The defendant was not party to this arrangement; indeed, he protested against it.[112] When subsequently the defendant did default and the bank resorted to the sum deposited by the plaintiff, the plaintiff made a claim for reimbursement from the defendant. The court understood the case to raise a conflict between two principles: the principle that where the plaintiff was subject to legal compulsion in paying off the defendant's debt he is entitled to be reimbursed by him, and the principle that an officious intervenor or volunteer is not entitled to payment for the officiously conferred benefit. It concluded that the latter principle should prevail in the circumstances and that the defendant was not liable. The decision was surely correct; not, however,

---

[108] Birks (1989*a*), 186; Mitchell (1994), 54ff.

[109] The plaintiff is intended to bear the risk of the defendant's default as against the creditor, not the defendant himself.

[110] Or a claim arising from the scheme of legal compulsion: see above at n 104.

[111] [1976] 1 QB 402.

[112] It is difficult to see how the security could properly be substituted without the defendant's consent, as opposed to being introduced as additional security.

because one principle prevailed over the other, but because, in the absence of any requirement under the general law for the plaintiff to act on behalf of the defendant, the principle governing cases of compulsory discharge was inapplicable.[113] In a surety case, the right of reimbursement, like the legal compulsion, arises from the contract of suretyship, and here there was no such contract between the plaintiff and the defendant.[114]

Thus the claim to reimbursement by a surety is contractual, arising from an implied term, not a restitutionary or non-contractual claim for payment (or reimbursement) as in the true compulsory discharge cases.[115] It has been argued that a contractual analysis is a manifestation of the implied contract heresy.[116] But, as noted previously, the implied contract heresy is really concerned with the analysis as a contractual claim of the restitutionary claim arising from a vitiated transfer, where there is clearly no agreement between the parties. Where there is actually an agreement between the parties, and a claim for payment or reimbursement arises out of it, the claim is contractual not restitutionary, and this is no less the case where the relevant term is not express but implied.[117]

Payments made with authority where no contractual claim arises

In a suretyship case, the debt is discharged because the plaintiff has authority under the contract of suretyship to discharge it, and the plaintiff at the same time acquires a claim for reimbursement from the defendant debtor under the contract. There are many other cases, of course, where the plaintiff has a contractual claim for reimbursement in respect of payments made on behalf of the defendant, whether to a creditor or otherwise. An example is where the plaintiff bank pays out in satisfaction of a cheque issued by the defendant, its customer, and then debits the defendant's account under his banking contract. It is possible in this type of situation that the plaintiff might make a payment by mistake, in circumstances such that he has no contractual right of reimbursement from the defendant: for example, where the defendant has cancelled the cheque and the plaintiff in error still pays out on it. Here the plaintiff can have no contractual claim against the defendant for reimbursement.[118] Instead it seems that the

---

[113] In fact the decision has been widely criticised: see e.g. Virgo (1999), 232.

[114] It may have been that the plaintiff was entitled to be reimbursed by X under an agreement with X, and that X was entitled to be reimbursed by the defendant on the basis that, so far as the defendant was concerned, the debt was discharged by the plaintiff acting in the name of X. If this was so, there may have been room to argue that the chain of liability could be circumvented, avoiding circuity of action, by giving the plaintiff a claim against the defendant: cf the cases concerning sub-lessees, e.g. *Moule v Garrett* (1872) LR 7 Exch 101. However the relationship between X and the defendant is not clear from the judgments.

[115] *Orakpo v Manson Investments* [1978] AC 95, 104; Mitchell (1994), 55. See further Chap. 8 with respect to subrogation.

[116] Birks (1989a), 29–39. It is sometimes said—e.g. Goff & Jones (1998), 401—that the issue is whether the claim is contractual or equitable, but this is to commit the fallacy discussed in Appendix 2.

[117] And this is still the case if the term is implied by law and so is really a rule of law regulating the contractual relationship.

[118] e.g. *Barclays Bank v Simms* [1980] QB 677.

plaintiff should have recourse against the payee, to recover the payment on the basis of his mistake.

Some difficulty arises where the payee is a creditor of the defendant and, although the plaintiff has no contractual right of reimbursement, he has authority to make a payment on behalf of the defendant in discharge of the debt.[119] This means that the creditor will have a defence of bona fide purchase and the payment will not be recoverable from him.[120] Thus the plaintiff will have neither a claim against the creditor to reverse the payment, nor a contractual claim for reimbursement from the defendant. Where the debt is discharged but no contractual right of reimbursement arises, it seems that the plaintiff should instead have a restitutionary claim for reimbursement from the defendant on the basis of an imputed contract, on the basis that the plaintiff was not officious and the defendant was incontrovertibly benefited.[121] This seems to be the basis for *Liggett v Barclays Bank*.[122]

Payments made to discharge a debt without legal compulsion or actual or apparent authority

In the cases above, where the debt is discharged it is either because this is a necessary implication of the legal compulsion or because the payment was made with the authority of the debtor. The traditional position is that in any other case where the plaintiff makes a payment to the creditor the payment will not be effective to discharge the debt (at least initially);[123] consequently, there can be no question of a claim arising against the debtor in respect of a benefit conferred on him. The plaintiff may instead have a claim against the creditor to reverse the payment to him if the payment was vitiated, for example by mistake (and there will be no defence of bona fide purchase where the debt is not discharged[124]). If the plaintiff was under the misconception that the effect of the payment would be to discharge the debt, it seems that he should have a claim against the creditor on the basis of mistake.

Where the payment was made by the plaintiff with a view to discharging the debt but did not initially do so, it seems that the debtor may subsequently adopt or ratify the payment, thereby discharging the debt. If the debtor knows that the

---

[119] Where the plaintiff pays but has no contractual right of reimbursement, one would think that there would also be no actual authority to pay on behalf of the defendant, but this is not necessarily the case: see e.g. *Lloyds Bank v Independent Insurance* [1999] 2 WLR 986. In any case, the plaintiff may have apparent authority, which will be sufficient to discharge the debt, as discussed in Chap. 7: it is arguable that *Re Cleadon* [1939] 1 Ch 286 and *Barclays Bank v Simms* were wrongly decided in this respect: Goode (1981); Friedmann (1983).

[120] Or in the nature of bona fide discharge: see Chap. 7.

[121] Or alternatively a restitutionary claim to reverse a vitiated transfer, the discharge of the debt operating to transfer wealth to the defendant: see Chap. 9 on subrogation.

[122] [1928] 1 KB 48; cf *Re Cleadon* [1939] 1 Ch 286. The issue was discussed in terms of subrogation: see Chap. 8.

[123] The case law is discussed in Mitchell (1994), chap. 1.

[124] As discussed in Chap. 7.

payment by the plaintiff was not intended to be gratuitous, it seems that by adopting the payment the debtor should be understood to have accepted a benefit offered by the plaintiff to him with a view to payment for it, and so should incur a liability to reimburse the plaintiff.[125] Such a liability is best understood as a contractual claim arising from the debtor's acceptance of an implicit offer by the plaintiff, although it has been argued to be a restitutionary claim based on free acceptance;[126] free acceptance is considered later in this chapter.[127] If the payment is not adopted by the debtor, it seems that there is no benefit to him, and no possibility of a claim against him. It may be also that there is no claim against the creditor, because the payment may have been free of any vitiating factor. For example, the plaintiff may have made the payment with a view to discharging the debt, but knowing that the payment would not be effective to do this without the debtor's adoption, and so unaffected by any mistake. Then the plaintiff will have no claim at all, unless he has (expressly or by implication) agreed with the creditor that the payment was to be conditional on adoption by the debtor, so that the creditor is liable to repay it if it is not adopted.[128] Such a claim against the creditor would be a contractual claim, although as considered elsewhere some would understand it to be a restitutionary claim based on total failure of consideration.[129]

The use claim

The use claim, which is considered separately in the next chapter, is another case where a claim for payment is allowed in the absence of a contract. Here the defendant uses the plaintiff's property without his permission and is liable to pay a reasonable fee.

INEFFECTIVE CONTRACTS

The restitutionary conditional transfer theory

The argument above has been that no claim arises for payment for a benefit conferred unless either there was a contract for payment or the two conditions—the

---

[125] See Birks & Beatson (1991), 190ff.

[126] Ibid., 192–3.

[127] However, even if the debtor knows that the payment was not intended to be gratuitous, his adoption of it should not necessarily generate a liability for reimbursement: in fact this appears to have been the position in *Owen v Tate*. Since the debtor was in effect forced to adopt the guarantee and deposit from the plaintiff instead of the original security, his adoption of it should not be understood to have implied an agreement to pay.

[128] There is much controversy surrounding this area: see e.g. Birks & Beatson (1991); Friedmann (1983).

[129] Birks & Beatson (1991), 193–4; see Chap. 2 at 54–6.

officiousness condition and the benefit condition—are met. But it is widely thought that a restitutionary claim for payment is available on a wider basis under the restitutionary conditional transfer theory or the restitutionary theory of "failure of consideration". As discussed in the last chapter, according to the theory if the plaintiff provided a benefit subject to a condition and the condition has not been fulfilled, the plaintiff is entitled to have the provision of the benefit reversed; this is how the quantum meruit is conceived. In reality this means that the plaintiff is entitled to be paid a reasonable price for the benefit. In the last chapter, there was a contract between the parties, and the theory was thought to operate on the basis that, as well as generating a liability in contract, the agreement entailed a condition subject to which the benefit was provided by the plaintiff, by virtue of which a non-contractual restitutionary claim for payment could arise as an alternative to the contractual claim if the plaintiff did not receive the expected reciprocal benefit.[130]

It appears to follow that, under the theory, where the agreement is not binding as a contract it can nevertheless serve to impose a condition on the defendant that will subject him to a restitutionary liability to pay. Furthermore, there seems to be no reason why, where there is no agreement at all, the plaintiff should not still be entitled to be paid for a benefit conferred, or imposed, on the defendant, if he intends to confer the benefit subject to a condition. More precisely, it seems that if the plaintiff confers a benefit on a stranger, meaning to be paid for it, he has conferred a benefit subject to a condition that he will be paid, and if the defendant does not pay him in accordance with this condition the plaintiff will in any case be entitled to a quantum meruit.

However such a wide operation of the theory is disavowed. Birks argues that the scope of the claim is limited as follows:

> If I do work for you, privately determined that you shall pay, I shall not by that alone persuade any court that I worked only in consideration that you would pay. I shall seem merely to have taken a risk. To avoid that charge I must communicate my intention to you so that you know the basis upon which I am working and can repudiate it if you wish. But if I know that you know my terms, I will be excused the need to tell you what they are.[131]

One suggestion here seems to be that a condition imposed purely privately and known only to the plaintiff could in principle be effective to generate a claim for payment, if the plaintiff could prove that he had had it in mind, the function of the agreement being simply to avoid the difficulty of proving this. This would mean that other forms of proof—maybe the evidence of a third party—would enable the plaintiff to enforce the condition even if the defendant was not notified of it, so that the plaintiff could simply impose benefits on strangers and demand payment provided that he had some evidence of his private intention to

---

[130] *Chillingworth v Esche* [1924] 1 Ch 97 is understood to be an example of the non-contractual claim, but there is no reason to doubt that the claim was contractual: see *Guardian Ocean v Banco de Brasil* [1991] 2 Lloyd's Rep 68, 87.

[131] Birks (1991*b*), 115.

charge. This would of course completely subvert the basic rule that denies a claim to officious intervenors or "risk-takers". In any case it is inconsistent with the second part of the passage, which suggests not that the problem is evidential, but that the purpose of the requirement of notice to the defendant is to give him the opportunity to reject the benefit.

The crucial question is really why it is necessary that the defendant should have an opportunity to reject, i.e. why he should know the basis on which the plaintiff is working and be able to repudiate it. The reason is surely that where the defendant has the opportunity to reject his failure to do so constitutes the acceptance of an offer; thus the claim is best understood as a contractual claim. This raises the issue of whether silence can amount to acceptance, which is indeed considered below,[132] but generally in the cases that are thought to involve failure of condition there has been a positive acceptance of an agreement, whether or not it is understood to give rise to a valid contract. In fact, it is very difficult to see how the legal relation established by the acceptance of (or acquiescence in) the provision of a benefit subject to a condition of payment can differ from an agreement to pay for the benefit. The agreement consists of a mutual understanding of the basis on which each party is prepared to make the exchange and a commitment to proceed on that basis, which is exactly what happens where there is an acceptance of a condition. The reason advocates of the restitutionary conditional transfer theory require that the condition be accepted, or that there is an opportunity to reject, is presumably exactly the reason why the plaintiff is required to seek agreement before conferring a benefit, viz. to protect the defendant's freedom to allocate his own resources in the light of his own tastes and resources.[133]

Furthermore, it seems generally to be thought that the communication and acceptance, or non-rejection, of a condition for the purposes of the restitutionary conditional transfer theory will *only* arise out of an agreement. Thus Burrows refers to the condition as arising from the fact that the plaintiff "[was] 'promised' (i.e., reasonably led to believe)" that he would be paid,[134] which seems to suggest that the claim can only arise through an agreement, and Birks appears to equate "failure of consideration" (meaning failure of a condition) and "requested benefits".[135] Consistently with this, Burrows expresses some doubt whether "failure of consideration" can ever operate outside a contractual context.[136]

---

[132] In connection with "pre-contractual claims".

[133] Possibly it might be thought that the plaintiff could have a claim because he acted on the basis of the agreement, i.e. he relied on the agreement, and that this would be different from enforcing the agreement. Maybe such a misunderstanding could be due to the same misconception that affects analysis of contracts, as discussed in the last chapter, viz. that an agreement is enforced in contract only through expectation damages and not by protecting the reliance interest directly. Whatever the reason, the argument is surely mistaken.

[134] Burrows (1993), 295.

[135] Birks (1991*b*), 109.

[136] He considers the possibility of a non-contractual sense of consideration as being of marginal significance, if any: Burrows (1993), 253, 320.

Thus, as concluded in the last chapter, where a claim arises that is understood to be based on "failure of consideration" in the sense of the restitutionary conditional transfer theory, it is really a contractual claim. With respect to valid contracts, the theory seems to make up for the limitations of the classical theory of contract, which appears to deny the possibility of a contractual claim in some circumstances where a claim is or ought to be available. The analogous problem in the cases considered in this chapter is the inflexibility of the orthodox contract rules on formation and validity, which appear to preclude a claim when one should be available, and the effect of the restitutionary theory is to allow what is in reality a contractual claim without appearing to subvert these contract rules.

The issue often arises in connection with "ineffective contracts", or contracts that are fully or partly unenforceable, which encompasses void, voidable and unenforceable contracts. In these cases, it is necessary to bear in mind the distinction between the claim to reverse a vitiated payment and the claim for payment for work done in conferring a benefit; these are generally conflated under the single head of restitution for unjust enrichment in accordance with the restitutionary conditional transfer theory, so that they appear to be available in principle on the same basis.[137] However, a payment made pursuant to an ineffective contract is liable to be vitiated, so as to generate a claim to reverse it (although there is some controversy over the vitiating factor);[138] but, if the contract cannot be relied upon, it seems that a claim for payment in respect of a benefit conferred should not arise unless the two conditions above are satisfied, and this will not generally be the case.[139] In some such cases, where it is said that there is no contract claim because there is no contract or the contract is invalid or unenforceable, a supposedly restitutionary claim for payment is nevertheless allowed, and is sometimes explained as a claim under the restitutionary conditional transfer theory. As the discussion above suggests, and as is argued below, despite appearances such a claim is in fact generally best understood as a contractual claim.

There is an alternative rationale for the requirement for an opportunity to reject, which will be considered further below. This is that in some circumstances, rather than constituting the acceptance of an offer, the defendant's failure to reject may constitute a wrongful act by him because it is a breach of a duty to save the plaintiff from wasting his time and money. Again such a claim would not be restitutionary; here it would in principle be tortious. The crucial question here is when, if at all, the defendant can incur such a duty. The issue arises in connection with free acceptance, which is considered separately below; indeed, as Birks defines the claim arising from failure of a condition in the passage

---

[137] The difference between the two is understood to relate only to the type of benefit and the way it is measured: see above 19.

[138] As discussed in Chap. 6.

[139] Sometimes the officiousness condition will be satisfied because the plaintiff is mistaken; but generally the benefit condition will not be satisfied.

above,[140] it is difficult to see how it differs from free acceptance, which is also said to occur where the defendant fails to reject a benefit provided to him when he has an opportunity to do so. In fact the difference appears to be that for the purposes of the restitutionary conditional transfer theory the plaintiff must have relied on the defendant's acceptance of the condition, or his failure to reject, so that there is a mutual understanding or agreement (and the claim is really contractual), whereas in cases where liability is supposed to arise only on the basis of free acceptance, the defendant's liability (if there is any liability) arises directly from his failure to act, as a breach of duty to the plaintiff, whether or not the defendant relied on it as indicating an agreement to pay. As discussed further below, the supposed doctrine of free acceptance is a misleading way of characterising such a liability.

Void contracts

A "void contract" often refers to a purported or apparent agreement where there was actually no agreement between the parties.[141] It is commonly argued that the plaintiff who has done work under such a void contract can make a restitutionary claim for payment. In *Rover v Canon*, which was discussed above, a claim for payment in the form of a quantum meruit was allowed for work done under a contract that was void because it was made before the plaintiff company had been incorporated. The quantum meruit was conceded, and so the basis for the claim was not considered, although it was said to be restitutionary and it has been argued that it should be understood in accordance with the restitutionary conditional transfer theory.[142] If, as argued above, the legal effect of the acceptance of a condition is only to generate an agreement, this would merely amount to resurrecting the void agreement by another name, or possibly finding a new agreement between the parties entered into during the course of the performance. Indeed, as argued above, something along these lines may be the best interpretation of the case, and if so there is no need to confuse matters by invoking restitution, or "failure of consideration" in the sense of failure of condition. The true issue in such a case is then the validity and scope of the rule that a pre-incorporation contract must be specifically ratified and does not take effect merely through tacit acceptance and performance after incorporation.[143]

---

[140] At n 131.

[141] "Void contract" is also used to refer to cases where there was an agreement between the parties, but there is an invalidating rule that renders the agreement void. Some such cases are "illegal contracts". In other cases this type of void contract appears to be similar if not identical to a contract that is "unenforceable" for failure to comply with a condition, typically a requirement for the agreement to be in writing. See further Chap. 6.

[142] Burrows, 311; Skelton (1998), 26.

[143] Cf Stoljar (1989), 235ff.

Another case with respect to which the restitutionary conditional transfer theory has been invoked is *Boulton v Jones*,[144] also mentioned above, where in fact no claim was granted at all. Here goods were ordered by the defendant and supplied by the plaintiff but there was no contract because the defendant meant to contract with the plaintiff's predecessor in business. Burrows argues that there was a failure of condition because the defendant "refused to perform his apparent contractual promise to pay".[145] Thus Burrows appears to argue that although the defendant's promise to pay did not generate any contractual liability for payment, it could nevertheless generate a claim for payment because the plaintiff acted on the basis of it. This surely shows very clearly that the restitutionary conditional transfer theory does no more than give effect to an agreement that under the rules of contract law does not generate a valid contract. It may be that a contract ought to have arisen, but if not there is no justification for giving effect to the agreement by subterfuge.

Voidable contracts

A voidable contract means an agreement that can be either affirmed or rescinded by one party, the plaintiff, on the ground that his agreement was affected by a vitiating factor. Commonly the plaintiff will be a party who has paid money under the agreement, rather than a party who has provided goods or services; for reasons considered below, the latter is less likely to seek rescission. If the plaintiff rescinds, the contract is treated as void from the start and the plaintiff is entitled to have his payment returned to him, as in the case of a void contract.[146] However, the rule is said to be that the plaintiff loses his right to rescind if "restitutio in integrum" becomes impossible, which means that it is impossible to restore the defendant to the position he was in before the contract, or, more broadly, that the defendant will be unfairly prejudiced by allowing rescission.[147] In a case where the defendant supplied property in return for the payment, and the property is still available and can be returned, there is no impediment to restitutio in integrum. Originally it was thought that a significant change in the condition of the property would preclude restitutio in integrum; but subsequently the courts accepted that it could be achieved even if the original property could not be returned in exactly the original condition, by making the plaintiff account for any change in its condition and for the profits made on the property during the period of the voidable contract.[148] More recently, the courts have gone further and allowed the plaintiff to rescind on the basis that he

---

[144] (1857) 27 LJ Ex 117.
[145] Burrows (1993), 306.
[146] See further Chap. 6.
[147] e.g. *Clarke v Dickson* (1858) EB & E 148; *Smith New Court Securities Ltd v Scrimgeour Vickers* [1994] 1 WLR 1271.
[148] *Erlanger v New Sombrero Phosphate Co* (1878) 3 App Cas 1218.

has to pay for work done by the defendant during the course of the voidable contract.[149] Thus the rule appears to operate less strictly than originally, and it is fair to say that its scope is in doubt.[150]

The widely accepted academic analysis of rescission in terms of unjust enrichment is broadly as follows.[151] Where the contract is voidable, each party has, prima facie, a restitutionary claim to reverse his performance of the contract; as it is said, the plaintiff has a restitutionary claim and the defendant a claim for counter-restitution. The plaintiff's vitiating factor is traditionally taken to be the factor vitiating the contract; for example, if the contract is voidable for the plaintiff's mistake, the vitiating factor is mistake. Nowadays, following the abrogation of the mistake of law bar,[152] it would be better to recognise that the claim is based on mistake as to the validity of the contract. The defendant is not affected by the factor that vitiated the plaintiff's assent to the agreement, and so it has been thought instead that there is an "unjust factor" behind his counterclaim, which is "failure of consideration", under the restitutionary conditional transfer theory. On this basis his performance was conditional and the condition failed when the contract was rescinded.[153] Again, in so far as the defendant has a restitutionary claim to reverse a transfer under the contract, it should now be recognised that it is based on mistake of law.

The "restitutio in integrum is impossible" rule is understood as follows. It is thought that the defendant's prima facie restitutionary counter-claim is denied where it is difficult to measure.[154] This is the case where it cannot be satisfied exactly through the return of goods supplied by him, because it then involves establishing the value of a benefit in the form of services or goods consumed. Where the defendant's counter-claim is denied on this ground, the plaintiff is also denied his claim, on the basis that the two claims must stand or fall together. Thus the defence of "restitutio in integrum impossible" is nowadays sometimes described as "counter-restitution impossible". The movement towards relaxing the strict restitutio in integrum rule is thought to be based on the recognition that the problem of measurement ought not to be insuperable.

---

[149] *O'Sullivan v Management Agency & Music Ltd* [1985] QB 428.

[150] Where the defendant also committed a wrong (i.e. the vitiating factor is derived from such a wrong, for example where there was a fraud by the defendant), the plaintiff has an alternative claim based on the wrong, for which the remedy will be compensation for his loss, but for present purposes it is assumed that the wrong is not relied on as such. In principle it should be possible for compensation for the wrong to be effected by a specific remedy, which would in effect involve rescission: see 348.

[151] e.g. Burrows (1993), 33.

[152] This is discussed in Chap. 5.

[153] Burrows (1993), 33. But in addition to the objections to the restitutionary conditional transfer theory that have already been made above and in the last chapter, and apply here as much as elsewhere, it is difficult to see, if the claim based on failure of condition requires the condition to have been accepted, how the plaintiff's acceptance of the agreement can be vitiated but his acceptance of the condition, by way of his acceptance of the agreement, still be effective for the purposes of the restitutionary claim.

[154] Birks (1989a) 421.

The same argument is used, as discussed in the last chapter,[155] in relation to total failure of consideration, and indeed total failure of consideration is equated with the requirement of restitutio in integrum.[156]

The main problem here is the failure to distinguish between the restitutionary claim arising from a vitiated transfer, and the restitutionary claim for payment for work and expenditure.[157] When a contract is voidable, the plaintiff has (prima facie) a claim for restitution for a vitiated transfer in respect of a payment under the contract, based on the vitiating factor of mistake as to validity.[158] At the same time the defendant has a claim for restitution for a vitiated transfer, also based on mistake as to validity,[159] if he has, say, transferred goods to the plaintiff. The difficulty arises where the defendant has provided work for the defendant, or goods that have been consumed. Here the problem is that normally the defendant needs to be able to rely on the contract in order to claim payment in respect of his work and expenditure, and rescission of the contract will deny him this. In the absence of a contractual claim, a restitutionary claim will arise only if the two conditions referred to above are met, and generally the benefit condition will not be satisfied.[160] The measurement problem here refers to the fact that the benefit condition for a restitutionary claim for payment is not satisfied. By contrast, where there is a valid contract, as in the cases considered in the last chapter, the problem of measurement is of course no basis for denying a claim for payment; the contract confers a claim for payment however difficult it may be to measure the claim.

Thus rescission, if it were allowed, would operate in favour of the party who made the payment, the plaintiff, at the expense of the party who provided the work and expenditure, by allowing the plaintiff's claim for restitution for a vitiated transfer but denying the defendant any claim for payment. The strict restitutio in integrum rule, by precluding rescission, protects the defendant's right to enforce the contract and recover payment for what he has done under it, even though the plaintiff's assent to the contract was vitiated. The plaintiff is allowed to rescind only where the defendant's position can be sufficiently protected by a restitutionary claim to reverse a payment or transfer, and he has done no work or incurred no expenditure for which rescission will deny him payment. The effect of the strict rule is to give full effect to the objective theory of contract,[161] in the sense that the contract is enforced because the plaintiff appeared to agree

---

[155] See Chap. 2 at 56.

[156] Birks (1989a), 417; Burrows (1993), 191; see also McKendrick (1995).

[157] Another objection to the restitutionary approach is that it gives no protection to the defendant who relied on the contract without giving a benefit to the defendant; it is said that the cases support the view that there is no protection for the defendant's reliance loss where it does not give rise to a benefit: Treitel (1999), 351–2.

[158] Or arguably the underlying vitiating factor affecting the contract. The vitiating factor applicable to a void contract is discussed in Chap. 6.

[159] The vitiating factor affecting the contract does not affect the defendant, and so mistake as to validity is the only plausible vitiating factor.

[160] The officiousness condition will usually be satisfied because of the mistake.

[161] Or, in other words, as considered in Chap. 7, bona fide purchase.

to it, notwithstanding the vitiation of his assent, unless the contract can be rescinded without prejudice to the defendant. One might reasonably argue that where the claim is based on the appearance of agreement rather than actual agreement one should not strictly regard it as a contractual claim, and that it would be better to treat it as restitutionary. But, first, the objective theory of contract is pervasive in the law of contract and it is hardly feasible to distinguish cases of true agreement and cases where there is merely an appearance of agreement, which are liable to merge into one another; and, secondly, if the claim is not a matter of contract it would have to be characterised as a claim based on estoppel or non-contractual reliance, not restitution.

Although this rule against rescission has the advantage of protecting the defendant in respect of his reliance on the appearance of agreement, it has the disadvantage of holding the plaintiff to an agreement that he did not properly assent to. It is not easy to reconcile these two considerations: the plaintiff has a legitimate interest in rescinding the contract and reversing his payment, and the defendant, who relied in good faith on the appearance of agreement, a legitimate interest in enforcing the contract, to the extent of being paid for what he has done under it.[162] The strict restitutio in integrum rule gives full protection to the defendant. A more flexible approach gives more protection for the plaintiff, by allowing him a claim in circumstances where under the original strict rule he would have been denied rescission altogether. This involves giving partial effect to the contract, in order to allow the defendant a claim for what he has done under the contract. (But the defendant does not have an expectation claim, as he would have if the plaintiff repudiated the contract in circumstances in which he was not entitled to rescind.) The remedies that arise may be similar to those that should be available on frustration, so as to protect so far as possible the plaintiff's interest in recovering his payment and also the defendant's interest in being paid for what he has done.[163] But it may also be necessary to impose a modified version of the contract on the parties, in order to take account of the fact that the plaintiff might not have agreed to the original contract in the absence of a vitiating factor.

Consider the case where the plaintiff agrees to give a guarantee to the defendant, but the plaintiff's agreement is vitiated because he was misled into thinking that the guarantee was limited to £15,000, whereas in fact it was not subject to any limit. Here the plaintiff seeks rescission in order to avoid a liability under the contract, not in order to recover a payment under it. It seems that rescission should be denied under the strict rule, unless the defendant has notice of the vitiating factor and so should be unable to rely on the appearance of agreement.[164] On such facts in *TSB Bank v Camfield*,[165] the Court of Appeal held that the contract was unenforceable because the defendant had notice of the vitiating factor.

---

[162] This assumes that the defendant has not behaved wrongfully.
[163] Frustration was considered in the last chapter.
[164] See Chap. 7 on bona fide purchase.
[165] [1995] 1 WLR 430.

But the first instance judge (who did not take the view that the defendant had the requisite notice) had held that the contract should be binding as a guarantee up to £15,000; i.e. he imposed a modified contract on the parties. Unfortunately the Court of Appeal thought that this outcome was not open to the court, which had either to enforce the contract in its original terms or to avoid it. However this seems to be inconsistent with *O'Sullivan v Management Agency and Music Ltd.*[166] Here the plaintiff transferred copyright in his songs to the defendant under a management contract that was voidable for undue influence. The plaintiff was entitled to the return of the copyright, but the defendant was entitled to reasonable payment for management services. The reasonable remuneration was less than the profit that the defendant made on the contract as agreed, which was considered to be unfairly advantageous to the defendant in the light of the undue influence.[167]

Thus, in conclusion, where the plaintiff's assent to a contract was vitiated, he has a prima facie restitutionary claim to recover a payment under the contract (or to disown a contractual liability as in *Camfield*). But where the contract has been partially performed by the defendant through work and expenditure (or, say, reliance on a guarantee), the strict restitutio in integrum rule at one time precluded rescission in order to protect the defendant's position under the contract. Nowadays the tendency in such a case is to allow the plaintiff to recover the payment or transfer, but subject to protecting the defendant's reliance under the contract. Here, although the plaintiff is said to rescind the contract, in reality the law gives partial effect to it, as a basis for the defendant's claim, adjusted as appropriate to take account of the way in which the terms agreed may have been affected by the vitiating factor. There is no restitutionary claim for payment for work done, and in particular no such restitutionary claim based on the restitutionary conditional transfer theory.

A distinction is generally drawn between a void contract, meaning here a case where there was no real agreement between the parties,[168] and a voidable contract, where the agreement was affected by a vitiating factor entitling one party to rescind. The void contract is said to be a nullity, whereas some effect can be given to the voidable contract to protect the party who relied on the appearance of agreement. But it is doubtful whether this distinction is really sustainable. For a voidable contract, it is not true to say that there *is* an agreement, but that it was vitiated, any more than for a void contract. In reality, where, say, the plaintiff's assent was given under duress or undue influence or mistake, there is no agreement, but there may be the appearance of agreement, which may justify holding the plaintiff bound as if there were an agreement. The great advantage of holding that a contract is voidable rather than void is that it makes it possible, in accordance with the restitutio in integrum rule, to provide some

---

[166] [1985] QB 428. See the discussion in Proksch (1996).

[167] There are other cases on rescission "on terms": e.g. *Solle v Butcher* [1950] 1 KB 671.

[168] The discussion here does not relate to a case where there *is* an agreement between the parties, but it is invalidated or prohibited as a contract: see further Chap. 6.

protection for the other party if he has relied in good faith on the appearance of agreement.[169] In fact there is one case where, although the contract is said to be prima facie void, it is enforceable if there is an appearance of contract: this is where an agreement would be void for lack of authority, but is actually enforceable on the basis of apparent authority.[170]

Unenforceable contracts

Sometimes there is an agreement between the parties that fails to comply with a condition imposed by law, for example a requirement for the agreement to be in writing or to be registered, failure to comply with which is said to render the contract unenforceable. The unenforceability is not based on the absence of an agreement, or on a vitiating factor.[171] The usual case, which will be discussed here, concerns a contract that was made without the required formalities. Following the original example of the Statute of Frauds, parts of which survive to the present day in other forms, a statute will sometimes provide that a contract is not to be enforceable (by one or both parties) unless it is in or evidenced in writing.[172] Similar provisions are found relating to the creation of trusts and the transfer of interests in land or under a trust, or agreements to do so.[173] The main purpose of such a provision seems to be to overcome evidential problems, and thereby to reduce the risk that a transaction will be falsely asserted, in error or by fraud, and mistakenly upheld by a court. Unfortunately, although such a provision can no doubt have a beneficial effect through the increased use of writing by those who are aware of it, it also creates a new danger of injustice, where one party carries out a transaction honestly but in disregard of the statute, and another party, having previously agreed to the transaction, and having now received the benefit of it, seeks to take advantage of the statute to deny the transaction, thereby not preventing an error or fraud but perpetrating one. For this reason the Statute of Frauds has always been controversial, and the courts have developed various techniques for getting around it.[174]

---

[169] This accounts for the movement towards treating agreements vitiated by mistake as being voidable rather than void, illustrated by e.g. *Solle v Butcher* [1950] 1 KB 671. The concept of voidability is also used to protect third parties, as discussed in Chap. 7 at 240 and Chap. 10 at 324.

[170] Furthermore, with respect to mistake, the contractual formation rules tend actually to incorporate the issue of apparent agreement into the determination of whether the contract is void: see further Chap. 5 at 178–80.

[171] Also, it seems that in such cases there is not necessarily any implication of wrongdoing on the part of either party if the condition is not met, and so no question of an illegal contract. Illegal contracts are considered in Chap. 6.

[172] See Furmston (1996), 207ff.

[173] e.g. the provisions now in Law of Property Act 1925 s.53; Law of Property (Miscellaneous Provisions) Act 1989, s.2.

[174] See Furmsten (1996), 209; Hayton (1996), 61ff.

Enforcing an "unenforceable" trust

Consider, for example, the case where the plaintiff transfers property to the defendant on trust for himself or a third party, but without using writing as required. Can the defendant, having accepted the transfer on trust, then invoke the statute, deny the trust, and keep the property for himself, free of any trust? This seems to be the undeniable effect of a statutory provision that declares a trust to be unenforceable unless evidenced in writing. However, the courts have adopted the principle that "equity will not allow a statute to be used as a cloak for fraud", by virtue of which the defendant is held to the trust, notwithstanding the statute, because he accepted the transfer on trust and it would be a fraud for him to go back on this.[175] On other occasions, the court has preferred to say that the original trust is unenforceable under the statute, but that to prevent fraud the property in the defendant's hands is subject to a constructive trust in favour of the plaintiff.[176] This formulation has the advantage that a constructive trust is not subject to the formality requirement,[177] but the better view is surely that the effect of the doctrine is in reality to enforce the express trust notwithstanding the statute.[178]

The Wills Act

A similar position arises in relation to the Wills Act 1837, which provides that a testamentary disposition is void unless in writing and witnessed. If the testator made an agreement with the defendant for the defendant to take a legacy under his will and pass it on to the plaintiff, the defendant will take the legacy on trust for the plaintiff, thereby giving effect to the agreement, even though it was not in writing and witnessed in accordance with the statute. It is usually argued that the agreement is altogether outside the terms of the statute, because it is not in itself a testamentary disposition: it is "dehors the will".[179] But this is unconvincing, because the agreement is clearly a means for disposing of property on death, and is capable of frustrating the objective of the statute, which is presumably designed to minimise the possibility of disputes by ensuring that clear evidence of the testator's intentions is available. Another view is that the court allows the agreement to be enforced in order to prevent the defendant from

---

[175] *Rochefoucauld v Boustead* [1897] 1 Ch 196.

[176] *Bannister v Bannister* [1948] 2 All ER 133. Constructive trusts are considered in Chap. 10.

[177] S.51(2) of the Law of Property Act 1925; s.2 of the Law of Property (Miscellaneous Provisions) Act 1989.

[178] This was the view of the court in *Rochefoucauld v Boustead*. This view appears to be widely supported by commentators. Where the plaintiff seeks to recover property transferred to the defendant, an alternative interpretation of the trust is that it represents a restitutionary claim arising from a mistake by the plaintiff as to the validity of the contract. Here the trust would be a genuine constructive trust.

[179] The approach is derived from the judgment of Lord Sumner in *Blackwell v Blackwell* [1929] AC 318.

using the statute to defraud the testator by going back on the agreement: this is the "fraud theory" of secret trusts, which is analogous to the "cloak for fraud" theory referred to above.[180]

Part performance

The courts have used similar techniques with respect to contracts affected by the Statute of Frauds. The Chancery courts developed the doctrine of part performance, according to which the plaintiff could enforce a contract that had been entered into without the required formalities, if he had part-performed it. For example, where the plaintiff gave up a secured tenancy under an oral contract according to which she was to have a secured tenancy of other premises, she could enforce the contract even though it was supposed to be unenforceable for lack of writing.[181] Again, the doctrine of part-performance was obviously designed to protect a plaintiff who had actually relied on the agreement by performing or starting to perform it, so that he would be prejudiced by its unenforceability. The rationale of the doctrine was controversial. One view was along the lines of the "cloak for fraud" principle; the defendant, who had agreed to the contract, would not be allowed to invoke the statute to escape his liability at the expense of the plaintiff.[182] Another view was that the doctrine of part performance did not in fact give effect to the contract at all:

> [T]he defendant is really "charged" upon the equities resulting from the acts done in execution of the contract, and not (within the meaning of the Statute) upon the contract itself.[183]

A similar case is where the defendant agrees to confer an interest in property on the plaintiff in return for work done by the plaintiff under an oral agreement. Although the oral agreement is supposed to be unenforceable for lack of formality, the plaintiff is allowed a claim in the form of a constructive trust or proprietary estoppel in respect of his reliance on the agreement.[184]

Thus one can see two differing approaches to avoiding the application of statutory formalities. The first is to say that, although the plaintiff's claim does enforce the agreement or trust, contrary to the letter of the statute, it should

---

[180] The fraud theory of secret trusts is associated with *McCormick v Grogan* (1869) LR 4 HL 82. The beneficiary is allowed to enforce the agreement although he is not privy to it.

[181] *Kingswood Estate v Anderson* [1963] 2 QB 169.

[182] Pollock on Contract (13th ed., 1950), 521; cited by Furmsten (1996), 226; *Steadman v Steadman* [1976] AC 536, 540 per Lord Reid.

[183] *Maddison v Alderson* (1883) 8 App Cas 467, 475 per Lord Selborne. Another view was that the statute was concerned with the difficulty of proof, and part-performance counted as evidence that could make up for the lack of writing: e.g. *Britain v Rossiter* (1879) 11 QBD 123, 130 per Cotton LJ. But it is doubtful whether the part-performance is itself evidence of an agreement, although possibly the fact that the defendant did not query the performance where he was aware of it may in some circumstances suggest that he had made an agreement.

[184] e.g. *Yaxley v Gotts* [1999] 2 WLR 1217; cf the "common intention" constructive trust of the matrimonial home.

nevertheless be allowed in order to prevent a fraud. If this justified at all, it must be based on a principle of statutory construction—a principle that a statute will be construed to avoid injustice, even if this is ostensibly contrary to the wording of the Act. The second approach is that, although the plaintiff's claim appears to give effect to the agreement or trust, in reality it is independent of it and so unaffected by the statute—for example, that it is a claim based on a constructive trust, or on "the equities resulting from the acts done" or that the agreement does not constitute a testamentary disposition and so operates "dehors the will".

A *restitutionary or contractual claim*

The discussion above is by way of a preamble to the issue mentioned above as to whether the claim for payment under an "unenforceable contract" is contractual or restitutionary. In relation to contract, the equitable doctrine of part performance mentioned above was one means of avoiding the effect of the statutory formalities. The same issue arose at common law. The plaintiff did work for the defendant under an agreement without first complying with a formality requirement of writing, and then the defendant refused to pay and invoked the formality requirement. At common law the courts also found the means to allow the plaintiff a claim, here a claim for payment for his work.[185] Two different routes to this outcome have been used at different times.[186] The first is that in the old common law, where a plaintiff completed his work under a contract and became entitled to the contract price, the claim was strictly speaking a claim in debt, not in contract, i.e. it was taken through a different form of action. Consequently, it was argued, the original Statute of Frauds, when it referred to an action on the contract, was not intended to cover a claim for the contract price, which was, in the language of the old forms of action, an action in debt. Even though the claim for the contract price was, in modern terms, contractual, the statute (or its successors) could be interpreted as permitting it.[187] The other argument was that the statute does preclude a claim in contract, but that in respect of work that he has actually carried out the plaintiff is entitled to a non-contractual, restitutionary quantum meruit, which is unaffected by the statute because it is not based on the contract. These again reflect the two different approaches mentioned above. The first argument involves enforcing the contract, notwithstanding the statute, here ostensibly by applying an historical argument for a restrictive construction rather than by reference to the fraud of going back on an agreement, but no doubt with this in view. The second argument is that the claim is unaffected by the statute because it is not based on the contract.

[185] In equity, under the doctrine of part performance the claim was not for payment, but typically for the transfer of an interest in land.

[186] See Ibbetson (1988), 319ff.

[187] Ibid., 319; Denning (1925); Stoljar (1989), 232ff; cf Atiyah (1986), 235ff.

The issue came up quite recently in *Pavey & Matthews v Paul*[188] in the High Court of Australia. The plaintiff builder had completed the renovation of a cottage for the defendant under an oral contract, which had provided for reasonable remuneration by reference to prevailing rates in the industry. A claim to reasonable remuneration based on the agreement would have been a contractual quantum meruit. A dispute arose over the amount due, and the defendant then denied any liability under the contract on the basis of section 45 of the Builders Licensing Act 1971 (NSW), which provided that a "building contract" (as defined) was unenforceable by the builder if not in writing. The court held that a claim for a contractual quantum meruit would be contrary to the statute. But it held that a claim for reasonable remuneration did lie in restitution or unjust enrichment, not in contract, and so was unaffected by the statute.[189] Deane J said:

> There is no apparent reason in justice why a builder who is precluded from enforcing an agreement should also be deprived of the ordinary common law right . . . to recover, in an action founded on restitution or unjust enrichment, reasonable remuneration for work done.[190]

Thus the court took the second of the two approaches mentioned above for avoiding the formality requirement.

But is there really any non-contractual basis for the claim? The problem is that in the absence of an agreement the general rule is that there *is* no "ordinary common law right" to payment for work done.[191] It is the function of the agreement to generate a claim to payment when one would not otherwise exist. This is why the builder made the agreement in the first place. In the absence of a contractual liability, the two conditions for an imputed contract must be satisfied. One might argue that the plaintiff was mistaken in thinking that he had a binding contract,[192] and so was not officious; but, as discussed above, there would be great difficulty in showing that the benefit condition was satisfied.[193]

It has been suggested that the restitutionary claim in *Pavey* was based on the restitutionary conditional transfer theory.[194] This would mean that the plaintiff builder is understood to have implicitly imposed on the defendant a condition that he would be paid, which, although conveyed through the agreement, operated independently of it; and that the plaintiff could enforce this condition even though he could not enforce the agreement. This approach has been rejected above. The court in *Pavey* found a non-contractual basis for the claim in the

---

[188] (1988) 162 CLR 221. A similar analysis applies to the leading Canadian case of *Degelman v Guarantee Trust Co of Canada and Constantineau* [1954] 3 DLR 785.

[189] At 256–7, per Deane J; at 227–8, per Mason and Wilson JJ.

[190] At 262.

[191] This is the fundamental rule discussed at the start of the chapter.

[192] If the contractual analysis is right he is not mistaken in this, or at least he has made a lesser mistake because it is only partly enforceable.

[193] One might say that it was obvious that the defendant had received a benefit; but see at n 88 above.

[194] Burrows (1988); Burrows (1993), 302; Birks (1991*b*), 111.

defendant's "acceptance" of the plaintiff's work under the agreement.[195] It is not clear what exactly was meant by "acceptance" on the facts of *Pavey*. If it meant accepting the benefit of the work once it was done, it is difficult to see that the defendant had any choice; the work could not be returned to the plaintiff.[196] Another interpretation might be that the defendant accepted by standing by and allowing the plaintiff to provide a benefit instead of intervening to stop him from doing so: this is free acceptance as usually defined, as considered below. Free acceptance is said to be based on unconscientiousness, and it might be thought that, by standing by without intervening, the defendant had acted unconscientiously, and that the plaintiff's claim was based on this unconscientiousness rather than on the agreement itself. Possibly this is plausible if the defendant knew all along that the statute would preclude any liability for payment (or ought to have known), and intended not to pay.[197] But this does not appear to have been the case, and there is in any case no suggestion that this is what the court meant. Alternatively it might be argued that, if the express oral contract between the parties is disregarded, the plaintiff's conduct in beginning to perform could be understood as an offer that was tacitly accepted by the defendant through his failure to intervene. But, whatever other objections there might be to such an analysis, on this approach the claim based on "acceptance" would be a contractual claim that would be affected by the statute in just the same way as the express oral agreement.

The better view is that, if *Pavey* was rightly decided, the claim was not restitutionary but contractual, and that the court ought to have adopted the first approach mentioned above to circumventing the formality requirement, according to which a contractual claim should be allowed, notwithstanding the statute, in circumstances where the denial of the claim would work an unacceptable injustice. As in the cases considered above, this might be the case where the defendant seeks to evade payment after the plaintiff has performed in accordance with the agreement, i.e. where the contract has been executed and is not executory. As discussed above, there is plenty of authority for this type of approach, although its legitimacy remains open to argument. The crucial issue is whether it is permissible to disregard the strict wording of the statute on the ground that the harshness of the outcome in particular circumstances shows that the statute could not have been intended to apply. The answer would depend on the relevant principles of statutory construction and a careful consideration of the statute's purposes.[198]

---

[195] At 227, per Mason and Wilson JJ; at 16262, 8 per Deane J.

[196] Burrows (1993), 302; Birks (1991*b*), 111.

[197] Unconscientiousness in connection with free acceptance is considered below, at 122–127.

[198] Another issue is whether, where the contract includes an agreed price rather than an agreement for reasonable remuneration, the statute gives the court the power to allow a claim for payment, but in a reasonable measure determined by the court rather than necessarily the agreed price, so that the agreement is enforced only so far as to avoid injustice and no further. In *Pavey*, there was no agreed price in the contract, merely a provision for reasonable remuneration.

The court seemed to assume that if the claim was contractual it was necessarily precluded by the statute. Where in cases of this sort there has been a reference to implied contract, Deane J said that it:

> should be recognised as but a reflection of the influence of discarded fictions, buried forms of action and the conventional conviction that, if a common law claim could not properly be framed in tort, it must necessarily be dressed in the language of contract.[199]

But a quantum meruit is usually contractual, not restitutionary. Where a quantum meruit was said to be based on an implied contract, this almost always meant a true implied agreement, not a fictional one, because the general rule is that a claim for payment does not arise except under an agreement—hence the traditional requirement for a request in order for a quantum meruit to arise. The real implied contract heresy concerns not claims for a quantum meruit, but claims for money had and received, arising from a vitiated transfer, where the claim is of course based on the receipt of the transfer.[200] Far from exposing a fiction, the court in *Pavey* adopted one: that "acceptance" is distinct from agreement and provides a non-contractual ground for a claim.

The contrast between the classical and reliance theories casts light on the decision in *Pavey*. Under the classical theory, a contractual claim is understood as based on a promise to perform, which would necessarily generate a claim in the expectation measure. This claim is distinguished from a restitutionary claim, which is supposed to be based on the benefit received through the agreement. There is no sound basis for a non-contractual, restitutionary claim; but it is fair to say that what the court had in mind was a simple contractual reliance claim, viz. a claim for payment for work done in reliance on the agreement, a claim that might not be thought of as contractual under the classical theory, because it did not represent the enforcement of a contractual obligation through the expectation measure.[201] Under the reliance theory, then, the effect of the statute is to deprive the plaintiff of the expectation measure presumption that would usually apply in favour of the plaintiff. Instead the plaintiff is confined to a proved reliance claim. Arguably this limited contractual claim is what is strictly necessary to avoid an obvious injustice, without going any further and giving the normal degree of protection provided by a contract by way of the expectation measure.

"Pre-contractual" claims

Often, whilst in negotiation for a contact, the plaintiff incurs expenditure and does work, for example in preparing a tender or a sample of work, or sometimes

---

[199] At 256, per Deane J.
[200] Above at 98.
[201] In fact on the facts of *Pavey* it seems that there would be no difference in the measures.

even in embarking on providing the work actually sought by the defendant in the negotiations. The usual rule is that he has no claim for payment for this work, because there was no contract.[202] This is an application of the basic rule that, because there was no agreement for payment, the plaintiff is an officious intervenor or "risk-taker". It is not necessarily irrational for the plaintiff to do work as a risk-taker. He may do the work in the hope that it will lead to a contract,[203] or that the defendant will pay him even though he is not bound to, or in order to impress the defendant and so get work in the future. However, there have been cases that appear to be exceptions to the rule, where the plaintiff has been able to recover payment for work done whilst negotiations are in course. Apparently there is no contract, and it is widely thought that these cases are examples of a non-contractual, restitutionary claim.[204]

One example is *British Steel Corporation v Cleveland Bridge & Engineering*.[205] Here the plaintiff and defendant were in negotiation for a contract by which the plaintiff would supply certain steel products to the defendant. Whilst negotiations over the terms of the contract were continuing, the defendant requested the plaintiff to make an immediate delivery, and the plaintiff did so. It was presumably envisaged that the contract would be concluded and that payment for the delivery would be governed by it. However, the expected contract was never made, and the plaintiff instead made a claim for payment in the form of a quantum meruit. It was held that there could be no contractual claim because no contract had been agreed, but that the request from the defendant generated a non-contractual, restitutionary liability for payment.

Clearly this was not a case where the two conditions stated above for an imputed contract were satisfied; in particular, the plaintiff was perfectly well placed to secure agreement before doing any work. The request is thought by some to be relevant to the application of the restitutionary conditional transfer theory. It is said to show that the work was provided subject to a condition accepted by the defendant, viz. that the plaintiff would be paid. Thus, as mentioned above, Birks regards "requested benefits" as the standard category of claims under the restitutionary conditional transfer theory,[206] and Burrows considers that in the absence of a contract there can still be a "loose bargain", which involves the imposition of a condition by the plaintiff of which the defendant is aware.[207] But, as discussed above, there are serious objections to the restitutionary conditional transfer theory, and in fact a supposed claim under the theory is best understood as a contractual claim in disguise. As a rule, a request to the plaintiff to provide work of the sort that he does for a living carries an implied agreement to pay a reasonable sum for it, simply on the basis of an

---

[202] e.g. *Regalian Properties v London Dockland Development Corporation* [1995] 1 WLR 212.
[203] As in *Regalian*, ibid.
[204] McKendrick (1998), convincingly criticised by Hedley (1998).
[205] [1984] 1 All ER 504.
[206] Birks (1991*b*), 109.
[207] Burrows (1993), 319.

inference of what was obviously intended. This is a standard example of the contractual quantum meruit,[208] and one would have thought that it was the obvious interpretation of *BSC v Cleveland*. The request would be expected to generate a preliminary informal agreement that would be subsumed into the formal contract on the conclusion of the negotiations.

It seems to have been thought that in this type of case the contractual interpretation is impermissible, because if the parties are in negotiation over the contract they cannot at the same time have made an actual contract with respect to the same subject matter. This was the view of Robert Goff J in *BSC v Cleveland*. But this is surely not a realistic picture of what happens in practice. It will be commonplace for parties to reach a preliminary understanding, or an agreement "in principle" or over the "heads of agreement", before the lawyers negotiate the formal contract, which will refine or vary the preliminary agreement. If the parties then begin performance along the lines provisionally agreed, before the formal contract has been finalised, and the court holds that a party is entitled to payment for such performance, the obvious inference is that the claim is based on the agreement actually reached by the parties, vague and incomplete as it may be.[209] Indeed, as discussed above, the application of the restitutionary conditional transfer theory actually depends on the existence of such an agreement.

It is true that lack of certainty in an agreement is said to preclude a contract from arising in law.[210] However, some lack of certainty must be acceptable; indeed, complete certainty can never be achieved. In particular, lack of complete certainty as to price, where it is implicit that a reasonable price will be paid, has never been an obstacle to a binding contract.[211] A more serious obstacle appears to be lack of certainty with respect to, say, the quality or specification of the goods or the time of delivery. Where the court is faced with an uncertain agreement, the choice is whether to disregard it as of no legal effect, or to attempt to "fill out" the agreement, such as it is, with implied terms determined in accordance with, say, custom and practice, or on the basis of "hypothetical contracting";[212] if the court does find a liability to pay, the obvious interpretation is that it has indeed adopted the latter approach.

The pros and cons of giving effect to an uncertain agreement differ according to whether the agreement has been performed or not. Where it is still executory, the parties are less likely to have incurred any significant reliance in respect of which they would suffer prejudice if the agreement is not enforced, whereas if one party has performed but is denied payment under the contract, he will certainly suffer prejudice. Thus it may be reasonable for the court to deny the enforceability of an executory contract on the ground of uncertainty even where it would enforce the contract by allowing a claim for payment if it had been

---

[208] See Chap. 2, at n 52.
[209] Such an analysis is explicitly adopted in *Way v Latilla* [1937] 3 All ER 759.
[210] See e.g. Furmston (1996), 44.
[211] This is the standard case of a quantum meruit: e.g. *Powell v Braun* [1954] 1 All ER 484.
[212] i.e. according to what the parties might reasonably have agreed.

performed. Furthermore, it is important to note that a restitutionary approach does not overcome the problem of uncertainty; if, for example, there should be no contract because the terms governing the quality of the work to be provided have not been settled, it cannot be a solution to allow a claim for payment in restitution, apparently irrespective of the quality of the work, and with no possiblity of a claim in respect of defective work.[213]

A non-contractual analysis was also adopted in the earlier case of *William Lacey Ltd v Davis*.[214] Here the plaintiff tendered for a building contract, and was told that he had been chosen. While the parties were negotiating the contract, the plaintiff carried out work requested by the defendant. The building contract was never concluded, however, and the judge held that no contractual claim for payment could arise in respect of the work requested. Furthermore, it was argued that not only was there no contract in respect of the work requested, there was an understanding between the parties that the plaintiff would be paid for it through the building contract, which, it was argued, was inconsistent with any contract to pay for the requested work as such. Barry J thought that the proposition that a claim for a quantum meruit would not be allowed in the absence of an actual agreement to pay, or where there was an agreement to the contrary, was based on the old implied contract heresy, according to which restitutionary claims were implied contractual claims that were necessarily precluded by a finding that there was no contract, or an inconsistent contract.[215] Thus he concluded that the finding of an inconsistent contract was no impediment to the liability for payment. This has been heralded as an important advance in escaping from the fiction of implied contract,[216] and a similar view was expressed in *Pavey* as mentioned above.

But, once again, the implied contract fiction does not generally relate to claims for payment on a quantum meruit, where the general rule, sound in principle and authority, is that no claim arises without an agreement. It follows a fortiori that there should be no claim where there is an agreement to the contrary. Indeed, even if a restitutionary claim for payment could arise in such circumstances in the absence of a contractually enforceable agreement, it has not been argued by even the most committed supporters of the restitutionary conditional transfer theory that such a claim can arise where there is a contract between the parties that provides to the contrary. In fact it seems that the parties *did* agree on payment, but the understanding was that payment should be by way of the building contract, in the mistaken expectation that the building contract would be agreed. In such circumstances, it is reasonable to conclude (as the judge must be taken to have done) that it would be more faithful to the

---

[213] This point was a matter of concern to Slade LJ and Bingham LJ in *Crown House Engineering Ltd v Amec Projects* (1990) 48 BLR 32.

[214] [1957] 2 All ER 712.

[215] Cf the discussion of *Sinclair v Brougham* [1914] AC 398 in Chap. 1.

[216] Birks (1989a), 273.

parties' agreement than subversive of it to give effect to the agreement by way of a separate liability in respect of the work requested.[217]

Another case discussed in this context is *Sabemo Ltd v North Sydney Municipal Council*.[218] Here the plaintiff incurred significant costs in the course of negotiations for a building contract, before the defendant decided to abandon the project. The plaintiff was allowed a claim for reasonable payment for its work. The basis for the decision was described as follows:

> where two parties proceed upon the joint assumption that a contract will be entered into between them, and one does work beneficial for the project, and thus in the interests of the two parties, which work he would not be expected, in other circumstances, to do gratuitously, he will be entitled to compensation or restitution, if the other party unilaterally decided to abandon the project, not for any reason associated with bona fide disagreement concerning the terms of the contract to be entered into, but for reasons which, however valid, pertain only to his own position and do not relate at all to that of the other party.[219]

As the claim is formulated here, by contrast with the cases above, it does not rely on a specific request to do the work in question, but merely on reliance on the assumption that a contract will in due course be entered into along the lines agreed in general terms. There has been some discussion of the nature of this claim. It is sometimes claimed to be a restitutionary claim, under the restitutionary conditional transfer theory.[220] Others have argued, as discussed below, that it is a claim based on a principle of non-contractual injurious reliance, or on "unjust sacrifice". The best analysis again is that it is a claim in contract in accordance with the reliance theory, i.e. that there is an agreement to assume responsibility for reliance on the assumption that the negotiations will come to fruition, or, more correctly, as the judge formulated his decision in *Sabemo*, reliance incurred on the assumption that the defendant was committed to the project and would not withdraw unless it became impossible to agree terms.[221] On this understanding the judge's formulation of the cause of action is peculiarly apt.

Privity and restitutionary claims against third parties to a contract

It has been argued by some commentators that where, pursuant to a contract between the plaintiff and X, the plaintiff confers a benefit on the defendant, who

---

[217] In *Brewer St. Investments v Barclays Woollen* [1954] 1 QB 428, there was an agreement governing the work, but Denning LJ thought that the claim had to be restitutionary because the agreed work was not completed, apparently by reference to the entire contracts rule. This argument was rejected in the last chapter, at 51–53.

[218] (1977) 2 NSWLR 880.

[219] At 902–3.

[220] Burrows (1993), 299.

[221] Cf *Waltons Stores (Interstate) Ltd v Maher* (1988) 164 CLR 387; see below at 128. The equivalent analysis under the classical theory would be that the parties have a duty to negotiate in good faith.

is not privy to the contract, and the plaintiff is unable to recover payment from X because of X's insolvency or default, the plaintiff should in the alternative have a restitutionary claim for payment against the defendant by virtue of his receipt of the benefit.[222] Say the plaintiff is contracted by X to send flowers to the defendant. The flowers are sent, but X is unable or unwilling to pay. It is difficult to see any basis for a claim for payment against the defendant. Sometimes it seems to be implied that the defendant should be subject to a restitutionary liability simply because he has received a benefit from the plaintiff, for which the plaintiff has not had anything in return.[223] But this simply contradicts the fundamental rule against liability for officiously conferred benefits.

It is argued, for the purposes of the restitutionary conditional transfer theory, that the benefit may have been conferred on the defendant conditionally.[224] As discussed above, it is usually acknowledged that under the theory the condition must be accepted by the defendant. This is thought to take effect through an agreement, but here the defendant is not party to any agreement with the plaintiff. In this case, it seems that the condition must be a privately imposed condition, not necessarily known to or accepted by the defendant. It would also be contrary to the contract with X, who, so far as the plaintiff was concerned, contracted to pay for the flowers to be given unconditionally to the defendant.

Possibly the position could be different where the defendant had contracted with X to receive the benefit, on the understanding that X would contract with the plaintiff to supply it. This is what happens when the defendant houseowner, say, contracts for building work with a head contractor, X, on the understanding that the head contractor is to sub-contract some of the work. If the plaintiff sub-contractor has done work on the owner's house for which the head contractor now cannot or will not pay him, should he not have a claim for payment against the owner? One might argue that the officiousness condition is satisfied by the fact that the plaintiff know that the defendant had contracted for the work, even though not with the plaintiff. And one might argue that the benefit condition is satisfied because the defendant's contract shows that it would be reasonable for him to pay the sub-contractor that part of the payment due to the head contractor that was attributable to the work in question. But this is the bargained-for benefit test that was rejected above:[225] the defendant's contract entails a valuation and an allocation of risk as between the defendant and X, but it does not constitute an objective measure of benefit or of a reasonable price for the purposes of a restitutionary liability. Furthermore, the contractual arrangements between the parties preclude a claim by the plaintiff against the defendant, and would be subverted by such a claim.[226] If the defendant could be liable

---

[222] Burrows (1994); Barker (1994); Barker (1995), 462; Virgo (1999), 345.

[223] This seems to be implicit, for example, in Barker (1994).

[224] Ibid.

[225] At 87 above.

[226] Just as they would be subverted by allowing a claim in tort in respect of the failure of the subcontractor to provide a benefit to the owner: thus *Junior Books v Veitchi* [1983] 1 AC 520, which recognised such a liability, has been discredited.

to pay the plaintiff, this would presumably replace his contractual liability to pay the head contractor for the same work. If the head contractor is unable to pay the sub-contractor because he is insolvent, his liquidator will want to recover any money due in respect of the work on behalf of the head contractor's creditors, who will include the sub-contractor, but also others. These creditors will be prejudiced by any attempt by the sub-contractor to claim directly from the owner, which will circumvent the due process for allocating the head contractor's assets amongst his creditors on bankruptcy.[227]

The privity issue arose in the recent case of *Pan Ocean Shipping v Creditcorp (The Trident Beauty)*.[228] Here the plaintiff contracted to hire a ship from the third party, X. An instalment of the hire price was paid, at X's direction, to the defendant, as a payment on behalf of X under a contract between X and the defendant. The ship turned out to be unavailable for hire in the period to which the instalment related, and the plaintiff sought to recover the sum for total failure of consideration. However, X was insolvent and so the plaintiff sought to recover the sum from the defendant. Some commentators have argued that the claim for total failure of consideration that would normally have arisen against the other contracting party (X) should arise in such a case against the defendant third party instead;[229] on the assumption that it is a restitutionary claim, it seems that it should apply against the recipient of the payment, even if he is not the other contracting party.

But there is no basis for such a claim. The claim arising on a total failure of consideration is best understood as contractual not restitutionary, as discussed in the last chapter. Even if the claim is understood to arise from a conditional transfer, it is generally thought that the condition must be accepted, and here the defendant did not accept any condition—he expected an unconditional payment in accordance with his contract with X. Furthermore, the imposition by the plaintiff of a condition would have been inconsistent with his contract with X, which envisaged an outright payment—if the payment to X was to be conditional, X could not have used it to make a payment pursuant to his contract with the defendant. The House of Lords rightly accepted that there was no restitutionary claim against the defendant.[230]

FREE ACCEPTANCE AND UNCONSCIENTIOUS RECEIPT

The idea of free acceptance was introduced above. There is said to be a free acceptance by the defendant where he "knows that a benefit is being offered to

---

[227] This does not mean that the parties necessarily intended to allocate the risk of insolvency, but this risk is a necessary incident of the arrangement that was chosen, for whatever reason. If a claim is allowed (as under US statutes), it should be regarded as a contractual claim against the head contractor that takes priority in the head contractor's insolvency.

[228] [1994] 1 WLR 161.

[229] Barker (1995), 462. See also Friedmann (1991), 273.

[230] If there had been a claim there would have been a defence of bona fide purchase, as considered in Chap. 7.

him non-gratuitously and where he, having the opportunity to reject, elects to accept",[231] and it is argued that as a result the defendant incurs a liability to pay a reasonable or market price for the benefit. An example might be where the plaintiff comes forward and cleans the defendant's car windows at traffic lights without any prior agreement. There seem to be cases of this sort where a liability to pay has indeed been found. For example, consider the case of *Lambe v Bunce*,[232] which is regarded by Birks as a case of free acceptance. A doctor attended to an injured man, responsibility for whose treatment lay with the parish. The parish officers visited the injured man and were aware, as the doctor knew, of the doctor's work, but there was never any explicit request to the doctor to provide his services. The doctor claimed payment from the parish and succeeded, the court observing:

> [T]he law raises an obligation against a parish where the pauper lies sick as casual poor, to look to the supply of his necessities; and if the parish officer stands by and sees that obligation performed by those who are fit and competent to do it, and does not object, the law will raise a promise on his part to pay for the performance . . . [T]the defendant, by not repudiating the plaintiff's attendance, did that which is equivalent to a previous request.[233]

The nature of the liability

The obvious interpretation of the liability is that it is contractual.[234] The difficulty seems to arise in cases like this from the supposed rule that silence cannot amount to acceptance in contract.[235] This seems also to be the reason the restitutionary conditional transfer theory is thought inapplicable, because in the absence of an agreement there is no acceptance of the condition. But nevertheless the best interpretation is that the liability is a contractual liability based on silent or tacit acceptance. The plaintiff has done the work, assuming, because the defendant is present and has not demurred, that his silence is intended to imply his agreement to pay. In *Lambe v Bunce*, the doctor had previously done work for the parish, and he thought, as the parish would have understood, that the parish was responsible for having the man treated.[236] In the circumstances, it was surely reasonable for him to treat the parish's silence as an agreement to pay. By contrast, the rule against silent acceptance should be understood to apply in circumstances where the plaintiff solicits the defendant out of the blue, as where he sends him a letter making an offer to clean his windows for £x and

---

[231] Birks (1989*a*), 104; also Goff & Jones (1998), 18.

[232] (1815) 1 M & S 275.

[233] Ibid., 277, cited and discussed at Birks (1991*b*), 117.

[234] The language of the decision might be thought to be consistent with a restitutionary approach on the basis that the "promise" and "request" were fictional.

[235] *Felthouse v Bindley* (1862) 11 CBNS 869; Mead (1989).

[236] In fact the parish denied responsibility, and this seems to have been the cause of the dispute.

saying that he will assume that the plaintiff has agreed if he hears nothing,[237] not where the circumstances are such as to justify an inference of acceptance in the absence of an explicit statement to that effect.[238] It may be that the parish deliberately refrained from accepting openly, not wishing to pay, and maybe hoping the work would be done nevertheless. But under the objective theory of interpretation in contract this does not in principle preclude the finding of a contract if the doctor's inference was reasonable in the circumstances.[239]

Similarly the dicta cited by Birks in support of free acceptance are consistent with a contractual analysis—for example the following passage from *Falcke v Scottish Imperial Insurance Co*:[240]

> It is perfectly true that the inference of an understanding between the parties—which you may translate into other language by calling it an implied contract—is an inference which will unhesitatingly be drawn in cases where the circumstances plainly lead to the conclusion that the owner of the saved property was laying out his money in the expectation of being repaid.

The interpretation of the claim in this type of case as contractual, even if this requires some refinement of the contractual rules on acceptance, is consistent with the general principles of contract, and is far less subversive of the established common law than the contrary position, which would undermine the general rule against liability to officious intervenors. It has been suggested that the contractual analysis resurrects the fiction of implied contract;[241] but, to the contrary, as discussed above principle and authority fully support an analysis of a claim for payment in terms of a real implied contract.

Unconscientiousness

Birks's argument is that free acceptance is a matter of unconscientiousness, not agreement inferred from silence, i.e. it is based not on the plaintiff inferring acceptance and acting in reliance accordingly, but on the wrongfulness of the defendant's behaviour, even if the plaintiff did not rely on him. But where the plaintiff is a risk-taker—i.e., where he knows that he has no contractual right to payment—it is difficult to see how there can be any unconscientiousness on the defendant's part. If the plaintiff has not approached the defendant to agree terms, the defendant knows that he is a risk-taker,[242] and if he knows the

---

[237] Cf *Felthouse v Bindley* (1862) 11 CBNS 869.

[238] Stoljar (1989), 191; Atiyah (1995), 69; Atiyah (1976).

[239] Beatson (1991), 37. One might argue that the evidence in that case disclosed no basis for finding an agreement; or that, if there was an agreement, nevertheless, in the interests of legal certainty, an agreement should not be enforced as a contract in law unless agreed to expressly rather than tacitly. This would imply that the case was wrongly decided, not that it was restitutionary.

[240] (1866) 34 Ch D 234, 249; Birks (1991*b*), 107.

[241] Burrows (1993), 295; Birks (1989*a*), 272–3.

[242] Leaving aside the case where the defendant knows that the plaintiff is acting under a mistake, which is considered below at 125–127.

plaintiff is a risk-taker, there is no reason why he should intervene. He is entitled to leave it to the plaintiff to approach him; he can assume, for example, that the reason the plaintiff has not tried to get an agreement from him is that he thought the defendant would not agree, and that the plaintiff is taking a risk, maybe in the hope of impressing him, or maybe because he thinks that the defendant may feel a sense of moral obligation to pay something.

The argument above is that the defendant is not unconscientious where the plaintiff is a risk-taker, and that the plaintiff is a risk-taker where he has not secured an agreement. One might object that the argument begs the question, and that if the defendant's liability can arise from his unconscientiousness, and does not depend on whether there is an agreement, then the plaintiff is not necessarily a risk-taker where there is no agreement: he may be entitled to payment because the defendant is acting unconscientiously in not speaking out if he is not intending to pay. This seems to create an unstable legal relation between the parties, under which the question whether the plaintiff is a risk-taker will depend on whether the defendant is unconscientious, and the question whether the defendant is unconscientious will depend on whether the plaintiff is a risk-taker. Presumably whether there is a liability to pay would then have to be settled according to some test of reasonableness, i.e. as to whether the defendant was unreasonable in keeping quiet and whether the plaintiff was unreasonable in thinking he would be paid. This would cause great uncertainty for both potential plaintiffs and potential defendants. In fact the best test of whether there is a liability to pay is whether an agreement has been made; or, in other words, the function of agreement is to enable the parties to deal with each other without such uncertainty. This is why (leaving aside the case considered next where the defendant knows the plaintiff is mistaken) agreement should be determinative and there is no room for a doctrine of free acceptance based on unconscientiousness.[243]

Defendant's knowledge of the plaintiff's mistake

The position is different where the plaintiff is mistaken and the defendant knows this; for example where, to the defendant's knowledge, the plaintiff is carrying out work on the defendant's land mistakenly thinking that it is his own. Here the plaintiff is not a risk-taker. There is good authority that the plaintiff

---

[243] See further in the section on "death of contract" below. Birks argues that the true test of free acceptance as a ground of liability lies in the case of "secret acceptance", where the plaintiff does not know that the defendant is aware that he (the plaintiff) is providing a benefit, as for example where the plaintiff window cleaner does not realise that the home-owner is watching him from inside the house: Birks (1991*b*), 119. The significance of secret acceptance for Birks seems to be that there is no possibility of the restitutionary conditional transfer theory applying, because this is understood to rely on an agreement or some looser dealing between the parties; more plausibly the significance is that there cannot be any contract, by silent acceptance or otherwise. But Birks does not appear to offer any example of any such claim, and it is difficult to see why any claim should be justified, unless the defendant has a duty to save the plaintiff from wasting his time.

has a claim if the defendant did nothing to warn the plaintiff. Traditionally the claim comes under the rubric of proprietary estoppel, however, not free acceptance. Under the "unilateral mistake" category of proprietary estoppel:

> [i]f a stranger begins to build on my land supposing it to be his own, and I, perceiving his mistake, abstain from setting him right, and leave him to persevere in his error, a Court of Equity will not allow me afterwards to assert my title to the land on which he had expended money on the supposition that the land was his own. It considers that, when I saw the mistake into which he had fallen, it was my duty to be active and to state my adverse title; and that it would be dishonest in me to remain wilfully passive on such an occasion, in order afterwards to profit by the mistake which I might have prevented.[244]

Unlike the usual case of proprietary estoppel, this claim does not arise from an agreement.[245] The passage implies that the claim is tortious in nature, arising from a breach by the defendant of a duty to prevent the plaintiff from suffering loss. Normally the law of tort is confined to imposing duties not to cause harm by positive act, and does not impose duties to act to benefit others or save them from incurring loss by their own hand. But it seems that there is an exception in this situation, possibly because so little is required of the defendant, and because he will profit through the mistake.[246]

If the claim is tortious, the plaintiff should be entitled to compensation for loss.[247] It is a separate question whether there should also be a claim for payment in respect of any benefit conferred on the defendant by the plaintiff by his mistake; the measure of liability for such a claim might exceed the plaintiff's loss, since it would generally take account of the benefit to the defendant and the work done by the plaintiff as well as just the plaintiff's loss. Such a claim does not seem to have been explicitly recognised in connection with proprietary estoppel. The best rationale for it would be as a use claim, i.e. on the basis that the defendant had appropriated the plaintiff's labour for his own purposes and should pay a fee for it, just as if he had made use of the plaintiff's property without his permission.[248] Such a claim might overlap with Birks's notion of free acceptance; but it is confined to cases where the plaintiff was mistaken and does not support the general doctrine of free acceptance stated above, which also allows a claim to risk-takers.

Where the plaintiff does work under a void or unenforceable contract, it is thought that there can be no claim for free acceptance because the defendant, thinking that the contract is valid and that he will be liable to pay, is not uncon-

---

[244] *Ramsden v Dyson* (1866) LR 1 HL 129, 140–1 per Lord Cranworth.

[245] Or representation. See below127–9.

[246] One might argue that because the defendant would certainly have acted if the plaintiff's activities had been damaging to his land, refraining from acting should be understood as a positive act resulting from the defendant's expectation of benefit.

[247] The usual remedy is the "minimum equity" to do justice, which may be pecuniary compensation, or may be an interest in land: see e.g. *Crabb v Arun DC* [1976] Ch 179, 198, per Scarman LJ.

[248] See Chap. 4 at 151–2.

scientious in failing to speak out.[249] But, in such circumstances, if the defendant knows that there is no valid contract and that the plaintiff mistakenly thinks that there is, it seems that the defendant may have a duty along the same lines as in the unilateral mistake cases of proprietary estoppel. Indeed it may be that some of the unilateral mistake cases of proprietary estoppel are of this sort.[250] Another example might be where the plaintiff sent a magazine to the defendant mistaking him for someone else and thinking that he had a contract with him, and the defendant kept and read it, knowing of the plaintiff's mistake. A tortious liability would be for the plaintiff's loss, which would be much less than the usual price of the magazine.[251] If a restitutionary claim (the use claim) were allowed, the measure would be greater, although still probably not the usual price.[252] On such facts in *Weatherby v Banham*[253] the defendant was held liable for the usual price of the magazine.

INJURIOUS RELIANCE AND UNJUST SACRIFICE

Injurious reliance

Some commentators, whilst denying that the claim in some of the "pre-contractual" cases, like *William Lacey v Davis*[254] and *Sabemo v North Sydney Municipal Council*,[255] can be contractual as argued above, have also argued that it cannot be restitutionary, because of the apparent absence of any benefit to the defendant; instead, it is argued that the claim is a claim for compensation for loss based on a non-contractual principle of injurious or detrimental reliance.[256]

One type of claim that is understood to be a non-contractual claim for reliance loss or injurious or detrimental reliance is proprietary estoppel. According to the doctrine of proprietary estoppel, where the plaintiff relied on an assurance given by the defendant, the defendant will be liable to the extent necessary to prevent injustice to the plaintiff. (This excludes the "unilateral mistake" line of cases which were considered above.)[257] In the typical case, the defendant has given the plaintiff to believe that the plaintiff owns land that

---

[249] Birks (1991*b*), 111. On this basis Birks criticises *Pavey & Matthews v Paul* (1986) 162 CLR 221, where the court considered that the restitutionary claim was based on acceptance of the benefit: above, n 196.

[250] For example it is arguable that in *Ramsden v Dysen* the plaintiff's mistake as to his entitlement to an interest in land arose from a false assumption by him that there was an agreement to this effect between him and the defendant.

[251] The tortious claim here would be liability for breach of the duty of preservation, or conversion, as discussed in later chapters.

[252] The measure of the use claim is considered in Chap. 4.

[253] (1832) 5 Car & P 228; cf Birks (1991*b*), 134.

[254] [1957] 1 All ER 932.

[255] (1977) 2 NSWLR 880.

[256] Beatson (1991), 38; cf Muir (1990) ; Stoljar (1987).

[257] Above, at n 244.

actually belongs to the defendant, or that the defendant will transfer land to him, and the plaintiff has acted in reliance, for example by building on the land in question or becoming dependent on it for access. The remedy is said to be whatever is necessary to satisfy the plaintiff's "equity", which amounts to relieving him of the detriment incurred through his reliance, or in other words satisfying his reliance interest.[258] Although the doctrine is referred to as proprietary estoppel, because in the typical case the assurance concerns an interest in land and the "equity" is satisfied by the recognition of an interest, there is no obvious reason why it should be confined to cases involving land. The modern tendency is to assimilate proprietary estoppel with a wider doctrine of estoppel that is not limited in this way.[259] The doctrine might also be thought to encompass *Hedley Byrne v Heller*,[260] where the defendant is subject to a liability for the plaintiff's reliance on a misstatement by the defendant.

The same principle of "injurious reliance" might be thought to lie behind these cases and also the pre-contractual cases mentioned above, like *Lacey v Davis* and *Sabemo*. It was suggested above that the latter cases were best understood in terms of contract, and it may be that the "injurious reliance" cases are also best explained as a manifestation of contract.[261] This is not how the cases have generally been interpreted. *Hedley Byrne* was decided as a case in tort, although it is explicit in the judgments that liability arose from an agreement to assume responsibility for reliance. Estoppel (whatever its true basis is understood to be) is generally regarded as distinct from contract, although again the usual formulation seems to require an agreement by the defendant to assume responsibility for the plaintiff's reliance on an expectation induced by the defendant.[262] The main reason why injurious reliance has not been interpreted as contractual is presumably the exchange doctrine of consideration. (This was explicit in *Hedley Byrne*.) But if the claim is based on an agreement it would be better to accept that the claim is contractual, and that (at least in this situation) the exchange doctrine of consideration does not apply.[263] Another reason why such cases might not have been interpreted as contractual is that they are not readily interpreted in terms of promising, but are explicitly agreements to assume responsibility for reliance, which under the influence of the classical theory one might be led to think could not be contractual.

It seems that an "injurious reliance" claim, if it is not contractual, must be understood to be a claim in tort arising from the breach of a duty not to behave in such a way, through words or conduct, as to induce reliance by the plaintiff to his detriment.[264] This would be a tortious claim in respect of what can be

---

[258] Above n 247.
[259] e.g. *Walton Stores (Intestate) v Maher* (1988) 164 CLR 387.
[260] [1964] AC 465.
[261] Beatson refers to reliance "requested, accepted, or acquiesced in": Beatson (1990), 34.
[262] See e.g. Collins (1997), 72.
[263] Atiyah (1986), 238ff; Collins (1997), 72; Jaffey (1998c), 122; cf Birks (1989a), 47.
[264] Or a strict liability for reliance on certain types of behaviour; it is not necessary to distinguish between these for present purposes.

called "voluntary reliance loss". Voluntary reliance loss is loss voluntarily incurred, by expenditure or opportunity cost (as opposed to loss caused through reliance but not voluntarily incurred, as for example where the plaintiff relies on the defendant's driving and suffers injury or harm as a result). The traditional principle seems to be that no claim arises in respect of voluntary reliance other than by virtue of an agreement to assume responsibility for reliance.[265] Such a principle preserves the defendant's freedom over his own behaviour by protecting him from any responsibility for the way in which others may choose to rely on him, in predicting his behaviour or otherwise, unless he has agreed to assume responsibility for it. Correspondingly the plaintiff knows that in choosing to incur an expense or other loss he relies on the defendant at his own risk unless he has secured an agreement.

The argument that there is a non-contractual claim for "injurious reliance" arising out of the reliance by the plaintiff on the words or conduct of the defendant during negotiations, in the absence of any agreement to assume responsibility for reliance, in cases like *William Lacey v Davis* or *Sabemo*, is contrary to this traditional principle, because it represents a liability for voluntary reliance. Perhaps there are cases where voluntary reliance should be protected without agreement, but it is difficult to accept that it is appropriate where parties are in a position to contract if they so choose. Such a rule would tend to undermine the practice of contracting, for just the reasons considered earlier in connection with free acceptance. Indeed the issue is the same, free acceptance also being based on a supposed duty to protect the plaintiff from his own voluntary reliance.[266] The plaintiff might see no need for contracting, hoping to recover instead on the basis that the defendant will be liable in tort if he fails to take action to stop the plaintiff from doing the work. Or, conversely, negotiations might be stultified by the defendant's fear of incurring a liability before any agreement had been reached.

Unjust sacrifice

It has also been suggested that the principle behind cases like *Lacey v Davis* and *Sabemo* is the principle of "unjust sacrifice".[267] Unjust sacrifice might be

---

[265] Or, if they are distinct, misrepresentation, estoppel or a fiduciary relationship. Before *Hedley Byrne*, the principle was reflected in the rule that there was no recovery for reliance incurred on a statement unless the statement was a term of a contract or a contractual representation, apart from cases of deliberate manipulation or deliberate inducement. The principle is usually expressed in terms of pure economic loss, that is to say that there is no recovery for pure economic loss. Voluntary reliance loss is a form of pure economic loss, but it seems that pure economic loss is recoverable when it is not in the form of voluntary reliance loss. Even after *Hedley Byrne*, the law is consistent with the principle if the rule in *Hedley Byrne* is based on an agreement, which seems now to be controversial; see generally Jaffey (1998c), 129–31.

[266] Free acceptance goes further because, as discussed above, it seems to imply the possibility of liability where the plaintiff did not rely on the defendant, i.e. through "secret acceptance".

[267] An "unjust sacrifice" approach has been advocated by Muir (1990), and Stoljar (1987).

understood to be the same thing as "injurious reliance". But it seems that unjust sacrifice is understood to be distinct from any recognised interpretation of injurious reliance, i.e. from contract and tort, and also estoppel, if this is a separate category. In fact although unjust sacrifice has attracted a certain amount of attention, it seems to have no plausible basis at all; certainly its basis has not been made clear.[268] The expression "unjust sacrifice" is attributed to Stoljar, but he appears not to have used it in relation to cases like *Lacey v Davis* or *Sabemo*. As discussed in the first section of the chapter, Stoljar used the expression to refer to the basis for a claim for payment for work done on the ground of necessitous intervention. His view seems to have been that claims in cases like *Lacey v Davis* and *Sabemo* were contractual.[269]

THE THEORY OF "DEATH OF CONTRACT"

It was assumed in the last chapter that contract law is concerned with enforcing agreements. In the usual case the purpose of the agreement is to effect an exchange. According to another view it is an illusion to think that contract law is concerned with enforcing agreements. Instead it concerns claims arising out of the exchange itself, or at least out of benefit or loss arising from the exchange. It may be that the parties make an agreement to regulate the exchange, but so far as the law is concerned it is not the agreement that determines the claims that arise, but the exchange itself. This is the "death of contract" theory.[270] On the death of contract approach, where parties embark on an exchange and it breaks down before completion, the claims that arise, although referred to as contractual, are in reality claims in tort or restitution; thus it can also be referred to as the theory of "contract-as-tort-and-restitution". The restitutionary claim is a claim for payment in respect of any benefit conferred before the breakdown.[271] The tort claim is a claim for loss incurred before the breakdown. This theory has a close connection to the issues discussed in the previous sections. If a tort claim were allowed in such circumstances it would be a claim for voluntary reliance as discussed above. If a non-contractual, restitutionary claim for payment were allowed, it would be a restitutionary claim for payment for a benefit conferred through the performance of an agreement, but not on the basis of the agreement as such, just like a claim under the restitutionary conditional transfer theory.

On the death of contract approach, whether a claim arises appears to depend on what is fair and reasonable. The claim in tort would arise, it seems, on the basis that the defendant encouraged the plaintiff to incur expenditure or an

---

[268] As pointed out by Birks (1992*a*), 100ff.

[269] Stoljar (1989), 239ff.

[270] "Death of contract" is usually associated with (amongst others) Gilmore (1974), Atiyah (1979), and Atiyah (1981), but the theory as formulated here is not intended as a faithful representation of these works.

[271] Or, as it might be put, reversing the unjust enrichment.

opportunity cost or failed to stop him from doing so. The availability of the restitutionary claim for payment for a benefit conferred would presumably depend on whether the plaintiff acted reasonably in conferring the benefit and on a judgement of its value to the defendant. The agreement is not the basis of the claims, but provides evidence of what is fair and reasonable. It is taken to indicate that the plaintiff acted reasonably in conferring the benefit, and that the defendant was responsible for the plaintiff's reliance loss; and the agreed price is taken to indicate a fair measure of liability.[272]

The death of contract theory is intended to overcome the problems of the classical promise-based theory of contract, some of which were discussed in the last chapter, including the rules on specific performance, mitigation and withdrawal, variation and duress, and consideration.[273] The inadequacies of the classical approach, based on the assumption that agreements are based on promising, are taken to show that contractual claims are not based on agreements at all. This approach might also be thought to gain some support from case law recognising a claim in restitution for payment for a benefit conferred in the absence of an agreement, as discussed above, which might suggest that when there *is* an agreement it is irrelevant to the liability for payment, and that the liability arises from the receipt of the benefit.[274]

There are serious objections to the death of contract theory. These objections are precisely those made above with respect to the non-contractual injurious reliance theory and the restitutionary conditional transfer theory, viz. the objection to liability for voluntary reliance and for payment for an unrequested benefit. Under the death of contract theory, instead of being able to rely on the agreement as determinative, the court has to make its own judgment of the reasonableness of the parties' behaviour and the fairness of the exchange. But agreement developed as the means of enabling parties to deal with these matters by exploiting their ability to determine what was best for them in the light of their tastes and resources, and so to effect exchanges to their mutual benefit. Surely this is the optimal basis for determining rights in connection with exchange (even if in some circumstances it may be appropriate to override the terms actually agreed).

There are certainly differences between the death of contract theory and the restitutionary conditional transfer theory (or the injurious reliance theory). According to the restitutionary conditional transfer theory, the restitutionary claim arises as an alternative to the contractual claim, whereas the death of contract theory holds that the restitutionary claim *is* the contractual claim that arises in respect of a benefit conferred (or at least one form that the contractual

---

[272] The theory distinguishes between compensation for loss and payment for, or reversal of, the benefit, although the contractual payment is intended to cover both.

[263] See Atiyah (1979), 764ff, Gilmore (1974), e.g. at 87.

[274] This might also be thought to gain support from the modern rules that override agreement on grounds of fairness.

claim can take). This was behind a difference of opinion between Birks and Atiyah on the relation between contract and restitution.[275] In response to the argument, supported by Birks, for a non-contractual restitutionary claim aris-ing as an alternative to a contractual claim on the termination of the contract,[276] Atiyah objected that the restitutionary claim should not be understood as an alternative claim, distinct from the contractual claim, but as a type of contrac-tual claim;[277] this is consistent with the death of contract theory as explained above. In fact, as the discussion above shows, the exchange between Birks and Atiyah belies the underlying close similarity of their positions, both of which are subversive of contract as based on agreement. There is at least a certain logic in the death of contract view, which rejects the agreement as the basis of contrac-tual claims in favour of restitution and tort. But the restitutionary conditional transfer theory, while purporting to accept that the legal relation governing the claim for payment arises from the agreement, and should not be subverted, also holds that a non-contractual claim for payment arises independently of the agreement. This is not coherent; contract and restitution cannot both serve the single purpose, in conflicting ways, of determining payment for the work done in providing a benefit.[278]

Atiyah put forward a refinement of the death of contract theory in terms of what he described as "promises as admissions". The argument was that although the parties' claims were in tort or restitution, the agreement between them operated as a "conclusive admission" of matters relevant to these claims, i.e. that the defendant was responsible for the plaintiff's reliance, or that the plaintiff acted reasonably in conferring the benefit, or that the agreed price was fair.[279] The conception of a promise or an agreement as an admission is flawed. The question whether a liability for reliance or for payment should arise is not a matter of fact about which an admission (in the usual sense) can be made; it is a normative issue, involving weighing up the respective interests of the parties. If the agreement is an "admission" that is conclusive of this normative issue, then in fact it constitutes the exercise of a normative power and is not merely a piece of evidence to be taken into account in assessing the existence and measure of claims in restitution and tort.[280] This is precisely equivalent to treating the contract as a conclusive measure of benefit for the purposes of a restitutionary

---

[275] Atiyah (1979), 764ff; Birks (1983); Atiyah (1986), 47ff.

[276] In the first edition of Goff & Jones (1966).

[277] Atiyah (1979), 768; also Atiyah (1986), 48.

[278] Another difference is that under the death of contract theory the plaintiff can in principle claim a fair price instead of the contract price even once he has completed his performance, but under the restitutionary conditional transfer theory it is thought that the plaintiff can claim a quan-tum meruit only in respect of part performance. This is supposed to be because only in the case of part performance is there no conflict with the contract. But it cannot be that the restitutionary claim subverts the law of contract before the contract is terminated but not after, as considered in Chap. 2.

[279] Atiyah (1981), 184ff.

[280] Cf Raz (1982), 924–927.

claim, as proposed under the "bargained-for benefit test", or through the application of the contractual ceiling, as discussed above and in the last chapter.

However, the problem that Atiyah was seeking to address through the concept of promises as admissions is clear. An agreement understood as involving promises as normally understood will generate obligations of performance, and Atiyah considered (as was also argued in the last chapter) that this understanding fails to account for the law. Thus he seems to have sought an explanation of the legal effect of an agreement that would attribute a real normative effect to it—i.e. altering the legal relation between the parties, rather than merely providing evidence—but without generating obligations of performance. The true answer is surely provided by the concept of an agreement to assume responsibility for reliance, as it was explained in the last chapter. This does indeed have a normative effect, since it generates the contractual relation between the parties, which gives rise to the contractual reliance claim, but it does not generally generate obligations of performance. Furthermore, it is not open to the objections made of the admissions theory. It does not presuppose that the claim for reliance or payment arises independently of the agreement, directly from reliance or benefit. The claim arises from reliance, but by virtue of the agreement. But the effect appears to be comparable to that envisaged by Atiyah for the theory of promises as admissions.[281]

---

[281] Save that the claim in respect of the reliance interest encompasses loss incurred in reliance and payment for work done, whereas the death of contract approach attempts to separate the claim for loss from the claim for work done, which is treated as a claim in respect of the benefit Thus the death of contract approach is presented with a problem in the case where work is done but has not yet conferred a benefit; the same problem has confronted more recent restitutionary analyses, as discussed in the last chapter.

4

The Use Claim

T HERE ARE A number of lines of authority that show that the plaintiff has
a claim against a defendant who has used his property without permission, in the measure of a sum that might reasonably have been agreed
for the use of the property. This will be described as the use claim, or claim
under the user principle.[1] For example, it is clear that the use of the plaintiff's
goods without permission can give rise to a liability to pay for the use at a rate
that might have been agreed for such use in a hire agreement. In *Strand Electric
& Engineering v Brisford*[2] items of electrical equipment belonging to the plaintiff came into the defendant's possession, and he refused to return them and
instead made use of them for his own purposes. In the circumstances the plaintiff could not show any loss caused by the absence of the items of equipment
from his possession, because he would not have used or hired them out, and
there was no damage to them, but the plaintiff recovered a sum that might reasonably have been agreed as a hire charge. The same approach has been adopted
with respect to the unauthorised use of the plaintiff's intellectual property, for
example the infringing use of a patented invention.[3] Similarly, with respect to
trespass to land, if the defendant has used a path over the plaintiff's land,[4] or has
used it as a dump,[5] or has lived in it, for example by staying on after the termination of tenancy,[6] without getting permission from the plaintiff, the plaintiff
can recover a reasonable licence fee for the defendant's use. Although these various claims are not compensatory, generally they take the form of a claim for
damages, nowadays often referred to in the academic literature as "restitutionary damages".[7]

The effect of the use claim is to bring about an exchange of payment for a
benefit, the benefit here being the use of the plaintiff's property. The claim is

---

[1] The expression was used by Nicholls LJ in *Stoke City Council v Wass* [1988] 3 All ER 394, 402;
see also *Inverugie Investments v Hackett* [1995] 1 WLR 713, 718 *per* Lord Lloyd.

[2] [1952] 2 QB 246; a similar case is *Penarth Dock Engineering Co Ltd v Pounds* [1963] 1 Lloyd's
Rep. 359.

[3] *Watson Laidlaw & Co Ltd v Pott, Cassels & Williamson* (1914) 31 RPC 104.

[4] *Phillips v Homfray* (1883) 24 Ch D 439.

[5] *Whitwham v Westminster Brymbo Coal & Coke Co* [1896] 2 Ch 538.

[6] *Ministry of Defence v Ashman* [1993] 2 EGLR 102.

[7] With respect to land, such damages are conventionally known as "mesne damages": see e.g.
Inverugie Investments v Hackett [1995] 1 WLR 713. A use claim has been awarded in other forms
e.g. money had and received: see the discussion of *Phillips v Homfray* below at 143–46.

analogous to the claim for payment for a benefit conferred by the plaintiff without agreement, as considered in the last chapter, in the sense that both give effect to an exchange that was not agreed. Thus the use claim can also be thought of as arising from an imputed contract in the sense discussed in the last chapter. No implied contract fiction is involved, because there is no implication of any actual agreement between the parties. The difference between the use claim and the claim for payment for a benefit conferred is that in the case of the use claim the benefit is appropriated by the defendant and not conferred by the plaintiff.

The first part of this chapter is concerned with distinguishing the use claim from other types of claim with which it is liable to be confused. Although the defendant may have committed a wrong by using the plaintiff's property, the claim is not a claim for compensation for harm caused through a wrong. It is not a claim for disgorgement, to strip away the benefit gained through the commission of a wrong, although this is how it is often characterised. And it is not a claim for restitution for a vitiated transfer, because there has been no transfer from the plaintiff to the defendant. The unauthorised use of the plaintiff's property involves the taking of a benefit, and it may cause the plaintiff a loss, but it is not a transfer from the plaintiff, any more than a benefit conferred through work or expenditure is a transfer.

THE USE CLAIM AND DISGORGEMENT COMPARED

Modern commentators have commonly conflated the use claim with disgorgement, assimilating them under the single head of "restitution for wrongs" or "restitutionary damages".[8] Thus the standard works and academic literature treat together the examples of the use claim mentioned above and the cases considered in Chapter 11 below as examples of disgorgement. But the two are quite distinct.[9] As pointed out in Chapter 1, they have quite different rationales. Disgorgement is a quasi-punitive sanction that arises as a response to a breach of duty. It reflects the principle that a wrongdoer should not benefit from his wrong, and its purpose is to promote the public interest, not to protect a private interest of the plaintiff. Thus the purpose of disgorgement is achieved if the defendant is deprived of the benefit received, and the same purpose is served by confiscation (as it is called) in criminal proceedings; it is an accident of civil procedure that gives the benefit to the plaintiff, for whom it is a windfall, as if it were a remedy.[10] A use claim on the other hand protects the private interest of the plaintiff in securing payment for the use of his property, just as a non-contractual claim for payment protects the plaintiff's private interest in being paid for his labour. The claim satisfies an interest of the plaintiff, like other civil

---

[8] Birks (1989*a*), 313ff; Burrows (1993), 376ff; Virgo (1999), 445ff. The approach is reflected in Law Commission (1997). A distinction along the lines in the text is found in Friedmann (1980).

[9] The distinction was pointed out in Jaffey (1995), (1996*a*).

[10] See further Chap. 11.

claims, and the satisfaction of the claim is not a windfall, but the plaintiff's entitlement. Because disgorgement is quasi-punitive and not remedial, it should be subject to special procedural requirements, as discussed in Chapter 11, whereas the use claim is a normal civil claim that need not be subject to any such special requirements.

The measure of disgorgement is liable to differ from that for the use claim. Disgorgement strips the defendant of any profit he has made through the wrong, whereas under the use claim the defendant must simply pay a reasonable fee for his use. A reasonable fee will generally be less than the value of the use to the user: the value of the benefit is merely relevant as a factor affecting the assessment of what is a reasonable fee. It is possible that in some circumstances a reasonable licence fee might be a convenient approximation for the value of the benefit for the purposes of disgorgement, so that the two claims would coincide; but this does not affect the fundamental proposition that the two claims are different and liable to generate different measures of liability. The measure of the use claim is considered later in this chapter.

Neither "restitution for wrongs" nor the use claim or disgorgement is a category recognised as such in the case law. Generally disgorgement and the use claim come in different forms in the case law. Typically disgorgement comes in the form of an account of profits, a constructive trust or punitive damages,[11] and the use claim in the form of damages or sometimes a claim for money had and received. In a disgorgement case, the court is liable to refer to the mischief of the defendant's keeping the proceeds of the wrong, and to consider whether it is acceptable for the plaintiff to receive a windfall, and whether the response is appropriate in civil proceedings;[12] in a use claim case, the issue will be whether the plaintiff is entitled to payment for the benefit received by the defendant. However, it seems that in some more modern cases, no doubt under the influence of academic discussion of "restitution for wrongs", the discussion tends to conflate the two types of case, as for example in one of the cases considered below, *Surrey County Council v Bredero*,[13] where the authorities cited were broadly concerned with the use claim, but some of the discussion, particularly in the judgment of Steyn LJ, was concerned with disgorgement.

Disgorgement is a response to a breach of duty or wrong by the defendant, whereas a breach of duty is not a condition for the use claim to arise. Usually the plaintiff's ownership of property entails both that others have a duty not to use the property and that the use of the property will generate a use claim. Thus usually unauthorised use of the property will be wrongful and also generate a use claim. But it is possible to have a form of ownership according to which there is no duty to refrain from using the plaintiff's property, but anyone who does use it incurs a liability to pay a reasonable fee. Such a regime has sometimes been advocated with respect to intellectual property rights, on the basis that the

[11] See further Chap. 11.
[12] A recent example is *Halifax v Thomas* [1996] Ch 217.
[13] [1993] 1 WLR 1361.

plaintiff should be entitled to a royalty in respect of the use of his idea or invention, but that, since the use of the idea or invention by others is not incompatible with the plaintiff's own use of it, he should not be entitled to restrict its use.[14] This shows that the use claim is in principle distinct from a claim arising from a breach of duty (whether for compensation or disgorgement).

The use claim may also arise in the absence of a breach of duty where in special circumstances the duty that would normally arise not to use the plaintiff's property is suspended. Consider, for example, the case where the defendant used the plaintiff's property in an emergency in order to avoid damage or injury. An example is provided by the American case of *Vincent v Lake Erie Transportation Co*,[15] where, because of the danger of leaving shore during a storm, the defendant moored his ship to the plaintiff's dock without the plaintiff's consent. As a result the dock was damaged and the plaintiff sought compensation. The court held that the defendant had not acted wrongfully because he had acted out of necessity, but nevertheless held the defendant liable to pay for the harm caused to the dock. This has given rise to some controversy, because the claim for compensation seems to be a claim in tort, and yet there was no tort because the defendant had a defence of necessity. It is now thought that the claim was restitutionary,[16] and this should be understood to mean a use claim. An appropriate measure of payment for the use of the dock (assessed after the event) would cover the loss caused.[17] The defendant had used the plaintiff's property so as to generate a use claim, but had not committed a breach of duty.

THE USE CLAIM AND COMPENSATION COMPARED

The "opportunity to bargain" argument

The use claim has sometimes been taken to be a form of compensation. This is unsurprising because compensation in the form of damages has always been the usual remedy at common law, and the use claim is usually awarded in the form of a claim for damages also. The use claim is not a claim for compensation, however, but a claim for payment for a benefit received through the unauthorised use. The appropriate payment will generally equal or exceed the measure of any loss caused to the plaintiff through the defendant's use, for example, loss through wear and tear or loss of use or loss of the opportunity to hire out the property; sometimes where a use claim is awarded there will be no loss at all.

---

[14] This is broadly the position under a compulsory licensing regime, as sometimes applies with respect to patents under the Patents Act 1977, although here the defendant must seek a licence, but the patentee is obliged to grant a licence at a reasonable price: see e.g. Cornish (1999), para. 7–43ff.

[15] 109 Minn 456, 124 NW 221 (1910).

[16] See the discussion in Friedmann (1980), 542ff.

[17] See further below at 147.

However, it has been suggested in a well-known article that the use claim can in fact be understood as compensatory.[18] The argument is that where the defendant uses the plaintiff's property without permission, in circumstances where the property is not damaged and the plaintiff incurs no other loss (because he would not have made any personal use of it and would not have licensed it for use) the plaintiff nevertheless "does suffer a real loss, namely, the opportunity to sell to the defendant"—or presumably to someone else—"the right to use the plaintiff's property",[19] or in other words a loss of the "opportunity to bargain" to grant a licence to use the property. The argument is unsatisfactory, because the value of this opportunity can only be the amount that the plaintiff would otherwise have made by exploiting the property but was prevented from making by the defendant's use, and ex hypothesi this is nil, since the argument is designed to show why the plaintiff should be able to recover a reasonable licence fee even when he would or could not have made such a fee by licensing.[20] If, to the contrary, the plaintiff was prevented by the defendant's use from making such a fee, then he could claim this amount as compensation in the normal way without relying on the user principle and the "opportunity to bargain" theory.

Another way of making the point is this. If the defendant had a duty to obtain a licence from the plaintiff—involving entering into negotiations to determine the licence fee—and failed to do so, then the plaintiff could claim the measure of a reasonable licence fee as determined by the court. This would be compensation: it would measure the plaintiff's loss with respect to the position he would have been in if the defendant had complied with his duty and taken a licence. This might be the position if the defendant contracted to take a licence and then failed to do so. Compensation here might (not very helpfully) be described as loss of the opportunity to bargain with the defendant. But in the situation to which the use claim relates, the defendant has no duty to take a licence. He may have a duty not to use the property, but no loss results from a breach of this duty unless the infringement causes damage or the plaintiff would otherwise have licensed it or used it and was prevented from so doing.

Thus the use claim is not a claim for compensation, but a restitutionary claim in the sense explained above. Although some judges have taken the view that the claim is compensatory,[21] the predominant view seems to be that it is restitutionary.[22] However, there is an element of truth in one argument used in support of a compensatory approach. If the use claim is regarded as a restitutionary

---

[18] Sharpe & Waddams (1982).

[19] Ibid., 290.

[20] Jaffey (1995), 33; Jaffey (1997), 80.

[21] e.g. Millet LJ in *Jaggard v Sawyer* [1995] 2 All ER 189, Lloyd LJ in *Ministry of Defence v Ashman* [1993] 2 EGLR 102, Lord Lloyd in *Inverugie Investments v Hackett* [1995] 1 WLR 713, Romer LJ in *Strand Electric and Engineering v Brisford Entertainments* [1952] 2 QB 246.

[22] e.g. Hoffmann LJ in *Ministry of Defence v Ashman* [1993] 2 EGLR 102, Lord Denning in *Strand Electric and Engineering v Brisford Entertainments* [1952] 2 QB 246 and in *Penarth Dock Engineering Co Ltd v Pounds* [1963] 1 Lloyd's Rep. 359, Steyn LJ and Dillon LJ in *Surrey CC v Bredero* [1993] 3 All ER 705, Lord Shaw in *Watson Laidlaw & Co Ltd v Pott, Cassels & Williamson* (1914) 31 RPC 104.

claim under the theory of unjust enrichment, it seems that it must be understood as a claim in the measure of the value received by the defendant, as is the case for a claim for disgorgement or a claim for restitution of a vitiated transfer. But it is clear that for the use claim the measure of liability is not the value of the unauthorised use to the defendant, but the amount that he might reasonably have paid for it, with respect to which the value obtained by him is merely a relevant factor in assessment, and this might be thought to preclude a restitutionary analysis.[23]

The restrictive covenant cases

A number of cases have involved a breach by the defendant of a restrictive covenant owed to the plaintiff. For the purposes of discussion, we can assume that the defendant has erected a building in breach of a restrictive covenant owed to his neighbour, the plaintiff. This constitutes a breach of duty and the cases suggest that it can also generate a use claim for payment. One might object that use by the defendant of his own property inconsistently with a restrictive covenant is not the same thing as use of the plaintiff's property.[24] But, as discussed further below, although the use claim is generally concerned with use of the plaintiff's property, nothing turns on this; the issue is whether the defendant incurs a liability to pay the plaintiff a reasonable fee such as would have been charged for a licence to do the act in question. For the purposes of discussion the breach of covenant will be referred to as a use of the plaintiff's property.

Support for a compensatory analysis of the use claim?

In the usual case of the use claim, there is a completed episode: the defendant has used the plaintiff's property but has now ceased to do so. But in the restrictive covenant case, it appears that the defendant continues to commit a wrong, and an unauthorised use, so long as the building remains standing. Thus one might expect the restrictive covenant case to be disposed of as follows. The defendant should be subject to an injunction to prevent him from continuing the breach of covenant, which would require him to demolish the building. Then, just as in the usual case, there would be a completed episode, and the defendant would be liable to a claim for damages for any loss caused to the plaintiff by the breach of covenant, while it lasted, and also to a use claim for payment for his temporary use of the plaintiff's property.

---

[23] See Bingham MR and Millett LJ in *Jaggard v Sawyer* [1995] 2 All ER 189 at 202 and 212 respectively; and Lord Lloyd in *Inverugie Investments v Hackett* [1995] 1 WLR 713, said at 718 that the claim is neither compensatory nor restitutionary but has elements of both.

[24] However, if a certain use of a property is inconsistent with some possible use of the neighbouring property, one can reasonably say that the use of one entails the use of the other.

However, in the cases in question, for example *Wrotham Park Estates v Parkside Homes*[25] and *Jaggard v Sawyer*,[26] the court refused an injunction on the ground that it would be oppressive, because the defendant constructed the building in good faith and requiring him to demolish it would impose an excessive cost on him compared to the loss inflicted on the plaintiff by allowing it to stand.[27] The issue remained what pecuniary claim the plaintiff should have. The plaintiff proved no loss in the form of disturbance of his own use, or actual loss of potential licence fees, but the plaintiff was allowed a use claim, in the measure of the fee that might reasonably have been agreed for a permanent waiver of the covenant. Now, in this type of case, it seems that a mistaken analysis of the effect of denying the injunction has provided some support for a compensatory analysis of the use claim. This faulty analysis is that at the time when the court makes its decision whether to grant an injunction the plaintiff has a subsisting right under the restrictive covenant against the continuing presence of the building, and therefore that in making its decision the court determines whether the plaintiff's subsisting right under the covenant is to be protected or not.[28] This seems to mean that the effect of the court's decision not to award an injunction is to destroy the plaintiff's subsisting right under the covenant to have the building demolished. This would be an extremely valuable right, because the defendant would pay a lot to avoid the loss of his investment in constructing the building, not to mention the cost of demolition. There is a tendency to think, therefore, that the function of the reasonable licence fee is to compensate the plaintiff for the loss of this right, and with it the valuable opportunity to bargain with the defendant over the right to keep the building.[29] (In fact, the value of such a bargaining opportunity would be much greater than the "reasonable licence fee", which is assessed on the basis of what would have been agreed before the defendant had begun to build.)

But it cannot be right to say that the court declines to enforce a subsisting right of the plaintiff in this way; if the plaintiff has such a right, the court would surely enforce it. In reality, in refusing the injunction the court merely gives effect to the existing legal position, the plaintiff having already lost his right to hold the defendant to the restrictive covenant under the oppression rule.[30] Thus the refusal of the injunction cannot itself be understood to cause loss and the plaintiff's right to compensation can only extend to loss caused by the

---

[25] [1974] 2 All ER 321.

[26] [1995] 1 WLR 269.

[27] *Shelfer v City of London Electric Lighting Co* [1895] 1 Ch 287. In *Wrotham Park* ([1974] 2 All ER 321, at 337 per Brightman J) it was thought that the ground for denying the injunction was wastefulness or inefficiency rather than unfairness to the defendant, but it is doubtful whether this is a proper ground if there is no unfairness.

[28] *Jaggard v Sawyer* [1995] 2 All ER 189, 212 per Millet LJ

[29] Ibid.

[30] Above n 27. Cf with respect to specific performance, where under the classical theory the court exercises a discretion to enforce or not to enforce a subsisting contractual right, whereas, under the reliance theory in the form set out in Chap. 2, by granting or not granting specific performance the court enforces the subsisting legal position.

construction of the building in breach of covenant. Ex hypothesi this does not account for the use claim. Just as in the usual case, the use claim can be justified only on the basis of an imputed contract, involving payment by the defendant for the use he has had, and more importantly the continuing right of use that he has effectively acquired under the oppression rule, although by way of a single lump sum licence fee, representing what would have been agreed for a permanent waiver of the covenant.

Lord Cairns's Act

A further issue in the restrictive covenant cases arises from the fact that the claim for damages has usually been in the form of a claim for damages "in lieu of an injunction" under Lords Cairns's Act,[31] rather than in the form of a claim for damages at common law. Lord Cairns's Act was a measure designed to enable the Chancery courts to award damages at a time when, before fusion, a plaintiff who sought but was denied an injunction in equity in respect of a common law claim would otherwise have had to restart proceedings at common law for damages. If, in accordance with the argument above, the refusal of the injunction is thought to be crucial to the use claim, in denying the plaintiff the right to bargain to have the building removed, it might also be thought that the use claim for damages in the measure of a reasonable licence fee could arise only as a claim for damages in lieu of an injunction under Lord Cairns's Act, and not as an ordinary claim for damages at common law. This is explicit in the judgment of Millet LJ in *Jaggard v Sawyer*,[32] and seems to be one of the reasons why a use claim was allowed in that case and in *Wrotham Park Estates v Parkside*[33] but not in *Surrey County Council v Bredero*,[34] where, because the plaintiff delayed in taking proceedings, no question of an injunction arose.

As argued above, Lord Cairns's Act and the injunction are not relevant in this way. It is true that if an injunction is awarded to stop the breach of a restrictive covenant, no question of a use claim can arise, at least with respect to future use, which will be prevented by the injunction. But the fact that the refusal of an injunction was an issue in the proceedings is not otherwise relevant to the use claim, which arises, as one would expect, on the same basis as in the ordinary cases at common law involving trespass to goods or land or intellectual property.[35]

---

[31] Chancery Amendment Act 1858, now s.50 of the Supreme Court Act 1981.

[32] *Jaggard v Sawyer* at 212, per Millet LJ.

[33] [1974] 2 All ER 321 at 338 per Brightman J, although the judge relied on common law authorities.

[34] [1993] 3 All ER 705 per Dillon LJ at 712, Rose LJ at 716.

[35] More generally, there is no difference between damages under Lord Cairns's Act and at common law. Lord Cairns's Act might be thought to differ from the common law in providing damages for a "future wrong", but in reality it provides for damages for future loss from a past wrong, as does the common law also. It should be accepted that since fusion the Act has had no purpose or effect, since its original purpose was to overcome a procedural problem that disappeared on fusion; see further Appendix 2.

THE USE CLAIM AND *PHILLIPS V HOMFRAY*

Phillips v Homfray as an authority against the use claim for land?

Phillips v Homfray[36] is possibly the most discussed case on "restitution for wrongs" or "restitutionary damages", which, as mentioned above, is a category that encompasses the use claim and disgorgement without differentiation. In fact the case concerned a use claim, not disgorgement. The defendant had mined coal from under the plaintiff's land and made use of tunnels that extended under the plaintiff's land in doing so. The defendant had died, and the action was brought against his estate. At that time actions against the defendant's estate after his death were governed by the abatement rule (actio personalis moritur cum persona), which, broadly speaking, provided that an action in tort would not survive the defendant's death. On these facts, the plaintiff would appear to have had a claim against the defendant in respect of the coal taken from his land and also a claim in respect of the use made of the tunnels passing under his land. In fact the first claim was not in issue in these proceedings, because it had been disposed of previously, although it was discussed in passing. The issue was whether a claim for payment for the use of the plaintiff's land would arise against the defendant, and if so whether it had survived his death or was subject to the abatement rule.

The court accepted, first, that the defendant had been liable before his death to pay "mesne damages" for trespass, meaning damages in the measure of a reasonable licence fee. The court characterised this claim as a claim for compensation for a wrong, but also accepted that the measure of the claim was necessarily a reasonable licence fee, without proof of loss.[37] Thus it was in reality a use claim, not a claim for compensation for a tort. Under the abatement rule, the court held that it would not bind the estate because it was based on the tort of trespass; understood as a use claim, however, it was not strictly based on the trespass as a wrong, and so should not have been held to lapse on the defendant's death.[38] Secondly, it was argued that the plaintiff could waive the tort of trespass and make a claim for money had and received for payment for the use made of the land.[39] It is not necessary for present purposes to consider the nature of the claim for money had and received arising from a waiver of tort, and in fact this was not a standard example of waiver of tort.[40] It is reasonably clear that here also the claim was actually a use claim. Thus the two claims identified by the court were in reality both forms of the use claim; the court considered that the claim arising from waiver was "similar in principle, though not

---

[36] (1883) 24 Ch D 439. See Birks (1992*b*), 65.

[37] At 454.

[38] Although it is not necessary for present purposes to consider the proper scope of the abatement rule.

[39] At 457.

[40] Waiver of tort is considered in Chap. 11.

identical, with an action for . . . use and occupation"[41] (meaning the action for mesne damages for trespass). However, the court held that the claim for money had and received arising from waiver of tort was not subject to the abatement rule,[42] because the claim was not based on the tort, which was waived, and therefore would not lapse on the defendant's death. This seems to be a correct understanding of the use claim, although it is of course a curiosity of the case that what was in reality a single claim was identified in two different forms, one of which was held subject to the abatement rule and one not.

With respect to this second version of the use claim, arising from the waiver of tort, which was capable of surviving against the estate, the court was unfortunately confused by the implied contract fallacy. The liability to pay for the use, which in reality arises from the unauthorised use itself, was thought to arise from a promise by the defendant to pay for his use, which it was necessary to show that the defendant had expressly or impliedly made when he used the plaintiff's property: the court said that the liability arose "upon the theory of an implied promise . . . to pay for what he had done".[43] As discussed in Chapter 1, the requirement to show that the defendant had promised to pay for the use was really a fictional requirement that had developed in order to enable the claim to be brought by way of assumpsit. But here, apparently oblivious to the fiction, the court rejected the claim because the circumstances were such as to "negative the idea that [the defendant] meant to pay for [his use]".[44]

Phillips v Homfray is regarded as an important case, but it has been misunderstood and its significance exaggerated. It is thought to be an authority against the availability of a use claim in relation to land, or, as it is put, a claim for restitutionary damages for trespass to land.[45] But to the contrary the court held that a use claim *was* in principle available, although it was identified in two different forms. In one form it was denied under the abatement rule, and in the other because of the effect of the implied contract fallacy. The abatement rule, which was crucial to the case, has long since disappeared. The influence of the case in perpetuating the implied contract fallacy in connection with a use claim with respect to land is found as recently as *Morris v Tarrent*.[46] But generally the implied contract fallacy has been overcome,[47] and it has not generally inhibited the recognition of the use claim, in relation to land or otherwise, because, as mentioned above, the claim has tended to take the form of a claim in damages in tort, which was never affected by the implied contract fiction, not a claim for money had and received.

---

[41] At 461.
[42] At 459–61.
[43] At 457.
[44] At 462.
[45] Burrows (1993), 390; *Re Polly Peck International* [1997] 2 BCLC 630, noted by Jaffey (1997), where the analysis differs slightly from that in the text; cf Birks (1989*a*), 323; Gummow (1990).
[46] [1971] 2 QB 143. Birks (1989*a*), 325.
[47] Chap. 1 above.

Phillips v Homfray and "negative benefit"

A second and related aspect of *Phillips v Homfray* concerns the concept of "negative benefit". There is a sensible sense of "negative benefit" to the defendant by which it means a benefit in the form of a cancellation or discharge of a liability of the defendant's.[48] But it is also used misleadingly by some commentators to refer to a benefit that does not leave the defendant with any additional wealth, as, for example, where he is provided with a "pure service" like training or entertainment, as discussed in the last chapter.[49] Such a benefit is described as a negative benefit because the benefit is understood to be the sum that the defendant would have paid to acquire the benefit, i.e. the saving of expenditure. In truth, however, the benefit acquired through a pure service is the pleasure or skill or knowledge or other positive benefit obtained from the service. The "negative benefit", meaning the price the defendant would have paid for the benefit, serves as a measure of the defendant's liability if he incurs a liability to pay for the benefit.[50] "Negative benefit" in this sense would therefore be more helpfully referred to as "non-wealth benefit".

Phillips v Homfray is often cited as authority for the proposition that a "negative benefit", meaning a non-wealth benefit or saving of expenditure, is not recognised as a benefit for the purposes of the law of restitution.[51] (The expression "negative benefit" is not actually used in the case.) In fact the case cannot possibly stand for the proposition that a use claim is not available in respect of a non-wealth benefit. As discussed above, the case did in substance recognise that a use claim arose on the facts, even though the defendant received a non-wealth benefit; the claim was denied for other reasons entirely, because of the mischaracterisation of the use claim as either contractual or tortious. In any case, there is no doubt that the use claim does arise from a non-wealth benefit as the usual examples show—for example, the defendant's pleasure in driving the plaintiff's car without permission, or the contribution to his business from his unauthorised use of the plaintiff's land for access, are non-wealth benefits that give rise to a use claim measured as a reasonable fee for the use of the plaintiff's car or land.[52]

In the passage relied on in *Phillips v Homfray*, the court contrasts the claim in trespass in respect of unauthorised use with the case where trespass is "in

---

[48] See Chap. 9 at 303–4.

[49] This understanding of a "negative benefit" is associated with Burrows: Burrows (1993), 8; cf Chap. 3 at n 77.

[50] Under the unjust enrichment theory this measure of liability tends to be confused with the measure of the benefit received, because the measure of the claim is equated with benefit: see Chap. 3, at 82.

[51] Birks (1989*a*), 323; Burrows (1993), 390.

[52] Even where the use generates wealth, the benefit received from the use is probably not the wealth itself. This is in any case not of any consequence.

substance brought to recover property, or its proceeds or value".[53] Such a claim is not actually based on the wrong and would survive the defendant's death. But here the defendant had not taken any property; as it was put:

> the deceased, by carrying his coal . . . over the Plaintiffs' roads took nothing from the Plaintiffs . . . Nor have the assets of the deceased Defendant been necessarily swollen by what he has done. He saved his estate expense, but he did not bring into it any additional property or value belonging to another person . . .[54]

The claim referred to here—the claim to recover property—is actually the restitutionary claim arising from a vitiated transfer.[55] In fact it is true to say that this claim arises only in respect of wealth-benefits; its function is to reverse transfers of wealth or property. But it is clearly not true that the defendant had not received any benefit—he would not have used the plaintiff's land if it was not of benefit to him to do so. It seems that the restitutionary claim to reverse a transfer of property was the only claim that was appreciated to be distinct from contract and tort, given the mischaracterisation of the use claim as either contractual or tortious, and therefore the only non-contractual claim available after the defendant's death under the abatement rule. This seems to account for the emphasis placed on the fact that no tangible property was transferred to the defendant.

THE MEASURE OF LIABILITY

A reasonable fee: the relevant factors

The measure of the use claim is a reasonable fee for the use made of the plaintiff's property. This should be assessed in broadly the same way as for imputed contracts in the last chapter, i.e. in terms of what the parties might reasonably have agreed. Here, however, there will often be no price that the parties would have agreed on: the plaintiff would not have accepted any price that the defendant was willing to pay. This is liable to be the reason the defendant acts without permission. An obvious example is where the defendant is a joy-rider who drives away the plaintiff's car. The plaintiff would certainly not have let the defendant use the car for any price that the defendant could have afforded. It seems that where this is the case the court must simply do its best to make the terms of the exchange as fair as possible in the light of the various factors that

---

[53] At 454. This implies the recognition of the non-tortious character of conversion or detinue in this context; see especially at 467 in the dissenting judgment, and see *Hambly v Trott* (1776) 1 Cowp 371; cf below, Chap. 10.

[54] At 462. By contrast there is the case where the defendant "saved his own pocket", and thereby made a benefit, by breaching a duty of repair owed in respect of the plaintiff's land: see at 455.

[55] Some would object that it is not a restitutionary but a proprietary claim, as to which see Chap. 9 below.

would be relevant to the parties in agreeing a price.[56] One might object that the defendant acted wrongfully and the court should not be even-handed in this way. But, as pointed out above, the commission of a wrong by the defendant is not material to the use claim, and if the defendant did commit a wrong the objective of stripping him of a benefit gained through it is a matter for disgorgement. The use claim is designed to secure reasonable payment for the benefit, which involves treating the parties even-handedly.

The price the parties would have agreed on depends on their particular circumstances, including the resources of the defendant, the benefit gained by him, the cost of alternative benefits, and the loss to the plaintiff.[57] In *Wrotham Park* the judge took the value of the benefit as the main guide to an appropriate fee, which was assessed as a small fraction of the profit that the defendant would make. The price should normally exceed the loss to the plaintiff. In a case where the defendant's use also constitutes a breach of duty, the breach will generate a liability for compensation anyway; but, as pointed out above, there can be cases where the defendant's is not a breach of duty. An example mentioned above was the case of *Vincent v Lake Erie Transportation Co Ltd*,[58] where the defendant made use of the plaintiff's dock in an emergency and caused damage in so doing. He was held liable to compensate the plaintiff for the damage. As discussed above, this is best understood as a use claim, because the defendant did not act wrongfully. If the use claim is conceived of as concerned with reversing unjust enrichment, it would seem perverse for the defendant's liability to be measured by the plaintiff's loss, rather than the value received or the value of a transfer from the plaintiff to the defendant.[59] But it makes sense as a measure for the use claim, because the measure of payment is the appropriate payment in the light of the defendant's gain and the plaintiff's loss, which may equal one of them but is not generally to be equated with either.

Where there is a market price, it may provide a good indicator of a reasonable price, but there may be reasons why the market price would be unfair to one of the parties. For example, say the defendant uses the plaintiff's land thinking that it is his own, in circumstances where he could have used his own land instead. Then he clearly would not have paid anything significant for the use in question, and this should be reflected in the measure of liability. A similar example is provided by *Ministry of Defence v Ashman*,[60] where there was a market rate but the court did not adopt it. The defendant was married to an RAF airman and living in RAF accommodation rented from the plaintiff MOD. Her husband left and the tenancy was terminated, but the defendant stayed on after the termination and the plaintiff MOD made a claim for rent at the market rate for equivalent

[56] See e.g. *Wrotham Park* [1974] 2 All ER 321, 341.

[57] The loss and benefit might not have been known if the parties had negotiated beforehand, but if they are known at the time of the hearing the court should take account of them.

[58] 109 Minn 456, 124 NW 221 (1910).

[59] e.g. Friedmann (1980), 543.

[60] *Ministry of Defence v Ashman* [1993] 2 EGLR 102.

accommodation in the area. The plaintiff offered no evidence of loss in the form of loss of rental income or otherwise; the claim was based on the user principle. The Court of Appeal rejected the market rate as a measure of liability. It was much greater than the rate that the defendant subsequently paid for local authority accommodation when she was rehoused. Because the defendant was entitled to be rehoused after she lost the RAF accommodation, she would not have agreed a rate with the plaintiff significantly higher than the rate she would have had to pay the local authority, and so this was indicative of the appropriate measure of liability.[61]

Must the plaintiff choose between the use claim and compensation?

One issue that has been discussed in relation to "restitution for wrongs" or "restitutionary damages" is whether the plaintiff has to choose between the restitutionary claim and compensation or whether he can have both. The general view is that the plaintiff must choose between them.[62] This rule is necessarily correct with respect to disgorgement. Disgorgement is designed to strip the defendant of the benefit of the wrong, and this must mean the benefit after the payment of compensation, because the payment of compensation reduces the amount that the defendant made out of the wrong.[63] The position is not quite as simple with respect to the use claim. The defendant's use may cause damage to the property, and, as discussed above, payment under the use claim will normally take account of this, so that one can say that the use claim will encompass compensation. Where the use also involves a wrong, the plaintiff is entitled to compensation for the loss as a remedy for the breach of duty. It does not seem to be of any consequence whether the compensation is treated as part of the use claim or as damages for the wrong, but it is clear that double compensation must be avoided. One might say that compensation for loss or damage that the plaintiff would normally expect as part of the use (e.g. wear and tear or opportunity cost) should be treated as part of the use claim, and compensation for other damage or loss covered by damages for the wrong. In any case, if the compensation is treated as based on the wrong, there is no reason why the plaintiff should not also recover payment for use, excluding any element of compensa-

---

[61] As noted above, some commentators equate the benefit with the saving of expense and regard the claim to be for the value of the benefit: this is the fallacy of "negative benefit".

[62] See Law Commission (1997), para. 3.64ff.

[63] This is consistent with *Mahesan v Malaysia Government Officers' Co-operative Housing Society Ltd* [1979] AC 374, where the plaintiff could recover either the value of a bribe (disgorgement) or the loss caused by the agent's breach of duty, and now *Tang Min Sit v Capacious Investments Ltd* [1996] AC 514. *United Australia Ltd v Barclays Bank Ltd* [1941] AC 1 is sometimes cited for this proposition, but actually concerned a claim for restitution for a vitiated transfer, as discussed in Chap. 11.

tion, and in this sense it is possible to have concurrent claims for compensation in tort and for payment under the use claim.[64]

The rationale

As argued above, the use claim is best understood as arising from an imputed contract, like the claim for payment for work done in conferring a benefit considered in the last chapter. In the case of the latter, a benefit is conferred without an agreement; in the case of the use claim, a benefit is taken without an agreement. In both cases the effect of enforcing a claim for payment is to give effect to an exchange of payment for benefit just as if there had been an agreement. In the case of the conferral of a benefit, the claim protects the plaintiff's interest in receiving the expected return on his work and expenditure; the use claim protects the plaintiff's right to the value of his property through use.[65]

In the case of the conferral of a benefit, the presumption is against any claim, because the claim is sought by the party who instigated the exchange without an agreement (deliberately or by mistake), and gives effect to an exchange for his benefit. The two conditions that have to be satisfied (the officiousness condition and the benefit condition) serve to protect the defendant against an exchange imposed on him against his interests, and the plaintiff who conferred the benefit should bear the risk that his work is wasted because the conditions are not met. By contrast, in the case of the use claim, the exchange has been instigated by the defendant, and the claim gives effect to an exchange for the benefit of the plaintiff. Of course the defendant did not intend to make an exchange—he did not intend to pay—but the plaintiff should be entitled to treat the unauthorised use as the first part of an exchange in order to protect his right to the value of his property through use. Here the plaintiff should be entitled to a claim as a matter of course, without having to satisfy any conditions designed to protect the defendant against the risk of an exchange that is not mutually beneficial.[66] The defendant must take this risk, because he instigated the exchange without agreement, although, as discussed above, the measure of liability should be assessed so far as possible as a fair price between the two parties.

One issue that arises is whether the use claim arises in respect of all types of property. One can approach this issue through the rationale of the plaintiff's ownership of the property, and in particular through a rough and ready

---

[64] Hoffmann LJ, dealing with a use claim in *Ministry of Defence v Ashman* [1993] 2 EGLR 102, considered that the restitutionary and compensatory claims were alternatives. See also Jaffey (1998b), commenting on Law Commission (1997), which unfortunately fails to take account of the distinction between the use claim and disgorgement.

[65] As noted below, this may state the scope of the use claim too narrowly.

[66] This has been referred to as the "reprehensible seeking-out" test of benefit: Burrows (1993), 15; in fact it is not strictly a test of benefit but of reasonable payment for a benefit.

distinction between two possible such rationales. The first is to give the owner the exclusive right to any value to be made through the property through use or licensing; and the second is to protect the owner from interference with his own use of the property. In the former case, one would expect the owner to have a use claim in respect of unauthorised use, to protect his right to the value of the property through use; in the latter case, by contrast, one would expect the owner to be entitled only to compensation for loss caused through any disturbance to the owner's own use, so that if his own use has not been disturbed in any way, he should not have any claim.[67] The difference between the two rationales is unlikely to make any practical difference in most cases, because the most important responses are likely to be compensation, injunction, and sometimes punishment, which would apply on either rationale. Nevertheless the distinction seems to provide some guide to the circumstances in which the use claim should be available. For example, a patent is awarded as a means of enabling the inventor to obtain a profit as a return on his invention, either by working the invention himself or by licensing it. Thus the patent seems to fall clearly in the category of property for which a use claim should be available. On the other hand, one can conceive of a case where land is held only for its use, whether for residential or business purposes, and not for financial exploitation, and where the owner's property right would fall into the category of property for which no use claim should be available.

Consider, in the light of this suggested distinction, the controversial decision in *Stoke City Council v Wass*.[68] Here the plaintiff council had what was referred to as a "market right", which gave it the exclusive right to hold and authorise markets in the city precincts. The defendant held an unauthorised market, which caused the plaintiff no loss in the form of damage or lost licensing fees or otherwise. The plaintiff obtained an injunction and also made a use claim for a reasonable licence fee. The claim was denied. Nicholls LJ said:

> [T]he application of the user principle in the case of the disturbance of a market right would not accord with the basic principles applicable to that cause of action. A market right confers a monopoly . . . but the protection which the law affords to the owner of a market right is limited to protecting him against being disturbed in the enjoyment of his right. If an unauthorised market is held without disturbing the lawful market, the owner of the lawful market has no remedy . . .[69]

This reflects the argument above, and Nicholls LJ explicitly distinguished the market right in issue from a patent. One might object that the council was not

---

[67] If the plaintiff has to prove loss, it seems that no use claim should be available because the rationale must be to protect the plaintiff in his own use. One might infer that if proof of loss is not required it must follow that the rationale is to allow exploitation by licensing as well as to prevent disturbance so that a use claim should be available. But even if the rationale is only to prevent disturbance, it may be reasonable to waive any requirement to prove actual loss in order to obviate the difficulty of proving it.

[68] [1988] 3 All ER 394.

[69] At 404.

expected to run the market itself, but to license others to do so, and therefore the market right should have been treated as designed for exploitation and not merely to prevent disturbance. In fact because the right-holder, the council, was a public authority, it may be that the rationale of the right was neither the exploitation of the precincts by the council nor the protection of the council in its use of the precincts, but the regulation of the city precincts in the public interest, and this rationale does not seem to justify a use claim.[70]

The use claim and property

As the use claim has been discussed above, it has been assumed that it is concerned with the use of property. Certainly it seems that most cases arise out of the use of property, and it is often said that the claim for "restitution for wrongs" or "restitutionary damages" arises only in relation to the infringement of property rights, like trespass to land, unauthorised use of chattels, and infringement of intellectual property rights, and not in relation to wrongs against the person like assault or libel or deceit.[71] This is consistent with the analysis above: a right against assault or libel or deceit is designed to protect against harm, not to secure to the right-holder the value to be obtained through the exploitation of his reputation or body for money. (By contrast, there would be no reason why disgorgement should be limited in this way.) But the plaintiff can have a right to exact payment from the defendant in respect of some benefit secured from the plaintiff that is not really the use of the plaintiff's property; use of the plaintiff's property is merely the most common way by which this can occur. For example, the defendant might make use of the plaintiff's labour by compulsion, as where the plaintiff is enslaved and forced to work for the defendant. This would involve a wrong, but in addition to a claim for compensation and disgorgement arising from the wrong, one would expect to see a claim for payment, which appears to be a use claim based on the plaintiff's right to the value of his labour. Another example might be where the defendant deceives the plaintiff into doing work for him. And, as considered in connection with free acceptance in the last chapter, where the defendant has a duty to alert the plaintiff to the fact that by mistake he is doing work that will benefit the defendant rather than himself, as where he is working on the defendant's land thinking

---

[70] Although the defendant in *Stoke City Council v Wass* was eventually prevented by injunction from continuing to hold a market in breach of the plaintiff's market right, it apparently kept all the profits that he had made while doing so and suffered no penalty, unless there were separate criminal proceedings. Thus the law failed to uphold the principle that a wrongdoer should not profit through a wrong. Academic criticism of the decision, as a decision on "restitution for wrongs" or "restitutionary damages", has concentrated on this factor, which is actually relevant not to the use claim but to disgorgement.

[71] *Stoke City Council v Wass* [1988] 3 All ER 394, at 402 per Nourse LJ; Goff & Jones (1998), 780–1; Jackman (1989), 305–11. Thus one clear indication that there should be no use claim is that a contract by which the plaintiff purported to license the defendant to do the act in question would be void on public policy grounds.

that it is his own, possibly the defendant's failure to do so should render him liable to pay for the plaintiff's work just as if he had deceived him into doing it.

The restrictive covenant cases

As mentioned earlier in the chapter, there is room for argument whether the breach of a restrictive covenant amounts to the use of the covenantee's property. But this is not determinative of whether there should be a use claim. The issue, according to the argument above, is whether the function of the restrictive covenant is to protect the covenantee from harm to his own property, or disturbance to him in his use of it, resulting from the way in which the neighbouring property is used or developed, or whether it is designed to give the covenantee a right to exploit the potential for development of the neighbouring property by exacting a fee for permitting it. This casts doubt on the appropriateness of a use claim arising from the breach of a restrictive covenant. In *Wrotham Park*, Brightman J noted that the covenant:

> is not an asset which the estate owner ever contemplated he would have the opportunity or the desire to turn to account. It had no commercial . . . value. For it cannot be turned to account except to the detriment of the existing residents who are the people the estate owner professes to protect.[72]

He regarded this as a factor that weighed in favour of a lower measure of liability under the use claim, rather than counting against a claim, or precluding one altogether. His insistence on finding a claim, however, seems to have been more to do with his objection to the defendant profiting from a wrong, which is properly a matter relating to disgorgement, not the use claim. But a true disgorgement claim would have led to a much higher measure of liability, encompassing the whole of the defendant's profits, not merely a fraction of them.

On the other hand, in *Surrey County Council v Bredero*, Dillon LJ accepted that:

> [the covenantee's] sole purpose in imposing the covenants . . . was that the defendant would have to apply for and pay for a relaxation if it wanted to build anything more.[73]

Thus here the purpose behind the covenant does seem to have been to exploit the potential for development of the defendant's property. If this is accepted as a legitimate purpose behind a restrictive covenant, then it seems that the use claim should have been available for an infringement of the covenant, although the claim was rejected, as discussed above.[74]

---

[72] [1974] 2 All ER 321 at 341.
[73] [1993] 3 All ER 705, 709. Dillon LJ considered the point in relation to the availability of an injunction.
[74] Above at 142.

The use claim and contract

A restrictive covenant arises out of a contract between neighbours, but becomes a property right because it becomes attached to the land in the sense that it remains enforceable by and against the owners for the time being of the plots of land, not just the original contractors. In *Surrey County Council v Bredero* the issue arose as between the original contractors, and was treated as a matter of contract. In *Wrotham Park* and *Jaggard v Sawyer* the issue was treated as a matter of property law, presumably because the parties were not the original contractors, and the use claim was allowed, partly by analogy with property cases. But surely it cannot be correct that the right of the contracting covenantee is more limited than that of his successor in title who inherits his position as covenantee through ownership of the land.

This raises the question whether the use claim should be available in relation to an ordinary breach of contract. The main reason for the rejection of the claim in *Surrey County Council v Bredero* seems to have been concern over the implications of recognising disgorgement as a response in the law of contract. But disgorgement and the use claim have to be considered separately.[75] It has sometimes been suggested, in relation to breach of contract, as an alternative to either holding the defendant liable for compensation and nothing more or holding him liable to disgorge the whole benefit from non-performance, that he should be liable to pay an intermediate sum, calculated as the amount that the parties would have agreed on as the plaintiff's price for a variation of the contract to permit the defendant not to perform.[76] This is equivalent to recognising a use claim in relation to the plaintiff's contractual right. It treats the plaintiff as having a right to performance in the sense that he is entitled to a share of the profit made by the defendant through his non-performance.[77] Other than the case of the restrictive covenant, there does not appear to be any authority for this approach. It seems that in principle there should generally not be a use claim, because generally contract is designed, at least under the reliance theory, to protect the plaintiff against loss in reliance on the agreement, not to secure to him some part of the value of the skill, labour and resources that the defendant would have used to perform the contract.[78] A contract like the one in *Surrey v Bredero*, where, as mentioned above, the

---

[75] Disgorgement for breach of contract is considered in Chap. 12.

[76] See Farnsworth (1985), 1389.

[77] But not necessarily a right to insist on performance.

[78] Chap 2, 29–34. Cf *Co-operative Insurance Society v Argyll Stores* [1997] 2 WLR 898, 906, where it is stated that the purpose of contract is not to enable a contracting party to profit by extracting more from the other party than the value of performance, i.e. compensatory damages (where damages are adequate). Possibly under the classical theory one might say that instead of having a right to rely on the expectation of performance the plaintiff promisee has a right to performance which includes the right to exploit it by waiver or licensing.

contract was designed to create an obligation that could be relaxed in return for payment, might be an exception.[79]

THE USE CLAIM AND "MISAPPROPRIATION"

The discussion above has mostly concerned the possibility of a use claim in relation to the use of well-defined types of property, in particular land or chattels. But the issue of the availability of a use claim has arisen in relation to less well-defined intangible things, in particular the intangible things that can be created through a business or other activities. Sometimes such intangible things are protected through statutory intellectual property rights, like patents, copyright and design rights. These forms of statutory property are generally understood to be concerned with enabling the plaintiff to exploit his invention or design or literary or artistic work by obtaining payment from third parties who make use of it in the form of a licence fee. The intellectual property right can be understood as a form of statutory use claim,[80] which serves to secure payment from a user for his use of the intangible. But there has been controversy over the general availablity of a common law claim to payment, or use claim, in respect of the use of ideas, information, ways of doing business or other intangibles that are not protected by a statutory intellectual property right. The issue has taken the form of a controversy over a supposed doctrine of misappropriation, which is understood to be a form of unfair competition,[81] requiring the defendant to pay for benefit that he has had from using the plaintiff's valuable intangible. Sometimes the issue is expressed in terms of whether the intangible is the plaintiff's property.[82]

Consider, for example, the American case of *International News Services v Associated Press*.[83] The defendant had been banned from reporting from Europe during the First World War. By relying on the plaintiff's newspapers in the East Coast, it could publish the news from the front in its West Coast editions in time to compete with the plaintiff's own West Coast editions. There was no infringement of copyright, because the form of expression was not taken, and there was no breach of confidence because the information was in the public domain after publication on the East Coast. But the Supreme Court held that the defendant had committed an unlawful misappropriation because it had

[79] Possibly because the use claim constitutes a delayed part of the sale price that takes account of the profit subsequently made by the purchaser from the property.

[80] Cf Gordon (1992), who argues that intellectual property rights are based on a principle of restitution. Generally the intellectual property right would be protected by an injunction (together with a use claim or a claim for compensation), but the principal underlying objective is to facilitate exploitation by licensing.

[81] See Cornish (1996), para. 1–13ff; Kamperman Sanders (1997), 12ff; Libling (1978); Terry (1988). There is a large literature on this topic.

[82] Libling (1978); Kamperman Sanders (1997), 79ff. It is not necessary for present purposes to consider whether the intangible should be described as a form of property.

[83] 248 US 215 (1918).

"[diverted] a material portion of the profit from those who have earned it to those who have not".[84] However, this doctrine has not developed strongly in the United States, and in the Commonwealth it seems to have been rejected entirely by the courts, although there has been some academic support for it.[85] For example, in the Australian case of *Victoria Park Racing v Taylor*,[86] the defendant erected a stand outside the plaintiff's racecourse to enable him to commentate on a race meeting, and, although the defendant thereby exploited for profit the fruits of the plaintiff's business, the plaintiff had no claim against him. The court denied that there could be in any property in "the intangible elements of value . . . which may flow from the exercise by an individual of his powers or resources",[87] unless a property right was created by statute. Thus in England and the Commonwealth property in intangibles is confined to property defined by statutory intellectual property rights.

There is a sound basis, at least in principle, for this traditional approach of denying any general use claim in respect of intangibles, or, in other words, any common law doctrine of misappropriation, and reserving to the legislature the exclusive power to define the scope of property in intangibles.[88] On one view,[89] someone who produces a valuable intangible should be entitled to the benefit to be made from it, i.e. he should have a right to be paid by anyone who uses it. This would justify the general availability of a use or misappropriation claim, and it would imply that the right should persist indefinitely (which is not of course the position for intellectual property rights).[90] On another view, someone who makes a valuable intangible is merely entitled to a reasonable return out of the benefits to be made from it, to cover his investment and give him a profit, and to provide an incentive to others to be similarly innovative. On this approach, whether the plaintiff has a claim against any particular person cannot be determined in isolation from the return that the plaintiff has made and is liable to make from others, in the light of the relevant market. Arguably, this can only be done through a statutory regime established by the legislature, which can set an appropriate term of protection with respect to a particular type of intangible, with a view to conferring a certain level of return.[91] This seems to be the main reason why in general there is no use claim in respect of intangibles except by way of an intellectual property right defined by statute.[92]

---

[84] At 240, per Pitney J.

[85] e.g. Libling (1978); Terry (1988).

[86] (1937) 58 CLR 479.

[87] At 509 per Dixon J. See also *Cadbury-Schweppes v The Pub Squash Co* [1981] RPC 429.

[88] But English law has a very wide concept of copyright that tends to give scope to the courts to achieve the effect of misappropriation: see e.g. Cornish (1999), para. 10.07.

[89] For a general discussion of these issues, see Hettinger (1989).

[90] Save for trade marks, which raise different issues.

[91] With respect to tangibles, an indefinite exclusive right is generally necessary to determine who can use the property, but for intangibles this is not necessary for this reason because the intangible can be used by more than one person at a time.

[92] There are also problems of defining the subject matter of an intangible property right and the circumstances in which it arises: Jaffey (1998e).

There is, however, the suggestion of a possible development out of the law of passing off that would represent the recognition of a non-statutory use claim in respect of an intangible, viz. fame or popularity. This is the right of celebrity or merchandising right in famous real or fictional people. Such a right would require any person who, for the purpose of promoting his business, makes some reference to the fame of the plaintiff, or of some fictional person in respect of which the plaintiff is taken to have a merchandising right, to pay a fee in respect of the benefit derived from it.[93]

[93] Ibid.

Part III

Reversing Vitiated Transfers: Restitution and Property

5

The Vitiating Factors

THE PLAINTIFF'S WEALTH is a store of value that he is entitled to control and apply for his own purposes. There are clearly circumstances in which a transfer of wealth from the plaintiff should not be recognised as legally effective on the ground that it would be inconsistent with the plaintiff's right to his own wealth: the most obvious case is where a transfer of wealth is effected by someone else without the plaintiff's permission. In such a case the plaintiff's right to his wealth generates a claim to reverse the transfer (subject to appropriate protection for the recipient). This is the claim for restitution for a vitiated transfer. Inevitably it is necessary to have criteria to determine what constitutes an effective application or disposition of the plaintiff's wealth by the plaintiff or someone acting on his behalf, or, in other words, when a transfer, or putative transfer, is vitiated so as to generate a restitutionary claim. This chapter is concerned with the various factors that vitiate a transfer of the plaintiff's wealth. There is a certain lack of consistency in the case law and literature over classification and description of the vitiating factors, reflecting disagreements over their precise nature. The vitiating factors identified below are lack of authority (the example given above), mistake, duress, incompetence, undue influence and inadequate bargaining ability.

These various vitiating factors are sometimes said to make the transfer involuntary or "non-voluntary", or to imply that that transfer was not genuinely consented to by the plaintiff.[1] If this is taken to mean that the plaintiff did not know or understand what he was doing, or what was being done in his name, it is not always true. It is not true, for example, of duress or of some cases of lack of authority. Thus, rather than saying that the vitiating factor vitiates the plaintiff's consent or makes the transfer non-voluntary, it might be better to say that the effect of the vitiating factor is that the transfer was not due to or derived from an autonomous decision of the plaintiff, or that it subverted the plaintiff's autonomy or his control over his wealth.

An agreement can be vitiated in just the same way as a transfer. There is no reason to doubt that the same vitiating factors should operate with respect to transfers and agreements, and some of the cases discussed concern agreements rather than transfers. The position with respect to agreements tends to be more

---

[1] Birks (1989a), 140. "Non-voluntary" is presumably preferred because it does not imply an automatic or unconscious act.

complex, because one has to distinguish between the effect of the vitiating factor on the agreement (which is, broadly speaking, to render it voidable or rescindable by the plaintiff, subject to the possibility of a defence based on reliance on the putative agreement)[2] and the implications of rescission for any transfers or work done under the voidable agreement.[3]

A vitiating factor is to be distinguished from the wrong of causing or exploiting the vitiating factor. For example, misrepresentation, which is the wrong of causing a mistake, is distinct from the mistake itself, which is the vitiating factor, and duress as a vitiating factor is distinct from the wrong of inflicting it, which may also be referred to as duress. The wrong may generate a claim for compensation for the loss incurred through the transfer caused by the wrong, and the claim may serve precisely the same purpose, in restoring the plaintiff's loss, as a restitutionary claim arising directly from the vitiating factor; this is the basis for the doctrine of waiver of tort, as considered in Chapter 11. If the transfer was to the party who committed the wrong, an appropriate remedy for the tortious claim might well be the reversal of the transfer,[4] which one might want to refer to as restitution. But, as discussed in Chapter 1, in the light of conventional usage it is better to use "restitution" to refer only to the claim arising from the vitiated transfer, and not to a remedy for the wrong.

LACK OF AUTHORITY AND INCAPACITY

Lack of authority

Lack of authority, not always identified as such, is the most important and common vitiating factor. A transfer of value from the plaintiff is vitiated where it was made by someone other than the plaintiff without the plaintiff's authority, or the authority of the law.[5] It is beyond doubt that in such circumstances the plaintiff must have a claim to have the transfer reversed. There cannot be a clearer case of a transfer of the plaintiff's wealth that subverts his right to determine how it is used. One can distinguish between two cases: first, where a stranger to the plaintiff effects the transfer by taking the plaintiff's money or goods in his absence or by force,[6] and secondly where someone empowered to act in relation to the plaintiff's property or to make transfers from him—an agent—makes a transfer that was outside the authority given to him.[7]

---

[2] Which might be referred to as the restitutio in integrum defence: see Chaps. 3 and 7.

[3] See Chap. 1.

[4] If the transfer is of a tangible asset, returning the asset avoids the problem of measuring its value for the purposes of damages; cf Chap. 10 at 348–49.

[5] e.g. a bailiff acting with authority under the law.

[6] e.g. *Neate v Harding* (1851) 6 Exch 349 (where money was stolen); *Holiday v Sigal* (1826) 2 C&P 176 (where money was lost and found).

[7] e.g. *Agip Africa v Jackson* [1991] Ch 547.

The vitiating factor of lack of authority, or something similar, has been recognised by Birks under the name of "ignorance".[8] The expression seems to be inapt; first, clearly it is possible for someone acting without the plaintiff's knowledge to make a transfer from the plaintiff that is not vitiated, because he was acting with the plaintiff's authority. Thus it is not ignorance that vitiates the transfer. Secondly, as Birks has pointed out, there are cases where the plaintiff is fully aware of a transfer, but is unable to stop it, as where a burglar ties him up while he takes his property, or takes the disabled plaintiff's bag while he sits impotent in his wheelchair. For these he requires a distinct vitiating factor, which he describes as "powerlessness",[9] or "helplessness",[10] but they fall comfortably into the category of lack of authority. Furthermore there are cases where the plaintiff wants to prevent a transfer and is powerless to do so, but it is not in consequence vitiated, as where a bailiff acts with legal authority to make a transfer from the plaintiff. Thus it is not surprising that the expressions "ignorance" and "powerlessness" are not known to the common law.

"Lack of authority", by contrast, *is* found in the case law as a vitiating factor. There have been cases where it is explicitly referred to as the vitiating factor with respect to a transfer,[11] but more commonly it is used in connection with agreements; its usual use is in connection with an agent's authority to make a contract for his principal. Often, however, the authority to make a contract is not explicitly distinguished from the authority to make a transfer under the contract, and the two are dealt with together. For example, where a payment is made by the plaintiff's agent under a putative contract made by the agent purportedly on behalf of the plaintiff but without authority, the question whether the payment can be recovered is often dealt with simply as part of the issue of whether the contract was authorised.[12]

There are other reasons why lack of authority is not more often explicitly referred to as the vitiating factor with respect to transfers. First, in many cases where lack of authority is the vitiating factor, it is more common to say that the plaintiff's claim arises from his retention of title to property or from the recipient's interference with his property. For example, where a stranger takes money or a chattel from the plaintiff and keeps it or passes it on, it is customary to say that the plaintiff's claim is based on his continuing ownership of the money or chattel, not from the fact that it was transferred without his authority, although it is clear that the fact that the stranger had no authority to make the transfer is a prerequisite to the claim, even if generally an unstated one. It is often thought that the claim based on ownership is quite distinct from the restitutionary claim,

---

[8] Birks (1989*a*), 140ff; Burrows (1993), 139ff.

[9] Birks (1989*a*), 174.

[10] Birks (1989*a*), 309–10; Birks & Chambers (1997).

[11] *Nelson v Larholt* [1948] 1 KB 339, 342, per Denning J; Re *Coltman* (1881) Ch D 64; *Blackburn & District Benefit BS v Cunliff, Brooks* (1885) 29 Ch D 902.

[12] e.g. *International Sales Agencies v Marcus* [1982] 3 All ER 551. The case concerned what is now s.35A of the Companies Act 1985, which deals with the authority of company directors to bind the company.

and generally precludes the need for any restitutionary claim arising from a vitiating factor of lack of authority.[13] This is a crucial issue in connection with the relation between restitution and property, and is considered in Chapter 9.

Secondly, the expression "authority" was traditionally used at common law, and not in equity. One very common type of transfer made without authority is where the plaintiff is the beneficiary under a trust,[14] and the trustee makes a transfer of trust property—i.e. in substance property belonging to the plaintiff—that is beyond his authority under the trust instrument. It is customary, however, to say that the trustee is acting beyond his powers, or that he is committing a breach of trust, rather than to say that he is acting without authority.[15] But there can be no objection to saying that he is acting without authority, meaning outside the authority derived from the trust instrument, so long as this is not misunderstood to imply that the trustee is an agent of the beneficiary with authority to bind him in contract.[16]

Thus the expression "breach of trust" is used in a way that disguises two distinct legal effects. It refers to a lack of authority to make a transfer, but more aptly it refers to a breach of duty committed by the trustee, which generates a liability to compensate the beneficiary for any loss resulting.[17] These two are distinct in principle. The breach of duty relates to the relation between the trustee and the beneficiary, and the lack of authority is relevant as a vitiating factor as between the beneficiary and a third party recipient.[18] It is generally assumed that an act in excess of authority is necessarily a breach of duty, but in principle this need not be the case. It would be possible for the law to provide that the trustee commits a breach of duty only where he is negligent; indeed, the trustee has statutory protection when he acted honestly and reasonably, which has much the same effect.[19]

Artificial entities and incapacity or *ultra vires*

An artificial entity like a company or local authority cannot act except through its agents, which means generally its officers and employees. The authority of an

[13]   Similarly, it might be said that where there is no authority there is not so much a vitiated transfer as no transfer, or an ineffective transfer.

[14]   Again the claim arising from such an unauthorised transfer is generally said to depend on a right of property rather than restitution. The trust is discussed in Chap. 9.

[15]   The equitable regime applies to fiduciaries as well as trustees, and a fiduciary will also be an agent, so that acting in excess of power or in breach of fiduciary duty would also be described in a common law context as acting without or in breach of authority.

[16]   This usage of "authority" in relation to breach of trust was adopted by Denning J in *Nelson v Larholt* [1948] 1 KB 339, 342–3.

[17]   i.e. equitable compensation; the breach of duty might generate a liability to disgorgement also, through an account.

[18]   Sometimes the recipient, in addition to being liable in restitution, may be liable through complicity in the trustee's breach of duty (knowing assistance), and then breach of trust (as opposed to exceeding authority) will also be the apt expression with respect to the action against the recipient.

[19]   S.61 of the Trustee Act 1925 gives the court the power to relieve the trustee of liability.

officer or employee to act for the entity will turn directly on whether he can derive authority from his appointment or otherwise by delegation from his superior. But ultimately all authority to act for an artificial entity must be derived from its constitution, which will be its memorandum and articles, or a charter or statute.

Often the constitution will limit the field or manner of activities of the body as a whole, and such a limitation is open to two different interpretations. The first is what can be described as the theory of limited capacity or ultra vires. On this approach, the entity's constitution defines its legal capacity, which is the range of acts that it is capable of having attributed to it. Any act outside its capacity, whether an agreement or a transfer, irrespective of the person who purported to act for the entity or the circumstances, will be vitiated, so that the agreement will not be binding and the transfer will be recoverable; the vitiating factor is incapacity or "ultra vires". The case where an agreement or transfer is ultra vires in this sense is to be contrasted, on this approach, with the case where it is within the constitution, but beyond the authority of the agent who purported to act for the entity, and so vitiated by lack of authority but not ultra vires. On the second interpretation, the theory of full capacity, the constitution does not limit the entity's capacity, but only the authority that can be delegated by the entity to its own agents. Thus there is no separate vitiating factor of incapacity, and the ground on which a transfer or agreement outside the constitution is vitiated is the lack of authority of the agent purporting to act for the entity, which is necessarily limited in accordance with the constitution. The same vitiating factor applies where the transfer or agreement is outside the constitution and where it is inside the constitution but beyond the authority conferred on the agent.

The crucial difference between the two approaches arises from the doctrine of apparent authority. Under the doctrine of apparent authority, the principal is bound by the agent, notwithstanding that the agent acts outside his actual authority, if he is within his apparent authority, unless the outsider dealing with the agent knew or ought to have known of the lack of actual authority.[20] Under the second interpretation, because the effect of the constitution is only to limit the authority of an agent who acts for the entity, the doctrine of apparent authority can operate to override any limitation in the constitution, so that the outsider can be protected by apparent authority even in relation to an agreement or transfer outside the constitution. The constitution merely has internal effect, just like other internal arrangements governing the authority of an agent. By contrast, under the first interpretation, which has always been the basis of the ultra vires doctrine, apparent authority cannot protect the outsider against ultra vires because the constitution is taken to define the entity's legal capacity and so precludes any transfer or agreement outside the constitution from being legally effective, irrespective of apparent authority.

---

[20] Apparent authority is equivalent to bona fide purchase, as considered in Chap. 7 below.

Partnerships and companies

In partnership law no doctrine of ultra vires is recognised. A partnership is recognised to have full capacity. Restrictions in the partnership agreement are understood only to limit the authority of the partners and other agents in accordance with the second approach above. In company law, however, the ultra vires theory was adopted by the House of Lords in the last century in *Ashbury Railway Co v Riche*.[21] Any contract outside the objects clause of the company's memorandum was held to be void, irrespective of any question of apparent authority, and any payment outside the objects was recoverable on the same ground.[22] Such cases were regarded as distinct from cases where an agreement or transfer was vitiated by lack of authority. The main reason for adopting the ultra vires theory for companies seems to have been the assumption that because the company has a separate legal personality its capacity must be derived from its constitution and so must necessarily be limited by its objects clause, by contrast with a partnership, which has no separate legal personality, so that the capacity of the partnership had to be the capacity of the partners themselves.[23]

But there is no reason of logic why the theory of ultra vires had to be adopted as the necessary consequence of separate personality, or of the statutory requirement for an objects clause. The company could have been held to have full capacity, in accordance with the second interpretation above, and the objects clause understood to have only internal effect, so that it would define only the limits of authority delegable to the board or other agents of the company. Indeed this view was adopted by Blackburn J in a lower court in *Ashbury Railway Co v Riche*.[24] It was at one time thought that the ultra vires doctrine was necessary to protect the interests of shareholders, on the basis that they had invested in the company on the understanding that its activities would be confined to those within the objects clause.[25] But in fact the two parallel doctrines of authority and capacity, with their vitiating factors of lack of authority and lack of capacity, seek to fulfil the same purpose of resolving the conflict between, on the one hand, the interest of the company (embodying the interests of its shareholders) in having the company's business conducted in accordance with its constitution, and, on the other hand, the interests of outsiders in being able to carry on business in reliance on the apparent authority of the company's agents. It is superfluous to have both doctrines. Furthermore, the ultra vires approach is crude, in simply striking down all agreements or transfers, without

---

[21] (1875) LR 7 HL 653.

[22] e.g. Re *Lee, Behrens and Co Ltd* [1932] 2 Ch 46.

[23] See Jaffey (1994), 73, n 25.

[24] (1874) LR 9 Ex 224, 264. Blackburn J's view was that traditionally "a corporation at common law has . . . the same power to contract . . . that a natural person has", notwithstanding any limitations in its constitution; and therefore that a company registered under the Companies Acts should be understood to have full capacity unless the statute explicitly provided to the contrary, and that there was no indication in the statute to that effect.

[25] *Ashbury Railway Company v Riche* (1875) LR 7 HL 653, 667 per Lord Cairns LC.

reference to the outsider's interests, whereas the doctrine of apparent authority provides the means for balancing the conflicting interests, through the proviso that the outsider cannot rely on the apparent authority if he knew or ought to have known of the lack of authority.[26] From the time of its first recognition, the ultra vires theory has been thought to have capricious effects on outsiders dealing with a company, and there has been an all too gradual process of abolition, eventually completed by the Companies Act 1989,[27] so that nowadays the position to all intents and purposes is in accordance with the second interpretation of the effect of the constitution.

Public authorities

By contrast with the developments in company law, the ultra vires doctrine remains in full force with respect to public authorities. A recent example is provided by *Hazell v Hammersmith & Fulham LBC*.[28] Here a local authority purported to make a "swap" contract, which is a sort of financial hedging contract.[29] The contract was held to be beyond the powers of the local authority as defined by statute,[30] and therefore ultra vires and void. The House of Lords relied on the company law authorities[31] in holding that "[a] corporation created by or under a statute has no power except the powers granted expressly or by implication by the statute".[32] But although the statute provides expressly for the powers of a local authority, there is no reason why this should not be understood to refer to the actual authority capable of being exercised by any person on behalf of the authority, and therefore subject to the doctrine of apparent authority.[33] The interest of the taxpayer, just like the interest of the shareholder, can be sufficiently protected through the doctrine of apparent authority.[34] There is no more reason to have two parallel doctrines of capacity and authority here than in relation to companies. A fuller consideration of the decline of ultra vires in company law might have led to this conclusion.

---

[26] The difficulty remaining is to determine the scope of the outsider's duty of inquiry, which affects the circumstances in which he can rely on apparent authority or change of position: see Chaps. 7 and 10 below.

[27] Amending Companies Act 1985, s.35.

[28] [1992] 2 AC 1. Cf *Auckland Harbour Board v R.* [1924] AC 318.

[29] See further Chap. 6 at n 15.

[30] The Local Government Act 1972.

[31] *Attorney-General v Great Eastern Railway Co* (1880) 5 App Cas 473.

[32] [1992] 2 AC 1, 39 per Lord Templeman.

[33] In fact the Local Government Act, Sched. 13, para. 20, does provide that outsiders shall not be prejudiced by irregularities, but this was held not to protect an outsider with respect to an ultra vires act.

[34] A strict "duty of inquiry", as considered in Chap. 10, will achieve the effect of ultra vires if this is thought appropriate.

Incapacity of people

Capacity is also used of real people. Certain categories of people, including children and the insane, are said to lack capacity to contract, or to make a transfer of money or property, by virtue of their inability to make a rational decision affecting their own interests. Here lack of capacity has a quite different meaning from its use in connection with ultra vires; it is not concerned with attributing acts to an artificial entity, but with the actual capability of a real person. Thus it might be better to refer to this vitiating factor, which is considered below, as lack of competence.

MISTAKE

The scope of mistake as a vitiating factor

The supposed liability test

It is well established that a transfer can be vitiated by mistake. However, there has been great controversy over the limits of mistake as a vitiating factor. At one time it was said that mistake was a vitiating factor only if it was such as to lead the plaintiff to think that he was liable to the defendant to make the payment to him: this was the "supposed liability" test. In *Kelly v Solari*[35] the plaintiff insurance company was allowed to recover where it paid out on an expired policy, which it mistakenly thought was still in force. If the plaintiff's understanding had been correct, the money paid would have been due to the defendant. By contrast in *Aitken v Short*[36] the plaintiff bank paid a debt owed to the defendant by a third party not because it thought it was liable to do so, but in order to release a charge that it mistakenly thought that the defendant had on property that the plaintiff had acquired from the third party. The plaintiff was denied recovery, and one judge at least seems to have justified the decision on the ground was that the plaintiff was never under the misapprehension that he was liable to make a payment to the defendant.[37]

The simple causation test

However, the supposed liability test was rejected in a leading modern case, *Barclays Bank v Simms*.[38] Here the plaintiff bank's mistake was to pay out on a cheque after it had received an instruction from the customer not to do so, and it was allowed a restitutionary claim notwithstanding that on the position as misapprehended it would have had no obligation to the defendant to pay him

[35] (1841) 9 M & W 54.
[36] (1856) 1 H & N 210.
[37] The defendant seems to have had a good defence in any case, as discussed in Chap. 7.
[38] [1980] QB 677.

(although it would have had such an obligation to the customer). As Goff J observed in *Simms*, there had been previous decisions in which a claim had been allowed where the supposed liability test was not satisfied.[39] He considered that the only requirement was that the mistake be shown to have caused the transfer—the simple causation test.[40] There is much to be said for this in principle, because it seems that the plaintiff's decision is equally vitiated whatever the nature of the mistake.

Possible qualifications to the simple causation test

Even if the supposed liability restriction is inapt, there is possibly, as the case law suggests,[41] some reason for disquiet over a simple causation test. An alternative limitation has been suggested, namely that the mistake must be "fundamental",[42] but this test is not sufficiently precise to be very helpful. Greene MR in *Morgan v Ashcroft*[43] suggested that a supposed liability mistake was an example of a fundamental mistake, and he gave the example of mistake as to identity as a fundamental mistake that was not a mistake as to supposed liability. He also suggested the following example of a non-fundamental mistake that should not ground recovery:

> [i]f a father, believing his son to have suffered a financial loss, gives him a sum of money, he surely could not claim repayment if he afterwards discovered that no such loss had occurred . . . To hold to the contrary would almost amount to saying that motive not mistake was the decisive factor.[44]

But the contrast between motive and mistake is misconceived. In all cases the plaintiff has a motive for the transfer, in the light of the facts as he understands them to be; it cannot be true to say that the payment results from motive as against mistake or vice versa.

However, the issue of motive does possibly reveal the reason for disquiet about a simple causation test. The important distinction seems to be between, on the one hand, payments made for an idiosyncratic or whimsical or private reason and, on the other hand, payments made for a reason that any reasonable person would recognise—an objective ground for payment, one might say—like a legal liability, or a moral responsibility.[45] The significance is evidential. Where a payment is made on an objective ground, there is normally circumstantial

---

[39] e.g. in *Larner v London CC* [1949] 2 KB 683 the facts as they were mistakenly taken to be would have generated a moral but not a legal obligation to make the payment. In *Jones v Waring & Gillow* [1926] AC 670, as in *Simms*, the supposed liability was not to the defendant but to a third party.

[40] Followed in Australia in *David Securities Pty Ltd v Commonwealth of Australia* (1992) 109 ALR 57.

[41] See also Krebs (1999).

[42] *Norwich Union Fire Insurance Society v WH Price Ltd* [1934] AC 455 per Lord Wright at 463.

[43] [1938] 1 KB 49.

[44] At 66.

[45] As in *Larner v London CC* [1949] 2 KB 683.

evidence to show the facts by virtue of which the reason for payment arises, and where such a payment is made by mistake, there is liable to be circumstantial evidence indicating that the payment was mistaken. But where the payment was private in the sense above, which seems to be the type of case that Greene MR regarded as a matter of the plaintiff's motive, there is liable to be no evidence apart from the plaintiff's own word to show what his reason was and that he made a mistake, rather than merely changing his mind afterwards and regretting the transfer. For example, a claim by the plaintiff that he gave £100 to a charity because he thought that a certain film star had endorsed it, when in fact the film star had endorsed a different charity, seems like the sort of claim that might easily be contrived.

Thus one might argue that, where the motive for the payment was private in the sense above, the plaintiff should be unable to recover because of the difficulty of disputing his evidence; or, in other words, that the plaintiff should be taken to have accepted the risk of a mistake relating to such a motive for payment. Indeed, someone who makes such a payment is liable to have a sense that he assumes this risk. This approach would tend to preclude recovery in some (but not all) cases of social, family or charitable payments, as opposed to commercial or arm's length payments. The problem of private payments in this sense may be behind the disquiet in the cases, but it might be doubted whether the distinction is sufficiently precise to work in practice. One might argue instead that the evidential problems that the plaintiff will have in establishing the mistake in such a case, together with the change of position defence where a mistake is recognised, are sufficient to protect the defendant without any need for a rule automatically excluding recovery in any category of case where a causative mistake is shown.[46]

Mistake of law

Until recently it was thought to be the case that a payment or transfer made by mistake of law rather than fact was irrecoverable.[47] This longstanding rule was overturned by the House of Lords in *Kleinwort Benson v Lincoln City Council*,[48] following many years of criticism and in the wake of similar decisions in other jurisdictions.[49] The objection to the mistake of law rule was

---

[46] In *Nurdin & Peacock v Ramsden* [1999] 1 WLR 1249, Neuberger J suggested, at 1273, that it might be appropriate to allow a claim only where there was a "close and direct connection between the mistake and the payment and/or [where] . . . the mistake impinges on the relationship between payer and payee".

[47] The authority usually cited for the old rule was *Bilbie v Lumley* (1802) 2 East 469.

[48] [1998] 3 WLR 1095.

[49] In Canada *Air Canada v British Columbia* (1989) 59 DLR (4th) 161, and in Australia *David Securities Pty Ltd v Commonwealth Bank of Australia* (1992) 175 CLR 353. There are various longstanding exceptions to the mistake of law rule: see the discussion in Law Commission (1994), paras. 2.9–2.15.

simply that the effect of the mistake as a vitiating factor is exactly the same as for a mistake of fact.[50]

Mistake of law and assumption of risk

One argument that was offered in support of the mistake of law rule is worth consideration, because, although not justifying a strict bar on recovery for mistake of law, it is still a factor that may restrict recovery in some such cases. With respect to mistakes of fact, it has always been the case that if the plaintiff was in doubt over the relevant facts, but made the payment nevertheless, he is taken to have accepted the risk of the mistake and has no claim.[51] Usually when the plaintiff is in doubt about a matter of fact he will be able to resolve the issue before deciding whether to make the payment. But doubt on a legal issue is likely to be more common and more difficult to resolve because of the inherent uncertainty and the expense of legal advice and legal proceedings,[52] and this may make it more common for the plaintiff to assume the risk of a mistake and pay without attempting to resolve the uncertainty. Thus it may be that in many cases of mistake of law non-recovery can still be justified on the basis of assumption of risk.[53] It will often be impossible to say whether the plaintiff was in doubt or not; his doubts may remain entirely private. But the plaintiff's doubts may be apparent from the fact that he consulted a lawyer.[54] The clearest case of assumption of risk arises in the form of the defence of "submission to an honest claim", which is considered below.

Mistake of private right

The idea of assumption of risk ties in with another distinction that was sometimes drawn in connection with mistake of law, viz. the distinction between a mistake of private right and a mistake as to the general law. It was sometimes said that the mistake of law rule applied only to the latter and not to the former. This is curious because the plaintiff will presumably always be concerned with the general law only in so far as it affects a private right. A proposition about a private right—for example as to ownership or contractual entitlement—is a matter of mixed law and fact, in the sense that to determine whether the proposition is true it is necessary to establish both the relevant facts and also the general law. Thus a mistake of private right may be attributable to an underlying mistake of fact or to an underlying mistake as to the general law. Where the

---

[50] The reason offered in *Bilbie v Lumley* (1802) 2 East 469 was that "ignorance of the law is no excuse". But as Lord Denning pointed out in *Kiriri Cotton Co Ltd v Dewani* [1960] AC 192, 204, this maxim is properly understood to mean that ignorance is not an excuse for the non-performance of one's duty, which has no application to the vitiation of intention.

[51] *Kelly v Solari* (1841) 9 M & W 54, 59; *Barclays Bank v Simms* [1980] QB 677, 695.

[52] Birks (1989a), 165.

[53] Goff & Jones (1998), 214.

[54] See the recent case of *Nurdin & Peacock v Ramsden* [1999] 1 WLR 1249.

plaintiff is aware of some doubt over his legal position, and so himself or through his advisers identifies a relevant issue of general law to be considered in reaching a conclusion about his private right, he should be denied a claim on the basis of assumption of risk; this is a case where the plaintiff would be understood to have made a mistake about the general law. Where the plaintiff makes a mistake without any such awareness or consideration, and therefore without considering any general issue of law, he will be regarded as having made a mistake as to private right, and so as having a claim, even if the underlying mistake is actually a mistake as to the general law rather than a matter of fact.

Two examples commonly given of mistakes as to a private right, where the mistake of law rule was avoided, are *Cooper v Phibbs*[55] and *Solle v Butcher*,[56] both contract cases. In *Solle v Butcher*, the plaintiff granted a lease over property, mistakenly thinking that it had ceased to be subject to rent control because of repairs and alterations made to it. Thus here there was a mistake of private right—viz. as to the entitlements of the parties with respect to rent—which was due to a mistake of law; there was no mistake over what had happened or what the material circumstance were, but over the general law that applied in the circumstances. In *Cooper v Phibbs*, the plaintiff's mistake was to think that the defendant owned property, which the plaintiff contracted to lease from him, when in fact the plaintiff owned it himself under the provision of a settlement of which he was unaware. The plaintiff's mistake resulted from a mistaken statement of a third party about the ownership of the property, which the plaintiff assumed to be correct, and it is not clear whether the original mistake was of fact or law. In neither case was there apparently any awareness or consideration of the general law that would have reflected some doubt and therefore assumption of risk, and this is reflected in the treatment of the mistakes as mistakes of private law, and consequently the availability of a claim.

Payments pursuant to a settled understanding of the law

A particular difficulty that arises in connection with mistakes of law, and which was at issue in *Kleinwort Benson v Lincoln CC*, is over payments made pursuant to a settled understanding of the law. In *Kleinwort Benson*, the plaintiff sought to recover a payment under a void "swap" contract,[57] on the ground that it had made the payment as a result of a mistake of law in treating the void contract as valid. As discussed above, such a mistake of law was held in principle to ground a claim for restitution. However, the defendant argued that at the time of the payment, according to expert opinion, the contract was not void, and that its voidness was due only to a later decision of the courts,[58] which changed the law. Thus it argued that in assuming the contract to be valid at the time of the pay-

---

[55] (1867) LR 2 HL 149.
[56] [1950] 1 KB 671.
[57] See Chap. 6, n 15.
[58] *Hazell v Hammersmith & Fulham LBC* [1992] 2 AC 1.

ment the plaintiff was not mistaken, but correctly understood the law at the time. Two of the judges in the House of Lords accepted this argument, but the majority rejected it.

This issue is unusual in explicitly raising an issue of legal theory. The traditional theory of the common law is that the courts discover and "declare" the law rather than make it. If this is true, the court never changes the law. If it overturns a previous decision precisely in point, or goes against expert opinion based on other decisions not precisely in point, this is because the previous decision or the opinion was false and misrepresented the law, which is now correctly declared in the new decision (subject to the possibility that this decision is itself mistaken). If the declaratory theory of law is correct, then a payment made according to an understanding of the law that is subsequently overturned is indeed a payment made by mistake. The original version of the declaratory theory was based on an explicit form of natural law; the underlying moral law was understood to be the true law by reference to which a decision or a prevailing understanding could be mistaken.[59] This conception of the law is nowadays widely regarded as untenable in the light of the positivist thesis that the law is distinct from morality, so that deciding an issue of law is a matter of consulting the authoritative sources of law, not of making any moral judgement. It is generally thought that the more common-sense and realistic view is that when a court makes a decision that is not covered by an earlier decision, or is inconsistent with an earlier decision or with the settled view of practitioners based on earlier case law, it is not restoring or discovering an underlying moral law but simply making law where there was none, or changing the previous law.

All the judges in the House of Lords thought that the declaratory theory was a fiction, even a fairy tale,[60] and seemed to adopt some version of this second approach. On this basis, it seems to follow that a payment made on the basis of a settled understanding of the law that is changed (or shown to be wrong) by a later decision is not mistaken because it was made in accordance with what was at the time a correct understanding of the law. Two of the judges did indeed reach this conclusion.[61] But the majority, even though they rejected the declaratory theory, held that there was a mistake in such a case. The reason arose from the retrospective effect of judicial decisions on the law. It seems to have been thought that, when a decision is made which changes the law, by a sort of pragmatic fiction the law is applied retrospectively, and so also, by the same or a parallel fiction, ought the understanding of the law at the time of the payment, although actually correct at the time, be treated as if it were mistaken. It is difficult to understand the rationale for this rather convoluted solution; if the judges were right in regarding the declaratory theory as a fiction, there seems to be much to be said for the minority's view, which seems to follow more

---

[59] The declaratory theory is traceable to Hale and Blackstone, who, as Lord Goff noted, held that "the decisions of courts are the evidence of what is the common law": [1998] 3 WLR 1095, 1117.
[60] At 1100.
[61] This was also the view of the Law Commission (1994), paras. 5.2, 5.3.

naturally from what the judges said about the nature of the common law. The majority's view follows more naturally from the declaratory theory, which all the judges rejected.

Although it is clearly true that the general understanding of the law will change following a decision like *Kleinwort Benson*, the second approach above also gives rise to serious difficulties. Why is the court entitled to change the law? If the court is entitled to do so, why does the law as changed apply retrospectively in respect of events that happened before the decision was made, including of course the case under adjudication?[62] It would appear fairer to apply the existing, unchanged law to the facts at hand (since ex hypothesi this was the law in force at the time), and then declare the law as changed to apply prospectively, rather than retrospectively to the events in dispute and other events that occurred before the decision. And if, as one would expect for a court bound by the rule of law, the court is understood to change the law only according to accepted criteria, so that, in principle at least, these criteria can be assessed at any time by anyone who wants to make his own judgement of what the law is, would it not be more sensible to say that these criteria form part of the law and that the court is then simply applying them rather than changing the law?[63]

Possibly the answer to *Kleinwort Benson* lies in a more sophisticated version of the declaratory theory. A court makes a decision by weighing up the relevant legal arguments on each side. These may be narrow arguments of precedent, or more wide-ranging theoretical arguments or arguments of principle or coherence. In weighing up these arguments and reaching a conclusion with respect to them, the court merely declares, without altering, the legal position as it is determined by the relevant legal arguments. Where it is swayed by the theoretical arguments, it may conclude that the previous understanding of the law based on narrower arguments of precedent is mistaken. Its decision may change some people's understanding of the law, even a widely settled understanding, but it is not changing the law (at least in one sense),[64] because before its decision the theoretical argument was just as much a valid legal argument, and therefore part of the law, as the narrow argument of precedent, and the previous understanding of the law was mistaken for placing too little emphasis on it.[65] This is a version of the declaratory theory of law, and supports the decision in *Kleinwort Benson*, although not the judges' reasoning. No doubt it is also open to criticism, but fortunately this is not the place to pursue the matter further.[66]

[62] It would also be necessary to distinguish between a decision changing the law and one that does not, and this would be as controversial as the decision itself.

[63] One might say that this is plausible only if the criteria relate to matters of principle rather than policy, in Dworkin's sense, because matters of principle are not contingent on varying circumstances in the same way as matters of policy and so can be thought of as subsisting implicitly in the law.

[64] See Finnis (1999).

[65] It was suggested that the wider theoretical arguments are arguments of principle as opposed to arguments of policy, apparently in Dworkin's sense: at 1139, per Lord Hoffmann.

[66] This seems to be consistent with the approach of Dworkin (1986); it may also be consistent with modern versions of positivism. "Theoretical argument" is not used in the same sense as in Dworkin.

The decision in *Kleinwort Benson* seems to give rise to the possibility of a claim arising many years after the payment in question, and this particularly concerned the dissenting judges. The problem arises because the limitation period for claims based on a mistake is provided by statute to run from the time when it became reasonably possible for the plaintiff to discover the mistake,[67] and the court held that this time was the date of the later decision overturning the previously settled law. In fact this was crucial to the case, because the limitation period as measured from the time of the original payment had expired. This may be correct on the approach adopted by the court, under which there was really no mistake at the time, but only a sort of deemed mistake when the law was changed retrospectively by the later decision, since on this view it seems that there was no possible way of discovering the mistake before the law was changed. But under some version of the declaratory theory, not only was there a mistake at the time of the payment, but also in theory the mistake was capable of being discovered at that time, or at least some time before the later decision overturning the previous decision or previous expert opinion, inasmuch as the legal arguments according to which the later decision was made were already available for consideration. It may be that the later decision became gradually more predictable in the light of other decisions or academic discussion, but it would be impossible to say precisely when a new understanding became reasonably discoverable in the light of such developments. Even if this will sometimes seem artificial, it should be assumed that the mistake was discoverable all along, and the limitation period should begin to run from the time of the payment. This would allay much of the disquiet of the minority.[68]

Misprediction

It is said that there can be no claim arising from a mistake as to the future.[69] It is not true to say, of course, that one cannot make a mistake about the future. A mistaken prediction is a mistake as to the future. But generally there can be no claim arising from such a mistake, because generally any assumption about the future is made with an awareness of doubt, and so a transferor who made a payment on the basis of such an assumption must be taken to have assumed the risk that it was wrong. As an exception that proves the rule, consider a mistake over some future event with respect to which there is no uncertainty, for example the date of an eclipse or the next leap year. There is no reason why such a mistake should not generate a claim, if for some reason a mistake on such a matter were

---

[67] S.32(1)(c) of the Limitation Act 1980.

[68] In any case, where the plaintiff consulted a lawyer at the time, he should be taken to have assumed the risk of a mistake, and where he has not done so, it is not easy to see why the settled understanding of the law at the time should have any bearing on the matter in any case: see Lord Hoffmann [1998] 3 WLR 1095, 1138.

[69] Birks (1989*a*), 147.

relevant to a payment. But generally where the plaintiff wants to make a payment to the defendant in reliance on a prediction about the future—typically a prediction about what the defendant will do, for example whether he will provide some reciprocal benefit, but sometimes also about other future events—he has to resort to the law of contract, by which he arranges with the defendant for the defendant to take responsibility for the plaintiff's reliance on an assumption about the future course of events, including the acts of the defendant.

Another supposed basis for recovery in respect of future events is said to be "failure of consideration", in the sense of failure of condition under the restitutionary conditional transfer theory. "Failure of consideration" is thought not to be a vitiating factor, because it does not relate to the plaintiff's decision-making, but an "unjust factor", which operates in an analogous way, to generate a liability for repayment if a condition attached to the payment is not fulfilled. If such a ground arose independently of contract on the basis of a unilaterally imposed condition, it would constitute a basis of recovery in respect of future events or acts of the recipient, and would effectively circumvent the exclusion of restitution for misprediction. Furthermore, if there were such a claim, it would be available instead of mistake in many cases. The effect of a mistake is often that the plaintiff's purpose in making the payment is not achieved: for example, if the plaintiff makes a payment to discharge a bill, but mistakenly pays the wrong person or forgets that he has already paid his bill, his purpose of discharging his bill will not be achieved. If the plaintiff's purpose in making a payment could be understood as a condition of the payment whose non-fulfilment would generate a claim to reverse it, there would be a claim based on failure of condition as well as mistake. In fact, it has been suggested that the restitutionary claim supposedly based on mistake as a vitiating factor is properly understood as an example of the claim based on failure of consideration or failure of condition.[70] In Chapters 2 and 3, however, it was argued that this theory of failure of consideration is misconceived. Furthermore, adherents to the theory generally take the view that the claim arises only where the defendant has accepted the plaintiff's condition,[71] and this means that in any case it would not be available merely because the purpose of a payment was not achieved.[72]

---

[70] Matthews (1980); Butler (1990); Krebs (1999). See also *Friends Provident v Hillier Parker* [1996] 2 WLR 123, 132.

[71] Chap. 3 at 102. As argued there, the claim is really contractual.

[72] The doctrine of estates in land allows for the creation of interests that are limited in time or conditional on a future event. Presumably the recipient of such an interest, which will be conveyed and defined in writing, can be expected to know of the limitation or condition and not be prejudiced by it. It may be that a transfer of a defeasible interest in property may be made without acceptance of the condition by the recipient, and merely by private condition, but this seems doubtful on principle; but see Watts (1995), 57.

Carelessness, assumption of risk and submission to an honest claim

It has already been pointed out above that where the plaintiff deliberately makes a payment when he is in doubt over the facts that provide the reason for the payment, or over his legal liability, he is generally denied a claim.[73] There are reasons why the plaintiff might make a payment in such circumstances: he may not be willing to bear the cost of establishing the law or facts in question, or the cost of litigation; or he may be concerned about the effect on his reputation if he does not pay promptly in response to a demand. Where the plaintiff was in doubt, one might say that he is not actually mistaken at all. Whether it is better to say that there was no mistake or that the plaintiff assumed the risk of a mistake does not seem to be of great consequence.[74] The argument of substance against recovery is that, where the plaintiff is aware of uncertainty over his position, to give him a claim is to allow him deliberately to impose the risk of a liability for repayment on the recipient. This will not usually be onerous for the defendant, because he is protected by the change of position defence, but it carries the risk of prejudice and it may cause inconvenience to him. There is no reason why the plaintiff should be able to choose to do this. On the other hand, where the plaintiff was not conscious of any doubt but was careless in reaching or acting on his mistaken view this has been held not to preclude him from making a claim.[75] Given that the defendant is protected by a change of position defence, it would presumably be unfair to the plaintiff to deny him a claim merely because of his carelessness.

Assumption of the risk of error is the basis for what appears to be a single rule (or closely related set of rules) expressed in different forms, viz. that the plaintiff has no claim in respect of a payment made "in submission to an honest claim", or "to close a transaction", or as a "voluntary payment".[76] As has been stated judicially, with respect to mistake of fact:

> If . . . the money is intentionally paid, without reference to the truth or falsehood of the fact, the plaintiff meaning to waive all inquiry into it, and that the person receiving shall have the money at all events, whether the fact be true or false, the latter is certainly entitled to retain it"[77]

and with respect to mistake of law:

> a payment may be said to be voluntary . . . when the payer makes it deliberately with a knowledge of all relevant facts, and either being indifferent to whether or not he be

---

[73] Above at 169; *Kelly v Solari* (1841) 9 M & W 54, 59; *Barclays Bank v Simms* [1980] QB 677, 695; *Nurdin & Peacock v Ramsden* [1999] 1 WLR 1249, 1270.

[74] Cf Arrowsmith (1991), 33.

[75] *Kelly v Solari* (1841) 9 M & W 54,59; *Scottish Equitable v Derby* (1999) unrep; Burrows (1993), 101.

[76] Cf Arrowsmith (1991), 25ff.

[77] *Kelly v Solari* (1841) 9 M & W 54, 59 per Parke B.

liable in law, or knowing, or having reason to think, himself not liable, yet intending finally to close the transaction.[78]

As noted above, assumption of risk is likely to be more common with respect to mistakes of law, and it may be that the mistake of law rule should always have been understood to be concerned with this rule (however expressed).[79]

On this understanding of the rule, the expression "submission to an honest claim" is not really apt, because the rule does not apply just because the payment was made in response to an honest claim or demand by the defendant, but only if in addition the plaintiff was in doubt over the validity of the demand, which one might typically be able to infer from a dispute over it. Similarly, the fact that the plaintiff made a payment intending to close a transaction, in the sense that he thought that the payment would bring a contract to completion by discharging his liability under it, cannot preclude a claim based on mistake; intending to "close a transaction" should be understood to refer only to the case where there was a dispute over liability in connection with the transaction and the plaintiff intended to bring this dispute, and thereby the transaction, to an end, by assuming the risk that the payment was not actually due rather than continuing the dispute or litigating over it. The formulation in terms of a "voluntary payment" is perhaps more defensible. To say that a payment was voluntary is usually understood to mean that there was no vitiating factor,[80] and it is a reasonable usage to say that where there was an assumption of risk there was no mistake. However, "voluntary" is arguably misleading for the reason given at the start of the chapter.[81] Generally it would be helpful to refer explicitly to assumption of risk, or perhaps waiver.

The description "submission to an honest claim" might seem more naturally to refer to a wider defence available only with respect to a claim based on mistake of law, and not based on assumption of risk, along the lines suggested in the minority judgment in *David Securities v Commonwealth Bank of Australia*:

> [I]t is a defence to a claim for restitution . . . [for] mistake of law that the defendant honestly believed, when he learnt of the payment . . . that he was entitled to receive and retain the money . . .[82]

This was described as the defence of receipt in satisfaction of an honest claim. Before the abrogation of the mistake of law rule, it would not have been important to determine whether this wider defence applied with respect to mistake of law or the narrower one based on assumption of risk, because the mistake of law rule would have precluded a claim in any case. The narrower rule based on

---

[78] *Mason v New South Wales* (1959) 102 CLR 108, 143 per Windeyer J; see also *David Securities v Commonwealth Bank of Australia* (1992) 175 CLR 353, 373.

[79] As argued in Goff & Jones with respect to the original case of *Biblie v Lumley* (1802) 2 East 469: Goff & Jones (1998), 214–5. See Arrowsmith (1991), 36.

[80] One might also say that a payment was voluntary, by way of denying a claim based on another vitiating factor, for example duress or undue influence.

[81] See at n 1.

[82] (1992) 175 CLR 353, 399 per Brennan J, dissenting.

assumption of risk is surely preferable, as the majority concluded in *David Securities*.[83] It is difficult to see why the fact that the defendant honestly believed he was entitled to receive the money, whether or not he also made an honest demand or claim for it, should negate the vitiating effect of the mistake, where there was no assumption of risk by the plaintiff.[84] If this were so, the abrogation of the mistake of law rule would be of little practical effect, because presumably payments made under a supposed legal obligation are almost always made in response to an honest demand of some sort from the defendant.[85] This supposed defence of "honest receipt" should not be confused with the well-established defence in respect of a payment made in discharge of a debt, which is best understood to be a form of bona fide purchase. This latter defence arises not merely because the defendant honestly thinks that he is owed the money in question, but because he is actually owed the money and relies on the receipt as discharging the debt.[86]

There may sometimes be grounds for a claim even where the plaintiff was in doubt when he made the payment. First, the plaintiff may be able to obtain the defendant's agreement to accept the payment on the condition that it is repayable if it subsequently transpires that it was not in fact due. Then the plaintiff will have a claim to recover the payment if he can subsequently prove that it was not due. Some would regard such a claim as a restitutionary claim based on "failure of consideration",[87] but it is better understood as a contractual claim.[88] The mere fact that a payment is made under protest does not justify an inference that the defendant agreed to such a condition;[89] he might reasonably assume that the plaintiff accepts the risk despite the protest, and he might prefer to settle the matter immediately rather than accept a conditional payment. Secondly, it may be reasonable to say that in some exceptional cases the recipient bears the responsibility, as between the parties, for establishing whether the payment is due, so that the plaintiff is free to make a payment and recover it simply on the ground that it was not due, without having to assume any risk if he was in doubt over the legal position. Where this is the case, it seems that the claim arises not from any factor vitiating the intention to pay, but simply from the fact that it was not due. This is possibly the explanation of the basis on which a mistaken overpayment of tax is recovered, as considered later in this chapter.

---

[83] At 373; Goff & Jones (1998), 215.

[84] It has been suggested that if the defendant made a threat to sue, to which the plaintiff capitulates, there is a defence even though there was no assumption of risk: Law Commission (1994), para. 2.34. It seems unlikely that proceedings would be begun without any prior dispute. In any case, it is difficult to see why the defendant should have a defence if the plaintiff did not make any assumption of risk.

[85] This was the view of the House of Lords in *Kleinwort Benson v Lincoln CC* [1998] 3 WLR 1095.

[86] Bona fide purchase is considered in Chap. 7.

[87] See Chap. 2, at 54–56.

[88] As held recently in *Nurdin & Peacock v Ramsden* [1999] 1 WLR 1249.

[89] Possibly this is an objection to the decision in *Nurdin & Peacock v Ramsden* [1999] 1 WLR 1249; cf below at n 231.

Mistake in contract

In principle there seems no reason why a factor that vitiates a transfer should not equally vitiate an agreement, and vice versa. But this appears not to be the position with respect to mistake: it is by no means the law that a contract is generally vitiated by a mistake that caused the plaintiff contractor to make it. The terms of a contract are the terms that would be reasonably inferred from the way that the parties have expressed and conducted themselves: this is the principle of objective interpretation in contract. Thus a party may find that he is bound by a contract whose terms he did not actually—i.e. subjectively—intend; he may have made a "unilateral mistake" about the terms of the contract.[90] For example, he may have misunderstood an expression used in the contract to describe the goods being sold.[91] Nevertheless, the mistaken party is bound by the contract unless the other contracting party was aware of the mistake.[92] However, the position for agreements is not inconsistent with that for transfers. When a transfer is made by mistake, if the defendant recipient received the transfer pursuant to a contract (whether with the transferor or a third party) he will have the benefit of the bona fide purchase defence;[93] this means that there will be no restitutionary claim unless he knew of the mistake,[94] just as for a mistake vitiating an agreement, by virtue of the principle of objective interpretation. The apparent difference in treatment arises from the fact that in the case of vitiation of an agreement the defendant necessarily has the benefit of the defence, in the form of the principle of objective interpretation,[95] so that he is affected by the mistake only with knowledge, whereas in the case of a transfer the defendant does not necessarily have the bona fide purchase defence because the transfer is not necessarily received under a contract.[96]

The position is different where a contracting party makes a mistake about a matter that is not governed by a term of the contract, but nevertheless affects his decision to make the contract because it relates to his assumptions or reasons for making the contract. For example, he may have thought that the product he was buying had a certain quality, or would be suitable for a certain application, although no reference to these matters appears in the contract, or he may have been ignorant of some matter that would be significant, like the presence of mineral deposits in the land he is selling. The rule here appears to be that the plaintiff's mistake does not vitiate the contract, even if the other contracting party

[90]   The approach to unilateral mistake is understood to follow Cartwright (1991), chap. 1.

[91]   *Smith v Hughes* (1871) LR 6 QB 597.

[92]   Ibid.; *The Hannah Blumenthal* [1983] 1 AC 854; Cartwright (1991), 5ff.

[93]   On bona fide purchase, see Chap. 7.

[94]   Or ought to have known of the mistake; but the same applies for contract: see Cartwright (1991), 19–21.

[95]   The principle of objective interpretation is equivalent to the bona fide purchase defence: see further Chap. 7.

[96]   The doctrine of apparent authority operates in the same way with respect to lack of authority; and see also with respect to inadequate bargaining ability and undue influence below.

does know that he has made the mistake.[97] The rule is less favourable to the mistaken plaintiff and more favourable to the defendant than in the case of the simple transfer or a mistake as to a term of a contract. Arguably this is justified in order to enable the defendant to exploit for profit, through a contract, secret information that he may have acquired through his own work and expense, and so should be entitled to make a return on.[98] On the other hand, it has been suggested that the rule is unfair or inefficient, since it may seem sometimes to permit the unfair exploitation of the plaintiff, and it has been suggested that the defendant should not be able to take advantage of a "deep secret", meaning information relating to some matter that it could not possibly have occurred to the plaintiff to investigate—possibly the presence of mineral deposits in the case mentioned above, where this possibility had never been suggested—as opposed to matters that the plaintiff might reasonably be expected to identify and investigate, or otherwise bear the risk of a mistake.[99] This would bring the rule closer to the assumption of risk approach for transfers, but the plaintiff in the contract case would still bear the risk of a mistake even when he was not aware of a doubt, with respect to a matter that he knew, or ought to have known, was relevant.[100]

There has been some discussion of the relationship between "submission to an honest claim" and contractual compromise. Where the defendant makes a demand and the parties then make an agreement compromising over the demand, the agreement will provide the defendant with a defence to a claim to recover the payment for mistake if the plaintiff subsequently discovers that the demand was unjustified and no payment was due. It has been suggested that wherever a defence based on "submission to an honest claim" arises, there is in any case a defence of contractual compromise, and therefore that there is no need for any defence apart from the contractual one.[101] This is clearly not the case if the defence is simply concerned with assumption of risk. Even in the case where the assumption of risk follows a dispute, it is surely possible for there to be an assumption of risk without a contractual compromise; the dispute may end in the plaintiff capitulating and satisfying the demand or simply paying over some lesser sum without any agreement over it. Where there *is* a contractual compromise, and not merely an assumption of risk, as the discussion above shows, the plaintiff accepts the risk not only of a mistake relating to a matter on which he was in doubt, but also the risk of a mistake relating to any other matter governed by the contract, which presumably means any other matter that

---

[97] Cartwright (1991), 6–7; unless it was due to a misrepresentation.
[98] See Trebilcock (1993), 106ff.
[99] Ibid.
[100] See the discussion in Trebilcock (1993), 109. This would also mean that the plaintiff's claim would arise in circumstances corresponding more closely to what might normally be described as a mistake. Such a rule requiring disclosure by the defendant would make it difficult for the defendant to know what he ought to disclose, and might enable the plaintiff to escape from a contract by falsely claiming to have been mistaken: Trebilcock (1993), 108.
[101] Andrews (1989), 437; cf Arrowsmith (1991), 29.

might affect his supposed liability, whether it was a matter that had occurred to him as being in doubt or not; whereas if the plaintiff merely makes an assumption of risk, it seems that a claim will still arise out of a mistake relating to some other matter that he did not actually advert to.[102]

DURESS

The nature of duress

There is a well-established vitiating factor of duress or coercion, but its nature and scope are controversial. Usually the person who inflicts the duress is also the recipient of the transfer or the other contracting party, and this will generally be assumed to be the case in the discussion below, and this person referred to as the defendant. Duress is said to arise from the pressure to which the plaintiff was subject when he made the agreement or transfer. But many decisions to make a transfer or agreement are made subject to some form of pressure, without any invalidating effect, and there has been great difficulty in defining the nature or degree of pressure that is necessary to vitiate the plaintiff's decision.

The main cases of duress are as follows. A long-established example is where pressure is imposed through a threat to cause physical injury to the plaintiff[103] or to take or damage his goods.[104] Another old line of cases holds that where a public official has threatened not to fulfil his public duty to the plaintiff unless the plaintiff makes him a payment, the plaintiff has a claim to recover the payment; this is the so-called doctrine of colore officii.[105] Similarly, where someone who is not a public official but has a statutory duty to provide a benefit to the plaintiff refuses to do so unless the plaintiff makes a payment that exceeds what is authorised by the statute, the plaintiff can recover the excess.[106] In a more modern line of cases a payment or a variation of an agreement induced by a threat not to perform a contract has been held recoverable or unenforceable;[107] these are generally referred to as cases of economic duress, because the execution of the threat would cause pecuniary loss or damage to the plaintiff's business. Lastly there are a number of cases where the plaintiff, or someone for whom the plaintiff is concerned, has committed a wrong against the defendant and the defendant threatens to take criminal proceedings, or to publish the fact of the wrongdoing or to disclose it to particular people, unless the plaintiff makes or agrees to make a payment to the defendant, and the plaintiff has a claim to recover the sum paid or set aside the agreement.[108]

---

[102] Cf Arrowsmith (1991), 31; Andrews (1989), 443.
[103] A modern case is *Barton v Armstrong* [1976] AC 104.
[104] Examples are *Astley v Reynolds* (1731) 2 Str. 915 and *Maskell v Horner* [1915] 3 KB 106.
[105] e.g. *Mason v NSW* (1959) 102 CLR 108.
[106] e.g. *Great Western Railway Co v Sutton* (1869) LR 4 HL 226.
[107] A number of example are considered below at 186–90.
[108] e.g. *Williams v Bayley* (1866) LR 1 HL 200.

Overborne will

At one time, it was thought that the distinguishing feature of cases where the pressure imposed on the plaintiff amounted to duress was that the plaintiff's will was "overborne".[109] This might be taken to mean that the plaintiff has lost his ability to make a judgement of his own interests, as if he had lost his capacity for rational thought. This might conceivably happen as a result of severe stress resulting from pressure. But this is a quite implausible interpretation of what generally happens in a case of duress, as opposed to cases of undue influence and lack of competence, which are considered below. In reality, duress is concerned with a situation where the plaintiff is in full control of his faculties and remains capable of judging his own best interests.[110] The "overborne will" theory of duress has been heavily criticised on this basis and has more recently fallen out of favour.[111]

Illegitimate pressure

Threats and warnings

More recently the question whether a decision taken under pressure is vitiated by duress has been addressed in terms of whether the pressure imposed on the plaintiff was "legitimate" or "illegitimate".[112] However, no very clear principle seems to have emerged to indicate when pressure is illegitimate. An important distinction, which seems not to have been recognised in the case law, is between threats and warnings.[113] Pressure induced by a warning is legitimate and non-coercive, but pressure induced by a threat is generally illegitimate and coercive. Sometimes, however, what appears to be a threat is not truly one, even if it might colloquially be so described.

In the case of both a threat and a warning, the defendant tells the plaintiff that a certain consequence will follow if the plaintiff does (or does not do) a specified act. One might think that the difference between a threat and a warning is whether the specified consequence is within the defendant's control. Certainly, a threatened act is an act that will be committed or procured by the defendant,

---

[109] *Pao On v Lau Yiu Long* [1980] AC 614, 635 per Lord Scarman.

[110] Atiyah (1982), 200. In making a threat the defendant presupposes that the payment is a rational response to it, and that the plaintiff is capable of this rational response: Lamond (1996), 219.

[111] *Director of Public Prosecutions for Northern Ireland v Lynch* [1975] AC 653, 695 per Lord Simon; *Cresendo Management Pty Ltd v Westpac Banking Corp* (1988) 19 NSWLR 40, 45–6 per McHugh JA; *The Evia Luck* [1992] 2 AC 152, 166 per Lord Goff.

[112] *Universe Tankships Inc of Monrovia v International Transport Workers' Federation (The Universe Sentinel)* [1983] 1 AC 366, 384 per Lord Diplock.

[113] That the crucial distinction in establishing whether there is duress or coercion is whether there is a threat or warning is generally assumed in the philosophical literature on coercion: see e.g.: Nozick (1972); Spector (1992).

whereas a warning will often relate to the act of a third party or a natural event, as for example where the defendant warns the plaintiff that he will be affected by bad weather if he goes out, or will be in danger if he goes to a certain part of town. But a warning can also relate to an act that the defendant will himself commit; for example the defendant might warn the plaintiff that if he does not arrive by dawn the defendant will leave without him.

Both a threat and a warning are designed to influence the plaintiff by subjecting him to a fear of the consequences of his acts. The difference between them is that when the defendant makes a threat he commits himself to carrying out an act that he has chosen for the very reason that it will be unwelcome to the plaintiff, whereas in the case of a warning the act warned of is either outside the defendant's control or is envisaged to be, as it were, the natural consequence of the plaintiff's behaviour, in the sense that if it occurs it will be due to the defendant's acting to protect his own interests (or otherwise acting for a legitimate reason) in the light of the plaintiff's behaviour.[114] Thus a warning merely provides information to the plaintiff about the consequences of his behaviour, including the effect that his behaviour will have on the defendant, and a warning and the plaintiff's response to it amount, overall, to a mutually beneficial interaction. But in the case of a threat the plaintiff is notified of a consequence that is contrived by the defendant for the purpose of securing a benefit to himself through the plaintiff's response, and there is only a benefit to the plaintiff relative to this contrived contingency. Thus there is no mutual benefit, merely the manipulation of the plaintiff to promote the defendant's ends. It follows that if a threat is carried out, it will involve the infliction of harm on the plaintiff for the purpose of causing harm, whereas if a warning is disregarded and the plaintiff suffers harm, the harm will be either out of the defendant's control, or, if within his control, will result incidentally from the defendant's pursuit of his own interests.

One situation where the defendant gives a warning rather than a threat is where he informs the plaintiff that unless the terms of a contract are changed he will be unable to perform because he is about to go bankrupt, or because his own contractors have let him down. The defendant's non-performance because of his bankruptcy or because of the default of others will be unwelcome to the plaintiff, but the defendant is not making a threat, because his non-performance is not something that he chooses to do because it is unwelcome to the plaintiff, in order to procure a revision of the contract.[115] Sometimes the issue is whether it is a threat or a warning for the defendant to say that he will disclose to a third party the fact that the plaintiff has an unsatisfied liability to the defendant. In the American case of *Silsbee v Webber*,[116] the defendant told the plaintiff he would inform the plaintiff's husband of the theft committed by their son from

---

[114] See e.g. Nozick (1972), 120.
[115] The defendant's financial difficulties were behind the contractual variation in *Williams v Roffey* [1991] 1 QB 1.
[116] 50 NE 555 (1898).

the defendant unless the plaintiff agreed to give security for the sum stolen. The husband was ill and, as the defendant knew, the plaintiff was afraid that the effect of discovering of the theft would be damaging to his health. The plaintiff gave the security but then succeeded in having it set aside, on the ground that the agreement was procured "solely by inspiring the plaintiff with fear of what he threatened to do".[117] The dissenting judge thought that the purpose of telling the husband was probably to see if he would be prepared to give security if the wife would not, which means that the defendant was giving a warning not a threat. It would also have been a warning if the purpose was to obtain the husband's influence in persuading the plaintiff or her son to pay.

Legitimate threats and the legal process

An important question is the effect of a threat of legal proceedings. (Rather awkwardly, for consistency with the rest of the discussion, here the defendant, as the person who makes the threat, would be the plaintiff in the threatened proceedings.) It is clear that the plaintiff cannot generally have a claim, even though he was subject to duress. A court clearly has the power to punish the breach of a legal duty and to threaten punishment in order to compel the performance of a legal duty. Thus if a party to legal proceedings makes a transfer in fulfilment of his legal duty in compliance with a court order and under threat of duly administered punishment—i.e. punishment for contempt—he is coerced but he has no claim based on duress as a vitiating factor; the availability of such a claim would entirely subvert the function of the courts.[118] Similarly, where the plaintiff makes a transfer under duress or "legal compulsion" arising from a threat of legal proceedings by the defendant, he can generally have no claim based on duress as a vitiating factor, because, although he acts under duress, the duress arises from the legitimate application of the legal process.[119] It seems that the threat of proceedings is legitimate only if it is designed to procure the fulfilment of the plaintiff's legal duty, and the proceedings are designed to establish and enforce the duty in question. Then the plaintiff has the opportunity to put his case so that it can be fairly established whether he truly has the legal duty that he is coerced into performing; and also the nature of the threatened act, which is the punishment that would be administered by the court for failure to satisfy judgment in the proceedings, can be presumed to be apt because it will be dispensed by the court in respect of the breach of duty in question.

Thus the payment of a debt in response to a threat of civil proceedings to enforce the debt, although made under duress, is not vitiated. Similarly, if the

---

[117] At 556, per Holmes J.

[118] The famous case of *Moses v Macfarlane* (1760) 2 Burr. 1005 is now acknowledged to have been mistaken in allowing a restitutionary claim to reverse a transfer made pursuant to a court order: see e.g. Friedmann (1991).

[119] As discussed in Chap. 3 at 95, "legal compulsion" is not a vitiating factor but a condition for liability under a scheme to facilitate enforcement.

plaintiff has a legal duty to provide some other sort of benefit to the defendant—as where the plaintiff is a public official whose duty it is to provide the defendant with assistance in some way—the plaintiff will have no claim based on duress if the defendant threatens civil proceedings to compel him to act, or even, it seems, if the defendant threatens criminal proceedings by which the plaintiff would be punished for failing to carry out his duty. On the other hand, if the defendant happens to discover that the plaintiff has committed a crime and threatens to report him or have him prosecuted unless he pays a sum to the defendant, clearly there is a claim for duress; the threat is not designed to compel the plaintiff to fulfil his legal duty. Similarly, if the plaintiff's son has committed a fraud against the defendant, and, as a result of a threat by the defendant to have the son prosecuted, the plaintiff pays the defendant the sum owed to him by the son as compensation, the plaintiff will have a claim for duress: this was the outcome in *Williams v Bayley*.[120]

If the defendant is owed money by the plaintiff, and the defendant tries to compel him to pay his debt by threatening him with civil or criminal proceedings relating to some quite different matter, the plaintiff again has a claim based on duress. Although the defendant is attempting to compel the plaintiff to fulfil a legal duty, the plaintiff can complain of duress because the defendant is not making legitimate use of the legal process: the plaintiff would not be able to have the existence of the duty to pay adjudicated on by the court in the threatened proceedings. A more difficult case might be where the plaintiff has committed a crime that is also a tort against the defendant, and the defendant threatens criminal proceedings unless the plaintiff pays compensation. The defendant is trying to compel the plaintiff to fulfil a legal duty to pay compensation to the defendant, but this duty is not precisely what would be in issue in criminal proceedings.[121] Lastly, it must follow that the fact that the act sought by the defendant through his threat was the plaintiff's duty does not mean that the plaintiff has no claim for duress, if the threat is not a threat of legal proceedings at all.[122]

In *Norreys v Zeffert*,[123] the plaintiff had failed to pay his betting debts and the defendant told him that unless they were paid he would be reported to Tattersalls, a trade association responsible for overseeing the conduct of the betting industry, and also to trade protection societies (which acted as credit reference agencies), and to the plaintiff's social club. All these seem to have been

---

[120] (1866) LR 1 HL 200. In fact the claim was said to be based on undue influence rather than duress, but is better interpreted as a case of duress, as pointed out by Birks & Chin (1995), 54. Undue influence is considered below at 193–98.

[121] It seems that a financial compromise over criminal proceedings is generally unenforceable, whether or not there is duress, on the ground that it interferes with the discretion of the public prosecutor to take legal proceedings in the public interest; cf Chap. 11 at 378, 381.

[122] A fortiori there must be a claim where the defendant honestly but mistakenly thinks that the plaintiff owes him money as in *CTN Cash & Carry Ltd v Gallaher* [1994] 4 All ER 714, but this was not the decision in that case. On the analysis here, in that case the defendant ought not to have made any threat other than a threat of legal proceedings in respect of the supposed debt.

[123] [1932] 2 All ER 187.

threats designed to coerce the defendant into paying. It was held that the threat to notify the plaintiff's social club and the trade protection agencies did give rise to a claim for duress, but the threat to notify Tattersalls did not. In making the threat to inform Tattersalls, the defendant was "merely taking a step in accordance with the recognised practice of bringing the matter before an independent committee", and using the "recognised procedure . . . for the protection of the interests of the creditor of this class",[124] Tattersalls being the appropriate body to deal with the matter. It seems that although the plaintiff was subject to coercion by a threat, there was no vitiating factor because the defendant was applying the coercion by way of a legitimate process, although not the legal process, to secure fulfilment of a duty of payment. The case appears to recognise that Tattersalls had a quasi-judicial power to make threats and impose punishment to compel compliance with its rules, and accordingly that the members had the right to threaten to refer matters to it.

It is an important issue concerning trade bodies and other private societies and associations whether they can indeed use threats in this way.[125] The issue also arose in *Thorne v Motor Trade Association*.[126] Here the plaintiff, a member of the defendant trading association, was fined for contravening the rules of the association, and was told that if he did not pay the fine he would be put on the "stop list" which would mean other members of the association would not trade with him. The plaintiff argued that a payment made in such circumstances would be recoverable for duress, and relied on an earlier case in which such a threat had actually been held to constitute blackmail (which is equivalent to duress in the context of criminal proceedings).[127] The House of Lords held that there was no duress (or blackmail), because the actions were taken in pursuance of the commercial interests of the association. This might be understood to suggest that the association was giving a warning rather than making a threat; but in fact the commercial interest in question seems to have been simply the interest in enforcing the association's rules through punishment and threats. The decision again appears to recognise a quasi-judicial power in an association to enforce its rules. It can presumably be justified on the ground that the members have agreed to submit to the power of the society to impose and threaten sanctions in accordance with its rules.[128]

---

[124] At 189–90, per Atkinson J.

[125] As opposed to, say, withholding unpaid-for benefits or excluding someone from the society in order to prevent that person from continuing to flout the rules as a member of the society, or giving a warning of such actions.

[126] [1937] AC 797.

[127] *R. v Denyer* [1926] 2 KB 258.

[128] One would accordingly expect the decisions of the society to be subject to the rules of natural justice.

Threats and offers and economic duress

Threats (and warnings) generally relate to a positive act that will cause harm to the plaintiff. Sometimes instead the defendant tells the plaintiff that he will not confer a certain benefit on the plaintiff unless the plaintiff pays or agrees to pay the defendant a specified sum. There seems to be no reason in principle why such a threat should not found a claim for duress, although it is presumably less likely to be effective. But often what might appear to be a threat not to do something unless a payment is made should be understood as an offer of a contractual exchange to do something in return for payment, which is unexceptionable. The distinction appears to turn on whether the defendant would in any case have conferred or have been bound to confer the benefit.[129]

Where the defendant has a duty to provide a benefit

Where the defendant has a duty to provide the plaintiff with a benefit, for nothing or for a specified or a reasonable price, and he offers to supply it only at an excessive price, the offer amounts to an implied threat by the defendant not to fulfil his duty. He makes a threat because he proposes to depart from his duty only in order to exact excessive payment. There are a number of examples of duress of this sort, as where a public officer abuses his public duty to provide a benefit, or a private person abuses his power contrary to a statutory duty to provide a benefit.[130] The common law does not generally recognise duties to provide benefits other than by contract; but one case at common law is where in an emergency the plaintiff needs the assistance of the defendant and is dependent on him because no one else is available, and the defendant exploits the circumstances to exact an excessive price; here the contract is treated as made under duress and the agreed price reduced to a reasonable sum.[131] The implication is that the defendant has a duty to provide the benefit, or at least to provide it for a reasonable sum if he provides it at all.

Economic duress

The so-called "economic duress" cases have arisen where there is an existing contract between the plaintiff and the defendant, and the defendant tells the plaintiff that he will not perform the contract with the plaintiff except on revised

---

[129] See e.g. Spector (1992). In *CTN Cash & Carry v Gallaher* [1994] 4 All ER 714, the defendant refused to continue a credit line unless the plaintiff paid a sum thought to be due. This was a threat rather than an offer because the sum was not understood to be the price of the credit line, which had already been arranged, although not irrevocably.

[130] Above at n 106.

[131] See below at n 158. Cf *Smith v Charlick* (1924) 34 CLR 38, which has been overtaken by statutory developments in competition law.

terms—for example extra payment.[132] With respect to contracts, it is necessary first to distinguish between the reliance and classical theories, as discussed in Chapter 2. Under the classical theory, the defendant has a duty to supply the benefit, and, on the argument above, a refusal to perform except on revised terms should count as a threat and vitiate the revised agreement, and an offer to perform on revised terms, if it implies a refusal to perform except on the revised terms, will imply such a threat.[133] But under the reliance theory, there is generally no duty to perform.[134] Unless such a duty has arisen, because the plaintiff has become dependent on the defendant for performance, it seems that the plaintiff commits no threat, and is merely making an offer to perform on the revised terms, just as if he were offering terms in initial negotiations.

For example, consider *Pao On v Lau Yiu Long*.[135] Here the defendant agreed to buy a company from the plaintiff for which it was to be paid in shares in B Co. The parties then made a subsidiary agreement by which the plaintiff agreed to buy back the shares in B Co at $2.50, in order to protect the defendant from a fall in the value of the shares in B Co. But the agreement had the effect of empowering the plaintiff to buy back the shares at $2.50 if the price was above that. The defendant, on realising this, refused to carry through the main agreement unless the subsidiary agreement was amended to apply only if the shares were worth less than $2.50. The plaintiff agreed but subsequently claimed, unsuccessfully, that the amended agreement was made under duress. The decision was unhelpfully formulated in terms of whether there was "coercion of [the] will" or "no true consent".[136] Lord Scarman said that the factors that might indicate that there was coercion of the will included whether there was a protest, whether a reasonable alternative course of action was open to the plaintiff, including an adequate legal remedy, whether the plaintiff was independently advised, and whether the plaintiff immediately attempted to avoid the new contract.[137]

The decision is surely inconsistent with the classical theory, according to which the defendant had a duty to perform and threatened to breach it, taking advantage of the lack of any means for compelling him to perform or punishing him for breach of duty, which would have inhibited him from making the threat. Under the reliance theory the decision is more plausible. The agreement was more or less executory, and it is doubtful whether the plaintiff could have become dependent on the defendant as a result of reliance on the agreement, so

---

[132] The issue of duress tends to be disguised behind the problem of consideration, because the revised agreement may be said to be unenforceable for lack of consideration, meaning lack of a reciprocal benefit. But where the problem of consideration is overcome, it is clear that the revised agreement is not necessarily vitiated: a recent example discussed in terms of consideration is *Williams v Roffey* [1991] 1 QB 1.

[133] Unless the defendant can show that he merely made a request for a variation, without implying that he would not otherwise perform, or that he gave a warning that he could not perform.

[134] See Chap. 2 at 31–32.

[135] [1980] AC 614. For consistency with the usage in this chapter, the plaintiff and the defendant have, as for some other cases, been reversed.

[136] Above n 109.

[137] At 636.

as to generate a duty of performance in the defendant. So the decision appears to be consistent with the reliance theory. This analysis tends to reflect the idea that there is duress if the plaintiff did not have any reasonable alternative course of action open to him.[138]

A recent example of a successful claim for duress is *B & S Contracts and Design v Victor Green Publications*.[139] Here the defendant was contracted to erect stands for the plaintiff at Olympia.[140] The defendant's employees refused to work unless they were paid an extra sum, and the defendant made it clear to the plaintiff that unless the plaintiff bore the cost of the extra payment the work would not proceed. The plaintiff paid the extra amount, but after the stand was erected succeeded in reclaiming it on the ground of duress.

> As the defendants' director said, he was over a barrel, he had no alternative but to pay; he had no chance of going to any other source of labour to erect the stands.[141]

The case is best explained on the basis that the defendant had become subject to a duty of performance because it was too late for the plaintiff to find anyone else to do the work, so that the plaintiff had become dependent on the defendant. Thus the defendant was making a threat to withhold a benefit it was obliged to provide, and the plaintiff was coerced into the extra payment. If the defendant had been unable to pay its workers, on the other hand, it would have been giving a warning and making an offer, not a threat.

In *North Ocean Shipping v Hyundai Construction Co*,[142] the defendant was contracted to build a tanker for the plaintiff. The price was fixed, but after a 10 per cent devaluation in the dollar the defendant refused to continue with the contract unless the plaintiff agreed to increase the price by 10 per cent. The plaintiff wanted delivery urgently in order to take advantage of a lucrative charter contract, and so agreed and paid the extra. The court held that the agreement was made under duress. First, it is doubtful whether, under the reliance theory, the plaintiff had become dependent on the defendant for performance, so as to put the defendant under a duty of performance, because it seems that there was no uncompensatable loss in the circumstances.[143]

This seems to be inconsistent with the reliance theory. But there are possible reasons why there might be duress even where, in accordance with the reliance theory, there is no duty to perform. First, although the defendant may not be under a duty to perform, if his liability is clear he is surely under a duty to pay

---

[138] And equally the argument that there is economic duress if the defendant was in bad faith (Birks (1989a), 183) can be understood to mean that he had incurred a duty of performance that he was threatening not to perform.

[139] [1984] ICR 419.

[140] The plaintiff and the defendant have been reversed.

[141] At 426, per Griffiths LJ.

[142] [1979] QB 705.

[143] It seems that the plaintiff declined to terminate and sue for damages not because it was dependent on performance to avoid uncompensatable loss, but in order to secure a lucrative but unforeseeable deal for which, it seems, it might not have been able to recover compensation from the defendant.

appropriate compensation promptly or to submit promptly to some process for settling the amount due if he chooses not to perform.[144] If he declines to do this, he should be understood to be making a threat. Such a threat may be effective if the plaintiff's resources are limited, because he may not be able to wait to succeed in litigation, or be able to bear the cost and risk of litigation. In fact in *Hyundai* the defendant refused the plaintiff's offer of arbitration, and the judge seems to have regarded this as significant.[145]

Secondly, one might distinguish between initial negotiations to form a contract and negotiations to revise a contract, as in *Hyundai*, in the following way. Consider first the possibility that in negotiating for a contract the parties have a duty to contract on fair terms, so that, if the defendant refuses to contract except on terms that are unfairly favourable to him, he should be understood to have coerced the plaintiff into contracting, on the basis that he has departed from his duty to contract fairly only in order to procure an additional benefit from the plaintiff. One might say that the defendant has made a threat in the sense that he refused to contract on terms that actually constituted a beneficial exchange to him, purely in order to procure an additional benefit. Of course, a contract is not actually vitiated by duress on this basis. Such a rule would be impracticable. There is liable to be a range of prices that represent a beneficial exchange, and, even if the range could be established, it seems unavoidable that there may be negotiations and threats in determining an agreed price.

On the renegotiation of a contract, since the defendant is entitled to withdraw, it seems, as suggested above, that the parties should be treated just as if they were negotiating for a fresh contract and so free to secure the best terms possible through negotiation in the same way. But, arguably, if the defendant wants to revise the terms of an existing contract, there should be a presumption that the original terms represented a fair exchange; then, if the defendant threatens not to perform except on revised terms, not because it will no longer be in his interests to perform on the original terms because of a change of circumstances,[146] but simply in order to divert to himself part of the plaintiff's profit on the original (and ex hypothesi fair) terms, the plaintiff should be understood to have been coerced. However, even if this is accepted, it seems that the defendant should still be able to threaten to withdraw in order to secure revised terms where the original terms were unfair, or possibly where, in the light of increased prospective profits for the plaintiff, the original terms would be unfair as the basis for the continuation of the contract.[147] Of course this analysis hardly

---

[144] i.e. as opposed to being subject to a liability: see Appendix 1. A duty to pay without delay where liability is clear is reflected in the US decisions imposing punitive damages on insurance companies for deliberately delaying in satisfying claims: see e.g. S.A. Smith (1997*b*), 375.

[145] At 719, per Mocatta J. But this would not have caused the plaintiff to agree to the new contract because it seems that damages would not have covered the loss of the lucrative contract: see above n 143.

[146] Which would amount to a warning.

[147] One might say again that in such circumstances the defendant was not in bad faith: see above n 138. Burrows has suggested that there is no duress where the original terms are unfair and the revised terms are not: Burrows (1993), 181. One might object that these risks were allocated in the

provides a certain basis for decision; but it may at least show why the issue is liable to be difficult to resolve.

Vitiation, wrongfulness and "illegitimacy"

Duress is generally defined, as mentioned above, as illegitimate or wrongful pressure. There has been controversy over the relation between the effect on the plaintiff—the coerciveness—and the defendant's wrongfulness. It is usually thought that there is coercion *because* the defendant's conduct was wrongful or illegitimate. It seems that the court has to examine the defendant's conduct in isolation from its effect on the plaintiff's transfer to establish whether it is wrongful and so coercive vis-à-vis the plaintiff. On this approach, it seems that the wrongfulness of the defendant's threat must depend on the wrongfulness of the threatened act.[148] Where, say, the defendant threatens to assault the plaintiff, this may appear plausible: it might be thought that it is because the assault is wrongful that the threat to assault is wrongful, and that it is because the threat is wrongful that it is coercive and vitiates the plaintiff's decision. If this were right, the implication would be that duress should be confined to cases where the threatened act is itself independently a wrong, which would generally mean a tort or breach of a contractual duty. As considered below, this seems to have been the position taken with respect to duress or "intimidation" in the law of tort.

In fact, as discussed above, it is clear that there can be duress where the defendant makes a threat to do something that is not wrongful. It is, for example, a standard case of duress for the defendant to threaten to disclose information about the plaintiff, even though disclosing the information is not wrongful.[149] But it seems that it was still thought that the issue of coerciveness turned on the quality of the defendant's conduct considered in isolation from its effect on the plaintiff. This is why, it seems, it came to be said that although it was apparently unnecessary for the defendant to have acted wrongfully, the pressure had to be "illegitimate".[150] The problem was to say when the defendant's conduct was "illegitimate", given that, as it was thought, it did not have to be wrongful in law, because the threatened act did not have to be wrongful. Also it was argued that in deciding what was illegitimate the court was making a judgment of social

original contract. But any revision of the contract would not enable the defendant to escape the application of the original terms, or reverse the risk of changes of circumstances, in respect of reliance already incurred, but only in respect of the future with respect to which he is entitled to withdraw.

[148] This appears to equate coercion with other cases where a wrong is used to impose pressure on the plaintiff, e.g. where a robber injures a bystander in order to force the police not to pursue him in order to take care of the bystander.

[149] The fact that it can be wrongful to threaten to do what is not wrongful has been described as the "paradox of blackmail": Lamond (1996), 215.

[150] *Universe Tankships Inc of Monrovia v International Transport Workers' Federation (The Universe Sentinel)* [1983] 1 AC 366; *CTN Cash & Carry Ltd v Gallaher* [1994] 4 All ER 714.

impropriety rather than legal wrongfulness,[151] which would be objectionable in principle. But, as the analysis above shows, the defendant's conduct is wrongful *because* it is coercive, just as misrepresentation and unconscionability (considered below) are wrongful because they vitiate the plaintiff's decision to transfer or agree.[152] It is not necessary to establish that the defendant's conduct was wrongful or illegitimate independently of its coercive effect. The test of whether the effect is coercive is generally whether the defendant makes a threat or a warning.[153]

The same issue, as to whether a threat can be wrongful even where the threatened act is not, is found in the law of tort and crime. Here what is in issue is not whether there was a vitiating factor, but whether a wrong was committed. In criminal law, for the purposes of the crime of blackmail, which amounts to a deliberate act of coercion, it is certainly recognised that a threat can be wrongful, notwithstanding that the act threatened is not independently wrongful. The threat or "menaces" can be to do anything "detrimental to or unpleasant to the person addressed".[154] But tort law, in connection with the tort of intimidation, reflects the view that a threat can only be wrongful where the threatened act is itself wrongful. The cases here have concerned not a claim by the person coerced, but a claim by another person, who has suffered from the action that the coerced person was compelled to take. In *Allen v Flood*,[155] for example, the defendant threatened to withdraw his labour in order to coerce the third party to cease using the plaintiff's labour. This was held not to be wrongful because the defendant was entitled to withdraw his labour, so the threatened act would not in the circumstances have involved a breach of contract or any other wrong.[156] In this the case is inconsistent with the law of duress and blackmail.[157]

---

[151] Birks (1989a), 177; *CTN Cash & Carry Ltd v Gallaher* [1994] 4 All ER 714, 718–19 per Steyn LJ, referring to "lawful act duress".

[152] With respect to duress there are cases where the coercion is justified, as in the case of a threat of legal proceedings.

[153] A rather different argument is that the threatened act is in fact always wrongful, because it is, by definition, an act causing harm for the very purpose of causing harm, and such an act is necessarily wrongful, even if the act can be lawfully carried out with some other motive: e.g. Finnis (1999), 237ff. This is convincing, although it seems that the common law does not actually accept that an act can be wrongful purely because of the motive behind it: see ibid. Nevertheless, it surely remains the case that the threat is wrongful because it is coercive, not because the threatened act, if carried out, would be wrongful. In any case, the wrongfulness of the threatened act does not on this analysis provide any guidance on whether there is coercion, because any threatened act would be wrongful.

[154] *Thorne v Motor Trade Association* [1937] AC 797, 817 per Lord Wright.

[155] [1898] AC 1.

[156] It was also said that duress is not necessarily tortious in *Universe Tankships Inc of Monrovia v International Transport Workers' Federation (The Universe Sentinel)* [1983] 1 AC 366, 385 per Lord Diplock. Traditionally, the restitutionary claim was said to be based on a "waiver of tort" which seems to suggest that a tort must have been committed, but that it is not relied on by the plaintiff. Waiver of tort is discussed in Chap. 11.

[157] *Allen v Flood* has been widely criticised, although not apparently on this basis: see e.g. Weir (1997), 21.

Duress of circumstances as a vitiating factor

As mentioned above, there are cases where because of an emergency the plaintiff is forced to pay the defendant a price for his services that is much greater than he would normally be able to charge. For example, if the plaintiff is drowning at sea and the defendant demands a fortune to save him, the plaintiff may have no choice but to accept, whereas if he were hiring a lifeguard beforehand he could negotiate for a reasonable price. In such a case, it seems that the court can reduce an agreed liability to pay an exorbitant price to a reasonable level.[158] In such circumstances, it seems that there is a duty to contract at a reasonable price, so that a threat not to contract except at an unreasonable price is wrongful and can constitute duress.[159] The duty arises out of circumstances that distort the usual relationship between potential contractors and make the plaintiff dependent on the defendant.

By contrast there is the case where there are no special circumstances interfering with the parties' contracting, but the plaintiff is simply so poor that a market price, or even the lowest price that it is worth the defendant's while to sell at, is an impossible burden to him. For example, the plaintiff might contract to pay for food at the normal market price and then after eating refuse to pay the agreed price on the basis that the agreement was made under duress because of his poverty. Here there is no basis for saying that the contract was entered into as a result of a threat; or if there was a threat it was a threat that is considered acceptable as part of negotiation. One cannot say that the defendant owed a duty to provide the plaintiff with the food at a price that was affordable to him. There is no authority to suggest that a court can set aside a contract on this basis: "mere impecuniosity has never been held a ground for equitable relief".[160]

---

[158] *The Medina* [1876] 1 P 272; *The Port Caledonia and The Anna* [1903] P 184.

[159] But it seems that the defendant has no duty to provide the benefit if he does not choose to contract at all, or at least no duty enforceable in damages or through criminal proceedings.

[160] *Alec Lobb (Garages) v Total Oil* [1985] 1 WLR 173, 189 per Dunn LJ. One might argue that in the light of the plaintiff's poverty it is an injustice for him to have to pay the full price, and that he should therefore be relieved of his liability under the contract. Whether this is so is liable to be controversial and will depend on many factors, including how the plaintiff came to be in his impecunious position and, most importantly, the basis on which resources are and should be allocated in the society. But in any case these considerations cannot be the basis for a claim against the defendant, because, whether or not there is an injustice of this sort, one cannot say that there is any injustice as between the plaintiff and the defendant; in other words, the defendant has no legal duty to provide for the plaintiff because of his poverty. Any injustice in the relation between the plaintiff and the community as a whole is surely a matter for the social security system, not for private law.

INCOMPETENCE, UNDUE INFLUENCE AND INADEQUATE BARGAINING ABILITY

Incompetence

As a general rule a transfer or contract made by a minor or by someone who is insane or drunk is vitiated on the ground that he is not competent to act. No difficulty arises in connection with the nature or justification of the vitiating factor, although there are other complexities in the law that will not be considered here.[161] The vitiating factor is often referred to as incapacity, and equated with incapacity as a vitiating factor in relation to artificial entities, which was considered above, but the two appear to have nothing in common.

Undue influence

A transfer or contract made under "undue influence" is vitiated. Undue influence has been described in broad terms as arising from:

> unfair or improper conduct, some coercion from outside, some overreaching, some form of cheating, and generally, though not always, some personal advantage obtained by a donee placed in some close and confidential relation to the donor.[162]

Some such cases are properly cases of duress; for example, *Williams v Bayley*[163] was a case of duress, but was decided as a case of undue influence.[164] Undue influence is now understood to arise where the plaintiff came under the influence of the defendant or a third party to the extent of surrendering his independence of mind. A distinction is drawn between cases of actual and presumed undue influence.[165] In a case of actual undue influence, the plaintiff proves that the stronger party in the relationship actually exercised his influence over him with respect to the particular transaction in issue. In the case of presumed undue influence, it is presumed that such influence was exercised because of the nature of the relationship between the two parties. The presumption is automatically made with respect to certain recognised categories of relationship, where the relationship is thought inevitably to subject the plaintiff to the risk of undue influence. The presumption can also be made if the plaintiff shows that, although the relationship in question does not fall within such a category, it is nevertheless such as to justify a presumption.[166] The relationships that have been held to attract the presumption automatically include parent and child, superior and member of a sisterhood, doctor and patient, and solicitor and

---

[161] See further Burrows (1993), 322–8.
[162] *Allcard v Skinner* (1887) 36 Ch D 145, 181.
[163] (1866) LR 1 HL 200; above n 120.
[164] Birks & Chin (1995), 54.
[165] *Allcard v Skinner* (1887) 36 Ch D 145; *BCCI v Aboody* [1990] 1 QB 923.
[166] *Barclays Bank v O'Brien* [1994] 1 AC 180, 189.

client.[167] In *Barclays Bank v O'Brien*,[168] the nature of the relationship between the husband and wife in that case was found to be such as to justify the presumption, even though the category of husband and wife relationships does not automatically attract it.

The essence of a relationship of undue influence seems to be that the plaintiff is open to the influence of the stronger party to the extent that his normal rational assessment of his own interests is suppressed. It seems that this might happen because of a reluctance to disagree, resulting from fear or insecurity,[169] or maybe because of an unquestioning assumption that the opinions of the other party are invariably correct, as a result of excessive deference or admiration. Such cases should be distinguished from cases where the plaintiff rationally chooses to defer to another party, because of that party's expertise, or because of a rationally agreed allocation of responsibility for matters of common interest. It is no doubt partly the difficulty of making such a distinction that justifies a presumption of undue influence for certain types of relationship.

Manifest disadvantage

There is some controversy over whether there is a requirement that the contract must be of "manifest disadvantage" to the plaintiff, which generally corresponds to an excessive or unreciprocated benefit to the stronger party. The expression is apt for a contract rather than a transfer; presumably a gratuitous transfer is necessarily of manifest disadvantage to the plaintiff. The manifest disadvantage requirement is due to *National Westminster Bank v Morgan*,[170] where it was explicitly applied only with respect to presumed undue influence, and not in relation to proved actual undue influence. It was subsequently thought to apply with respect to actual undue influence as well,[171] but more recently, in *CIBC Mortgages v Pitt*,[172] it was said that the manifest disadvantage condition certainly does not apply to cases of actually proved undue influence, and some doubt was expressed whether there was any place for it all.

The requirement seems ostensibly inappropriate, because once it is established that the plaintiff's decision was vitiated, one would think that it should follow immediately that he should not be held to it,[173] just as for mistake or duress or lack of authority, whatever the nature of the transaction. However, in a case where undue influence is merely presumed, because of the difficulty of proof, there is a good reason for imposing a further condition of manifest disadvantage as a form of corroboration of the undue influence. As Lord Scarman put it:

---

[167] *Goldsworthy v Brickell* [1987] Ch 378,401; *Barclays Bank v O'Brien* [1994] 1 AC 180, 189.
[168] [1994] 1 AC 180.
[169] Some such cases might tend towards duress.
[170] [1985] AC 686.
[171] *BCCI v Aboody* [1990] 1 QB 923.
[172] [1994] 1 AC 200, 206.
[173] As Lord Browne-Wilkinson argued in *CIBC Mortgages v Pitt* [1994] 1 AC 200, 206.

the Court of Appeal erred in law in holding that the presumption of undue influence can arise from the evidence of the relationship of the parties without also evidence that the transaction was wrongful in that it constituted an advantage taken . . . which was explicable only on the basis that undue influence had been exercised.[174]

Furthermore, the use of a presumption raises the risk of some unjustified prejudice to the defendant because there may in fact have been no vitiating factor, and arguably the mitigation of this risk justifies imposing the further requirement.

Bona fide purchase and independent legal advice

The presumption of undue influence can be rebutted by evidence of independent legal advice. Now in fact it seems unlikely that the influence of a strong and well-established relationship of undue influence will always, or even generally, be overcome by a discussion with a lawyer. As it has been put, "[t]he problem is not lack of understanding but lack of independence".[175] But it appears that, where the issue is whether a contract with the defendant is vitiated, the defence of bona fide purchase[176] will be available to the defendant provided that he has taken reasonable steps in response to the danger of vitiation, and this he is taken to have done if has arranged for independent legal advice.[177] The defendant is in effect entitled to pass responsibility to the plaintiff's solicitor for ensuring that the plaintiff does not act under undue influence, or possibly for ensuring that the transaction is nevertheless not unfair to the plaintiff. On this approach, legal advice is generally relevant in determining whether there is a defence, not whether there was a vitiating factor.[178]

Undue influence as a wrong?

Undue influence is sometimes described as if it were a wrong rather than a vitiating factor.[179] There has been some controversy on the point.[180] As mentioned at the start of the chapter, there can certainly be no objection to a claim based on a wrong by the defendant that caused the plaintiff to act under a vitiated intention, or exploited the plaintiff's vitiated intention. Such a claim would be

[174] *National Westminster Bank v Morgan* [1985] AC 686, 704. And in *Royal Bank of Scotland v Etridge (No 2)* [1998] 4 All ER 705, 712, the Court of Appeal said: "[w]hatever the true position . . . the presence of manifest disadvantage is obviously a powerful evidential factor".

[175] *Royal Bank of Scotland v Etridge (No 2)* [1998] 4 All ER 705, 714.

[176] Or in the nature of bona fide purchase: see Chap. 7.

[177] *Barclays Bank v O'Brien* [1994] 1 AC 180, 196–7; *Royal Bank of Scotland v Etridge (No 2)* [1998] 4 All ER 705, 720ff. If there is no reason to suspect undue influence, it seems that it is sufficient merely to advise the plaintiff to see a lawyer.

[178] Although no doubt one might also be able to show that the legal advice meant that there was no vitiating factor. The two effects of legal advice are distinguished in *Royal Bank of Scotland v Etridge (No 2)* [1998] 4 All ER 705, 714.

[179] This is implicit in the language of *Barclays Bank v O'Brien* [1994] 1 AC 180, although the point was not in issue.

[180] See e.g. Birks & Chin (1995); Bigwood (1996); Capper (1998).

for compensation in tort. There are certainly examples of such wrongs: for example misrepresentation is the wrong of inducing mistake, and duress refers not only to the vitiating factor but also the tort of inducing and exploiting it.[181] No doubt where the defendant exploits the plaintiff's position of weakness under a relationship of undue influence he commits such a tort. Of course, since undue influence arose in equity it would not be conventional to refer to the wrong as a tort, but as an equitable wrong, or more particularly as unconscionability,[182] or fraud,[183] or exploitation.[184] The remedy for the wrong would normally be pecuniary compensation; but it may be that compensation can best be effected by reversing the transfer to the defendant. One might say that this is a restitutionary remedy for the wrong: compensation for the wrong is effected by reversing the transfer, i.e. by restitution in a remedial sense. But, as discussed in Chapter 1,[185] it is more helpful, and consistent with normal usage, to reserve "restitution" to refer to a claim to reverse a transfer arising from the fact that the transfer was vitiated, not a claim to reverse a transfer on the ground that it was caused by a wrong.[186] Perhaps there are reasons for arguing that in particular circumstances there should be no restitutionary claim based directly on the vitiating factor, merely a tort claim, although it is difficult to see what the justification could be for having an actionable wrong of inducing or exploiting a vitiating factor, but no restitutionary claim arising from the vitiating factor itself. In any case, what is necessarily misconceived is to say that the restitutionary claim (in the usual substantive sense) itself depends on the commission of a wrong.

It will often be the case that where the plaintiff's decision has been vitiated by undue influence the stronger party will indeed have committed a wrong. If the stronger party has deliberately exploited his influence he will clearly have acted wrongfully, and it may be that he has a duty to ensure that he does not inadvertently take advantage of his influence. It is unclear whether, where the stronger party contracts with the plaintiff, he acts wrongfully when he knows or ought to know of the undue influence but makes, or tries to make, a fair contract.[187] As mentioned above, if the plaintiff's claim is based on the vitiation of a contract with the defendant (where he is a third party to the relationship of undue influence),[188] the defendant is likely to have a defence of bona fide purchase. He will be denied the defence if he has actual or possibly constructive knowledge of the vitiating factor;[189] and it may be that if the defendant has such knowledge he

---

[181] See above at 160.

[182] e.g. *Dunbar Bank v Nadeem* [1998] 3 All ER 876, 883–4.

[183] e.g. *CIBC Mortgages v Pitt* [1994] 1 AC 200, 206.

[184] This expression is used in Burrows (1993), 189ff.

[185] See also Chap. 1 at 22–23.

[186] The discussion here does not of course relate to disgorgement arising from a wrong.

[187] According to Millett LJ in *Dunbar Bank v Nadeem*, there is no wrongfulness in such a case, and so apparently no claim: [1998] 3 All ER 876, 883–4.

[188] Presumably the stronger party would not have the benefit of the defence; but compare the "fair dealing" rule at n 200 below.

[189] The knowledge requirement depends on the relevant "duty of inquiry": see Chap. 10 at 342–6.

will also generally have acted wrongfully by exploiting the plaintiff's position of weakness.[190] This would mean that, in such cases, undue influence as a vitiating factor will generally be actionable only where the defendant has also acted wrongfully.

In *Dunbar Bank v Nadeem*[191] the defendant was a bank which had taken a charge from the plaintiff and her husband over their house. The court accepted that the plaintiff's decision to contract was vitiated, to the extent that "although . . . the pen may have been the pen of [the plaintiff], the mind was the mind of [her husband]".[192] But it nevertheless held that there was no undue influence because there was no wrongdoing by the husband, since he did not exploit his influence over his wife, but did his best for her in difficult financial circumstances. It is curious that, according to Millett LJ, the undue influence requires the commission of a wrong by the stronger party in the relationship of undue influence with the plaintiff, even if (as in that case) this party is not the defendant. This wrongfulness requirement cannot be justified on the basis that the claim is for compensation for the wrong of inducing or exploiting the vitiating factor, rather than for restitution based on the vitiating factor itself, because of course the wrong in question has not been committed by the defendant. Conversely, if the claim is restitutionary, and the plaintiff's intention was vitiated, it is difficult to see how it can be of any consequence, as against the defendant, whether the vitiation was induced or exploited by some third party.[193]

Undue influence and fiduciary relationships

Undue influence seems to have a strong connection with the law of fiduciary relationships, which is considered in Chapter 13. Broadly speaking, a fiduciary relationship is a form of contractual relationship in which the principal has entrusted the fiduciary with a job on his behalf which is imprecisely defined, so that inadequate performance is likely to be difficult to detect. Because a breach by the fiduciary is liable to be difficult to remedy, the plaintiff has become dependent on the fiduciary. Although the principal has become dependent in this sense, a fiduciary relationship it is not necessarily such as to render the principal emotionally susceptible to the fiduciary. The principal's dependence is a practical matter arising from the nature of the fiduciary's job, not from the nature of the personal relationship between the parties, and it does not imply that the principal has in any way lost his ability to assess his own interests and act rationally in the light of the information available to him. By contrast it is clear that for undue influence it is the personal relationship that is crucial, and

---

[190] This raises the issue whether a defendant commits a wrong in dealing with the plaintiff if he knows that there is a vitiating factor, but acts fairly to the plaintiff: see above at n 187.

[191] [1998] 3 All ER 876.

[192] At 883–4.

[193] Possibly the wrongfulness requirement should be understood as a requirement of fairness in the contract, which would amount to the manifest disadvantage condition discussed above.

consequently the character of the parties is liable to be crucial as well. For undue influence, but not with respect to a fiduciary relationship, it will be important, for example, whether the plaintiff is "strong-willed, autocratic, and generous"[194] or whether he is a "failing and vulnerable old man".[195]

However, it will often be the case that a fiduciary relationship will arise at the same time as a relationship of undue influence. Although most fiduciary relationships arise in a commercial context,[196] for example between business partners, or a principal and his commercial agent, or an investor and investment manager, where a relationship of undue influence is unlikely to arise, some will involve the management of affairs for someone who cannot act for himself, in particular a minor. In such a case, a presumption of undue influence is likely to be appropriate. This may account for the fact that the fiduciary relationship has often been confused with the relationship of undue influence, but it would be helpful to keep them distinct.[197] Thus it would be desirable to avoid describing a relationship that attracts the presumption of undue influence as a relationship of "trust and confidence",[198] because this expression is more commonly used in connection with fiduciary relationships.[199]

A fiduciary who deals with his principal is subject to the "fair dealing rule",[200] which is liable to render voidable a contract made between the fiduciary and the principal. The vitiating factor underlying the fair dealing rule is not clear. In some cases where the fair dealing rule has been applied there is likely to have been a relationship of undue influence.[201] But the fair dealing rule does not appear generally to depend on any impairment of the principal's independence of mind through emotional dependence, since this is not a general feature of a fiduciary relationship. In other cases, the vitiating factor may be lack of authority or mistake,[202] or the principal's claim may strictly be a claim for compensation for a wrong rather than a restitutionary claim based on a vitiating factor.[203]

---

[194] Re *Brocklehurst's Estate* [1978] Ch 14, 36; Cartwright 181.

[195] Re *Craig*, decd. [1971] Ch 95, 107.

[196] See Chap. 13.

[197] Sometimes it is argued that relationships of undue influence are a distinct category of fiduciary relationship: e.g. Millet (1998), at 219–20. This may be so as a matter of usage, although there are surely many cases of undue influence that do not make any use of the expression, and this is surely the better practice.

[198] The expression was used in this context in *Barclays Bank v O'Brien* [1994] 1 AC 180, 196 per Lord Browne-Wilkinson.

[199] *Tate v Williamson* (1866) LR 2 Ch App 55 is sometimes regarded as a case of undue influence but was actually a case of breach of fiduciary duty.

[200] *Tito v Waddell (No 2)* [1977] Ch 106. See further Chap. 13.

[201] As where the principal is a minor. Under the "fair dealing" rule the contract is set aside only if not proved fair; this seems to be analogous to the manifest disadvantage rule in qualifying the effect of the vitiating factor. It may be particularly desirable here because of the effect of the no-conflict rule in allowing a presumption of a breach of duty or excess of authority, as discussed in Chap. 13.

[202] There is room for argument whether there is a mistake when the fiduciary conceals information that he ought to reveal.

[203] i.e. where the principal has acted contrary to his fiduciary duty of loyalty. As considered in Chap. 13, the no-conflict rule may provide the plaintiff with a presumption of breach of duty.

Inadequate bargaining ability and "unconscionable bargains"

There is a line of cases in which a court has set aside a contract as "unconscionable". The criteria for the claim seem to be, first, that the terms are clearly unbalanced to the plaintiff's disadvantage, and, secondly, that the plaintiff is disabled in some degree from promoting his own interests in relation to the contract in question, because of an inadequate ability to understand the contract in issue, or its effects or risks, by virtue of a lack of intelligence, education, experience or other relevant skills or knowledge;[204] in short, one might say, the plaintiff has an inadequate bargaining ability with respect to the contract in question.

Examples in the cases

An early example is *Fry v Lane*,[205] where a plumber's assistant and a laundryman each sold a reversionary interest under a will for a price that was actually many times less than the price that such an interest would have been independently valued at or would have been reasonably expected to make. The court held that it could set aside a sale made by a "poor and ignorant man at a considerable undervalue".[206] More recently the case was directly followed in *Cresswell v Potter*[207] where, after leaving her husband, a woman made a clearly bad bargain by giving up her half share in the matrimonial home in return for being relieved of any liability on the mortgage loan. The judge held that the plaintiff, a telephonist, could "properly be described as 'ignorant' in the context of property transactions in general and the execution of conveyancing documents in particular".[208] Given that the value of her share of the equity was considerable, and assuming that she did not mean to make a gift, the terms of the arrangement show that she failed to understand the effect of the transaction. The judge held that, by modern criteria, the plaintiff was "poor" as well as "ignorant", but it is difficult to see that poverty is relevant except to the extent that it suggests a lack of experience of or familiarity with the type of transaction in question, particularly, one would have thought, at the time of *Fry v Lane*.

Similarly, in *Commercial Bank of Australia v Amadio*,[209] the two parents of a businessman in financial difficulty agreed to give a mortgage over their property to secure loans to the son's business, and the court set aside the contract on the basis that the bank took advantage of "a person [with] a special disability", the special disability here being:

---

[204] "Poverty or need of any kind, sickness, age, sex, infirmity of body or mind, drunkenness, illiteracy or lack of education, lack of assistance or explanation where assistance or explanation is necessary": *Louth v Diprose* (1992) 175 CLR 621 quoting *Blomely v Ryan* (1956) 99 CLR 362, 405. Some of these seem to relate to incompetence or undue influence rather than the ability to contract.

[205] (1888) 40 Ch D 312.

[206] At 322.

[207] [1978] 1 WLR 255.

[208] At 258, per Megarry J

[209] (1983) 151 CLR 447.

the combination of their age, their limited grasp of written English, the circumstances in which the bank presented the document to them for signature and, most importantly, their lack of knowledge and understanding of the contents of the document.[210]

In *Boustany v Pigott*,[211] the plaintiff's affairs, including the renting of certain properties, were managed by her cousin because, although apparently not generally incompetent to contract, she was not fully capable of managing them herself. The defendant tenant approached the plaintiff in her cousin's absence, although she knew that the plaintiff did not usually manage her own affairs, and secured a new lease on terms that were clearly unduly favourable to her. A lawyer drew up the agreement at the plaintiff's direction, after pointing out to her aspects of the agreement that he thought might be against her best interests. It was clear from the evidence, as it must have been clear to the defendant, that the plaintiff was under a "total misapprehension of the facts" relating to the property. The lease was set aside.[212]

Procedural and substantive unfairness

The plaintiff's weakness or "special disability" does not amount to general incompetence; he may be perfectly capable of dealing with some other transactions. Neither does it imply that the plaintiff was subject to the defendant's undue influence. Furthermore, it is said that no claim arises just on the basis of "substantive unfairness" or "contractual imbalance", in the absence of "procedural unfairness", i.e. a vitiating factor.[213] The ground of claim is generally thought to be based on the wrongdoing of the defendant—hence the designation in terms of "unconscionability". If this is so, as discussed above, the claim is really a claim for compensation in tort, not a restitutionary claim at all.[214] But again it is surely the case that any wrong committed by the defendant is parasitic on a vitiating factor, in the sense that the wrong consists of exploiting the plaintiff's weakness. Although no doubt it is wrongful in the circumstances to take advantage of the plaintiff's weakness, the weakness itself, as a vitiating factor, will surely also generate a restitutionary claim. However, this vitiating factor by its nature arises only in relation to a contract rather than a transfer, and the defendant, being the other party to the contract, will always have a defence of bona fide purchase[215] unless he knows (or possibly ought to know) of the plaintiff's weakness, and where he has this knowledge it seems that he will generally, if not always, be acting wrongfully in exploiting the plaintiff.

---

[210] At 477, per Deane J.

[211] (1995) 69 P & CR 298 (PC).

[212] Two other recent cases ostensibly concerned with this line of cases seem really to be concerned with undue influence (*Louth v Diprose* (1992) 175 CLR 621 (Aust)) and incompetence (*Hart v O'Connor* [1985] 2 All ER 880 (PC)).

[213] *Hart v O'Connor* [1985] 2 All ER 880, 892.

[214] Except in the remedial sense discussed in Chap. 1.

[215] i.e. under the principle of objective interpretation in contract or of restitutio in integrum: see Chap. 7.

Consequently it seems that the restitutionary claim will not arise unless the defendant also acts wrongfully. Nevertheless the plaintiff's claim should be regarded as primarily restitutionary, because the crux of the claim is the plaintiff's weakness.[216]

This vitiating factor has always been problematic and the jurisdiction is apparently under-developed. The problem is that every contractor to some extent falls short of fully understanding the implications of a contract, even to the extent that it is ascertainable and determinate in theory. The problem is where to draw the line. The difficulty is partly overcome by the requirement for the contract also to be clearly substantively unfair or unbalanced. As has often been observed, substantive unfairness or "contractual imbalance", although distinct from procedural unfairness, is indicative of it. In particular, where the vitiating factor is the inability to weigh up the consequences of the contract, substantive unfairness is direct evidence of the vitiating factor.[217] Substantive unfairness is not merely a factor that is indicative of an inadequate bargaining ability for the purposes of a finding that the contract was vitiated. It may also be the *defendant's* only indication of the plaintiff's inadequate bargaining ability, so that without it he is likely to have the benefit of the bona fide purchase defence.[218] In addition (as with respect to "manifest disadvantage" in relation to undue influence), because of the difficulty in establishing the vitiating factor it may be reasonable sometimes to disregard cases where it is possible that the plaintiff may have had inadequate bargaining skills if the contract is not also unbalanced. But there may be cases where it should not be necessary to show that there is anything wrong with the terms of the contract as well. For example, in a case like *Amadio*, involving the mortgaging of a house to support a business, it would be clear to both the defendant and the court that the contract involved a great gamble that most old people would not be prepared to take, even if there was nothing wrong with the terms of the contract (in the sense that a better bargain could have been achieved by a more able contractor). It is not out of the question that a couple might be willing to take such a risk for their son, but it is important that the risk has been properly understood and assessed.[219]

A point should be made about substantive unfairness or contractual imbalance. As the latter expression implies, it seems generally to be understood to refer to a case where the benefit received by the plaintiff is out of proportion to

---

[216] It will be the unfairness of the contract that will generally put the defendant on notice. It seems that the defendant can usually escape liability if he has ensured that the plaintiff has legal advice: cf above 195. In *Boustany v Pigott* (1993) 69 P & CR 298, where it was clear that the defendant knew that the plaintiff remained unable to act properly in her own interests notwithstanding the involvement of a lawyer, whose advice was rejected, the legal advice did not preclude a claim.

[217] Cf Collins (1997), 261.

[218] Or the principle of objective interpretation in contract: see Chap. 7 on bona fide purchase. Cf the case where the plaintiff is of unsound mind but ostensibly sane, where the defendant can rely on the agreement: *Hart v O'Connor* [1985] 2 All ER 880 (PC).

[219] A similar example might be *Cheese v Thomas* [1994] 1 WLR 129.

the benefit received by the defendant. However, when a contract is made, each party is principally concerned not so much that his benefit will be comparable to the other party's, but that the value of the benefit he will receive will exceed the measure of his own reliance interest by as much as possible. This is behind the "contractual valuation",[220] which equates the benefit and the measure of the reliance interest, and is based on the presumption of the plaintiff's competence at assessing the implications that the contract will have for him. Substantive unfairness in this sense is tied more closely to the vitiating factor, because it is concerned only with what the plaintiff would have had to assess, and not with the relative positions of the parties in an objective sense.[221]

"Inequality of bargaining power"

Lord Denning made a famous attempt to identify a general principle to draw together various grounds for setting aside a contract.[222] The general principle he identified was "inequality of bargaining power", and to support it he drew on common law duress (i.e. duress of goods and duress to the person), "undue pressure" (equitable cases of duress traditionally treated as actual undue influence), undue influence, unconscionable transactions, and salvage agreements. Lord Denning's attempt does not seem to have attracted judicial support.[223] It covers what have been treated here as three distinct vitiating factors: duress, including economic duress, undue influence and inadequate bargaining ability. These are distinct types of vitiating factor and, although they may sometimes arise together, there is no reason to disregard the distinctions between them and subsume them under a single head.

More narrowly, it has been argued that the law of undue influence should be assimilated with the law of unconscionability.[224] Now, although there is no real consistency in usage or interpretation, it seems that in this context "unconscionability" is usually used not to refer to a the wrong of exploiting undue influence, but in connection with the distinct jurisdiction to set aside "unconscionable bargains", which, on the approach adopted here, is concerned with the vitiating factor of "inadequate bargaining ability", not the vitiating factor of undue influence. Apart from questions of usage it is helpful to distinguish these two vitiating factors, and also to distinguish between a vitiating factor and the wrong of causing or exploiting the vitiating factor, although there is perhaps no objection to using "unconscionability" to refer to the wrong of causing or

---

[220] See Chap. 2.

[221] Of course if the contract is more beneficial to the defendant than to the plaintiff, one might think that the plaintiff could have achieved better terms, but in cases of unconscionability the issue will be not that a contract that is beneficial to the plaintiff is even more beneficial to the defendant, but that it was a bad contract for the plaintiff.

[222] *Lloyd's Bank v Bundy* [1975] QB 326, 339.

[223] It was rejected by Lord Scarman in *National Westminster Bank v Morgan* [1985] AC 686, 708.

[224] e.g. Capper (1998).

exploiting any vitiating factor, including both undue influence and inadequate bargaining ability.[225]

PAYMENTS OF TAX

It has recently been held by the House of Lords in *Woolwich Building Society v Inland Revenue*[226] that "money paid to a public authority in the form of taxes . . . pursuant to an ultra vires demand . . . is prima facie recoverable . . . as of right", and probably that a tax "wrongly exacted . . . not because the demand was ultra vires but for other reasons, for example because the authority has misconstrued a relevant statute" would be recoverable on the same basis.[227] This has been referred to as the "*Woolwich* principle". In *Woolwich*, the demand was excessive because it was made under subordinate legislation that was void as ultra vires the primary legislation. It had apparently been the practice of the Inland Revenue to return overpaid tax in what it considered to be an ex gratia payment, but the plaintiff sought to establish its right to repayment in order to recover interest, which the Inland Revenue would not have paid ex gratia. It is not easy to say what exactly the *Woolwich* principle is and whether it can be explained in terms of established vitiating factors. A number of possible factors were mentioned in the judgments or have been suggested by commentators.

It is often said or implied that the *Woolwich* principle is concerned with ultra vires tax demands. This has no connection with the "ultra vires doctrine" or incapacity as a vitiating factor, which was considered above; in *Woolwich*, the relevance of ultra vires was that the tax regulation was void, and this is what caused the mistaken demand. Unfortunately it seems sometimes to have been thought that, in a case where the demand is excessive because of a mistake in asssessment rather than an ultra vires regulation, the claim will arise under the *Woolwich* principle only if the demand was an ultra vires administrative act, which would be the case if the mistake in assessment was a mistake of law going to jurisdiction.[228] But in *Woolwich* ultra vires did not provide the taxpayer with a vitiating factor in itself; its relevance was only that in that case the reason for the mistaken demand was the void regulation. It surely cannot make any difference to the plaintiff's position whether a sum that was not due was demanded because a regulation was ultra vires, or because of a mistake of construction or for some other reason.[229] This was the provisional position of the House of

---

[225] In *Commercial Bank of Australia v Amadio* (1983) 151 CLR 447 at 474, Deane J said: "[u]ndue influence looks to the quality of the consent or assent of the weaker party . . . [Unconscionability] looks to the conduct of the stronger party in . . . dealing with a person under a special disability".

[226] [1993] AC 70.

[227] Per Lord Goff [1993] AC 70, 177.

[228] e.g. Law Commission (1994), para. 6.39.

[229] No doubt the difference would be significant if the taxpayer had to seek judicial review of a tax assessment as an administrative act to have it quashed. But the claim under the *Woolwich* principle is not based on having a tax assessment quashed by judicial review or otherwise.

Lords in the passage quoted above, and there is no plausible analysis of the case that suggests that the claim is tied to ultra vires.

One argument mentioned by Lord Goff and strongly relied on by Birks is the principle that "taxes should not be levied without the authority of Parliament".[230] But it is doubtful that this offers an independent basis for recovery. The effect of the principle is that taxes may not be raised by the executive except under an authorising statute: there is no Crown prerogative to impose taxes. This principle may be relevant to determining whether a tax is due (without it a public authority would presumably have no need to bring its tax raising regulations within the terms of primary legislation). But it does not seem that the principle, in itself, establishes that a payment made by a taxpayer that was not due should be recoverable, any more than that the fact that a sum paid to a private citizen was not due means that it is necessarily recoverable. In *Woolwich*, the issue was not whether the tax was due but whether, not having been due, it could be recovered.

If a taxpayer, suspecting that a demand is excessive, secures an agreement from the Inland Revenue to repay any excess, it will have a contractual claim for repayment of the excess. This was accepted in principle in *Woolwich*, but there was held to have been no such agreement on the facts. In particular, it was held that one could not infer an implied agreement to this effect purely from the fact that the parties were in dispute when the payment was made or that the payment was expressly made under protest.[231] In such circumstances the taxpayer might have chosen not to pursue the dispute without necessarily seeking an agreement, and the public authority might of course have merely accepted the payment noting the protest but without intending to accept any condition attached to it.

A plausible argument on the facts is that the *Woolwich* principle is really an example of a vitiating factor of duress.[232] This argument was apparently not pressed by the plaintiff in the House of Lords and was not taken up by Lord Goff,[233] although he did refer to the "coercive power" behind the Inland Revenue.[234] As discussed earlier in this chapter, although a payment made under threat of legal proceedings is made under duress, duress of this sort is sanctioned by the law as the legitimate use of the legal process. Normally where there is a threat of proceedings to recover a debt, the threatened act is the punishment that will be inflicted by the court on the debtor if at the trial he is ordered to pay and does not do so. This means that the threatened punishment will not be imposed unless the plaintiff's claim has been adjudicated on by the court and the plaintiff has still refused to pay. There is no threat of punishment of the debtor for his refusal to pay the debt when the demand was first made of

---

[230] Per Lord Goff, citing the Bill of Rights 1688, at 172; Birks (1992c).

[231] Cf *Nurdin & Peacock v Ramsden* [1999] 1 WLR 1249, at 177 above.

[232] Burrows (1991), 41.

[233] [1993] AC 70, 173; but it was the ground principally relied on by Lord Slynn: [1993] AC 70, 204.

[234] At 171.

him, even if the court determines that the demand was valid. It would be inappropriate for the court to impose any such punishment, or for the creditor to be able to take advantage of a threat of such punishment, because the effect would be to undermine the debtor's right to have the debt adjudicated on. The debtor would be inclined to pay the debt, even when he genuinely thought that it was not due, for fear of the penalties that would be imposed on him for his failure to pay on demand, if it turned out that he was mistaken and the debt was actually due, and thus sometimes the debtor would end up paying when no debt was actually due, or paying more than was actually owed.[235]

But this latter position seems actually to be the position that applies with respect to tax demands by the Inland Revenue. If proceedings are taken against a taxpayer for non-payment of a demand, and it is found that the demand was valid and the tax due, it appears that the taxpayer is liable to a penalty for his failure to pay on demand, even if he honestly doubted his liability to pay. This was apparently the main reason why the plaintiff in *Woolwich* paid first and then sought restitution instead of refusing payment and forcing the Inland Revenue to sue.[236] The rationale for punishment for non-payment on demand is presumably to facilitate tax collection and discourage delay in paying; but its effect will often be, as in *Woolwich*, to compel a taxpayer to satisfy an excessive demand in order to avoid the risk of a penalty. This suggests a justification for the taxpayer's right to restitution. Although a threat of legal proceedings is usually a legitimate form of duress that does not generate a restitutionary claim, a creditor makes an illegitimate use of the legal process, and so imposes duress that does vitiate the debtor's payment, if he takes advantage of a regime that allows for the debtor to be coerced into paying without any prior adjudication of the debt, unless it agrees with the debtor, before the debtor pays, to repay any excess over what is subsequently found to be due. This means also that there is good reason to infer the existence of such an agreement if the payment was made under protest.[237]

On the facts of *Woolwich*, there was no claim based on a vitiating factor of mistake. There might often be a mistake of fact or law in the case of an excess payment of tax, but here the taxpayer knew or at least suspected that the amount demanded was not due, and so on normal principles would be assumed to have accepted the risk of a mistake. However, the *Woolwich* principle can be understood as an extension of recovery for mistake to exclude the normal principle of assumption of risk, on the basis that the authority has a responsibility to act on behalf of the taxpayer as well as for the state. On this basis, the authority takes primary responsibility for determining the tax due, at least so far as it

---

[235] It might, however, be appropriate for the court to punish the refusal to pay on demand where it is shown that the debtor did not doubt that the debt was due, particularly if delay in payment is likely to be damaging to the creditor: see above n 144.

[236] One reason why the plaintiff in *Woolwich* chose to pay first and then take proceedings rather than withhold payment was that it "feared that if it failed in its legal arguments it might incur penalties": [1989] 1 WLR 137, 142–3 per Nolan J at first instance.

[237] As Nolan J thought at first instance [1989] 1 WLR 137, 147.

depends on matters of law, and the taxpayer need not concern himself with whether the sum demanded is correct, and can pay, even knowing or suspecting a mistake, and leave it to the authority to determine the position and to return any excess payment.[238] This would amount to a rule that in these circumstances a payment is recoverable simply if it was not due, without the need to show a vitiating factor, which one might describe as a claim based on "no consideration";[239] or alternatively that the taxpayer can make a payment subject to a unilaterally imposed condition that is binding on the authority irrespective of whether it was accepted.[240] Where the legal arrangements for recovering tax due are such that the taxpayer can be penalised for failing to pay on demand, even when he honestly and reasonably doubts the validity of the demand, it is easy to infer that the taxpayer is entitled to hold the authority responsible for assessing the amount owed.

OTHER SUPPOSED VITIATING AND "UNJUST" FACTORS

A number of other vitiating factors have been suggested by commentators, including legal compulsion and moral compulsion, which were rejected above. It seems also to be widely thought that there can be "unjust factors", which operate in an analogous way to justify a restitutionary claim.[241] As discussed in Chapter 1, there is room for confusion over the nature of unjust factors and their relation to restitution. If restitution is used in a purely remedial sense to refer to the remedy of reversing a transfer, then torts and breach of contract can be unjust factors, because reversing a transfer can be the appropriate remedy for a breach of contract[242] or tort.[243] But it seems that restitution is generally intended in a substantive sense, by which it is necessarily distinct from other substantive categories like contract and tort. However, this leaves unclear what this category is, if it extends beyond restitution for vitiated transfers. One supposed "unjust factor" is where a transfer is "qualified", which means it was made subject to a condition. A restitutionary claim is said to arise if the condi-

---

[238] With respect to this ground, one would expect a payment made under an agreement settling the dispute between the taxpayer and the authority not to be recoverable, on the basis that by making the agreement the taxpayer now assumed responsibility for protecting his own interest in the dispute; but in so far as the duress ground applied in the circumstances, it would vitiate the agreement just as much as the simple payment.

[239] Lord Goff, at 166, and Lord Browne-Wilkinson, at 197, mentioned "no consideration", but not clearly in this sense. There is an analogous case where a payment is made under an illegal contract, the defendant having the principal responsibility for compliance with the invalidating rule in question: see Chap. 6, at n 218.

[240] This would be an application of the restitutionary conditional transfer theory: see below at 208.

[241] For a breakdown of the various unjust factors, see Birks & Chambers (1997).

[242] On the preferred analysis in Chap. 3, the claim arising on total failure of consideration is the reversal of a payment as a remedy in contract.

[243] A remedy of reversing a transfer can be available as the response to unconscionability as discussed above.

tion fails; this is the restitutionary conditional transfer theory or theory of failure of consideration, which was considered and rejected in Chapters 2 and 3 above. Another supposed unjust factor is "free acceptance" or "unconscientious receipt". This concept also was considered and rejected as the basis for a restitutionary claim in Chapter 3.

It is even thought that "policies calling for restitution" can constitute unjust factors,[244] although here it is difficult to see that "restitution" can be used in anything other than a simple remedial sense, from which some cases of contract and tort could not be excluded. These policies include "constitutional legality", "encouraging help" and "regulation of sensitive transactions".[245] Some of these have been considered in this chapter or elsewhere, although not as policies calling for restitution. Policy is presumably used here to refer to utilitarian considerations of general welfare as opposed to matters of private justice as between the two parties. In fact, as Lord Goff recently said in connection with the law of restitution, "[the court's] task is essentially to do justice between the parties in the particular case before us".[246] It is difficult to accept that the common law imposes on the defendant a liability to make a payment to the defendant merely in order to promote the public interest, and there do not seem to be any recognised claims that need to be interpreted in this way.[247]

Absence of juristic basis

There has been some discussion over what is supposed to be an alternative approach to the basis for a restitutionary claim, viz. that a claim arises not where there is a vitiating factor affecting the transfer, but where there is no "juristic basis" for it. This latter formulation has ostensibly been adopted in Canada and is said to be the approach in civil law systems.[248] It is said that the juristic basis approach is quite distinct from and foreign to the vitiating factor approach of English law.[249] The concept of juristic basis seems to be open to different interpretations. First, juristic basis might be understood as simply the converse of vitiation, so that there is a juristic basis for a transfer where the transfer is based on a properly formed—i.e. unvitiated—intention. Then it is clear that there is no fundamental difference between the two approaches, merely a difference of terminology. The vitiating factor formulation is preferable, because an issue arising in relation to vitiation tends to be specific to the type of vitiating factor in issue.

---

[244] Birks (1989*a*), 294ff.
[245] Ibid., 294ff. See at 203–206 above, Chap. 3 at 82, and Chap. 6 at 217–23.
[246] *Woolwich v IRC* [1993] AC 70, 174.
[247] Leaving aside disgorgement and punishment, which include some cases of "private illegality". Of course this involves a controversial assumption about the nature of the common law.
[248] L.D. Smith (1992); Krebs (1999); Birks (1993), 231ff.
[249] Birks (1993), 232.

Secondly, there seems to be a possible interpretation that does make the jurisitic basis approach substantively different from the vitiated intention approach. This is that whether there is a jurisitic basis depends not on whether the plaintiff's intention was vitiated, but on whether his purpose was achieved. For example, the purpose might be to discharge a debt, to make a gift, or to make a payment with a view to a reciprocal benefit, as in the case of a payment under a contract, and if the purpose is not achieved there is no juristic basis. This approach seems to be equivalent to the "failure of consideration" or "failure of condition" theory of restitution, which was considered in Chapters 2 and 3.[250] The transfer is conditional on the success of the plaintiff's purpose, and if the purpose is not achieved the transfer must be repaid. As noted above,[251] this approach would deal satisfactorily with many cases of mistake; for example, if a payment is made with a view to discharging a debt, and because of a mistake it fails to do that, it would be recoverable. The effect of allowing a claim on this basis would be to eliminate any defence based on assumption of risk, because where the plaintiff is in doubt about the position he can simply make a conditional payment for the specified purpose, to be returnable if it turns out not to be due. This approach cannot however apply generally to replace the vitiating factor approach. (In other words failure of condition cannot encompass all vitiating factors.) For example, in a case of duress the plaintiff's purpose is to prevent the defendant from carrying out the threat, and this would presumably usually be achieved by the payment. But the claim for restitution should not of course turn on whether this is so or not.

More importantly, it is at the very heart of restitution, or at least restitution for vitiated transfers of wealth, that it is concerned with protecting the plaintiff against transfers of his wealth that are inconsistent with his right to decide on the application if his wealth, i.e. that do not result from an autonomous decision made by him or with his authority. This provides a convincing moral underpinning to the law of restitution, and distinguishes it clearly from that part of the law that provides facilitative rules that enable the plaintiff to make transfers on terms of his own choosing. The theory of failure of consideration or failure of condition, if it were valid, would fall into the latter part of the law; and, as argued in Chapters 2 and 3, it is not in fact a valid part of the law because it is inconsistent with the well-established rule that the plaintiff should not be able to subject the defendant to a liability without the defendant's agreement.[252] It is sometimes argued that the vitiating factor approach is not sufficiently coherent or general, consisting merely of various distinct and unrelated grounds for restitution. But the various vitiating factors are unified by their effect in subverting the plaintiff's decision-making, and the number of different grounds is a contingent fact determined by the nature of human decision-making.

[250] See also Chap. 6 below.
[251] At 174 above.
[252] As discussed in Chaps. 2 and 3, in fact the requirement that the condition be accepted avoids this danger but at the expense of showing that the liability is actually contractual.

One possible example of the jurisitic basis approach is "no consideration" as the basis for a claim in *Woolwich*. Here the plaintiff has made a payment where he knows or suspects that it is not due, so that he is not mistaken (or has assumed the risk of a mistake), but he does not mean to make a gift. There is still a claim, however, even though there is strictly no vitiating factor (leaving aside the possibility of duress). As argued above, one approach is to say that this is an exceptional case where the claim might be justified on the basis of a special responsibility of the defendant in relation to the determination of the amount due. The special responsibility would mean that the plaintiff has a power to make a payment for a specified purpose, viz. the discharge of the true tax liability, and on the condition that any surplus is to be repaid, the condition to be binding on the authority irrespective of its agreement. This is consistent with the juristic basis approach, in the second sense above. There may be good reason to apply this approach in the special circumstances of tax payment, because of the relationship between the parties. One might argue that it should apply more widely in relation to payments made for the purpose of discharging a debt. But, even if this is so, it does not mean that the juristic basis approach is generally preferable or that it provides a general alternative to the vitiating factor approach, for the reasons given above.[253]

---

[253] See also the discussion of *Westdeutsche Landesbank Girozentrale v Islington LBC* [1994] 4 All ER 890 in the next chapter.

6

Vitiated Transfers and Contracts

VITIATED TRANSFERS UNDER VALID CONTRACTS

I T IS POSSIBLE in principle for a party to a valid contract to make a vitiated transfer pursuant to it. For example, he might intend to pay half the amount due under the contract, and by mistake pay the full amount due. Prima facie, he should have a restitutionary claim to recover the overpayment. However, the other party will usually be able to resist the claim, either by way of a counter-claim for the amount due, or by way of a defence of bona fide purchase to the restitutionary claim.[1] Often such issues are likely to be settled as if they were purely a matter of contract law, and without any reference to the law of restitution. It is also possible that the parties to a continuing contract may have an understanding that payments in excess, whether mistaken or deliberate, should be credited to the payer and set against future liabilities. Then the issue truly would be purely a matter of contract.[2]

It is widely thought that payment or other performance under a valid contract, even though not affected in any way by a vitiating factor, can generate a restitutionary claim on the termination of the contract as a result of breach or frustration. This is the restitutionary theory of failure of consideration, or the restitutionary conditional transfer theory. The failure of the contract to go to completion is regarded as the failure of a condition on which the plaintiff rendered his performance, which is taken to generate a right to have the performance reversed. This theory was discussed and rejected in earlier chapters.[3]

TRANSFERS UNDER VOID CONTRACTS

The basis of the restitutionary claim

There can surely be no doubt that a claim for restitution must arise when a transfer is made under a void contract, and there was good authority to this effect, even before the recent controversial case of *Westdeutsche Landesbank Girozentrale v Islington LBC*.[4] In this case such a right to restitution was recognised, but there was some difficulty in determining the relevant vitiating factor,

---

[1] Or a variant of *bona fide* purchase: see further Chap. 7.
[2] e.g. under a standing arrangement with a utility or credit card company.
[3] Chaps. 2 and 3.
[4] [1994] 4 All ER 890 (Hobhouse J and CA), [1994] 2 All ER 961 (HL).

and the case has caused controversy in the literature.[5] The obvious and surely the true vitiating factor where a transfer is made under a void contract is mistake. The plaintiff makes the payment under the mistaken understanding that the contract is valid and that he is therefore protected in respect of the transfer by his rights under the contract.[6] Unfortunately, as discussed in the last chapter, mistake of law was not explicitly recognised as a basis for restitution until the recent decision in *Kleinwort Benson v Lincoln City Council*,[7] which was decided after *Westdeutsche*.

Traditionally, it seems that the basis for restitution has been understood to be the voidness of the contract in itself, although sometimes there may have been a hint that mistake as to voidness is the underlying ground.[8] This is unsurprising—it is surely a natural assumption that the voidness of a contract vitiates a transfer under it, and it must often have gone without saying. As was once said:

> [where] . . . the defendant [has] received moneys belonging to the [plaintiff] under a transaction which had no validity of any sort or kind . . . I should have thought it plain that there being no contract an action for money had and received would lie.[9]

But voidness cannot strictly be a vitiating factor, because a vitiating factor must be something that bears on the way in which the decision to transfer was made, and it is not the voidness but the mistake by the plaintiff as to voidness that affects the decision to transfer. However, to treat voidness as the vitiating factor generally has the same effect and is perhaps an understandable subterfuge if mistake cannot be explicitly relied on.

Where the voidness of a contract was relied on (which strictly should be understood to mean a mistake as to voidness), it has sometimes been said that the basis of the claim was that there was a failure of consideration, or that there was no consideration for the contract.[10] It is not entirely clear, however, how this should be understood. It seems at one time to have been simply a manner of saying that the agreement or purported agreement was void or unenforceable,[11]

---

[5] See e.g. Birks (1993); Burrows (1995); Swadling (1994).

[6] A mistake about whether an agreement is legally enforceable is a mistake of law, whereas a mistake about whether an agreement has been reached is a mistake of fact.

[7] [1998] 3 WLR 1095.

[8] e.g. "it followed that the contract which the directors thought they were making was not a contract at all, but was simply a transaction which in point of law did not exist. . . It was an action brought for money lent under a transaction which was thought to be valid but which was in fact not valid": per Lush J., *Brougham v Dwyer* (1913) 108 LT 504, quoted by Hobhouse J in *Westdeutsche Landesbank* [1994] 4 All ER 890, 926.

[9] Per Lush J, *Brougham v Dwyer* (1913) 108 LT 504, 505, quoted and adopted by Hobhouse J at 926.

[10] e.g. Re Phoenix Life Assurance, *Burges & Stock's* case (1862) 2 J & H 441, 448; *Flood v Irish Provident Assurance Co* [1912] 2 Ch 597; *Sinclair v Brougham* [1914] AC 398. See also Burrows (1993), 305–12. It is not always clear whether "failure of consideration" refers to voidness or lack of reciprocation, as required by the conditional transfer theory. Sometimes the basis for the claim is said to be "ultra vires", referring to the defendant's lack of capacity, which can only mean voidness of the contract so far as the plaintiff is concerned.

[11] See Stoljar (1959), 53; Atiyah (1979), 181. An example discussed in *Westdeutsche Landesbank* is *Hicks v Hicks* (1802) 3 East 16; 102 ER 502.

which is consistent with the old sense of consideration, by which it meant a ground for enforcing a contract.[12] Unfortunately the argument that there is a claim for restitution arising from the voidness of a contract in the form of "failure of consideration" faces the immediate difficulty that "failure of consideration" or "total failure of consideration" is best known as a claim for restitution arising from a valid contract, when the defendant has not performed the contract at all, i.e. where there has been a "total failure" as considered in Chapter 2. This seems to suggest that failure of consideration cannot refer to the voidness of the contract. An explanation for this was proposed in Chapter 2.[13] It was suggested there that the claim arising on total failure of consideration in the case of a valid contract should be understood as originally based on the idea that a valid contract that had not been performed to any extent should be treated as being of no effect, and so equated with a void contract.[14] This is plausible on the basis that a contract was understood to protect the contracting parties' reliance on it. It would also imply, of course, that the total failure requirement applies only with respect to valid contracts and not with respect to void contracts. As argued in Chapter 2, this theory seems to account for the existing law and terminology, although it is not ultimately defensible as a matter of principle.

The problem came to a head in *Westdeutsche Landesbank* and the literature that followed the case. In *Westdeutsche Landesbank* the parties had entered into a "swap contract",[15] which was held void as ultra vires the defendant local authority.[16] The plaintiff bank, which had paid more than it had received under the contract, sought to recover the difference. Presumably in the light of the difficulty concerning failure of consideration and valid contracts, it seems to have been assumed that the doctrine of failure of consideration had to be interpreted in accordance with the restitutionary conditional transfer theory, according to which a claim arises from the fact that the contract was not performed as agreed, whether the contract is valid or void. The theory makes no distinction between valid and void contracts, and it seems to follow that in both cases the claim must be governed by the total failure requirement, so that no claim can arise if the defendant has partly performed. This would have meant, however, that there could be no claim on the facts of *Westdeutsche Landesbank*, because

---

[12] Cf above Chap. 2 at 61–63.

[13] Chap. 2 at 60–63.

[14] This is consistent with the following passage quoted by Hobhouse J in *Westdeutsche Landesbank*: "I should have thought it plain that there being no contract an action for money had and received would lie. The case appears to me to be on all fours with one in which money has been advanced on something which was thought to be a contract, but as to which there has been a complete failure of consideration", from *Brougham v Dwyer* (1913) 108 LT 504, 505 per Lush J, quoted by Hobhouse J at 926.

[15] A swap contract is a financial hedging contract that provides for each party to be liable at regular intervals to pay the other a sum measured as the interest on a notional sum, the different parties' payments being determined by different interest rates on the same notional sum, one of the interest rates being variable and the other fixed. Thus there is a net liability from one party to the other, which will depend on how the variable interest rate has changed. For a discussion of swap contracts, see Burrows (1995).

[16] *Hazell v Hammersmith & Fulham BC* [1992] 2 AC 1.

the void contract had been partly performed by the defendant as well as the plaintiff. At the same time, the case showed that the total failure requirement was unjustifiable, because a claim was clearly justified on the facts.[17] This approach in terms of the restitutionary conditional transfer theory seems to have been the approach of Lord Goff when the case reached the House of Lords,[18] although by that stage the point was not in issue, and it was thought that for the lower courts the total failure requirement was not open for reconsideration. The restitutionary conditional transfer theory has of course been criticised and rejected in previous chapters, with respect to both valid and void contracts.[19]

Hobhouse J did, however, find that a claim arose. He relied on *Hicks v Hicks*[20] and the so-called annuity cases as showing that a claim for restitution could arise out of a partly performed void contract. In *Hicks*, the parties had made a contract for an annuity which was void for failure to comply with a statutory requirement for registration. The party who had paid the lump sum was entitled to recover it on the basis of the voidness of the contract, subject to a deduction for the annuity payments he had received. It was held that:

> This was either an annuity or not an annuity. If not an annuity, the sums paid on either side were money had and received by the one party to the other's use.[21]

However, Hobhouse J described the basis of the claim in *Westdeutsche Landesbank*, which he took to be the voidness of the contract, as "absence of consideration" or "no consideration", rather than failure of consideration.[22] Although it is not clear exactly how he understood the concept of "failure of consideration", he took the view that it was a purely contractual doctrine that allowed a claim where a valid contract had not been performed, and that it was not relevant to the claim based on the voidness of the contract. If the claim was based on the distinct ground of absence of consideration, arising from the voidness of the contract, the total failure requirement relating to failure of consideration was inapplicable; and in principle it should not apply because the performance of a contract in whole or in part does not affect its voidness.[23] Thus Hobhouse J held further that in a case of a "closed swap", where the term of a swap contract had expired, and all the payments under it made, a claim for restitution to unwind the void contract and recover payments under it could still arise.[24] By contrast, the restitutionary conditional transfer theory would not

---

[17] Especially because there is no problem in measuring the balance of claims where both parties' performance consists in the payment of money. Cf the recent case of *Goss v Chilcott* [1996] AC 788.

[18] *Westdeutsche Landesbank*, per Lord Goff [1994] 2 All ER 961, 968.

[19] Chaps. 2 and 3 respectively.

[20] (1802) 3 East. 16; 102 ER 502.

[21] (1802) 3 East 16, at 17; 102 ER 502 at 502; cited by Hobhouse J at 923.

[22] At 925ff.

[23] [1994] 4 All ER 890, 924. Similar views were adopted in the Court of Appeal. Under the restitutionary conditional transfer theory the requirement is also unjustified in principle, but the theory implies that the established rule applies to void contracts.

[24] [1994] 4 All ER 890, 936.

permit such a claim, because there is no failure of condition when there has been complete performance of the contract as agreed.

Hobhouse J's decision was criticised on the ground that "absence of consideration" is a new and alien concept to the common law.[25] But in fact "absence of consideration", although a new expression, was used by the judge to refer to a well-established ground for restitution, viz. voidness; unfortunately he was denied the traditional expression to describe it—"failure of consideration"—by the distracting effect of the restitutionary conditional transfer theory. In fact it is this theory and the concept of failure of consideration as an unfulfilled condition that is new and alien to the common law (apart from being untenable). Hobhouse J's decision is consistent with the approach suggested above, according to which failure of consideration has traditionally referred to a void contract, and also by extension to a completely unperformed valid contract.

There was particular criticism of the decision with respect to closed swaps. Partly this was because of inconsistency with the conditional transfer theory; but also it was thought that as a matter of principle a plaintiff could have no complaint arising from a void contract if the contract, although void, had actually been completed as agreed.[26] But the judge's decision was surely correct in this respect. If the claim is based on the voidness of the contract (or a mistake as to its validity), the fact that the defendant has completed the performance specified under the void contract cannot affect the claim to restitution, because the contract remains void even if the performance specified by it has been completed. And it cannot be right to say that a party has no genuine complaint if the void contract has actually been performed as agreed, because if the contract is void it cannot be assumed that the contract represents what the plaintiff truly agreed to, or that it is fair to hold him to what he agreed: this is generally why the contract is void.[27] The decision concerning closed swaps was confirmed in *Guinness Mahon v Kensington & Chelsea RBC*,[28] and furthermore here the court reverted to the traditional expression, "failure of consideration", to refer to the voidness of the contract, Morritt LJ saying,[29] "it is the very fact that the contract is ultra vires which constitutes the total failure of consideration justifying . . . restitution".[30]

---

[25] Birks (1993), 213ff; Swadling (1994), 75ff. It was suggested also that Hobhouse J had adopted a ground for restitution that was equivalent to the civil law concept of "absence of juristic basis". In fact the only plausible sense of "absence of juristic basis" in which it differs from the vitiating factor approach is the sense in which it means failure of a condition (Chap. 5 at 208), and this approach was not adopted by Hobhouse J. Obiter in the House of Lords Lord Goff gave some support to the critics of Hobhouse J: [1996] AC 669, 683.

[26] Birks (1993), 214. Swadling (1994), 80.

[27] This depends on the basis for the voidness. It may be that the law will give some partial effect to an agreement that has been performed that otherwise would be held void. This is the position with respect to some "unenforceable contracts", as discussed in Chap. 3.

[28] [1998] 2 All ER 272.

[29] At 282.

[30] See also *Kleinwort Benson v Lincoln CC* [1998] 3 WLR 1095, 1125, per Lord Goff. It seems that Lord Goff's view was that the claim based on total failure of consideration might lapse, but a separate claim based on mistake would lie anyway; see also Birks (1993).

In the future, the recognition in *Kleinwort Benson* that mistake of law can ground a claim arising from a void contract means that it will be unnecessary to refer to the voidness itself, whether under the label of "failure of consideration" or "absence of consideration", as the basis of the claim. And, as discussed in Chapter 2, the claim arising on total failure of consideration where a valid contract has not been performed should be understood as a contractual reliance claim, not as a restitutionary claim at all, and here also it will be possible to abandon the expression "failure of consideration".

Categories of void contract

"Void contract" tends to be used in two different senses.[31] First, it is often used to refer to a case where there is actually no agreement between the parties, although one or other party thinks that there is. This would include the case where the contract was purportedly entered into on behalf of one party by someone who had no authority, or where one party had no capacity to make the contract; thus it would include *Westdeutsche Landesbank*.[32]

In a distinct sense, "void contract" is also used to refer to a case where there *is* an agreement between the parties, but it is not recognised, or fully recognised, as a valid contract. One type of case is where the contract is "illegal", meaning that the making or performance of the contract involved a wrongful act.[33] Illegal contracts will be discussed briefly below. But there are other cases, where there is apparently an unvitiated agreement, and apparently the making and performing of the agreement is not regarded as wrongful, but the contract is nevertheless void. One example mentioned above is *Hicks v Hicks*, where a statute provided that the contract was void unless duly registered. Again it seems that mistake as to the validity of the contract should provide the basis for a restitutionary claim in respect of a transfer under the contract.[34]

However, there are some void contracts of this sort where no restitutionary claim has been allowed, apparently on the basis that to give effect to it would subvert the invalidating provision. For example, it has been held that a rule rendering a loan contract void must necessarily also exclude a restitutionary claim on the part of the lender to recover the money lent, on the basis that the restitu-

---

[31] Cf Chap. 3 on void contracts.

[32] As suggested in Chap. 3, at 109, there is much to be said for assimilating this type of void contract with the category of voidable contracts. This would mean that the defence of "restitutio in integrum impossible" would be available with respect to both. With respect to a voidable contract, it appears that the restitutionary claim to reverse a transfer traditionally arose not as a claim for money had and received, but as an incident of the claim for rescission: Burrows (1993), 33.

[33] Although, as will be seen below, in the text at 217–18, such a contract is not necessarily void in all cases.

[34] In other cases a contract is said to be unenforceable rather than void as, typically, where there is a formal requirement of writing, although it is not clear whether this is intended to have a different effect. Here also there is presumably a restitutionary claim in respect of a payment under the contract.

tionary claim is exactly equivalent to a contractual debt, and so the restitutionary claim merely resurrects the contract that was supposed to be void. The most notorious example of this is *Sinclair v Brougham*.[35] Here the plaintiff made what it assumed to be a deposit under a banking contract—i.e. a loan contract—with the defendant, which turned out to be running an ultra vires banking business. The plaintiff's claim for money had and received was held to be inconsistent with the ultra vires rule.[36] But reversing a payment under the contract is not the same thing as enforcing the contract; a restitutionary claim is not equivalent to a contractual debt-claim, even apart from the difference in the way the two claims arise.[37] There is surely no reason to deny the restitutionary claim beyond protecting the defendant in respect of any change of position. A further curiosity of the case is that an in rem tracing claim in equity was allowed, and was not regarded as being inconsistent with the ultra vires rule, apparently because the claim was in rem rather than in personam. As argued in Chapters 9 and 10, this reflects a misinterpretation of the relation between the common law and equitable restitutionary claims.[38]

ILLEGAL CONTRACTS

The effect of illegality

Great difficulty has arisen in connection with illegal contracts. Broadly speaking, some contracts are said to be illegal because the making or performance of the contract is wrongful.[39] The law governing the consequences of illegality is complex and disordered.[40] The law will never recognise that a contract can give rise to a duty to commit a wrong, so as to justify an order of specific performance. Furthermore, it seems that generally a wrongdoing party to an illegal contract cannot enforce it by way of a claim for the price of work or goods, or

---

[35] [1914] AC 398; see also *Orakpo v Manson* [1978] AC 95. See the discussion in Mitchell (1994), 149ff.

[36] One ground was based on the implied contract theory, which is now recognised to be insupportable, as noted by Lord Browne-Wilkinson in *Westdeutsche Landesbank* [1996] 2 All ER 961, 993.

[37] The restitutionary claim is a claim to surviving value, which as discussed in Chap. 9 is distinct from a debt claim.

[38] There is a line of cases that permit a plaintiff lender under an ultra vires loan to be subrogated to the claim of a previous lender who was paid off with money lent by the plaintiff, as an exception to the rule denying the restitutionary claim. The rationale may be that in so far as the money was used to pay off previous lending the aggregate debt of the borrower will not exceed its borrowing limit and so will not be ultra vires: see Mitchell (1994), 153.

[39] Sometimes this is because the contract involves the commission of a wrong that is separately recognised as a tort or crime. In other cases, a contract is said to be illegal because it relates to some activity that is regarded as wrongful, at least in this particular context, although it may not be criminal or tortious, e.g. contracts that subvert marriage or the administration of the law: see Law Commission (1999), para. 1.6ff. Such contracts are said to be contrary to public policy.

[40] Prompting Law Commission (1997).

a quantum meruit for payment under the contract, or damages for non-performance.[41] But a party to the illegal contract may not himself be a wrong-doer, and then it seems that he may sometimes be able to enforce it.[42]

It might appear that where a payment or transfer of goods was made under an illegal contract it should be recoverable through a restitutionary claim on the basis that the payment or transfer was vitiated by the voidness of the contract, or by a mistake as to its voidness. But again the general rule is that the claim will be refused on the basis that it is a claim arising out of a wrong.[43] For example, in *Parkinson v College of Ambulance Ltd*[44] the plaintiff had paid the defendant in advance to procure an honour for him, the defendant having represented falsely that he could do so. No honour was forthcoming, but the plaintiff was denied any claim to recover his prepayment, whether on the basis of misrepresentation, which would have made the contract voidable, or under the contract. This is sometimes said to be the defence of illegality to the restitutionary claim.[45]

However, there are some cases where a restitutionary claim will be allowed. First, there are various types of case where the plaintiff is said not to have been in pari delicto, i.e. the plaintiff was not complicit in the wrongdoing, which was attributable only to the defendant. Here a restitutionary claim is allowed, but not, it seems, on the basis that the plaintiff's innocence of the wrongdoing is itself a ground of restitution,[46] but on the basis that, because of the plaintiff's innocence, the illegality does not exclude a restitutionary claim if he can show a vitiating factor. For example, in *Oom v Bruce*,[47] the plaintiff took out a policy of insurance in respect of goods in Russia that was illegal because war had been declared between Russia and Britain, but the plaintiff was entitled to recover the premium paid on the basis of mistake because he did not know of the state of war.

Where a contract is rendered void by statute, the statute may be construed to place the responsibility for compliance on one party, so that the other party can claim not to be in pari delicto when a contract is entered into contrary to the statute. For example, in *Re Cavalier Insurance Co Ltd*,[48] the plaintiff took out insurance from an insurer that was prohibited from offering the type of insurance in question, so that the insurance policy was held illegal. The insured sought to recover the premiums he had paid, and the judge said that:

[41] This is something of a simplification; see generally Enonchong (1998), 32ff. In *Mohammed v Alaga* [1999] 3 All ER 699 it was held that a quantum meruit could be awarded in respect of work done under an illegal contract, because the claim was restitutionary not contractual.

[42] The question seems to be whether that party was actually subject to duty under the invalidating rule, and whether the duty can arise without knowledge.

[43] Enonchong (1998), 74; Treitel (1999), 452.

[44] [1952] 2 KB 1.

[45] Birks (1989a), 424.

[46] Innocence of wrongdoing cannot itself be a vitiating factor because it discloses nothing that affects the plaintiff's decision to transfer.

[47] (1810) 12 East 225.

[48] [1989] 2 Lloyd's Rep. 430.

where the statutory duty was laid exclusively on the shoulders of the insurer for the protection of insured persons and the insured had no reason to suspect that he was being asked to enter into a void contract [the circumstances] amply justify treating the insured as not equally delictual . . . and therefore entitled to recover the premiums.[49]

A similar, earlier case is *Kiriri Cotton Co Ltd v Dewani*[50] which concerned regulations that prohibited landlords from demanding a premium from tenants in addition to the rent. The plaintiff tenant paid a premium and was then successful in a claim to recover it. It was held that the defendant landlord was the party upon whom the statute laid the duty not to enter a contract requiring a premium from the tenant, and the plaintiff was accordingly not in pari delicto and was entitled to make a restitutionary claim. Although in *Kiriri* the judgment implied that the vitiating factor was mistake, the plaintiff having been ignorant of the prohibition on charging a premium, and the same vitiating factor could explain *Re Cavalier Insurance*, where a statute prohibits a contract for the benefit of one of the contracting parties, it seems that a contracting party may be able to recover a payment under the contract even where he made no mistake.[51] It seems that an alternative basis for the plaintiff's claim is to remove the defendant's wrongful profit, irrespective of whether the plaintiff's transfer was vitiated, i.e. disgorgement rather than restitution for a vitiated transfer.

Secondly, there is a rule that if the plaintiff repudiates the illegal purpose before the contract has been performed he can recover his payment, although the scope of the rule is controversial.[52] The rationale for the claim seems to be that the plaintiff is not conclusively a wrongdoer merely by virtue of having paid over the money with a dishonest purpose in mind, if the dishonest purpose has not yet been carried out and it is still possible to step back from it. Thus if he does seek to withdraw from the contract before any wrong has been committed he should be treated as an innocent party.[53] However, this does not make clear exactly what the basis of the claim is; it does not appear that there is necessarily a vitiating factor, or any basis for a contract claim, even leaving aside the illegality. Again it seems that the rationale for the claim is disgorgement, to remove the defendant's wrongful profit through the receipt of a payment made for a wrongful purpose. It may be that it is justifiable to give the plaintiff a claim as a means of removing the defendant's wrongful profit, provided that the plaintiff is himself innocent. At the same time, the claim serves to encourage the plaintiff to repudiate the contract before the wrongful purpose is carried out.[54]

---

[49] Ibid., 450 per Knox J.

[50] [1960] AC 192.

[51] It seems that non in pari delicto is then itself the ground for recovery: Treitel (1999), 453. Another possible vitiating factor is duress. In *Kiriri*, the defendant had a duty to lease the property without charging a premium, and procured the contract by refusing to contract except wrongfully, which amounts to duress: see above, Chap. 5 at 186.

[52] This is the doctrine of locus poenitentiae.

[53] Just as normally a party is not regarded as a wrongdoer until he has committed himself to the act as opposed to having made preparatory moves towards it.

[54] It is sometimes argued that the claim is based on complete failure of consideration; but on the analysis in Chaps. 2 and 3 such a claim would amount to enforcing the contract.

Lastly there is a rule that a party can assert his title to money or goods and thereby recover them or their value, even if the title was acquired through an illegal transaction. For example in *Bowmakers Ltd v Barnet Instruments Ltd*,[55] there was a hire purchase agreement under which goods were acquired and vested in the plaintiff and then hired by the defendant. The agreement was illegal under regulations governing hire purchase agreements. The defendant failed to pay the instalments under the agreement and disposed of the hire goods without authority from the plaintiff. The plaintiff was successful in a claim for conversion in respect of the disposal of the goods, because for this he needed only to assert his title to the goods in the possession of the defendant.[56]

More difficulty has arisen in connection with equitable title under a resulting trust. In *Tinsley v Milligan*,[57] the plaintiff and the defendant purchased a house jointly but put it in the name of the defendant only, in order to enable the plaintiff to claim social security benefits that she was not actually eligible for, given her half share of the house. The defendant subsequently sought to deny the plaintiff's interest, but the plaintiff was allowed to assert her interest notwithstanding that it arose in connection with an illegal transaction, viz. the fraudulent arrangement between the parties, because the claim was simply based on her equitable title under a resulting trust.[58] But it was said that if the plaintiff had had to invoke the illegal transaction to prove her title she could not have claimed. This would be the case where to evade his creditors the plaintiff transfers property to his son, and, in the absence of proof of the plaintiff's true purpose, there is a presumption of advancement, to the effect that the transfer was for the benefit of the son, and not on resulting trust for the father. In such a case the father could not assert an equitable title under a resulting trust because to rebut the presumption of advancement he would need to prove the wrongful purpose.[59] But in *Tribe v Tribe*[60] it was held that the plaintiff could indeed assert his equitable title, notwithstanding that he had to prove his wrongful purpose in order to rebut the presumption of resulting trust, if the wrongful purpose had not yet been put into effect—i.e. if no creditors had been deceived—on the basis that the plaintiff could repudiate the illegal purpose as discussed above. These cases, it should be noted, are not restitutionary. They involve the assertion of title that was created or transferred voluntarily, not through a vitiated transfer, and the effect of the rule is to recognise the transfer or creation of title

---

[55] [1945] KB 65.

[56] The curious effect is that, although the regulation of hire purchase agreements is presumably designed to protect the hirer/debtor, not the owner/creditor, the owner-creditor is protected by his title to the hire goods.

[57] [1994] 1 AC 340.

[58] Resulting trusts are considered in Chap. 10.

[59] e.g. *Chettiar v Chettiar* [1962] AC 294. There is no obvious reason why the availability of the presumption of advancement should be so significant, as pointed out by Nourse LJ in *Silverwood v Silverwood* (1997) 74 P & CR 453.

[60] [1996] Ch 107.

notwithstanding that it was made pursuant to or in connection with an illegal agreement or arrangement.[61]

The problem with illegal contracts

The important principle behind the rules on illegality is that the law cannot recognise a claim that enables someone to profit through wrongdoing.[62] This certainly appears to provide the basis for denying a claim to be paid for doing something that was wrongful. So far as the law gives effect to this principle it is an aspect of the law of disgorgement (including forfeiture), which is considered in Chapter 11. In other cases the effect of the illegality rules is not to prevent the plaintiff from profiting, but to prevent him from recovering losses incurred when the contract is stopped half way through after he has made a payment, or incurred expenditure, without having received anything in return. This is the case where the claim is a restitutionary claim to reverse a transfer and also where it is a contractual claim to recover a payment made under the contract, or compensation for expenditure. The effect is simply to inflict a loss on the plaintiff relative to the position that he would have been in if the contract had been completed or enforced in the normal way. This seems to be explicable only as punishment of the plaintiff for his involvement in wrongdoing. Thus here the law is an aspect of the law relating to punishment, and in particular punishment in civil proceedings, of which the law of disgorgement is really a part.[63] (In the following discussion "punishment" will be used to encompass disgorgement and forfeiture.)

The infliction of punishment on either the plaintiff or the defendant does not serve to do justice as between the two of them, but to promote the public interest in compliance with the law.[64] Thus if illegality is invoked to frustrate the plaintiff's claim it is not aptly described as a defence, because it is not designed to safeguard an interest of the defendant, but to punish the plaintiff. And if the defendant succeeds in the objection he receives a windfall relative to the just position as between the two parties themselves. As it was put many years ago by Lord Mansfield:

> It is not for [the defendant's] sake . . . that the objection is ever allowed; but it is founded in general principles of policy, which the defendant has advantage of, contrary to the real justice, as between him and the plaintiff, by accident, if I may so say.[65]

---

[61] There is the possibility of a clash with the rule denying a restitutionary claim arising out of an illegal contract, where the restitutionary claim takes the form of an equitable interest under a constructive trust.

[62] And it cannot recognise a contractual duty to do a wrong.

[63] See Chap. 11.

[64] See the discussion in Chap. 11.

[65] *Holman v Johnson* (1775) 1 Cowp 341, 343.

Lord Mansfield expressed the policy in this way: "[n]o Court will lend its aid to a man who founds his cause of action upon an immoral or an illegal act".[66] This should be understood to express the punitive rationale advanced above, that wrongdoing should be punished by preventing the wrongdoer from gaining a benefit from his wrong, or from recovering for losses incurred by him with a view to profiting through the wrong, through a legal claim, i.e. by founding a cause of action on a wrong.[67] Conversely, in pursuance of the same policy it may be justified to *confer* a claim for disgorgement on the plaintiff, as arguably in a case like *Kiriri* as suggested above, or in a case of repudiation of an illegal purpose.

This seems to suggest that the court should approach its function in the following way: it should determine what the plaintiff's position would be if the position were resolved purely on the basis of what is fair as between the parties, assuming the contract to be valid, but to have been terminated by agreement or frustrated. This might be referred to as the baseline position. Then it should assess what the appropriate punishment of the plaintiff should be in pecuniary terms for the wrong that he has committed; and then it should deny the plaintiff's claim just in so far as necessary to leave him out of pocket, relative to the baseline position, by the measure of appropriate punishment.[68] On the law as it stands, one way in which the law departs from this model is that the general rule against enforcing illegal contracts or restitutionary claims arising out of illegal contracts may have the effect of punishing a party who did not himself commit a wrong at all.[69] But often the general rule is qualified to protect a party who was not himself guilty of any wrongdoing; thus the general rule denying any restitutionary claim is subject to exceptions where the plaintiff is not in pari delicto. Secondly, the law is inconsistent with the model above in stipulating always for an all-or-nothing outcome: either the plaintiff is allowed his claim in full or he is not. This means that the punishment may be excessive, because if the plaintiff is not allowed a claim the loss inflicted relative to the baseline position may exceed the appropriate measure of punishment.[70] For example in *Parkinson*, where the plaintiff paid a sum in advance for an honour, the loss of the whole

---

[66] Ibid.

[67] There is an alternative interpretation, that the claim should be denied because it is undignified or unseemly for a court to be involved in determining rights under illegal contracts: see the discussion in Enonchong (1998), 17. But this is a weak argument. The court's task is to determine the rights of the parties. No doubt it would be unseemly for a court to hold that a plaintiff wrongdoer could enforce a contractual claim that enabled it to profit through a wrong, but this is simply to say that this should not be the law. The reason is not that it is unseemly, but that the plaintiff should not be allowed to profit from his wrong. The problem is that sometimes the court does not appear to have the necessary measures open to it to deal properly with the issue.

[68] This accommodation (so far as it is possible) between punishment and justice as between the parties is "sterring the middle course": *Saunders v Edwards* [1987] 1 WLR 1116, 1134, per Bingham LJ; Enonchong (1998), 19.

[69] e.g. where an insured is not allowed to enforce an insurance contract because the insurance company was in breach of regulatory rules: *Re Cavalier Insurance Co Ltd* [1989] 2 Lloyd's Rep. 430.

[70] See Coote (1972).

of this sum may have been an excessive penalty in the light of the extent of his culpability.

It has been suggested that the courts should have a discretion.[71] This might appear to enable the court to allow partial recovery, in just the way that the principle above prescribes, and this will indeed often be the case. Normally a discretion is inappropriate as a means of resolving civil claims, because the legal relation between the parties should be a matter of well defined rules or principles. But the determination of punishment is customarily discretionary, and if it is justified at all for punishment to be relevant to the determination of civil claims, it seems that it must be justified to provide for a discretion. But, even with a discretion, the court would be left with an intractable problem. In the usual case where punishment is imposed in civil proceedings, in the form of punitive damages or disgorgement, there is a defendant wrongdoer and an innocent plaintiff, the victim of the wrong. Punishment of the wrongdoer will take effect by way of a pecuniary liability to the plaintiff, who receives a windfall. In the case of an illegal contract, punishment takes effect by way of the denial of a restitutionary or contractual claim rather than a pecuniary liability. The problem is that where, as will often be the case, the plaintiff and the defendant are both wrongdoers, it will be impossible to inflict punishment on *both* parties, because the imposition of punishment on one party constitutes a benefit to the other. To take *Parkinson* again, denying the plaintiff a remedy may have been an appropriate response to the plaintiff's wrongdoing considered in isolation, but it left the defendant, who was also a wrongdoer, with a profit from the half-performed contract. It is in this type of case, in particular, that "[t]he objection, that [the] contract is immoral or illegal . . . sounds . . . very ill in the mouth of the defendant".[72] Thus a general regime that deals satisfactorily with illegal contracts, i.e. that inflicts appropriate punishment on both parties, cannot be achieved purely through the clumsy instrument of withholding civil claims. It will require a power to impose fines or to order confiscation payable to the state (or to some third party victim of the wrong).[73] This part of the law has to be addressed as part of the wider issue of the role of disgorgement and punishment in civil proceedings, which is discussed in Chapter 11.

---

[71] This is the position under s.7 of the New Zealand Illegal Contracts Act 1970, and has been recommended in England: Law Commission (1999), Part 7. In *Tinsley v Milligan*, the House of Lords rejected the "public conscience test", which Lord Goff equated with a judicial discretion: [1994] AC 340, 362–4. The public conscience test, which requires the court to determine the availability of a claim in terms of whether it would be an affront to the public to allow it, is objectionable (if it is to be taken literally) on the distinct ground that it is an abdication of the court's responsibility to make its own judgment in favour of consulting public opinion, quite apart from whether it involves the exercise of discretion.

[72] *Holman v Johnson* (1775) 1 Cowp 341, 343 per Lord Mansfield. It is presumably less objectionable to allow a windfall to a defendant who is not a wrongdoer.

[73] Other objections to punishment and disgorgement in civil proceedings are discussed in Chap. 11 below.

7

Change of Position, Surviving Value and Bona Fide Purchase

STRICT LIABILITY

RESTITUTION FOR A vitiated transfer reverses a vitiated transfer from the plaintiff to the defendant in order to protect the plaintiff's interest in control over his wealth. To require the defendant to pay back what he has received is no injustice to him because he is merely relieved of what he ought not to have received; he cannot be said to have suffered a loss. By the nature of the claim it arises from the defendant's receipt of the transfer: given that the transfer was vitiated, the claim against the defendant is justified once he has received the transfer. Sometimes the defendant has committed a wrong in procuring the transfer to him, as where he induces it by deceit or duress, but the restitutionary claim (as opposed to a claim for compensation for the wrong) arises merely from the receipt of the vitiated transfer and not from any breach of duty.[1] The restitutionary claim, in other words, is necessarily a matter of strict liability. It follows, furthermore, that it is immaterial whether the defendant knew, or ought to have known, that the transfer was affected by a vitiating factor. The transfer may even take effect and the liability arise without the defendant's being aware that he has received anything. The traditional common law claim for money had and received arising from a vitiated transfer has indeed always been based on strict liability. It has been thought that in equity the restitutionary claim is not based on strict liability. This is not so, however, as will be seen in Chapter 10;[2] indeed, it cannot rationally be so for a restitutionary claim to reverse a vitiated transfer.[3]

CHANGE OF POSITION AND SURVIVING VALUE

Change of position

A defendant may receive a vitiated transfer and, on the assumption that he is to that extent wealthier, spend money that he would not otherwise have spent. If

---

[1] See Chap. 1 at 8, Chap. 5 at 160.

[2] See Chap. 11 at 340–42.

[3] Cf where restitution is used in a purely remedial sense to refer to a remedy in contract and tort: see Chap. 1.

the defendant remains liable for the full value that he received, he will be worse off than if he had never received the payment. This would be unjustified (unless, as will be seen below, one can say that the defendant ought to have known that he was liable to return the money received). The restitutionary liability is based on the fact that the defendant has received a windfall—that he is in surplus, as it were—and therefore that overall he will not be prejudiced by the restitutionary liability; if it would prejudice him, it should be reduced accordingly.[4] This is the "change of position" defence: the plaintiff's claim diminishes to the extent that the defendant's position has changed in consequence of the receipt.

The change of position defence was explicitly recognised for the first time in *Lipkin Gorman v Karpnale*.[5] There Lord Goff gave as a clear example a case where the defendant pays part of the money received to charity: to the extent of the payment to charity the defendant is protected from the plaintiff's claim.[6] The application of the defence to the actual facts in the case, which will be considered below, was less convincing. The main difficulty in applying change of position is evidential: how to establish to what extent there has been a change in the defendant's position that would not have occurred in the absence of the receipt. It is usually said that the defendant's expenditure must be exceptional or extraordinary. The position is sometimes clear, as where the defendant has incurred expenditure that he would never ordinarily spend his money on; but it will be more difficult if the defendant simply raises his standard of living by spending more on the things he usually spends his money on. This is an issue of fact that a court has to grapple with as best it can. In principle, one would think that doubt should be resolved in favour of the defendant, and in some circumstances, as considered below, there is an evidential presumption in his favour.

The change of position defence is usually formulated in terms of reliance on receipt: for example, "the central element [of the defence of change of position] is that the defendant has acted to his or her detriment on the faith of the receipt".[7] Change of position through reliance is no doubt the most common form of the defence, but it is not the only form of change of position, and this formulation is consequently too narrow. In accordance with its rationale stated above, the defence should apply where the change of position results from the receipt, even if not by way of the defendant's reliance. For example, the defendant might receive £1,000 by mistake, which is paid into his bank account, and then lost in the bank's insolvency.[8] Here the defendant has lost £1,000 in the insolvency that he would not have lost but for the receipt, and if he remains liable to repay the £1,000 he will end up worse off by £1,000 than if had not received anything. Clearly the change of position defence must apply. Another

---

    [4] Cf Simester (1997), 126.
    [5] [1991] 3 WLR 10; *Baylis v Bishop of London* [1913] 1 Ch 127 exemplifies the old position denying change of position.
    [6] [1991] 3 WLR 10, at 34.
    [7] *David Securities v Commonwealth Bank of Australia* (1992) 175 CLR 353, 385, citing Birks (1989a), 410; original italics excised.
    [8] Birks (1992a), 141.

example of non-reliance change of position might arise where the defendant receives £100, and then loses £100 to a pickpocket. Change of position applies if he would not have lost £100 to a pick pocket if he had not had the receipt, which might depend on whether the same notes or coins received by the defendant were taken from him.[9] In general there is change of position whenever a loss is caused by the receipt, in the sense that it would not have occurred without the receipt. This may give rise to very difficult issues of fact, and the outcome may be fortuitous.[10] But this reflects the nature of the situation, not any incoherence of principle.[11]

Surviving value

As Birks has pointed out,[12] the change of position defence can be expressed in two different ways. On the orthodox formulation, the plaintiff has a prima facie claim for the value received by the defendant, but the defendant has a defence to the extent of his change of position. This is the form of expression adopted above. The other formulation combines the two elements of the overall measure of the claim by saying that the plaintiff has a claim to "surviving value". At the time of receipt, surviving value is the value received, but surviving value changes according to the defendant's change of position, i.e. with any loss in the defendant's estate that would not have occurred without the receipt. The two formulations seem to be exactly equivalent. It might seem that there is a difference in that the first formulation seems to present change of position as a defence and the second as an element of the claim. This would appear to be of consequence with respect to the onus of proof. In fact, as will be seen below and in Chapter 9, the second formulation is the correct one, because (quite apart from evidential matters) surviving value is a fundamental concept that is crucial in cases where third party rights are involved. However, there is no reason why this should determine the issue of onus of proof.[13] Whether or not change of position is properly understood as a defence, it is convenient for the purposes of exposition sometimes to express it as such (as with respect to bona fide purchase which is considered below).

---

[9] It is possible that even though the notes received were taken, the defendant would have lost the same sum anyway, say because he would have put £100 from another source in the pocket from which the notes were taken if he had not received the £100 in question.

[10] Birks (1996), 61; cf Chap. 9, at 295.

[11] Birks notes the case where a loss is caused by the receipt in the strict but-for sense, but would not usually be taken to be a cause in law, as for example where the defendant receives £1,000 and then suffers a loss in an accident on the way to depositing the money in the bank. The receipt would not be regarded as a cause of the loss because the link is incidental and so there is no change of position: Birks (1992*a*), 142.

[12] Birks (1996), 52, 71ff.

[13] Cf below at n 131.

The transfer to the defendant will often take the form of the transfer of property, or an asset.[14] The initial value received will be the value of the asset. It may be that a change of position takes place through a loss of the asset received or a loss in its value, so that surviving value continues to correspond to the value of the asset in the defendant's estate; but it is equally possible for a change of position to occur by expenditure that leaves the value of the asset unaltered. Surviving value is not necessarily value embodied in a particular asset; it is such value in the defendant's estate as is attributable to the receipt, in the sense that the defendant would not have had it but for the receipt.

Proprietary tracing claims

The conventional view is that, before any question of a claim for restitution for a vitiated transfer arises, there is a separate issue of whether ownership in an asset transferred into the defendant's possession or control has passed to the defendant; if it has not, the plaintiff will have a claim arising in respect of his ownership of the asset rather than in restitution for a vitiated transfer. It is also thought that this claim based on ownership can arise not only in respect of the original asset transferred, but in respect of other assets that, under the doctrine of tracing, are deemed to take the place of the original asset so far as the plaintiff's claim is concerned.[15] The subject of such a claim is referred to as the traceable proceeds of the asset received. Thus it appears that an important distinction must be drawn between surviving value in the defendant's estate, which is the subject of the restitutionary claim and may sometimes be represented by the value of a particular asset, and "traceable proceeds", which form the subject of a claim to ownership. However the "traceable proceeds" are also sometimes described as surviving value; thus Birks has described the subject of the restitutionary claim as "abstractly surviving value" and the subject of the claim to ownership based on tracing as "traceable surviving value".[16] The complex issues arising from the relation between restitution and property will be dealt with in Chapters 9 and 10. The view reached there is that the distinction between the two concepts identified by Birks is spurious, and that there is in reality only a single concept of surviving value. This does not for the most part affect the discussion in this chapter, which can be understood to relate to the restitutionary claim to "abstractly surviving value".

Surviving value and consequential value received

The measure of surviving value is the increase in value to the defendant's estate due to the vitiated transfer, less loss to the defendant's estate that would not

---

[14] It is not necessary for present purposes to establish what counts as property or an asset.

[15] There is fierce controversy, as discussed in Chaps. 9 and 10, about whether the "ownership claim" is restitutionary or proprietary.

[16] Birks (1996), 52, 71ff; Birks (1997*b*); cf Nolan (1995), 183–4.

have occurred but for the receipt, i.e. that was caused by the receipt. The loss could be the loss of an asset, by destruction or loss or consumption or transfer to someone else, or opportunity cost, in the sense of value that would have been acquired but was not, as where as a result of the receipt the defendant refrained from exploiting an opportunity he would otherwise have taken up.[17] Conversely, in principle the defendant should bring into account any value that he acquires in consequence of the receipt, to offset any loss resulting from the receipt. Thus, for example, if the defendant receives £1,000 and uses it to buy an asset worth £500, the value of the asset acquired is surviving value, so that the surviving value is £500.[18] The asset bought is usually referred to as an exchange product.[19]

Exchange products

No difficulty arises in measuring the value of the exchange product where it is an investment or a commodity having a reasonably well-defined, uniform value.[20] But the product could be land or goods having a special value to the defendant, differing from both the market value of the product and the value to the plaintiff. What then is the surviving value due to the exchange product? The difficulty is avoided if the defendant has the option of handing over the exchange product to the plaintiff in satisfaction of the liability for the value received and used to buy the product.[21] If the defendant has the option of handing the product over but prefers to keep it, he should be liable for the amount that he paid for the exchange product (which is the value received, or that part of it that was used in the purchase). Only to the extent that the plaintiff has recovered the value of the transfer should the defendant be entitled to profit from the additional value of the exchange product to him.[22]

---

[17] As in the recent Australian case of *Gertsch v Atsas* [1999] NSWSC 898, para. 98.

[18] See *Lipkin Gorman v Karpnale* [1991] 3 WLR 10, 16 per Lord Templeman. This assumes that the defendant would not have bought the asset in the absence of the receipt. See also *Gertsch v Atsas*, [1999] NSWSC 898, para. 96.

[19] Some people would object to this label on the basis that it is concerned with "traceably surviving value" rather than "abstractly surviving value". See further the section on tracing in Chap. 9.

[20] As one can say for a second hand car in the example given by Lord Templeman, above n 18.

[21] Cf the discussion of specific restitution in Chap. 9 at 287. The alternative seems to be to estimate the price of the exchange product on an immediate forced resale, but this also may be very difficult to measure.

[22] A more difficult case is where the defendant has bought an asset that is not a marketable commodity partly with surviving value and partly with other money. If the asset has a special value to the defendant, there may be great difficulty, because the option of transferring the product to the plaintiff cannot arise. This may be a case of wealth that cannot be measured and treated as surviving value because its realisation is liable to prejudice the defendant, so that no claim should be available at all. There was a complicating factor in *RBC Dominion Securities v Dawson* (1994) 111 DLR (4th) 230, where the defendant sold old furniture in order to buy new furniture with the value received through the vitiated transfer. The best measure of the surviving value seems to be the resale price of the new furniture less the cost of acquiring an equivalent to the old furniture. This would be very difficult to measure, and the claim was denied. See also Bryan (1996), 83; and Nolan (1995), 139ff.

Value received used in buying a service

Where the defendant uses up the value received in buying a service, for example a haircut or a meal or visit to the cinema, the defendant will be said to have consumed or dissipated the value received; there will be no surviving value and no restitutionary claim to surviving value.[23] Posssibly one might argue that instead one should attempt to determine the value of the benefit to the defendant, and require him to account for that value to the plaintiff. But if a claim is to arise in respect of such a benefit, it must be not a claim to recover surviving wealth, which has been dissipated, but a claim for payment for a benefit conferred on the defendant under an imputed contract, for which, as discussed in Chapter 3, the two conditions—the officiousness condition and the benefit condition—must be satisfied.[24]

The claim for restitution for a vitiated transfer protects the plaintiff's interest in his own wealth, and it operates in respect of wealth in the defendant's estate; surviving value, in other words, is a measure of wealth attributable to the vitiated transfer. The difficulties that arise are difficulties of measurement, either measuring loss of wealth, or measuring wealth-benefits received. These issues are considered further in connection with tracing in Chapter 9.

A wider unfairness defence?

Thus change of position is an issue of fact, and more precisely an issue of causation, concerned with loss and gain in wealth to the defendant resulting from the receipt. The issue is relevant because of the unfairness of allowing the defendant to be prejudiced by the receipt. There has been some consideration of whether the change of position defence can go further than this, and deny or reduce recovery on broader fairness grounds. The formulation of the defence in *Lipkin Gorman* seems to provide some scope for this:

> [T]he defence is available to a person whose position has so changed that it would be inequitable in all the circumstances to require him to make restitution, or alternatively to make restitution in full.[25]

It might be argued that change of position cannot be concerned merely with the causation question of loss and gain, because it sometimes leaves the defendant

---

[23] e.g. per Lord Templeman in *Lipkin Gorman v Karpnale* [1991] 3 WLR 10, 16.

[24] The officiousness condition is certainly satisfied, because far from having been conferred officiously, the plaintiff's wealth, in the form of surviving value in the defendant's estate, is applied by the defendant not the plaintiff in conferring the benefit. It is likely to be more difficult to show that the benefit condition is satisfied. Thus, for example, where the plaintiff's surviving value is used to make improvements to the defendant's property, there will generally be no claim for payment, just as where the plaintiff mistakenly confers such a benefit himself: Re *Diplock* [1948] Ch 465, 547–8; cf Nolan (1995), 139ff. Cf. Chap. 9 at 311.

[25] [1991] 3 WLR 8, 35 per Lord Goff, following American Law Institute (1937), Art. 142(1).

with surviving value.[26] It is true that in certain types of case where it is very difficult to measure the gain, a rule that gives the benefit of the doubt to the defendant may have the effect that he will be left with a clear benefit even whilst the plaintiff is left with his loss unrestored.[27] However, this is due not to any distinct consideration of unfairness, but simply to the difficulty of measuring loss and gain precisely.

It has also been suggested[28] that the defence might apply where there has been an adverse change in the defendant's position unrelated to the receipt, as for example where he has lost his job.[29] Such a defence would clearly be quite unrelated to surviving value. If hardship of this sort should provide a defence to a restitutionary claim, it should equally provide a defence to a claim in contract or tort, and of course no such defence is recognised (save through the law of bankruptcy). Even if there were such a defence, it would serve no purpose to conflate it with the change of position in the sense in which it is concerned only with causation and surviving value.

Change of position on the facts of *Lipkin Gorman*

Change of position was recognised by the House of Lords in *Lipkin Gorman*, but there has been some difficulty in explaining the actual application of the defence on the facts of the case. The plaintiff's money was used without authority by X, a rogue, to gamble in the defendant's casino. Thus there was a transfer from the plaintiff to the defendant, via X, vitiated by X's lack of authority.[30] Simplifying slightly for convenience, let us say that X took £100,000 of the plaintiff's money. He bet and lost all this at the casino. In the course of losing the £100,000, he won £50,000 through a number of winning bets, and also bet and lost this £50,000. Thus altogether X bet and lost £150,000. The defendant received £150,000 from X altogether, but paid out £50,000 to him. The House of Lords held that the defendant's prima facie restitutionary liability was for the sum received, £150,000, but that it could rely on the change of position defence to the extent of the £50,000 paid out, and so was liable only for £100,000.[31]

---

[26] Nolan (1995), 174.

[27] See above n 22; cf Chap. 3 at 86, 93 with respect to mistaken improvements.

[28] The possibility is considered in Birks (1991), 488–9, but doubted in Birks (1992*a*), 143–4 and Birks (1996), 62–4. The issue is said to be whether the defences are "unjust-related" or "enrichment-related". Birks also considers that where the defendant receives a bundle of notes that are lost in a fire there is no change of position unless the defence applies in an "unjust-related" way: Birks (1991), 489. But this is not so unless the same amount of money would have been lost in the fire anyway.

[29] A hardship defence was recently rejected in *Scottish Equitable v Derby* (1999) unrep; see also the recent Australian case of *Gertsch v Atsas* [1999] NSWSC 898.

[30] On lack of authority as a vitiating factor, see Chap. 5.

[31] There was no bona fide purchase defence because the gambling contract was unenforceable. Bona fide purchase is considered below at 239–253.

However it is very difficult to explain this outcome in terms of change of position.[32] When the defendant made a payout, it was made in consequence of a bet, in the sense that the defendant would not have paid out if X had not laid a bet, because it was paid out under an obligation arising from the bet (although not an obligation enforceable in law, because of the unenforceability of a gambling contract). But the payout was not caused by the receipt of the stake itself, or, in other words, it was not made as a result of an accretion to the recipient's wealth resulting from the receipt. If the payout had been caused by the receipt in this sense, which is the necessary sense for the change of position defence, it could not have exceeded the amount of the receipt, whereas of course the payout on a bet invariably exceeds the amount of the receipt, which is the stake. In *Lipkin Gorman*, the payout in respect of one bet was effectively used to offset the restitutionary liability in respect of other bets by X, and this is inexplicable as change of position.[33]

The better view is that there was no significant change of position in *Lipkin Gorman*.[34] Nevertheless the decision was correct, because the value transferred from the plaintiff to the defendant was £100,000. The plaintiff lost £100,000 and the defendant received £100,000, and to reverse this transfer required a restitutionary liability of £100,000. At first sight this might appear too simple. When a payout is made to X, it might be thought that this money in X's hands belongs to the plaintiff, or at least represents surviving value in X's hands,[35] so that when X subsequently lays it out on further bets there is a further transfer to the defendant of wealth of the plaintiff's. This is presumably why it was thought that the prima facie measure of the plaintiff's restitutionary claim included the value of any winnings that were bet again.[36] But if the winnings constituted surviving value in X's hands, the effect of the payout is to restore surviving value previously lost. Thus if the surviving value is bet again and lost, this does not constitute the transfer of additional surviving value to the defendant, but the re-transfer of the same surviving value that had previously been transferred and restored. Alternatively, it may be that a payout received by X does not

---

[32] As Lord Goff acknowledged, [1991] 3 WLR 10, 36–7, and others have also noted, e.g. Nolan (1995), 169. But Lord Goff accepted change of position in preference to the alternatives. The first was that change of position should be confined to cancelling the liability on a particular winning bet. This is a strictly correct application of change of position on the assumption that a payment is only made in reliance on the receipt of the stake, but it would not have significantly reduced the defendant's liability from the full amount received. The second was that the risk of having to pay out incurred on acceptance of the bet was itself a change of position; but this would amount to bona fide purchase, enforcing the contractual assumption of risk.

[33] Nolan (1995), 169. Nolan says, *ibid.*, that "[a] series of gaming transactions are treated as one because *in the absence of better evidence*, a certain level of winnings has to be regarded as the product of the total amount of gambling" (original italics). But it is not by virtue of lack of evidence that one assumes that the winnings on a bet exceed the amount staked. See further at n 135 below with respect to anticipatory expenditure.

[34] See n 5 above.

[35] As considered in Chap. 9, these are actually equivalent statements.

[36] The court may also have had in mind the benefit received by the defendant rather than the plaintiff's loss as the basis of the claim, in accordance with some concept of unjust enrichment.

constitute the plaintiff's property or surviving value, so that further bets would not be transfers of surviving value at all.[37] This would not mean that, if X had exhausted the surviving value derived from the plaintiff, but had stopped gambling while he was in profit from payouts from the defendant, the plaintiff would not have been able to recover anything from X; X would of course have been liable to the full extent of his estate in respect of the money taken from the plaintiff, although not in this case by way of a claim for restitution for a vitiated transfer.[38]

The duty of inquiry

If the defendant is aware of his restitutionary liability in respect of a transfer received, because he knew of the vitiating factor, he clearly cannot take advantage of the receipt by spending it, and then also claim a defence of change of position. The question also arises whether he should be able to claim change of position when he did not actually know of the restitutionary liability, but might have realised it in the light of the facts known to him, or discovered it if he had made inquiries. In other words, does the defendant have a duty of inquiry,[39] and if so what is required of him?

If the defendant has no duty of inquiry, he will lose the benefit of change of position only if he actually knew of the existence of the restitutionary liability. A slightly weaker position for the defendant would be that he has a weak duty requiring him to consider what inferences he can make from known facts. An even weaker position for the defendant would be where he has a stronger duty requiring him to make inquiries to establish whether a transfer was vitiated. One could go further, to a position where the defendant is "strictly liable as to a vitiating factor", or "at risk", so that he is presumed to know of the restitutionary liability, or in other words is taken to act at his own risk in respect of the transfer. In such a case the defendant would in effect be denied the change of position defence altogether. ("Strict liability as to the vitiating factor" must be distinguished from the strict liability that governs the restitutionary claim, as mentioned above, which relates to the accrual of the restitutionary liability, not the change of position defence.) And one can go further at the opposite end of the scale as well, to an even stronger position for the defendant, where he would not be affected even by actual knowledge of the vitiating factor. Not all the points on this series are aptly described as representing a duty of inquiry, but it

---

[37] Whether the payout constituted surviving value would have been of consequence if X was insolvent.

[38] The claim would have been for compensation or disgorgement arising from a wrong, assuming X acted wrongfully, as in *Lipkin Gorman*. Cf the discussion of *Trustee of the Property of FC Jones and Sons v Jones* [1996] 3 WLR 703 in Chap. 11, at 316–17.

[39] The "duty of inquiry" is not strictly a duty, but a condition governing the accrual of the duty of preservation: see Appendix 1, n 9. However the expression is convenient and established in certain contexts.

is generally convenient to refer to this issue in terms of the level of the defendant's duty of inquiry, or alternatively in terms of a scale of "constructive knowledge", which is knowledge that the defendant would have had if he had fulfilled his duty of inquiry.[40]

The old law, according to which no change of position defence was recognised at all, can be understood as holding the defendant to be always at risk in the sense above, and indeed this is how the law was sometimes expressed.[41] It is now usually said that there is a requirement of "good faith" for change of position.[42] This appears to mean that the defence is lost only if there is actual knowledge of the restitutionary liability, reflecting the absence of any duty of inquiry. There has been some discussion, however, as to whether the defence should be lost where the defendant did not appreciate that he had a restitutionary liability but might have done—i.e. what level of duty of inquiry or constructive knowledge should apply—but there seems to be no explicit authority on the point.[43] The question of the applicable duty of inquiry arises not just for change of position, but for bona fide purchase (which is considered below), where there is a long history of case law on the point. Here the issue is traditionally expressed in terms of constructive knowledge.[44] The case law shows, not surprisingly, that the relevant point on the scale will depend on the nature of the transaction in issue, and this suggests that it is misconceived to think that a single position should apply generally for change of position any more than for bona fide purchase. The duty of inquiry, which is often the crucial issue in practice, will be considered more fully in Chapter 10.[45]

Surviving value and the duty of preservation

The usual analysis is to say that to the extent that the defendant knew (or ought to have known) of the vitiating factor, his change of position is disregarded in determining the measure of his restitutionary claim. It would be better, however, for reasons that will emerge, to use an alternative formulation based on the concept of the duty of preservation. On this formulation, the defendant's liability has to be resolved into two distinct components. First, there is a restitutionary liability for surviving value, which is independent of the defendant's actual or constructive knowledge, and depends purely on causation. If expenditure would not have happened but for the receipt, the surviving value—the measure of the restitutionary claim—is reduced accordingly, even if the defendant has actual or constructive knowledge of the restitutionary liability when he incurs

---

[40] See further Chap. 10 at 327 ff., 343.
[41] See Chap. 10 at 323.
[42] *Lipkin Gorman* [1991] 3 WLR 10, 34 per Lord Goff.
[43] e.g. Nolan (1995) 151ff; Birks (1996), 58; Bryan (1996) 80.
[44] See Chap. 10 at 327 ff.
[45] Chap. 10 at 342–46.

the expenditure. Secondly, however, once the defendant has actual or constructive knowledge of his restitutionary liability, he incurs a "duty of preservation" to preserve or repay the surviving value, and any expenditure contrary to the duty of preservation generates a liability for the amount spent. The two separate liabilities are together equivalent to the liability determined by the first approach.

One might think that the difference between these two formulations is merely semantic, and that the first one should be preferred as a matter of simplicity. It is true that often it is unnecessary to distinguish between them. But, although the first formulation is often convenient, the second formulation is correct, and the difference is crucial in some situations, as will emerge in Chapter 9. The second formulation distinguishes between two claims that are distinct in principle and sometimes need to be treated differently. The first claim is the restitutionary claim to surviving value, which is value attributable to the defendant's receipt as a matter of causation. The second claim is not a restitutionary claim at all, but a claim for compensation for breach of the duty of preservation, which is in nature tortious.[46] The duty of preservation is a duty not to cause harm to the plaintiff by reducing the value surviving. It is analogous to the more readily recognisable tortious duty not to take property, or value, from the plaintiff without his authority, or otherwise to cause him to make a vitiated transfer.[47] In that type of case the defendant procures the vitiated transfer, whereas a breach of the duty of preservation occurs when the defendant fails to preserve value received through a vitiated transfer for which he was not necessarily originally responsible. The first and orthodox formulation fails to distinguish between these two types of liability, and therefore obscures important issues, as will become clear in later chapters. The composite claim, if it is expressed as a claim to surviving value, requires a concept of surviving value that is not just based on causation; it is in effect a claim for a deemed surviving value, which includes value that has actually been lost from the defendant's estate.

MINISTERIAL RECEIPT

Where the plaintiff makes a vitiated transfer to an agent for the account of his principal, in certain circumstances the agent is said to have a defence of ministerial receipt to a restitutionary claim by the plaintiff. The effect is that the plaintiff has to sue the principal and not the agent. The most common example is where the agent is the principal's bank, which receives a payment on behalf of the principal and credits his account. There is some controversy over the defence, and some inconsistency in the cases, which do not seem to support any

---

[46] But a duty of preservation can also arise by agreement or assumption, as a fiduciary duty: see Chap. 9 at 290.

[47] e.g., some or all manifestations of trespass, conversion, duress, misrepresentation, "unconscionability", knowing assistance.

single analysis. Nowadays there is particular controversy about whether ministerial receipt is merely a manifestation of change of position. Ministerial receipt pre-dates the explicit recognition of change of position in *Lipkin Gorman*, but it was thought by Lord Goff in *Lipkin Gorman* to be a specific manifestation of or precursor to the defence of change of position.[48]

It is sometimes said that "payment over" to the principal is a condition of the defence,[49] i.e. the agent must have paid over the value received to the principal, as where the principal makes a withdrawal based on sums credited to his account by the agent-bank in respect of the receipt. Where there is a payment over, it is clear that the defence of change of position is available to the agent and precludes any liability to the plaintiff, the agent having changed his position in the full measure of the receipt. The plaintiff will have to make a claim against the principal, who is now the indirect recipient of the vitiated transfer.

Is ministerial receipt an independent defence?

The interpretation of ministerial receipt as an application of change of position seems to require that there must be a payment over. But there are cases where the defence has been allowed in the absence of payment over,[50] which might suggest that ministerial receipt is distinct from change of position. It might be argued, however, that change of position can apply even when there has been no payment over, for the following reason. From the moment of receipt of the payment, the agent incurs a liability to pay over the sum received to the principal.[51] Thus the agent automatically incurs a loss at the moment of receipt in the form of this liability, exactly cancelling out the value of the receipt, so that the surviving value in the agent's estate is nil.[52] This is a case where change of position operates without any act of reliance by the recipient.[53] By the same token, there is effectively a transfer of value through the agent to the principal from the time of receipt by the agent, so that the principal is immediately liable to the plaintiff's restitutionary claim whether or not the agent has actually paid over.[54] One might say that this is a fiction because the money is really with the agent until

---

[48] [1991] 3 WLR 8, 33.

[49] As held in *Buller v Harrison* (1777) 2 Cowp. 565.

[50] e.g. *Sadler v Evans* (1766) 4 Burr. 1984.

[51] As noted in *East India Co v Tritton* (1824) 3 B & C 280, 289. This is so whether or not the receipt is recorded in a written account, as will happen where the agent is the principal's bank.

[52] In equity, where the agent receives the payment on trust he does not retain any surviving value, according to Millet J in *Agip Africa v Jackson* [1990] Ch 265, 292. In general the analysis in the text here does not differ according to whether the receipt is on trust or not, although the position with respect to "recalling" the transfer may differ.

[53] Above at 226–27.

[54] *Sorrell v Finch* [1977] AC 728. It might be argued that the plaintiff should not be affected by a contract between the agent and the principal to which he is not a party; but the contract does not affect the plaintiff's legal position directly as if he were party to it; he is affected by it in a factual way, because it alters the effect of the receipt on the agent's wealth.

actual payment over.[55] But it is no more a fiction to say that the value has moved to the principal than it is a fiction to say that I own £100 if I have £100 in my account at the bank, although it is true of course that where it comes to enforcing a debt and recovering money (either by the principal or the plaintiff) a debt is not worth any more to the creditor than the resources of the debtor.

This argument is good, however, only if it is true to say that if the agent repays the plaintiff he remains liable to account to the principal for the original sum received. If the agent's liability to account to the principal is cancelled if the agent repays the plaintiff, then the agent can in effect recall the transfer from the principal by repaying the plaintiff. If this is the legal position, then the agent has no change of position defence without an actual payment over. If nevertheless the agent has a defence of ministerial receipt in the absence of payment over, ministerial receipt must be a distinct defence.

Does the agent remain liable to account to his principal if he repays the plaintiff? It has been said in one or two cases, involving a bank as agent, where the liability to the principal has been recorded in the form of a credit in the principal's account, that the agent can simply cancel the liability to the principal by striking out the credit:

> [I]t was not true that the sum had been used and could not be recalled. The defendants had only got to run a pen through some private entries in their own books and the matter would then have stood in precisely the same position as it stood before the mistake was made.[56]

This seems misconceived, because in principle one would think that once an agent had incurred a liability to his principal he could not unilaterally cancel it by his own act without the principal's assent. Whether the liability was recorded or not is, in this respect, beside the point.

However, where the agent's liability to account is based on the receipt of a vitiated transfer, so that, when the receipt is relayed to the principal through the liability to account, the principal becomes subject to a restitutionary liability, if the agent repays the plaintiff the agent's liability to account to the principal should lapse because the effect will be to discharge the principal's restitutionary liability to the plaintiff. In other words, although value passed to the principal, the agent can in effect recall the transfer to the principal in order to reverse the vitiated transfer from the plaintiff. This seems to imply, once again, that the agent should have no defence of change of position unless there has been actual payment over (so that again if the agent has a defence of ministerial receipt in the absence of payment over, ministerial receipt is an independent defence).

But this line of argument also faces a difficulty, because the principal may himself have a defence of change of position to the plaintiff's claim, even though there has been no actual payment over, because he may have relied in some other

---

[55] Swadling (1995), 254.
[56] *Colonial Bank v Exchange Bank of Yarmouth* (1885) 11 App Cas 84, 89 per Sir John Hobhouse.

way on his receipt in the form of the agent's liability to account to him.[57] This is the relevance of the recording of the agent's receipt in an account, at least if the principal has been given a statement of the account, which he may have relied on.[58] If the principal has changed his position in reliance, it seems that if the agent repays the plaintiff he will nevertheless remain liable to the principal to the extent of any such defence. On this basis, the agent should equally have a defence of change of position to the plaintiff's claim against him, to the extent of the principal's change of position.

From the agent's point of view, the principal's position vis-à-vis the plaintiff may sometimes appear clear—for example, the vitiating factor may be indisputable, and the principal may not have been notified of the receipt, so there can be no question of his having relied on it—but there is no reason why in general the agent should know the position as between the plaintiff and the principal, and no reason why he should bear any risk in respect of it.[59] For this reason, the agent should be entitled to refuse to repay the sum, and require the plaintiff to take proceedings against the principal. One might say that the agent should in all cases simply drop out of the picture, leaving the plaintiff to pursue the principal. As Bryant says, this would "[save] the agent from the predicament of having to balance the duty to make restitution against the obligation to account to the principal".[60]

On the other hand, even though the agent should not be liable to the plaintiff until the plaintiff's case has been proved against the principal, the agent should not be free actually to discharge his liability to account to the principal by paying over the sum to him. This is so because if the plaintiff's claim is established against the principal, and the agent has not actually paid over, the plaintiff will be able to get satisfaction from the agent; in effect the agent's debt to the principal can be a form of security for judgment for the plaintiff. Once the agent has notice of the plaintiff's claim he should not able to deprive the plaintiff of this security;[61] he should be required to pay the money into court, or to give an undertaking not to pay over. If the agent nevertheless pays over, he should be liable to the plaintiff in so far as the plaintiff is unable to realise a proved liabil-

---

[57] Thus it cannot be right to place importance on actual withdrawal as the test of whether the agent can recall the transfer: see Bryant (1998), 175.

[58] Or the principal may have some other defence with respect to part or all of the plaintiff's claim.

[59] Where the principal is undisclosed, it is likely that the only type of defence or counterclaim that he will have is change of position, and the agent will know that there is in fact no such defence if the principal has not been notified of receipt. Thus arguably there should be no defence of ministerial receipt for the agent where there has been no notification of the principal in the case of an undisclosed principal, but a defence in all cases of a disclosed principal. This would partly account for the distinction sometimes drawn between disclosed and undisclosed principals, e.g. Swadling (1995), 251; *Kleinwort Sons & Co v Dunlop Rubber Co* (1907) 97 LT 263.

[60] Bryant (1998), 180. Bryant's useful article distinguishes between the reversibility model and the mandate model of ministerial receipt. The reversibility model allows the plaintiff a claim against the agent where the liability to the principal is reversible, and the mandate model precludes a claim wherever the agent has simply received it on behalf of the principal (and possibly where it been recorded).

[61] As ever the issue arises whether constructive notice suffices.

ity against the principal. Sometimes, at least if the principal is amenable to proceedings and solvent, the plaintiff may agree that the agent should be able to account to the principal and leave the matter to be settled between the plaintiff and the principal. Where the agent is merely a functionary and poor compared to the principal, it is understandable that the courts should be inclined to require the plaintiff to sue only the principal and allow the agent to pay over and drop out,[62] by contrast to the position where the agent is the principal's deep-pocketed bank.

Ministerial receipt as a procedural constraint

The change of position defence should certainly be available to the agent. But because his position with respect to change of position cannot generally be determined independently of the position of the plaintiff as against the principal, he is allowed an independent defence of ministerial receipt, not requiring change of position to be established, which enables him to resist the plaintiff's claim pending the determination of the position as between the plaintiff and the principal. Thus ministerial receipt is essentially a procedural constraint.[63] By the same token, the plaintiff should be able to prevent the agent paying over until the determination has been made. The doctrine of subrogation, which is considered in Chapter 8, concerns similar problems arising from the difficulty of resolving the position as between the plaintiff and defendant when it is dependent on the position of the defendant with respect to a third party.

TRANSFER RECEIVED UNDER A CONTRACT: *BONA FIDE* PURCHASE

The defendant has a defence to a restitutionary claim when he receives the vitiated transfer pursuant to a contract in good faith, i.e. without actual or constructive knowledge (given his duty of inquiry) of the fact that the transfer was vitiated. There are a number of variants of the defence, not all conventionally recognised as such, and going by various labels. It is sometimes convenient to refer to the generic defence of "bona fide purchase", although it may be closer to conventional usage to use this expression to refer only to certain variants of it.

---

[62] As in *Sadler v Evans* (1766) 4 Burr. 1984.

[63] This is consistent with the view that the doctrine of ministerial receipt "is not so much a defence as a means of identifying the proper party to be sued": *Portman Building Society v Hamlyn Taylor Neck* [1998] 4 All ER 202, at 207 per Millet LJ.

The standard case

One example of the defence concerns the sale or purchase by a trustee for or from the trust fund. Here the plaintiff's trustee, acting beyond his authority under the terms of the trust, transfers trust money or property—in substance belonging to the plaintiff—to the defendant under a contract with the defendant to buy or sell property to or from the trust.[64] There is a transfer from the plaintiff to the defendant vitiated by lack of authority,[65] and so prima facie a restitutionary claim against the defendant. But the defendant has a complete defence to the claim because the money or property was received by him as payment or performance under a contract with the trustee. This defence is traditionally known as the "equity's darling" defence, which is understood to be an example of bona fide purchase, and it applies provided that the defendant has no actual or constructive knowledge of the vitiating factor, i.e. the breach of trust or lack of authority. "Constructive knowledge" depends on the duty of inquiry, which in this context has been the subject of much debate.[66]

Traditionally the bona fide purchase defence also arose at common law, here explicitly described as bona fide purchase, as a defence to a claim for money had and received.[67] An example is where money is taken from the plaintiff by his agent without authority and used by the agent as his own money to buy property from the defendant.[68] A similar case might be where the plaintiff has a voidable contract with a third party, X, to hire a ship from X, and, before the contract is avoided by the plaintiff, the plaintiff transfers advance hire charges ostensibly due to X under the contract to the defendant at X's direction. X so directs the plaintiff because X has assigned its contractual right of payment to the defendant as security for a loan. After rescission, the plaintiff claims restitution from the defendant, but bona fide purchase is a good defence to the claim, the defendant having received the payment under his contract with X.[69]

It is sometimes said that bona fide purchase applies only in three party cases, or, more precisely, in intermediary cases, where X, with whom the defendant has a contract, is an intermediary through whom an indirect transfer from the plaintiff comes to the defendant; and not in three-party non-intermediary cases

[64] The standard authority is *Pilcher v Rawlins* (1872) 7 Ch App 259.

[65] Lack of authority as a vitiating factor is discussed in Chap. 5.

[66] See Chap. 10 at 331–34, 343. The defence also applies where the trustee's transfer in breach of trust was made to an intermediate party, who then transferred surviving value on to the defendant. Thus it is said that a tracing claim is lost if the traceable proceeds reach a bona fide purchaser: *Re Diplock* [1948] Ch 465.

[67] *Millar v Race* (1758) 1 Burr. 452; *Lipkin Gorman v Karpnale* [1991] 3 WLR 10.

[68] Cf *Lipkin Gorman v Karpnale* [1991] 3 WLR 10.

[69] Such a defence is sometimes described as "third party rights": see Barker (1995), 203; below n 127. The facts are adapted from *Pan Ocean Shipping v Creditcorp (The Trident Beauty)* [1994] 1 WLR 161. In that case, the contract was valid, not voidable, and so there was no restitutionary claim at all, although there was argued to be a claim based on complete failure of consideration. The case is discussed in Chap. 2 at 58 and Chap. 3 at 122. The House of Lords held that the defendant was in a position "analogous to that of a bona fide purchaser for value": at 166, per Lord Goff.

where the contract is with the third party, X, but the payment comes straight from the restitutionary plaintiff,[70] or in two-party cases, where both the contract and the transfer are between the same two parties. But, although there are differences between the cases, a defence in the nature of the generic defence defined above arises in all such cases, as discussed further below. In fact there is one two-party case that is generally accepted as an archetypal example of bona fide purchase; this is where the equity's darling defence involves a transfer not by a trustee but by a fiduciary, who in equity is equated with a trustee for most purposes. Here the restitutionary plaintiff is the fiduciary's principal, whose money was transferred by the fiduciary, and the contract is also often with the principal himself, having been made by the fiduciary as his agent.[71] (By contrast, in the case of the trustee, the trustee does not contract on behalf of the beneficiary but on his own behalf, in the sense that he and not the beneficiary is liable on the contract.)

Some commentators take the view, with respect to the intermediary cases, that no restitutionary claim can arise out of an indirect transfer, and that the only claim arising out of an indirect transfer is a proprietary claim.[72] It follows from this point of view that bona fide purchase in this type of case is a defence to a proprietary claim, and not to a restitutionary claim at all; furthermore, if it is right that bona fide purchase is confined to the intermediary cases, then on this view bona fide purchase is always a defence to a proprietary claim and never to a restitutionary claim. In fact, it seems to be because it is thought, by reference to the intermediary case, that bona fide purchase is a defence to a proprietary claim and not to a restitutionary claim, that it is also thought that the same defence cannot be in issue in non-intermediary cases, where the claim in question is thought not to be proprietary but restitutionary. These issues turn on the analysis of the relation of restitution and property, which will be considered in Chapters 9 and 10. The conclusion there will be that the distinction between restitutionary and proprietary claims is illusory, which is consistent with the approach here of identifying variants of the same defence.

The rationale of *bona fide* purchase and its relation to change of position

In the standard case of bona fide purchase, the defendant has performed under his contract with the third party, X, after receiving the payment or transfer from X, which is actually an indirect vitiated transfer from the plaintiff, and generates a prima facie restitutionary claim in the plaintiff. The defendant would in any case have a defence of change of position to the plaintiff's restitutionary

---

[70] e.g. *Aitken v Short* (1856) 1 H & N 210, 156 ER 1180, *Barclays Bank v Simms* [1980] 1 QB 677, both considered below, and the example above adapted from *The Trident Beauty*.

[71] The fiduciary may sometimes purport to act for himself.

[72] e.g. Swadling (1997); Virgo (1999), 674; cf Segal (1998), 109–12; Barker (1995), 213. These issues are considered in Chap. 9.

claim, arising from the loss incurred by him through the performance of his contract with X in response to the receipt. The defence of bona fide purchase also protects the defendant in respect of the reliance incurred by him through his contractual performance, but it goes beyond the change of position defence.[73] Where the defendant receives the vitiated transfer under a contract, in rendering performance himself he relies not only on the receipt (as required for change of position), but also on the contract. Consequently he can take advantage of the protection provided by the law of contract to a contractor who has relied on a transfer received under the contract as being performance of the contract by the other party. This is the bona fide purchase defence.[74]

Under the change of position defence, the court has to measure the loss to the defendant and reduce his restitutionary liability accordingly. Thus it might find that the loss incurred by the defendant through his contractual performance fell short of the value of the transfer received, leaving the defendant with a net restitutionary liability. But under the bona fide purchase defence, the defendant's loss through performance in reliance on the contract is presumed to be no less than the value of the transfer received, so that there is a complete rather than a pro tanto defence. This is an application of the "contractual valuation", which equates the plaintiff's reliance interest with the value of the benefit received under the contract.[75] In the ordinary non-contractual case of change of position, by contrast, there is no reason generally to presume that the defendant's reliance interest will correspond to the payment received by him, and a general presumption of reliance in the full measure of the receipt would be unfair to the plaintiff in the majority of cases.

If the defendant receives notice of the vitiating factor before he has performed, it seems that he cannot continue with performance on the basis that he will be protected by bona fide purchase;[76] in other words, he incurs a duty of preservation. Similarly, where the defendant is a bank and the payment made by X (and derived from the plaintiff) is made as a deposit for X's account, i.e. in return for accepting a liability to X for the same sum, the bank should be able to rely on bona fide purchase as a defence only to the extent that it cannot cancel the liability to X.[77] As considered above, however, the bank may have a defence of ministerial receipt which would force the plaintiff to sue X first, on

---

[73] Some commentators have argued that bona fide purchase is merely a variant of change of position: e.g. Millet (1991); Birks (1991a); others have argued that the two are distinct: per Lord Goff in *Lipkin Gorman* [1991] 3 WLR 10, 35; Burrows (1993), 474–5. Barker (1995), 197 suggests that bona fide purchase differs fundamentally from change of position in being concerned with efficiency rather than fairness, as to which see Chap. 10, at 345–6.

[74] This reflects the assumption that contract law protects the reliance interest as discussed in Chap. 2.

[75] See Chap. 2 at 31.

[76] *Story v Windsor* (1743) 2 Atk. 630; Birks (1998). One might argue that there should be a presumption of reliance, and that the defendant should be able to proceed with the contract. But some small risk to the defendant is maybe acceptable; cf restitutio in integrum impossible, at 249 below.

[77] As stated by Lord Goff in *Lipkin Gorman v Karpnale* [1991] 3 WLR 10, 31. Here bona fide purchase would be equivalent to change of position.

the basis that the bank's liability will depend on the extent of any defence that X may have to a restitutionary claim by the plaintiff in respect of the value received by X through the bank in the form of the credit to its account.

One might ask why the defendant should be able to invoke the contract as against the plaintiff, even though his contract is with X.[78] The answer is presumably that, given the difficulty in determining the relative measures of the defendant's reliance loss and the value of the benefit received by him, it is reasonable simply to apply the contractual valuation, even though the plaintiff was not a party to the contract, given that in principle doubt should be resolved in favour of the defendant as the innocent recipient.[79]

Bona fide purchase and services

The bona fide purchase defence applies equally where the defendant's reliance in the form of his contractual performance is to provide services rather than incur expenditure or transfer land or goods.[80] It may seem difficult to justify a complete defence in this case, rather than a defence limited to the actually measured change of position. An example of this type of case is discussed in the literature.[81] The defendant owns an expensive restaurant and X pays £1,000, derived from the plaintiff, for a meal which he consumes. The defendant asserts bona fide purchase as a complete defence to a restitutionary claim by the plaintiff. It may be that the defendant's actual reliance loss is much less than £1,000, and that much of the value goes to paying him for his work rather than compensating for a loss.[82] One might also think that £1,000 represents an over-generous rate of pay, although this is a notoriously difficult issue to evaluate.[83] It has been suggested that here the defendant should be protected only to the extent of a reasonable price for the meal,[84] and that he should be liable to the plaintiff for the difference.[85] The defendant would have to make up the difference by suing X under the contract.

But it would be very difficult to operate such a rule. To require the court to determine actual reliance loss or a reasonable measure of payment in some or all cases would be liable to cause unfairness to the defendant in some cases because

---

[78] In the two-party case, including the case of the agent or fiduciary, the plaintiff is himself party to the contract and cannot of course complain about the contractual valuation.

[79] The problem is relying on the "contractual valuation" with respect to allocation of risk as opposed to valuation itself.

[80] e.g. it would have applied for the service of gambling in *Lipkin Gorman v Karpnale*, but for the statutory unenforceability of gambling contracts. Cf the reliance interest, Chap. 2, 30–31.

[81] Birks (1991), 490; Key (1994).

[82] This will depend on his opportunity cost, as has been pointed out: Key (1994), 423, n.10. It is perhaps less justifiable for the defendant to rely on his interest in payment for work done, as opposed to an interest in compensation for loss, as against the plaintiff's interest in recovering for his loss.

[83] Furthermore, the effect on the plaintiff is likely to be more severe because, by contrast with the position with respect to land or goods under the exchange product rule, the defendant's performance may not give rise to anything to take the place of the payment as surviving value in X's estate.

[84] Or even the opportunity cost.

[85] Key (1994), 423.

of the difficulty of determining the appropriate measure, even if in others it would prevent unfairness to the plaintiff. One might say that the defendant will not lose out because he can always make up the difference by suing X; but often the defendant would not have agreed to perform without first being paid, in order to avoid the difficulty of having to recover from X, and to reduce him now to that position imposes on him the risk that he sought to avoid and will certainly inconvenience him and may cause him significant prejudice. Thus, in general, if the benefit of the doubt is to be given to the defendant, it is reasonable to apply the bona fide purchase rule as a complete defence, even where the defendant has done work rather than having disposed of or expended money or goods.[86]

Discharge of debts: bona fide purchase and "good faith discharge"

Often the defendant will carry out his contractual performance in favour of X and become entitled to payment before he receives the payment or transfer; then he has not incurred any reliance on the receipt of the payment through his own performance. If he is obliged to return the value received to the plaintiff, he is left as he was before, having carried out his contractual performance, but still owed a debt for payment under the contract. It might seem, therefore, that the fact that the payment was made under the contract should not provide any defence in these circumstances. But in fact there does appear to be a defence in such a case. For example, there seems to be no suggestion that the equity's darling defence does not apply if the trustee pays after the defendant has supplied goods or services to him.

Furthermore, the defence applies where the defendant is a creditor of X, whether the debt arose out of a contract or otherwise,[87] and money belonging to the plaintiff is paid to the defendant in satisfaction of X's debt.[88] As it was put in the leading case of *Barclays Bank v Simms*,[89] which will be considered below, there is a defence where:

> the payment is made for good consideration, in particular if the money is paid to discharge, and does discharge, a debt owed to the payee . . .

An example is provided by *Aitken v Short*.[90] The plaintiff wanted to discharge a debt owed by X to the defendant, and secured by a charge on property that it

---

[86] Another difficulty with work or work and materials contracts is that the defendant may have received full payment but only part-performed by the time he gets notice of the vitiating factor. There is something to be said here for attributing part of the payment to the work already done and limiting the defendant's defence to that part of the payment.

[87] The debt may not have accrued out of a contract; but this should not affect the principles governing its discharge by voluntary arrangement, which is essentially a contractual matter.

[88] See also Chap. 3 on compulsory discharge.

[89] Per Goff J at [1980] 1 QB 677, 697.

[90] (1856) 1 H&N 210, 156 ER 1180.

had just acquired from X. The plaintiff made a payment of its own money to the defendant with a view to satisfying the debt. But the payment was made by mistake because in fact there was no charge over the property, and so there was prima facie a restitutionary claim to recover the payment. However, the claim was defeated by a defence:

> The money which the defendant got . . . was actually due to her and there can be no obligation to refund it.[91]

In this discharge type of case, the defence is sometimes described as "good faith discharge".[92] *Aitken v Short* and *Barclays Bank v Simms* are non-intermediary three-party cases, and this has some significance in the present context as considered below.

The explanation for the discharge defence might appear to be that the discharge of the debt alters the defendant's position, so that if he were still subject to a liability to return the payment he would be left without either the benefit of the debt owed to him or the money received. This seems to be what is meant by saying that the discharge of the debt is good consideration. On this basis, however, the defence is best understood as an example of the non-reliance form of change of position, where the defendant's position has changed other than through his reliance on the receipt.[93] But this explanation is unsatisfactory. It must be right that, if the debt is indeed discharged, the defendant has a good defence. But the question whether the debt is discharged is an aspect of the law in issue. If one could be sure that the defendant has not relied in any way on the receipt, it would surely be better to reverse the payment and hold the debt to remain outstanding. This would reflect the normal approach of allowing the plaintiff his restitutionary claim so far as possible without prejudicing the defendant.

In fact the defendant *is* liable to have incurred reliance on the receipt, by refraining from taking action to recover what would remain due to him if the payment had not discharged the debt. This may be a very significant form of reliance, at least if there has been any delay by the plaintiff in making the restitutionary claim. On the other hand, particularly if the mistake or other vitiating factor is immediately discovered and the defendant notified, there may have been no significant reliance by the defendant at all.[94] Furthermore, in the nature of the case it is very difficult to say whether and to what extent there has actually been reliance. The best way of dealing with the difficulty is surely to allow the defendant a defence as a general rule, without proof of actual reliance, and also to treat the debt as discharged. This means that to the extent that the defendant has actually incurred reliance he is protected, but that there is no risk of a

---

[91] Per Platt B, (1856) 1 H & N 210, 215, cited by Goff J in *Barclays Bank v Simms* [1980] QB 677, 688; and see now *Lloyds Bank v Independent Insurance* [1999] 2 WLR 986.

[92] e.g. American Law Institute (1937), §14; Goff & Jones (1998), 204.

[93] See Goff & Jones (1998), 205; *Lloyds Bank v Independent Insurance* [1999] 2 WLR 986.

[94] This was thought to be the position in *Lloyds Bank v Independent Insurance* [1999] 2 WLR 986.

windfall to him if he has not actually incurred reliance, because the debt is discharged.[95] On this basis, contrary to the usual understanding, the discharge of the debt is the legal *consequence* of the availability of the defence, which is based on the reliance, or presumed reliance, of the defendant; the defence is not the legal consequence of the discharge of the debt. The defence is a manifestation of, or at least a variant of, bona fide purchase,[96] because it is based on reliance on a payment as being contractual performance, or, more broadly, as being payment in discharge of a debt owed to the defendant.

Authority to pay the debt

In order for the defendant to be protected in respect of his reliance on the payment as being made in discharge of the debt (so that, as argued above, the payment does indeed discharge the debt), the payment must be made by some person who has the authority to make the payment on behalf of the debtor. In the case where the payment is made by the debtor himself (using money derived from the plaintiff), it is clear that the debtor has authority to discharge his own debt. This is the position in the intermediary cases, where a trustee transfers trust money to the defendant in discharge of a debt due under the defendant's contract with the trustee, or at common law where the plaintiff's money is taken by the intermediary and used to pay the defendant under a contract with the intermediary. But in *Aitken v Short*, the payment was made by the restitutionary plaintiff not the debtor. The issue then is whether the plaintiff had authority to make a payment on behalf of the debtor in discharge of his debt. It seems that such authority can be either actual or apparent, and in *Aitken v Short* it seems that there was actual authority under the arrangement between the plaintiff and the debtor.

Consider also the standard case where the defendant relies on a contract with the plaintiff made through the plaintiff's agent or fiduciary, who makes a payment to the defendant in discharge of the plaintiff's debt under the contract. It may be that the contract is made with apparent but not actual authority, and also that a payment is made with apparent but not actual authority.[97] In either case the defendant is protected in respect of his reliance on the payment as being in discharge of the plaintiff's debt. However, this type of case can cause confusion because it is liable to be dealt with in equity or at common law. At common law, one would refer to an agent rather than a fiduciary, and it would normally be said that the plaintiff has no claim because the defendant can enforce the

---

[95] The defendant has benefited to the extent that actual payment is better than a claim for payment.

[96] The defence arises only if there is actually a valid debt; otherwise there is no prejudice through reliance: cf the supposed defence of "honest receipt", in Chap. 5 at 176–7.

[97] It may be that the contract was made with apparent authority, but the payment is made with actual authority, given that the contract is now binding on the principal.

contract by virtue of the agent's apparent authority to act on behalf of the plaintiff. Generally there is no explicit reference to the plaintiff's claim as a restitutionary claim, the whole issue being treated as a matter of contract.[98] In equity, it would be said that the defendant has the equity's darling defence to the plaintiff's equitable restitutionary claim.[99] The expression "apparent authority" is a common law expression and is not found in equity. But, in reality, equity applies the concept of apparent authority as an element of the equity's darling defence. Thus it is said that the defendant does not have a defence if he knew or ought to have known of a breach of fiduciary duty, which amounts to saying that he knew or ought to have known that the agent was exceeding his authority in making the payment. It is only a failure to appreciate the nature of the relationship between common law and equity that has prevented the equity's darling defence in equity and reliance on the contract by way of apparent authority at common law from being recognised as different formulations of the same defence. This is an example of the confusing effect of the fallacy of law and equity as distinct bodies of substantive law.[100] Perversely there have been cases where the court first considers whether there is apparent authority so as to preclude a claim at common law, and then separately considers whether the defendant has sufficient notice to preclude a claim in equity.[101]

The role of apparent authority

One situation where the issue of apparent authority has been controversial is illustrated by *Barclays Bank v Simms*.[102] Here the third party, X, who was a contract debtor of the defendant, issued a cheque to pay the defendant against its account at the plaintiff bank. Before the plaintiff had paid out on the cheque, X cancelled it. But by mistake, and now without authority under the banking contract with X, the plaintiff did pay out. The plaintiff then sought to recover the payment in a restitutionary claim against the defendant, and its claim succeeded. The judge held that the defendant would have had a good defence if the plaintiff had made the payment with authority; the case would then have corresponded to *Aitken v Short*, where it appears there was actual authority to discharge the debt.[103] But because the plaintiff had no authority to make the payment on behalf of X the defence was not available. As has been observed,[104] the decision is surely mistaken for failing to take account of the plaintiff's continuing apparent authority to make the payment on behalf of X, the defendant

---

[98] Cf Chap. 5 at 162.

[99] Some would say that this is a proprietary claim, as to which see Chaps. 9 and 10.

[100] This is of course the fusionist position: see Appendix 2.

[101] *International Sales & Agencies v Marcus* [1982] 3 All ER 551; see also Chap. 10 at 341–2.

[102] [1980] QB 677.

[103] On the argument here it is really always apparent authority that is relevant so far as the defendant is concerned.

[104] Goode (1981); Friedmann (1983).

having had no reason to suspect that the cheque had been cancelled and that the plaintiff was not fully authorised to pay out on it in the normal way.[105]

Simms has been defended, and the apparent authority argument rejected, on the basis that although the customer, X, the debtor, held the plaintiff bank out as its agent for the purpose of making the payment by the issue of the cheque, the representation bound only X itself and not the bank, and so in an action by the bank against the creditor the creditor could not rely on it and so should have no defence to the bank's action.[106] This argument is surely misconceived. Apparent authority is relevant to the question whether the defendant can rely on the payment as being paid in discharge of the debt owed to him, i.e. the question is whether the payment is made with the apparent authority of the debtor, X. Thus it is certainly true that the immediate effect of the apparent authority is that the debtor himself is bound by the payment as being made on his behalf in discharge of the debt. But, provided the defendant can rely on the payment, he has the benefit of the bona fide purchase defence, and this protects him in respect of his reliance on the payment as against the restitutionary plaintiff, even where, as is usually the case, the restitutionary plaintiff is not the same person as the debtor or other contracting party: the standard case of bona fide purchase is a three-party case. The apparent authority, in binding the debtor, operates against the plaintiff indirectly rather than directly, by giving the defendant the benefit of the bona fide purchase defence.[107]

Two-party cases

It was mentioned above that it is thought by some that the bona fide purchase defence applies only with respect to three-party intermediary cases, as in the standard case of purchase of trust property from a trustee.[108] At least on the analysis here of the defence as arising from receipt under a contract, the defence, or at least a variant of the defence, also arises in non-intermediary three-party cases and two-party cases as the examples above show.

Nevertheless it is worth considering the point further in relation to a simple two-party case. Consider the case where the plaintiff and the defendant are parties to a valid contract. Say the plaintiff makes a payment to the defendant, ostensibly in performance of the contract, but vitiated by mistake (or some other vitiating factor). Perhaps he has a number of similar contracts and means to make a payment under one but mistakenly makes a payment under another; or

---

[105] This seems to be the basis for *Liggett v Barclays Bank* [1928] 1 KB 48; cf Chap. 3 at 99–100.

[106] Matthews (1982); and see now the obiter remarks of Waller LJ in *Lloyds Bank v Independent Insurance* [1999] 2 WLR 986, 995–6.

[107] The point may sometimes be concealed by the fact that the debtor is the same person as the restitutionary plaintiff, or by the fact that the debtor pays on his own behalf. Of course this raises the broader issue of why bona fide purchase can in effect bind the plaintiff even though he was not party to the contract, but this is undoubtedly the case as discussed above.

[108] Barker (1995b), 193; Birks (1995), 334, Birks (1998b), 5.

he makes a mistake over the stage of performance reached by the other party and so makes a payment before it is due.[109] The plaintiff might seek to recover the payment so that he can subsequently make the payment as and when he intended to make it; or if he recovered the payment he might be able to with-draw from the contract and never make the payment. If the plaintiff had an accrued liability, the defendant would in any case have a counterclaim. But it may be that there was no accrued liability when the payment was made, as where the plaintiff was paying in advance to trigger the performance of the con-tract. Nevertheless, it is surely the case that the plaintiff would not have a claim, unless the defendant knew or ought to have known of the mistake. But is this because in the circumstances "[a] valid contract for the receipt and retention of the benefit remains in being, thereby ousting the plaintiff's restitutionary rights"[110]—or is it because there is a defence to a restitutionary claim arising from the vitiated transfer?

Say the defendant knew or ought to have known that the plaintiff had paid by mistake. Surely the plaintiff should then have a claim, and this would presum-ably be a restitutionary claim.[111] This shows that in the ordinary case the plain-tiff has a prima facie restitutionary claim to which the defendant has a good defence. This defence, that the defendant received the transfer under his con-tract with the plaintiff,[112] is clearly of the same nature as the defence that arises where the contract is with another party. In both cases reliance on a contract is invoked to defeat a restitutionary claim. There is no reason why the defence should not be referred to as bona fide purchase in the two-party case (as is the practice in the fiduciary case), although often the issue is likely to be submerged in a contractual claim, and no reference made to restitution or a restitutionary defence.[113] This is not to say that the two- and three-party cases are the same. In particular, as discussed above, some further justification may be called for in relation to the three-party case, where the defendant is allowed to invoke the contract as against the plaintiff who was not party to it.

Bona fide purchase and the "restitutio in integrum impossible" rule

Another type of two-party case where the defence is in effect that the defendant received the transfer under a contract with the plaintiff is where the plaintiff

---

[109] This is a possible interpretation of *Banque Financière de la Cité v Parc (Battersea) Ltd* [1998] 2 WLR 475, which is considered in Chap. 9.

[110] Barker (1995*b*), 200–1. See also *Portman BS v Hamlyn Taylor Neck* [1998] 4 All ER 202, 208, per Millett LJ. There seems to be some confusion here between a mistake as to a transfer and a mis-take vitiating the agreement.

[111] Although the defendant might have a counterclaim for an amount owing under the contract.

[112] Generally the defence would be based on a presumption of reliance on the receipt of a pay-ment under the contract.

[113] Some commentators prefer to use the expression "good faith exchange" to refer to the defence in the two-party case, but there does not seem to be any consistency of usage in this respect: see e.g. Chambers (1997), 237.

wishes to set aside an agreement that he made with the defendant under a vitiated intention—i.e. a voidable agreement—and recover a payment made under
it. Here the basic rule is that if the defendant has relied on the agreement by
beginning performance, the plaintiff is denied rescission under the "restitutio in
integrum impossible" rule (unless the defendant's performance is also a
reversible transfer). This type of case was considered in Chapters 3 and 5
above.[114] Again, the defendant's defence based on his acting in reliance on the
voidable agreement is not generally described as bona fide purchase, although
clearly it is based on the same principle of denying a claim in order to protect the
defendant's reliance on the agreement. It is sometimes thought of as the application of the principle of objective interpretation in contract,[115] which is true,
but not inconsistent with the analysis here or the description in terms of bona
fide purchase. An important distinguishing feature of this example of the
defence is that the defence validates the contract (i.e. it overrides the vitiating
factor), as opposed to merely invoking a normal valid contract as a defence to
the restitutionary claim. Because the contract is voidable, it seems that the
defence may operate less favourably to the defendant than in the usual case of
bona fide purchase.[116]

Barclays Bank v O'Brien

Sometimes the plaintiff may seek to rescind the agreement not in order to make
a restitutionary claim in respect of a transfer under the agreement, but to avoid
the enforcement of the contract against him. This was the issue in the case of
Barclays Bank v O'Brien,[117] and the case is interesting, and has caused confusion, because, although it concerns the enforcement of a vitiated agreement,
Lord Browne-Wilkinson's judgment adopts not the usual language of rescission
and restitutio in integrum but, more or less, the language of bona fide purchase.

In *O'Brien*, a wife joined her husband in making a contract with the husband's bank to grant security over the matrimonial house in return for a loan to
the husband's business. However, the wife had made the contract under the
influence of a vitiating factor in the form of undue influence exercised by her
husband. It was held that the bank could enforce the contract against the wife if
it did not have notice of the vitiation of the wife's assent to the agreement. This
was expressed in the language of bona fide purchase or equity's darling or, more
precisely, the language of the equitable doctrine of notice, of which the equity's

---

[114] Chap. 3 at 105–10, and Chap. 5 at 195, 200.

[115] See Chap. 3 at 107–8.

[116] The defence may be partial, not complete, and there is no presumption of reliance if the defendant has not actually performed. This is justifiable on the basis that, since the plaintiff's assent to
the contract was vitiated, the defendant should not be able to invoke it unless it is strictly necessary
to protect him.

[117] [1994] 1 AC 180. For a similar analysis see O'Dell (1997). In *Royal Bank of Scotland v Etridge
(No 2)* [1998] 4 All ER 705 it was said, at 718: "[t]his is not, we think, a true application of bona fide
purchase, but the effect appears to be much the same".

darling rule forms a part. The case has been controversial, and there are a number of complicating factors which account for this. First, it was actually a two-party case, the plaintiff and the defendant being parties to the same vitiated or voidable agreement. However, it seems to have been taken for a three-party case, because of the presence of the husband. But the husband was relevant merely as the cause of the vitiating factor, not as a contracting party.[118] Secondly, as compared to the usual two-party case the roles of the parties were reversed, because the plaintiff was seeking to invoke "restitutio in integrum impossible" or bona fide purchase in order to sue on the agreement, rather than as a defence against a claim to reverse a transfer based on rescission. Conversely, the wife, who was effectively seeking rescission, was not doing so in order to make a restitutionary claim, but in order to avoid a contractual liability; thus the case was not actually concerned with restitution at all.[119]

The most controversial feature of the decision has been the so-called "two-transaction" analysis.[120] Lord Browne-Wilkinson said, first:

> [I]f the creditor bank has notice, actual or constructive, of the undue influence exercised by the husband (and consequently of the wife's equity to set aside the transaction) the creditor will take subject to that equity and the wife can set aside the transaction against the creditor.[121]

And later he said:

> The doctrine of notice lies at the heart of equity. Given that there are two innocent parties, each enjoying rights, the earlier right prevails against the later right if the acquirer of the later right knows of the earlier right (actual notice) or would have discovered it had he taken proper steps (constructive notice).[122]

The first formulation is apt. It describes a limitation on the operation of a claim of "restitutio in integrum impossible" or bona fide purchase to resist a claim for rescission. But the second formulation, which is the source of the "two-transaction" tag, has caused confusion. It is apt only in some cases, in particular where bona fide purchase is invoked to resist a claim for restitution for a vitiated transfer in an intermediary case, or more precisely in an intermediary case in equity, where the restitutionary plaintiff's claim takes the form of an equitable interest in property or surviving value in the hands of the intermediary as trustee, which is then transferred to the defendant.[123] Then the effect of the equity's darling defence or, in other words, in this context, the equitable

---

[118] In this respect the case is like apparent authority, which is also treated as a standard case of bona fide purchase or equity's darling in equity, even though it is really a two-party case, apparently because of the third party's role as the cause of the vitiating factor.

[119] Cf *TSB Bank v Camfield* [1995] 1 WLR 430, discussed in Chap. 3 at 108–9.

[120] See McKendrick (1996), 101; Battersby (1995), 42–6.

[121] [1994] 1 AC 180, 191.

[122] [1994] 1 AC 180, 195.

[123] See further Chap. 9 at 289–91.

doctrine of notice or priorities, can be understood to be to extinguish the plaintiff's equitable interest or restitutionary claim to surviving value.[124]

In *O'Brien*, the issue was not whether the bank received a transfer of property or surviving value free of a claim by the plaintiff, but whether the bank could enforce the agreement against the attempt by the plaintiff to rescind it for undue influence. The issue here is simply whether there was notice of the vitiating factor so as to preclude reliance on the contract by the bank. But because Lord Browne-Wilkinson adopted the language of the equitable doctrine of notice or equity's darling in its usual three-party form, it seems that he was forced to try and construct a prior right to be overridden. In the absence of a pre-existing equitable interest or claim to surviving value, as in the three-party intermediary case, he found this in the idea that the wife had a pre-existing equity against her husband that the bank was seeking to override. The equity was thought to be the contractual right against the husband, who was party to the contract between the bank and the wife. But this was quite inapt. The husband was a party to the contract between the wife and the bank, but this was not a necessary feature of the case. The issue arose as between the bank and the wife, and the enforcement of the agreement as between the husband and the wife was irrelevant, except that the vitiating factor affecting the agreement between the bank and the wife happened to be the undue influence of the husband, which would also have vitiated an agreement between the husband and the wife. But the bank was in no sense attempting to override an interest or equity of the wife's that had arisen from her agreement with her husband, as if the bank had received a transfer of trust property held by the husband on trust for the wife and transferred to the bank in breach of trust.[125]

Variants of the defence

It is reasonable to think in terms of a number of variants of a generic defence that the transfer was received under a contract. It is reasonable to refer to the generic defence as bona fide purchase, although conventionally bona fide purchase tends to be used to refer to one or certain variants only.

In the standard case, bona fide purchase stricto sensu,[126] which includes the equity's darling defence, the plaintiff's claim is for restitution for a vitiated

---

[124] This formulation presupposes the approach adopted in Chap. 9 to restitution and property.

[125] In any case, even if a contractual right of the wife against the husband had been relevant, the contract between the wife and the husband did not arise before the time at which the bona fide defence had to operate, which is when the single contract was made between all three parties. A very similar type of case to *O'Brien*, curiously neglected in *O'Brien* and elsewhere, is where the plaintiff company makes a contract with the defendant company, and a director of the plaintiff also has an interest in the defendant. The contract is vitiated by the director's personal interest as a fiduciary, but only if the defendant has notice of it. An example is *Transvaal Lands Co v New Belgium (Transvaal) Land & Development Co* [1914] 2 Ch 488, where the defence was clearly treated as a form of bona fide purchase.

[126] Bona fide purchase at common law and the equity's darling defence or the doctrine of notice or priorities in equity.

transfer, and the defendant has relied on a contract with a third party, typically, although not always, an intermediary through whom the vitiated transfer from the plaintiff has reached the defendant.[127] In a second case, the plaintiff's vitiated payment is made to discharge a debt owed to the defendant by a third party, and the payment is taken to be received under the defendant's contract with the third party because the plaintiff has the actual or apparent authority of the third party to make the payment. This is sometimes referred to as bona fide discharge.[128] In a third case, the defendant receives a vitiated transfer of value from the plaintiff under a contract with the plaintiff himself. It seems that this is sometimes referred to as bona fide exchange.[129] In a fourth case, the plaintiff seeks to rescind a voidable contract, in order to make a restitutionary claim, and the defendant invokes the contract, or appearance of a contract, in his defence. This is a typical example of "restitutio in integrum impossible". In a fifth case, illustrated by *O'Brien*, the roles are reversed and the plaintiff invokes "restitutio in integrum impossible" or bona fide purchase to enforce a voidable contract against the defendant's attempt to rescind to avoid liability under the contract. The last two cases might also be said to be based on the principle of objective interpretation in contract.[130]

All these cases illustrate the application of the same underlying principle. There are significant differences between the different variants, for example as to whether the contract is with the restitutionary plaintiff as in two-party cases or with a third-party as in three party cases; as to whether the vitiating factor affects a transfer or an agreement; and as to whether, in the latter case, it is invoked as a defence to a restitutionary claim to reverse a transfer under the agreement, or in order to enable a contracting party to enforce a claim under the contract as in *O'Brien*. The different contexts may give rise to differences, for example as to the relevant duty of inquiry. It may be that it would be desirable to maintain or develop different labels for the variants, but the more important objective is to establish the underlying similarity between them.[131]

ESTOPPEL

Before the change of position defence was explicitly recognised, it was said that the defendant could resist a restitutionary claim only if he could show that he

---

[127] Where the vitiated transfer was by way of a voidable contract between the plaintiff and X, then relayed to the defendant, the defence is sometimes referred to as "third party rights", although this tends to be confused with X's defence of "restitutio in integrum impossible" to a claim by the plaintiff: see Barker (1995), 203.

[128] Above n 92.

[129] Above n 113.

[130] See Chap. 3 at 107–8.

[131] There has been no attempt to discuss whether, when the defendant raises bona fide purchase or any of the variants, he should be understood as denying the existence of an element of the plaintiff's claim, or as raising a defence to a claim whose elements have been established. The point seems to be purely a matter of proof, which may vary for different variants, and does not seem to bear the significance attributed to it, for example in Barker (1998*b*).

had relied on a statement by the plaintiff confirming that the payment was due. This was described as the defence of estoppel. It was suggested in Chapter 3 that estoppel could be described as arising from an agreement to assume responsibility for reliance;[132] then the question is whether there has been a statement by the plaintiff amounting to an assumption of responsibility for reliance. This may be a difficult issue of fact; a mere statement of account would presumably not count, but a letter in response to a specific inquiry presumably would.

The ostensible non-recognition, until recently, of the change of position defence implied that the defendant was "at risk" with respect to receipts in the sense explained above. To secure his position in respect of a receipt, he had to seek an agreement from the plaintiff transferor to assume responsibility for reliance on the receipt, so as to have the benefit of a defence of estoppel. It has been suggested that there remains no role for estoppel after the recognition of change of position, because the defendant is no longer at risk;[133] but there could presumably still be cases where, by virtue of the nature of the transfer, the defendant is at risk with respect to a vitiating factor, and so normally cannot rely on change of position and would have to rely on estoppel.[134]

Estoppel also remains of importance with respect to anticipatory expenditure. Say that before the plaintiff makes a mistaken payment to the defendant, he informs the defendant that he is about to make the payment, and, in reliance on the expectation of receipt rather than the receipt itself, the defendant incurs exceptional expenditure. For example, the defendant may be informed that he has won the lottery and in anticipation treat himself to an expensive meal that he would not otherwise have had. If the mistaken payment is then made, it seems that the defendant's restitutionary liability should be reduced by the amount of his expenditure. It has been suggested that this should be explained in terms of change of position.[135] But it is difficult to see on what basis change

---

[132] See Chap. 3 at 128, and Jaffey (1998c), 129.

[133] Key (1995).

[134] Similarly, a defendant recipient might suspect a vitiating factor, so that he could not rely on change of position. But if he makes an inquiry and receives a statement he can rely on he may now be able to assume his entitlement to the receipt. But this could equally well be understood as discharging the duty of inquiry for the purposes of change of position.

[135] Nolan (1995), 163ff; Burrows (1995), 21; Birks (1995), 329. It has been suggested that *Lipkin Gorman* is a case where the change of position defence covered loss incurred in anticipation of receipt: *South Tyneside Metropolitan BC v Svenska International plc* [1995] 1 All ER 545, 566 per Clarke J; although Clarke J considered that in general change of position would not cover anticipatory expenditure. The argument is that because the defendant could bring into account all his payouts on winning bets, even though they exceeded the value of the stake for the bet in question, he must have been allowed to set off the loss incurred through the payout against the restitutionary liability in respect of subsequent receipts. But a payment on a winning bet is in no sense made in anticipation of future receipts; each bet may be the last. A better explanation of this aspect of *Lipkin Gorman* was offered above. A stronger case for anticipatory expenditure to be covered by change of position arises where a recipient bank receives a direction to pay from another bank on the understanding that the recipient will be immediately put in funds, and the recipient relies on the understanding and make the payment to a third party: cf Chap. 9 at n 95. But here there is effectively an undertaking to pay a certain sum which should be understood as a form of wealth in itself which is in effect transferred.

of position could apply. Change of position is concerned with surviving wealth due to the receipt, and this cannot be affected by loss of wealth that was not caused by the receipt at all, but by a statement made before receipt.

Estoppel is entirely apt to meet the case. The issue is whether the defendant was entitled to rely on the statement or, in other words, whether the statement entailed an agreement to assume responsibility for reliance. Normally one would think that a statement made by the person who was responsible for the subsequent payment would be a statement that implied an agreement to assume responsibility, but this might not be so. If the defendant was not entitled to rely on the statement, or if he incurred anticipatory expenditure without any statement having been made, then there is no reason why he should be entitled to any reduction in his liability through change of position as a result of anticipatory expenditure. Furthermore, where estoppel is allowed it should not strictly be understood as a defence to the restitutionary claim, like change of position, but as a claim or counterclaim arising from the plaintiff's statement.[136] Then if the defendant was entitled to rely on the statement, he should have a claim for his reliance loss even if the plaintiff discovers the mistake before payment and the payment is never made.[137]

An important issue is whether estoppel gives the defendant a complete defence to the claim, as for bona fide purchase, or merely a defence in the measure of his proven reliance, as for change of position. In *Avon County Council v Howlett*,[138] the plaintiff overpaid the defendant, an employee, over a period of months, and then sought to recover the overpayment. The defendant relied on estoppel, and the main issue was whether the defence protected the defendant only to the extent of his proved reliance, or whether it was a compete defence. On the facts of the case, the court was of the view that the defence should be a complete one, but it was accepted that there might be cases where estoppel would operate pro tanto in respect of actual reliance only. The difficulty was essentially one of proof. The defendant may have:

> altered his general mode of living or undertaken commitments or incurred expenditure or entered into other transactions which it may be very difficult for him subsequently to recall and identify retrospectively in complete detail . . . If the pecuniary amount of his prejudice has to be precisely quantified by a defendant in such circumstances, he may be faced with obvious difficulties of proof.[139]

The same issue has arisen in connection with claims for proprietary estoppel: the measure of recovery is said to be the reliance measure, and sometimes, though not always, this is equated with the expectation measure, which is

---

[136] The same might sometimes be said of bona fide purchase.

[137] In some contexts estoppel is said to be "a shield and not a sword", but this is not always the case. It is not true of proprietary estoppel, for example, or of the recent Australian version of equitable estoppel: *Waltons Stores (Interstate) Ltd v Maher* (1988) 164 CLR 387.

[138] [1983] 1 WLR 605.

[139] At 621–2, per Slade LJ.

equivalent to allowing a complete defence to a restitutionary claim.[140] Recently it has been held that estoppel does not provide a full defence, at least in a case where change of position is available to do precise justice between the parties.[141]

If estoppel is properly understood to arise from an agreement, it has this in common with bona fide purchase. Bona fide purchase does generally provide a complete defence, whereas estoppel does not necessarily do so. This seems to be because bona fide purchase arises from an agreement for an exchange, so that, in the nature of the exchange, one can equate the defendant's reliance loss with the value of the receipt. In the case of estoppel, however, as for change of position, there is no reason to presume that the defendant's reliance loss is comparable to the receipt, and so the court should have to measure the change of position unless in a particular case there is good reason to allow a presumption in favour of the defendant.[142]

---

[140] The remedy is said to be whatever is necessary to do justice to the plaintiff in the circumstances: see e.g. *Crabb v Arun DC* [1976] Ch 179.

[141] *Scottish Equitable v Derby* (1999) unrep; see also *RBC Dominion Securities v Dawson* (1994) 111 DLR (4th) 230.

[142] There is another difference, which is that the bona fide purchase defence operates where the other contractor is not the restitutionary plaintiff, although this is not as easy to justify as where they are the same parties. This raises the issue whether an estoppel based on a statement by a third party, X, and not by the restitutionary plaintiff can provide a defence to the plaintiff's restitutionary claim or only a claim against X. But, whereas in the bona fide purchase case to deny the defence to the restitutionary claim might mean that the exchange between the defendant and X would have to be unravelled, here it is possible to require the defendant to recover for his reliance from X. The defendant could be protected by subrogating the restitutionary plaintiff to the estoppel claim against X.

8

Indirect Recipients, Three-Party Cases and Subrogation

I N A STRAIGHTFORWARD case of restitution for a vitiated transfer, the transfer goes from the plaintiff to the defendant and only the two parties are involved. But in some cases there can be three (or more) parties involved in one way or another. These three-party cases are gathered together in this chapter not because they are linked by any common principle, but partly for convenience, and partly to deal with a tendency to confuse different types of three-party case.[1]

THE THIRD PARTY AS THE CAUSE OF VITIATION

Sometimes a third party becomes involved, because, although he is neither the plaintiff nor the defendant to the restitutionary claim, he was responsible for the vitiated transfer. One example is where a transfer of value from the plaintiff to the defendant is effected by the plaintiff's agent acting without authority, or even by a stranger acting without the plaintiff's authority. Similarly, a transfer of value from the plaintiff may be made by a trustee holding property on trust for him, acting beyond his authority under the trust instrument.[2] Another example is where the third party made the misrepresentation or exercised the undue influence or duress that vitiated the transfer, without being the defendant to the restitutionary claim.[3] The role of the third party here is likely to be significant only in connection with the question whether the defendant had notice of the vitiating factor, so as to render him subject to a duty of preservation and deny him the defence of change of bona fide purchase. But the presence of a third party in the analysis has sometimes caused confusion.[4]

THE THIRD PARTY AS AN INTERMEDIARY

Sometimes the plaintiff makes a vitiated transfer to a third party, X, who then relays the value received to the defendant. X might receive £100 from the

---

[1] These categories are not mutually exclusive.
[2] See above Chap. 5 at 162.
[3] See above, Chap. 5.
[4] As in *Barclays Bank v O'Brien* [1994] 1 AC 180; see Chap. 7 at 250–2.

plaintiff, and then, thinking himself £100 the richer, give £100 to the defendant.[5] (X may or may not also be responsible for the vitiating factor.) Here one can say that there has been an indirect transfer of value from the plaintiff to the defendant, in the sense that the transfer of value to the defendant was the direct consequence of the transfer from the plaintiff, or in other words the transfer from the plaintiff was the cause of the transfer to the defendant. The issue here is whether, and if so in what circumstances, the plaintiff can have a restitutionary claim against the defendant based on an indirect rather than a direct transfer. As a matter of principle, it seems that a restitutionary claim ought to arise in respect of an indirect transfer just as for a direct transfer. The justification for a claim applies in the same way for the two cases: in both cases there is a vitiated transfer of value from plaintiff to defendant, involving a loss to the plaintiff and a windfall to the defendant. The difference is only evidential, i.e. in showing, in the indirect case, that a particular transfer from the intermediary to the defendant constitutes the transfer of value derived from the plaintiff. A further problem for the plaintiff may be that the defendant is less likely to have notice of the vitiating factor affecting the transfer from the plaintiff, because it was made to an intermediary and not directly to him, and so less likely to incur a duty of preservation. In particular, he may have a defence of bona fide purchase arising from a contract with the intermediary.

However, it seems to be generally thought, to the contrary, that a restitutionary claim arises against an indirect recipient only if the transfer to the defendant by the intermediary, X, was a transfer of the plaintiff's property, and not if there was merely a transfer of value in the sense that the transfer from X was caused by the earlier transfer from the plaintiff.[6] In other words, the plaintiff must identify the asset in the hands of X that was transferred to the defendant as his property. Thus Tettenborn argues that:

> where [X] lawfully transfers to the defendant his own unencumbered property or money, the defendant's title to keep what he gets should be indefeasible, save only in respect of claims by [X] himself.[7]

Some commentators infer that where the plaintiff does have a claim against the defendant it is not a restitutionary claim at all, but a claim arising in the law of property.[8]

But further consideration makes clear that this supposed rule, according to which a claim arising from an indirect transfer can arise only from the transfer of the plaintiff's property, is misleading. In a case where a particular asset

---

[5] X might be a stranger to the plaintiff; but a case where X is the plaintiff's trustee or agent and himself procures the transfer from the plaintiff to himself and then to the defendant would also be a case of this sort.

[6] See e.g. Burrows (1993), 48–9; Tettenborn (1997); L.D. Smith (1997), 299; Birks (1995), 311.

[7] Tettenborn (1997), 1.

[8] e.g. Swadling (1996a), (1997a). It is thought that if title passes to the defendant on receipt the claim will be restitutionary, but that this will not be the case where the transfer is without authority. See further Chap. 9.

derived from the plaintiff is relayed to the defendant, it seems plausible to say that the claim against the defendant arose not because of a transfer of value, but because of the transfer of property of the plaintiff's.[9] But in many cases where a claim is allowed it is not an asset derived from the plaintiff that reaches the defendant from X. Instead, the plaintiff's argument is that his property right in or title to the asset originally transferred from him was transmitted to a different asset in X's estate under the doctrine of tracing, and that the transfer of this substitute or traced asset to the defendant then constituted the transfer of his own property to the defendant. Thus there is an obvious objection. The argument that the plaintiff has a claim only when an asset belonging to him reaches the defendant becomes empty if any asset representing a transfer of value derived from the plaintiff is deemed to belong to him under the doctrine of tracing. If this were the case, then the true position would be that an indirect transfer of value always generates a restitutionary claim, although the formulation of the claim in terms of a transfer of the plaintiff's property might suggest otherwise. It is argued in Chapter 9 that this is, more or less, the correct understanding of tracing. But if this is wrong, it is certainly necessary to give an alternative account of how and why an asset not originally belonging to the plaintiff is deemed to be his, if there is to be any content to the argument that a restitutionary claim arises only from the transfer of the plaintiff's property and not from a mere transfer of value.[10]

There is a further argument for the orthodox view that no claim arises against an indirect recipient just by virtue of a transfer of value, but only by virtue of the receipt of the plaintiff's property. Tettenborn argues that this position is justified because such a rule protects "the freedom of a property owner to do as he wishes with his own, and of others to deal with him on that basis".[11] But it can hardly be said that the direct recipient is free to dispose of his own unencumbered property to third parties if property that would otherwise be his own unencumbered property is deemed not to be by the application of a special set of rules (the tracing rules) that apply in this type of situation, ostensibly for the very purpose of determining whether a claim can arise against an indirect recipient of such property.

It is no doubt true that to allow a claim in respect of indirect transfers as well as direct transfers increases the element of uncertainty involved in dealings with X, which means dealing with anyone, since anyone might be in X's position. But, first, the uncertainty is not of course reduced by an exercise in deeming an indirect transfer to be a transfer of the plaintiff's property. Secondly, the contrary position, limiting claims to arise only from direct transfers, would give far less protection to an owner of wealth, who would often have a restitutionary claim only against the first recipient and no restitutionary claim as soon as the value transferred was disposed of by the first recipient. Furthermore, the

[9] Although the statement disguises complications that will be considered in Chaps. 9 and 10.
[10] And, as concluded in Chap. 9, no such argument is available.
[11] Tettenborn (1997), 6–7.

owner's protection would be limited in an arbitrary way, since as between the plaintiff and the defendant it makes no difference in principle whether the defendant is a direct or indirect recipient. And thirdly, and most importantly, the crucial issue in protecting the defendant recipient, whether he is a direct or indirect recipient, is whether he has a defence of change of position or bona fide purchase. The underlying issue of principle is how to balance the plaintiff's interest in the preservation of his wealth against the interest of a recipient of a transfer in being able to rely on the receipt. This balance is set principally through the level of the duty of inquiry to which recipients are subject.[12] These issues, which raise difficult questions concerning the relation between restitution and property, are discussed further in Chapters 9 and 10. Indeed this section is really a preamble to that discussion.

THE THIRD PARTY AS A CONTRACTOR

As considered in the last chapter, the defendant may have a defence of a bona fide purchase arising from a contract with a party other than the restitutionary plaintiff. In fact this is usually the position with respect to the bona fide purchase defence. Often the other contracting party will also be an intermediary through whom an indirect transfer came from the plaintiff, but this is not necessarily so.

NON-INTERMEDIARY THIRD PARTIES AND "INTERCEPTIVE SUBTRACTION"

Interceptive subtraction

Another type of three-party case is where the third party, X, makes a payment to the defendant that does not consist of value derived from the plaintiff (or of the plaintiff's property), but which nevertheless generates a claim for the plaintiff in the amount of the payment. One would think that such a claim could not be a restitutionary claim to reverse a vitiated transfer, on the basis that it does not arise from a transfer from the plaintiff to the defendant. But Birks has argued that in some such situations the transfer from X to the defendant is in effect a transfer from the plaintiff to the defendant because "the wealth in question would certainly have arrived in the plaintiff if it had not been intercepted by the defendant en route from the third party".[13] The transfer is said to be by way of "interceptive subtraction", by contrast with the ordinary transfer from the plaintiff to the defendant, including the three-party intermediary case, which involves a direct subtraction from the plaintiff's existing wealth. It will be argued below that most, if not all, of the cases that Birks places in his category

---

[12] See further Chap. 10 at 342–6.

[13] Birks (1989a), 133–4, and generally 133–9, 142–6. For a valuable critique of the theory of interceptive subtraction, see L.D. Smith (1991).

of interceptive subtraction can be better explained on some other, non-restitutionary basis.[14]

The mere fact that X makes a payment to the defendant that he would otherwise have made to the plaintiff cannot by itself give rise to a restitutionary claim. This is so because there is no transfer from the plaintiff. For example, say the plaintiff makes an offer to do business with X, but before X accepts the defendant makes a better offer, which X does accept. Even if it is assumed that X would have accepted the plaintiff's offer if he had not accepted the defendant's, so that the defendant received from X what would otherwise have gone to the plaintiff, the plaintiff clearly has no claim against the defendant, restitutionary or otherwise,[15] unless the defendant was under a duty not to interfere, or a duty to act on behalf of the plaintiff. Another example might be where X has offered a prize for the fastest 100 metres run before a certain date, and just before the date the defendant beats the previous fastest time by the plaintiff, thereby diverting to himself the reward that would otherwise have gone to the plaintiff. Here again there is of course no claim. These examples reflect the crucial distinction between the plaintiff's existing wealth, which he can be deprived of only by an unvitiated transfer, and the plaintiff's expectation of future wealth, which can be defeated by the diversion to the defendant of wealth that the plaintiff expected to receive, which is objectionable only where it involves a breach of duty by the defendant.[16]

One might argue that where the defendant incurs a liability to account to the plaintiff for the value received by him from a third party (such a liability does arise in some circumstances, as discussed below), his failure to do so constitutes a diversion of value to himself, and therefore the claim is based on interceptive subtraction.[17] But here the important question is of course the basis on which the defendant incurred the liability to account in the first place. The fact that the defendant incurred a liability to account to the plaintiff—in effect to relay the value received to the plaintiff—does not mean that the liability arose because the value would have reached the plaintiff. Furthermore, the defendant's failure to satisfy the liability to the plaintiff is not relevant to the accrual of the liability to the plaintiff in the first place.[18] One might say that the defendant's failure to satisfy his liability to the plaintiff leaves him unjustly enriched. It must be true that if a defendant does not satisfy a liability to the plaintiff he is in a sense unjustly enriched at the plaintiff's expense, but this is true of any remedial liability, whatever its nature, whether in contract or tort or otherwise, and this does not turn it into a liability in restitution or unjust enrichment.[19]

---

[14] Smith reaches the same conclusion: L.D. Smith (1991).

[15] Leaving aside the question whether the benefit received by the plaintiff from X involved a transfer of wealth to him.

[16] It is beside the point to ask whether there was a vitiating factor in such cases because there was no transfer.

[17] The vitiating factor would presumably be lack of authority.

[18] This seems to correspond to the circularity objection made in L.D. Smith (1991), 486.

[19] Cf below, 273.

Receipt of a profit by a fiduciary from his position

A fiduciary is liable to account to his principal for a profit made from his position, as for example where he is a director who takes personal advantage of a corporate opportunity.[20] The fact that the claim is based on the receipt of value might suggest that it is restitutionary, and it has been argued that it can be explained as a restitutionary claim arising from interceptive subtraction.[21] Now, in some (but not all) cases of this sort the benefit would have ended up with the plaintiff if the defendant fiduciary had not taken it. But, even in such cases, the claim is based on the plaintiff's loss of an expectation of future wealth, not on loss through a transfer of pre-existing wealth, and as argued above the restitutionary claim arising from a vitiated transfer can only arise in respect of pre-existing wealth. Furthermore, there is no difficulty in explaining the claim on more orthodox lines. Sometimes the claim will be best understood as a claim for compensation for loss caused by a breach by the defendant of his fiduciary duty.[22] Where the breach of duty consists of diverting to the defendant an opportunity that would otherwise have gone to the plaintiff, the profit made by the defendant is a reasonable measure of the loss caused to the plaintiff.[23] In other cases, where the profit would not have gone to the plaintiff, even if the defendant had fulfilled his duty,[24] the claim is explicable as a claim for disgorgement.[25]

By contrast, there is clearly a restitutionary claim arising from a vitiated transfer (in addition to a claim arising from a breach of duty) where a director, acting without authority, transfers the company's existing money or property to himself or another party.[26] Some confusion has resulted from the description in some cases[27] of the corporate opportunity as the company's property, which is conceived of as being transferred to the defendant when the defendant takes the

---

[20] e.g. *Cook v Deeks* [1916] 1 AC 554; *Canadian Aero-Services v O'Malley* (1973) 40 DLR (3d) 371. Fiduciary relationships are considered in Chap. 13.

[21] Birks (1989a), 137,145.

[22] See further Chap. 13 at n 18.

[23] Even where the remedy is in the form of a constructive trust, it may be best explained as a compensatory remedy: see e.g. *LAC Minerals Ltd v International Corona Resources Ltd* (1989) 61 DLR (4th) 14, 17 per Wilson J. See further Chap. 10 at 348. There may similarly be circumstances where a defendant can be liable in the measure of the value of a benefit received as the measure of the plaintiff's loss where the tortious duty was not to interfere in the plaintiff's acquisition of the benefit: e.g. possibly a duty against intimidation, or conspiracy, or abuse of a dominant position.

[24] e.g. *Industrial Development Consultants v Cooley* [1972] 1 WLR 443, where X refused to deal with the plaintiff and this prompted the defendant to breach his duty and take the contract for himself.

[25] Disgorgement is considered in Chap. 11. With respect to a claim arising in respect of a receipt by the fiduciary, the no-conflict rule can be helpful to the plaintiff as considered in Chap. 13.

[26] e.g. *Guinness v Saunders* [1988] 1 WLR 863. This might include a case where X already had an accrued contractual liability to the company, and the director, acting beyond his authority, transferred it to himself or another party.

[27] e.g. *Cook v Deeks* [1916] 1 AC 554.

opportunity for himself,[28] but in fact an opportunity merely represents an expectation of wealth, not a form of existing wealth, and the claim in such cases must be based on a breach of duty.

Receipt by an agent on behalf of the plaintiff

Another situation where the payment by X generates a claim for the plaintiff, which may well overlap with the last type of situation and the next, is where the defendant is the plaintiff's agent who receives a payment paid to him for the account of the plaintiff.[29] When the defendant receives such a payment, he incurs a liability to the plaintiff for the sum received. Again the liability is not restitutionary; here it is contractual, arising out of the agreement between the plaintiff and the defendant governing the defendant's agency.[30] It may be true to say that if the payment had not been made to the defendant it would have been made to the plaintiff (or to someone else for the plaintiff) so that if the defendant fails to account to the plaintiff he has effectively diverted the transfer to himself. But this fact does not generate the liability, which arises from the arrangement between the plaintiff and the defendant, and from the unvitiated intention of X in making the transfer to the defendant.

Trust, attornment and privity

Trust and attornment

In another type of case X makes a payment to the defendant for him to hold for or pay over to the plaintiff, but the defendant is not the plaintiff's agent and the receipt is not governed by any existing agreement between the defendant and the plaintiff. Nevertheless the plaintiff may have a claim against the defendant. Most commonly the claim is a claim under a trust, on the basis that the payment by X was made to the defendant on trust for the plaintiff. The constitution of the trust by the transfer of the money and the declaration of trust immediately generates a claim for the plaintiff for the money paid to the defendant. There is an analogous claim at common law. Here, a claim accrues to the plaintiff in the

---

[28] This seems to have been in order to enable the shareholders to sue by bringing the case within the exception to the proper plaintiff rule in company law ("the rule in *Foss v Harbottle*"), which was thought to require a transfer of property from the company.

[29] This type of case is not separately identified by Birks in connection with interceptive subtraction.

[30] The defendant will take the payment on trust if this is the understanding with the plaintiff. One might argue that there is not necessarily any contract behind an agency relationship, because of the absence of consideration (meaning an exchange). But the reason the liability arises is the agreement between the two parties governing the appointment of the agent, and if the liability does in fact arise, it arises by virtue of the agreement, and it is perverse to deny that it is contractual; cf Chap. 3 at 128.

measure of the sum received, but only when the defendant "attorns" to the plaintiff by acknowledging such a liability to him.[31]

Birks considers the plaintiff's claim arising from attornment at common law to be a restitutionary claim based on interceptive subtraction.[32] He argues that the function of attornment is as a conclusive indicator of the fact that the value received by the defendant would certainly have reached the plaintiff, so as to establish interceptive subtraction. No doubt if X had not made the transfer to the defendant he would generally have arranged by some other way to make a transfer to or for the benefit of the plaintiff; but it is difficult to see why the attornment should be indicative of this. And even if the payment would have gone to the plaintiff, this is not in itself, as argued above, enough to justify a claim, and so even if the attornment were an indicator of this it would not explain why the claim arose. Furthermore, it is surely clear that attornment is the exercise of a legal power, which changes legal relations, not merely an act whose significance is as evidence of what did or might have happened.[33]

Both attornment and trust are generally understood to be part of the law of property, and in particular to provide a means of transferring or creating a right of property or an interest in property or a fund of property.[34] But, although a claim arising out of a trust or attornment may generate rights or interests in or relating to property, the true basis for the plaintiff's claim here is surely the agreement made by the defendant with X to relay the payment to the plaintiff. Attornment is concerned with the question who can enforce the defendant's undertaking to X to account to the plaintiff. In the normal way one would expect the agreement by the defendant with X to be enforceable only by X under the privity doctrine.[35] But it is clearly convenient for both X and the plaintiff if the liability is enforceable by the plaintiff, although a difficulty could arise if the liability were enforceable by both of them. The function of attornment is to determine when the defendant's liability to X lapses and is replaced by a liability to account to the plaintiff.[36] In equity the plaintiff has the right to enforce, and X's right lapses, from the moment when the trust is constituted and declared.

Secret trusts

Birks considers that a claim under a trust is not in the normal course a restitutionary claim arising from interceptive subtraction, but that sometimes it can be

---

[31] The claim arising from attornment is said to be a personal claim for money had and received, but the claim is said to relate to a fund in the hands of the defendant: Goode (1976), 366, 384.

[32] Birks (1989*a*), 134.

[33] For another example of treating the exercise of a legal power as if it were a conclusive indicator of a matter of fact, see above, Chap. 3 at 132, in connection with Atiyah's "promises as admissions".

[34] e.g. L.D. Smith (1991), 504–11.

[35] See Jaffey (1998*c*), 128. There would be a difficulty over the appropriate remedy; cf *Beswick v Beswick* [1968] AC 58. The doctrine of privity will not be considered here, nor will the effect of the recent statutory reform of the doctrine.

[36] Just as if there were a novation.

so explained. He identifies one such case in the secret trust.[37] A secret trust arises where the defendant agrees with X that if X leaves a legacy to the defendant in his will, the defendant will pay over the legacy to the plaintiff. The agreement is given effect to in equity by way of a trust of the legacy that is binding on the defendant and enforceable by the plaintiff.[38] The trust is known as a secret trust, because the arrangement is designed to prevent X's provision for the plaintiff from being published, as it would be if X simply left the legacy to the plaintiff in his will. Secret trusts have caused some controversy because the agreement giving rise to the secret trust is enforceable even though it does not comply with the requirement for testamentary dispositions to be in writing, signed and witnessed, under the Wills Act 1837, section 9. Birks argues that here the agreement made by X and the defendant cannot be enforceable as such because of non-compliance with the Wills Act, and that instead the plaintiff's claim is a restitutionary claim based on interceptive subtraction. The defendant intercepts a transfer from X to the plaintiff, in effect resulting in a transfer from the plaintiff to the defendant, which the plaintiff's claim reverses. But, as already seen, the claim cannot arise from the mere fact that the transfer would have reached the plaintiff by some other route; there is no transfer of wealth from the plaintiff and, for that matter, no vitiating factor affecting any of the parties.

Again, a better analysis is that the plaintiff's claim arises from the defendant's agreement with X, which the plaintiff is allowed to enforce by way of a trust, notwithstanding that he is a third party to it, and notwithstanding the formality requirements. The trust is not fully constituted at the time of the agreement, but only when the defendant receives the legacy. It is particular clear here that the plaintiff should be able to enforce the agreement, even though he is not a party to it, because X has died having relied on the agreement with the defendant and can no longer act to protect his reliance under it.[39] It is the defendant's reneging on his agreement with X that the courts have characterised as fraud under the fraud theory of the secret trust.[40] Whether it is justified to give effect to the agreement notwithstanding the Wills Act is a difficult question; a similar issue was considered in Chapter 3.[41]

Mistaken payment by the third party

Consider the case where X makes a payment to the defendant by mistake, intending to pay the plaintiff. X might have mistaken the defendant for the

---

[37] Birks (1989*a*), 135–6.

[38] The leading cases are *McCormick v Grogan* (1869) LR 4 HL 82 and *Blackwell v Blackwell* [1829] AC 318.

[39] Jaffey (1989*c*), 128.

[40] The fraud theory was adopted in *McCormick v Grogan* (1869) LR 4 HL 82. It is the unfortunate effect of the division between law and equity to disguise the contractual basis of the claim: see Appendix 2 and Chap. 13 at 408; see also Chap. 3 at 111–12.

[41] In the section on "unenforceable contracts".

plaintiff, say, or he might have meant to make a payment to the plaintiff, and thought that the defendant was the plaintiff's agent, when in fact he was not and had no apparent authority as such. X clearly has a restitutionary claim based on mistake to recover the payment from the defendant.

It could be argued that in this type of case also it would be convenient for all parties if the plaintiff had a claim against the defendant to give effect to the original intention of X, which has been frustrated by his mistake. Correspondingly, X's claim against the defendant would have to lapse in order to protect the defendant against a double liability for the same receipt. But the usual rule appears to be that X has the claim to recover the payment for mistake, so that X can then decide, if he wishes, to make the payment to the plaintiff, or not now to make it and to keep the money instead.[42] If he had not made a mistake the payment would now be with the plaintiff and irrecoverable; but where, even if fortuitously, the payment has not taken effect, X retains the right to change his mind. This reflects the traditional equitable doctrine that "equity will not perfect an imperfect gift"[43] where the plaintiff has attempted to make a gift but failed, by mistake or otherwise, to take the appropriate steps to carry out his intentions.

But suppose X died before he had had time to recover the gift from the defendant. Then it seems that his executors would be able to recover the money for the estate, but they would not be able to make the originally intended gift, because they would be bound by the terms of the will or intestacy. Possibly here the plaintiff should be able to recover the payment for himself. There is some slight authority to suggest that the plaintiff might acquire a claim in such circumstances.[44] If there is such a claim, it is justified as an exception to the rule against perfecting an imperfect gift, by which the intention of the donor will be effected by operation of law after his death where his true intention is known and he took the appropriate steps to implement it while he was alive on the facts as he understood them. In such circumstances, contrary to the assumption behind the usual rule against perfecting an imperfect gift, the donor is not in a position to perfect the gift himself. The claim in such a case is not a restitutionary claim to reverse X's vitiated transfer to the defendant, or not merely such a claim; it might be understood as having the effect of first reversing the vitiated transfer and then substituting the intended transfer. One might say that the plaintiff has a "derivative" claim by which he enforces X's restitutionary claim for his own benefit and thereby gives effect to X's interest in the fulfilment of his original intention. The claim is derivative in the sense that it is based on protecting X's right to make the payment rather than a right of the plaintiff's to receive it.[45] One might also reasonably say that the claim arises because the

---

[42] See L.D. Smith (1991), 516.

[43] Or "equity will not assist a volunteer": *Milroy v Lord* (1862) 4 De GF & J 264.

[44] Birks so argues: Birks (1989a), 137, relying on a dictum in *Lister v Hodgson* (1867) LR 4 Eq 30, 34.

[45] One could say that the derivative claim should be implemented by subrogating the plaintiff to X's restitutionary claim against the defendant: see at n 72 below.

defendant intercepted a transfer on its way to the plaintiff, although this description does not fully convey the nature of the claim (if such a claim arises at all).

Usurpation of office

The usurpation of office cases are also invoked as examples of interceptive subtraction.[46] In these cases, the defendant has usurped an office that the plaintiff is entitled to occupy, and receives a payment made to him as office-holder by the third party, X. It seems here that the payment ought to have been made to the plaintiff and not the defendant, and that, having paid the wrong person, X should remain liable to the plaintiff for the amount due to the office-holder. X would then have a restitutionary claim to recover his payment from the defendant, based on his mistake in paying the wrong person. The plaintiff's position, on this analysis, seems to be quite unaltered by the mistaken payment by X: he continues to have a claim against X for the amount due to the office-holder.

But in fact the position is that X's liability to the office-holder is discharged. Although as between the plaintiff and the defendant the plaintiff is entitled to hold the office, as against third parties the defendant has the rights and powers of the office-holder: he is the de facto office-holder, and can give a good discharge for a debt owed to the office-holder.[47] Correspondingly, the defendant is liable to account to the plaintiff for the amount of the payment.[48] The claim is based on the fact that, although the defendant may be the de facto office-holder, the plaintiff and not the defendant is the true office-holder, ultimately entitled to the benefits of the office.[49] This rule that the de facto office-holder gives a good discharge is obviously designed to protect X from being prejudiced by the dispute between the plaintiff and the defendant. In the absence of such a rule, X would still have to pay the plaintiff, and he would have to recover the payment mistakenly made to the defendant if he was not to end up paying twice over. If he had notice of the possibility that the defendant might not be the true office-holder, he might have the dilemma of whether to pay the defendant (or even the plaintiff), possibly without any right of recovery if the payment proved not to discharge his liability to the true office-holder,[50] or not to pay until the dispute

---

[46] Birks (1989*a*), 134.
[47] See the discussion in L.D. Smith (1991), 494.
[48] e.g. *Arris v Stukely* (1677) 2 Mod 260.
[49] Ibid. An alternative basis is that the claim is for compensation for the loss caused to the plaintiff by a wrong committed through the usurpation. There may be such a claim, but there may not always be a wrong, and in any case the claim has always taken the form of a claim for money had and received rather than damages. One might argue that it is a claim for disgorgement arising from the wrong. Sometimes the claim has involved a waiver of tort, and this is sometimes equated with disgorgement, but this view is rejected in Chap. 11.
[50] On the basis of assumption of risk: see Chap. 5 at 175–7.

is resolved, risking the consequences that might follow from non-payment of the sum due to the office-holder (which might be, e.g., loss of a licence).

Thus the rule by which the defendant, as the de facto office-holder, gives a good discharge, and the rule that the defendant becomes liable to the plaintiff for sums paid to him as office-holder, go together to avoid circuity of action and to force litigation onto the most appropriate parties to conduct it.[51] The law here is procedural in the sense that it is designed not to alter the final distribution of wealth—the value in question should end up with the true office-holder—but the manner by which this final position is attained.[52] The final outcome (if all claims are pursued, and subject to the vicissitudes of litigation) is the same as would be achieved by the alternative legal position, according to which X would have to recover the payment and then pay the plaintiff, but the law as it is does not impose the same risk of prejudice to X, who should not be affected by the dispute. Smith denies that a procedural principle of this sort can determine who has a cause of action.[53] Certainly considerations of this sort should not determine the final allocation of wealth, but there is no reason why they should not determine the means by which it is achieved. Again there is no need to invoke interceptive subtraction as the basis for the claim.

Re Diplock

The claim in Re *Diplock*[54] has also been argued to be an example of interceptive subtraction.[55] Here, a testator's executor made a payment out of the estate to a charity ostensibly in accordance with the terms of the will. However, it transpired that the relevant clause of the will was invalid and the payment was therefore outside the authority of the executor under the will. The payment ought to have been made to the plaintiff, the beneficiary in default, who inherited on the invalidity of the clause. The plaintiff was permitted a claim against the defendant charity, but it was held that he had first to exhaust his claim against the executor.

Two interpretations of the case have been suggested.[56] On the first interpretation, the executor, X, controls wealth belonging in substance to the beneficiary; thus when X makes a transfer outside the terms of the trust he is an intermediary who transfers wealth from the plaintiff to the defendant. This is the normal analysis of a claim by a beneficiary arising from a payment made by a trustee beyond his authority under the terms of the trust.[57] On this approach

---

[51] This principle was cited in a similar case concerning payment of rent, *Official Custodian for Charities v Mackey (No 2)* [1985] 1 WLR 1308, 1314–15.

[52] It is not procedural in the sense of pertaining merely to the procedure governing a particular claim as opposed to the substantive law. In this sense, the rule is substantive, not procedural.

[53] L.D. Smith (1991), 491.

[54] [1948] Ch 465.

[55] Birks, 143.

[56] L.D. Smith (1991), 497ff; Burrows (1993), 52.

[57] But the conditions for the claim in Re *Diplock* differed from the usual equitable claims arising from breach of trust, as discussed in Chap. 10 at 334.

it is difficult to see why the plaintiff should be obliged to sue the executors first: he would simply have concurrent claims for compensation for breach of trust against the executors and in restitution against the defendant charity. No such requirement exists in the normal case of payment in breach of trust.

On the second interpretation, which corresponds to Smith's analysis,[58] this is not an intermediary case. The legal relation between the executor and the plaintiff is that the executor merely has a liability to account to the plaintiff for the amount owing to him under the intestacy; the executor does not hold the estate or any part of it on trust for the plaintiff (at least in the normal sense), or in other words he does not control wealth belonging to the plaintiff and does not transfer wealth from the plaintiff to the defendant, so as to generate a restitutionary claim for the plaintiff against the defendant. Thus the plaintiff and the defendant are linked not by the fact that there was a transfer of wealth from the plaintiff to the defendant going via the executor as an intermediary, but by the fact that the payment was made to the defendant when it ought to have been made to the plaintiff, just as in the usurpation of office or mistake cases above.

On this second interpretation, it seems that the plaintiff's legal position is unaffected by the payment to the defendant; he retains his claim against the executor, X, for the amount owed to him. There is no rule that payment to the defendant discharges the executor, X; by contrast with the case of usurpation of office, there is no basis for saying that the executor should be protected from the consequences of the mistake, and the plaintiff left to resolve the position as between him and the defendant. It is X who is responsible for making the claim against the defendant, and who has the restitutionary claim against the defendant arising from the mistaken payment. However, one might argue that in so far as X fails to recover the payment from the defendant, and in so far as in consequence he is unable to satisfy the plaintiff's claim against the estate, the defendant has been enriched at the expense of the plaintiff, and so should be liable to a claim by him. Such a claim by the plaintiff against the defendant can on this approach arise only once the plaintiff's claim against X is exhausted, as the court actually decided in Re *Diplock*. One might think that the plaintiff's claim against the defendant in these circumstances would inevitably be futile because if X could not recover from the defendant there would be nothing for the plaintiff to recover either. But Smith argues that in Re *Diplock* X's claim (but apparently not the plaintiff's) would have been precluded by the mistake of law bar.[59]

There are problems with this approach, however. Ex hypothesi (on this approach), X is not an intermediary transferring value from the plaintiff. Any loss to the plaintiff resulting from the inability of the estate to satisfy his claim as a result of the mistaken payment is equivalent to loss suffered in just the same way by anyone with a claim against the estate that the executors cannot satisfy

---

[58] L.D. Smith (1991), 497.

[59] L.D. Smith (1991), 497. (The bar has now been abolished, as discussed in Chap. 5.) But it seems that the mistake of law bar was not applied in equity: see Law Commission (1994), para. 2.13. If the bar did apply, it is not clear why it would not equally have affected the plaintiff's claim.

as a result of the mistaken payment. Thus any legatee or even any creditor of the estate could have a claim against the defendant on the same basis. This surely cannot be correct. If the wealth in the estate is not the wealth of the plaintiff or any other claimant from the estate, it follows that any claim in respect of the mistaken payment must be made by X for the benefit of the estate, so that the sum recovered is available to be allocated amongst claimants to the estate according to the rules governing the winding up of the estate. A direct claim by the plaintiff would be liable to subvert these rules.[60] The plaintiff can have a claim against the defendant in his own right only in the intermediary case, where the transfer is from the plaintiff, not merely out of the estate. Thus the better view is that Re *Diplock* should indeed be understood as an intermediary case, and the requirement to sue the executors before the recipient should be abandoned, as has been widely suggested.[61]

SUBROGATION

Subrogation is a doctrine by which, it is said, the plaintiff stands in the position of a third party, X, for the purposes of a claim against the defendant.[62] In the usual case, the three parties are the plaintiff, the creditor and the defendant debtor. The liability of the debtor to the creditor—the "pre-existing" liability—may have arisen in contract, or tort, or out of a vitiated transfer, or otherwise. The plaintiff pays the creditor in respect of the pre-existing liability of the debtor to the creditor. The plaintiff is then subrogated to the position of the creditor, in the sense that he has a claim against the debtor in the precise terms of the creditor's pre-existing claim. The effect is that, overall, the creditor's claim is satisfied at the debtor's expense; but this is achieved not directly through a transfer from the debtor to the creditor, but in two stages, first by a payment to the creditor by the plaintiff and then by way of a claim by the plaintiff against the debtor.

There are two interrelated issues with respect to cases like this. First, there is the question why it is that a payment by the plaintiff to one person should give him a claim against another person; why it is, in other words, that the plaintiff can pay the defendant's debt and thereby acquire a claim against him. This depends on the type of case in issue—i.e., the nature of the pre-existing liability—and the various cases have nothing in common in this respect. Secondly, there is the question why it is apt to express the plaintiff's claim against the debtor as if it were the creditor's original claim. This is in reality a fiction: the

---

[60] Cf the rule in company law that a creditor cannot sue a director because this would subvert the winding up rules: Jaffey (1996*b*), 43. Furthermore, the second interpretation is impossible to reconcile with the availability to the plaintiff of an in rem claim against the defendant, as recognised in Re *Diplock* [1984] ch 465.

[61] e.g. Hayton (1996), 836; Goff & Jones (1998), 702. This means that the case should be assimilated with the normal claim arising from a breach of trust: see further Chap. 10, at 334.

[62] Mitchell (1994), 3.

claim is not the creditor's pre-existing claim, but a new claim of the plaintiff's.[63] The crucial point is that the plaintiff's claim exactly simulates the pre-existing claim of the creditor, in the sense that the measure and the validity of the plaintiff's claim are determined by the measure and the validity of the pre-existing claim. By expressing the plaintiff's claim by way of subrogation, the measure and validity of the pre-existing claim are automatically brought into issue. Thus subrogation is a legal device, or more precisely a compendious way of formulating a claim, which is apt where the plaintiff acquires a claim that exactly simulates the pre-existing claim of a third party, to which the plaintiff is subrogated. It can be appropriate in various contexts; it is not itself a type of claim in the sense of being contractual or tortious or restitutionary.

One example of subrogation arises in the case of compulsory discharge. Here, as considered in Chapter 3, the plaintiff is compelled to satisfy the defendant debtor's liability to the creditor as a means of facilitating the satisfaction of the creditor's claim and protecting him from having to take proceedings against the defendant himself, and, as a corollary, to ensure that the plaintiff does not bear the final burden of the defendant's liability, the plaintiff acquires a claim against the defendant to recover the amount paid to the creditor. In Chapter 3, this claim was discussed without mention of subrogation.[64] But subrogation is an apt way of formulating the claim because (or, at least, subrogation is apt in so far as it is true to say that) the defendant should be liable to the plaintiff only if and to the extent that he would have been liable to the creditor, i.e. only if there was in fact a pre-existing liability, and in its measure.[65] Another case of subrogation is where the plaintiff is the defendant's surety, who pays the creditor because he is contractually bound to do so on the defendant's default under the contract of suretyship, and acquires a contract claim for reimbursement under the same contract.[66] Again, the claim was discussed in Chapter 3 without mention of subrogation, but subrogation is an apt form for the plaintiff's claim because the defendant should be liable to reimburse the plaintiff only if and to the extent that the defendant was actually in default, and a claim expressed by way of subrogation will naturally incorporate this condition.

Another standard example of subrogation is the indemnity insurer's subrogation right.[67] Here the pre-existing liability is the liability of a tortfeasor (the

---

[63] Birks (1989a), 375. But see below at n 69.

[64] It seems that such cases are not usually disposed of in terms of subrogation except in the case of sureties, but see Mitchell (1994), Chap. 5.

[65] It is sometimes said that in cases like this there are alternative claims, directly at common law, and indirectly by subrogation in equity: Mitchell (1994), 51. But there is in reality only one claim, although expressed in a different form in equity and at common law. It is impossible to identify two different bases for a claim.

[66] See Mitchell (1994), Chap. 5. It has been argued (e.g. Mitchell (1994), chap. 10) that the surety's claim is a restitutionary claim arising from failure of consideration, the default of the defendant debtor constituting the failure of consideration, in accordance with the restitutionary conditional transfer theory rejected in earlier chapters. The better view is that the right of subrogation is contractual, arising from a term, actual or implied, in the surety contract; cf Chap. 3 at 97–98.

[67] See Mitchell (1994), Chap. 6.

defendant debtor) to compensate a tort victim (the creditor), and the creditor is also the insured under a policy of indemnity insurance with the plaintiff insurer, who is liable to indemnify the creditor in respect of his loss resulting from the tort. As between the plaintiff insurer and the creditor-insured, the plaintiff is liable to indemnify the insured for his net loss,[68] but the net loss depends not only on the cost to the creditor-insured of the injury caused by the tort, but also on the value to him of the claim that has accrued to him against the tortfeasor as a result of the injury. The problem is that it is very difficult to make any judgement of the value of the cause of action, which will depend on the likelihood that the insured will be able to take proceedings and get judgment. But this seems to mean that the position as between the plaintiff and the creditor cannot be resolved until after such proceedings. The difficulty can be overcome if the insured pays for the full cost of the injury but acquires from the insured the cause of action against the tortfeasor, or at least the right to any benefit obtained through it. Thus again the measure and validity of the plaintiff's claim against the defendant tortfeasor are determined by the measure and validity of the creditor's pre-existing claim against him.[69]

A further example of subrogation is where the plaintiff has made a vitiated transfer to the defendant and the defendant uses the surviving value to discharge a debt to the creditor. It seems that the plaintiff has a restitutionary claim to surviving value against the defendant in the measure of the debt discharged, on the basis that the discharge of the debt represented a receipt of wealth to the defendant.[70] If the debt was not in fact due to the creditor, the defendant should not be regarded as having received a transfer of wealth or as otherwise having been benefited through the payment to the creditor, and this is the effect of treating the plaintiff's restitutionary claim as being a subrogated claim.[71] This example of subrogation is discussed in Chapter 9 in connection with tracing.

The claim arising from usurpation of office discussed earlier in this chapter might be formulated in terms of subrogation, but according to a different pattern from the cases discussed above. Again there are three parties, the creditor, the debtor and a third party, X, but here the plaintiff is the creditor, not X as in

---

[68] This is an aspect of the "principle of indemnity" (see e.g. Mitchell (1994), 68), or, one might say, the principle against over-compensation.

[69] This is said to be "simple subrogation", rather than "reviving subrogation". In a case of reviving subrogation, the plaintiff's payment discharges the debtor's liability because the plaintiff acts or is taken to act on behalf of the debtor, and the liability to the creditor is replaced by an equivalent liability to the plaintiff. By contrast, in a case of simple subrogation the plaintiff acts on behalf of the creditor and the payment does not discharge the debtor's liability; but, as between the plaintiff and the creditor, it is the plaintiff, not the creditor, who has the benefit of the claim. Thus proceedings against the defendant must be in the creditor's name, but the plaintiff is entitled to control the proceedings and to take the proceeds. In reality the claim is the plaintiff's, not the creditor's, although it has to be made in the name of the creditor.

[70] *Banque Financière de la Cité v Parc (Battersea) Ltd* [1998] 2 WLR 475; *Boscawen v Bajwa* [1996] 1 WLR 328.

[71] If this is not the case, the claim should not be expressed through subrogation. Alternatively the plaintiff has a restitutionary claim to payment in respect of an incontrovertible benefit non-officiously conferred through the discharge of the debt, as discussed in Chap. 3.

the standard pattern above. Under the standard pattern there is first a payment by X to the creditor and then a subrogated claim by X against the debtor. In the usurpation of office case there is first a payment by the debtor to X, who is the de facto office-holder, which generates a claim against X by the creditor, who is the true office-holder. The overall effect is to achieve the movement of value from the debtor to the creditor, but by a different route from the usual form of subrogation. As in the compulsory discharge cases, the rationale for the rule is to release a party from further litigation or dispute, but here it is the debtor who is protected rather than the creditor. In fact it is not customary to refer to this as an example of subrogation, but it seems that expressing the claim in terms of subrogation would be apt because the effect would be to preserve any defence of change of position that X might have had to a restitutionary claim by the debtor.[72]

Subrogation is thought by some to be in essence a restitutionary doctrine.[73] It is argued (in terms of the standard pattern again) that, once the plaintiff has made a payment to the creditor, if he is not subrogated to the creditor's claim against the debtor either the creditor will be unjustly enriched (if the pre-existing liability of the debtor is not discharged by the payment so that the creditor can in effect recover twice over),[74] or the debtor will be unjustly enriched (if the pre-existing liability is discharged, but without the debtor incurring a new liability to the plaintiff).[75] It is true that where there is a rule designed to shift wealth or benefit between the debtor and the creditor through the intervention of the plaintiff by way of subrogation, if the plaintiff has paid and then the process is not completed, the creditor or the debtor will be unjustly enriched and the plaintiff unjustly impoverished. Indeed, as noted above,[76] in any situation where, as a result of some act or event, the defendant incurs a remedial liability to the plaintiff, whether the remedial liability arises in contract, or tort, or restitution for a vitiated transfer, or otherwise, the plaintiff will be unjustly impoverished and the defendant unjustly enriched if the remedial liability is not in due course satisfied. But this cannot mean that the remedial liability is restitutionary or that it arises to prevent unjust enrichment, or all claims would be subsumed into restitution. As the examples above show, subrogation is a technique that can arise in various types of case, and neither the subrogated claim nor the pre-existing liability necessarily falls into any particular field of law.

---

[72] e.g. if X was not to know that he was not the true office-holder and had changed his position in reliance on receipt. Another case that might be described in terms of subrogation following the same pattern as the usurpation of office case is where a gift intended for the plaintiff is misdirected to X. The plaintiff can be said to be subrogated to the donor's restitutionary claim to recover the payment: see above at n 45.

[73] Millett LJ took this view in *Boscawen v Bajwa* [1995] 4 All ER 769, 777; Mitchell (1994), 4; Burrows (1993), 92.

[74] i.e. in a case of simple subrogation: Mitchell (1994), 9.

[75] i.e. in a case of reviving subrogation: Mitchell (1994), 10.

[76] Above 261.

9

Restitution and Property: A Rational Scheme

T HE RELATIONSHIP BETWEEN the law of restitution for vitiated transfers and the law of property has been a matter of great controversy. This is the subject of this chapter and the next. For the most part this chapter will concentrate on general principles and concepts. The objective is to find a rational approach to this difficult area of law,[1] without for the moment concentrating too closely on the cases or accepted doctrine. The approach proposed is at odds with certain widely held assumptions about property and restitution. In the next chapter the law will be considered in more detail to see to what extent it can be explained, and how it might be developed, in accordance with the approach suggested in this chapter.

The restitutionary claim to surviving value protects wealth or transferable value.[2] In previous chapters, it has generally been assumed that the vitiated transfer is, as it were, a transfer of disembodied value, or of value in the abstract. But the plaintiff's wealth, or transferable value, can take a number of different forms. It may be what might be called "pure wealth", which is held purely as a store of value, in the form of cash, or money in the bank or investments, which are usually in law contractual rights to payment; or it may take the form of a tangible thing like land or a chattel, or an intangible thing, like a company share or intellectual property. In some or all of these cases, the plaintiff's wealth would also be said to be his property; as will become clear, it is not for present purposes necessary to consider what types of wealth are properly described as property or as an asset.[3] In many cases a transfer of value will also be a transfer of property.[4]

There is taken to be an important distinction between proprietary and restitutionary claims arising from transfers of the plaintiff's property or wealth, or

---

[1] This approach was set out in a paper to the Restitution Section of the SPTL Conference 1998.

[2] Cf *Nelson v Larholt* [1948] 1 KB 339, 342, *per* Denning J: "[a] man's money is property which is protected by law. It may exists in various forms, such as coins, treasury notes, cash at bank, or cheques, or bills of exchange".

[3] It is not necessary to consider whether, for example, a contractual right to payment counts as property.

[4] A transfer of wealth by way of an instruction to the bank to deduct a sum from the customer's account and credit it to someone else's account would not normally be described as a transfer of property even if the contractual right to the money in the account were so described.

in other words between claims arising in the law of property and claims arising in the law of restitution. ("Proprietary" is used here in this sense, and not to mean "in rem", which is defined below.) A proprietary claim is understood to be a claim arising from the defendant's receipt of property still belonging to the plaintiff. The plaintiff retains ownership or title, although the asset transferred enters the defendant's possession or control; it is sometimes said that there is an ineffective transfer. In other words, the asset remains in the plaintiff's estate rather than the defendant's, a person's estate being the sum of all his property or wealth. A restitutionary claim, by contrast, is understood to arise where title to the asset is effectively transferred to the defendant, and the asset becomes part of his estate, but nevertheless the transfer of value is vitiated so that the plaintiff has a claim to surviving value out of the defendant's estate.

However, the thesis put forward here is that the distinction between restitutionary and proprietary claims arising from the transfer of wealth or property is entirely spurious, and that the failure to perceive this has been the source of enormous confusion. The simple reason why the two should be equated is that both are concerned with protecting the same interest—viz. the plaintiff's interest in his wealth or transferable value, which includes, or is equivalent to, his property—against a vitiated transfer.[5] It might be thought that property law in some sense protects a distinct interest in a tangible thing, rather than mere value or the value of a thing, which is what the claim to surviving value protects. But this would be a misunderstanding. First, there are forms of wealth other than tangible things that are said to be the subjects of property law and proprietary claims. In many cases where a claim is said to be proprietary the transfer is a transfer of money, even a transfer taking effect by way of an electronic credit transfer. More importantly, whatever forms of wealth are correctly described as property, by definition the interest of an owner in his property must be measured by its value to him, provided that all aspects of value are taken into account, and there is no distinction to be drawn between protecting the right to an asset and protecting the right to its value. This is true not only of pure wealth but also of forms of property that have special value to the plaintiff. It may be that in such a case the best way of ensuring that the full value of the property is restored is by returning the asset through specific restitution, as considered below, rather than by making a payment of its assessed value, but this does not mean that there is a proprietary right distinct from the right to the value of the property protected through the restitutionary claim.[6]

What should be regarded as a single category of claim, which will be referred to here as the restitutionary claim to surviving value arising from a vitiated

---

[5] The approach here is consistent with Stoljar (1989), 5–6; see also Kull (1995), 1214; Dietrich (1998), 209ff; cf Rudden (1997).

[6] Compare this with the position in tort. Here a pecuniary claim arises from damage to person or property, although of course the restoration of the person or property to its original state would be preferable if it were possible. But this does not imply that in some sense the pecuniary claim protects the value of the person or property but not the person or property itself.

transfer, tends to be identified in different contexts as either proprietary or restitutionary. It may be that traditionally claims arising out of vitiated transfers of
wealth consisting of the ownership of things held for their use or possession, not
as a store of value, were described as proprietary, and transfers of wealth in the
form of a store of value, whether money or rights to payment of money (at least
in modern times) as the subject of the law of restitution,[7] although there is certainly no consistency in this. It may be that there are good grounds for treating
these types of case differently for certain purposes. But this does mean that they
concern different types of claim.

Rejecting the distinction between restitutionary and proprietary claims
clearly requires some reinterpretation of the concept of title, because the difference between the two is understood to be that proprietary claims are based on
the plaintiff's continuing title to a specific asset that comes into the control or
possession of the defendant, and restitutionary claims not on a continuing title
(title having passed to the defendant) but on a right to value in the abstract. If
the two are equated, the analysis must be that title relates not to a specific asset,
but to value, or surviving value (although, as considered below, this sometimes
amounts to the same thing), and that this is the case whether or not what is
transferred is a specific asset. On this analysis, no distinction can be drawn
between the question, conceived of as a matter of property law, whether a transfer or purported transfer was ineffective to transfer title to an asset, and the
question, conceived of as a matter of the law of restitution, whether the transfer
of the value embodied in the asset was vitiated. Conventionally this is taken to
be a fundamental distinction; for example, it might be said in a particular case
that title to money passed but that the transfer was nevertheless vitiated.[8] Of
course this concept of title is quite inimical to conventional thinking; but the test
of its validity, and of the validity of this general approach, lies in whether they
succeed in dissolving the confusion and complexity that surround the area and
in providing a coherent framework for the law.

This understanding of title will in turn require some reconsideration of other
matters. These include the concept of "separation of title", which is discussed
later in the chapter, and the concept of the in rem claim. As noted above, there
is some inconsistency in the usage of "proprietary" as between the sense of "in
rem" and the sense of a claim "in property law" rather than in restitution; here
"proprietary" it is used to refer to the law of property; "in rem" is defined in the
next section.

---

[7] Although in fact traditionally such claims were often thought of as proprietary, as illustrated
by the disputes over *Lipkin Gorman v Karpnale* [1991] 3 WLR 10; Fox (2000): see further Chap. 10
at 313–15.

[8] Furthermore, there is only one decision to transfer by the plaintiff and it is difficult to see how
there can be two different tests to determine whether the decision was vitiated. One might argue that
different criteria should be applied because the nature or effect of the transfer is different—hence
the tendency to say that title in property law passes more easily in order to protect third parties, who
are not protected when title does not pass. But this is to misunderstand the nature of the protection
of third parties, which is based on change of position and bona fide purchase.

The equivalence of the restitutionary and proprietary claims arising from a vitiated or ineffective transfer may have been obscured by the theory of unjust enrichment. The theory purports to assimilate the claim for restitution for a vitiated transfer with the claim for payment under an imputed contract and the claim for disgorgement, and a supposed category of claim that includes claims for payment and disgorgement appears clearly quite distinct from a proprietary claim arising to reverse an ineffective transfer. It is only when the relevant restitutionary claim is distinguished and identified as being concerned with transfers of wealth that the equivalence of the proprietary claim to reverse an ineffective transfer and the restitutionary claim to reverse a vitiated transfer becomes apparent.

One might suggest that it would be a reasonable usage to refer to the primary legal relation that subsists between the owner of wealth or property and other people as "proprietary", and the remedial relation arising from a vitiated or ineffective transfer as "restitutionary". A primary relation consists of the primary right and the correlative primary duty or liability that exist as between parties before any claim has arisen, and by virtue of which, on the occurrence of a "causative event", a remedial right or claim can arise in favour of one party against the other. The remedial relation consists of the remedial right or claim and the correlative remedial duty or liability that arises on the occurrence of the causative event.[9] It is certainly true that "proprietary", and not "restitutionary", is used to describe the primary relation constituting ownership of property. But both restitutionary and proprietary are used to refer to the remedial claim to reverse a transfer; as discussed above, the problem is that these are wrongly supposed to refer to different claims. The important point of substance is that there is a single remedial claim arising from a vitiated or ineffective transfer, not distinct restitutionary and proprietary claims.

Another approach should be briefly mentioned. As discussed in Chapter 1, on one view "restitution" refers to a remedy that can arise in response to different types of claim rather than to a substantive field of law or category of claim. Thus, for example, where the defendant has committed a wrong that has induced the plaintiff to make a transfer, the reversal of the transfer might be the appropriate means of effecting compensation for the defendant's wrong, quite apart from whether a claim to reverse the transfer arises as a response to a vitiating factor, and one might say that this tortious remedy to reverse the transfer should be described as restitutionary. Apparently along the same lines it is argued that restitution is a remedy that can arise either in response to a proprietary claim based on the receipt by the defendant of property still belonging to the plaintiff, or in response to an unjust enrichment claim, based on a vitiated transfer of value.[10] The difference between this approach and the orthodox approach above is merely terminological; it does not challenge the distinction

---

[9] See Appendix 1.
[10] Birks (1998*a*), Virgo (1998*a*).

between proprietary and restitutionary claims in the sense set out above, which it preserves as the distinction between proprietary claims arising from retention of title and unjust enrichment claims arising from a vitiated transfer, merely shifting the use of restitution to refer to the remedy rather than the nature of the claim in the case of the vitiated transfer.[11]

RIGHTS IN REM AND IN PERSONAM

Primary relations in rem and in personam

Primary relations (as described above)[12] can be classified into relations in rem and relationships in personam. An in rem primary right (under an in rem primary relation) is a primary right that correlates to a primary duty on or liability of "all the world", which means anyone at all, without the need for a prior connection with the right-holder through an agreement or other relationship. In other words, a relation in rem is a relation that subsists between unconnected parties. For example, a right against assault is an in rem right, because it arises as against "all the world". Any two people at all are subject to a primary legal relation by which each has a right against assault and the other a duty not to assault; there need be no connection between the two people other than through the act of assault itself.[13] A primary relation in personam, by contrast, is a relation that arises as between parties who are linked by an agreement (or possibly by some other connection); thus a contractual right is in personam.

The standard example of an in rem primary relation, and the relevant one for present purposes, is ownership. Ownership is an in rem primary relation between the owner and any other person, whether or not connected with the owner in any way, because the owner's right to his property is enforceable against any such person. Commonly the very concept of the in rem right is equated with ownership. The concept of the estate (meaning the aggregate of what a person owns, i.e. his wealth and property) presupposes the concept of an in rem primary right, because the estate consists of wealth and property that is exclusively available to the owner vis-à-vis everyone else. The primary relation that generates the restitutionary claim arising from a vitiated transfer is also in rem: the recipient of a vitiated transfer need have no prior relationship or

---

[11] Another position is that the proprietary claim arising from retention of title is a type of restitutionary claim, based on a vitiating or "unjust" factor of "retention of title": Burrows (1993), chap. 13. But a vitiating factor must be something that affects the decision-making of the plaintiff, like lack of authority or mistake, whereas (even on an orthodox approach) retention of title is the consequence of the presence of a vitiating factor, which in most cases where there is thought to be a proprietary claim is lack of authority. To treat retention of title as a vitiating factor in itself is to deny the need for a vitiating factor altogether and to beg the question when title passes.

[12] See also Appendix 1.

[13] It is unnecessary for present purposes to consider generally which primary relations are in personam and which in rem or whether there is a hard and fast distinction between the two.

connection with the plaintiff transferor; indeed, if it is accepted that there is no distinction between restitutionary and proprietary claims, the primary relation from which the restitutionary claim arises is the same primary relation that constitutes the ownership of property and wealth.

Remedial relations and insolvency

In practice the distinction between in rem and in personam rights is taken to be important with respect to remedial relations rather than primary relations, and in particular in connection with claims in insolvency. It may not at first blush be apparent how the distinction applies with respect to remedial relationships, because one might think that all remedial claims are necessarily in personam according to the definition above, on the basis that the remedial claim is against a particular identified person, viz. the defendant, rather than "all the world".

Consider first an ordinary claim for damages in tort, or for damages or debt in contract. These are claims for sums of money exigible against the defendant's estate. Where the defendant is insolvent, there is a conflict between the plaintiff's claim against the defendant and the claims of third party creditors against the defendant, who also have claims for sums of money exigible against the defendant's estate. The obvious solution (and the one actually adopted) is that the plaintiff's claim and the competing claims are to be treated equally and each must take a proportionate share of the burden of the defendant's inability to satisfy all his liabilities; thus each gets the same proportion of the full amount owed to him.[14]

Now consider a claim arising out of a transfer into the possession or control of the defendant of property belonging to the plaintiff, as it is usually analysed. Because the asset remains in the plaintiff's estate, and does not become part of the defendant's, it is not available to satisfy any other claims against the defendant. This follows from the in rem nature of ownership in binding the whole world as well as the defendant, presupposed by the concept of the estate.

> Since the asset never belonged to [the insolvent recipient], creditors cannot complain of its removal by [the plaintiff], for this does not in any way diminish [the insolvent's] estate and his general creditors are unaffected.[15]

By contrast, the claim for damages or debt is a claim to value from the defendant's estate, and is in personam because it is a claim only against the defendant's estate and so diminishes in insolvency in competition with other claims against the estate. This shows the connection between the sense of in rem in primary relationships, and the sense it has in relation to remedial claims.

---

[14] i.e. the aggregate value of the assets in the estate as a proportion of the aggregate liabilities. Sometimes the loss will cause more hardship to one creditor than another: this is presumably the basis for the preferential treatment given to employees in their employer's insolvent liquidation. But equality of treatment is surely the only workable presumption for the general case.

[15] Goode (1998), 65; For the same point, see Goode (1992), 141; Goode (1987), 439.

But consider now the position with respect to the restitutionary claim to surviving value against an insolvent defendant. This is a claim to a part of the value of the insolvent defendant's estate, being that part of the value that would not have been in the estate in the absence of the receipt. The accepted law is that such a claim is generally a claim to value out of the estate and is, therefore, like a claim for damages or debt in contract or tort, necessarily in personam and liable to diminish in insolvency in competition with other claims. But in principle this should not be so. Assume for the moment, as argued elsewhere,[16] that a restitutionary claim can arise through an indirect transfer, simply by virtue of the transfer of value. Then if the direct recipient of a vitiated transfer from the plaintiff transfers some part of the surviving value in his estate to an indirect recipient, that indirect recipient will also be subject to a restitutionary claim by the plaintiff. It follows that where the plaintiff has a claim to surviving value against an insolvent, then with respect to any part of the surviving value that is transferred to a creditor of the insolvent, the grounds for the plaintiff's claim against the insolvent equally require that he should, in principle, have a restitutionary claim against the creditor as an indirect recipient. But this simply amounts to saying that the surviving value should be withheld from the insolvent's estate so far as third parties are concerned, or in other words that a claim to surviving value should have priority in the insolvency. On this basis, the restitutionary claim to surviving value is an in rem remedial claim, which should attract priority in insolvency, notwithstanding that it is not a claim in respect of (or necessarily in respect of) a specific asset. It is a misconception, in other words, to think that an in rem remedial claim is to be equated with a claim to a specific asset, or, conversely, that a claim to value is the same thing as an in personam claim.[17]

The argument above in favour of priority for the restitutionary claim to surviving value does not apply to claims for damages or debt in contract or tort. Such claims do not involve a claim to surviving value, or to some part of the value of the defendant's estate that could be relayed to an indirect recipient. It is true that a contract creditor may have made a transfer of value to the insolvent, but his claim in contract does not arise from a vitiated transfer and is not a claim to the surviving value of the transfer in the defendant's estate. Accordingly there is no question of the plaintiff acquiring any claim against indirect recipients of value from the defendant's estate, or having priority in the defendant's insolvency. To put it another way, a plaintiff contractor who makes an unvitiated decision to transfer value to the defendant under a contract in return for a future benefit bears the risk that the defendant's estate will be insufficient to satisfy the claim.[18]

---

[16] See the section on tracing below, and Chap. 8 at 257–60.

[17] Cf Sherwin (1989), 332.

[18] It follows that the remedy arising in a claim for restitution for a vitiated transfer is not the same remedy as in the case where the plaintiff has a claim to reverse a transfer in contract and tort: cf Chap. 1 at n 82.

THE ALTERNATIVE THEORY OF RESTITUTION AND PROPERTY

The alternative theory

The argument above has been, first, that there is no genuine distinction between a restitutionary claim and a proprietary claim, and, secondly, that the single restitutionary (or proprietary) claim to surviving value is an in rem claim, although not an in rem claim to or "in" a specific asset in the orthodox sense. On what might be referred to as the integrated or alternative theory of property claims, every claim thought to arise from an ineffective or vitiated transfer of wealth or property is either a manifestation of this claim or is a claim for breach of the duty of preservation of surviving value. As discussed in Chapter 7, a recipient of surviving value incurs a duty of preservation in relation to surviving value at the time when he knows or (in the light of his duty of inquiry) ought to know of the restitutionary liability, and he breaches the duty by dissipating or disposing of surviving value. The claim arising from a breach of the duty of preservation is not a claim to surviving value, and is not an in rem or priority claim; it is a tortious claim arising from a duty not to cause harm to the plaintiff by reducing surviving value.

The orthodox theory

The orthodox approach, by contrast, is based on a fourfold classification of claims, based on two distinctions: the first is between proprietary and restitutionary claims; and the second is between in rem claims, understood to mean rights "in" an asset,[19] and in personam claims, understood to mean rights to value. In fact, strictly there seems to be an eightfold classification, because the orthodox view envisages a third independent distinction, between claims at common law and claims in equity, which will be considered below. The "orthodox theory" or "orthodox approach" will be used to refer to any approach that is based on these assumptions. This seems to encompass the positions of most commentators, although there is great diversity and controversy within this.

Thus, first, under the orthodox theory it is thought that there can be both a restitutionary claim in rem and a proprietary claim in rem.[20] Where an asset is transferred to the defendant, but the plaintiff retains title, he will sometimes have a proprietary claim in rem. But it is said that where an asset is transferred into the defendant's estate, so that the plaintiff does not retain title (i.e. title to the specific asset in the orthodox sense), the transfer of value involved in the

---

[19]   A distinction is drawn between a right "in" an asset and right to or relating to an asset which is a claim "in personam ad rem": Goode (1987), 437.

[20]   Sometimes described as "restitutionary proprietary" and "pure proprietary" claims: see e.g. Burrows (1997), 112.

transfer of the asset can nevertheless be vitiated so that there is a restitutionary claim to reverse the transfer of value rather than to protect the original title; and it is thought that sometimes this restitutionary claim takes the form of an in rem claim in the original asset or in a different asset identified through tracing,[21] or in other words a claim based on a new title as opposed to the original retained title. This claim then appears to be a restitutionary in rem claim.[22] But, in the light of the discussion above, there is, first, no basis for distinguishing between cases where title does not pass and cases where title does pass but the transfer is vitiated; and, secondly, the claim is necessarily in rem, since it is a restitutionary (or proprietary claim) and there is no need to use the device of identifying an asset to which the plaintiff has a title in order to establish an in rem claim.

On the orthodox theory, also, it is thought that where title does not pass, so the claim is proprietary, the plaintiff may have no in rem claim, but instead an in personam claim, i.e. a proprietary in personam claim. This is conceived of as a claim arising from interference with the plaintiff's title or ownership.[23] But in fact the claim is generally a simple restitutionary claim, as is clear if the distinction between an ineffective transfer of title and a vitiated transfer of value is rejected, although sometimes it will be a claim for breach of the duty of preservation. These various cases will be considered further in the next chapter.

Defences

The availability of the defences of change of position and bona fide purchase to a claim arising from a transfer from the plaintiff is a crucial matter, but it is very difficult to see what principles determine the issue as the law is currently formulated. The usual analysis of the incidence of the defences is in terms of the fourfold or eightfold analysis mentioned above.[24] Thus, for example, it is sometimes said that the bona fide purchase defence necessarily applies only to a proprietary claim,[25] typically a proprietary in rem claim in equity (in the form of the equity's darling defence). But at common law it appears to apply as against a proprietary in personam claim when the claim is money had and received,[26] but not when it is conversion.[27] And similarly it is said that change of position applies only to restitutionary claims and not to proprietary claims, or possibly only to restitutionary in personam claims and not to in rem claims, whether

---

[21] Tracing is considered below at 293–311.
[22] e.g. Birks (1989*a*), 378; Swadling (1997*a*), 131; Goode (1991), 225.
[23] With respect to chattels this is understood to be conversion or detinue, which is regarded as tortious, and with respect to money it is the claim for money had and received; these are considered in the next chapter.
[24] These cases are considered further in the next chapter.
[25] e.g. Swadling (1997*c*).
[26] *Lipkin Gorman v Karpnale* [1991] 3 WLR 10 is authority for this on one view of the case.
[27] See Chap. 10 at 323–5.

restitutionary or proprietary.[28] But not surprisingly there is great controversy over the correct classification of the claim in some cases, and no consensus over the availability of the defences.[29]

On the alternative theory, the restitutionary (or proprietary) claim to surviving value is in principle always subject to change of position or bona fide purchase, on the basis set out in Chapter 7. The crucial issue in practice is whether, in the light of the level of his duty of inquiry, the defendant recipient has incurred a duty of preservation, as explained in Chapter 7. Where he incurs a change of position, but is in breach of the duty of preservation, his restitutionary liability diminishes and the liability for breach of the duty of preservation increases in the same measure, and he remains liable vis-à-vis the plaintiff as if he had not changed his position (although often no distinction is made between the restitutionary claim and the claim for breach of the duty of preservation). Similarly, where the defendant is in breach of the duty of preservation, he cannot rely on bona fide purchase as a defence; more precisely "bona fide" should be understood to mean that the defendant has not incurred a duty of preservation. Where the level of the defendant's duty of inquiry is such that he is "at risk" or strictly liable with respect to the vitiating factor, in effect he will never have a defence to the plaintiff's claim for the full value of the transfer. This is the better analysis of cases where, according to the case law, the defendant has no defence to the plaintiff's claim, as in the case of the receipt of chattels transferred without authority at common law,[30] and the absence of a defence is attributed to the fact that the claim is proprietary or that it is in rem. By contrast, where the defendant is not "at risk", and consequently will have the practical benefit of change of position and bona fide purchase, the claim is generally regarded as restitutionary or in personam or both. Whether it is right that the defendant should be at risk in one type of case and not the other is the crucial question, which is merely obscured by the analysis in terms of the fourfold or eightfold classification.[31]

Insolvency

It was argued above that the claim to surviving value is an in rem claim, although not an in rem claim to a specific asset in the orthodox sense. The conclusion was based on the argument that if any part of the surviving value in the insolvent's estate derived from the vitiated transfer from the plaintiff reached a creditor of the insolvent, the plaintiff would have a claim in respect of such value

---

[28] See e.g. Smith (1997), 384; Segal (1998), 107; Nolan (1995), 175; but see now *Gertsch v Atsas* [1999] NSWSC 898, para. 22.

[29] Ibid.

[30] See Chap. 10 at 325–7.

[31] In Chap. 7 there was some discussion of the scope of the bona fide purchase defence, and in particular whether it is confined to intermediary cases. The present discussion is confined to intermediary cases, and so the point is not directly in issue.

against the creditor, and so the surviving value should be regarded as outside the insolvent's estate. Now, if some part of the surviving value were actually transferred to a creditor, the creditor might have a defence of change of position or bona fide purchase. But even if no transfer is actually made to a creditor of value derived from the plaintiff, it is quite possible that, in giving credit to the insolvent, or refraining from withdrawing credit, a contract creditor has already relied on the receipt by the *insolvent* of value derived from the plaintiff, because he may well have relied on the apparent wealth of the insolvent, which will include any wealth received from the plaintiff through the vitiated transfer. If so, the creditor should have something in the nature of a change of position defence as against the plaintiff, although relating to the insolvent's receipt rather than his own, the effect of which would be to negate the priority of the plaintiff's claim to surviving value in the insolvent's estate. This counter-argument to the argument for priority will be referred to as the "apparent wealth" argument.[32]

It would be very difficult in practice to determine in a particular case to what extent the receipt from the plaintiff increased the insolvent's apparent wealth vis-à-vis a particular creditor, and to what extent the creditor relied, or reasonably relied, on any such increase. Many factors would be relevant to such a determination, including the time of the receipt relative to the time of the creditor's transaction, the nature of the insolvent's wealth, the nature of the transfer from the plaintiff to the insolvent, the nature of the creditor's transaction, and the extent of the creditor's duty of inquiry, if any, with respect to the origin of wealth in the insolvent's estate. The apparent wealth and the degree of reliance on it would be likely to differ as between different creditors in the insolvency. Perhaps it will be possible to develop a sufficiently precise rule that takes account of the conflict between the plaintiff's restitutionary claim and the interests of the insolvent's creditors under the apparent wealth argument.[33] Failing that, it seems that the only practicable way of resolving the conflict is to adopt an arbitrary rule in favour of one or the other, i.e. treating the restitutionary claim as either having priority or not having priority. One might think that the creditors, whose position is analogous to that of innocent recipients, should be given the benefit of the doubt, and the plaintiff's priority denied. But the better argument seems to be, to the contrary, that the benefit of the doubt should be

---

[32] There is a similar argument in Sherwin (1989), 360. The argument against priority applies in favour of a contract creditor of the insolvent, but not a tort creditor, who does not rely on the apparent wealth of the tortfeasor. But a tort creditor has an analogous argument to the extent that surviving value derived from the plaintiff was used in the insolvent's business and thereby contributed to the commission of the tort.

[33] One might argue that the court should be left free to weigh up the conflicting interests in each case to see whether priority is appropriate or not on the facts, making a judgment of the degree of reliance by creditors or other relevant factors. This would amount to a discretion to determine property rights, in the form of what is sometimes described as the "remedial constructive trust". Such an approach would surely be undesirable because it would cause enormous practical difficulties in the administration of insolvency and in the resolution of disputes over priority. The remedial constructive trust is considered further in Chap. 10.

given to the plaintiff, because generally the surviving value will constitute only a small proportion of the insolvent's estate, so that if it influences the creditors at all the effect is likely to be marginal.[34]

Even if the apparent wealth argument were accepted as denying the restitutionary plaintiff's priority in the usual case, there are circumstances where it seems that the argument would not be applicable, so that the plaintiff's argument for priority should certainly prevail. One example is where the assets representing the surviving value of a vitiated transfer from the plaintiff, although within the insolvent's possession or control, are kept segregated from the rest of his wealth and not used for his own purposes or for his business, and so do not contribute to his apparent wealth. Thus it might happen that the insolvent received a vitiated transfer, and, knowing of the vitiating factor, and therefore of his restitutionary liability, placed the value received in a separate account for the plaintiff, or in other words on trust for him.[35] More commonly, this is surely one reason for the express trustee's duty to keep the trust assets separate from his own. Here the trust fund is not the result of a vitiated transfer, but arises from a voluntary arrangement, but the nature of the plaintiff's interest is the same, as considered in the next section, and so is the relevance of segregation to priority. Another case where the apparent wealth argument would not apply is where it is clear that there were no significant transactions affecting the insolvent's estate between the receipt of the transfer from the plaintiff and the insolvent's bankruptcy, so that one could say that there was no time for the transfer to contribute to the insolvent's apparent wealth vis-à-vis creditors before everyone dealing with the insolvent was put on notice of his insolvency by his bankruptcy.[36] In these cases the legitimacy of the plaintiff's claim to priority seems clearest. But, in any case, as argued above, the best position seems to be that the restitutionary claim should in any case generally prevail over the apparent wealth argument and have priority.

---

[34] Where value attributable to the plaintiff entered the recipient's estate with the consent of the plaintiff, there will be no restitutionary claim, but there may be a contractual claim or a claim arising under a trust or bailment. In the case of contract the claim does not have priority because the plaintiff does not retain a claim to surviving value, but may be given security. Here creditors are sometimes protected by registration to overcome a form of the apparent wealth argument. In the case of trust the claim does have priority. In the case of bailment, under the old doctrine of reputed wealth the plaintiff was taken to have assumed the risk that others would rely on the goods transferred as being the apparent wealth of the recipient: see e.g. Re *Florence*, ex parte *Wingfield* (1879) 10 Ch D 591.

[35] It is an important practical question whether the duty of preservation requires the defendant to act in this way.

[36] e.g., in *Chase Manhattan v Israel British Bank* [1981] Ch 105 the plaintiff made a payment by mistake and almost immediately sought repayment, but in the meantime the defendant had become insolvent. The plaintiff was allowed to recover the payment in full. *Taylor v Plumer* (1815) 3 M & S 562 is similar. But this argument would not provide the basis for a precise rule of the sort that is desirable in insolvency.

Specific restitution

It is sometimes thought that an order for the return of a specific asset can be justified only if the plaintiff has retained title to it in the orthodox sense by which title signifies an in rem claim to or "in" a specific asset. Thus it is sometimes thought that an in personam claim, which is thought to be equivalent to a claim to value rather than to a specific asset, cannot generate such a "specific remedy". But where a restitutionary claim to surviving value arises from a transfer of a tangible asset like land or goods, there is no reason why the restitutionary claim cannot be satisfied through an order to return the asset in question, notwithstanding that the claim is a claim to surviving value rather than an in rem claim in a specific asset in the conventional sense.[37]

A remedy of specific restitution has certain advantages as a means of satisfying a restitutionary claim. First, where the thing transferred is unusual or has an unusual significance to the plaintiff, it may be very difficult to value it, and its value to the plaintiff and the defendant may be very different. A pecuniary remedy for the restitutionary claim would be difficult to quantify, and might be inadequate where the value to the defendant is less than the value to the plaintiff. (It would be unfair to the defendant if he were liable for the full value to the plaintiff where this exceeded the value to him). In such a case the fairest way of satisfying the restitutionary claim is through specific restitution of the thing.[38] Secondly, if the plaintiff has a claim for specific restitution, he may be able to avoid having to take legal proceedings by recovering the thing in question without having to go to court for determination of the pecuniary claim.

Specific restitution should be available, if appropriate, where the defendant has, on the facts, no change of position defence, so that the surviving value corresponds to the value of the asset received; or where the surviving value has fallen below the value received only as a result of the defendant's breach of his duty of preservation, so that the defendant's aggregate liability, under the restitutionary claim and the claim for breach of the duty, remains no less than the value of the asset. Where the defendant is insolvent, whether specific restitution remains possible depends on whether the plaintiff's claim retains priority; if it does the measure of the plaintiff's claim will not have fallen below the value of the asset. (This is the opposite of the orthodox understanding of priority in insolvency, by which the claim to priority is taken to depend on the right subsisting in the asset.) Where the plaintiff has a claim for specific restitution because of the absence of any defence, his title to surviving value might appear to amount to a title to the asset itself in the orthodox sense. But although one might refer to title to the asset, the title is in principle contingent on the persistence of surviving value.

---

[37] Cf the claim "in personam ad rem": Goode (1991), 223. Goode assumes in the orthodox way that an in rem claim must be a claim in an asset, not a claim to value.

[38] Cf Chap. 7 at 229.

Indirect transfers

As discussed in Chapter 8 above, the orthodox view is that a claim against an indirect recipient of a transfer of value arises only if the indirect recipient has received property belonging to the plaintiff, which is to be understood to mean where the plaintiff has an in rem claim in the orthodox sense in the specific asset transferred to the indirect recipient by the direct recipient. Under the alternative theory, however (as assumed above), the question can only be whether surviving value derived from the plaintiff has reached the defendant (which has been presumed above to be the case). This issue turns on the correct understanding of tracing, which is considered later in this chapter.

THE TRUST AND SEPARATION OF TITLE

The trust is closely connected with the law of restitution, but the relation has been controversial. The approach to restitutionary claims suggested above provides a new way of understanding the trust and its relation to restitution.

The trust and separation of benefit and management

The trust is an arrangement by which the power of management of specified property—the trust property—is separated from the right to benefit from it through use, occupation or income from investment or licensing.[39] The power of management is given to the trustee and the right to benefit, or beneficial interest, to the beneficiary or beneficiaries. The historical origin of the trust in English law lies in the division of the law into the separate jurisdictions of common law and equity.[40] For this reason, the beneficiary is known as the equitable owner, with equitable title, and the trustee is said to be the legal owner, with legal title. The trust—in the case of an express or deliberately created trust—is established by a settlor, who transfers the trust property to the trustee and declares the terms of the trust, which provide for how the benefit of the property is to be allocated.[41]

The beneficiary has an in personam right against the trustee, which is correlated to a duty in the trustee to keep the trust fund separate from his own

---

[39] By giving the power of management to a trustee, the settlor can use a trust to provide for a beneficiary who is incompetent to manage his own property, or to provide for a complex allocation of benefit from property whilst allowing the property to be kept undivided under the control of the trustee for the purposes of management and investment.

[40] See Appendix 2.

[41] Here we are generally concerned with the case where the trustee holds property for the beneficiary absolutely, free of any condition, under a "bare trust", and the beneficiary is entitled to direct the trustee to transfer the trust property to him or account to him for the value of the fund.

property and preserve and, if appropriate, invest it, and to pay the beneficiary in due course in accordance with the trust instrument.[42] The beneficiary also has an in rem right in the trust fund. This means that the trust fund is kept outside the trustee's insolvency, so that the beneficiary's claim to the value of the fund or any part of it is unaffected by the insolvency. The trustee has the power to sell trust property and buy new property for the trust as part of the management of the trust fund, which might be described as a dispositive power; it is understood to go with his legal title to the trust property. If the trustee makes a transfer from the trust fund in breach of trust—i.e. outside his authority under the trust instrument—the beneficiary may have a claim against the recipient of the transfer. However, whereas an absolute owner (i.e. where there is no trust) is thought to have an absolute in rem right that necessarily prevails against any recipient who receives it through a transfer without authority,[43] the beneficiary under a trust is said to have a lesser form of in rem right (an equitable interest) which will not prevail against a recipient of trust property if the recipient is a bona fide purchaser (i.e. equity's darling). To put it another way, the trustee's legal title or dispositive power enables him to dispose of trust property to a bona fide purchaser.

The trust under the alternative and orthodox theories

The trust, and the nature of the beneficiary's interest, are explained straightforwardly by the alternative theory set out above. Consider, first, not the standard case of the express trust as outlined above, but the situation where a direct recipient is in receipt of a vitiated transfer from the plaintiff. The plaintiff will have a restitutionary right to the surviving value in the direct recipient's estate, which is, in principle, in rem. Thus the plaintiff's claim should have priority in insolvency, and if the direct recipient transfers surviving value to an indirect recipient, the plaintiff should have a restitutionary claim to surviving value against the indirect recipient unless he is a bona fide purchaser. If the direct recipient knows or ought to know that the transfer to him was vitiated, so that he has a liability for surviving value in his estate, he is subject to a duty of preservation in relation to the surviving value, so that if he consumes or disposes of any part of it he will be liable in personam to the plaintiff for his breach of duty.

The position of the plaintiff in such a case is very close to that of the beneficiary under a trust.[44] The beneficiary's interest under a trust is in effect a right to what is the equivalent of surviving value in the direct recipient's estate, viz. the value of the trust fund in the trustee's estate.[45] The beneficiary's position as

---

[42] There may be a trust of specific property rather than a fund, but this makes no difference to the analysis.

[43] In fact at common law this is true with respect to chattels but not money.

[44] Although the settlor and the beneficiary may be different people, whereas the plaintiff will be both the transferor and the claimant.

[45] Or the beneficiary's share of the fund.

against indirect recipients of trust property follows naturally. A transfer by the trustee in breach of trust is a transfer of value from the beneficiary, vitiated by the trustee's lack of authority, which gives the beneficiary a restitutionary claim to surviving value against the indirect recipient, unless the indirect recipient can claim bona fide purchase. In the case of the trust, the "surviving value" is transferred to the trustee by arrangement with him for him to hold on trust, rather than through a vitiated transfer, and so the trustee necessarily has a duty of preservation. The duty of preservation, here a fiduciary duty, arises from the trustee's acceptance of the position, not under the general law in consequence of notice of the vitiated transfer. The fiduciary duty is stricter than the duty of preservation arising from a vitiated transfer,[46] and certainly requires the trustee to invest the trust property in the case of a fund, or to look after and return it in the case of a trust of a specific asset; it will also require him to segregate the trust property, to make it easier to account for.[47]

The discussion shows that the nature of the beneficiary's interest under a trust is in principle the same as that of a restitutionary plaintiff to surviving value in the recipient's estate. Conversely, a restitutionary claim can be understood in terms of a trust or, in other words, a separation of title: the plaintiff's restitutionary claim to surviving value is a beneficial title and the recipient acquires a dispositive title to the asset transferred through the vitiated transfer. The beneficial title or restitutionary claim relates to surviving value in the recipient's estate, and the dispositive title to the specific asset transferred. As considered below, this interpretation of a restitutionary claim has certain advantages. In fact the restitutionary claim arising from a vitiated transfer has been understood in these terms, but only in certain situations, viz. where the issue has traditionally been dealt with in equity, which means, broadly speaking, where the vitiated transfer was a transfer by a trustee acting without the authority of the trust instrument or by a fiduciary acting without the authority of his principal, the plaintiff. In these cases, the court has treated the plaintiff's claim arising from a vitiated transfer as an equitable interest under a trust. The trust is said to be a constructive rather than an express trust, because it arises by operation of law in response to the vitiated transfer, rather than by arrangement.[48] Traditionally an analysis in terms of separation of title was possible only in equity because separation of title was understood in jurisdictional rather than functional terms, i.e. in terms of legal and equitable title rather than dispositive and beneficial title. But separation of title should be dissociated from the old jurisdictional division, which was concerned with a procedure for enforcement that no longer

---

[46] This is to say that the duties of an express trustee are stricter than the duties of a constructive trustee, even if the constructive trustee has incurred a duty of preservation; see Pettit (1997), 356ff.

[47] As discussed in connection with the apparent wealth argument this also strengthens the argument for priority.

[48] There is some controversy over this terminology; some say that although there is a separation of title there is strictly no trust, and others say that there is a trust but it is a resulting trust not a constructive trust. This is discussed in Chap. 10.

applies.[49] This would mean that separation of title would be available generally as the appropriate framework for a restitutionary claim.

Under the traditional analysis of the trust, by which it is regarded as intrinsically a creature of the jurisdictional divide between law and equity, it is thought that the reason a recipient from the trustee has a defence of bona fide purchase to a claim by the beneficiary, whereas, say, the recipient of a chattel belonging absolutely to the plaintiff has no such defence to the claim based on the plaintiff's legal title, is something to do with the equitable nature of the beneficiary's ownership as compared to the absolute legal ownership of the owner of the chattel. Thus in this context the bona fide purchase defence is referred to as the "equity's darling" defence. But, in reality, as the analysis above shows,[50] the difference must be understood to lie not in the nature of the plaintiff's interest in his wealth or the asset transferred, but in the extent of the duty of inquiry of the recipient, which (rightly or wrongly, and for historical reasons) is generally weaker in equity than at common law. And this is consistent with the fact that a claim at common law arising from the transfer of money is subject to the bona fide purchase defence, even if the plaintiff had absolute legal ownership and not merely the beneficial interest under a trust of the money: here the nature of the plaintiff's interest cannot be different in nature from his interest in the chattel, but there may be good reasons why the level of the duty of inquiry should differ as between money and chattels.

Furthermore, in accordance with the orthodox theory, the equitable interest under a trust is thought to consist of an in rem right in the orthodox sense, subsisting in a specific asset or assets, whereas under the alternative theory the equitable interest is an in rem claim to value in the estate, viz. the value segregated in the trust fund, which consists of a fluctuating body of assets having a collective identity. Under the alternative theory it is clear that the fluctuating body of assets can represent the value to which the plaintiff is entitled. But the orthodox theory faces the difficulty that the in rem claim, although supposed to subsist in specific assets, is apparently transmitted to new assets as the assets in the fund are bought and sold. In the case of an express trust, the trustee might be understood to have a power under the trust to revest the plaintiff's in rem right as he buys and sells; but the difficulty cannot be overcome in this way with respect to the surviving value of a vitiated transfer. This issue is considered below in connection with the doctrine of tracing.

---

[49] See Appendix 2. There seem to be cases analogous to the trust purely at common law. An example is the case where the plaintiff entrusts a fund of money to the defendant for him to hold for or at the direction of the plaintiff, which was enforced through the doctrine of money had and received and attornment. It seems that here the concept of the fund was also recognised: Goode (1976), 366, 385. At common law attornment was necessary for the right to the fund to vest in a third party.

[50] See above at 284.

The advantages of separation of title as the response to a vitiated transfer

The in rem nature of the claim to surviving value is made explicit by expressing it in the form of a title to part of the recipient's estate. Title signifies that the subject of the claim is a part of the estate, which can be withdrawn from it in insolvency and relayed to an indirect recipient. At the same time, separation of title means that the plaintiff's title to value in the recipient's estate—the beneficial title—is compatible with the existence of a dispositive title in the recipient, signifying that the asset transferred has entered the recipient's estate, in the sense that the recipient has the power to dispose of the asset in favour of indirect recipients free of any claim: it is the trustee's dispositive or legal title that is understood to be the basis of the equity's darling defence. Thus in equity separation of title provides a framework under which an asset can enter the direct recipient's estate so far as third party indirect recipients are concerned, whilst its value remains attributable to the plaintiff as surviving value in the direct recipient's estate.[51]

At common law where the claim to surviving value generally takes the form of a claim for money had and received, the absence of any recognition of the trust or separation of title has meant that the claim to surviving value has been equated with a claim to damages or debt and treated as an in personam claim to a sum of money exigible against the estate, and not as representing a continuing title or in rem claim to any part of the recipient's estate. By contrast, with respect to chattels at common law, the plaintiff's claim is understood to be based on retention of title, and, because of the non-recognition of any separation of title, the direct recipient is understood not to acquire a title of any sort. On one view this means that there can be priority in insolvency.[52] At the same time it is understood to preclude any defence of bona fide purchase for an indirect recipient under the doctrine of nemo dat quod non habet.[53] The lack of separation of title at common law thus tends to encourage a crude choice between, on the one hand, denying priority, as for money claims, and, on the other hand, denying any bona fide purchase defence, as for chattel claims. Separation of title provides a framework that accommodates both a priority claim based on a beneficial interest and protection for recipients based on a dispositive title. If, under this framework, the bona fide purchase defence is denied, the explanation lies in the fact that the indirect recipient is "at risk" with respect to the vitiating factor, not in the absence of any dispositive title in the direct recipient.

---

[51] Cf the discussion in L.D. Smith (1997), 320ff.
[52] On one view, the priority in such cases is due to equity: see Chap. 10 at 322.
[53] See Chap. 10 at 323–5.

Tracing under the orthodox theory

A distinction is drawn, in terms of the orthodox theory, between "following" and "tracing" with respect to an asset in a recipient's estate to which the plaintiff is understood to have an in rem claim.[54] The plaintiff can "follow" his asset through the hands of the recipient to an indirect recipient so as to assert a claim against the indirect recipient. Alternatively, it is thought, the plaintiff's title to his original asset can be transmitted to a different asset giving the plaintiff an in rem claim in the substitute asset, just as if it were the original one.[55] The exercise of identifying the substitute asset for the purpose of asserting an in rem claim in it is called tracing,[56] and the tracing rules are the rules of identification.[57] The principal tracing rule is the exchange product rule, which holds that if the recipient exchanges an asset in which the plaintiff has an in rem claim for another asset, then the plaintiff's in rem claim is transmitted to the other asset, the exchange product, which is typically the pecuniary proceeds of sale of the asset received from the plaintiff.[58] The plaintiff can follow the exchange product or "traceable proceeds" for the purposes of a claim against an indirect recipient, just as if it were his original asset, or trace again into a further exchange product.

Tracing is understood to be important in two ways. First, in the recipient's insolvency, in order to get priority, the plaintiff will seek to assert an in rem claim, understood in the orthodox way as an in rem claim in a specific asset, and this may mean asserting an in rem right to traceable proceeds. Secondly, it is generally said that no claim arises against an indirect recipient purely by virtue of a transfer of value to him, and that only if the indirect recipient has received the plaintiff's property—i.e. an asset to which the plaintiff has an in rem claim—can a claim against him arise.[59] Sometimes this will be by way of the receipt of the plaintiff's original asset, but sometimes it will be by way of the receipt of traceable proceeds.

---

[54] In terms of the orthodox theory, this might be a restitutionary or proprietary claim: see Chap. 10 at 330–1.

[55] There is some controversy over the nature of the traced in rem claim: see Chap. 10 at 330–1.

[56] Thus there is a distinction between tracing as the process of identification and the claim to the asset so identified: e.g. Birks (1989*a*), 358; L.D. Smith (1997), 10ff; followed in a dictum of Millet LJ in *Boscawen v Bajwa* [1996] 1 WLR 328, 334. The traditional usage is to refer to the "equitable tracing claim", which tends to merge the two.

[57] See, generally on the tracing rules, L.D. Smith (1997); Hayton (1995).

[58] The concept of tracing is foreshadowed by the concept of the fund, consisting of a body of fluctuating assets, as assets are bought and sold by the trustee.

[59] As discussed in Chap. 8. See Burrows (1993), 58; Birks (1991*a*), 476; Birks (1992*c*), 158; Tettenborn (1997), 1; L.D. Smith (1997), 30.

Justifying tracing as the transmission of an in rem right in a specific asset

A number of different justifications have been offered for the conventional view of tracing as the transmission of an in rem right (in the orthodox sense) in one specific asset to another. One view is that it is justified because otherwise, if the recipient acquired an in rem right to the traced asset instead, he would be unjustly enriched; in other words, the in rem claim arises to reverse the vitiated transfer of value, and so is a restitutionary in rem claim.[60] But the in rem claim to a specific asset is unnecessary to reverse a vitiated transfer, because an in personam claim to value will serve this purpose. The new in rem claim to a specific asset might be understood to be justified as a means of preserving priority (on the orthodox assumption that the in rem claim to a specific asset is necessary for priority). But this cannot be a sufficient answer, because it is assumed for the purposes of the argument that it is the existence of the in rem claim to a specific asset that justifies priority, not vice versa. If, as the orthodox approach assumes, continuing priority depends on first establishing an in rem claim to the exchange product, this argument cannot be relied on without circularity.

It is also said that allowing the transmission of the in rem claim to the exchange product is justified because creditors of the insolvent recipient should not have access to the exchange product in insolvency, since the exchange product never belonged to the recipient, and so the creditors are not prejudiced by allowing the plaintiff to trace into it.[61] But as it stands this argument also fails, because one could equally well say that, if the exchange product did belong to the recipient, and it was accordingly made available to the recipient's creditors (in other words, if the in rem right could not be traced into it), the plaintiff could have no complaint because the exchange product never belonged to him.

Another argument is that the recipient should not be able to thwart the plaintiff's claim in rem to a specific asset simply by exchanging that asset for another one, and so in consequence the plaintiff should be able to transfer his in rem claim to the exchange product.[62] This argument seems to be that the recipient has committed a wrong against the plaintiff by disposing of his property,[63] and that the plaintiff should not suffer by the recipient's wrong. But the wrong by the recipient against the plaintiff has significance only as between recipient and the plaintiff, and where only their interests are at stake and no others, the in rem claim is in any case unnecessary—the plaintiff can be protected by an in personam claim. Where the interests of other parties are at stake, in the recipient's insolvency, there is no reason why the plaintiff should be protected in preference to third parties from the consequences of the recipient's wrong to the plaintiff.[64]

---

[60] Birks (1997a), 661; Birks (1995), 318–19.

[61] Goode (1991), 226.

[62] e.g. Moriarty (1995), 73.

[63] The wrong in question is a breach of the duty of preservation.

[64] In fact the claim to traceable proceeds or surviving value, which can be in rem, does not depend on whether the recipient acted wrongfully, but purely on whether there is surviving value, and the claim arising from the wrong is a claim for compensation, which is not in rem.

Smith argues in favour of allowing the in rem claim to be traced into substitute assets on other grounds.[65] One argument is based on the specificity of rights in rem. It is a characteristic of an in rem claim on the orthodox view, i.e. an in rem claim in a specific asset, that it has specificity—its subsistence depends on the subsistence of the asset. The specificity of in rem rights means that events can have fortuitous effects on such rights.[66] Consider the case where R has two identical assets in his possession, one belonging to P1 and one to P2. P1's asset is destroyed in an accident; P2's is unscathed. It is in the nature of in rem rights that P1 suffers a loss and P2 does not. P1 is unlucky and P2 is lucky: this is the fortuity or "unfairness" of in rem rights.[67] Now consider the case where the plaintiff's asset in the recipient's hands is exchanged for another asset. Smith seems to argue that the fortuity of in rem rights supports the right to trace. He argues that because in rem rights necessarily carry a risk of fortuity, one cannot object to allowing the plaintiff to acquire an in rem claim to the exchange product by tracing on the ground that it adversely affects third parties, because that sort of adverse effect is just the sort of fortuitous effect that results from rights in rem. But, to the contrary, one would think that the loss of an in rem claim to a specific asset on the disposal of the asset by a recipient of it, at least vis-à-vis the recipient, is, as in the case of its destruction, simply a consequence of, or an illustration of, the specificity or fortuity of in rem rights in the orthodox sense; it in no way explains why the plaintiff should acquire a new in rem right instead.

The orthodox approach to tracing is no more convincing with respect to claims against indirect recipients. Here the argument that no restitutionary claim arises unless the indirect recipient receives an asset in which the plaintiff has an in rem claim (in the orthodox sense) entirely begs the issue at stake in the absence of some explanation of why an asset received by the direct recipient from a third party and transferred to the indirect recipient, which was never the plaintiff's, is deemed to be his under the exchange product rule of tracing for the purposes of the plaintiff's claim against the indirect recipient.[68] (Under the usual rules for acquiring title, the exchange product would belong to the direct recipient rather than the plaintiff because the third party would have intended to transfer title to the direct recipient). The orthodox position is again caught in a circular argument: it holds that the claim against the indirect recipient arises from the in rem claim in a specific asset and not simply from a transfer of value per se, but the accrual of the in rem claim seems to be explicable only on the basis that it represents the location of value moving from the plaintiff to the indirect recipient.

---

[65] Smith (1997), 303ff.

[66] Under the alternative theory, surviving value can be affected fortuitously, but tracing does not depend on this argument.

[67] The argument does not seem to imply that in rem rights are unfair, but rather that they can have fortuitous consequences. See also Rogers (1990).

[68] The same point was made in Chap. 8 at 259.

Smith also argues that a reason for allowing tracing (with respect to both priority and indirect transfers) is that it is a means of making the in rem right more durable.[69] He argues that the problem that arises in connection with in rem rights is how to balance the owner's interest in his asset against the interest of a recipient of it; the more durable and better protected the in rem right is, the better is the owner's position as against that of recipients. The effect of allowing tracing is to enhance the durability of the in rem right and shift the balance in favour of the owner. But in fact one would think that the durability of an in rem right in a specific asset in the orthodox sense would follow from its specificity: it should persist as against the recipient for just so long as the asset remains in the recipient's hands. The argument for durability possibly makes sense under the alternative approach to tracing, considered below: the durability of the plaintiff's wealth depends on the extent to which the tracing rules and presumptions allow him to locate his surviving value in the estates of direct or indirect recipients. But, more importantly, one might say that the durability of the plaintiff's wealth increases with the level of the duty of inquiry of direct or indirect recipients, because a higher level of duty means that they are more likely to become subject to a duty of preservation that will induce them to preserve the plaintiff's wealth, or give the plaintiff an alternative claim for breach of duty.[70]

Tracing under the alternative theory

Thus the orthodox approach to tracing is open to serious, if not insuperable, objections. Tracing is much easier to explain under the alternative theory. Here the plaintiff's claim is to surviving value, not necessarily to a specific asset, and tracing is concerned with determining whether there is surviving value in the recipient's estate for the purposes of the claim. Surviving value, it will be recalled, is the value that the recipient has received, less any change of position, which means any loss in the recipient's estate due to the receipt. So surviving value is determined as a matter of causation: it is that part of the value of the recipient's estate that would not have been there if the recipient had not had the receipt. Where there is a loss or transfer of some part of the recipient's estate, the question whether it consists of surviving value depends on whether or not the loss or transfer would have occurred in the absence of the receipt of the vitiated transfer.[71] The best guide to this will often be the intention of the recipient: did he mean to transfer or consume some part of the value derived from the vitiated transfer; or, in other words, did he regard the asset transferred or consumed as being derived from the vitiated transfer?[72] This contradicts what appears to

---

[69] Smith (1997), 307.

[70] See further Chap. 10 at 342–6.

[71] See Oesterle (1983), 190; Fennell (1994), 45; Hayton (1995), 2; Bant (1997), 87; Millet (1995), 12; cf Birks (1991), 481, and Birks (1995), 311.

[72] Per Millet LJ in *Boscawan v Bajwa*: "[i]t is not necessary to apply artificial tracing rules where there has been an actual appropriation": [1996] 1 WLR 328, 336. An actual appropriation of funds

be the usual view that intentions are irrelevant to tracing, and that it operates purely by reference to the movement of assets, in particular exchange, irrespective of the accompanying intentions of the parties involved.[73]

The alternative theory requires the integration of two parts of the law that are currently regarded as distinct, viz. the law of change of position and the law of tracing. Even where change of position is analysed in terms of a concept of surviving value, this form of surviving value is thought, in accordance with the orthodox position, to be distinct from traceable value or proceeds, or, in other words, there is thought to be a difference between "abstractly surviving value" and "traceably surviving value".[74] Surviving value is the measure of the restitutionary in personam claim (the value received subject to change of position), whereas the traceable proceeds are the subject matter of a restitutionary or proprietary in rem claim arising through tracing from the plaintiff's original asset in the sense of transmission of the in rem claim in a specific asset.[75] But the alternative theory, in denying the distinction between restitutionary and proprietary claims, and in recognising the in rem nature of the claim to surviving value in the abstract, eliminates the distinction and equates traceably surviving value and abstractly surviving value. The difference between the two is merely that change of position (which has only recently been explicitly recognised at all) has developed in connection with claims raising only issues as between the plaintiff and the recipient, whereas tracing has developed in circumstances where third party rights, and therefore the in rem nature of the restitutionary claim, are relevant, i.e. in connection with priority and indirect transfers.

The exchange product rule under the alternative theory

Some revision of the existing tracing rules would be necessary to make the law consistent with the alternative theory. The effect of the law of following, and the exchange product rule of tracing, is that the original asset received through the vitiated transfer is deemed to embody surviving value, and its exchange product is deemed to embody surviving value also. But, although it is a reasonable presumption, it is not necessarily the case that the asset received continues to embody surviving value—in other words that the recipient necessarily consumes or transfers value derived from the vitiated transfer when he consumes or transfers the original asset received. It may be that another asset of the same value would have been consumed or transferred in the absence of the receipt.

---

from a mixture means a decision to use funds from a certain source or attributable to a certain person.

[73] Smith (1997), 136.

[74] See Chap. 7 at 228.

[75] Birks (1996), 52, 71ff; Birks (1997*b*). There is some controversy over whether the claim is restitutionary or proprietary: see Chap. 10 at 330. Previously Birks distinguished between the "first measure" of receipt or "value received", which (subject to change of position) is equivalent to abstractly surviving value, and the "second measure" or "surviving value" which generally referred to traceable proceeds: Birks (1989*a*), 75.

Where this is the case, it should be recognised that there is no loss of surviving value, even though the original asset or its exchange product is no longer in the defendant's estate. Conversely, it may be that the receipt has caused the recipient to consume or transfer a different asset from the one received (or its exchange product), and this should be recognised as a loss of surviving value, even though the asset received (or its exchange product) is still in the estate. Thus the rule of following, and the exchange product rule, should be understood as presumptions of intention only, subject to contrary evidence, including evidence of intention, the fundamental issue being causation.

This reflects the accepted position with respect to change of position. Although a rule in the nature of the exchange product rule has been recognised in connection with change of position,[76] it is also clear that a change of position is possible where a different asset from the one received (and not its exchange product) is lost, if this was the result of the receipt; and conversely that there may be no change of position even when the asset received or its exchange product is lost, if the same loss would have been incurred in some other form in the absence of the receipt. It is clear in other words that here the exchange product rule must be contingent on a finding, or a presumption, subject to contrary evidence, that in the circumstances the asset exchanged did actually constitute surviving value, under a test of causation.

The swollen assets test

Under the orthodox theory, tracing necessarily involves identifying a specific asset in which the in rem right subsists; this is so by virtue of the orthodox conception of the in rem right as necessarily a right in a specific asset. But under the alternative theory it is not necessary to locate surviving value in a particular asset. Surviving value is part of the recipient's estate, not necessarily embodied in any particular asset. It is strictly necessary to establish whether surviving value is embodied in a specific asset only where the issue is whether the consumption or transfer of that asset caused a loss of surviving value or a transfer of surviving value to another party. However, it may also be helpful to treat the surviving value as embodied in a particular asset for the purposes of measurement, as where the asset received is exchanged for another and the value of the exchange product is taken to be the measure of surviving value.

Consider a case where the insolvent recipient received a vitiated transfer, but it is impossible to identify the original asset or its exchange product in his estate. Applying the conventional rules of tracing, the plaintiff cannot claim priority because he cannot identify the proceeds of the vitiated transfer in the form of a specific asset;[77] but it may nevertheless be quite clear that there is still surviving value from the receipt in the recipient's estate, because it may be quite clear that

---

[76] *Lipkin Gorman v Karpnale* [1991] 3 WLR 10, 16 per Lord Templeman.
[77] Or in a mixture under the mixture rules mentioned below at 300–302.

the recipient would certainly not have incurred any net expenditure as a result of the receipt. There is some limited judicial support for the view that the plaintiff should have priority in such a case,[78] even though a specific asset cannot be identified: this is the so-called "swollen assets" theory of tracing.[79] But the theory has been criticised and generally rejected mainly on the ground that it is inconsistent with the conventional understanding of tracing as requiring the identification of a specific asset to which an in rem claim in the orthodox sense can attach.[80] Also it seems that it may have been mistakenly thought that the swollen assets theory gives the plaintiff priority merely in consequence of the receipt of the vitiated transfer, without any requirement for the surviving value to persist in the recipient's estate, as if it were a secured debt in the measure of the value received.[81]

On the analysis under the alternative theory, the swollen assets theory is already recognised at common law in the sense that surviving value as defined by change of position is merely a part of the value of the estate as a whole, defined under a test of causation, and does not have to be located in a particular asset. The alternative theory requires this concept of surviving value to be adopted for the purposes of establishing priority under the tracing rules.

Indirect recipients

Under the existing tracing rules there can be a restitutionary claim against an indirect recipient only if the direct recipient or intermediary transferred the plaintiff's original asset or its exchange product to the indirect recipient. This is understood to reflect the rule that a restitutionary claim arises only from the transfer of the plaintiff's property, and not merely from an indirect transfer of value under a test of causation.[82] But, under the alternative theory, the question is whether there has been a transfer of surviving value to the indirect recipient and this is a matter of causation, i.e. whether the transfer to the indirect recipient would have happened without the receipt of the vitiated transfer by the direct recipient.[83] The transfer of the plaintiff's original asset, or its exchange product, to the indirect recipient does not necessarily indicate a transfer of value, because the direct recipient might have made a transfer of the same value if he had never had the receipt; similarly the direct recipient might relay value

---

[78] *Space Investments Ltd v Canadian Imperial Bank of Commerce (Bahamas) Ltd* [1986] 1 WLR 1072, 1074 per Lord Templeman.

[79] See also Taft (1939), 172; Oesterle (1983), 190. The version of the swollen assets theory consistent with the alternative theory is the "augmentation version" in Smith's terminology: L.D. Smith (1997), 315ff.

[80] e.g. L.D. Smith (1997), 310, 311.

[81] This is the "strong version" of the swollen assets theory in Smith's terminology, above n 79, which is inconsistent with the alternative theory as well as the orthodox approach to tracing. This understanding of the swollen assets theory seems to be the basis of the adverse reaction to *Space Investments* and the doubts expressed in Re *Goldcorp Exchange* [1994] 2 All ER 806.

[82] See Chap. 8 at 257–60.

[83] Oesterle (1983), 190; Sherwin (1989), 332. See also Rogers (1990).

derived from the plaintiff through a transfer that is not of the plaintiff's original asset or of an exchange product. Again the existing strict tracing rules should be replaced by rebuttable presumptions as to causation, and again the direct recipient's intention is the best guide as to the movement of surviving value.

The alternative theory resolves a tension that is clear in existing attempts to rationalise tracing. On the orthodox view, the in rem claim is specific to the asset in which it subsists; it is a right in an asset, not a right to the value of the asset. (If the claim were just to the value of the asset, then it would be just a right to value from the recipient's estate, measured by the value of the asset,[84] and on an orthodox view it would be an in personam claim and would not have priority.) Thus under the orthodox theory tracing must involve creating a new in rem claim, specific to the substitute asset, in place of the original in rem claim in the original asset. But explicitly or implicitly it is recognised that tracing is concerned with following value, because it is clear that it is only the following of value that can relate the assets linked through tracing.[85] This is consistent only with the alternative view, because here the claim is a claim to value out of the defendant's estate, not a claim to or in a specific asset as such.

Mixtures and "parallel tracing"

Different tracing rules apply where the vitiated transfer from the plaintiff is of money that is mixed with the recipient's own money. The basic rule here is the pari passu rule, according to which ownership of the mixture is apportioned between the plaintiff and recipient in the proportions in which the mixture consists of value derived from the two parties. Typically the issue arises in connection with mixtures of money in investments or bank accounts.[86] A withdrawal from such a mixed account is taken to consist of surviving value in the proportions of the surviving value and the recipient's own money in the account as a whole. This is possibly understandable, and consistent with the alternative theory,[87] in the absence of any other evidence of causation, i.e. as to whether the recipient intended to use surviving value, or in other words whether the same withdrawal would have been made in the absence of any surviving value in the mixture. But it should be subject to contrary evidence, viz. evidence to the effect that the same sum would have been withdrawn if only the recipient's money was

---

[84] As in the case of the claim "in personam ad rem", above n 37.

[85] L.D. Smith (1997), 15; Birks (1995), 292.

[86] But a different rule, the "first in first out" rule, or rule in *Clayton's case* (1817) 1 Mer. 572 is said to apply to a mixture in a current active bank account.

[87] Whether it is consistent with the orthodox theory is difficult to say because of the difficulties, discussed above, in understanding the nature of the in rem claim in a specific asset and its transmission to other assets.

in the account, or evidence that no money at all would have been withdrawn if there had been no surviving value in the account.[88]

The pari passu rule is said not to apply as against a wrongdoer (i.e. a recipient in breach of the duty of preservation). For example, in Re *Hallet*[89] the recipient had mixed money representing surviving value derived from the plaintiff with his own money in a bank account, and then withdrawn and dissipated part of the mixture in the account. It was held in favour of the plaintiff, who sought priority in the recipient's insolvency, that it should be presumed that the money drawn out was not made up of the two sources of value under the pari passu rule but instead consisted entirely of the recipient's own money, so that correspondingly more of the money left in the account was surviving value of the plaintiff's (i.e. traceable proceeds). The rationale was said to be that the recipient should be presumed to have acted honestly in intending to withdraw and dissipate his own money rather than the plaintiff's. By contrast, in Re *Oatway*[90] the wrongdoer recipient drew out money from a mixed fund and invested it, and subsequently dissipated the money that had been left in the mixed account. Following Re *Hallet* it might seem that the money withdrawn should be treated as the recipient's own, so that it was the plaintiff's money that was left in the account and dissipated and the recipient's that was preserved in the investment. But here the contrary presumption was made, and in the plaintiff's favour it was presumed that the investment consisted of traceable or surviving value from the account, and that the money left in the account and dissipated was the recipient's own money.

These cases are thought to give rise to a paradox: where exactly is the surviving value or traceable proceeds? Surely it is either left in the account, or withdrawn, or the withdrawal is a mixture of surviving value and the recipient's money? But the cases seem to hold that the plaintiff can treat either the money withdrawn or the money left in the account as surviving value, depending on which is more favourable to him in the light of subsequent events. The apparent paradox is the possibility of "parallel tracing", where the plaintiff can trace the movement of value derived from him along more than one possible path, which seems to imply that surviving value can be in two or more places at once. This seems to create the possibility of an exponential expansion in the measure of the surviving value as assets embodying surviving value multiply. In fact this is not what happens, because the plaintiff must, it seems, ultimately designate one asset as the repository of his surviving value, which he will do in the light of which path is more fruitful. But nevertheless the position seems to be objectionable in recognising, even provisionally, that each of two or more different assets can represent surviving or traceable value at the same time, and allowing the

---

[88] A case that seems to illustrate such contrary evidence is Re *Tilley's WT* [1967] Ch 1179, where the trustee was taken to have used her own money from the mixture in the account because this was her intention.

[89] (1880) 13 Ch D 696.

[90] [1903] 2 Ch 356.

plaintiff a choice of which asset to treat as representing his surviving value. Birks has offered an explanation in terms of an "in rem power", which the plaintiff can exercise to vest in himself an in rem claim (in the orthodox sense) in one of the two or more assets in question.[91] But this seems simply to describe in formal terms (consistent with the orthodox theory) what the cases appear to decide, rather than to provide any theoretical basis for them, and without explaining what appears to be the crucial difficulty for the orthodox theory of what happens to the in rem claim before the power is exercised.

In fact the paradox arises only under the orthodox theory and not under the alternative theory. Under the alternative theory, although it is true to say that surviving value cannot be in two places at once, because this would be inconsistent with the laws of causation, surviving value need not actually be identified as being embodied in any particular asset at all. Where the issue is whether and to what extent surviving value that is known to have entered the recipient's estate is still there, the issue is whether surviving value survives in the account as a whole: this is the swollen assets theory discussed above. There is no paradox in the fact that it may be impossible to say at any particular time where the surviving value is located.

However, if it is possible to show that the recipient intended to withdraw the plaintiff's money rather than his own, this will be indicative of the movement of surviving value under the causation test. This is reflected in the approach in terms of a presumption of intention adopted in Re *Hallet*, although in the circumstances of that case it is clear that the presumption of honesty was fictional: the recipient was obviously dishonest. Where the recipient is a wrongdoer, it seems reasonable to apply a presumption in the plaintiff's favour; but here the plaintiff will in any case have a claim for breach of the duty of preservation, and as between the two parties it is unnecessary to distinguish between the restitutionary liability and the liability for breach of the duty of preservation. The difference is important only where third party interests are concerned, in the recipient's insolvency or where there has been a transfer to a third party, and here there is no basis for a presumption that favours the plaintiff over creditors of the defendant.

Subrogation and tracing through the discharge of a debt

One controversial case is where the recipient of a vitiated transfer applies surviving value in discharge of a debt. Now, it is surely the case that the discharge of a debt of the recipient increases his wealth. Subject to a qualification below, the discharge of a debt of £100 owed by the recipient constitutes the addition of £100 to his wealth, because it frees £100-worth of assets for use for some

---

[91]   Birks (1992*f*); Birks (1995), 307; Birks (1997*a*), 662.

purpose other than the discharge of debt.[92] Thus if surviving value is used to discharge a debt, there is, overall, no change in the measure of surviving value in the estate. On the alternative theory the plaintiff should be able to trace into the recipient's estate. On a causation test, there is surviving value in the estate in the measure of the debt discharged, because without the original receipt, which led to the discharge of the debt, the recipient's estate would be worse off by the value of the debt discharged. This would be an example of the swollen assets theory, because, after the discharge of the debt, the surviving value in the estate is not represented by the value of any specific asset in the estate, but is simply a part of the value of the estate as a whole.

On the orthodox view, however, it is impossible to trace through the discharge of a debt, because of the requirement on the orthodox view to identify a specific substitute asset to take the place of the original asset under the exchange product rule. There is no such specific asset in this case, the discharge of the debt merely going to augment the estate as a whole. Thus it appears that the use of the surviving value to discharge the debt extinguishes the plaintiff's claim to surviving value, and this is usually said to be the position.[93]

A variation of the orthodox view is proposed by Smith. He argues that where a debt is discharged there *is* (or can be) an identifiable exchange product. He argues that where the recipient uses surviving value to discharge a debt incurred in taking a loan, and the money borrowed was used to purchase an asset, the plaintiff can invoke "backwards tracing" and treat the asset purchased as the exchange product of the surviving value, even though it was already in the recipient's estate at the time of the receipt of the vitiated transfer.[94] However, as argued above, the only plausible basis of the exchange product rule is that it operates as a proxy for the causation test; i.e. it is presumed that the exchange product would not have been acquired without the vitiated receipt, and so the value of the exchange product represents surviving value under the causation test. If this is the rationale for the exchange product rule, backwards tracing is not generally justified. If the recipient receives £100 through a vitiated transfer and uses it to buy a painting to give his wife, it is likely to be the case that the wife would not have received the painting if the recipient had not received the vitiated transfer. But if the recipient buys a painting for his wife on credit and then subsequently receives a vitiated transfer and pays off the debt with surviving value, there is no reason to infer that the wife would not have received the painting in the absence of the vitiated transfer, unless, it seems, one can say that

---

[92] See *Lacey v Hill* (1876) 4 Ch D 537, 545 per Jessell MR, cited by Smith (1997), 297. One might argue also that the discharge of the debt does not constitute a wealth benefit, but that there is instead a restitutionary or non-contractual claim for reimbursement (i.e. under an imputed contract in the sense explained in Chap. 3) on the basis that the plaintiff's money has been used to confer an incontrovertible benefit on the defendant without any officiousness on the part of the plaintiff; cf Birks (1989a), 373. It is doubtful whether such a claim would attract priority, however.

[93] Re *Diplock* [1948] 1 chap. 465, 521. *Bishopsgate Investment Management Ltd v Homan* [1994] 3 WLR 1270; Hayton (1995), 16.

[94] L.D. Smith (1995b).

the debt was incurred with the intention of subsequently paying it off with surviving value received or to be received. Only in the latter case is the causation
test (in a sense)[95] satisfied; and in *Bishopsgate Investment Management Ltd v
Homan*[96] the Court of Appeal was prepared to allow "backwards tracing" only
in that type of case, if at all.[97] In such a case backwards tracing might be relevant to establish that a particular asset in the recipient's estate represents surviving value after the discharge of the debt.[98]

The subrogated claim and the role of subrogation

Although it is said that the plaintiff cannot trace through the discharge of a debt,
so that his in rem claim is extinguished by the use of surviving value to discharge
a debt, it seems that generally the plaintiff does acquire a claim to be subrogated
to the debt-claim of the discharged creditor; i.e. the plaintiff is treated as if he
were owed the debt that his surviving value was used to discharge.[99] The justification for the subrogated claim and its relation to the restitutionary claim and
tracing are not clear under the orthodox theory or in the case law. Under the
alternative theory, as argued above, after the discharge of the debt there is surviving value in the estate due to the discharge, and the subrogated claim is the
form taken by the restitutionary claim to surviving value in the recipient's estate
after the discharge of the debt. The subrogated claim is a claim to surviving
value, but, in accordance with the alternative theory and the swollen assets
theory, it is not a claim to a specific asset in the estate. The role of subrogation
here follows from the nature of subrogation as discussed in Chapter 8.

When the recipient's debt is discharged, it seems that the surviving value in
the estate due to the discharge—the measure of wealth received by the debtor
through the discharge—is equal to the face value of the debt. This is not always
the case, however; and, in particular, it is not the case where the debtor whose
debt was discharged is insolvent or in danger of insolvency. In an insolvent liquidation the debt is worth only whatever fraction will be paid out in the insolvency; and if the debtor is in danger of becoming insolvent the creditor will be
willing to accept less than the face value to sell or discharge it. One might say
that the debt has a real value and a face value, although, apart from the case of

---

[95] The chain of causation involves the defendant's reliance on his expectation of receipt. Cf above
Chap. 7, at n 135.

[96] [1994] 3 WLR 1270.

[97] See Hayton (1995), 16. Smith (1995a) objects on the ground that the intention of the defendant
is irrelevant to the exchange product rule, and in particular that it is irrelevant what his intention
was when he took out the loan.

[98] The best example of backwards tracing seems to be where the recipient is a bank that pays out
in advance of the receipt of the vitiated transfer, under an instruction to pay from a reputable bank,
as happens as a matter of course through the clearing system. But one might argue that the instruction, carrying with it an undertaking to pay, itself generates a right to payment, which constitutes
wealth that can be relayed. See also Chap. 7 at n 135.

[99] e.g. *Boscawen v Bajwa* [1996] 1 WLR 328, considered below at 306–7. See also Chap. 8 on subrogation and Chap. 3 on compulsory discharge.

actual insolvent liquidation, the real value is a matter of speculation as to the prospects of the debtor.[100] Now, where a debt is discharged, the increased value thereby added to the estate is the real value, not the face value. Thus if a recipient of a vitiated transfer uses surviving value to pay off a debt at its face value, the surviving value in the estate after the discharge will be the real value of the debt, not the face value, even if the face value was paid. The difference will constitute the dissipation of surviving value.

Unfortunately the difficulty in measuring the real value presents a problem for the plaintiff, since this is the measure of his claim to surviving value. What is needed is some means of settling the measure of the plaintiff's claim without any knowledge of the real value of the debt discharged. The doctrine of subrogation provides the solution. As discussed in Chapter 8, subrogation is a technique that enables a dispute between the plaintiff and the defendant to be resolved in circumstances in which the legal position as between the two parties is dependent on the present or past legal relation between the defendant and some other party. This is the position here because the measure of the plaintiff's claim depends on the real value of the discharged debt owed by the defendant recipient to the creditor. Thus the plaintiff is said to be subrogated to the position of the creditor who was paid off. When the plaintiff takes over the precise position of the creditor who was discharged, although the measure of surviving value cannot be determined, it is clear that the plaintiff's claim cannot exceed it, because the value of the recipient's estate apart from the surviving value has not been altered by the discharge of the debt.

It was argued earlier in this chapter that a restitutionary claim should in principle have priority in the recipient's insolvency. If the surviving value is used to discharge a debt, the priority should in principle continue with respect to the surviving value in the estate after the discharge. Now, the surviving value is the real value of the debt that was discharged, and this is, as it were, simulated through subrogation. In the recipient's insolvency, the value of the subrogated claim, which is the value that the discharged creditor's debt would have had, declines in insolvency. Thus, although in principle the plaintiff's claim, as a restitutionary claim, is still an in rem or priority claim, it behaves as if it were an in personam claim.[101] This means that other creditors are in just the position they would have been in if (all else being the same) the surviving value had not been received and the debt had not been discharged. This is as it should be, because it means that the plaintiff's claim is confined to that part of the estate that was due to the vitiated receipt.

Although the restitutionary claim takes effect by way of subrogation, it is still a claim to surviving value in the recipient's estate, although not a claim to a specific asset or the value of a specific asset in the recipient's estate. The subrogation serves to measure the surviving value by equating it with the real value of

---

[100] It might have a market price if tradable.

[101] Strictly speaking the argument implies that the plaintiff's claim diminishes pro rata with existing claims, but has priority over claims accruing after the discharge of the debt.

the debt as explained above. The effect of the subrogation is to give the impression that, rather than having a claim in respect of surviving value in the recipient's estate (not localised in a specific asset), the plaintiff has acquired a quite different claim, viz. the discharged creditor's claim. This appears to fit in with the orthodox position that it is impossible to trace through the discharge of a debt into the estate. But the discharged creditor's claim to which the plaintiff is subrogated is a fiction:[102] the debt has been discharged, not transferred to the plaintiff. The claim is consistent only with the alternative theory.

Subrogation to a secured debt

The recipient may use surviving value to discharge a secured debt. Here the position is different, because here the surviving value is necessarily the face value of the debt—the real value and the face value coincide. This is so because, by virtue of the security, the discharged creditor could certainly have recovered the face value, and accordingly the discharge of the debt necessarily increases the wealth of the estate by the face value of the debt. Thus here the plaintiff's claim is always in the measure of the face value, and so does have priority as against the other creditors of the recipient, and this will be the effect of treating the plaintiff as subrogated to the discharged secured debt. But it is important to be clear about the reason for priority. The plaintiff's claim is a restitutionary claim to surviving value in the recipient's estate, which in principle attracts priority because it is a restitutionary claim. The priority is lost when the surviving value is used to discharge an unsecured debt, but it is preserved when the debt is secured, because the wealth conferred on the estate through the discharge is the face value of the debt, and this value does not decline in insolvency, since the discharged debt would not have done. The plaintiff's priority is not of course based on the security itself, in the sense that the discharged creditor's priority was, because the security no longer exists and the plaintiff does not *actually have* any such security.

The recent case of *Boscawen v Bajwa*[103] involved subrogation of a restitutionary claim to a discharged secured creditor's claim. The defendant owned a house secured by a mortgage with the Halifax Building Society. He made an agreement to sell the house, and the purchaser arranged a mortgage with the plaintiff building society. The plaintiff transferred the money that was to be borrowed by the purchaser to the purchaser's solicitors. Just before the conveyance of the house was due to take effect the purchaser's solicitors transferred the money to the defendant's solicitors, who were to hold it on trust for the plaintiff until the conveyance was executed, when it was to be used as the purchaser's purchase price and then paid to the Halifax on behalf of the defendant in discharge of the loan secured on the house. Unfortunately the defendant's

---

[102]   Chap. 8 at 270–1; cf Birks (1989a), 375.
[103]   [1996] 1 WLR 328.

solicitors mistakenly paid off the Halifax before the conveyance had taken place, thereby discharging the defendant's loan from the Halifax. The agreement subsequently fell through and the sale was never completed. The transfer of the money to the Halifax by the defendant's solicitors was without authority (in breach of trust).[104] Instead of having a loan contract with the purchaser secured on the house, as it had expected, the plaintiff found that its money had simply been transferred without authority to the defendant and used to discharge his mortgage. Furthermore, it seems that the defendant's building society had a good defence of bona fide purchase to a restitutionary claim, the payment having been made with the apparent authority of the defendant in discharge of his debt.[105] The plaintiff successfully claimed to be subrogated to the Halifax's mortgage over the defendant's house, in order to obtain priority over other creditors of the defendant. It seems that the right to subrogation followed directly from the fact that the plaintiff "did not intend its money to be used at all" in the circumstances as they turned out,[106] or, in other words, it would appear from the mere fact that the payment was vitiated.[107] The implication is that subrogation is available wherever a debt is discharged with the surviving value of a vitiated transfer.

The decision is inconsistent with the orthodox view of tracing, and consistent with the causation or swollen assets theory of tracing adopted above. This is so because, as argued above, given that subrogation is fictional and that the plaintiff did not genuinely acquire a charge over the defendant's house, in reality the plaintiff's claim was merely to surviving value out of the defendant's estate, not to a specific asset as the orthodox theory requires, and yet the claim was allowed priority. As mentioned above, it seems that the incompatibility of this type of case with the orthodox approach to tracing has been concealed by the fiction that the plaintiff *actually has* a mortgage or other security, as opposed to being treated as if he did.

Subrogation in respect of payments under a void or valid contract

One type of vitiated payment that is prone to give rise to a restitutionary claim by way of subrogation, because the payment will inevitably be used to discharge a debt, is a payment that is vitiated because it is made under a void loan contract, in a case where the void contract provided that the money lent would be used to discharge existing borrowing.[108] Before considering this type of case,

---

[104] i.e. the vitiating factor was lack of authority, as discussed in Chap. 5.

[105] *Aitken v Short* (1856) 1 H & N 210, 156 ER 1180; Chap. 7, at 247–8.

[106] At 339, per Millett LJ.

[107] Ibid., Millett LJ unfortunately expressed the condition for subrogation in terms of a fictional intention to be imputed to the vendor's solicitors, viz. that they intended to keep the charge alive for the benefit of the plaintiff. The requirement for an intention to keep the charge alive is derived from the cases on contractual subrogation as considered below.

[108] As discussed below at 308–9, the significant fact is that the payment *was actually* used to pay off the debt; the fact that the void contract provided that it was to be so used is not relevant.

however, it is helpful to refer briefly to the case of subrogation arising from a transfer under a *valid* loan contract of this sort, since there seems to have been some confusion between the two types of case. A contract for borrowing that provides that the loan will be used to discharge an existing loan is likely to provide that the plaintiff lender will take over the discharged creditor's security as security for his own loan to the defendant. In effect this means that the defendant borrower agrees to give the plaintiff security exactly equivalent to the security discharged; it is really a fiction to say that the plaintiff acquires the previous security.[109] The advantage of expressing this in terms of subrogation is that it makes clear that existing creditors are not prejudiced by the grant of a new security, as would be the case where the defendant granted security for an existing unsecured loan. Where the new loan is used to discharge an existing secured loan, the value of the estate available for distribution to creditors is unaffected by the grant of security to the plaintiff because he simply takes the place of the discharged secured creditor. This is presumably the reason why subrogation of a lender to the discharged security is normally presumed to have been intended, even if it was not explicitly provided for in the contract, if the loan was made for the purpose of enabling an existing secured debt to be discharged.[110] In cases of this sort, arising from a valid contract, the plaintiff's claim for repayment is contractual, not restitutionary. The subrogation takes effect under an express or implied term of the contract, and so operates as part of the law of contract.[111]

The position is different where the contract is void. Here the payment by the plaintiff (the putative lender) will be vitiated,[112] and if it is used to discharge a debt a claim for subrogation should arise, as discussed above, from the fact that the payment was vitiated, and not by virtue of the subrogation provisions in the void contract. The same should be the case where the contract is valid, but the payment under it was nevertheless vitiated, say by a mistake. The issue arose recently in *Banque Financière de la Cité v Parc (Battersea) Ltd*,[113] where the plaintiff had lent money to the first defendant to enable it to pay off a secured creditor, C.[114] It was clear from the contract terms that the contract did not confer on the plaintiff a right to be subrogated to C's security.[115] However, the agreement did contain a subordination provision purportedly made on behalf of the second defendant, who was also a creditor of the first defendant, by which the second defendant agreed not to enforce its claim for payment until the plaintiff's loan had been fully repaid. It was found, however, that the contract, and

---

[109] But provision may be made for the assignment of existing security: see Mitchell (1994), 139ff.

[110] This was the view taken by Lord Diplock in *Orakpo v Manson Investments Ltd* [1978] AC 95 at 104; cf Mitchell (1994), 146.

[111] *Banque Financière de la Cité v Parc (Battersea) Ltd* [1998] 2 WLR 475, 483 per Lord Hoffmann.

[112] *Westdeutsche Landesbank Girozentrale v Islington LBC* [1994] 4 All ER 890.

[113] [1998] 2 WLR 475.

[114] In fact only part of the secured debt was discharged, but this makes no difference to the analysis.

[115] This was implicit in the subordination provision.

in particular the subordination provision, was not binding on the second defendant because it had been made without its authority. The plaintiff made the loan, and, when the first defendant went into insolvent liquidation, a dispute arose over whether the plaintiff's claim had priority over the second defendant's. Because the plaintiff could not rely on the subordination provision in the contract, it argued instead that it was subrogated to C's security on the discharged debt. The claim was successful, but the decision has been controversial.[116]

One might argue that the contract was void because of the invalidity of the subordination provision, which was clearly a crucial term as far as the plaintiff was concerned.[117] If this was the case, the plaintiff would appear to have had a restitutionary claim based on its mistake about the validity of the contract.[118] This is at least a plausible account of the case, but the judgments contain no discussion of whether the contract was void, or of the nature of the vitiating factor if it was void, and yet these would surely have been controversial issues.[119] Alternatively, it may be that the contract was valid as between the plaintiff and the defendant, even though there was no binding contract between the plaintiff and the second defendant, and that the plaintiff's payment to the defendant was vitiated by its mistake in assuming that the second defendant was bound by the subordination provision.[120] On either basis, the plaintiff would acquire a restitutionary claim to surviving value, which, on the argument above, should be subrogated to C's security in respect of the discharged debt and so attract priority in the defendant's insolvency, just as C's secured debt would have done.[121] On the other hand, if the contract was valid, and the payment took effect under the contract, so as to generate a contractual debt, there should have been no claim to subrogation, because the contract did not provide for subrogation, expressly or by implication: the plaintiff implicitly took the risk of insolvency, save to the extent that he was protected by the subordination provision. The fact that the subordination provision was ineffective could not give the plaintiff a right of subrogation *under the contract*, because this would involve simply rewriting the contract.[122]

---

[116] e.g. Watts (1998*a*); Friedmann (1999); Bridge (1998).

[117] Possibly on the basis that there was a misrepresentation of authority, or because there was no consensus ad idem with respect to the major terms.

[118] Or "failure of consideration": see Chap. 6 with respect to *Westdeutsche Landesbank Girozentrale v Islington LBC* [1994] 4 All ER 890.

[119] Ibid.

[120] Or as to whether a precondition for the contract to come into effect had been fulfilled. But this approach requires some consideration of whether the defendant had a defence of bona fide purchase to the restitutionary claim on the basis that the payment, although vitiated, was received as payment under a valid contract, as considered in Chap. 7, at 244–8.

[121] In fact the debt to C was only partly discharged, and so the security persisted in favour of C to the extent of the unpaid debt. But this does not affect the argument. As Lord Hoffmann noted, there is no question of the plaintiff and C sharing the security: the security was C's, and the plaintiff was treated *as if* it were secured to the extent that surviving value was used to discharged the debt. Lord Hoffmann noted that C retained priority over the plaintiff, but this would not be in issue if the original debt to C was adequately secured, and was not in issue in the proceedings.

[122] As discussed in Chap. 2, it is sometimes argued under the restitutionary conditional transfer theory that there can be a restitutionary claim even though the contract is valid. However, that raises

Lord Hoffmann thought that the claim was restitutionary, not contractual,[123] although there was no discussion of a vitiating factor.[124] He held accordingly that it was irrelevant whether subrogation was provided for in the agreement, or what the intentions of the parties were with respect to subrogation.[125] But he also held that, although the claim was restitutionary, the plaintiff should have priority only as against the second defendant and not other creditors, i.e. that he should be subrogated to C's security only as against the second defendant, apparently because by virtue of the subordination agreement the plaintiff expected to have priority only over the second defendant.[126] But only the subordination provision could give rise to a position in which the plaintiff had priority with respect to the second defendant but not with respect to other creditors, and the subordination provision had no legal force.[127] The fact that surviving value of a vitiated transfer was used to discharge the secured loan could not justify discriminating between parties on the basis of a void agreement and would necessarily give priority as against all creditors.

It is argued by some that where a payment is made under a void lending contract, and used to discharge a debt, and the void contract does not provide for subrogation, the plaintiff should not be entitled to be subrogated, because he has taken the risk of being unsecured: "it would be quite wrong to put [the plaintiff] into such a favourable position", because "this would have the effect of giving [the plaintiff] more than he originally bargained for".[128] This would imply that the decision in *Banque Financière* was mistaken. But this argument cannot be correct, because in the case of a vitiated transfer[129] under a contract or putative contract subrogation does not arise from the contract, but from the fact that the transfer was vitiated.[130] The terms of a contract, or the risk implicit in those terms, cannot be relevant to a claim whose basis is that the payment was vitiated because the contract was void.[131] Even if the contract was valid, its terms cannot be relevant to a restitutionary claim that arises from a mistaken payment that did not take effect as a payment under the contract. The contractual terms

---

considerable difficulty and requires consideration of the doctrine of complete failure of consideration.

[123] This was the view of the whole house; Lord Hoffmann's was the leading judgment.

[124] The clearest indication of a vitiating factor was in the judgment of Lord Steyn, who referred to the plaintiff's mistake in thinking it was protected by the subordination agreement.

[125] He said, at 485, that the idea that subrogation was based on intention was derived from the cases on contractual subrogation, and that it is fictional to base subrogation on intention when it arises out of a restitutionary claim: cf above at n 107. See D Wright (1999).

[126] Possibly this could be thought to give support to the restitutionary conditional transfer theory, above n 122, on the basis that the payment was made on this condition even though the condition was not part of a contract binding the second defendant; however there was no reference to any such issue.

[127] Watts (1998*a*), 344.

[128] Mitchell (1994), 158; Goff & Jones (1998), 157.

[129] Whether the contract was void or not.

[130] See above at n 118.

[131] This was Millett LJ's view in *Boscawen v Bajwa* [1996] 1 WLR 328, 338.

would be relevant only if the plaintiff's payment constituted contractual performance so as to generate a debt governed by the contract.[132]

Claims to appreciated value and consequential benefits

The in rem claim, in the original asset or a substitute asset through tracing, is understood to have a further advantage, in addition to its significance in insolvency and as against indirect recipients. If the asset received by the recipient from the plaintiff, or its exchange product, has appreciated in value, or has generated a return through interest or dividends or licensing fees, the plaintiff's claim encompasses the appreciated value and the return generated. A claim to appreciated value or consequential profits is taken to be justified under the orthodox theory because the claim is an in rem claim to a specific asset. The in rem claim necessarily attaches to the whole appreciated value of the asset, and it is assumed that the plaintiff can trace into its "fruits" by virtue of his in rem claim in the asset.[133]

Under the alternative theory, the plaintiff's claim is always a restitutionary claim to recover his loss by reversing the transfer of value, subject to change of position, which limits the claim to surviving value.[134] Where the original asset transferred has appreciated in value in the hands of the recipient, it is reasonable to assume that the plaintiff would have benefited from the same appreciation in value, and so the value of the asset remains the correct measure of surviving value; this argument is presupposed by the argument for specific restitution above. There are two arguments that can account for claims to consequential benefits. First, if the recipient is a wrongdoer, he may be subject to a claim for disgorgement. This will sometimes explain why the tracing rules operate adversely to wrongdoers. Alternatively, there may be scope for a claim under an imputed contract for payment for the use of surviving value attributable to the plaintiff. Tracing has often had the effect of allowing these additional claims without proper consideration of their justification, but the alternative theory identifies the nature of such claims and requires them to be explicitly justified.[135]

---

[132] Cf Chap. 10 at 339.

[133] e.g. a dividend paid on shares.

[134] This is consistent with the award of an equitable charge rather than a proportional share as a remedy. The position appears to be that the plaintiff has a choice between these remedies, at least as against a wrongdoer: Re *Hallet* (1880) 13 Ch D 696; cf Hayton (1996), 848. As against an innocent party he presumably cannot get more than a proportionate share and may be forced to accept a charge even if less, as in *Foskett v McKeown* [1997] 3 All ER 392 where the plaintiff's surviving value was used to pay the premiums on an insurance policy, and the claim to the proceeds was limited to the amount of the surviving value spent on the premiums, and did not extent to a proportionate share. *Foskett v McKeown* (CA) has been overturned by the House of Lords (2000).

[135] See e.g. the discussion in Chap. 10 of *Trustee of the Property of FC Jones and Sons v Jones* [1996] 3 WLR 703. See also Chap. 7 at n 24.

SUMMARY

The orthodox understanding of this area of the law is based on three spurious or misunderstood distinctions. The first is between claims arising in the law of restitution for vitiated transfers and claims arising in the law of property, or in other words restitutionary and proprietary claims. This distinction is spurious, because there is only one relevant interest of the owner at stake. The second distinction is between in rem claims and in personam claims. There is such a valid distinction, but it has been wrongly equated with a distinction between claims to or in a specific asset and claims to value. The restitutionary (or proprietary) claim to surviving value is an in rem claim, having (in principle) priority in insolvency, but it is not an in rem claim in a specific asset in the orthodox sense. The third distinction is between claims in equity and claims at common law. There is no substantive or principled basis for this distinction, and it has obscured the practical function of separation of title. These three distinctions are the basis for an over-complex classification of claims that has no sound foundation and has not surprisingly caused confusion and controversy and left the law cluttered with a multiplicity of apparently different claims dealing with substantively the same issues.

The best approach would be to recognise that all claims arising from a vitiated or ineffective transfer of wealth or property are examples of either the restitutionary claim to surviving value or the claim for breach of the duty to preserve surviving value. This approach provides a clear and coherent framework for addressing the real issues that arise in connection with vitiated transfers of value. These include the use of presumptions in the law of tracing or change of position to determine the measure of surviving value; the availability of specific restitution; the relevant duty of inquiry of the recipient; the content of the duty of preservation, for example whether it requires the defendant to segregate surviving value; and the position with respect to priority, in terms of the issues considered above. Unfortunately different manifestations of the claim to surviving value and the claim for breach of the duty of preservation have developed in different contexts, with their own terminologies and rules, and their underlying uniformity has been obscured. The next chapter will deal with some of these different contexts, and attempt to explain their rules and terminologies in terms of the framework set out in this chapter.

10

Restitution and Property:
The Rational Scheme in Action

INTRODUCTION

T HE LAST CHAPTER set out what was described as the integrated or alternative theory of property claims, and contrasted it with the orthodox
approach to the area. The orthodox approach represents not the case
law as such, but the preconceptions and the terminology governing its interpretation and expression, as identified in the last chapter. This chapter will address
the application of the alternative theory to particular areas of law, with a view
to showing that in general it provides a better account of the law and a better
framework for its development.

MONEY PAYMENTS AND MONEY HAD AND RECEIVED

Money had and received is the standard form of the claim for restitution at
common law in respect of vitiated payments of money. It is generally accepted
to be an in personam claim, not attracting priority in insolvency,[1] and to be subject to the defences of bona fide purchase[2] and change of position.[3]

Proprietary or restitutionary?

There has been much discussion of whether, or in what circumstances, the claim
for money had received is restitutionary rather than proprietary.[4] As discussed
in the last chapter, it is thought, on an orthodox approach, that there is a proprietary claim if the money passes into the hands of the defendant recipient
without title first passing to him,[5] and a restitutionary claim if title passes under
the transfer but the transfer is nevertheless vitiated. Thus, for example, it is said

---

[1] See e.g. *Chase Manhattan v Israel-British Bank* [1981] Ch 105.

[2] *Miller v Race* (1758) 1 Burr. 452, 97 ER 398.

[3] *Lipkin Gorman v Karpnale* [1991] 3 WLR 10.

[4] e.g. Smith (1997), 333; Swadling (1996a); Fox (2000); Virgo (1998), 314. Some commentators
take the view that there are both restitutionary and proprietary versions of money had and received
(or even three versions, including two types of proprietary claim).

[5] Title to money will pass after receipt once the money is mixed and becomes untraceable at
common law: see below at 35.

that if a payment is made under a "fundamental mistake" title does not pass, and so a proprietary claim arises; but a lesser mistake can vitiate the payment and generate a restitutionary claim without preventing the passing of title.[6] In fact, as considered in Chapter 5, there has been some uncertainty over the type of mistake that will vitiate a payment and generate a restitutionary claim,[7] and little judicial discussion of the difference between the type of mistake that will prevent title passing and the type of mistake that will vitiate a payment, or of what the rationale might be for the difference. The alternative theory denies any distinction between proprietary and restitutionary claims, and this is consistent with the fact that the two claims go by the same name of money had and received. Furthermore, even those who distinguish between the two claims do not appear to think that there are any differences between the proprietary and restitutionary versions of money had and received with respect to any issue of substance—for example, with respect to priority, or to the defences of change of position or bona fide purchase. It seems that the difference is really assumed because of an unreflective commitment to the orthodox distinction between restitutionary and proprietary claims.[8]

One type of case where it is thought, on an orthodox approach, that title cannot pass and so the claim will be proprietary is where the transfer is without authority, as where the plaintiff's agent has paid the plaintiff's money to the defendant in excess of authority, or the defendant has stolen and kept the plaintiff's money, or a stranger to the plaintiff has found or stolen the money and paid it to the defendant, or the plaintiff's money has been lost and found by the defendant. Thus some commentators deny altogether that there can be a restitutionary vitiating factor of lack of authority,[9] preferring to say that the claim is a proprietary claim based on retention of or interference with title.[10] It is understandable that in such cases the vitiating factor should not receive any attention because the lack of authority is so palpable (although clearly, even on an orthodox approach, there must be a lack of authority to justify the claim). Instead the emphasis is likely to be on whether it is possible to trace the movement of value, or in other words to establish the location of title,[11] which

---

[6] See Fox (1996), 64; Fox draws a similar distinction with respect to other vitiating factors like duress.

[7] In fact one view has been that the mistake must be fundamental: *Norwich Union Fire Insurance Society v W.H. Price Ltd* [1934] AC 455 per Lord Wright at 462; Chap. 5 at 167.

[8] For the same reason a well-known dictum to the contrary has been dismissed as obviously mistaken: *Norwich Union Fire Insurance Society v W.H. Price Ltd* [1934] AC 455 per Lord Wright at 462. It is surely doubtful whether the distinctions now discerned in the old case law between restitutionary and proprietary forms of money had and received would have been recognised by the judges at the time.

[9] Or ignorance, as it is usually described in the restitution literature: Chap. 5 at 160–66.

[10] Swadling (1996a); Bant (1998); Goff & Jones (1998), 77ff; Virgo (1999), 129; Grantham & Rickett (1997).

[11] e.g. *Lipkin Gorman v Karpnale* [1991] 3 WLR 10; *Banque Belge pour l'Etranger v Hambrouck* [1921] 1 KB 321.

might on an orthodox approach suggest that the claim is proprietary not restitutionary.[12]

This issue has been discussed in connection with the recent decision of the House of Lords in *Lipkin Gorman v Karpnale*.[13] Here a rogue, Cass, who was a partner in the plaintiff firm of solicitors, drew money from the partnership account and lost it by gambling at the defendant's casino. The plaintiff was allowed to recover the money from the casino. The case was ostensibly decided as a case in restitution and has been generally accepted as such.[14] But some commentators argue that because Cass had no authority to use partnership money for gambling there was no question of title passing from the plaintiff to the defendant when it was received, so that the claim was based on the defendant's receipt of property belonging to the plaintiff and was proprietary, not restitutionary. This seems to be consistent with the fact that the decision involved no discussion of a vitiating factor, the main issue indeed being whether the defendant received money belonging to the plaintiff, i.e. in which the plaintiff had title. If it is right to distinguish between restitutionary and proprietary claims with reference to title, it seems difficult to deny that the claim in *Lipkin Gorman* was proprietary and not restitutionary. But according to the alternative theory there is no distinction to be drawn between the two, and the claim in *Lipkin Gorman* was a restitutionary (or proprietary) claim to surviving value, based on a vitiating factor of lack of authority. To say that the plaintiff had title to the money transferred to the defendant was, as argued in the previous chapter, simply to say that this money represented surviving value, and therefore that there was a transfer of surviving value to the defendant. On the alternative theory, this is how reference to retention of title should be understood in cases concerned with claims for money had and received.

Priority and separation of title

As noted above, the claim for money had and received is in personam and does not attract priority in insolvency. As argued in the last chapter, in principle it should attract priority because it is a restitutionary claim. It is usually said that the common law does not recognise any in rem claim at all;[15] this is associated with the failure of the common law to recognise the possibility of separation of

---

[12] Commentators who on an orthodox view consider the claim to be a restitutionary claim, arising from lack of authority or ignorance, will generally require that the plaintiff has title to the money in the intermediary's hands, but that the title will pass to the indirect recipient on receipt.

[13] [1991] 3 WLR 10.

[14] Especially Birks (1991*a*).

[15] e.g. Birks (1997*a*), 646. Where the plaintiff's money remains identifiable as a tangible chattel, like coins in a bag or bars of gold bullion, and has not "passed into currency", then it seems that the claim can have priority, just like a claim in respect of a chattel, as considered below. It seems that such a claim is a claim in conversion rather than money had and received, although on one view the claim can take the form of a distinct version of money had and received: Fox (2000).

title, which would have allowed the plaintiff's claim for money had and received to be expressed in the form of beneficial title to some part of the defendant's estate, rather than a claim in the nature of damages or debt in the measure of value received.[16] What is necessary is the recognition that the restitutionary plaintiff's claim to surviving value, defined in terms of change of position, is equivalent to title to a part of the defendant's estate, meaning title to value in the abstract and not to a specific asset.

There are cases that give some support to the idea of title to value in the defendant's estate. For example in *Banque Belge pour l'Etranger v Hambrouck*,[17] where the plaintiff's money was paid without authority to the defendant through an intermediary and then deposited in the defendant's account, the claim was limited to the amount remaining in the account from the sum transferred, and was not for the amount received, as one would expect on the normal understanding of the claim for money had and received. The language of the decision suggests that the court conceived of the plaintiff as having title to the money left in the account. This seems to be inconsistent with the usual understanding that the claim for money had and received is in personam, and so should be, it seems, a claim for the value received, rather than being a claim to any part of the defendant's estate. The approach was more like that for chattels, where title to the chattel does not pass to the recipient, as considered below.[18]

A similar, more recent case is *Trustee of the Property of F.C. Jones and Sons v Jones*.[19] Here money in the account of a partnership that had been declared bankrupt was paid out to the defendant, who was the wife of one of the partners, without the authority of the plaintiff trustee in bankruptcy, in whom the money in the account had vested from the time of the bankruptcy. The defendant made a speculative investment with the money, about £10,000, and ended up with about £70,000, which she paid into her own account. Following the plaintiff's claim, the £70,000 was paid by her bank into court. The defendant admitted liability to the tune of £10,000, but asserted a right to the rest of the £70,000. The defendant's argument was that title to the money had passed to her, leaving the plaintiff with only a restitutionary in personam claim for money had and received, in the measure of the value of the transfer, £10,000. But it was held that the plaintiff had retained legal title to the money transferred, which could be traced into the £70,000 proceeds as its exchange product, and consequently that he could claim the whole of the proceeds as money had and received. It seems a small step from this to say that, because the £70,000 belongs to the plaintiff, his claim should have priority.[20]

---

[16] See Chap. 9 at 292.

[17] [1921] 1 KB 321.

[18] It seems that in so far as this approach is permissible at common law it depends on the money not having been mixed, as in *Banque Belge* and *Jones*.

[19] [1996] 3 WLR 703.

[20] As would be the position for a chattel, as considered below at 322. At common law, the exchange product rule is attributed to *Taylor v Plumer* (1815) 33 M & S 562, but on one view this aspect of the decision was a matter of equity: see Khurshid and Matthews (1979), Smith (1995a).

Jones demonstrates the difficulty arising from the lack of separation of title. Because the £70,000 was in the defendant's bank account, the plaintiff's title to it actually took the form of title to the defendant's bank account in which the £70,000 had been deposited, as a chose in action. But it is very difficult to see how the plaintiff can be understood to acquire (through tracing) the legal title to a bank account in the defendant's name. The defendant surely has the legal authority to withdraw money from the account, which presumably goes with legal title to the account. The position would be conveniently dealt with in equity through separation of title: the defendant as account holder would have a legal or dispositive title that would protect the bank or third parties dealing with her as account holder (subject to notice of the restitutionary claim), and the plaintiff the equitable title representing the claim to surviving value in the defendant's estate. Perhaps the decision in *Jones* should be regarded as moving the common law towards the recognition of a separation between dispositive and beneficial titles.[21] The problem of lack of separation of title and third parties is considered further below.

Another difficulty with *Jones* is that in principle, as argued in the last chapter, the restitutionary claim to surviving value is for the value of the transfer subject to change of position, and does not cover the fruits of an investment, which should be covered separately, if at all, by way of a claim for disgorgement or a use claim. Disgorgement, but not the use claim, would encompass the whole of the profits, but there was no discussion of the culpability of the defendant in this connection. If the defendant made money through her skill and knowledge in good faith there was no basis for requiring her to pay over the whole of her profits, although she should have paid for her use of the money.

Tracing against indirect recipients and separation of title

Because of the absence of priority, for money had and received the issue of tracing generally arises with respect to claims against indirect recipients. It is said that it is not possible to trace through a mixture,[22] and that at common law it is not possible to trace through an electronic transfer.[23] These rules seem inexplicable under the orthodox theory, and are also incompatible with the alternative theory in the light of the function of tracing as determining the movement of value as a matter of causation.[24] However, if no mixing is involved, tracing against an indirect recipient is apparently allowed, even tracing through (unmixed) bank accounts.[25]

[21] For similar criticisms of *Jones* and also *Lipkin Gorman*, below at 318, leading to rather different conclusions, see Smith (1997), 335ff.

[22] *Banque Belge pour l'Etranger v Hambrouck* [1921] 1 KB 321.

[23] *Agip (Africa) Ltd v Jackson* [1991] Ch 547.

[24] Furthermore, the common law tracing rules are inconsistent with the rules adopted in equity, and yet, as discussed in the last chapter, there is no difference in principle between the restitutionary claim to surviving value in law and in equity.

[25] *Banque Belge pour l'Etranger v Hambrouck* [1921] 1 KB 321; *Lipkin Gorman v Karpnale* [1991] 3 WLR 10.

As discussed in the last chapter, there is a problem at common law concerning claims against indirect recipients, resulting from the absence of the concept of separation of title. The point is illustrated by *Lipkin Gorman*. To establish a claim against the defendant, the plaintiff had to be able to trace into the money received by him, i.e. he had to show that he had title to it.[26] In the absence of any concept of separation of title—with only one title to play with, as it were—the issue was whether the single legal title to the money withdrawn by the rogue Cass vested in Cass or in the plaintiff. Lord Goff refused to overturn a previous authority to the effect that title vested in Cass, not the plaintiff. This would seem to settle the matter in favour of the defendant, on the basis that the money transferred to the defendant was not the plaintiff's; but Lord Goff also appeared to hold that the plaintiff did have title in some different sense, and that this title was sufficient to justify a restitutionary claim. It seems, in other words, that there were two titles involved, although this is not stated explicitly.[27]

The judgment can be understood to involve the recognition of separation of title in the common law, between a dispositive title, or power in relation to an asset to dispose of it in favour of an indirect recipient, and a beneficial title, or right to benefit from the value of the asset, which, in the context of a restitutionary claim, is the claim to surviving value. In the previous authority faced by Lord Goff, *Commercial Bank of Sydney Ltd v Mann*,[28] the defendant recipient of the transfer from the rogue had given consideration for it and the decision can be understood to be based on the fact that the rogue had a dispositive title, by virtue of which he could give title to the defendant as a bona fide purchaser.[29] On this basis it is distinguishable from *Lipkin Gorman*, where the issue was whether the plaintiff had the right to benefit, or beneficial title, or in other words whether the money withdrawn and transferred to the defendant represented surviving value due to him. This treatment, by which a title signifying the claim to surviving value was with the plaintiff but a title signifying the power of disposition in favour of a bona fide purchaser was with Cass, is exactly the approach that equity would take, in the form of a constructive trust or equitable tracing claim, the power of disposition being the legal title and the right to benefit the equitable title. On this interpretation, *Lipkin Gorman* is consistent with the argument in the last chapter, that separation of title should be recognised as

---

[26] Under the alternative theory, this means that it was necessary to use the tracing rules to show that the transfer represented surviving value, and so a transfer of value from the plaintiff. Under the orthodox theory, it meant that the plaintiff had to show that it had an in rem claim in the orthodox sense in the money transferred.

[27] Birks has argued that Lord Goff should be understood to mean that the plaintiff did not have title, but had instead a power to reclaim title or revest it in himself: Birks (1989a) 393; Birks (1991), 478. The "power *in rem*" is used by Birks in his analysis of tracing, as considered in the last chap. But the approach is unconvincing. If there is a power *in rem* but it has not been exercised before the money reached the defendant, the plaintiff has no *in rem* claim to the money and should have no claim against the defendant: see L.D. Smith (1997), 325. More generally, the power *in rem* theory seems to be no more than an *ad hoc* device lacking any underlying rationale.

[28] [1961] 1 AC 1; also *Union Bank of Australia Ltd v McClintock* [1922] 1 AC 240.

[29] This was by virtue of the statutory bona fide purchase defence.

functional and not jurisdictional, and detached from its misleading historical origin in the law and equity divide.

Bona fide purchase

The claim for money had and received is subject to the defence of bona fide purchase.[30] The availability of the defence follows naturally from the alternative theory, because in principle it applies wherever there is reliance on a receipt under a contract. In the archetypal case of bona fide purchase, the defendant is an indirect recipient who receives the vitiated transfer through an intermediary, the direct recipient.[31] There is something slightly anomalous about the bona fide purchase defence to the claim for money had and received in such a case. In equity, as mentioned above, the bona fide purchase defence is associated with separation of title.[32] It is the legal or dispositive title of the direct recipient that is conceived of as providing the basis for the bona fide purchase or equity's darling defence in favour of an indirect recipient. Conversely, with respect to chattels at common law the general rule is that an indirect recipient of a chattel does not have any defence of bona fide purchase, and this is directly related to the absence of any separation of title. With respect to chattels, the only claim is understood to arise from the plaintiff's retention of title to the chattel,[33] and the fact that the direct recipient has received no title is understood under the principle of nemo dat quod non habet to preclude the indirect recipient from acquiring any title under the bona fide purchase defence (except where there is a statutory bona fide purchase defence, as for cheques).[34]

Under the orthodox theory, with respect to money had and received, where the plaintiff's claim against the direct recipient is conceived of as a restitutionary claim, title is understood to pass on receipt. This seems to mean that there can be no question of a subsequent claim arising against an indirect recipient, or any issue of bona fide purchase in favour of an indirect recipient. If the claim against the direct recipient is conceived of as a proprietary claim, title does not pass on receipt, but generally title will pass soon afterwards as the money received is mixed in with the recipient's money, so that again no risk is posed to indirect recipients.[35] But it seems that there are circumstances in which title to

---

[30] *Miller v Race* (1758) 1 Burr. 452; 97 ER 398.

[31] See generally Chap. 7 on bona fide purchase. The concern here is with intermediary cases. In two-party cases the plaintiff has both a beneficial title and a dispositive title in the sense that he is the absolute owner of the wealth transferred.

[32] See Chap. 9 at 292.

[33] i.e. what is understood to be a proprietary in personam claim or claim in the tort of conversion.

[34] See below at 323–5.

[35] Thus it seems that coin passes into currency either where it is mixed and ceases to be identifiable as a chattel, or where it is received in good faith for good consideration even if still identifiable: *Lipkin Gorman v Karpnale* [1991] 3 WLR 10, 27ff.

the money in the direct recipient's possession is retained so that there can be a claim against an indirect recipient of it, as in *Lipkin Gorman*.[36]

Where a claim does arise against an indirect recipient, because the plaintiff has retained title to the money transferred to him, it might seem that, by analogy with the position for chattels, there should be no possibility of a bona fide purchase defence based on the indirect recipient's contract with the direct recipient, on the basis that the direct recipient has no title to dispose of the money in favour of the indirect recipient.[37] But in fact the common law does recognise a defence of bona fide purchase. However, it is understood not to depend on the direct recipient's having acquired any title empowering him to dispose of the money in favour of the indirect recipient as for the equity's darling defence; instead it is said that the title acquired by the defendant is a new title, not a derivative title.[38] It would be an advance in coherence, and a step towards the fusion of common law and equity, if the defence of bona fide purchase to the claim for money had and received at common law were understood in terms of a separation of title, as in equity, and therefore based on a dispositive title in the direct recipient, while the plaintiff retains a beneficial title. As argued above, this is also a plausible way of interpreting *Lipkin Gorman*.

The claim for breach of the duty of preservation?

The distinction has been drawn between the restitutionary claim to surviving value and the claim for breach of the duty of preservation.[39] As discussed below, the two claims are clearly identifiable in equity, and discernible though obscured in the law on chattels at common law, but in the law of money had and received no such distinction is apparent. As discussed previously,[40] it is common to aggregate the claims for surviving value and for breach of the duty of preservation into a single claim. Then the liability is for the value received, adjusted for change of position, but disregarding any change of position caused by the defendant when he knew or ought to have known of the vitiating factor, i.e. due to a breach of the duty of preservation. This approach is deficient only when it is necessary to identify the true surviving value, which is independent of the defendant's actual or constructive knowledge and is based purely on causation, or in other words excludes liability due to breach of the duty of preservation. The

---

[36] [1991] 3 WLR 10; *Miller v Race* (1758) 1 Burr. 452, 97 ER 398. This can be the case, it seems, if the money is not mixed, even if it passes unmixed through a bank account. e.g. *Banque Belge pour l'Etranger v Hambrouck* [1921] 1 KB 321.

[37] This is the position at common law with respect to a cheque, which is treated as if it were a chattel and subject to the law of conversion, although now subject to a statutory bona fide purchase defence, as illustrated by *United Australia Ltd v Barclays Bank Ltd* [1941] AC 1, as discussed in Chap. 11.

[38] See e.g. Fox (1996), 62.

[39] Chap. 7 at 234–6; Chap. 9 at 282–4.

[40] Ibid.

usual reason for identifying the true surviving value is to establish priority for the purposes of a claim to surviving value; the priority will not extend to the liability for breach of the duty of preservation. But the claim for money had and received is not recognised as attracting priority, and so there is no need to distinguish between the two types of liability on that score. The development of the common law and its integration with equity will require the recognition of the distinction, as in equity.

CONVERSION AND TRANSFERS OF GOODS OR CHATTELS

Where the defendant receives a chattel belonging to the plaintiff, he is liable in damages in conversion for the value of the property received.[41] Conversion is said to be a tort; thus it seems to be generally thought that the law governing ineffective transfers of chattels is not part of the law of restitution at all, and certainly it is not generally discussed in books on restitution. But, as considered below, excluding conversion from the law of restitution on the ground that it is a tort is rather like excluding money had and received from the law of restitution on the ground that it is contractual: conversion is often, although not always, a fictional tort,[42] just as money had and received used to be based on a fictional contract. In fact it is widely observed that there is an anomaly in treating conversion as a tort, and that it should be understood as a proprietary claim,[43] which, as argued above, is synonymous (in this context) with a restitutionary claim.

In terms of the orthodox theory, conversion (whether or not understood as being a genuine tort) is a claim based on interference with the plaintiff's title in his chattel, i.e. the claim is thought to be proprietary in personam. Under the alternative theory, the claim is based on the vitiated transfer of value through the transfer of the chattel. In the typical case, where a chattel is stolen or lost, the vitiating factor is lack of authority. Under the orthodox theory, it seems that there should be a distinct restitutionary claim where title passes but the transfer is vitiated. But it is difficult to find any line of authority of this sort.[44]

Specific restitution

The usual remedy in conversion is damages in the measure of the value of the chattel. At one time this was the only remedy, but for a long time the court has

---

[41] Subject to the condition that the defendant has refused to return the chattel, or otherwise acted inconsistently with the plaintiff's rights of ownership: see e.g. Bridge (1996), 45. The law is complex and intricate and a simplified picture is presented here.

[42] See at 326 below.

[43] "Trover [sc conversion] is in form a tort, but in substance an action to try property": *Hambly v Trott* (1776) 1 Cowper 371, 98 ER 1136 per Lord Mansfield; Weir (1996), 491.

[44] See the very short section in Goff & Jones (1998), 253.

had a discretion to order the return of the chattel, i.e. as it is described, specific restitution.[45] The fact that the normal remedy is damages follows naturally from the alternative theory, because it implies that the plaintiff's title is to surviving value rather than to the asset itself in the orthodox sense, specific restitution being appropriate where the value of the asset transferred is difficult to measure.[46] It is perhaps not as easy to understand such a discretion under the orthodox theory, where one would think that title to the asset in the orthodox sense would generate an automatic right to its return.[47]

Priority

If the defendant is insolvent, the plaintiff's claim has priority if the defendant still has the chattel or its exchange product.[48] This is understood, under the orthodox view, to follow from the fact that the plaintiff retains title, but this is not easy to reconcile with the idea that the plaintiff has only a proprietary in personam claim for damages through conversion and does not necessarily have a right to the asset itself. It has been argued that the common law claim does not in itself attract priority, and that priority is conferred only through the effect of equity, which keeps the chattel outside the insolvency by virtue of the in rem claim recognised by equity.[49] Under the alternative theory, priority is (prima facie) justified in the nature of the claim, as a restitutionary claim.

Change of position

The defendant is not understood to have any change of position defence. If he incurs expenditure on the assumption of increased wealth, or if he disposes of the chattel itself, the traditional rule is that he will still be liable for its full value.[50] This seems to be taken to follow from the fact that the claim is tortious

---

[45] Common Law Procedure Act 1854, s.78; now Torts (Interference with Goods) Act 1977, s.3(3)(b).

[46] See Chap. 9 at 287.

[47] The original reason for the lack of any specific remedy was the institutional deficiency of the common law courts, in the sense that a specific remedy was not available to it.

[48] e.g. *Taylor v Plumer* (1815) 33 M & S 562, 105 ER 721.

[49] Goode (1976), 564; Smith (1995a). If this is the explanation, one wonders why the plaintiff cannot rely on this equitable in rem right to recover his asset in the usual case. Alternatively it has been said that the claim in conversion does not itself attract priority, but that the plaintiff can secure priority indirectly by way of a claim in conversion against the defendant's trustee in bankruptcy for the full value of the chattel if the trustee in bankruptcy does not return it: Goode (1976), 401. This is a curious argument, because the trustee in bankruptcy should in principle take over the defendant's estate as it stands. If the defendant, at the moment of insolvency, is subject only to an in personam claim it is difficult to see how the position can be any different vis-à-vis the trustee.

[50] But there is now a limited statutory defence of change of position under s.3(7) of the Torts (Interference with Goods) Act 1977, although it has not been recognised as such: see Chap. 3 at 92 in connection with *Greenwood v Bennett* [1973] QB 195.

or proprietary[51] rather than restitutionary. It is consistent with the alternative theory on the basis that the defendant is "at risk" with respect to the vitiating factor,[52] and indeed this is how the position is sometimes described: "persons deal with the property in chattels or exercise acts of ownership over them at their peril".[53] This means that the defendant is taken to know of the vitiating factor, or at least is taken to accept the risk that the transfer to him was vitiated, and accordingly that he incurs an immediate duty of preservation in respect of the chattel. Then if the defendant disposes of the chattel or otherwise fails to preserve the surviving value, he will incur a liability for breach of the duty of preservation instead of or in addition to the restitutionary liability for surviving value.

Tracing into the proceeds of sale

If the defendant sells the chattel, it is said that the plaintiff has a claim in respect of the proceeds of sale. This is traditionally characterised as a claim for money had and received arising from a waiver of tort—i.e. waiving the claim for damages for the tort of conversion in respect of the sale—and nowadays this is often taken to mean that it is a claim for disgorgement. But, as argued below in Chapter 11, the claim for money had and received arising from a waiver of tort is not a claim for disgorgement for a wrong; and, in any case, the wrong in this case is thought to be the tort of conversion, and (as considered below) it is often a fiction to say that conversion is a wrong at all. The better interpretation is that the rule is an example of the tracing of surviving value into the proceeds of sale under the exchange product rule.[54] This seems to be supported by the fact that the plaintiff's claim to the proceeds appears to have priority in insolvency,[55] and there is no reason why a claim for disgorgement should do so.[56]

Bona fide purchase and claims against indirect recipients

The plaintiff has a claim in conversion against an indirect recipient of the chattel. Under the orthodox theory, this is taken to follow from the plaintiff's retention of title to the chattel as it passes through the hands of the direct recipient. Under the alternative theory, it means that (by way of a rule of tracing or following) surviving value is deemed to be embodied in the chattel in the hands of

---

[51] Although it seems also to be thought that the claim for money had and received is subject to the defence even when it is a proprietary claim: on one view *Lipkin Gorman v Karpnale* was itself a proprietary claim.

[52] See Chap. 7 at 233, Chap. 9 at 292.

[53] Per Cleasby B in *Fowler v Hollins* (1872) LR 7 QB 616.

[54] As discussed in the section on tracing in the Chap. 9.

[55] *Taylor v Plumer* (1815) 33 M & S 562, 105 ER 721.

[56] As discussed below at 349–50 in connection with constructive trusts.

the indirect recipient.[57] An indirect recipient who acquires the chattel by purchase from the direct recipient has no defence of bona fide purchase. This is taken to follow from the fact that the plaintiff has retained title, so that the direct recipient has no title to pass on to an indirect recipient, even a bona fide purchaser: nemo dat quod non habet. As argued above,[58] the problem here is that, in the absence of any concept of separation of title, if the plaintiff has a claim at all against a direct or indirect recipient, it is taken to be based on his retention of title, but if he has retained title it seems to follow that there can be no defence of bona fide purchase.

Through what are regarded as various exceptions to the general principle, however, the common law does often give protection to a bona fide purchaser of a chattel.[59] One case is where the recipient can show that he received the chattel under a contract made by an agent of the plaintiff on behalf of the plaintiff with his apparent authority. Even without apparent authority, there is protection for a purchaser from a bailee, and for a purchaser from a buyer who has taken possession by consent before ownership has passed. A bona fide purchaser is also protected where the owner negligently allows an "indicium of title" to come into the possession of the person who sells it without authority, by way of an extension of apparent authority. Similar protection is given to a purchaser from someone who received a chattel from the plaintiff under a vitiated or voidable contract. Here the law adopts the idea of a provisional or voidable title[60]; the plaintiff can cancel or rescind the voidable title, thereby revesting his own title to the chattel and giving him a claim for its value, but so long as the direct recipient has the voidable title he can give a good title to a bona fide purchaser. In these various cases, the purchase is from a direct recipient or intermediary who received the chattel with the plaintiff's consent, or as a result of some carelessness on his part in allowing it to come into the hands of the direct recipient. A claim in respect of a cheque, which is technically treated as a chattel and protected through the law of conversion, is subject to a bona fide purchase defence introduced by statute, and this applies, as for money under the claim for money had and received, even if the cheque came into the hands of the direct recipient without the plaintiff's consent or any carelessness by him, as where it was lost or stolen.[61] Furthermore, there was at one time a defence of market overt, which protected a bona fide purchaser of a chattel who bought it at a recognised market, again even if the chattel had been lost or stolen.[62]

It would be more coherent if the real issue here, which is the conflict between the plaintiff's interest in his property and the indirect recipient's interest in relying on the direct recipient's apparent ownership of it, were addressed in the

[57] See Chap. 9 at 297–8.
[58] See above 319–20.
[59] For an outline of these exceptions, see Bridge (1996), 98ff.
[60] Thus the concept of a voidable contract is used both to protect third parties and to protect the other contracting party, as discussed in Chap. 7.
[61] Under the Bills of Exchange Act 1880, ss.60 and 80, or the Cheques Act 1957, s.4.
[62] Bridge (1996), 98.

same way as in equity by way of a separation of title. In other words, these various exceptions should be understood as incipient manifestations of separation of title, according to which the direct recipient has a form of dispositive title equivalent to legal title where there is a separation of legal and equitable title. As in equity, a recipient of the chattel, who is in possession or control of it, however he came to be so, should be understood to have a dispositive title, the plaintiff retaining a beneficial title, which is the restitutionary claim to surviving value if it was received through a vitiated transfer. Whether the indirect recipient has a defence of bona fide purchase in a particular case would depend on his duty of inquiry. This raises explicitly the question of the appropriate level of the duty of inquiry, and whether it is justifiable for the recipient of a chattel generally to be "at risk". Another important issue is the significance with respect to some of these exceptions of the plaintiff's responsibility for the fact that the chattel is in the direct recipient's estate. These issues are considered further below.[63]

Conversion and the "at risk" rule

The law of conversion is crude, not only with respect to the absence of separation of title, but also because of the absence (as with money had and received) of any distinction between a restitutionary claim to surviving value and a tortious claim for breach of the duty of preservation. A restitutionary claim is in principle a strict liability claim, subject to change of position, which would generally mean in relation to the transfer of a chattel that the claim would lapse on the loss of the chattel, since this would generally constitute a loss of surviving value. A claim for breach of the duty of preservation, on the other hand, should in principle be subject to a requirement of actual or constructive knowledge (in the light of the appropriate duty of inquiry), but should not lapse on the loss of the chattel. The actual claim in conversion does not adequately serve either purpose. It is a strict liability claim, in order to serve as the restitutionary (i.e. proprietary) claim, but there is no change of position defence or (in general) any bona fide purchase defence, and this is because of its function as a tortious claim. If it is to be a tortious claim, however, there should be a requirement of actual or constructive knowledge; but then the claim would fail to serve as a restitutionary claim.[64] This tension in the law has been remarked upon, and conversion is thought to operate harshly in some circumstances, where the defendant is in effect denied protection for change of position or bona fide purchase.[65]

---

[63] See below at 342–6.

[64] As the law of money had and received shows, it is possible to give some effect to change of position and bona fide purchase without the explicit recognition of a distinction between a restitutionary claim and a tortious claim for breach of the duty of preservation.

[65] Bridge (1996), 45; *Hollins v Fowler* (1875) LR 7 HL 757, 764 per Blackburn J. *Elvin and Powell Ltd v Plummer Roddis Ltd* (1933) 50 TLR 158 is a case where an innocent defendant was allowed what amounts to a change of position defence to a claim in conversion.

It seems that at one time the distinction between the restitutionary claim and the tortious claim was recognised in the law in relation to chattels; the restitutionary claim was detinue, which arose from the receipt and continuing possession of a chattel, and the tortious claim was conversion, which was, in its original sense, the wrongful disposal or appropriation of the chattel or failure to return it,[66] and amounted to what has been described here as breach of the duty of preservation. In addition, where the defendant committed a wrong in acquiring the chattel, for example by taking the chattel by force or stealth, as opposed to committing a wrong after receipt by breach of the duty of preservation, he committed trespass. Detinue, conversion and trespass in these senses would make, or would have made, a rational classification of claims.[67]

The origin of detinue was in the case where the defendant had taken possession of the chattel by arrangement with the plaintiff owner, i.e. under a bailment, so that the liability for failing to return it arose from the agreement and was by nature contractual; hence the common etymological origin of "detinue" and "debt".[68] Later, detinue came also to apply as against a stranger who came into possession, and by its origin it is clear that the claim was based on a liability arising from receipt and continuing possession, and not from a wrongful act.[69] Thus it seems that the liability in detinue would lapse if the defendant no longer had the chattel.[70] This would have been an example of the change of position defence, on the assumption that the loss of the chattel would entail the loss of surviving value. Where a defendant disposes of a chattel before he knows or ought to know of the vitiating factor—in other words before he becomes subject to a duty of preservation—he should be free of liability in conversion (in the true and original tortious sense) as well. This may more or less have been the position a very long time ago, before the conflation of detinue and conversion.[71] Unfortunately, the distinction between the two has long been blurred, and was then lost entirely, detinue having been subsumed into conversion.[72]

The present position, by which the recipient is denied any defence of change of position or bona fide purchase, is justified in principle only if it is justified for the recipient of a chattel to be held to be "at risk" with respect to the receipt. Where this is the case, the recipient incurs a duty of preservation on receipt and there is no need to distinguish between the restitutionary claim and the tortious claim (unless priority is in issue). But it is doubtful whether there is any good reason for the recipient to be at risk; the present position is better understood to be the capricious result of the mistaken conflation of conversion and detinue. As

---

[66] Bridge (1996), 39.

[67] Ibid.

[68] Milsom (1981), 262ff; Ibbetson (1999), 33–6.

[69] Milsom (1981), 269ff; Ibbetson (1996), 107ff. The refusal to deliver up might be wrongful, but a duty to deliver up presupposes a pre-existing liability based on receipt itself.

[70] Milsom (1981), 274; Ibbetson (1996), 107. This was true with respect to the finder, not the contractual bailee.

[71] Milsom (1981), 377; Ibbetson (1996), 112.

[72] Ultimately by the Torts (Interference with Goods) Act 1977; Milsom (1981), 377–9.

Milsom says: "[w]e tell ourselves that [the innocent converter] is a victim of a policy of discouraging theft; but in truth he is a victim of history".[73] On this understanding, conversion is a fictional tort in any case where there is no legitimate basis for saying that the recipient knew or ought to have known of the vitiating factor. But, whereas the fiction of implied contract has now been exposed, and there is constant vigilance against any recurrence, the fiction of a tort is allowed to persist,[74] subject only to the occasional acknowledgement that it is incongruous or irrational.[75]

THE EQUITABLE *IN REM* CLAIM AND THE EQUITABLE CLAIM FOR KNOWING RECEIPT

Receipt from a trustee acting in breach of trust

A recipient of property transferred in breach of trust can be subject to two types of claim, which will be referred to as the equitable in rem claim and the claim for knowing receipt. The equitable in rem claim is usually described as the "equitable proprietary claim", but in this context it seems that "proprietary" is used to convey that it is an in rem claim, having priority in insolvency, and "in rem" will be preferred in accordance with the usage adopted in the last chapter.[76] In accordance with the orthodox theory, the claim is understood to be a claim to a specific asset, which can be transmitted to other assets under the law of tracing. Where tracing is involved the claim is traditionally described as the equitable proprietary tracing claim. The equitable in rem claim is subject to a defence of bona fide purchase, known in this context as the equity's darling defence: the recipient takes the trust property free of any claim by the plaintiff beneficiary if he receives it under a contract with the trustee, without actual or constructive knowledge of the breach of trust. The equitable in rem claim arises against a subsequent indirect recipient of traceable proceeds, subject again to the bona fide purchase defence.

The claim for knowing receipt is an in personam claim, not having priority in insolvency. Its measure is normally the value of the property received. It arises when the defendant recipient has actual or possibly constructive knowledge that he has received property transferred in breach of trust;[77] as discussed below,[78] it is a controversial question whether constructive knowledge suffices for liability. If the recipient acquires actual or constructive knowledge of the breach of trust

---

[73] Milsom (1981), 379.

[74] And has even in effect been consolidated by statute as recently as by the Act of 1977.

[75] e.g. Weir (1996), 491.

[76] In the sense of "proprietary" adopted in the last chapter there is controversy, as with respect to money had and received, whether the claim is proprietary or restitutionary: see below at 330–1.

[77] Where the duty of preservation is incurred after receipt, the claim is sometimes said to arise from "knowing dealing" rather than "knowing receipt".

[78] See at 331–4.

at some time after receipt, the measure of recovery is limited to the value of the property remaining at this time, as discussed below.[79]

Some difficulty has arisen from the use of inconsistent terminology in connection with these two claims. It is customary to say, and it has been assumed above, that to say that there is a trust, or that the recipient is a trustee, is just to say that there is a separation of title, or in other words that the plaintiff has an equitable in rem claim. Where the trust arises from a transfer in breach of trust, as opposed to having been deliberately created, the trust is said to be a constructive trust (and the recipient a constructive trustee). But there seems to be another usage, according to which it is not correct to say that there is a trust, or that the recipient is a constructive trustee, merely because there is a separation of title and an equitable in rem claim, but only if the recipient has the necessary knowledge to be liable for knowing receipt. Furthermore, sometimes "knowing receipt" is used to refer to the equitable in rem claim. Generally in this section the discussion will refer to the two claims only as the "equitable in rem claim" and "knowing receipt". The terminological issue is considered again in the discussion of constructive trusts below.

The claims under the alternative theory

These two claims are readily explained in accordance with the alternative theory.[80] The equitable in rem claim is the restitutionary claim to surviving value. It arises here because the trustee effects a transfer of value from the plaintiff to the defendant recipient that is vitiated for lack of authority; there is no authority because the trustee acts in excess of his authority under the trust instrument.[81] The transfer by the trustee constitutes a transfer of value from the beneficiary because it is a transfer from the trust fund, which constitutes value attributable to the plaintiff although under the control of the trustee. The claim is subject to the bona fide purchase defence as one would expect for a restitutionary claim.

The equitable in rem claim attaches to traceable proceeds in the defendant recipient's estate, and this should be equated with surviving value for the purposes of the restitutionary claim, as discussed in the last chapter. (As discussed there, this is at odds with the current understanding, which distinguishes between surviving value, or "abstractly surviving value", and traceable proceeds.) The claim is in rem because it is a restitutionary claim to surviving value, but the claim is not an in rem claim in a specific asset in the orthodox sense. Surviving value should be defined independently of the actual or constructive knowledge of the recipient, so that any loss in surviving value caused by the recipient when he has actual or constructive knowledge does reduce the measure

---

[79] See at 329–30.
[80] This follows from the discussion of the trust in Chap. 9. Cf Nicholls (1998), 245.
[81] See Chap. 5 at 162.

of the restitutionary claim, but generates instead a claim for breach of the duty of preservation. This is broadly speaking the position here: the traceable proceeds are reduced if they are consumed or disposed of by the recipient, whether or not he has actual or constructive knowledge. Instead the plaintiff has to rely on the claim for knowing receipt, which, on the alternative theory, is the claim for breach of the duty of preservation.

Unlike the equitable in rem claim, the claim for knowing receipt is not in rem and does not attract priority in insolvency. This is as one would expect for a liability for breach of the duty of preservation, which is a liability in tort. Whereas the equitable in rem claim arises on receipt, but subject to bona fide purchase or change of position (meaning loss of traceable proceeds), the claim for knowing receipt can arise only once a duty of preservation has arisen, which is why the claim arises only once the defendant recipient knows or, in accordance with his duty of inquiry, ought to know of the breach of trust. The measure of the claim ought to be the extent of the loss to surviving value or traceable proceeds due to the breach of duty. This will indeed be the measure of a knowing receipt claim where a separate equitable in rem claim to surviving value is also made. But often, if no priority is sought, there will be a single claim for knowing receipt, whose measure will incorporate the measure of the equitable in rem claim, and so will be for the measure stated above, viz. the surviving value at the time when the recipient acquired his actual or constructive knowledge and became subject to the duty of preservation.[82]

A defendant may know of and assist in the breach of trust without receiving any trust property. Then he can commit a breach of duty, which (because he is not a recipient) is not a duty of preservation, but a duty not to cause harm to the beneficiary by interference in the trust. Traditionally the recipient and the assister have been associated with each other in the case law, and treated together as constructive trustees under the heads of knowing receipt and "knowing assistance".[83] It is clear from this analysis that the two types of liability have something in common, viz. they arise from breach of a duty not to cause harm to the beneficiary, and so are by nature tortious. More recent analyses of knowing receipt, which characterise it as a restitutionary claim (as considered below), make less sense of the traditional association between the two.

The expression "knowing receipt" might appear inapt to refer to the commission of a wrong. It seems that, strictly speaking, "knowing receipt" refers to the legal relation that arises when the defendant recipient becomes subject to the duty of preservation, before he has actually committed a breach of the duty. This is explicable on the basis that, as noted above, the sum of the restitutionary claim and the claim for breach of the duty of preservation will be the value

---

[82] Some commentators have identified the knowing receipt claim as analogous to conversion: e.g. Swadling (1997a); cf L.D. Smith (1998); Penner (1998), 333. But this appears to be because it is thought that the claim arises from interference with title rather than from a vitiated transfer, i.e. that the claim is proprietary rather than restitutionary.

[83] *Barnes v Addy* (1874) 9 Ch App 244.

surviving at the time when the recipient became subject to the duty of preservation. But where it is necessary to distinguish the claims, as where there is a claim for priority, the claim for knowing receipt should be measured by the loss of surviving value caused by the breach of duty.

Problems under the orthodox theory

The equitable in rem claim

The various attempts to explain the two claims under some version of the orthodox approach have caused great difficulty and controversy. Some of these difficulties were referred to in the last chapter. Take the equitable in rem claim first. One issue that has been controversial (as with respect to money had and received) is whether the equitable in rem claim is restitutionary or proprietary, i.e. whether it arises from a vitiated transfer of value or from the retention by the plaintiff of title in the asset (here an equitable title). As mentioned previously in connection with money had and received, on one view there can be no question of title passing in the case of a transfer without authority, and so the claim must be proprietary in rem.[84] Some commentators think that although the plaintiff's title to the asset first received by the recipient is the plaintiff's original title, so that the claim is proprietary at this stage, the claim to a traced asset is based on a new title, not the original one, and so is restitutionary in rem.[85] On another view, the claim is always proprietary, whether in respect of the original asset or a traced asset, because the plaintiff's same original title is preserved and transmitted from asset to asset.[86] Some commentators think that, even with respect to the original asset transferred, the title can be a new one, not the original one, so that the claim is restitutionary, not proprietary.[87] Some accept that the claim is based on the plaintiff's original title, whether with respect to the original or a traced asset, but nevertheless argue that the claim is restitutionary.[88] Unfortunately, although these disagreements are vigorously pursued, it is very difficult to see exactly what turns on them, and in particular what turns on whether a claim is restitutionary or proprietary. This is not surprising, because, as the alternative theory shows, there is no valid distinction to be made between a restitutionary and a proprietary claim.[89]

---

[84] e.g. Swadling (1997a); Goff & Jones (1998), 77ff.

[85] e.g. Birks (1997), 664ff; L.D. Smith (1997), 300; Burrows (1993), 58.

[86] e.g. Swadling (1996a), 65; Bant (1998); Pearce & Stevens (1995), 539–43; Grantham & Rickett (1997); Virgo (1999), 595.

[87] e.g. Birks (1997a), 632; see also Chambers (1997), 102–4.

[88] Burrows (1993), 362ff; and in a different sense see Virgo (1999), 129, discussed in Chap. 9 at 278.

[89] See Chap. 9 at 276–9. On this view the controversy over the classification of the claim in *Macmillan v Bishopsgate* [1995] 3 All ER 747 as restitutionary or proprietary was misconceived.

There is more agreement on the in rem nature of the claim, but as argued in the last chapter the orthodox conception of the in rem claim as necessarily a right in a specific asset is mistaken, and impossible to reconcile with the doctrine of tracing. Also, one would think that an in rem claim in a specific asset in the orthodox sense would be, by its nature, good against "all the world", and yet this is clearly not the case for the equitable in rem claim, which is subject to the equity's darling defence. Of course, there is said to be a difference between an in rem claim in law and in equity. But this is more of a restatement of the anomaly, or at the most an ad hoc rationalisation, than an explanation or argument. The rational explanation for when bona fide purchase is available is in terms of the level of the recipient's duty of inquiry under the alternative theory.[90]

Another difficulty is how to explain why the equitable in rem claim is subject to the bona fide purchase defence, but not, apparently, to the change of position of defence.[91] In principle they should both arise in respect of a restitutionary claim. Under the alternative theory, the change of position defence is indeed available: it corresponds to the limitation of the claim to traceable proceeds (although, as discussed in the last chapter, the equation of surviving value assessed in terms of change of position with traceable proceeds would require some revision of the tracing rules). But under the orthodox theory the issue arises whether there is a distinct change of position defence to the equitable in rem claim. The availability of such a defence has been discussed,[92] but there seems to be no sign of it (separately from tracing) in the case law.

The claim for knowing receipt

There has been particularly intense controversy over knowing receipt and the most discussed issue has been the degree of actual or constructive knowledge necessary for liability.[93] The traditional position,[94] which is consistent with the alternative theory, is that the recipient is liable for knowing receipt only if he has actual or constructive knowledge, constructive knowledge being determined exactly as for the equity's darling defence to the equitable in rem claim, i.e. according to the same duty of inquiry. In the terms of the alternative theory, when the recipient has actual or constructive knowledge according to the duty of inquiry to which he is subject in the circumstances, he becomes subject to a duty of preservation, and in consequence can be liable for knowing receipt, and at the same time is denied the equity's darling defence.

---

[90] It is also said that bona fide purchase is in principle or by origin a defence to an in rem claim, so that an issue arises concerning its availability as against a restitutionary in personam claim where such a claim arises instead of or in parallel to a restitutionary in rem claim: see e.g. Barker (1995), 213.

[91] There has been some controversy over the availability of change of position as against the equitable in rem claim: see e.g. Nolan (1995), 175.

[92] See e.g. ibid.

[93] See e.g. Birks (1991); Birks (1992a), 26; Harpum (1994); Millet (1991).

[94] Millet (1991); Harpum (1986); *Belmont Finance v Williams Furniture (No 2)* [1980] 1 All ER 393; *International Sales & Agencies v Marcus* [1982] 3 All ER 551.

A second position is represented by Re *Montagu*.[95] The plaintiff was the eleventh Duke of Manchester, grandson of the ninth Duke of Manchester. Under the will of the ninth Duke, certain chattels were to be held by his trustee-executors for the plaintiff grandson, but, misinterpreting the will and therefore acting in breach of trust, the trustees transferred them to the defendant, the tenth Duke, the plaintiff's father. The mistake came to light after the death of the defendant, when the chattels had been disposed of and were no longer in the defendant's estate. The plaintiff brought a claim against the defendant's estate as the recipient of the chattels transferred to the defendant in breach of trust. Megarry VC held that the equitable in rem claim to the chattels would have been available if the chattels had still been in the estate (because the defendant, not having given consideration, could not be equity's darling). With respect to the claim for knowing receipt, the judge held that the defendant was liable only if he actually knew or suspected that there had been a breach of trust, and not on the basis of constructive knowledge. In this respect the decision might be understood simply to reject the traditional position with respect to the recipient's duty of inquiry, i.e. to hold that a recipient incurs a duty of preservation only if he has actual knowledge or suspicion of a breach of trust, and that he does not have any actual duty to make inquiries, at least with respect to the type of transfer in question there, without otherwise challenging the traditional analysis.[96]

Less convincingly, the judge held that although for the purposes of the claim for knowing receipt the defendant's liability depended on actual knowledge, constructive knowledge was sufficient to negate the bona fide purchase defence to the equitable in rem claim. The basis for this was that in personam liability for knowing receipt was more onerous than liability to the equitable in rem claim, so that although the latter could reasonably be determined according to "the cold calculus" of constructive knowledge, which can render the recipient liable in the absence of any dishonesty,[97] the former should require actual knowledge, implying some degree of dishonesty.

It is true that knowing receipt is a potentially onerous liability in the sense that it is liable to leave the defendant worse off than if he had never had the receipt, whereas the equitable in rem claim, being limited to surviving value, cannot (subject to the point in the next paragraph) leave the defendant worse off than if he had not received the transfer. This is justified because liability for knowing receipt (as interpreted under the alternative theory) is based on a wrongful act,[98] but the restitutionary claim is based on the receipt and retention of surviving

---

[95] [1987] Ch 264. The facts are slightly simplified.

[96] This is the position that should be attributed to a number of recent cases that appear to follow Re *Montagu*: see e.g. *Eagle Trust v SBC Securities* [1992] 4 All ER 488; *Cowan de Groot Properties v Eagle Trust* [1992] 4 All ER 700. There has been considerable discussion of this line of cases: see e.g. Birks (1994c). *Twinsectra v Yardley* (1999) unrep and *Bank of America v Arnell* (1999, CA) unrep take the same line, but attribute it to *Royal Brunei Airlines v Tan* [1995] 2 AC 378, which was actually concerned with knowing assistance.

[97] [1987] Ch 264 at 273, 278.

[98] i.e. breach of the duty of preservation.

value. But where a defence of bona fide purchase to the equitable in rem claim is denied because of actual or constructive knowledge, notwithstanding that the defendant has incurred reliance, for example by paying for what he received, the defendant is in effect held liable for more than actual surviving value, because the defendant's loss in reliance in the form of his expenditure is not taken into account. Thus the liability is justifiable only as a liability for breach of the duty of preservation, and so must depend on the defendant's having incurred a duty of preservation. It may be that in the circumstances no actual knowledge should be necessary for a duty of preservation to arise, merely constructive knowledge, but it is simply contradictory to require actual knowledge for liability for knowing receipt, but also to deny the defence of bona fide purchase where there is only constructive knowledge. This would imply that the defendant had two different levels of the duty of inquiry at one and the same time.

Lastly, in connection with Re *Montagu*, it is worth noting also that the case shows the importance of integrating the tracing rules with the rules on change of position. On the facts of that case, the tracing and following rules provided that the surviving or traceable value was the value of chattels remaining in the defendant's possession. But the change of position rules recognise that in such circumstances surviving value may have been reduced by the disposal of some other asset in reliance on the receipt, and so can fall below the value of the chattels still in the defendant's possession. In Re *Montagu*, if the chattels had still been in the defendant's estate, the failure to recognise this in applying the tracing rules could also have rendered the defendant liable in a measure exceeding the actual surviving value, in the absence of any duty of preservation.

A third position is that liability for knowing receipt should not in principle depend on actual or constructive knowledge, but should be based on strict liability. This is Birks's position.[99] On his view, in accordance with a version of the orthodox theory, there should be, in addition to an equitable restitutionary in rem claim (the equitable in rem claim), an equitable restitutionary in personam claim, analogous to what is understood to be the common law restitutionary in personam claim, the claim for money had and received, and this is the role of knowing receipt. On this approach, knowing receipt, being a restitutionary claim, must in principle be a strict liability claim, and not based on actual or constructive knowledge at all. If there were such a restitutionary claim, the measure would be surviving value, or "abstractly surviving value", conceived of as distinct from traceable proceeds.[100] There would be two parallel claims, one relating to traceable proceeds and the other to abstractly surviving value, and traceable proceeds and abstractly surviving value would be distinct, the former a measure of an in personam claim, the latter a part of the recipient's estate, and the two would be identified or measured by different criteria. As discussed in the last chapter, there is no rationale for such a distinction, and there is certainly no sign of it in the case law.

---

[99] Birks (1989*b*); Birks (1992*a*), 26ff.
[100] See at Chap. 9 at 297.

There seems to be no authority for Birks's strict liability position in the case law explicitly concerned with knowing receipt, but he invokes support from what appears to be an analogous equitable claim, the so-called Re *Diplock*[101] in personam claim. In Re *Diplock* the defendants were charities that had received payments from the executors of the will of Diplock. It turned out that the payments were unauthorised by the will, because the provision pursuant to which the payments had been made was invalid. The plaintiff, the default beneficiary, had an equitable in rem claim against the defendants, but sought in addition an in personam claim against them in respect of any value received that could not be recovered through the equitable in rem claim. It was held that the defendants had no actual or constructive knowledge for the purposes of a claim for knowing receipt, but that they were nevertheless liable in personam in respect of any value not recovered through the in rem claim. The claim was said to be a claim peculiar to the winding up of estates.[102] On Birks's view, the Re *Diplock* claim is an in personam restitutionary claim that provides a model for knowing receipt.[103] In accordance with the alternative theory, on the other hand, the Re *Diplock* claim should be understood on the basis that in the particular situation in which the claim arises the recipient is taken to be "at risk", so that he necessarily incurs a duty of preservation on the receipt of a vitiated transfer, and will remain liable for the value received, to the extent that it exceeds the actual surviving value or traceable proceeds for which there is an in rem claim. It is another question whether there is any justification for the recipient to be "at risk" in this situation, and if so how the circumstances in which the claim is available are to be distinguished from the ordinary case of receipt from a trustee in breach of trust where the duty of preservation arises only if there is actual, or possibly constructive, knowledge.

Transfers by fiduciaries or agents

In the archetypal case in equity, the vitiated transfer is a transfer by a trustee in breach of trust, as, for example, in Re *Montagu*. But equity has always treated a transfer by the plaintiff's fiduciary in breach of fiduciary duty in exactly the same way as a transfer by the plaintiff's trustee in breach of trust. Thus the plaintiff will have an equitable in rem claim, subject to the equity's darling defence,[104] and a claim for knowing receipt. Many of the recent cases on the equitable in rem claim and knowing receipt have concerned company directors, who are fiduciaries, rather than trustees. A typical example is *Belmont Finance*

---

[101] [1948] Ch 105. The case was discussed in a different connection in Chap. 8.

[102] *Ministry of Health v Simpson* [1951] AC 251, 266 per Lord Simonds, on appeal from the Court of Appeal decision in Re *Diplock* [1948] Ch 465. In fact the jurisdiction has subsequently been extended to other types of case e.g. Re *J. Leslie Engineers Ltd* [1976] 2 All ER 85.

[103] Above n 99.

[104] Here the equity's darling doctrine is equivalent to the doctrine of apparent authority: see Chap. 8 on bona fide purchase.

v Williams Furniture (No 2),[105] which concerned a payment by directors of a company that was beyond their authority because it was contrary to statutory restrictions on using company money to facilitate the purchase of the company's shares.

There is some controversy over how to identify a fiduciary,[106] although there are standard cases, which include, in addition to company directors, partners and senior managers or agents.[107] In general, it seems that for present purposes a fiduciary is someone who, by arrangement with the plaintiff principal, exercises a power on his behalf to manage or dispose of his property. Thus the fiduciary in equity, in this context, will be an agent at common law, although agency is used more commonly to refer to the power to contract on behalf of the principal rather than the power to dispose of property. It is worth noting that in the fiduciary case, unlike the trustee case, the plaintiff does not have an equitable interest under a trust before the transfer, and the equitable in rem claim against the recipient cannot be thought of as an equitable interest persisting from a pre-existing trust.

Transfers by stranger-intermediaries

The equitable in rem claim and the claim for knowing receipt also arise where the defendant received a transfer, not from the trustee or agent, but from a stranger who received from the trustee or agent, provided that the plaintiff can trace the passage of surviving value to the defendant. In such a case it is generally less likely that the defendant will have constructive knowledge, because there is less likely to be any indication of the vitiating factor, which did not affect the transfer to the defendant himself. Although the equitable regime can apply even though the defendant did not receive the transfer from a trustee or agent, the traditional view is that it cannot apply if there was not originally a transfer in breach of trust or fiduciary duty.[108]

Fusion, overlap and the fiduciary relationship requirement

Traditionally the equitable and common law regimes have generally operated in separate spheres, the equitable claims in cases concerned with transfers in breach of duty by a trustee or fiduciary, and the common law typically in two-party cases not involving a fiduciary or trustee. Thus the equitable regime is

---

[105] [1980] 1 All ER 393.

[106] See further Chap. 13.

[107] *Agip (Africa) v Jackson* [1991] Ch 547 provides an example of a fiduciary who was an employee but not a director.

[108] Re *Diplock* [1948] Ch 465.

traditionally delimited by the requirement of a fiduciary relationship.[109] There has sometimes been pressure for the equitable regime to expand into the common law sphere, to give the plaintiff the advantages of the equitable claim, in particular priority. For example, in *Chase Manhattan Bank v Israel-British Bank*,[110] the plaintiff made a payment to the defendant by mistake, an earlier payment having been ignored as a result of a clerical error. Because the payment was not made in breach of trust or fiduciary duty, the restitutionary claim would normally have been a claim for money had and received at common law. However, because the defendant had gone into insolvency almost immediately after the receipt, it was now crucial to the plaintiff to establish priority, and it therefore sought an equitable in rem claim. The judge allowed the equitable in rem claim on the basis that the defendant became a fiduciary on receipt and itself committed a breach of fiduciary duty by failing to return or segregate the money received from the plaintiff. But the defendant was certainly not a fiduciary for the plaintiff according to any plausible definition, because he did not by arrangement with the plaintiff exercise control over his property, and the finding that he was was surely no more than an ad hoc device by which to allow the equitable in rem claim in a situation where traditionally it was not available. On the approach in this case, it seems that *any* vitiated transfer can be understood to generate a fiduciary relationship and therefore an in rem claim on exactly the same basis.

The earlier case of *Sinclair v Brougham*[111] concerned a transfer made under a void contract. The plaintiff had deposited money with the Birkbeck Building Society under a contract that turned out to be void because the building society had no statutory power to carry on a banking business. When the plaintiff sought to recover the sum it had deposited, it was held that it could not recover in contract, because the contract was void, nor by way of a claim for money had and received, because, it was held, this would be to give effect to the contract indirectly.[112] However it was held instead that there was an equitable in rem claim. The decision is objectionable, first, because it is inconsistent to treat the common law restitutionary claim, but not the equitable restitutionary claim, as subverting the contractual claim.[113] Secondly, the equitable in rem claim is understood to have arisen on the basis that the directors of the building society became fiduciaries for the depositors because they received money paid to them under void contracts of deposit.[114] Again it is difficult to see that there was genuinely any fiduciary relationship between the directors and the plaintiffs,

---

[109] Ibid., recently affirmed in various cases including *Boscawen v Bajwa* [1996] 1 WLR 328, 335 per Millet LJ, and *Westdeutsche Landesbank Girozentrale v Islington BC* [1996] 2 All ER 961, 998 per Lord Browne-Wilkinson.

[110] [1980] 2 WLR 202.

[111] [1914] AC 398.

[112] See Chap. 6 at 217.

[113] This is surely so even on the orthodox view in which the common law claim is in personam and the equitable one in rem.

[114] This was the interpretation in Re *Diplock* [1948] 1 Ch 465, 540.

because there was no arrangement for the directors to manage or control the plaintiffs' money or property.[115]

It has been widely argued that the limitation of the equitable regime to transfers involving a breach of fiduciary duty should be abandoned.[116] It is difficult to defend what seems to be an arbitrary limitation on the availability of the in rem claim, arising, it seems, purely from the historical remit of the Chancery courts. Thus it seems generally to be thought that the equitable regime should expand into the traditional territory of the common law claim, so as to allow for an equitable claim as an alternative to the common law claim, the two regimes operating in parallel. But although the fiduciary relationship requirement should be abolished, this should not be to allow the two regimes to operate in parallel, but to make way for the uniform recognition of a restitutionary claim as an in rem claim, as part of the integration of the common law and equitable regimes. The alternative theory (which entails the argument for fusion) necessarily precludes the co-existence on the same facts of what are in reality equitable and common law manifestations of the same claim: it requires that the division of restitutionary claims between law and equity be abolished and the claims integrated. As it was put by Denning J:

> The principle [sc of restitution] has been evolved by the courts of law and equity side by side. In equity it took the form of an action to follow moneys impressed with an express trust, or with a constructive trust owing to a fiduciary relationship. In law it took the form of an action for money had and received or damages for conversion of a cheque. It is no longer appropriate, however, to draw a distinction between law and equity. Principles have to be stated in the light of their combined effect.[117]

This means that where a claim arises the court should look to both law and equity in developing the law, so as to move towards uniformity. The major steps required to eliminate unnecessary divisions, within the common law as well as between the common law and equity, are set out at the end of this chapter. If, to the contrary, the argument for fusion is denied, it is difficult to see what the justification is for abandoning the breach of fiduciary duty requirement for an equitable claim, since this is the historical basis for the equitable jurisdiction,[118] which, one would think, would have for the proponents of the jurisdictional divide exactly the force and validity of the divide itself.

Westdeutsche Landesbank *and the scope of the equitable in rem claim*

Westdeutsche Landesbank Girozentrale v Islington BC,[119] which was discussed in Chapter 6, involved a payment by the plaintiff bank under a void contract

---

[115] The intention was not to retain any interest in the money paid, but to create a loan contract.
[116] e.g. Smith (1997), 120ff; Worthington (1996), 184. Friedmann has noted that where subrogation confers security the effect can be to circumvent the requirement for a breach of fiduciary duty, as in *Banque Financière de la Cité v Parc (Battersea) Ltd* [1998] 2 WLR 475: Friedmann (1999), 198.
[117] *Nelson v Larholt* [1948] 1 KB 339, 343 per Denning J.
[118] As noted, e.g., in *Agip (Africa) v Jackson* [1991] Ch 547, 566; see Smith (1997), 120.
[119] [1996] 2 All ER 961.

with the defendant local authority. It was recognised that the plaintiff bank had a claim in money had and received to recover the value of the vitiated payment, and this was not in issue in the House of Lords. What remained in issue was whether the plaintiff was entitled to compound interest on the amount of the payment over the period since it was made. Compound interest, it was held, was available only in equity, and so the plaintiff had to show that he was entitled to an equitable in rem claim, not merely the claim for money had and received. In fact the plaintiff did not need the in rem claim in itself, because there was no insolvency, and in any case under the tracing rules it seems that there were no traceable proceeds. The case was similar to *Sinclair v Brougham* in that both cases concerned transfers under void contracts. But the court in *Westdeutsche Landesbank* did not follow *Sinclair v Brougham*, and held that the plaintiff had no equitable in rem claim.

The first point to note about the case, although it is not directly relevant to the present discussion, is that, even if it is right that some claims should attract compound interest and not others, it surely cannot be right for the distinction to be based on whether the claim in question would have been pursued through the Chancery courts before the court systems were fused (or whether it has evolved from such a claim). The decision illustrates the fact that, when a court makes a decision in terms of whether a matter arises in equity or at law, it is liable to take account of factors that, according to any principled analysis, are irrelevant to the issue at hand, and also to lay down the law with respect to matters that were not actually in issue at all, including here the question of priority.[120]

As regards the question whether an equitable in rem claim arose, it is curious, first, that the court did not approach the question at all in terms of whether there was at any time a breach of fiduciary relationship.[121] Instead, Lord Browne-Wilkinson held that whether the defendant recipient received the payment subject to a trust depended on whether he had knowledge of the relevant facts, which would mean here the fact that the contract was ultra vires and void. Now this might be understood to mean that, in accordance with the usage preferred by some, separation of title and an in rem claim should not be described as a trust, and that one should refer to a trust only where the recipient has incurred a duty of preservation by virtue of his knowledge of the vitiating factor, and so can be liable for knowing receipt. As mentioned above, this is contrary to the usage adopted here, which is to equate a separation of title with a trust. But in fact it appears that Lord Browne-Wilkinson meant to say here that there could be no equitable in rem claim unless there was knowledge of the vitiating

---

[120] See further Appendix 2.

[121] It seems that this was because it was thought that the breach of fiduciary duty requirement applied only where there was a requirement to trace, and not in order to make an equitable in rem claim if tracing was unnecessary for the claim. Until relatively recently, however, the distinction between the two was not generally made, and for the requirement to apply with respect to tracing is, one would think, even more difficult to justify than for it to apply with respect to the equitable in rem claim.

factor.[122] It is hard to see how this can be correct:[123] according to the most famous rule of equity, the equity's darling rule, the recipient is subject to the equitable in rem claim provided that he is not a bona fide purchaser, and this means that where he is a donee he is subject to the claim even in the absence of any actual or constructive knowledge. Furthermore, as a matter of principle, the question whether the recipient knew or ought to have known of the breach of trust is not relevant to the restitutionary claim—which is the in rem claim—but only to the tortious claim for breach of the duty of preservation, which is in personam. There is no reason why the fact that the recipient has behaved wrongfully as against the plaintiff should mean that the plaintiff's position should be stronger as against a third party (which is the effect of allowing an in rem claim).[124]

According to the argument in the last chapter, a restitutionary claim to surviving value is by nature in rem; in other words, at least as a matter of principle, an equitable in rem claim should always arise from a vitiated transfer, giving the plaintiff priority in insolvency to the extent of surviving value, and a claim against indirect recipients of surviving value, subject to the bona fide defence for indirect recipients who are contractors. This position is based on the arguments of principle set out in the last chapter.

The House did consider arguments of principle concerning priority. Lord Goff argued that the plaintiff should not have priority because "[a]fter all, it has entered into a commercial transaction, and so taken the risk of the defendant's insolvency, just like other creditors who have contracted with it".[125] But the plaintiff made the payment by mistake, thinking that it had the benefit of an enforceable contract. It cannot be right to hold the plaintiff to a risk incidental to a void contract. Whenever a plaintiff makes a restitutionary claim the basis of the claim is that his decision to make the transfer was vitiated, and this necessarily means that he is not bound by any assumption of risk that would have been involved in making the payment if it had not been vitiated. This includes the assumption of the risk of insolvency that is necessarily involved when a payment is made pursuant to a contract in reliance on the receipt of some future rec-

---

[122] [1996] 2 All ER 961, 988–9. See also *Bank of America v Arnell* (1999), unrep.

[123] Chambers (1997), 208; Worthington (1996), p. xiv; Swadling (1998), 231ff. It is possible that Lord Browne-Wilkinson was concerned only with personal liability, i.e. liability arising from a duty of preservation.

[124] Cf Chap. 9 at 294.

[125] [1996] 2 All ER 961, 968.

[126] Cf Chap. 9 at 310. This point would surely be clear if the true basis of the claim in *Westdeutsche Landesbank* were recognised as the plaintiff's mistake in thinking that his payment was made pursuant to an enforceable contract; but, as discussed in Chap. 6, the vitiating factor was thought by Lord Goff at least to be "failure of consideration" in the sense of the restitutionary conditional transfer theory, and this is thought not to be based on mistake or any other vitiating factor. On this approach, furthermore, it follows naturally that the plaintiff should have an in rem claim whenever a contract terminates early, for breach or frustration. Birks is forced to make an artificial exclusion of priority for contractual creditors, as noted by Lord Browne-Wilkinson in *Westdeutsche Landesbank* at 992: Birks (1992e), 356–9 and 362.

iprocal benefit.[126]

Lord Browne-Wilkinson noted that if an equitable in rem claim arose in respect of a transfer under a void contract, an indirect recipient of traceable proceeds of the transfer could incur a restitutionary liability to the plaintiff and would be subject to the plaintiff's priority. He said:

> I can see no moral or legal justification for giving such priority to the right of [the plaintiff] to obtain restitution over third parties . . . If [the plaintiff's] arguments are correct, a businessman . . . could find that assets which apparently belong to one person in fact belong to another; that there are "off balance sheet" liabilities of which he cannot be aware; that these property rights and liabilities arise from circumstances unknown not only to himself but also to anyone else who has been involved in the transactions. A new area of unmanageable risk will be introduced into commercial dealings.

But exactly this conflict between the plaintiff and the indirect recipient or creditor of the direct recipient, and the possibility of "unmanageable risk" or the risk of "off balance sheet" liabilities arise whenever there is a restitutionary claim arising out of a vitiated transfer. Lord Browne-Wilkinson gives no reason to distinguish the position of a creditor of the recipient, or an indirect recipient, in the case of a transfer under a void contract from the position of a creditor or indirect recipient in any other case, and yet there are many cases in which a creditor is subject to the restitutionary plaintiff's priority, and an indirect recipient is held subject to a restitutionary claim. In particular this is the case with respect to a transfer made in breach of trust or fiduciary duty, as discussed above.[127] Traditionally, this conflict between the interest of an owner of wealth, some part of whose wealth has been lost through a vitiated transfer, and the interest of an indirect recipient or a creditor, is not explicitly addressed. Often it is resolved in favour of the owner or recipient on the arbitrary basis of whether the claim was traditionally dealt with in law or equity. It is certainly desirable for this underlying issue to be addressed, but it has to be addressed with respect to restitutionary claims in general, not merely claims under void contracts.[128]

Lipkin Gorman *and the scope of the common law claim*

Lipkin Gorman involved, not the expansion of the equitable regime to achieve priority, but what appeared to be an extension of the common law claim for money had and received to a situation traditionally dealt with in equity.[129] As considered above, the case involved a transfer by an agent from his principal, the plaintiff, to the defendant recipient. There was clearly a breach of fiduciary duty by the agent, and initially the case was pursued in equity. But in the House of

---

[127] And also with respect to chattels at common law, where there is no bona fide purchase defence.

[128] Another difficulty in *Westdeutsche Landesbank* was that the court described the trust as a resulting and not a constructive trust. This point is considered in the last section below.

[129] See generally Fox (2000).

Lords the equitable claims were abandoned and the claim for money had and received successfully pursued instead. The claims in equity were presumably abandoned because, first, the money received by the defendant recipient was not traceable into a specific asset, so there was no equitable in rem claim under the tracing rules; and, secondly, because on the facts the recipient did not have the actual or constructive knowledge necessary for liability for knowing receipt. The claim for money had and received, by contrast, was a strict liability claim, not requiring actual or constructive knowledge, and it did not require tracing of surviving value into a specific asset. Thus it is usually said, making a comparison between money had and received and knowing receipt as the two in personam claims, that the common law claim has the advantage of strict liability. But this is not the appropriate comparison between the equitable and common law regimes, and does not reveal the true advantage of the common law regime in *Lipkin Gorman*. The equitable counterpart to the restitutionary claim for money had and received is the equitable in rem claim, and the advantage of the common law claim is that it is unnecessary at common law to locate surviving value in a specific asset; the issue is only what the measure of surviving value is in the estate, surviving value being the value received adjusted for change of position. In other words, for the purposes of the claim for money had and received the common law adopts the swollen assets theory of tracing, and the deficiency in the equitable regime exposed by *Lipkin Gorman* was the tracing requirement to identify a specific asset.[130]

Under the alternative theory, the common law and equitable claims for restitution (the claim for money had and received and the equitable in rem claim) are in principle different forms of the same claim. On this approach it is perverse that, under the present position as illustrated by *Lipkin Gorman*, the tracing rules and the rules on change of position, which in principle both serve the single purpose of identifying surviving value, can give different outcomes, on the same facts, to what is in principle the same restitutionary claim. The same difficulty has arisen with respect to bona fide purchase. On the present position it is possible that the two claims in law and equity can both arise, prima facie, on a particular set of facts, but that the defence of bona fide purchase arises with respect to one but not the other, because of a difference between law and equity with respect to the duty of inquiry. This possibility is illustrated by *International Sales and Agencies v Marcus*.[131] Here a company director paid out company money in breach of fiduciary duty. The company made a claim to recover the value of the payment, and the defendant invoked what is now section 35A of the Companies Act 1985, which is intended to protect a person dealing with a company by providing, in effect, that he is entitled to a defence of bona fide pur-

---

[130] On the alternative approach, *Lipkin Gorman* should be understood as a step towards integration. On a more conventional understanding the case raises the question whether the common law claim is now available wherever the equitable claim is available.

[131] [1982] 3 All ER 551.

[132] See Chap. 7 at 247.

chase, or apparent authority,[132] provided that he is in good faith, i.e. it sets a low level for the duty of inquiry for people dealing with a company. Lawson J held that the defendant was in good faith because he did not know that the payment was not authorised,[133] and so could rely on the defence under section 35A to resist a claim at common law.[134] But the judge then held that the defendant was liable in knowing receipt in equity to repay the sum received because he had constructive knowledge of the director's lack of authority.[135] This outcome is seen to be perverse under the alternative theory, because what is in reality the same claim in different forms is treated differently on the same set of facts.[136]

THE LEVEL OF THE DUTY OF INQUIRY AND THE BALANCE OF INTERESTS

Examples of the duty of inquiry

The level of the duty of inquiry, which determines when a recipient (whether direct or indirect) becomes subject to a duty of preservation, is a crucial practical issue. The higher the level of the duty of inquiry, the more likely it is that the plaintiff will be able to recover his loss, either through a restitutionary claim (on the basis that the presence of a duty of preservation is likely to cause the recipient to preserve surviving value) or through a claim for breach of the duty of preservation. At common law, where the tortious claim for breach of the duty of preservation is not explicitly distinguished from the restitutionary claim, the duty of inquiry is expressed in the form of a condition attaching to a defence to the restitutionary claim; if the recipient has the requisite actual or constructive knowledge, he loses the defence. In equity, the duty of inquiry is expressed both as a condition attaching to the equity's darling defence, and also as a condition attaching to the claim for knowing receipt.

The alternative theory provides a framework which exposes for comparison the different levels of the duty of inquiry that have been adopted in different contexts. One can distinguish roughly between three levels of the duty of inquiry:[137] where the recipient is "at risk", so that he automatically incurs a duty

---

[133] This has been overridden by statute: s.35A(2b) of the Companies Act 1985, as amended.

[134] Presumably a claim for money had and received, although this was not discussed.

[135] i.e. his breach of fiduciary duty.

[136] Even on an orthodox approach, it is difficult to see why s.35A was not understood to apply to both the common law and equitable claims; it was clearly designed to confer a general protection on an outsider dealing with the company.

[137] Cf above, Chap. 7 at 233–4. The most intensive consideration of the level of the duty of inquiry has been in connection with cases in equity on knowing receipt. The so-called *Baden Delvaux* scale, which was much cited at one time, sought to distinguish five different levels of the duty of inquiry: (1) actual knowledge, (2) wilfully shutting one's eyes to the obvious, (3) wilfully and recklessly failing to make such inquiries as an honest and reasonable man would make, (4) knowledge of circumstances which would indicate the facts to an honest and reasonable man, and (5) knowledge of circumstances that would put an honest and reasonable man on inquiry: *Baden Delvaux and Lecuit v Société Générale pour Favouriser le Développement du Commerce et de l'Industrie en France* [1983] BCLC 325, 407–8 per Peter Gibson LJ.

of preservation on receipt; where he incurs a duty of preservation in circumstances where he would have discovered the vitiating factor if he had made reasonable inquiries or if he had made reasonable inferences from facts that he knew or ought to have discovered, i.e. the duty arises with constructive knowledge;[138] and where he is subject to a good faith test, which means that the duty arises only with actual knowledge or suspicion of the vitiating factor.[139]

With regard to money at common law,[140] until recently the position with respect to a donee was that he was at risk. Now, with the introduction of the change of position defence, it seems that he is subject to a good faith test. A purchaser of money—i.e. someone who receives it under a contract—has always been subject to a good faith test. With respect to chattels at common law,[141] normally a recipient is at risk, whether he is a donee or a purchaser. On the occasions where a bona fide purchase defence is available, it seems that the recipient is subject to a constructive knowledge test.

In equity, the traditional rule is that the recipient is subject to a constructive knowledge test.[142] With respect to transfers of land, the conventions of conveyancing established reasonably precisely what the duty of inquiry was, i.e., what the recipient was deemed to know: the purchaser might have to call for and examine the documents of title, or inspect the land, or carry out searches of the register. But a distinction is drawn between the purchase of land and commercial transactions; it is thought incompatible with the normal conduct of commercial transactions for the recipient to be required to make any inquiries unless there is something about the transaction that is actually suspicious or at least anomalous or incongruous,[143] so here the test here seems to amount to a good faith test.[144] As mentioned above, it appears that with respect to the so-called Re *Diplock* in personam claim in equity a recipient from a trustee-executor is at risk, whereas in Re *Montagu* a recipient from trustee-executors was held not to be liable for knowing receipt without actual knowledge, i.e.

---

[138] This would also include a case where the recipient incurs a duty of preservation unless he has taken certain steps to ensure that the transfer is not vitiated where there is an apparent risk of vitiation, e.g. by advising the plaintiff to take legal advice in a possible case of undue influence.

[139] The issue of the level of the duty of inquiry is distinct from, although related to, the question (which will not be pursued here) whether the level of the duty of inquiry should be defined in terms that take account of the personal qualities of the recipient, i.e. in what are inaptly called "subjective" or "objective" terms. e.g., should an obtuse recipient, subject to a good faith test, incur a duty of preservation when he did not realise that the circumstances were suspicious, but a reasonably perceptive person would have done? Or, similarly, should he incur a duty when he is subject to a constructive knowledge test but would not himself have realised what was happening even if he had made the requisite inquiries, although a reasonably perceptive person would have done? And should reasonable inquiries depend on what it is reasonable to expect of the recipient himself, with his own knowledge and experience?

[140] See above Chap. 7 at 234.

[141] See above at 322–5.

[142] Megarry VC in Re *Montagu* distinguished between constructive knowledge and constructive notice: [1987] Ch 264.

[143] e.g. per Vinelott J in *Eagle Trust plc v SBC Securities Ltd* [1992] 4 All ER 488, 507.

[144] See above at 332.

under a good faith test.

With respect to a transfer from a company, the recipient used at one time to be subject to a constructive knowledge test, based on a duty of inquiry that required him to inspect the Companies' Register to establish whether the transfer was outside the authority of the memorandum or articles.[145] In many cases, especially with respect to small transactions, this placed a disproportionate burden on the recipient, who was forced either to incur a disproportionate expense in inspecting the register or to take the risk that a transfer was vitiated by lack of authority, so that he was in effect subject to an at risk test. Usually he was safe, but sometimes the rule would work capriciously against him.[146] The position now by statute is that generally an outsider is subject only to a good faith test.[147]

Determining the level of the duty of inquiry

It is surely right that the level of the duty of inquiry should vary according to the circumstances. But the brief survey above suggests that the actual variation is sometimes arbitrary. In principle, the appropriate level of the duty of inquiry depends on the appropriate balance between the interests of the plaintiff and the defendant, or in other words between owners of wealth and recipients of it through vitiated transfers.[148] The stricter the duty of inquiry, the greater the burden on the recipient in terms of having to make inquiries with respect to his receipts, or to bear a risk of liability, or to avoid transactions that might generate an unpredicted restitutionary liability. Conversely, the weaker the duty, the less likely the owner is to recover in full the loss caused to him through a vitiated transfer of his wealth, and accordingly the more likely he is to have to take precautions against the risk of vitiated transfers, in particular mistaken or unauthorised transfers, including theft or fraud, which may involve expensive or time-consuming procedures and may lead him also to adjust his business to avoid certain types of transaction. It may even make it less worth his while to build up wealth because of the risk of losing it.[149]

The appropriate level of the duty of inquiry—the appropriate balance between the two classes of people, owners and recipients—will vary.[150] For

---

[145] The position was actually more complicated than this.

[146] e.g. Re *Jon Beauforte (London) Ltd* [1953] Ch 131; in this case as in others the doctrine of constructive notice tended to become intertwined with the ultra vires doctrine.

[147] S.35A of the Companies Act 1985, as amended. There remains controversy over the meaning of good faith in this context.

[148] As Denning LJ said: "[i]n the development of our law, two principles have striven for mastery. The first is the protection of property: no one can give a better title that he himself possesses. The second is for the protection of commercial transactions: the person who takes in good faith and for value without notice should get a better title": *Bishopsgate Motor Finance Corp v Transport Brakes Ltd* [1949] 1 All ER 37, 46.

[149] Beatson & Bishop (1991), 139.

[150] i.e. people in their capacities as such.

example, with respect to the purchase of land, it seems that the nature of land means that it is possible to develop practices and procedures, including the use of title documents and registration of ownership and interests, which enable standard inquiries to be made without great expense or inconvenience and which can avoid the risk of serious loss to the owner, and accordingly it seems justified for the duty of inquiry to encompass such practices and procedures.[151] But in commercial transactions it seems that there are no standard inquiries that are likely to be useful, and any genuine attempt to investigate is likely to be very burdensome to the recipient; thus here there tends to be only a good faith test, both in equity and at common law.[152] It might be justified to hold the recipient to be at risk with respect to the receipt of an asset through one possible channel of supply if there is an alternative reasonably convenient channel of supply by which to acquire the asset which can provide significant protection to the plaintiff. This seems to have been the position at one time with respect to the receipt of chattels, where the defendant was at risk unless he bought through a market overt.[153] The rationale was to enable the plaintiff to go to the market himself to try and retrieve his stolen or lost property, and to protect him at the recipient's expense where the owner was not able to do that because the sale was not through market overt.[154] A recipient could avoid any risk by buying through the market overt.[155]

The issue of the balance behind the level of the duty of inquiry, which determines when the tortious duty of preservation arises, is an aspect of the broader question of how to determine when a duty arises in tort, in the light of the conflicting interests of the potential tortfeasor and the potential victim. The issue is more commonly addressed in connection with the duty not to cause damage or injury in the tort of negligence. There the issue is what precautions are required of the defendant in the performance of an activity that may harm the plaintiff, whereas in connection with the duty of inquiry and the duty of preservation the issue is what measures are required of the defendant to establish whether property or value received by him represents surviving value derived from a vitiated transfer (or, more crudely, whether it belongs to someone else). There is a large body of literature that approaches the issue, in connection with negligence, on the assumption that the appropriate measure should be determined as a matter of efficiency, i.e. with a view to minimising aggregate social cost, which means, with respect to the duty of preservation, the aggregate cost incurred

---

[151] Registration has the advantage over documents of title that it makes the duty of inquiry easier to fulfil. The confinement of minor interests in land to equity and the defence of bona fide purchase can operate with respect to them.

[152] Although not for chattels at common law, as considered above.

[153] The defence of sale by market overt has now been abolished by the Sale of Goods (Amendment) Act 1995, s.22(1).

[154] Milsom (1981), 271.

[155] It may have been reasonable to say with respect to any sale not by market overt that the buyer had good reason to be suspicious of a vitiating factor, in particular that the chattel had been stolen, and so would actually be liable under a constructive knowledge or good faith test; cf Milson (1981), 271.

through precautions taken by owners against loss through vitiated transfers and precautions taken by recipients in connection with the risk of receiving a vitiated transfer.[156] But one might argue instead that the issue is a matter of fairness as between different people or classes of people, rather than efficiency: to what extent is it fair to require one person to incur expense or inconvenience in order to protect another from a risk of loss? Clearly this depends on the extent to which the expense or inconvenience is likely to be effective, and the extent to which the other party can protect himself, and at what expense and inconvenience. The considerations that would be relevant to an efficiency calculus are likely also to be relevant on a fairness approach.[157] In practice, judgements of the appropriate level are inevitably impressionistic. For present purposes what is most important is to establish a framework, such as would be provided by the alternative theory, within which cases can be compared and the duty of inquiry assessed.

A final issue arises where the plaintiff's careless or unreasonable behaviour has contributed to his loss, as where, say, his mistake was due to carelessness or he was reckless in entrusting his wealth to an unknown agent. This should not affect the plaintiff's restitutionary claim, because the defendant recipient is not adversely affected by it (provided that the claim is properly confined to actual surviving value).[158] But with respect to the liability for breach of the duty of preservation, which, as mentioned above, is potentially onerous (because the recipient can end up worse off that if he had never had the receipt), if the plaintiff has also acted carelessly or unreasonably there is every reason to apply a principle of contributory negligence by which some part of the loss due to the breach of the duty of preservation is borne by the plaintiff. This provides a further reason for distinguishing between the restitutionary claim and the tortious claim; and, indeed, once the two claims are distinguished, and the tortious claim characterised as such, the law of contributory negligence in tort should apply as a matter of course.[159]

---

[156] Beatson & Bishop (1991).

[157] Barker argues that fairness is behind the change of position defence, whereas efficiency is behind the bona fide purchase defence: Barker (1995), 196ff. On the approach set out in Chap. 7, the difference between the two lies in the extra protection normally given to a contractor in respect of reliance under a contract; possibly one could argue that efficiency contributes to justifying the protection of contractual reliance as against a third party not privy to the contract, but given the importance of protecting the innocent recipient of a vitiated transfer against being prejudiced by a restitutionary liability it is arguable that fairness can fully account for this also.

[158] See also Chap. 5 at 175. The plaintiff at common law is in a weaker position where he has entrusted his property to a bailee or agent, because the level of the duty of inquiry is lower: the recipient is not at risk, but can have a bona fide purchase defence: see above at 324–5. But in principle the plaintiff's risk-taking should not affect the level of the duty of inquiry, but the measure of the defendant's liability for breach of the duty of preservation.

[159] Civil Liability (Contribution) Act 1978; this analysis appears to correspond to "strict liability with comparative fault" in Beatson & Bishop (1991), 143.

CONSTRUCTIVE AND RESULTING TRUSTS

The constructive trust

A trust, as considered in the last chapter, is a relationship in which the power to manage or dispose of property is separated from the right to benefit from the property, the former conventionally designated by legal title and the latter by equitable title. Where the separation of title arises by deliberate arrangement between the settlor and the trustee, the trust is an express trust. An express trust constitutes a primary legal relation between the parties involved. By contrast, a separation of title can arise not by arrangement, but by operation of law in response to a breach of duty or other "causative event" defined by the primary relation between the parties.[160] Here the trust constitutes a remedial relation between the parties. Such a trust is traditionally known as a constructive trust.

The main example of a constructive trust for present purposes is the trust under which the plaintiff has an equitable in rem claim against the recipient of a transfer made by the plaintiff's trustee or fiduciary in breach of trust or fiduciary duty.[161] Here the causative event is the receipt of the transfer made without authority. The response to the causative event is the remedial restitutionary liability for surviving value, which in such a case is recognised as an equitable in rem claim under a constructive trust. As argued in Chapter 9, an in rem claim or constructive trust should arise in respect of all vitiated transfers, because the restitutionary claim is by nature in rem. Traditionally, however, a constructive trust has arisen only in cases falling within the jurisdiction of equity, i.e. where there was a breach of trust or fiduciary duty. At common law the remedial relation is understood to be an in personam liability.

A problem of usage mentioned above should be reiterated here. The usage adopted in Chapter 9 is that any separation of title is a trust, and where the separation of title has arisen as a remedial relation, the trust is a constructive trust. (The discussion above simply referred to the equitable in rem claim.) Thus any recipient of a transfer in breach of trust who is not equity's darling takes subject to a constructive trust and is a constructive trustee.[162] But this is denied by some; it is said instead that the recipient is not properly described as a constructive trustee unless he has actual or constructive knowledge of the breach of trust, i.e. in the terms adopted here, once a duty of preservation has arisen.[163] On this approach, to say that the recipient is a constructive trustee or that there is a constructive trust is to say that the recipient can be liable for knowing receipt. This is consistent with the usage according to which liability in knowing receipt is

---

[160] See Appendix 1.

[161] In the case of the trustee, the equitable in rem right is conceived of as simply persisting from the original trust, and in the case of the fiduciary it seems to have been recognised simply because the case arose in equity.

[162] e.g. Millet (1998), 202–4.

[163] Per Lord Browne-Wilkinson in *Westdeutsche Landesbank* [1996] 2 All ER 961, 986; per Megarry VC in Re *Montagu* [1987] Ch 264, 277.

described as "liability as a constructive trustee for knowing receipt". This is purely a terminological difference over the usage of "constructive trust" and "constructive trustee". As argued above, those who deny that a constructive trust arises in the absence of actual or constructive knowledge cannot plausibly consider that the plaintiff whose property has been transferred in breach of trust does not have an equitable in rem claim unless the recipient has actual or constructive knowledge; this would be inconsistent with the well-established effect of the equity's darling rule.[164]

The variety of constructive trusts

The constructive trust arising from a transfer in breach of trust is not the only recognised example of a constructive trust. For example, where the defendant makes a profit through the commission of a wrong he is probably subject to a constructive trust of the profit in favour of the plaintiff.[165] Where the plaintiff contracts to buy land or goods from the defendant, and the contract is specifically enforceable, the defendant is said to hold the land or goods on constructive trust for the plaintiff.[166] A constructive trust arising as the remedial response to the non-performance of an agreement also accounts for the secret trust,[167] the interest in land awarded as a remedy for proprietary estoppel, and probably the common intention constructive trust of matrimonial property. Where the defendant takes an asset for himself in breach of a fiduciary duty to procure the asset for the plaintiff, the defendant is said to hold the asset on constructive trust for the plaintiff.[168] It may also be possible to have a constructive trust as a remedy in tort: for example, if the defendant has tortiously taken an asset from the plaintiff, the most apt way to achieve compensation may be to impose a constructive trust of the property in favour of the plaintiff.[169]

In these various cases, the constructive trust serves different functions, and in principle the incidents of the remedial relation should differ accordingly. In the case of a restitutionary constructive trust arising in response to a vitiated transfer, the function of the constructive trust is to give effect to the plaintiff's in rem claim, which gives him priority and entitles him to pursue a claim against an indirect recipient through tracing, and also to allow for specific restitution where appropriate to avoid measurement problems, i.e. because specific restitution most aptly restores the plaintiff's loss without prejudice to the defendant. In the tort case, if a constructive trust is imposed as a response to the wrongful taking or diversion of property, it is a compensatory remedy, and its function is

---

[164] See above at n 123.

[165] *Attorney-General for Hong Kong v Reid* [1994] 1 AC 324.

[166] *Lysaght v Edwards* (1875) 2 Ch D 499.

[167] Unless this is properly an express trust.

[168] e.g. *LAC Minerals v International Corona Resources* (1989) 61 DLR (4th) 14; *Cook v Deeks* [1916] 1 AC 554; Chap. 8 at 262–3; Chap. 13 at 403–4.

[169] In fact, being a claim in conversion at common law the constructive trust would not traditionally be available; but see *Taylor v Plumer*, above at 322.

to provide a specific remedy to avoid measurement problems in determining pecuniary compensation. There is no justification here for an in rem claim conferring priority on the plaintiff. In the contract case also, the constructive trust generally serves to effect compensation,[170] and again the advantage of the constructive trust is to provide a specific remedy to avoid measurement problems. Again it is doubtful whether the plaintiff should have an in rem claim; certainly an in rem claim would have to be justified according to a different argument from the one advanced in Chapter 9 for restitutionary claims.[171] Unfortunately it has generally been assumed that the constructive trust has a uniform set of characteristics, and in particular that it necessarily generates an in rem claim.[172] This means that in a case where the constructive trust is really designed to provide a specific remedy as a means of effecting compensation it will also give the plaintiff priority in insolvency where this is unjustified.

The problem is further illustrated by the use of the constructive trust to effect disgorgement.[173] Here, the purpose of the constructive trust is to remove the profit obtained wrongfully by the defendant. The profit is given to the plaintiff as a means of achieving this, not because the plaintiff has any right to it, except in this incidental or parasitic sense; thus to the plaintiff disgorgement provides a windfall.[174] In the defendant's insolvency, there is no justification for giving the plaintiff's claim priority, or indeed giving him any claim at all, because in insolvency the defendant will lose all his wealth anyway, including the wrongful profit, which will be distributed amongst his creditors if the plaintiff has no claim.[175] It is true that if the wrongful profit is used to satisfy creditors' claims in insolvency they will in a sense also be receiving a windfall, inasmuch as the profit ought never to have been in the defendant's estate. But this seems to be a better way to deprive the defendant of the wrongful profit than giving it to the plaintiff, since in this way it will serve to offset the creditors' losses in the insolvency. This is particularly the case where the creditors may have to some extent relied on an appearance of wealth in the defendant's estate contributed to by the wrongful profit.[176]

---

[170] Elias would regard the function as "perfectionist" rather than compensatory: Elias (1990), 50ff. This would be apt under the classical theory of contract.

[171] Possibly where the contract provides for the defendant to hold the property temporarily and to keep it separate, there should be an in rem claim, although here one might say that the trust was an express trust.

[172] This is often the import of the assertion that English law recognises only the institutional or substantive constructive trust and not the remedial constructive trust, as considered below at 350–52.

[173] As noted in Chap. 1, disgorgement is not strictly a remedy at all.

[174] See Chap. 11 at 378.

[175] i.e. far from having priority, the disgorgement claim should be subordinated to the claims of creditors. The plaintiff may however have a claim for loss; and sometimes it may not be clear to what extent a claim for a constructive trust (or an account of profits) will serve to compensate, since the plaintiff's loss may not be easy to establish: see Chap. 13 in connection with the "no-conflict rule".

[176] The Canadian case of *Soulos v Korkontzilas* [1997] 2 SCR 217 illustrates the conflation of different types of constructive trust, in that case disgorgement and a specific remedy to effect compensation: see paras. 14, 43.

In *Lister v Stubbs*[177] it was indeed held that no constructive trust should arise to effect disgorgement because the plaintiff should not have priority over the defendant's creditors in the defendant's insolvency; instead it was held that the plaintiff should be confined to the in personam remedy of an account of profits. The problem with the account, however, is that it is understood to be limited in measure to the value of the initial wrongful profit, so that if the defendant makes a further profit through investing the original wrongful profit the further profit cannot be subject to the account. This is what happened in the recent case of *Attorney-General for Hong Kong v Reid*,[178] and to ensure that the defendant could not retain the consequential profits of investing the original wrongful profit the court insisted that a constructive trust was the appropriate remedy. Unfortunately, this means, as the constructive trust is understood, that the plaintiff will also have priority in insolvency.[179]

Thus it would be helpful to distinguish between what are really distinct remedial relations that are inaptly forced together under the label of the constructive trust. There is, first, the true constructive trust, which gives effect to an in rem right, carrying with it priority and claims against indirect recipients, and which will be the appropriate form for a restitutionary claim arising from a vitiated transfer and possibly sometimes a contractual claim. Secondly, there is the remedy of specific restitution or specific compensation, where an order to transfer specific property is appropriate as the best way to compensate the plaintiff or restore a loss to him, but without giving him an in rem claim. Thirdly, there is the disgorgement response,[180] which will remove the defendant's wrongful profit, including consequential profits, but again without giving him an in rem right or priority.[181]

The "remedial constructive trust" and the "institutional constructive trust"

There has been much discussion in recent years over what are understood to be two rival conceptions of the constructive trust, referred to as the "remedial constructive trust" and the "institutional" or "substantive" constructive trust. "Remedial constructive trust" is an entirely inappropriate expression because, as argued above, the constructive trust is on any conception a remedial trust, but the usage is unfortunately very well established. The remedial constructive trust is said to be the version of the constructive trust recognised in the United States, and English law is said to recognise only the institutional constructive trust,

---

[177] (1890) 45 Ch D 1.

[178] [1994] 1 AC 324.

[179] It has been suggested (Birks (1989*a*), 394) that it should be possible to have an in personam claim "in the second measure" determined through tracing, which would be equivalent to a constructive trust not conferring priority: see also Goode (1991).

[180] Disgorgement is not strictly a remedy: see Chap. 11.

[181] And arguably the claim should be subordinated to the claims of creditors, subject to the point at 175 above.

although there have been suggestions that the remedial constructive trust should be introduced.[182]

It is said that whereas the institutional constructive trust arises on the occurrence of the event that generates the remedial relation—the transfer in breach of trust, or the breach of contract or fiduciary duty—the remedial constructive trust does not arise until the time when the court makes its decision and pronounces that a trust should exist.[183] This implies that the court has a discretion whether to find a constructive trust or not, in the light of the circumstances of the case, which amounts to a discretion to vary existing property rights, apparently according to what the court considers just in the circumstances.[184] A constructive trust as so conceived is open to objection on the ground that it involves excessive uncertainty for the parties involved and for third parties who do not know and cannot ascertain whether the plaintiff has an in rem claim carrying priority. It might even be argued that the whole concept is incoherent, and there does seem to be some difficulty in understanding exactly what the legal relation between the parties is during the period between the events that gave rise to the plaintiff's claim and the court order.[185]

But nevertheless the remedial constructive trust conceals an important truth. This is that, as argued above, in the various circumstances in which a constructive trust is presently recognised it should not always have the same incidents, and the effect of the discretionary remedial constructive trust may be to allow to the court to recognise this. Thus, for example, in a case of disgorgement or where a specific remedy is called for to avoid measurement problems, it may be that a court that understands itself to have a discretion whether to declare a constructive trust would award it to effect a specific remedy in the usual case but not if the defendant is insolvent, to avoid giving priority where it is not justified. It would be better, of course, for the different forms of response that go by the name of constructive trust to be distinguished and the appropriate one identified in the light of the circumstances, as suggested above. This would eliminate the impression of uncertainty, and the impression that the court exercises a discretion or varies property rights.

---

[182] e.g. *Westdeutsche Landesbank*, per Lord Browne-Wilkinson [1996] 2 All ER 961, 999; Re *Goldcorp Exchange* [1995] 1 AC 74, 104 per Lord Mustill; Goode (1991), 224.

[183] Re *Polly Peck (No 2)* [1998] 3 All ER 812 per Nourse LJ at 830–1; *Fortex v Mackintosh* [1998] 3 NZLR 171, 173.

[184] Ibid. There are a number of other supposed differences between the institutional and remedial constructive trusts. It is said that the remedial constructive trust, but not the institutional constructive trust, is concerned with restitution or unjust enrichment; that personal obligations attach to the trustee under the institutional version but not the remedial version; and that the remedial but not the institutional constructive trust can arise in the absence of a pre-existing fiduciary relationship. These are no doubt important issues, but it is difficult to see why they are related to the controversy as between the two conceptions of the constructive trust.

[185] For various criticisms of the remedial constructive trust see e.g. Gardner (1994); Birks (1994a); Birks (1997a), 641; Millet (1998), 199; Grantham & Rickett (1999). The remedial constructive trust was rejected in Re *Polly Peck (No 2)* [1998] 3 All ER 812. It was also noted that the creation of rights in rem would be inconsistent with the insolvency legislation.

There are other circumstances where one might argue that the court has or ought to have a genuine discretion, as envisaged for the remedial constructive trust. One possibility concerns the restitutionary claim arising from a vitiated transfer. As discussed above, the traditional position was that broadly speaking a vitiated transfer gave rise to a claim in rem only if the matter arose in equity. But this is now recognised to be an unjustifiable basis for determining the availability of an in rem claim, and in the absence of a clear alternative the position is uncertain. It might seem appropriate that the court should exercise a discretion to determine whether in the particular circumstances an in rem claim is justified,[186] and this would appear to amount to a discretion to declare a remedial constructive trust. On the argument in Chapter 9, a restitutionary claim to surviving value is always in principle an in rem claim, giving priority. The possibility was also mentioned that in insolvency the plaintiff's priority might be overridden by the apparent wealth argument.[187] If a court were permitted to assess the weight of the apparent wealth argument on a case-by-case basis it would more or less have a discretion to recognise an in rem claim under what would amount to a remedial constructive trust. But it would certainly be preferable for a clear and certain rule to be adopted, which it was suggested should be in favour of priority.[188]

The resulting trust

Trusts are usually divided into three types: express, constructive and resulting. But the analysis above seems to suggest a simple two-fold classification of trusts into primary and remedial trusts, corresponding to express and constructive trusts. What then is a resulting trust? The resulting trust is also said not to be an express trust, but to arise by operation of law, which suggests that it is a form of remedial trust. Recently it has been argued that the resulting trust is a restitutionary remedial trust,[189] whereas it was argued above that such a trust was properly referred to as a constructive trust.

---

[186] See e.g. Goff & Jones (1998), 81.

[187] Chap. 9 at 285.

[188] Ibid. Another type of case where it appears that the court has exercised a discretion to award a remedial constructive trust is in the case law on Lord Denning's "new model constructive trust", which was thought to give the courts the power to reallocate property rights as between married and co-habiting couples in the light of what was fair in all the circumstances: e.g. Pettit (1997), 61–3. The position is now governed by the common intention constructive trust, and although the new model constructive trust is supposed to have been entirely discredited, there remains considerable uncertainty in the application of the law. The common intention constructive trust appears to be a remedial trust arising from a breach of an agreement, in a broad sense, arising from the relationship between the parties. Here the constructive trust might be best understood not as an in rem claim but as a specific remedy, whose function is to facilitate measurement, and on this basis there is no reason for disquiet about the consequences of uncertainty for third parties.

[189] Birks (1992e); Chambers (1997).

Traditionally the resulting trust is said to arise in two types of case.[190] The first is where a settlor transfers property on trust but fails to dispose of the whole of the beneficial interest. For example, he might transfer the property to trustees to hold for X for life without providing for what should happen after X's death. The rule is that the remaining beneficial interest is held for the settlor himself under a resulting trust. The second type of case is where the settlor makes a gratuitous transfer of property to X, and the court presumes, in the absence of evidence to the contrary, that it was not intended as a gift to X, but as a transfer to X to hold on trust for the plaintiff transferor. But, in this latter type of case, if the transfer is to someone for whose welfare the transferor is responsible, there is a contrary presumption in favour of the transferee, the so-called presumption of advancement, which precludes a resulting trust. Similarly, where one person buys property in the name of another, or where two people buy property that is put in the name of one or other of them, or in their joint names, there is a presumption that there is a trust of the property in favour of the person who provided the purchase money or for the contributors in shares proportionate to their contributions to the purchase price.

In these cases the beneficiary is the transferor or settlor, and the expression "resulting trust" originates in the Latin *resalire* meaning to "jump back", which seems to describe the movement of the beneficial interest in the property back to the transferor or settlor. The first type of resulting trust above is said to be an "automatic" resulting trust. The location of the beneficial interest is thought to be based not on the intention of the settlor or transferor, but simply on his failure to dispose of it. The second type is said to be a "presumed" resulting trust, because the location of the beneficial interest is thought to be based on a presumption of the intention of the settlor or transferor. In either case, the resulting trust is subject to evidence of an actual intention as to the beneficial ownership, which will displace the resulting trust in favour of absolute ownership or an express trust.[191]

The resulting trust as a trust based on a default rule

Whenever there is a transfer of the possession or control of property, the law must determine who has ownership of the property transferred. As discussed above, although the recipient will normally acquire title to the property in the sense that he can dispose of the asset as part of his estate—i.e. legal title—it is not necessarily the case that he will acquire the beneficial title to the value transferred: he may take the property on trust. The fundamental rule is that it is the intention of the pre-existing owner of the property, from whom the transfer to the recipient was made (or the person who supplied the purchase price, by whom or at whose direction the transfer was made) that determines ownership.

---

[190] Re *Vandervell's Trusts (No.2)* [1974] 1 All ER 47, 63ff per Megarry VC; *Westdeutsche Landesbank* [1996] 2 All ER 961, 1000 per Lord Browne-Wilkinson.
[191] *Westdeutsche Landesbank* [1996] 2 All ER 961, 1000 per Lord Browne-Wilkinson.

Sometimes, as discussed above, the transfer will be vitiated, by lack of authority or otherwise; then the transferee will acquire a legal title to the assets transferred, but the transferor, the previous owner, will retain an equitable or beneficial title to surviving value in the transferee's estate under a constructive trust.[192] But there is another type of case. Here the transfer is voluntary (i.e. unvitiated), so no constructive trust arises, but the transferor's intention is in doubt because it was not expressed, or, where the intention was to establish some form of complex ownership, the transferor may by oversight have failed to form or express an intention with respect to some aspect of it. The issue then is how to determine ownership in so far as it has been left uncertain.

It seems here the court must operate on the basis of a default rule or presumption that applies in the absence of, and subject to, evidence of actual intention, which would be determinative if formed and expressed.[193] The obvious presumption is one in favour of the settlor or transferor himself, for two reasons. First, it is likely that often this would have been his intention if he had considered the matter and formed an intention. Secondly, to hold the ownership to stay with him is the prudent approach in the absence of clear evidence of what his intention actually was, because it means that he can now dispose of it as he actually intended.[194] It is understandable that the default rule should be expressed in the form of a presumption of intention imputed to the transferor or settlor, because it is his intention that determines ownership in the usual case; and also because often this presumed intention will be his actual but unexpressed intention to be inferred from the nature of the transaction. It follows that a resulting trust is not restitutionary. It does not arise from a vitiated transfer, but from a voluntary or unvitiated transfer whose terms are not explicit. The resulting trust, like the express trust, constitutes a primary relationship, not a remedial or secondary relationship.[195] This analysis makes sense of what appear to be inconsistent features of the law, viz. that the resulting trust is based on intention,[196] and yet it cannot be based on an actual proved intention, because then there would be an express trust, or no trust at all.[197]

---

[192] As discussed above, this is actually the position only with respect to claims in equity.

[193] Cf the analysis in Rickett & Grantham (2000).

[194] This may mean he can change his mind, but this is unavoidable where his original intention cannot be properly ascertained.

[195] See Appendix 1. It follows that the line between an express trust and a resulting trust, corresponding to the distinction between inferring a real intention and imputing an intention in accordance with a presumption, will often be blurred.

[196] *Westdeutsche Landesbank* [1996] 2 All ER 961, 1000 per Lord Browne-Wilkinson.

[197] Both presumed and automatic resulting trusts fit this analysis, but one might distinguish between them in the following way. In the case of a presumed resulting trust, it is more likely that the transferor formed a relevant intention, even if it was not expressed, and the presumption of intention operates to give effect to it; whereas in the case of an automatic resulting trust, it is more likely that by oversight the transferor did not form any relevant intention at all, so that the presumption operates to impute to him an intention where there was none. But neither generalisation is invariably true, and it is doubtful whether there is any advantage in distinguishing between them in terms of the role of intention. One might object that in Re *Vandervell's Trusts (No.2)* [1974] 1 All ER 47 the transfer was clearly intended to dispose of the whole of the transferor's beneficial

This analysis reveals an analogy between a resulting trust and an implied term in contract. An agreement will never provide for all possible contingencies: sometimes the parties will have reached an actual agreement on a certain matter without expressing it; sometimes they will not even have given any consideration to an issue that then arises in connection with the agreement. In such cases, the court has to imply a default term, i.e. a term not actually agreed but introduced to fill out the contract by inference or extrapolation from what was actually agreed. Similarly, a resulting trust is based on a default rule that operates in circumstances where intention is determinative, but where evidence of actual intention is absent. One might object that on this analysis the resulting trust involves the use of a fictional intention, rather like the fictional implied contract in the restitutionary implied contract theory. But a default term does not itself involve a fiction with respect to a trust, any more than with respect to a contract, although possibly one could take exception to the formulation of the presumption in terms of a deemed intention. But this is maybe forgivable, because of the function that intention normally plays in determining ownership of property transferred. By contrast, with respect to the implied contract theory of restitution, intention and agreement have nothing whatsoever to do with the restitutionary claim that was supposed to be explained in terms of the fictional contract.

On this analysis of resulting and constructive trusts, there is a clear distinction between the two. The constructive trust arises as a remedial relation; in the case of the restitutionary constructive trust, the remedial relation arises to protect the plaintiff from loss of his property as a result of a vitiated transfer; in other circumstances, as discussed above, it arises in response to a breach of contract, or some other type of "causative event".[198] The resulting trust, by contrast, arises as a primary relation, like an express trust, in accordance with an intended arrangement, like the rights and liabilities under a contract, and not as a remedy to protect the plaintiff's interest in the light of a breach of duty or other causative event.

The theory of the resulting trust as a restitutionary remedial trust

Recently a quite different analysis of the resulting trust has been advanced by Birks and Chambers, which gives the resulting trust an important role in restitution. Birks's argument is that the presumption of intention behind a resulting trust is really a presumption of a vitiating factor, typically a mistake, so that the resulting trust is properly understood as a restitutionary remedial trust.[199]

---

ownership, and that the effect of the resulting trust was to frustrate this clear intention. However, an intention not to retain any part of the beneficial interest does not provide any basis for determining who should acquire any part of the beneficial interest not actually provided for; one can still say—in fact one is bound to say—that there is no relevant intention.

[198] See Appendix 1.
[199] Birks (1992e).

Chambers argues that a resulting trust arises wherever there is an "absence of intention" to benefit the recipient.[200] This is understood to cover the case where the plaintiff had an actual intention not to benefit the defendant, or where the plaintiff had no relevant intention at all, or where he had an intention that was vitiated.

The problem with this approach is that, by the use of the concept of "absence of intention", or by the presumption of a vitiating factor where there is none, it obscures the distinction between a vitiated intention and an incomplete or tacit intention, and therefore also the distinction between a vitiated transfer and a voluntary transfer, unaffected by any vitiating factor. Thus it also subverts the classification of constructive and resulting trusts based on the distinction between remedial and primary relations. The analysis adopted here is surely preferable because it preserves this fundamental distinction. Furthermore, the case law provides strong support for the distinction. The only very well established authority for a trust arising in response to a vitiated transfer is the constructive trust arising from a beach of trust or fiduciary duty; and the vast majority of resulting trust cases, in accordance with the rules described above relating to automatic and presumed resulting trusts, do not involve vitiated transfers. No doubt some support in the case law can be found for the view that a resulting trust arises from a vitiated transfer.[201] Any such support is explicable on the basis that a trust arising from a vitiated transfer will be a trust in favour of the person from whom the transfer came, and there is no doubt a tendency to describe any such trust as a resulting trust, whether the trust arises by virtue of a default rule or a vitiating factor.[202] Any such general usage would, however, controvert the well-established usage in relation to transfers in breach of trust or fiduciary duty, which have always been said to generate constructive trusts; and in any case the location of the beneficial interest is a superficial matter compared to the basis on which the trust arose, which should determine usage and classification.

The principal significance of the Birks and Chambers analysis is understood to be that it shows that a trust arises, or ought in principle to arise, in response to any vitiated transfer, so that a restitutionary claim always is, or ought to be, a claim in rem, with priority in the recipient's insolvency. This has been one ground of objection to the analysis by some commentators.[203] In this respect, however, the implication of the analysis is consistent with the position adopted

---

[200] Chambers (1997), 3.

[201] Some possible examples are given by Chambers (1997), 21ff. Also where a trust arises as a result of a transfer on trust when the express trust turns out to be invalid, there is said to be a resulting trust, although it appears to be a remedial restitutionary trust. There are also certain other cases where judges have used "resulting trust" to describe what is properly (on the analysis here) a constructive trust, including *Westdeutsche Landesbank* [1996] 2 All ER 961 at 994 per Lord Browne-Wilkinson, and *Sinclair v Brougham* [1914] AC 398, 420 per Lord Haldane LC.

[202] Birks distinguishes between trusts that are "resulting in pattern" in the sense of involving a trust in favour of the settlor or transfer, and trusts that are "resulting in origin", meaning in terms of the basis on which they arise: Birks (1989a), 60.

[203] Swadling (1996b), 126.

here. But the advantage of the argument for an in rem claim advanced here is that it is based on principle, i.e. it is based on an assessment of the nature of the interests of the parties, whereas the Birks and Chambers approach is a rather narrower doctrinal argument, which offers no principled basis for the general availability of the in rem claim and, therefore, even if it were accepted, it would be unlikely to settle the controversy in the face of contrary arguments of principle.

MOVING TOWARDS A RATIONAL SCHEME

The various claims considered above, including the claims for conversion, and money had and received, the equitable in rem claim, and the claim for knowing receipt, are under the integrated or alternative theory advanced here manifestations of a single related pair of claims, the restitutionary claim to surviving value and the tortious claim for breach of the duty of preservation. There may be grounds for the conditions governing these claims to vary in different contexts, in particular with respect to the level of the duty of inquiry, so giving the impression that the claims in different contexts are different types of claim altogether. But the discussion above suggests that more often the differences in the case law are not justifiable but are due to historical accident or to misconceived arguments arising from the orthodox approach. The recognition of the alternative theory and the framework it lays down would force differences between the different manifestations of the claims to be justified by the differences in context. The steps necessary to achieve integration have emerged in the discussion in this chapter and the last, and can be listed here. They include the rejection of the three distinguishing features of the orthodox approach, viz. the distinction between restitutionary and proprietary claims, the conception of an in rem claim as necessarily a claim to a specific asset and not a claim to value, and the division between law and equity.[204]

Seven steps forward

Proprietary and restitutionary claims

The supposed distinction between restitutionary and proprietary claims should be abandoned. There is a single restitutionary (or proprietary) claim to surviving value arising from an ineffective or vitiated transfer. It follows that title (or beneficial title) must be understood to relate to value, not to a specific asset, and that what is understood as the vitiation of a transfer of value in the law of restitution corresponds precisely to the ineffectiveness of a transfer of title in property law.

---

[204] It should be noted that there are other matters for which the restitutionary theory has implications that have not been considered, including non-ownership interests in property and security.

Surviving value, traceable proceeds and the subject of title

The surviving value in the recipient's estate in the light of his change of position must be equated with traceable proceeds in the recipient's estate. The law of change of position and the law of tracing have served the same purpose in different contexts, viz. to identify the subject matter and the measure of the restitutionary (or proprietary) claim. The test of whether there is surviving value is a test of causation, as is accepted with respect to change of position. The exchange product rule of tracing should be understood accordingly as a presumption or convention that is indicative of causation. Under the causation test it is not necessary to identify surviving value in a specific asset. This is consistent with the swollen assets theory of tracing, which corresponds to the effect of change of position.

The restitutionary claim to surviving value as an in rem claim

It is wrong to think that an in rem claim is necessarily a claim to or "in" a specific asset, or conversely that a claim to value is necessarily a claim in personam. The restitutionary claim to surviving value is in rem notwithstanding that it is not a claim in a specific asset in the orthodox sense. Specific restitution can nevertheless be an appropriate remedy.

Duty of preservation and duty of inquiry

Surviving value depends purely on causation, and not on whether the recipient knew or ought to have known of the vitiating factor. To the extent that the recipient consumes or disposes of surviving value where he knows or ought to know of the vitiating factor, he commits a breach of his duty of preservation, which requires him to preserve and return surviving value to the plaintiff. The recipient cannot rely on the bona fide purchase defence if he is acting in breach of his duty of preservation. The liability for breach of the duty of preservation is by nature tortious, not restitutionary, and in personam, not in rem. The tortious liability, but not the restitutionary liability, should in principle be subject to reduction in accordance with the plaintiff's contributory negligence.

The circumstances in which a recipient incurs a duty of preservation are determined by the level of his "duty of inquiry". The level of the duty of inquiry is the principal factor in determining the relative weight given to the interest of a recipient in relying on his receipt as against the interest of owners of wealth in having restored to them wealth that has been lost through a vitiated transfer. For the sake of uniformity, the alternative theory requires the determination of the level of the duty of inquiry to be explicitly addressed and comparisons made between cases from different contexts, including cases that are traditionally considered in isolation from each other.

Separation of title

Separation of title is a functional rather than a jurisdictional concept, and legal and equitable title represent what would be better described in functional terms as dispositive and beneficial title. The remedial relation arising from a vitiated transfer is helpfully described in terms of separation of title. The plaintiff's restitutionary claim to surviving value is equivalent to a beneficial title. The formulation of the claim to surviving value in terms of beneficial title will allow the in rem nature of the claim to be recognised. The recipient acquires a dispositive title in relation to an asset received, which means that an indirect recipient from him will be able to rely on bona fide purchase in relation to the receipt of the asset. Separation of title arising from a vitiated transfer is recognised in equity in the form of the constructive trust (not the resulting trust), and there are incipient signs of it at common law that will provide the basis for developing the common law towards the position in equity.

Law and equity

In the light of the procedural nature of the relation between law and equity, following fusion there is no justification for the existence of different manifestations at law and in equity of the same restitutionary claim to surviving value, i.e. the claim for money had and received (or conversion) and the equitable in rem claim. The common law and equitable claims should be integrated.[205] The existence of the different forms in law and equity is particularly objectionable given the significant differences between them, for example with respect to tracing, priority in insolvency and bona fide purchase, which means that there are arbitrary differences in the legal position between cases that differ only in terms of whether they would originally have been dealt with by the courts of equity or the common law courts. These differences, which are mistakenly thought to follow from the nature of claims as being claims in law or equity, should be eliminated if they cannot be explicitly analysed and justified in substantive terms. For example, this will be the case with respect to the argument that the bona fide purchase defence is available in equity, but not with respect to a chattel at common law, because of the nature of the plaintiff's right as being legal or equitable, or that the availability of a priority claim in equity and not at law results from the in rem nature of a claim in equity and the in personam nature of a claim at common law.

Appreciated value and consequential benefits

The restitutionary claim is designed to recover only the surviving value of the vitiated transfer, which will generally include the appreciated value of an

---

[205] See further Appendix 2.

asset transferred. Whether there should be a claim to consequential benefits, derived from the recipient's investment or exploitation of the surviving value, should be settled as a distinct issue, in terms of whether a claim for payment or disgorgement is available, and not subsumed into the tracing rules and disposed of by default.

Part IV

Disgorgement

11

Disgorgement

INTRODUCTION

D ISGORGEMENT IS THE legal response to a wrong consisting of the transfer to the plaintiff of the benefit obtained by the defendant through the wrong.[1] Its rationale is the principle that a wrongdoer should not be allowed to profit from the wrong, whether because it would be inherently wrong to allow him to profit or in order to remove any incentive for others to commit wrongs. The principle seems to be indisputable, and one might expect to see it well established in the common law. But this is not the case at all, and the main reason seems to be the "procedural objection", viz. the argument that, even if disgorgement is desirable in principle, it ought not to be imposed in civil proceedings. The procedural objection will be considered later in the chapter. The first part of the chapter deals with various actual or supposed examples of disgorgement in the case law. Disgorgement is not a term of art in the law; these various examples are in the form of various different traditional causes of action or remedies, including damages, the account of profits and the constructive trust, whose nature and function are not always clear. Modern commentaries have combined disgorgement with the use claim under the category of "restitution for wrongs" or "restitutionary damages"; the distinction between the two was discussed in Chapter 4.

DISGORGEMENT IN THE CASE LAW

Damages

"Exemplary" or punitive damages as disgorgement?

"Damages" usually means a pecuniary compensatory remedy—a sum of money representing the measure of the plaintiff's loss. But damages (despite the connotation of the word) are not always compensatory. "Exemplary" or punitive damages, imposed on the defendant as a punishment for a wrong, are available in certain circumstances. According to *Rookes v Barnard*,[2] they are not available unless the wrongdoer acted with governmental authority, or where "the

---

[1] But see Chap. 13 at 404–7 in connection with the fiduciary "no-conflict rule".
[2] [1964] AC 1129.

defendant's conduct has been calculated by him to make a profit for himself which may well exceed the compensation payable to the plaintiff".[3] This "profit motive" category , which is the relevant one for present purposes, is difficult to justify. Why should the defendant be subject to punishment if he committed a wrong in order to make money, but not if he committed a wrong out of spite or malice or revenge? A wrong committed out of a profit motive is surely not necessarily morally worse or otherwise more apt for punishment. In Lord Reid's view in the later case of *Cassell v Broome*,[4] there is no logical reason for the distinction. In his view, punitive damages should have been abolished entirely, on the ground that punishment should not be administered through civil proceedings; the profit motive category of cases was entirely arbitrarily defined, and was simply forced on the court in *Rookes v Barnard* by previous case law. In Lord Wilberforce's minority view in *Cassell v Broome*, punitive damages should not be limited to the profit motive category, but should always be available, for example for a deliberate defamation, whether the defendant's motive was profit or malice.[5]

The profit motive category makes more sense if it is re-interpreted to provide, not for punishment in a case where there was a profit motive, but for disgorgement whenever the defendant actually made a profit from a deliberate wrong. Although it is difficult to see any sound reason for distinguishing between a profit motive and other motives with respect to the justifiability of punishment, there is a good reason to distinguish cases where the defendant made a profit from a wrong from the generality of cases, because in these cases the punitive damages can serve to remove the profit. As considered below, it is arguable that disgorgement may be justified in civil proceedings, even if it is not justified to impose punishment, which will go beyond merely removing the profits of the wrong and may of course apply with respect to wrongs that do not generate a profit. In fact Lord Diplock pointed out in *Cassell v Broome* that punitive damages in the profit motive category "would seem to be analogous to the civil law concept of enrichessement indue".[6]

"Restitutionary damages"

As discussed in Chapter 4, where the defendant used the plaintiff's property without permission, the plaintiff is usually entitled to a sum measured as a reasonable licence fee for the unauthorised use of his property. Traditionally the award is in the form of damages for trespass or interference with goods. Academic commentators have described these damages as restitutionary damages, which are taken to be an example of "restitution for wrongs" or disgorge-

---

[3] Per Lord Devlin at 1226.
[4] [1972] 1 All ER 801, 838.
[5] At 865. For a recent restatement of the profit motive requirement see *John v MGM Ltd* [1996] 2 All ER 35, 58.
[6] [1972] 1 All ER 801, 872–3.

ment.[7] However, as discussed in Chapter 4, restitutionary damages here are the remedy for a use claim, not disgorgement; the category of restitution for wrongs conflates the two.

Account of profits

An account, or account of profits, is a pecuniary liability in respect of a benefit received by the defendant.[8] It became established as an equitable remedy.[9] A trustee is liable to account to the beneficiary for the value of the trust fund. An account arises from the receipt of money by an agent or fiduciary on behalf of his principal, where it generally amounts to a remedy for a claim in contract.[10] A stranger in receipt of a vitiated transfer, made by a trustee or fiduciary without authority, is liable to account "as a constructive trustee", where the claim is in substance restitutionary or tortious, as considered in Chapter 10. But the account is also awarded to effect disgorgement, as where a trustee or fiduciary makes a profit through a breach of duty, in circumstances where the profit received was not paid for the benefit of the principal or beneficiary, and does not represent any loss to him.[11] A good example is where the trustee or fiduciary takes a bribe from a third party.[12] It has been made clear in cases of this sort that the function of the account is to effect disgorgement; it is said, for example, that an account of profits serves to remove any incentive to commit a breach of duty and to maintain the standards of conduct of fiduciaries.[13] However, it is worth noting that it is often not easy to say whether a profit received by a trustee or fiduciary represents a benefit that would otherwise have gone to the beneficiary or principal, and so whether the account is justifiable only on the basis of disgorgement, or also as a liability in contract or restitution. Breach of fiduciary duty is considered further in Chapter 13.

The account is also used to give effect to disgorgement for other equitable wrongs, including knowing assistance,[14] breach of confidence,[15] passing off[16] and infringement of a statutory intellectual property right (patent, copyright or trade mark).[17] In *A-G v Guardian Newspapers (No 2) (Spycatcher)*,[18] the House

---

[7] e.g. Birks (1989*a*), chap. X; Burrows (1993), 386ff; Jackman (1989).

[8] The account traditionally referred to the right to an examination of the defendant's accounts to establish the amount owing.

[9] Meagher, Gummow & Lehane (1992), para. 2502. There was previously a common law version of account.

[10] Ibid., para. 2503.

[11] Cf Chap. 8 at 262–3.

[12] As in *A-G for Hong Kong v Reid* [1994] 1 AC 324.

[13] e.g. *Bray v Ford* [1986] AC 44, 51–2; see further Chap. 13.

[14] e.g. *Warman v Dwyer* (1925) 128 ALR 201; Jaffey (1995).

[15] *Peter Pan Manufacturing Corp v Corsets Silhouette* [1963] 3 All ER 402; *A-G v Guardian Newspapers (No 2) (Spycatcher)* [1990] 1 AC 109.

[16] *My Kinda Town v Soll* [1982] FSR 147.

[17] Cornish (1999), para. 2.43.

[18] [1990] 1 AC 109.

of Lords attributed the availability of the account to "the principle that no-one should be permitted to profit from his own wrongdoing".[19] Because it originated in equity, the account has not been awarded for common law torts or for a breach of contract that is not a breach of fiduciary duty.

The usual position seems to be that, apart from disgorgement by a trustee or fiduciary under the no-conflict rule,[20] the defendant can be liable to account, where the effect is disgorgement, only where he knew that he was committing a wrong, reflecting a requirement that the defendant should have acted dishonestly or unconscionably.[21] This is consistent with the position taken with respect to punitive damages at common law as mentioned above.[22]

The intellectual property cases demonstrate the difference between disgorgement and the use claim which, as mentioned above, are customarily conflated under the head of "restitution for wrongs". Generally the use claim is allowed by way of a claim in damages, and disgorgement through an account. In the case of a use claim, the measure of liability is a reasonable licence fee, which might be a certain fraction of the selling price of each infringing article, i.e. a notional royalty.[23] But the measure of liability under an account of profits is, in principle, the whole net profit made on each sale.[24]

Constructive trust

The constructive trust is, like the account of profits, an equitable response in origin, and its availability is also still regarded as limited on this basis. It is thought of as the in rem or proprietary counterpart to the account, giving the plaintiff an equitable title to the profit received. Under the orthodox view of property discussed in Chapter 9, this is understood to give the plaintiff various advantages, including priority in insolvency and a right to consequential profits.[25] As with the account, in the standard case of the constructive trust it is not concerned with disgorgement, but with claims in contract or in restitution, as discussed in Chapter 10. But the constructive trust is clearly an instrument of disgorgement in some cases; a leading recent example is *A-G for Hong Kong v Reid*.[26] As discussed in Chapter 10, the problem in connection with disgorgement arises from the inflexibility of the orthodox conception of the constructive trust.[27]

---

[19] Ibid., 262 per Lord Keith; cf per Lord Goff at 286.

[20] Considered in Chap. 13.

[21] *Colbeam Palmer Ltd v Stock Affiliates Pty Ltd* (1968) 122 CLR 25, 34 per Windeyer J.

[22] The position is different where the account arises by statute for the statutory intellectual property rights; see Law Commission (1997), para. 3.19ff.

[23] *Watson, Laidlaw & Co Ltd v Pott, Cassels & Williamson* (1914) 31 RPC 104; above, Chap. 4.

[24] Cornish (1999), para. 2–43; *My Kinda Town v Soll* [1982] FSR 147.

[25] The alternative theory advanced in Chaps. 9 and 10 undermines the existing understanding of the distinction between the constructive trust and the account of profits.

[26] [1994] 1 AC 324.

[27] Disgorgement is also sometimes effected through the tracing rules concerning wrongdoers: see Chap. 9 at 311 and the discussion of *Trustee of the Property of F.C. Jones and Sons v Jones* [1996] 3 WLR 703 in Chap. 10 at 317.

Forfeiture of rights acquired by wrongdoing

Generally with respect to disgorgement the issue is whether the defendant has received a tangible benefit through his wrong. But sometimes the benefit is in the form of a right to receive a payment. The standard example is where the defendant kills someone and ostensibly becomes entitled to a legacy or inheritance out of his victim's estate, or to a payment on a life insurance policy. Under the "forfeiture rule",[28] the defendant cannot enforce his claim and so is in effect required to disgorge it.[29] In the *Spycatcher* case, where the defendant published a book in breach of a duty of confidentiality owed to the Crown, it was suggested that the defendant might forfeit his copyright in the book to the Crown,[30] although no mention was made of the traditional forfeiture rule. Also, as discussed in Chapter 6, in some circumstances the rules governing illegal contracts, by which a contractual or restitutionary claim is sometimes denied or forfeited on the ground that the making or performance of the contract was wrongful, are best understood as being designed to prevent a contracting party from profiting through a wrong, or to punish him for his involvement in it.

Money had and received and waiver of tort

The nature of waiver of tort

Under the doctrine of waiver of tort, a plaintiff who has a claim in tort is said sometimes to be able to waive the tort and instead make a claim for money had and received in respect of a sum received by the defendant through the commission of the tort. In recent years it seems to have been widely thought that the claim for money had and received arising from a waiver of tort is a form of restitution for wrongs or disgorgement.[31] However, it is very doubtful whether this is the way the doctrine should be understood. The better view is that the claim arising from waiver of tort is a claim for restitution for a vitiated transfer (or sometimes a use claim). This is clear from the judgments in the leading modern case, *United Australia Ltd v Barclays Bank Ltd*.[32] In his judgment Lord Atkin

---

[28] See Virgo (1998). A recent example is provided by *David v Titcumb* [1990] Ch 110. Forfeiture in this sense must be distinguished from forfeiture as a measure open to a sentencing court, which involves stripping the defendant of any property used for the purposes of the crime.

[29] There has been some discussion about whether preventing someone from receiving something, as opposed to removing it once it has been received, is really disgorgement: see e.g. Virgo (1998), 46. As Virgo notes, the two are equivalent because the same principle is at stake. In any case, in a forfeiture case the defendant *is* stripped of an asset in the sense of the right to benefit.

[30] [1990] 1 AC 109, 263 per Lord Keith.

[31] Birks (1989*a*), 314; Burrows (1993), 381; Jackman (1989), 309; Law Commission (1997), para. 3.6.

[32] [1941] AC 1.

referred first to cases of money had and received "where the defendant had received money from the plaintiff to which he was not entitled". He went on:

> These included cases where the plaintiff had intentionally paid money to the defendant, e.g., claims for money paid on a consideration that wholly failed and money paid under a mistake: cases where the plaintiff had been deceived into paying money, cases where money had been extorted from the plaintiff by threats or duress of goods. They also included cases where money had not been paid by the plaintiff at all but had been received from third persons, as where the defendant had received fees under colour of holding an office which in fact was held by the plaintiff: and finally cases like the present where the defendant had been wrongfully in possession of the plaintiff's goods, had sold them and was in possession of the proceeds.[33]

These are cases of restitution for a vitiated transfer.[34] Lord Atkin then concluded:[35]

> But while it was just that the plaintiff in such cases should be able to recover the money in the possession of the other party, he was not bound to exercise this remedy: in cases where the money had been received as the result of a wrong he still had the remedy of claiming damages for tort in action of trespass, deceit, trover, and the like. But he obviously could not compel the wrongdoer to recoup him his losses twice over. Hence he was restricted to one of the two remedies: and herein as I think arose the doctrine of "waiver of the tort".

Thus waiver of tort cases were a sub-category of the cases where a claim for money had and received, meaning here a claim for restitution for a vitiated transfer, was available. The sub-category consisted of those cases where the vitiated transfer was caused by the defendant's wrong, so that the defendant had a choice between the restitutionary and the tortious claims. The two claims were clearly alternatives because they served to compensate the plaintiff for, or restore to him, the same loss. Where the tort was waived, the plaintiff would rely for the purposes of the restitutionary claim on the vitiating effect, rather than the wrongful character, of the defendant's conduct. Nowadays, the plaintiff might advance both claims in the alternative, but under the old forms of action it seems that he would have had to choose between the claims because they would have to be pursued by way of different forms of action in different proceedings.[36] The disgorgement analysis, by contrast, makes no obvious sense of the idea of "waiver", or of choosing between different causes of action, since disgorgement is a different response to the tort claim, not a different type of claim.

---

[33] At 27.

[34] Conversion is considered below. The claim arising from complete failure of consideration is not best understood as restitution for a vitiated transfer, although this is a plausible interpretation of how it was actually understood: see Chap. 2 at 60; the same might be said of the claim arising from usurpation of office: see Chap. 8. In any case they are clearly not examples of disgorgement.

[35] At 28; see also above Chap. 4 at 143–4.

[36] See per Viscount Simon LC in *United Australia* [1941] AC 1, 11; see also Hedley (1984), 656.

In the same case, Viscount Simon LC noted, "[a] learned author includes among torts which can be waived, conversion, trespass to land or goods, deceit . . . and the action for extorting money by threats".[37] And he added,[38] "it is clear that there are torts to which the process of waiver could not be applied; the tort of defamation, for example, or of assault". It is the fact that the tort is also a cause of vitiation that means that it is capable of being waived—this is true of extortion (duress), deceit (mistake), and conversion and some cases of trespass (lack of authority). (Conversion raises particular difficulties, which will be discussed below in connection with the facts of *United Australia*.) Defamation and assault are not torts that vitiate a transfer by the plaintiff or from his estate. Trespass to land or goods includes cases of unauthorised use as well as unauthorised taking. Unauthorised use is not a vitiated transfer, but can generate a use claim; in such a case the claim for money had and received on a waiver of tort is the use claim. But, whether the claim arising from waiver was a use claim or a claim for restitution for a vitiated transfer, it was not based on the wrong as such; as the court said in *Phillips v Homfray*,[39] which involved trespass in the form of unauthorised use and unauthorised taking, in a case of waiver:

> the plaintiff is entitled . . . to abstain from treating as a wrong the acts of the defendant in cases where, independently of the question of wrong, the plaintiff could make a case for relief.[40]

By contrast, the disgorgement analysis makes no sense of the limited range of torts for which waiver was possible. If disgorgement is the rationale for waiver of tort, one would expect it to apply in principle to any tort, not to the limited range of torts with respect to which the doctrine was recognised to apply.

Waiver of tort and conversion

Many cases of waiver of tort have concerned conversion by the disposal of the plaintiff's chattel (the example is mentioned by Lord Atkin in the quotation above). When the plaintiff's chattel comes into the defendant's possession as a result of a vitiated transfer, and the defendant sells it, the plaintiff has always been able to make a claim for the amount of the defendant's proceeds of sale.[41] This was in the form of a claim for money had and received, waiving the tort of conversion, the conversion being the unauthorised selling of the chattel.[42] This is again sometimes thought to be a claim for disgorgement.[43] But, again, the

---

[37] At 13, referring to Winfield (1931), 169.
[38] At 14.
[39] (1883) 24 Ch D 439. The case was considered in detail in Chap. 4.
[40] At 461.
[41] See Chap. 10 at 323. The advantage of the claim for money had and received was to avoid any difficulties in valuing the chattel for the purposes of the claim in conversion.
[42] *Lamine v Dorrell* (1701) 2 Ld Raym. 1216, 92 ER 303; *United Australia v Barclays* [1941] AC 1.
[43] Birks (1989*a*), 317; Virgo (1999), 490.

claim is far better understood as a claim for restitution for a vitiated transfer: the proceeds of sale restore the surviving value in the defendant's estate—in other words, the plaintiff can trace his surviving value from the chattel to the proceeds under the exchange product rule.[44] In this type of case, by contrast with cases involving duress or deceit, say, the tortious act may not actually be the cause of the original vitiated transfer, because the defendant may dispose wrongfully of a chattel that reached him as a result of some other vitiating factor; but sometimes the conversion will also involve a taking from the plaintiff as well as a disposal, and so constitute a vitiating factor as well as a wrong. In either case, again it is clear that the two claims cannot both be available, and that the plaintiff must choose between them, or in other words that he must waive the tort if he wishes to pursue the restitutionary claim. As it was put in an early case:

> In bringing an action for money had and received, instead of trover [sc conversion], the plaintiff does no more than waive any complaint, with a view to damages, of the tortious act by which the goods were converted into money, and takes to the neat proceeds of the sale as the value of the goods.[45]

The position is complicated by the fact that, on the theory put forward in Chapters 9 and 10, conversion plays the role of both the restitutionary claim and the tort of breach of the duty of preservation. If it cannot be said that the defendant knew or ought, in the light of the appropriate duty of inquiry, to have known that the chattel belonged to someone else, his retention or disposal of it is not a real tort. If the tort and the restitutionary claim were distinguished, there would be no claim in tort in such a case as an alternative to the restitutionary claim in respect of the proceeds of sale, and no question of waiver would arise. In such a case, the strange position in the traditional common law is that a fictional tort of conversion was waived in order to allow a fictional claim in contract (the claim for money had and received). In fact in such a case there is genuinely only one claim, viz. the restitutionary claim to surviving value in the defendant's estate, which conventionally took the form of a fictional tort before the sale of the chattel and a fictional contract afterwards.

Further confusion has been introduced by the ratification analysis of waiver of tort, exemplified by the decision in *Lamine v Dorrell*.[46] When an agent, acting in accordance with his principal's instructions and with his authority, sells his principal's chattel on behalf of the principal, the plaintiff principal has a claim under the agency contract against the defendant agent in the measure of

---

[44] In the sense explained in Chap. 9. Burrows rejects this interpretation: Burrows (1993), 384. In theory, if the surviving value is restored, the plaintiff should have no tortious claim, only his restitutionary claim to the traceable surviving value. But it is understandable that the plaintiff should be understood to have either a claim for the loss of the value of the chattel, disregarding the proceeds as surviving value, or a restitutionary claim for the surviving value in the form of the proceeds.

[45] *Hunter v Prinsep*, 10 East. 378, 391 per Lord Ellenborough, adopted by Viscount Simon LC in *United Australia* [1941] AC 1, 18.

[46] (1701) 2 Ld Raym. 1216, 92 ER 303; *United Australia* [1941] AC 1, 27–8 per Lord Atkin.

the proceeds of sale.[47] The argument in *Lamine v Dorrell* was that when the defendant (a stranger to the plaintiff) sells the plaintiff's chattel without authority, the plaintiff can adopt or ratify the sale so that the defendant is treated as if he had made an authorised sale on behalf of the plaintiff as his agent, thereby becoming subject to a fictional contractual claim, as if under the agency contract. On the ratification analysis, the claim for money had and received arising from the waiver of the tort of conversion is this fictional contract claim, and the waiver of tort is the fictional adoption or ratification.[48] The ratification analysis of waiver of tort clearly relates only to the tort of conversion: normally there would be no reason why the waiving of the tort should generate a claim, as opposed to merely cancelling the claim in tort and confining the plaintiff to another claim, and this is sufficient, apart from any objection to the fiction, to disqualify it as an analysis of waiver of tort in general. There would be no reason to mention it, if it had not led to certain remarks in *United Australia v Barclays Bank* that have been taken to support the disgorgement analysis of waiver of tort.

United Australia v Barclays Bank

In *United Australia* a cheque in favour of the plaintiff was endorsed over without authority by the plaintiff's secretary to a company, MFG. MFG deposited the cheque with its bank, which collected on it and credited MFG's account at the bank. The plaintiff originally brought an action for money had and received against MFG in respect of the money received through the cheque, but then, when MFG went into liquidation, it brought an action for conversion against the bank instead. The bank's act of conversion was accepting the cheque and collecting on it: a cheque is treated in the law of conversion as if it were a chattel worth the amount payable on the cheque. The crucial issue for present purposes is the nature of the original, discontinued claim for money had and received against MFG. The bank's argument was that in making the original claim for money had and received against MFG, the plaintiff had implicitly waived any claim in respect of MFG's conversion of the cheque. Under the ratification analysis, this implied that the plaintiff had authorised MFG's cashing of the cheque. Consequently, it was argued, the bank could not have committed a conversion in accepting and collecting on the cheque. The House of Lords rightly rejected the argument, and held that the claim against the bank was not affected by the prior action against MFG.

The House of Lords rejected the ratification analysis; it held that, in reality (as explained above), waiver is concerned with avoiding double recovery; thus a

---

[47] The claim would presumably have traditionally taken the form of a contractual claim for a debt owing or a claim for account.

[48] By contrast, in the case of an actual agent, there is the possibility of genuine ratification: *United Australia* [1941] AC 1, 28 per Lord Atkin. In *Marsh v Keating* (1834) 1 Bing. NC 198 the defendant actually purported to sell on behalf of the plaintiff.

claim against MFG to recover compensation for loss caused by the wrong of conversion would not have been precluded by the claim actually taken for money had and received, waiving the tort, unless the claim for money had and received had been successfully completed and the loss recovered. The ratification was a fiction, and the waiver did not in any way validate MFG's action of depositing the cheque, which remained wrongful, leaving open the option of a claim in conversion against MFG or the bank. As Lord Romer said, referring to the effect of the action for money had and received against MFG:[49] "[t]he plaintiff in no way affirms the tortious act so as to treat it as having been a rightful one".

Now, MFG's action in depositing the cheque had two quite distinct legal effects. It constituted a wrong to the plaintiff;[50] but it also constituted a transfer of value without authority from the plaintiff to itself (via the bank). The claim for money had and received, being a restitutionary claim, was based on the latter effect, and the claim in conversion on the former. Unfortunately the court failed to distinguish between these two distinct legal effects. In rejecting the argument that the claim for money had and received validated MFG's wrong, it insisted that the claim was actually based on it. Thus Lord Romer said, following the passage above, "[t]he action [for money had and received] would not lie if it were understood that no tort had been committed". But although the claim for money had and received does not deny the wrongful character of the defendant's action, neither is it based on it. Lord Romer's dictum is only true to the extent that where the tort is committed there is also a lack of authority; and it is possible in principle that there could be a transfer without authority that did not constitute a wrong because of the innocence of the defendant. Similarly Lord Atkin said:[51]

> If I find that a thief has stolen my securities and is in possession of the proceeds, when I sue him for them I am not excusing him. I am protesting violently that he is a thief and because of his theft I am suing him: indeed he may be in prison upon my prosecution.

But in principle the claim in money had and received to recover the proceeds of a conversion by a thief does not depend on showing that the thief acted wrongfully in any real sense, or still less that he was sufficiently culpable to be criminally punishable, but merely that there was a vitiated transfer from which the proceeds of the sale are traceable. The confusion is due to the failure to distinguish in principle between conversion as a wrongful act and as a transfer without authority.

---

[49] At 35.

[50] As noted above, conversion is not always genuinely a wrong. In *United Australia*, it seems that the bank, and presumably also MFG, did behave wrongfully (possibly because it had notice of the connection between MFG and the secretary), because the bank appears to have accepted that it could not take advantage of the statutory bona fide purchase defence in respect of cheques and bills of exchange.

[51] At 29.

Unfortunately, the emphasis on the wrongfulness of MFG's action rather than its vitiating effect as the basis for the discontinued claim for money had and received has been misinterpreted to imply that it was a claim to disgorgement, i.e. a response to the defendant's wrong. Thus Birks argues that the case shows that "on these facts the tort was just as much the cause of action whether the damages sought were restitutionary [sc disgorgement] or compensatory".[52] But the analysis above shows that the claim for money had and received is not based on the defendant's wrong as such, and that *United Australia* does not imply that it is. Furthermore, as noted above, conversion is often not genuinely a wrong, and in such a case there can be no question of disgorgement.

In conclusion, the doctrine of waiver of tort does not concern disgorgement at all, but restitution for a vitiated transfer (or a use claim). This is consistent with the authorities. It explains the restricted range of cases for which waiver is available. It explains the concept of waiver, because the restitutionary and tortious claims are alternative claims in respect of the same loss. Lastly, it explains the absence in the judgments of any discussion of the factors that one would expect to see considered in connection with disgorgement (and are considered where disgorgement is effected by way of an account, constructive trust or punitive damages): i.e. the principle that the defendant should not profit from a wrong, or the objection that disgorgement gives the plaintiff a windfall.

This is not to say that there are no cases in which waiver of tort has been invoked to give effect to disgorgement. One example might be the controversial case of *Reading v A-G*,[53] where a claim for disgorgement of a bribe to a Crown employee was recoverable as money had and received.[54] Recently in *Halifax v Thomas*,[55] which concerned an unsuccessful claim for disgorgement for fraudulent misrepresentation, the claim was framed in the alternative as a claim for waiver of tort, although no issue of restitution for a vitiated transfer was at stake (or any other issue that has traditionally been addressed through waiver of tort); no doubt this was the result of the influence of academic writing that treats waiver of tort as a means of disgorgement.

A summary of the position under the case law

The law of disgorgement as it appears from the case law is far from satisfactory. Although it is widely thought that money had and received based on waiver of tort and restitutionary damages are examples of disgorgement, in fact they are generally concerned with restitution for a vitiated transfer or the use claim.

---

[52] Birks (1989*a*), 316; also Birks (1992*b*), 68.

[53] [1951] AC 507.

[54] The use of money had and received for this purpose is apparently quite modern: see *Mahesan v Malaysia Government Officers' Co-operative Housing Society* [1979] AC 374, 380 per Lord Diplock. The alternative ground relied upon by some of the judges was an account in equity on the basis that the defendant was a fiduciary, as discussed in Chap. 13.

[55] [1995] 4 All ER 673.

Disgorgement, where it is allowed, is effected at common law in the form of punitive damages, and in equity through an account of profits or a constructive trust. The attitude of the courts is very different at common law and in equity. At common law, punitive damages are regarded as anomalous, understandably because here the association of disgorgement with punishment has brought into consideration the procedural objection to the imposition of disgorgement through the civil courts. In equity, on the other hand, the use of the account or constructive trust to effect disgorgement seems to have evolved from its use as a normal civil remedy to enforce a claim arising in restitution or contract or under a trust, and often there is a strong overlap with these types of case, and probably for this reason there have been no apparent scruples over disgorgement, with respect to fiduciaries or more generally.

The upshot is that no general principle of disgorgement is recognised. Disgorgement is available only by reference to specific lines of authority governing certain types of case. There have been attempts to explain the established incidence of disgorgement,[56] but much of this discussion is marred by the conflation of disgorgement with the use claim and restitution for a vitiated transfer, and accordingly by a preoccupation with restitutionary damages and waiver of tort. In fact there is surely no basis for distinguishing between different wrongs with respect to disgorgement. Any wrong must come within the terms of the principle that a wrongdoer should not profit through his wrongdoing.[57] It is strange that where disgorgement is allowed it is treated as justified simply on the basis of the principle that a wrongdoer should not profit from his wrong,[58] and yet disgorgement is denied in other cases even though the principle is equally applicable. In recent years there have been attempts to expand the availability of disgorgement, with limited success.[59] At the root of the controversy is the procedural objection, which is considered next.

DISGORGEMENT, PUNISHMENT AND THE PROCEDURAL OBJECTION

The "quasi-punitive" nature of disgorgement

The crucial issue with respect to the law of disgorgement is its relation to punishment. Punishment consists in the infliction of harm on the defendant as a response to his breach of duty, not because the harm is the incidental consequence of providing a remedy for the wrong vis-à-vis the plaintiff (as for compensation or an injunction), but because of the value or beneficial effect that the

---

[56] e.g. Birks's three tests for "restitution-yielding" wrongs: Birks (1989a), 326; Jackman (1989).

[57] Subject to the conditions discussed below at 383–7 and the procedural problem.

[58] As in *Spycatcher* [1990] 1 AC 109, above n 19, and *Rookes v Barnard* [1964] AC 1129, above 364.

[59] e.g. *Halifax v Thomas* [1996] Ch 217; *Stoke CC v Wass* [1988] 1 WLR 574; *Surrey CC v Bredero* [1993] 1 WLR 1361; cf *A-G v Blake* [1998] 2 WLR 805, discussed in Chap. 12.

infliction of harm is understood to have as a response to the breach of duty. There is great controversy over the nature of this value or beneficial effect—as to whether punishment is to be justified in terms of its deterrent or retributive effect, or otherwise—but it would surely be uncontroversial to say that at a more abstract level (encompassing these various conceptions of punishment) punishment is inflicted for the purpose of upholding the community's interest in the performance of the duty broken and of legal duties in general.[60]

On any conception of punishment, it seems clear that due punishment must exceed or encompass the removal of any benefit received by the wrongdoer.[61] On a utilitarian approach to punishment, the harm inflicted on the defendant must exceed the benefit obtained by him through the wrong, so as to ensure that on a cost-benefit calculus it is not worth committing the crime.[62] On a retributive approach, it is surely the case also that the harm inflicted on the defendant, to purge him of his guilt, as it were,[63] should at least exceed the benefit obtained. It follows that punishment encompasses disgorgement, or in other words that disgorgement is merely an element of punishment. In so far as the defendant has received a pecuniary benefit, or possibly more broadly a measurable benefit, punishment should include the removal of the benefit, and this element of punishment is disgorgement.[64] This is what should be understood by references to the "quasi-punitive" nature of disgorgement.[65]

The argument suggests that disgorgement calls for no separate justification from punishment and involves no separate considerations from punishment; disgorgement should be disposed of simply as an aspect of punishment. Nevertheless, there are good reasons why sometimes disgorgement should be isolated for separate consideration from the larger issue of punishment. First, where punishment is being administered, given that punishment should

---

[60] Commonly punishment is defined simply as harm imposed as a response to a breach of duty, which fails to distinguish it from compensation.

[61] A liability for compensation may have the effect of removing part or all of the benefit obtained through a wrong. This does not mean that these claims are forms of disgorgement, because their purpose is not to prevent the defendant from profiting from a wrong, and the measure of recovery is not determined by the measure of profit. However, in so far as the defendant's profit is reduced by a remedial liability, the need for disgorgement is reduced also. This is consistent with the rule against cumulative recovery in damages and by an account: *Tang Min Sit v Capacious Investments* [1986] AC 514; see Chap. 4 at 148.

[62] As Bentham said: "the value of the punishment must not be less in any case than what is efficient to outweigh that of the profits of the offence", cited in Hodgson (1984), 7. The same principle is the basis for the modern economic analysis of punishment.

[63] On a retributive view, it seems that punishment serves as a sort of quid pro quo that negates or neutralises the defendant's guilt.

[64] Cf Ashworth (1995), 72–3, who treats "deprivation of profits" as an aspect or rationale of punishment, and suggests that this is the position under the jurisprudence of the European Convention of Human Rights. One might argue that sometimes, if not generally, liability to punishment should require a greater degree of knowledge than a liability to disgorgement. This may be so, but it is not a valid objection to the argument; it is merely an aspect of the principle that the severity of punishment should depend on the nature and extent of the defendant's knowledge of his wrong, which would surely not be denied in relation to punishment, and is consistent with the position that disgorgement is an element of punishment.

[65] The expression "quasi-punitive" is used in Law Commission (1993), para. 7.18.

necessarily involve the removal of any benefit received, it may be sensible to address disgorgement explicitly as a distinct element in the determination of punishment, to ensure that the function of punishment has been properly effected with respect to any identifiable benefit; thus in setting a pecuniary penalty the court should determine the measure of any such benefit and ensure that the pecuniary penalty exceeds it. In criminal proceedings it seems that in principle the measure of a fine is indeed set with a view to ensuring that the defendant's profits are removed; however, for various reasons it was necessary also to introduce a specific power of confiscation to enable the court to remove the pecuniary profits of wrongdoing.[66] Secondly, although the "procedural objection" applies to disgorgement, as well as to punishment in full, it is arguable that, as discussed below, the objection is weaker with respect to disgorgement dispensed on its own, and this may also justify the separate treatment of disgorgement.

The "procedural objection"

It was mentioned above that one would expect to see the general recognition and implementation of the principle that a wrongdoer should not profit from his wrong (as an aspect of the broader principle that a wrong should be duly punished). But, as the discussion of the case law above showed, this is not generally the case in civil proceedings, and the main reason is surely the procedural objection. The procedural objection arises from the different functions of punishment and disgorgement on the one hand and remedies on the other.[67] A remedy is designed to protect the plaintiff's private interest in the performance of the duty owed to him,[68] by putting him in the position he would have been in if the duty had been performed,[69] whereas punishment and disgorgement are justified as a means of upholding the community interest in the performance of the duty broken.[70] Thus disgorgement, like punishment, is not strictly a remedy, although

---

[66] Confiscation orders are a modern phenomenon (now in the Criminal Justice Act 1988 and the Drug Trafficking Offences Act 1986) introduced following concern about the failure to deprive the defendants of the benefits of drug dealing in *R v Cuthbertson* [1981] AC 470. It seems that fines were sometimes inadequate to achieve this because of a specified maximum for the fine. Also the usual criterion for the severity of a fine is the gravity of the offence, and it seems to have been thought that this precludes taking account of the measure of profit because crimes of similar gravity can give rise to very different profits. In fact, the gravity of the offence should be reflected in the excess of the fine over the benefit, and the maximum should be specified in terms of the excess also: see the discussion in Wasik (1984).

[67] Jaffey (1995). For a similar distinction, see MacCormick (1982). Sometimes a duty is owed to the community and there is no plaintiff or private remedy. This does not affect the analysis.

[68] A remedy can also arise from a causative event that is not a wrong: see Appendix 1.

[69] This may be by injunction requiring the defendant to perform the duty, or to undo the effects of his non-performance, or it may be by an award of damages as compensation, measured by the cost of the defendant's breach of duty to the plaintiff.

[70] By contrast, the use claim, which is often confused with disgorgement, is a genuinely remedial claim designed to satisfy the plaintiff's private interest in payment for the use of his property.

often referred to as such when dispensed in civil proceedings. Disgorgement (or punishment) and remedy are different forms of "legal response" to a breach of duty. The two types of response—punishment and remedy—are normally implemented through different channels. This is the basis for the division between civil proceedings, which are instigated by the plaintiff, as the person to whom the duty was owed, in order to secure a remedy, and criminal proceedings, whose purpose is to inflict punishment on the defendant at the instigation of a prosecutor acting on behalf of the state.

The reason for the two types of proceedings is that the type of response determines not only the appropriate person to instigate the proceedings, but also the appropriate form of procedure and the evidential requirements for determining whether there has been a breach of duty and what the precise form of the response should be. Thus criminal proceedings provide a greater degree of protection for a defendant against the possibility of a mistaken verdict, for example through the higher standard of proof required in criminal proceedings.[71] This is the procedural basis for the division between civil and criminal justice.[72] It follows that where the defendant in civil proceedings has made a profit through his wrong, or has otherwise committed a wrong for which he should be punished, prima facie disgorgement or punishment should not be imposed because the proceedings are not designed to provide him with the degree of protection in evidential and procedural matters that he is entitled to in relation to such a legal response and would receive through criminal proceedings. This is the main aspect of the "procedural objection" to punishment or disgorgement in civil proceedings. The procedural objection was clearly behind the decisions of the House of Lords in *Rookes v Barnard*[73] and *Cassell v Broome*,[74] concerning punitive damages.[75] In *Cassell v Broome* Lord Reid said that imposing punishment

---

[71] See Jaffey (1995*a*). With respect to a claim for compensation, a mistaken decision by the court in favour of one party is usually comparable, in terms of the injustice caused, to a mistaken decision for the other. To minimise the risk of injustice to either party, the proceedings should be even-handed. Thus civil procedure does not discriminate between the parties, for example with respect to pleading and evidence, including the standard of proof on the "balance of probability". In the case of punishment the procedure should be weighted in favour of the defendant. A mistakenly inflicted punishment is a serious injustice. A mistaken failure to punish is an injustice to the victim and, in a sense, to the community, but the injustice in either case is not comparable in gravity. This asymmetry is reflected in the position in criminal proceedings, where the prosecuting authority is subject to stricter rules governing disclosure and evidence, and the standard of proof is "beyond reasonable doubt".

[72] The procedural analysis implies that the distinction between civil and criminal law does not lie in the nature or content of legal duties. For example, it implies that it would be mistaken to think that there are two distinct duties not to assault, one in criminal law and one in civil law, as opposed to a single duty not to assault capable of generating two different types of response through two different systems.

[73] [1964] AC 1129.

[74] [1972] 1 All ER 801.

[75] The procedural objection is also apparent in the decisions refusing to enforce penalty clauses in contracts, on the ground that the clause is intended to operate "in terrorem of the offending party": *Dunlop Pneumatc Tyre Co Ltd v New Garage and Motor Co Ltd* [1915] AC 79, 86 per Lord Dunedin.

in civil proceedings is "highly anomalous", and that "[it confuses] the function of the civil law which is to compensate with the function of the criminal law which is to inflict deterrent and punitive penalties".[76]

The procedural objection to punishment in civil proceedings is not only that it jeopardises the defendant's procedural rights. A further objection is that it operates by way of a requirement to pay over the wrongful profit to the plaintiff rather than the state, which gives the plaintiff a windfall, because ex hypothesi it goes beyond what is necessary to remedy the wrong the plaintiff has suffered.[77] Also it will mean that the parties can negotiate over the defendant's punishment. Moreover, it may create a risk of double punishment of the defendant because of duplication with criminal proceedings; and it may involve the imposition of punishment by a judge who lacks experience of determining sentence.[78]

In other common law countries, the procedural objection appears to have been widely ignored or overridden, and the courts seem to have moved towards a position where punitive damages are generally available in civil proceedings, more or less wherever the wrong the court is dealing with deserves punishment.[79] No doubt this is because of disquiet at the possibility that the defendant will escape due punishment altogether. Recently the Law Commission has suggested that English law should follow suit.[80] As discussed below, there may be circumstances in which the procedural objection can legitimately be overcome. Unfortunately, often the argument for the general availability of punishment and disgorgement in civil proceedings seems to reflect a mistaken understanding of the relation between civil and criminal justice, i.e. that civil proceedings deal with a different category of wrong from criminal proceedings, which might suggest that if due punishment is to be achieved at all it must be through the civil proceedings; or that punishment in civil proceedings is in some sense not real punishment and so does not raise any question of special procedural safeguards or safeguards against double punishment.[81]

Disgorgement in civil proceedings

It may be unnecessarily inflexible to insist on the complete segregation of remedy and punishment between civil and criminal proceedings, and its corollary, the procedural objection to punishment or disgorgement in civil proceedings.[82]

---

[76] At 837. And he described it as "palm tree justice", at 837–8.

[77] This was a point of concern in *Halifax v Thomas* [1985] 4 All ER 673, 682 per Glidewell LJ.

[78] See the concerns expressed in *John v MGN* [1996] 2 All ER 35, 51 per Sir Thomas Bingham MR, in the light of Art. 10 of the European Convention of Human Rights.

[79] Law Commission (1997), para. 4.5.

[80] Ibid., para. 5.42.

[81] As argued in Jaffey (1998*b*), discussing Law Commission (1997).

[82] For example, compensation orders are now sometimes available in criminal proceedings, but only for small and straightforward claims, where the issues will not distract from the normal

It may be that it is possible to dispense punishment in civil proceedings in some cases without unfairness to the defendant, and if so this would have the advantage of achieving the necessary legal response—both remedy and punishment—through only one set of proceedings, and at no public cost. If punishment is minor and pecuniary, it may be that it can be dispensed without procedural unfairness by some adaptation of civil proceedings to provide appropriate additional protection to the defendant, without the need for the full panoply of protection that criminal proceedings provide for more severe types of penalty. It may be sufficient only to require a higher burden of proof, and even then it may be that the full rigour of proof beyond reasonable doubt can be relaxed to a lower requirement of "clear and convincing" evidence (which is still more demanding than the ordinary civil "balance of probabilities" test).[83]

Furthermore, there is much to be said for allowing disgorgement in civil proceedings even if full punishment is excluded. Disgorgement is limited in extent, and in its nature involves no exercise of discretion by the court, which means that the absence of any sentencing expertise does not cause any difficulty and there is no risk of capricious over-punishment. It may also be that, by contrast with full punishment, knowledge or intention should not be a necessary requirement for disgorgement,[84] so that no expertise on or judgment of intention or "mens rea" would be called for. In these respects, disgorgement has more in common with compensation than punishment, and would fit more easily into civil proceedings than criminal proceedings.[85] Furthermore, it would require a considerable expansion of the criminal justice system to effect disgorgement or confiscation through criminal proceedings wherever it is necessary,[86] since it would have to deal with cases where traditionally there have been no criminal proceedings (i.e. where the wrong is not recognised as a crime), possibly including, as mentioned above, cases where the defendant has committed a wrong without the necessary mens rea for full punishment. Allowing disgorgement in civil proceedings even if punishment in full is not permitted will at least prevent the conspicuous retention of an identifiable benefit, which is liable to be particularly corrosive of respect for the law.

---

criminal procedure and undermine the defendant's safeguards, or give the plaintiff any influence over the proceedings: s.35 of the Powers of Criminal Courts Act 1973; *R. v Inwood* (1974) 60 Cr App Rep 70.

[83] This standard is sometimes used in the United States for punitive damages: see Sebert (1986), 1668. In *John v MGN* it was said for exemplary damages the proof must be "clear": [1996] 2 All ER 35, 58 per Sir Thomas Bingham MR.

[84] See below at 386–7.

[85] A further advantage relates to future profits. Sometimes, as discussed below at 384–6, the wrongdoer may be able to make profits at some time in the future, after criminal proceedings have been concluded, for example where he publishes a book about the wrongdoing. It would be possible in principle to allow for re-application to the court to obtain disgorgement of later profits. In practice, this might be best achieved through civil proceedings, because the plaintiff could monitor the defendant's activities and re-apply if necessary.

[86] Especially if disgorgement is appropriate in the absence of knowledge.

But there remain difficulties with disgorgement in civil proceedings. Even if the defendant's procedural rights can be protected, the general availability of disgorgement would have the drawback that control over the promotion of the public interest would be in the hands of a plaintiff who might, for whatever reason, choose not to pursue proceedings (although presumably this is better than no disgorgement or confiscation at all). This consideration seems to have been behind the reluctance of the Hodgson Committee to recommend any expansion of disgorgement in civil proceedings.[87] Also the problem remains that it is undesirable that the law should confer a windfall if this can be avoided.[88] It might be possible for the defendant's profit to be paid over to the state or to a charity, even though the order is obtained by the plaintiff in civil proceedings. But if the public interest is to be implemented by the plaintiff, it might be necessary to give the plaintiff the windfall, or at least part of it, to encourage him to take proceedings. Difficulties may also arise in multiple plaintiff cases, where the defendant has made a profit through an act that is a wrong to a number of people, as in the case of a public nuisance.[89] Possibly the first plaintiff to get to court should get the whole of the profit;[90] this might be convenient, but would create an unsatisfactory distinction between victims in similar positions. Alternatively it might be possible to require a class action in order to share the windfall around and ensure that the plaintiffs are treated in the same way.[91]

A possible alternative to civil disgorgement at the instigation of the victim of the wrong, involving a greater departure from the traditional framework, would be for a public authority to be empowered to take disgorgement or confiscation proceedings through the civil courts. This would achieve disgorgement without a windfall, and through the agency of a public authority. It might take advantage of civil law expertise in certain types of case. It might also provide a means for disgorgement where criminal proceedings would be oppressive, or where there is insufficient evidence for full punishment through a criminal conviction, but still sufficient for disgorgement, or where the defendant's state of knowledge does not justify full punishment through a criminal conviction. However, it would expand the role of the Crown at great expense, and there would be difficulties of co-ordination with respect to civil proceedings by the plaintiff where he is also seeking compensation, and with respect to separate criminal proceedings in respect of the same wrong.[92]

---

[87] Hodgson (1984), 27.

[88] Hodgson (1984), 26–7; *Halifax v Thomas* [1995] 4 All ER 673, 682 per Glidewell LJ.

[89] The problem is noted by Stuart-Smith LJ in *A.B. v South West Water Services* [1993] QB 507, 527; see also Law Commission (1997), 5.31ff with respect to punitive damages.

[90] Ibid., para. 5.31ff.

[91] The issue arises how to allocate the windfall amongst the plaintiffs.

[92] In Australia and the United States there are examples of a public power to sue for what are described as civil penalties or civil forfeiture (confiscation) in respect of certain types of wrong: Hodgson (1984), 30ff. Although the proceedings go through the civil courts, they are not remedial but punitive or quasi-punitive, and it is surprising that the defendant seems to get no extra procedural protection or protection against double jeopardy.

Priority as between civil and criminal proceedings

With respect to full punishment, as opposed to disgorgement, one would think that punishment should be left to the criminal process where criminal proceedings are available. Normally criminal proceedings would take place first, and if they have been completed, there could be no justification for the civil court to impose any further punishment, or to impose punishment where the criminal court declined to.[93] If no criminal proceedings have been taken, for the civil court to impose punishment would appear to usurp the discretion of the public prosecutor not to act, or to pre-empt the judgment of the criminal court if proceedings are underway.[94]

However, it is doubtful whether disgorgement would ever be an inappropriate response to a wrong (if the conditions for disgorgement are met), so no question of discretion should arise. It may then be more convenient for the civil court always to have the responsibility of imposing disgorgement where a wrongful profit is established in civil proceedings. This would mean that the criminal court should not generally effect disgorgement or confiscation except where there are no civil proceedings, typically in the case of "non-victim" crimes.[95] Given that (under the present arrangements) civil proceedings will often be possible but not criminal proceedings, a rule giving priority to civil proceedings with respect to dispensing disgorgement, where criminal proceedings *are* possible, would have the advantage of uniform treatment of plaintiffs with respect to windfalls.

In *Halifax v Thomas*,[96] the defendant had bought a house with the help of a mortgage fraudulently obtained from the plaintiff building society, and made a profit through the increased value of the house. A confiscation order was made in criminal proceedings to deprive the defendant of his profit, but had not yet been executed. In civil proceedings, the plaintiff argued that it was entitled to disgorgement. In fact the disgorgement claim failed, but it was apparently assumed without argument that if the plaintiff did have a claim to disgorgement it would necessarily take precedence over the Crown's confiscation order. No doubt a remedial claim, whether in rem or in personam, would take precedence over the confiscation order, on the basis that the function of the confiscation order is achieved if it merely catches any surplus left after the satisfaction of the defendant's remedial liabilities in respect of the wrong.[97] But the plaintiff's claim was no more a remedial claim than the Crown's. Under the procedural analysis of the relation between civil and criminal justice, the claims were

---

[93] *Archer v Brown* [1985] 1 QB 401, 423 per Peter Pain J.

[94] In practice, this argument may be artificial, because no doubt criminal proceedings are often not taken purely because of a lack of resources.

[95] e.g. drug trafficking. Difficulties might of course arise when it is unclear whether there are or will be civil proceedings.

[96] [1995] 4 All ER 673; Jaffey (1996*a*).

[97] See Chap. 4 at 148.

exactly equivalent in function. On the Crown's side is the argument that the plaintiff should not receive a windfall, and on the plaintiff's is the argument of uniformity mentioned above.

Attorney-General v Blake[98] is also a recent example of the failure to appreciate the equivalence of disgorgement in civil proceedings and confiscation in criminal proceedings in accordance with the procedural distinction between civil and criminal justice. The defendant had published an account of his work in the secret services. It was argued, in an action by the Attorney-General on behalf of the Crown as the defendant's ex-employer, that he should be subject to disgorgement for breach of contract or fiduciary duty in a civil action.[99] Secondly, and quite separately, although in the same proceedings, it was argued by the Attorney-General, this time acting in the general public interest, that the court could exercise a power in the nature of confiscation in criminal proceedings to prevent the defendant from profiting, because the publication was a criminal offence under the Official Secrets Act 1989.[100] Apparently the special status of the Attorney-General meant that both a civil and criminal jurisdiction were open to the court. But only one wrong by the defendant was in issue, namely the wrongful publication of his story. It is understandable that the wrong might have led to both civil proceedings for compensation and criminal proceedings for punishment. It is also understandable that disgorgement, or even punishment, could be administered in civil proceedings rather than criminal proceedings. But it makes no sense for civil disgorgement and criminal confiscation both to be available as alternative measures in a single set of proceedings. This reflects a failure to understand the true relation between civil and criminal justice.

The same failure to appreciate the procedural nature of the division between civil and criminal law is reflected in the identification of a topic of "benefits of crime" as part of the civil law of disgorgement.[101] The assumption here seems to be that crimes are a substantive category of wrong distinct from civil wrongs, so that it is plausible to consider whether disgorgement should be available for this particular type of wrong. The same misconception lies behind the fact that the treatment of disgorgement or "restitution for wrongs" usually makes no reference to punishment or confiscation in criminal law.

Thus the issue of the availability of punitive damages and disgorgement in civil proceedings is complex. The underlying difficulty is the tension between the procedural objection and the desirability of achieving punishment and disgorgement where it is appropriate. Various factors have to be taken into account, including the desirability of achieving punishment as cost-effectively as possible, the importance of safeguards for the defendant against mistaken

---

[98] [1998] 2 WLR 805; Jaffey (1998*d*).

[99] In fact the action was for an injunction to prevent the defendant's publisher from paying over the defendant's profits to him.

[100] Although the defendant had not actually been convicted of an offence.

[101] e.g. Virgo (1999), 556ff.

punishment and double punishment, the desirability of public control over the promotion of the public interest through punishment, and the desirability of uniform treatment of the victims of wrongs, even with respect to windfalls. The question whether disgorgement or punitive damages should be imposed in a particular civil case is not simply a matter of establishing the justice of the case as between the plaintiff and the defendant, as in the standard case of a remedial claim in the common law. It goes further even than recognising the validity of the principle that a wrongdoer should not profit from a wrong. It involves institutional considerations that are difficult for a judge to address in a particular case. A sensible regime can be developed only through legislative provision, based on a proper appreciation of the relation between civil and criminal justice.[102]

CONDITIONS FOR DISGORGEMENT

Aside from the procedural problem, certain other general issues arise in connection with disgorgement.

The nature of benefits subject to disgorgement

In the light of the analysis above, the question what type of benefit should be subject to disgorgement is a practical matter of identifiability or measurability. It is clear, first, that disgorgement should apply to any identifiable wealth in the form of an asset or fund of money acquired through the wrong, as where the defendant is paid £100 for committing an assault, or for supplying drugs. Secondly, it seems reasonable that it should also apply to any reasonably easily quantifiable contribution to the defendant's business, even where there is no wrongfully acquired asset or fund, or "money-making in the strict sense".[103] In many cases of intellectual property infringement, the plaintiff has been awarded an account of profits in the measure of the proportion of the defendant's profits due to the infringement, as, for example, where the defendant constructs a building part of which infringes copyright,[104] or publishes a book aspects of which infringe copyright or are in breach of confidence.[105] Another example is provided by the American case of *Edwards v Lee's Administrators*,[106] where the

---

[102] In this respect, on this analysis, the Law Commission's discussion in Law Commission (1997) was flawed.

[103] *Rookes v Barnard* [1964] AC 1129, 1227 per Lord Devlin, in connection with punitive damages; also Bingham MR in *A.B. v South West Water Services* [1993] QB 507, 529.

[104] e.g. *Potton v Yorkclose* [1990] FSR 11, 16 per Millett J. Also the account seems not to extend to an intangible benefit like an enhanced position in the market: *Redrow Homes v Bett Brothers plc* [1999] AC 197, 209 per Lord Clyde.

[105] As noted by Millett J in *Potton v Yorkclose* [1990] FSR 11, 18.

[106] (1936) 265 Ky 418.

defendant charged people to be shown around a cave that opened onto the defendant's land but extended under the plaintiff's, and was liable to account for a proportion of the profits, assessed on the basis of the contribution made by the part of the cave under the plaintiff's land.[107] In these cases, although the wrong is part of a wider activity, it is reasonably well-defined and the benefit from it reasonably quantifiable. There may be greater difficulty in a case where the wrong consists in failing to meet a general standard for the conduct of an activity or a business that can be carried on legitimately. In principle, here the relevant profit is the defendant's gain relative to his position if he had carried on the activity to the appropriate standard. The measure may be difficult to determine, and this may justify leaving disgorgement and punishment to a criminal court. This might be the position with respect to wrongs like negligence or nuisance, which may also constitute particular criminal offences.[108] Certainly there should not be disgorgement of the whole profit of the activity, which would be an arbitrary response to the wrong, and would be liable to deter people from carrying on legitimate and useful activities.[109]

Indirect benefits

Sometimes a benefit is the indirect product of a wrong. There seems to be no reason in principle why this should affect the liability for disgorgement, provided that causation can be established and the benefit is measurable. The issue has arisen in connection with the indirect or consequential profits of investing the original wrongful receipt. As discussed in Chapter 10 in connection with *A-G for Hong Kong v Reid*,[110] it seems to be thought that a constructive trust rather than an account of profits is necessary to catch such consequential profits. But, whatever the form of liability, the indirect profits through investment are clearly subject to disgorgement.

The disgorgement of indirect profits was considered in passing in *A-G v Guardian Newspapers (No 2) (Spycatcher)*.[111] The defendants were the publishers in the United Kingdom of the memoirs of Wright, an ex-MI5 agent. The original publication abroad had been in breach of Wright's duty of confidentiality to the Crown, but now that the information had been published and was no longer confidential, the House of Lords accepted that the defendants could not be subject to any duty of confidentiality, although they could be liable to account in respect of profits made through disclosures in breach of confidence at the time when the information was still confidential. In passing, Lord Goff

---

[107] In the case of intellectual property infringement or trespass to land, the plaintiff might also have a use claim, in the lesser measure of a reasonable licence fee for use of the plaintiff's property, but it seems that such a claim would not be available in a case like *South West Water*: see Chap. 4 at 151.

[108] e.g. driving, or health and safety, or environmental safety offences.

[109] Cf Birks (1992*b*), 88, discussing *Stoke v Wass* [1988] 3 All ER 394.

[110] [1994] 1 AC 324.

[111] [1990] 1 AC 109.

also considered the position of Wright himself, who was not party to the proceedings.

It had apparently been assumed by the parties to the litigation that Wright remained subject to a duty of confidentiality, although as Lord Goff noted it was no more plausible for him to be subject to such a duty with respect to information that had become public than it was for the defendants, notwithstanding that he had been responsible for the original disclosure. According to Lord Goff, the assumption that Wright remained subject to a continuing obligation of confidence may have been partly induced by the assumption that he would otherwise be free to profit from the continuing sale of his book.[112] But Lord Goff said:

> [I]t is doubtful whether the answer . . . lies in artificially prolonging the duty of confidence in information which is no longer confidential. Indeed, there is some ground for saying that the true answer is that the copyright in the book . . . [is] held by him on constructive trust for the confider, so that the remedy lies not in breach of confidence, but in restitution or in property . . .[113]

Although Lord Goff may not have had this precisely in mind, the claim "in restitution or property", whether by way of forfeiture of copyright or constructive trust, or account, should, on the argument above, be understood to mean a claim for disgorgement of the profits of continuing publication as the indirect profits of the original breach of confidence, rather than disgorgement based on the wrongfulness of continuing publication. The mistaken argument for a continuing duty arose from the failure to recognise the possibility of disgorgement of the indirect benefits of the earlier wrong.

Another case of an indirect profit is where the defendant makes a profit through the publication of the story of his wrongdoing. For example, a criminal may come out of gaol and then be paid by a newspaper for an account of his crime.[114] It seems to be generally assumed that disgorgement cannot extend to cover the profits of publication.[115] Again a distinction has to be drawn between the question whether the criminal has a duty not to publish and the question whether he incurs a liability to disgorge his profits. Generally there will be no duty not to publish, save with respect to a part of the publication that involves a breach of confidence, but the fact that the publication is not wrongful does not mean that there cannot be a liability to account for the profits as the indirect profits of the original wrongdoing. It is difficult to see that the indirect nature of the profit can be an objection in itself, as the examples above show. A bigger problem might appear to be the difficulty of measurement: a well-known

---

[112] At 288.

[113] At 288.

[114] An example considered by Lord Goff in *Spycatcher* [1990] 1 AC 109, 289.

[115] *Spycatcher* [1990] 1 AC 109, at 289 per Lord Goff; cf *A-G v Blake* [1998] 2 WLR 801, 823, where the court appears to confuse the jurisdiction to confiscate profits with the jurisdiction to freeze "proceeds of crime" which is surely concerned with restoring lost property or wealth not disgorgement or confiscation: see Jaffey (1998*d*).

criminal's autobiography might relate to many matters other than his wrong-doing, although presumably the sales will be largely due to the wrongdoing. But it must be common for an autobiography to refer to a legal wrong committed by the author, maybe a minor one, mentioned incidentally, and it is doubtful whether in any such case the author should be liable to surrender some small fraction of the profits of the book. It might seem that to extend disgorgement to the profits of publication of accounts of wrongdoing would involve an exces-sively wide and uncertain rule of disgorgement; but it would surely be possible to develop a rule that confined disgorgement to cases where the wrongdoing is serious and the book is designed to cater principally to interest in the wrongdo-ing or in the author because of his notoriety as a result of the wrongdoing.[116]

The issue is also obliquely relevant to *Attorney-General v Blake*,[117] which was discussed above. It was held that the defendant should forfeit his right to receive the profits of the publication of his book, because publication was in breach of duty to his employer, the Crown, and also contrary to the Official Secrets Act. But it is surely open to doubt whether the publication was prohibited by the Act, and certainly whether it ought to have been, because it did not apparently involve the disclosure of any secret information.[118] The real concern of the Attorney-General and the court was surely that the profits were attributable to the original wrongdoing described in his book. This is implicit in the court's observation that "[i]t is obvious that, if the [defendant] had not been a notori-ous spy who had also dramatically escaped from prison, royalties of this order would never have been paid to him for his autobiography". Furthermore, if the Attorney-General was really concerned that the publication was itself wrongful, it is difficult to see why proceedings were taken against the publishers only as third parties, to stop them from paying over any profits to the defendant, and not in respect of their own profits from complicity in the supposed wrong of publication.[119] But no attention was given to the possibility that the profits could be forfeited as the indirect profits of the original wrongdoing, without the need to show that the publication was itself wrongful.

The relevance of intention

Where disgorgement is in principle available, an important issue is whether it should be subject to a condition that the defendant knew that he was acting wrongfully. Where disgorgement is available on the authorities (either by way of punitive damages or an account of profits or constructive trust), as noted

[116] A further difficulty is likely to be that there may be many different wrongs and victims involved. There are statutory provisions in Australia and the United States that enable the victims of crime to claim the criminal's profits from marketing his account of the crime: see e.g. Okunda (1985).

[117] [1998] 2 WLR 805.

[118] See Jaffey (1998d).

[119] As in *Spycatcher* [1990] 1 AC 109.

above the usual position seems to be that knowledge is a requirement.[120] The issue is analogous to the question whether knowledge or intention, or a "mens rea", is a prerequisite of a criminal offence, or, in other words, of punishment, the infliction of punishment being the objective of the criminal process. This question is of course controversial in criminal law. Normally mens rea is required for serious offences, but there are many minor offences that do not have any such requirement. Although full punishment should at least sometimes be precluded by the absence of knowledge, it is difficult to see why in principle the defendant should ever profit from a wrong, whether or not he knew or suspected that he was committing it. However, if disgorgement is applied without a requirement for intention it is all the more important that the measure be strictly confined to the actual profit of the wrong, for example with respect to activities that can be carried on legitimately. There would otherwise be a risk of suppressing the activity altogether.[121]

The innocent donee of wrongful profits

It appears that someone who profits from a wrong without having committed it cannot be subject to disgorgement; this would cover the earnings of crime journalists or legal writers. But where a wrongdoer makes a profit from his wrongdoing and makes a gift of it to someone else, the donee should surely be subject to disgorgement.[122] This might be thought to present a problem for the argument that disgorgement is an aspect of punishment, because the donee is not himself guilty of any wrong. One might say that the profits received by the wrongdoer and passed on by him are tainted because they came through a "corrupt, polluted channel";[123] but this is more of a figure of speech than a justification. The true reason is surely that removing the benefit from the person to whom the wrongdoer gave it is an aspect of the punishment of the wrongdoer. One of the benefits of wealth is the power to dispense it, and making donees liable to surrender such receipts denies the wrongdoer this power with respect to his wrongful profit. However, the donee should be protected with respect to any change of position and a purchaser for value should be fully protected.[124]

---

[120] Other than where disgorgement arises under the no-conflict rule for fiduciaries, as considered in Chap. 13. In connection with punitive damages, the requirement is said to be for a profit motive, but this means intending to obtain a profit by deliberately acting wrongfully. The Law Commission also recommends that disgorgement should be available, along with punitive damages, in the case of a "deliberate and outrageous disregard of the plaintiff's rights": Law Commission (1997), para. 3.49.

[121] See above at 383–4.

[122] This is the position with respect to confiscation orders: Criminal Justice Act 1988, s.74(1)(b). See also Hodgson, 126.

[123] *Bridgeman v Green* (1757) Wilm 58, at 65, 97 ER 22, at 25 per Lord Commissioner Wilmot, cited by Virgo (1999), 557. Although the phrase is apt, in this case the claim was not actually for disgorgement but for restitution in respect of a transfer vitiated by undue influence.

[124] As argued by Hodgson (1984), 126.

12

Disgorgement for Breach of Contract

THE LEGAL RESPONSE TO BREACH OF CONTRACT

T HE RULE IS said to be that no disgorgement or punitive damages are available for a breach of contract.[1] In English law, this might be understood to reflect the procedural objection discussed in the last chapter.[2] But other factors suggest that there are additional reasons for disallowing disgorgement for breach of contract. There are cases where disgorgement or punitive damages have been awarded for torts, but not for breach of contract. Many torts are also crimes and attract punishment by that means, but a breach of contract is not a crime. In the United States and other countries where punitive damages are generally available for a deliberate tort, they are not generally available for a breach of contract.[3]

This is ostensibly anomalous, at least according to the classical theory of contract (as explained in Chapter 2), under which the contracting parties are understood to be subject to a duty to perform as agreed. Non-performance is a breach of duty, and should therefore attract disgorgement, at least where the breach was deliberate. The same anomaly appears to arise with respect to an order to perform a contract: an injunction, although said to be discretionary, will invariably be granted to prevent the commission of a tort if it is possible to do so, and yet for contract specific performance is available only exceptionally.[4] The implication appears to be that there is a systematic shortfall in the enforcement of the law of contract as compared with the law of tort. There have accordingly been calls for the wider availability of specific performance and disgorgement or punitive damages for breach of contract.[5] However, even then the calls tend to be for disgorgement for egregious cases of breach of contract,[6] and do not seem

---

[1] *Tito v Wadell (No 2)* [1977] Ch 106; *Surrey CC v Bredero* [1993] 1 WLR 1361; *Addis v Gramophone Company Ltd* [1909] AC 488. As discussed in Chap. 11, the position of disgorgement is comparable to that for punitive damages.

[2] The procedural objection seems to be behind the rule against enforcing penalty clauses: Chap. 11 at n 75. There seems to be no clear authority on the enforceability of a "disgorgement clause". *Reid Newfoundland Co. v Anglo-American Telegraph Co Ltd* [1912] AC 555 (discussed Birks (1987), 433) might suggest that such a clause is valid, but the clause in that case appears to have provided for a liability to account in respect of a permitted activity, not disgorgement for a prohibited activity.

[3] See e.g. Linzer (1981); Sebert (1986); see below 395–6.

[4] As discussed in Chap. 2 at 34.

[5] See, e.g. Jones (1983); Birks (1987); L.D. Smith (1994), 135–40; Friedmann (1989); Fried (1981), 17–21; McBride (1995).

[6] e.g. Birks (1987) argues that disgorgement should be available for a "cynical" breach of contract.

to envisage that all breaches of contract, even deliberate breaches, should attract disgorgement, or that a breach of contract should generally be treated in the same way as a tort.[7] Sometimes it has been suggested that disgorgement should be available in circumstances where specific performance would have been granted.[8] This makes sense because both should arise where there is a duty to perform[9]; but the classical theory suggests that there is always a duty to perform. The apparent anomaly in the legal response to breach of contract has prompted many different analyses, some of which will be discussed briefly below.

THE POSITION UNDER THE RELIANCE THEORY

Breach of contractual duty or wrongful non-performance

The explanation preferred here is in terms of the reliance theory of contract as set out in Chapter 2.[10] On this approach, an agreement generally consists of the assumption of responsibility for reliance on the expectation of the specified performance, not promises of performance. Consequently there is generally no duty to perform and no ground for compelling performance or imposing disgorgement for non-performance as a wrong.[11] Sometimes, however, the assumption of responsibility for reliance will generate a duty of performance, on the ground that actual performance is the only way of satisfying the reliance interest. This is the basis for the rule that specific performance is available if damages are inadequate.[12] In principle disgorgement should be available according to the same criterion,[13] at least where the breach was deliberate. A deliberate breach means here a breach committed in the knowledge that the plaintiff is dependent on performance because of the loss that he will otherwise incur.[14] This is not the recognised rule in English law, but there is some support for it, in addition to the theoretical arguments; and recently the Court of Appeal suggested that disgorgement should be available for breach of contract where "compensatory damages are an inadequate remedy if regard is paid to the

---

[7] An exception is McBride (1995), who takes the classical theory to its logical conclusion.

[8] Law Commission (1993), paras. 7.19–21; Beatson (1991), 16–17; Waddams (1991), 209.

[9] Although it is not clear that this is why the analogy between specific performance and disgorgement has been made. Beatson and the Law Commission take the view that disgorgement represents the cost of specific performance to the defendant, or is "monetised specific performance". Disgorgement represents the cost of specific performance where the defendant's profit from non-performance is his saving from non-performance, but not where it is a profit made from a third party through a breach of contract. With respect to Waddams, see below at 394–5.

[10] There is no discussion here of the position under other versions of the reliance theory, e.g. as in Raz (1982), or the death of contract theory as discussed in Chap. 3.

[11] One way by which it might be inferred that a contract is intended to create a duty is if there is a penalty clause; but penalty clauses are not enforceable.

[12] See Chap. 2.

[13] Subject to the procedural justice objection considered in the last chapter.

[14] See below at n 19.

objects which the plaintiff sought to achieve by the contract".[15] This is consistent with the reliance theory, and it is not clear what other basis it might have.

Examples of contractual duty

Various types of case where the defendant incurs a duty of performance were considered in connection with specific performance in Chapter 2. The cases where disgorgement is appropriate are similar cases, where specific performance is no longer possible and the uncompensatable damage has been inflicted and cannot be properly remedied.

Fiduciary relationships

There is one very clear category of contract where the defendant has a duty to perform because of the inadequacy of damages, and disgorgement is in fact routinely imposed: this is where the contractual relationship is fiduciary. Fiduciary relationships raise particular questions, however, and indeed are generally thought not to be merely a type of contractual relationship. They are dealt with separately in the next chapter.

Dependence on source of supply

Where the plaintiff has carried on business in reliance on a contract for supplies from the defendant that cannot be obtained from elsewhere, the defendant will incur a duty to supply. Damages are inadequate because there is no substitute performance that damages would enable the plaintiff to procure. If the defendant fails to perform in such circumstances, he should be liable to punitive damages or disgorgement in respect of any profit he makes as a result of the breach of contract.

An illustration is provided by *Seaman's Direct Buying Service v Standard Oil*,[16] a decision of the Supreme Court of California on punitive damages. The essence of the case was that the defendant had contracted to supply oil to the plaintiff, and had then failed to supply it in circumstances that, to its knowledge, meant that the plaintiff's business would fail because it could not obtain supplies from any other company. As it was subsequently put by Mosk J in *Freeman & Mills v Belcher*,[17] a later decision of the Supreme Court of California:

because of the unusual combination of market forces and government regulation . . . [the defendant's] conduct had a significance beyond the ordinary breach: its practical

---

[15] *A-G v Blake* [1998] 2 WLR 805, at 819; Jaffey (1998d).
[16] 686 P.2d 1158 (Cal. 1984) A similar English case, which concerned specific performance rather than disgorgement, is *Sky Petroleum Ltd v VIP Petroleum Ltd* [1974] 1 WLR 576.
[17] 900 P.2d 669 (Cal. 1995).

effect was to shut [the plaintiff] out of the oil market entirely, forcing it out of business.[18]

It was not possible for the plaintiff to make alternative arrangements to obtain supplies, and damages could not feasibly compensate for the complete loss of the business. Mosk J went on to argue that punitive damages should be imposed where:

> a party intentionally breaches a contractual obligation with neither probable cause nor belief that the obligation does *not* exist *and* when the party intends or knows that the breach will result in severe consequential damages to the other party that are not readily subject to mitigation, and such harm in fact occurs.[19]

This is consistent with the analysis in terms of assumption of responsibility for the reliance interest of the other party.

Negative obligations

Another type of case where disgorgement should be available on the same analysis is where the defendant's performance is negative, i.e. the contract specifies that he will refrain from doing something. Where performance is negative, damages are generally inadequate because, in contrast to the usual case of positive performance, it is not possible to find someone else to provide substitute performance. The plaintiff contracted with the defendant for the very reason that the defendant was in a special position by virtue of which he could do something that might harm the plaintiff, which the plaintiff wanted him to refrain from doing, and it is not possible for anyone to do this on behalf of the defendant. An example of negative performance is provided by *Reading v Attorney-General*,[20] in which the defendant, an army sergeant, took a bribe in return for using his uniform to assist smugglers to avoid discovery, and was held liable to disgorge the bribe to his employer, the Crown. Clearly the Crown's reliance on the defendant could only feasibly be satisfied by fulfilment of the negative contractual duty to refrain from using his uniform for personal profit.[21]

Another example of negative performance is where the defendant acquires information in the course of performing a contract with the plaintiff—say an employment contract—and the contract specifies that, say, the defendant is not to publish it or use it outside his work. Here the plaintiff becomes dependent on the defendant as a result of taking him into employment and allowing him access to the information, because the defendant's contractual performance in this respect cannot be carried out by anyone else. Thus the defendant incurs a

---

[18] At 689.
[19] Ibid.
[20] [1951] AC 507.
[21] The plaintiff and defendant are reversed. The court said that the defendant was a fiduciary of the Crown, but, as suggested in Chap. 13, this was really a fiction.

duty to comply with the contractual restriction. In *Attorney-General v Blake*,[22] the defendant had published information gleaned from his time in the secret service, contrary to his employment contract, and the court suggested obiter that disgorgement should be available for breach of contract in such a case. More generally, it said, disgorgement should be available where "the defendant has obtained his benefit by doing the very thing which he contracted not to do".[23]

A further example of failure of negative performance is breach of a restrictive covenant.[24] Here the plaintiff has incurred reliance, typically by transferring property to the defendant, on the understanding that (inter alia) the restrictive covenant entered into by the defendant will be observed. Again, only the defendant can provide the performance in question, and damages will not enable the plaintiff to arrange for substitute performance. Thus generally the defendant will incur a duty to comply with the covenant, and a deliberate breach should attract disgorgement of any profit made through the breach.[25] Where the issue has arisen, however, there is clearly some confusion between the use claim and disgorgement. In *Wrotham Park v Parkside Homes*,[26] one reason for awarding damages was that the defendants should not be left "in undisturbed possession of the fruits of their wrongdoing"; and yet the damages did not cover the whole of the defendants' profit, but merely a small proportion, measured as if it were a licence fee.

Contracts to reduce a risk of harm

Another situation where disgorgement is appropriate is illustrated by another American case, *City of New Orleans v Firemen's Charitable Association*.[27] Here the defendant had contracted to provide certain safeguards against fire damage, but it had failed to provide all the safeguards specified. Fortunately for the parties, although the plaintiff was subject to a greater risk of loss than it would have been if the contract had been performed as specified, the risk did not materialise into any actual loss, and so there was no claim for compensation.[28] The

---

[22] [1998] 2 WLR 805.

[23] At 818. Where the information is confidential, disgorgement through an account of profits is available because the action for breach of confidence arises in equity, as noted in the previous chapter, and this is so whether the obligation of confidence arises by contract or otherwise; but it seems that, as in *A-G v Blake*, a contract can sometimes impose an obligation in respect of information that is not strictly confidential.

[24] Cf the discussion of the use claim in connection with restrictive covenants in Chap. 4.

[25] This is subject to the oppression rule discussed in connection with restrictive covenants in Chap. 4.

[26] [1974] 2 All ER 321, 339, per Brightman J.

[27] (1891) 9 So 486; discussed in *A-G v Blake* [1998] 2 WLR 805, 818. The court in *Blake* characterised *City of New Orleans* as a case of "skimped performance", where "the defendant fails to provide the full extent of services which he has contracted to provide and for which he has charged the plaintiff"; but this seems to describe an ordinary breach of contract, and not to identify what was distinctive about *City of New Orleans*.

[28] In any case it would not be easy to prove that such a loss would not have occurred if additional precautions had been taken.

defendant was, however, forced to disgorge the profit it had made in the form of the amount it had saved by not performing as agreed. Where the defendant's contractual performance is designed to obviate a risk to the plaintiff, he has a duty of performance. By definition, only performance and not damages in lieu will satisfy the plaintiff's reliance interest, because the purpose of the contract is to reduce or eliminate the risk, not to obtain insurance to cover the loss caused if the risk materialises.

The rule prescribed by the reliance theory

The recognised rule in English law is that disgorgement is not available for breach of contract. But the discussion above shows that there is some support for the rule prescribed by the reliance theory, that disgorgement is appropriate where the defendant has not performed a contract in circumstances where the plaintiff is dependent on him for performance, in the sense that he is liable to suffer uncompensatable reliance loss as a result of non-performance. This means, in other words, that disgorgement should be available where the defendant committed a breach in circumstances where specific performance would in principle have been available. In practice, the most common example of such circumstances is where the contractual relationship is a fiduciary relationship, where disgorgement is in fact recognised as available. If, as argued in the next chapter, fiduciary relationships are merely a category of contractual relationship, it is clear that disgorgement is available in principle for breach of contract and should be awarded in other cases where it is justified on the same grounds.

OTHER ANALYSES OF THE LEGAL RESPONSE TO BREACH OF CONTRACT

Many other analyses have been offered, in the literature and in the case law, to explain the apparent shortfall in the legal response to breach of contract, including the absence of disgorgement or punitive damages.[29]

Contractual rights as property rights

Waddams argues that disgorgement should be available in just those cases where specific performance is in principle available, because, he suggests, "[i]t may usefully be said . . . that the plaintiff has a proprietary interest in the promised performance", and disgorgement should be available either on the basis that "the defendant has derived profit from the plaintiff's property", or that "the plaintiff has been deprived of her right to bargain for the sale of her

---

[29] A recent such analysis not discussed here is offered in S.A. Smith (1997*b*).

interest", and that this right is worth the amount the plaintiff would have charged the defendant for permission not to perform.[30] One might interpret this, first, as an argument for a use claim rather than disgorgement for non-performance of a contract.[31] Alternatively, it is surely true, as argued above, that the availability of disgorgement and specific performance should correspond, because both should arise where the defendant has a duty to perform. But it is unhelpful to say that this is because the plaintiff has a proprietary right. Waddams uses "property" to refer to a right of the plaintiff that corresponds to a duty, as opposed to a right that corresponds to a primary liability.[32] Thus it is implicit in the argument that a contracting party does not always incur a duty of performance, but Waddams gives no explanation of why or when this should be, which is the crucial issue.

Contract and tort: the voluntary nature of contract

Another suggestion is that disgorgement and punitive damages are inappropriate for breach of contract because contractual obligations are voluntary, rather than arising under the general law.[33] This argument is difficult to follow, because it is not clear why the fact that an obligation arose from the exercise of a power to subject oneself to an obligation rather than under the general law means that a breach of the obligation should attract a lesser response from the law. An American judge, Kozinski J, put the objection in this way, in rejecting punitive damages for breach of contract:

> Perhaps the most troubling, the willingness of courts to subordinate voluntary contractual arrangements to their own sense of public policy and proper business decorum deprives individuals of an important measure of freedom. The right to enter into contracts—to adjust one's legal relationships by mutual agreement . . . is too easily smothered by government officers [sc judges] eager to tell us what's best for us.[34]

But this is a perverse response to the breach of a contractual duty. Freedom to contract free of legal constraint is hardly the same thing as—indeed it is opposed to—freedom to breach a contract without legal constraint. A breach of contractual duty is contrary to what the parties agreed, and to impose punitive damages for it is to uphold freedom of contract, not to curtail it, because it gives legal effect to what was freely agreed.[35] Again the crucial issue is what the parties have agreed, and whether it has generated duties of performance.

---

[30] Waddams (1991), 208–9.

[31] Cf Chap. 4 at 138–40.

[32] See Appendix 1.

[33] Law Commission (1997), paras. 5.70–72.

[34] *Oki America, Inc v Microtech Intern Inc* 872 F.2d 312, 316 (9th Cir.1989).

[35] One might say it upholds sanctity of contract rather than freedom of contract, but freedom to determine the terms of contracting presupposes the sanctity of the contract as agreed.

Kozinski J's view may be explicable in terms of the way in which punitive damages for breach of contract have been rationalised in the United States. Punitive damages are generally available for "bad faith" or deliberate torts, but there has been great controversy over their availability for breach of contract.[36] Where punitive damages have been allowed for breach of contract, they seem to have been based on treating a breach of contract as a tort or "tortious breach of contract" in order to take advantage of the established power to impose punitive damages in tort.[37] Thus it has been argued that in committing the breach of contract the defendant also breached an extra-contractual or tortious duty to comply with a certain standard of business ethics. The judge's indignation seems to have been at the introduction into the contract of a duty to comply with a standard of business ethics that was not derived from the contract as agreed by the parties.[38] Whether a contract should be subject to mandatory rules that override the agreed terms can of course be controversial, although it is surely common in American law as it is in English law. But the imposition of a mandatory term is not the issue in relation to punitive damages. The supposed extra-contractual duty of business ethics is in reality a duty to comply with the terms of the contract, which in fact adds nothing to the contractual duty to perform. Thus the claim for punitive damages arises from a breach of the contract, which will generally be a term actually agreed by the parties. The idea that punitive damages for breach of a duty to perform a contract are really for a breach of a tortious duty is a fiction, adopted to enable punitive damages to be imported from tort, and the judge's objection shows that he was deceived by it.[39]

The need for certainty

It has been argued that the need for certainty in contract makes punitive damages inappropriate, because punitive damages involve the exercise of a discretion.[40] The implication appears to be that a contracting party should be able to assess his likely liability and then work out whether it is worth his while to breach the duty. Now, where the defendant has no duty to perform a contract, it is legitimate for him to work out his potential liability in compensation and then decide whether it is in his interests to perform.[41] But the law should not be designed to allow a contracting party to assess whether it is worth his while to break a duty; to the contrary, it is at least part of the function of punitive damages, and, with less efficacy, of disgorgement, to ensure that it is never worth-

---

[36] See e.g. Sebert (1986).

[37] See Chutorian (1986).

[38] 872 F.2d 312, at 315.

[39] The subterfuge is equivalent to that of characterising a breach of contract as fiduciary for the same purpose: see Chap. 13 at 413–14.

[40] Law Commission (1997), para. 5.72; Steyn LJ in *Surrey County Council v Bredero* [1993] 3 All ER 705, 717.

[41] i.e. where there is a primary right–liability relation: see Appendix 1.

while to do this. Thus the uncertainty in the measure of punitive damages is not objectionable in this sense.[42]

However, under the reliance theory a contracting party may well be faced with a significant problem of uncertainty about whether a contractual duty has arisen. This is of course liable to be the source of dispute and litigation. If punitive damages are available for a breach of duty, a contracting party is liable to perform in circumstances in which he is not strictly required to, from fear of the possibility that they will be imposed in any event. This may even tend to discourage people from making contracts at all because they cannot be sure that a contract on the terms that they are willing to accept will be enforced as such. In other words, in imposing punitive damages, "courts must be cautious not to fashion remedies which overdeter the illegitimate and as a result chill legitimate activities".[43]

Uncertainty of this sort is not of course confined to contract—for example, there is liable to be some uncertainty in determining whether the defendant has acted unreasonably so as to be in breach of a duty of care in tort, and, on the same basis, this might discourage people from undertaking legitimate activities in the course of which a tort might inadvertently be committed. For breach of contract or for tort, the uncertainty may be reduced to some extent by the requirement of intention or knowledge of the uncompensatable damage.[44] The "chilling" effect of such uncertainty may also be smaller if the breach of a duty is punished only through civil proceedings, so that the extra stigma of criminal punishment is avoided.[45] Also it will be smaller if there is some reassurance that punitive damages will not be excessive; thus the risk of "overdeterrence" is presumably much less for disgorgement than punitive damages. But, in any case, this uncertainty does not justify excluding punitive damages or disgorgement, because, even if the legal position would be more certain, the absence of punitive damages or disgorgement would mean that a contracting party who is owed a duty of performance would be inadequately protected. This can also have a chilling effect, because contracting parties may be less likely to make a contract on terms that make them dependent on the other party, because of the risk of inadequate enforcement.

The economic theory of efficient breach

The most widely discussed attempt to explain the apparent shortfall in the legal response to breach of contract is the economic theory of efficient breach,[46]

---

[42] But a difficulty remains in settling proceedings if the measure of punitive damages is unpredictable, which is a difficulty with punishment in civil proceedings. The objection would not apply with respect to disgorgement, which has a reasonably determinate measure.

[43] *Freeman & Mills v Belcher* 900 P.2d 669, 684 (Cal. 1995).

[44] Cf Chap. 11 at 387.

[45] Chap. 11 at 380.

[46] See e.g. Posner (1992), 117–19; Cooter & Ulen (1997), 219; cf O'Dair (1993).

which has received some judicial recognition in the United States.[47] The efficient breach hypothesis seeks to account for the general absence of disgorgement, punitive damages and specific performance on the basis of efficiency, or "wealth maximisation". A contract is a means by which wealth is increased because it enables each party to receive something that he or she values more highly than whatever it is he or she has to do in return, so the net effect is to increase wealth (defined as what people are willing and able to pay for).[48] On the economic approach, the legal enforceability of contracts is justified because their performance increases aggregate wealth, and the rules of contract law should be designed to promote the practice of contracting and its wealth maximising function.

In general, the performance of a contract as agreed will maximise wealth; but sometimes it may happen that, in the light of circumstances that have arisen after the contract was made, wealth will be maximised by applying resources in a manner contrary to that specified in the contract. For example, where a supplier has contracted to provide a benefit to a recipient, and it now appears that a third party values the benefit more highly than the recipient, or that it will be more costly for the supplier to perform than it would be for another person who is offering the recipient an equivalent benefit, it seems that efficiency requires that the supplier should not perform, but simply pay compensation instead. The compensation will allow the recipient to procure the same performance from someone else, so that he is no worse off, and the supplier will be better off than if he had performed, because he can make more by providing the same benefit to someone else, or because the compensation he has to pay is less than what it would have cost him to perform. Thus Posner J has said:

> Even if the breach is deliberate, it is not necessarily blameworthy. The promisor may simply have discovered that his performance is worth more to someone else. If so, efficiency is promoted by allowing him to break his promise, provided he makes good the promisee's actual losses. If he is forced to pay more than that, an efficient breach may be deterred, and the law doesn't want to bring about such a result.[49]

The position is more complex than this, however, because even if the supplier can be compelled to perform by court order or threat of punishment, if he wants to avoid performing it is still open to him to negotiate with the recipient for a release from performance. Clearly the recipient is favoured by an arrangement by which a release is required, because he can ensure that he is properly compensated before granting the release, and he may also be able to negotiate for a share of the profit made by the supplier through non-performance. By contrast, in the other case, where the supplier does not need a release and simply chooses

---

[47] e.g. *Freeman & Mills v Belcher* 900 P 2d 669, 682 (Cal. 1995); *Patton v Mid-Continent Systems* 841 F 2d 742 (7th Cir. 1988), 750; see also Law Commission (1997), paras. 5.70–72.

[48] Wealth here does not correspond to "transferable value", as elsewhere in this book.

[49] *Patton v Mid-Continent Systems* 841 F 2d 742 (7th Cir. 1988), 750. It is of course the same Posner who is quoted non-judicially above.

not to perform and to incur liability for compensation, the recipient bears the risk of an inaccurate assessment of due compensation by the court and has no prospect of sharing in any profit made by the supplier. But it seems that either legal position could produce an efficient outcome, according to which the supplier does not perform when it is not efficient for him to do so.[50] In fact, the question which legal rule is more efficient will turn on the extent of "transaction costs" in either case, i.e. the cost of negotiating a release from performance, and the costs of negotiating a settlement with respect to the compensation due to the recipient, or of litigating over it where no release is required. It is far from easy to say which position is likely to generate lower transaction costs,[51] but in theory on the economic approach the court should choose the appropriate legal response according to its best judgment of this issue.[52]

There is, first, an apparent contradiction in the efficient breach hypothesis that arises from the way in which it is customarily expressed. It seems that commentators have assumed for the purposes of the economic analysis that a contract generates mutual obligations of performance, in accordance with the classical model—this is implicit in the quotation from Posner J above. But it is surely inconsistent to argue both that the parties have made an agreement by which one of them has incurred an obligation to perform and also that that party may breach the obligation without being compelled to perform or being treated as if he had acted wrongfully by the imposition of punitive damages or disgorgement.[53] This is not to be dismissed as mere semantics, because the very basis of the economic approach is that the law of contract should promote the confidence of contractors in the practice of contracting, and whether the law bolsters or undermines this confidence depends on the true nature of the understanding of contracting parties and whether the response of the law to non-performance is consistent with it. This is not a point against the substance of the economic theory, but about the misleading way in which it has been expressed in terms of the classical theory.

[50] Cooter & Ulen (1997), 217. This is an application of the "Coase theorem", according to which the efficient outcome will always be reached by agreement if there is no impediment to negotiation. See also L. D. Smith (1994). Whether the rule favours the supplier rather than the recipient or vice versa is a matter of distribution of wealth and not aggregate wealth.

[51] Macneil (1982). Different commentators have used this approach to reach different judgments of what is likely to be efficient: see Cooter & Ulen (1997), 219–20, who argue that, if the court judges that it would be easy for the parties to negotiate, specific performance should be awarded, because this will secure the promisee's right to full compensation whilst still allowing for the exploitation of new opportunities, and in other cases damages should be awarded because although the promisee will take the risk of undercompensation this is outweighed by the value of preserving the promisor's freedom to exploit new opportunities.

[52] Strictly, it seems that the court should adopt the rule that the parties would have chosen if they had addressed the issue—i.e. on the basis of hypothetical contracting—which in theory is the same rule, because the parties would choose the rule that minimises aggregate costs. Cases where disgorgement is appropriate are cases where the parties would have agreed on disgorgement, because of the difficulties in determining the compensation and the risk of undercompensation.

[53] This is the basis of the argument in Friedmann (1989); L.D. Smith (1994). To put it another way, in terms of hypothetical contracting, one cannot plausibly say that the parties would have agreed on a term that is implicitly inconsistent with what they have actually agreed.

Instead, one might argue that the economic theory should be understood not to explain why the parties are free to breach their obligations, but why the parties make assumptions of responsibility rather than promises, so that their non-performance is not generally wrongful.[54] It is no doubt true that because contracting parties will generally agree terms that promote their interests, a legal response that reflects the parties' expectations will appear to be justified by a criterion of wealth maximisation. If the parties judge it to be in their interests so far as possible to avoid binding commitments as to their future behaviour, they will generally reach understandings in the form of assumptions of responsibilities rather than promises. But this does not mean that giving effect to what the parties have agreed is justified in terms of wealth maximisation rather than fairness to the parties who made the agreement in these terms and acted in reliance on it.[55]

[54] This is consistent with Posner's description of a breach as not blameworthy: above at n 49. An alternative might be to understand the theory to envisage the parties as constructing a set of incentives and disincentives for each other, in the form of the legal response to performance or non-performance, rather than any sort of normative regime. But this is implausible as an interpretation of how parties understand their agreement, because contracting parties think in terms of a normative relationship. Also it makes no sense of the fact that agreements can be made without any reference to the law.

[55] And an evaluation of wealth maximisation may give a good indication of what the parties did or might have agreed. Hypothetical contracting is surely as justifiable on the basis that it is fair as on the basis that it is wealth maximising.

13

Fiduciary Relationships

INTRODUCTION

THE PRINCIPAL SIGNIFICANCE of fiduciary relationships is that a breach of fiduciary duty generates a claim to disgorgement, in the form of an account of profits or constructive trust. Thus fiduciary relationships are dealt with here, although they also raise other issues relating to restitution.[1]

The nature of a fiduciary relationship is notoriously controversial. Many types of relationship are recognised to be (at least prima facie) fiduciary: for example, trustee–beneficiary, director–company, agent–principal, partner–partner, solicitor–client. But there is no exhaustive list of fiduciary relationships. There must presumably be a definable concept of a fiduciary relationship to justify the uniform treatment of these various types of relationship, but despite many suggestions the issue remains unsettled. What is reasonably clear is that a fiduciary relationship has the following features.[2] First, in a fiduciary relationship the fiduciary has a duty to his principal to advance the principal's interests, in so far as they relate to the subject matter of the relationship, at the expense, if necessary, of his own interests.[3] This will be referred to as the fiduciary duty, although it is often described as a duty of loyalty or a duty of good faith.[4] The fiduciary duty may require the fiduciary to refrain from undertaking ventures on his own or someone else's behalf that would damage the principal's interests.[5] Secondly, the principal is entitled to claim any profit made by the fiduciary in breach of duty, and is not limited to claiming compensation for loss caused by the breach of duty.[6] Thirdly, the fiduciary is subject to the "no-conflict rule", which makes him liable to the principal for the value of any benefit acquired by him from a position in which there was a reasonable possibility of a conflict between his own interests and his fiduciary duty, and renders unenforceable by him any contract with the principal made when the fiduciary was in such a

---

[1] Cf Chap. 8 at 262–3 and Chap. 10 at 334–7.

[2] These seem to be found in most treatments of the fiduciary relationship.

[3] e.g. *Bristol and West Building Society v Mothew* [1998] Ch 1; Hayton (1996), 333; Millett (1998), 219–20; this is the first of three categories of fiduciary relationship identified by Millett, the others being relationships of confidentiality and relationships of undue influence; but it would be more helpful to say that only the first is truly a fiduciary relationship: see below at 413–14 and n 50.

[4] In the sense adopted here the fiduciary duty encompasses what are distinguished in company law as the duty of good faith, the duty of care, and the duty to pursue the right objectives or purposes (the proper purposes rule).

[5] *Bray v Ford* [1896] AC 44; see e.g. Meagher, Gummow & Lehane (1992), para. 501.

[6] e.g. *Boardman v Phipps* [1967] 2 AC 46; Meagher, Gummow & Lehane (1992), para. 549.

position, even if the principal cannot prove that the fiduciary actually acted contrary to his fiduciary duty by acting against the principal's interests.[7] There is some variation in the way in which these rules are expressed; the justification for the formulation adopted here will emerge below.

THE FIDUCIARY RELATIONSHIP AS A CONTRACTUAL RELATIONSHIP UNDER THE RELIANCE THEORY

The fiduciary relationship is sometimes defined in terms of the features of the relationship set out above.[8] Thus it is offered as a definition of a fiduciary relationship that it is a relationship in which one party "is subject to a duty of loyalty to another",[9] or, to put it another way, in which one party "is entitled to expect that [the other party] will act in [the first party's interest] to the exclusion of his own".[10] This is true as a description of a fiduciary relationship but is flawed as a definition because it provides no basis for determining when such a relationship arises or why. It is liable to give rise to a circular argument: there is a fiduciary relationship when there is a duty of loyalty, and a duty of loyalty arises when the relationship is fiduciary.[11] The same objection lies against the suggestion that a fiduciary relationship is a relationship generating a duty the breach of which attracts the response of disgorgement.[12] Again this is true but trivial because it gives no indication of how to determine whether a relationship is fiduciary and so should attract disgorgement.[13]

The distinctive feature of a fiduciary contract

It seems clear that a fiduciary relationship is a form of agreement between the principal and the fiduciary, by which the fiduciary "undertakes or agrees to act for or on behalf of" the principal.[14] The issue is how to distinguish an agreement that constitutes a fiduciary relationship from other agreements, which are treated as ordinary contracts, and to explain the distinct rules that apply in the case of a fiduciary relationship. It seems that the characteristic feature of a fidu-

---

[7] *Boardman v Phipps* [1967] 2 AC 46; Meagher, Gummow & Lehane (1992), para. 549.

[8] There have been many attempts to provide a definition of a fiduciary relationship: see e.g. the discussions in Shepherd (1981) and Easterbrook & Fischel (1993). These various theories will not be considered here.

[9] Waters (1964), 4; and above n 3.

[10] Finn (1992), 9.

[11] Weinrib (1975), 5; Easterbrook & Fischel (1993), 435.

[12] "[A fiduciary relationship] is one in respect of which . . . the same remedy exists . . . as would exist against a trustee": Re *West of England and South Wales District Bank ex p Dale & Co* (1879) 11 Ch D 772, 778 per Fry J.

[13] Weinrib (1975), 5; Easterbrook & Fischel (1993), 435. See below at n 62.

[14] As it was put in *Hospital Products Ltd v United States Corporation* (1984) 156 CLR 41, 96 per Mason J; cf *Bristol and West Building Society v Mothew* [1998] Ch 1, 18 per Millet LJ.

ciary agreement is that it requires the fiduciary to carry out a general task on behalf of the plaintiff involving the exercise of judgement as to how to carry out the task in the way that will best serve the principal's interests in circumstances that cannot be known in advance.[15] This might be, for example, managing the principal's property, or his investments, or his business, or acting as his agent or conducting his litigation. The agreement cannot specify what the fiduciary's performance is, beyond stipulating that it consists of acting in the principal's best interests in relation to the subject matter in question, and this will normally go without saying, as a term implicit in their agreement.[16]

The reliance theory in the form advanced in Chapter 2 shows why this type of agreement receives special treatment. Under the reliance theory, the fiduciary assumes responsibility for the principal's reliance on the understanding that the fiduciary will provide performance in the form of advancing the principal's interests. The principal acts in reliance by transferring power to the fiduciary or by refraining from taking other measures to protect his interests. Here, because of the difficulty in specifying the fiduciary's performance it is difficult to estimate the expectation measure or otherwise to protect the reliance interest of the principal by compensation. Consequently, as discussed in connection with specific performance, the fiduciary's assumption of responsibility generates a duty of performance. This duty of performance is the duty to promote the principal's best interests with respect to the matters entrusted to the fiduciary—viz. the fiduciary duty. By contrast, under the classical theory a duty of performance arises out of all agreements and no sense can be given to the distinction between the fiduciary relationship where there is invariably such a duty and the ordinary case where there is not. In connection with a breach of fiduciary duty, however, specific performance will be beside the point. The principal's grievance will normally be that the duty has already been broken by the fiduciary in the way he has carried out his responsibilities so far, and it will not be possible for the fiduciary now retrospectively to perform them as they ought to have been performed. Thus the main significance of the duty here is that a breach of the duty can generate a response of disgorgement. This is the why the distinctive feature of breach of fiduciary duty is that the principal is entitled to claim the benefit received by the fiduciary, not merely compensation.

There are two other distinct grounds for allowing the principal a claim to the fiduciary's profit in some cases of breach of fiduciary duty.[17] First, it is often true of a fiduciary position that it involves procuring benefits for the principal, say by investment or contracting, and so may well give the fiduciary the opportunity to make benefits for himself instead. Sometimes where the fiduciary makes a profit for himself through a breach of duty he ought instead in accordance with his duty to have made it for the principal. Where this is the case the principal can

---

[15] Easterbrook & Fischel (1993).

[16] "When one party hires the other party's knowledge and expertise, there is not much they can write down": Easterbrook & Fischel (1993), 426.

[17] See also Chap. 8 at 262–3.

claim that the fiduciary's profit is also his own loss resulting from the fiduciary's breach of duty, and that the claim in respect of the fiduciary's benefit is a compensatory claim.[18] The compensatory analysis will be unavailable where, although the fiduciary committed a breach of duty in not attempting to procure the opportunity for the principal, in fact the opportunity could not have been procured for the principal—say because the third party did not want to deal with the principal.[19]

Secondly, sometimes the fiduciary's job involves receiving payments made to him for the benefit of the principal. Then the receipt can itself generate a liability to the principal in the measure of the receipt independently of any breach of duty by the fiduciary. Here there is some room for argument over how the claim should be characterised; the most obvious interpretation is that the claim arises from the agreement according to which the fiduciary has agreed to take receipt of benefits on behalf of the principal and account for them to him. Thus there are three distinct but overlapping reasons why the fiduciary might be held liable for a benefit received. The usual form of the claim is the account of profits, and it seems likely that the origin of the account is in the last of the three types of claim, where the defendant received a sum on behalf of the plaintiff, and was liable to hold it for the plaintiff or account to him for it.[20]

THE NO-CONFLICT RULE

The rationale for the no-conflict rule

Because of the general way in which the fiduciary duty is defined, it is often difficult to prove a breach of duty. It may be easy to say that the fiduciary's duty is to manage the principal's business in the best possible way, but it is more difficult to specify what that involves in any particular respect, in order to show that the duty has not been fulfilled. A systematic difficulty in proving a breach of duty means that there is a danger of systematic underenforcement of fiduciary relationships,[21] with respect to both providing the principal with a remedy and imposing a penalty on the fiduciary. The no-conflict rule serves to alleviate this problem, at least with respect to cases where there is a possibility that the fiduciary may have acted in his own interests at the expense of the principal (as opposed to the case where he is incompetent or misguided).

Under the no-conflict rule, where the fiduciary receives a profit in circumstances evincing a possibility of a conflict between his fiduciary duty and his own

---

[18] e.g. *LAC Minerals Ltd v International Corona Resources Ltd* (1989) 61 DLR (4th) 14, 17 per Wilson J; see Chap. 8 at n 22.

[19] e.g. *Industrial Development Consultants v Cooley* [1972] 1 WLR 443.

[20] Meagher, Gummow & Lehane (1992), para. 2504.

[21] This is the theme of various economic analyses of fiduciary relationships, including Cooter & Freedman (1991).

interests—in other words, a possibility that the profit came to him as a result of the pursuit of his own interests at the expense of the principal's—the fiduciary is presumed to have committed a breach of duty by preferring his own interests. Consequently the principal can recover the profit received by the fiduciary, as deemed disgorgement.[22] Thus it has been said that the no-conflict rule addresses the problem that "no court is equal to the examination and ascertainment" of the facts;[23] that the court:

> is not entitled . . . to receive evidence, or suggestion, or argument as to whether the principal did or did not suffer any injury . . . the safety of mankind requires that no agent shall put the principal to the danger of such an inquiry as that[24];

and that in a position of conflict:

> it is neither wise nor practicable for the law to look for a criterion of liability. The consequences of such a conflict are not discoverable. Both justice and policy are against their investigation.[25]

It is also commonly said that the function of the no-conflict rule is to remove the fiduciary's incentive to breach his fiduciary duty as a matter of public policy.[26] Strictly speaking this is the function of disgorgement rather than of the no-conflict rule itself. As argued in the last chapter, disgorgement is or ought to be available in cases of breach of contract other than fiduciary cases, where the no-conflict rule does not apply.[27]

This argument shows the rationale for the rule, but to say that a breach of duty is presumed is to use a fiction. To be more direct, the no-conflict rule imposes on the fiduciary a liability for the value of the profit received irrespective of any breach of duty, in the specified circumstances. The principal need not in fact establish a breach of duty (and still less a deliberate breach of duty): the no-conflict rule:

> in no way depends on fraud, or absence of bona fides; or upon such questions or considerations as whether the profit would or should otherwise have gone to the plaintiff, or whether the profiteer was under a duty to obtain the source of the profit for the plaintiff, or whether he took a risk or acted as he did for the benefit of the plaintiff, or whether the plaintiff has in fact been damaged or benefited by his action . . . The liability arises from the mere fact of a profit having, in the stated circumstances, been made.[28]

---

[22] Or, as discussed above, deemed compensation, in circumstances where the profit received might have represented the principal's loss as well as the fiduciary's benefit.

[23] Ex parte *James* (1803) 8 Ves. 337, 345 per Lord Eldon LC.

[24] *Parker v McKenna* (1874) LR 10 Ch 96, 124–5 per James LJ.

[25] *Furs Ltd v Tomkies* (1936) 54 CLR 583, 592.

[26] e.g. *Bray v Ford* [1986] AC 44, 51–2.

[27] Conversely, as mentioned above, the application of the no-conflict rule can in principle be used for the purposes of a claim for compensation rather than disgorgement based on a deemed breach of duty.

[28] *Regal (Hastings) v Gulliver* [1942] 1 All ER 378, 386 per Lord Russell.

The no-conflict rule does not impose a duty on the fiduciary, but subjects him, in the specified circumstances, to a liability irrespective of the fact that he has not committed a breach of duty (because of the difficulty of proving a breach of duty).[29]

It is usually said, however, that the no-conflict rule imposes on the fiduciary "[a duty not] to put himself in a position where his interest and duty conflict",[30] or where there is a possibility that they might conflict. On this approach, the fiduciary's liability under the no-conflict rule is a response to a breach of duty. But this is a quite implausible formulation of the no-conflict rule.[31] Many fiduciaries are often in a position of conflict of interest, and have to be in order to carry out their job. A company director often has to search out work for his company, even though this may present the temptation to take the work for himself contrary to his duty, and it is part of the finance manager's job to make transfers of money that he might be tempted to pay to himself. By contrast the rule that a fiduciary must not "advance his own interests (e.g. by making a profit) at [the principal's] expense"[32] is entailed in the fiduciary duty to advance the principal's interests. Under the no-conflict rule if the fiduciary has received a profit from a position of conflict he is treated as if he had advanced his own interests at the principal's expense even if this cannot be shown to be the case.

Table A, Article 85 and section 310 of the Companies Act 1985

The distinction between a breach of fiduciary duty and liability under the no-conflict rule provides the solution to a longstanding controversy in company law. This controversy concerns the rules on "self-dealing" and "fair dealing", which are a manifestation of the no-conflict rule. Because of his special knowledge of the principal's affairs and his power to contract on behalf of the principal and determine the terms of contracting, there is a risk that the fiduciary will be able to use his position to make a contract between himself personally and his principal that is unfair to the principal. If the fiduciary does this he will have committed a breach of fiduciary duty, but again it may be difficult to show that a contract is not in the principal's best interests even if it also benefits the fiduciary. Under the no-conflict rule, any contract between the principal and the fiduciary is presumed to have been made in breach of duty. The contract can be set aside at the instance of the principal and the fiduciary must return any profit he has made through it.[33]

---

[29] i.e. the no-conflict rule establishes a primary right–liability relation: see further Appendix 1.

[30] e.g. *Bray v Ford* [1896] AC 44, 51 per Lord Herschell.

[31] At least as a general rule; no doubt there could be a case where this is a plausible understanding of what the relationship requires.

[32] *Bray v Ford* [1896] AC 44, 51–2 per Lord Herschell.

[33] e.g. *Guinness v Saunders* [1990] 2 AC 663; *Hely Hutchinson v Brayhead* [1968] 1 QB 549. In some circumstances the fiduciary can resist rescission on the ground that the contract is fair, i.e. where the "fair dealing" rule applies rather than the "self-dealing" rule.

With respect to companies, this is taken to mean that a contract between the company and a director cannot be made by another director on behalf of the company, or even the whole board of directors,[34] without the endorsement of the company's general meeting of shareholders. But it is liable to be highly inconvenient if the general meeting is required to sanction an ordinary contract of employment or service contract with a director. Thus most companies include in their articles of association a provision in the form of Article 85 of Table A, which provides, in part, as follows:

> [P]rovided that he has disclosed to the directors the nature and extent of any material interest of his, a director notwithstanding his office—
>
> (a) may be a party to . . . any transaction or arrangement with the company . . .;
> . . . and
> (c) shall not, by reason of his office, be accountable to the company for any benefit which he derives from any such . . . transaction or arrangement . . . and no such transaction or arrangement shall be liable to be avoided on the ground of any such interest or benefit.

The effect is to oust the operation of the no-conflict rule with respect to such contracts. It has been argued, however, that an article in the form of Article 85 must be void by virtue of section 310 of the Companies Act 1985,[35] which invalidates any article that purports to exempt a director from "any liability which by virtue of any rule of law would otherwise attach to him in respect of any negligence, default, breach of duty or breach of trust of which he may be guilty in relation to the company".[36] The argument seems correct on the orthodox understanding of the no-conflict rule, under which the rule imposes a duty on the fiduciary not to put himself in a position of conflict of interest, and Article 85 purports to relieve the director of a liability arising from a breach of it. There have been a number of attempts to reconcile Article 85 with section 310, and thereby to avoid the inconvenience that would follow from its invalidity.[37] In *Movitex v Bulfield*,[38] Vinelott J held that Article 85 was not inconsistent with section 310, because the no-conflict rule did not generate a fiduciary duty, but instead rendered the fiduciary subject to a "disability", and that excluding the disability by contract did not amount to excluding a fiduciary duty or exempting the director from liability for breach of fiduciary duty.[39] Vinelott J's analysis has sometimes been regarded as a clever but contrived device to circumvent a statutory anomaly, but in fact it is sound in principle and consistent with the argument above.[40]

---

[34] But cf *Queensland Mines v Hudson* [1978] ALJR 379.

[35] S.310 was originally introduced to deal specifically with provisions of the articles that relieved directors of liability for negligence, as in Re *City Equitable Fire Insurance Co* [1925] Ch 407.

[36] Or at least that the provisions are irreconcilable e.g. Davies (1997), 624, discussing *Movietex v Bulfield* [1988] BCLC 104, where the argument was rejected.

[37] See the discussion in Watts (1987).

[38] [1988] BCLC 104.

[39] At 120–1.

[40] "Disability" must be understood in the sense of "primary liability" in Appendix 1.

IS THE FIDUCIARY RELATIONSHIP CONTRACTUAL?

It has been argued above that a fiduciary relationship is a type of contractual relationship, viz. where one party's performance is to promote the interests of the other with respect to the subject matter of the contract. The fiduciary duty is the contractual duty to promote the interests of the other party. There might be an express term requiring one party to promote the interests of the other, but generally such a term will be implied from the context. Where one party entrusts his business or investments to another, it hardly needs to be stated that the other is intended to manage them in the first party's interests, although there may be other types of case where there is room for confusion between the parties about whether the understanding was that one should act in the interests of the other with respect to some aspect of an arrangement. (An example is considered below.)[41]

The "parallel relationship" fallacy

The main reason it has been assumed that a fiduciary duty is non-contractual, even when it is acknowledged that it is based on or arises from a contract, is probably that a fiduciary duty is equitable, whereas contract law is part of the common law. It seems that fiduciary duties were enforced in equity because of the association with the trust and because to obtain an adequate remedy the plaintiff needed to claim the defendant's receipt through the equitable remedies of account of profits or constructive trust.[42] Thus it is thought that the fiduciary relationship exists in equity, distinct from and parallel to the contractual relationship at common law. But although a fiduciary agreement is distinguishable from other agreements in the way explained above, a fiduciary duty is no more than a type of duty arising from an agreement, in circumstances that, as explained above, also justify the application of the no-conflict rule.[43] The idea that the fiduciary relationship exists in parallel to the contractual relationship is an illusion brought about by the procedural requirement to seek disgorgement through equity. The parallel relationship approach is no more correct for fiduciary relationships that it would be for specific performance: it is clear that it would be misconceived to say that specific performance is never available for breach of contract, but that in certain circumstances another relationship arises concurrently with the contractual relationship by virtue of which a party is entitled to specific enforcement of what was agreed.[44]

---

[41]   At 412.

[42]   Sealy (1962), 72; above n 12.

[43]   There are other agreements not recognised as such and enforced in equity—e.g. in connection with secret trusts and proprietary estoppel; cf Chap. 3 at 128, Chap. 8 at 264.

[44]   See further Appendix 2.

The parallel relationship fallacy is illustrated by *Hospital Products Ltd v United States Surgical Corporation*.[45] Here the defendant was an exclusive distributor whose due contractual performance was to "devote its best efforts to distributing [the plaintiff's products], and building up the market for those products, in Australia", and not to deal "in any products competitive with [the plaintiff's products].[46] It seems clear that the nature of the defendant's contractual performance was such that the relationship was fiduciary, because the performance was to promote in general terms the interests of the plaintiff.[47] Here the duty to act generally in the interests of the principal was stated explicitly, rather than being implicit in the circumstances, but this surely cannot affect the nature of the relationship as fiduciary. However, when the defendant began to build his own business in competing products, it was held that although the defendant had committed a breach of contract and was liable to pay compensation, there was no fiduciary relationship and therefore no liability to disgorgement. It is an example of the parallel relationship fallacy to suppose that where there is a contractual duty to promote the interests of the other party there may or may not also be such a parallel fiduciary duty in equity.

The effect of the parallel relationship fallacy is that the courts misunderstand their function with respect to fiduciary relationships. The proper approach, on the analysis set out above, is to interpret an agreement, in the light of its explicit terms and the context and other relevant factors, in order to determine whether, as part of his contractual performance, one party is to promote the interests of the other in some general and unspecified way, so that the agreement is fiduciary. But under the influence of the parallel relationship fallacy, the court attempts to determine, applying criteria that remain obscure, whether an agreement is fiduciary in the light of its general nature or category, and then, if it is fiduciary, it recognises a duty, distinct from and in addition to any contractual duties, requiring one party to promote the interests of the other.[48]

A mandatory rule?

One objection that might be made to a contractual analysis is that a fiduciary relationship is based on a mandatory rule,[49] imposed irrespective of the agreement of the parties. This argument seems to be derived from the idea that the fiduciary duty is imposed on the parties by the general law rather than being a

---

[45] (1984–5) 156 CLR 41.

[46] At 120, per Deane J.

[47] Notwithstanding that in some respects the defendant was entitled to act in his own interests: the arrangement was not a partnership or joint venture.

[48] The economic approach to contract, which was considered briefly in the last chapter, also treats a fiduciary relationship as a type of contract, and denies the parallel relationship fallacy. The concept of the fiduciary relationship as a contractual relationship involving performance that cannot be specified precisely appears to be due to law and economics writers: see above n 15.

[49] i.e. rules that override actual agreement to the contrary.

term of their own contract, which reflects the parallel relationship fallacy. In fact the fiduciary duty is not in itself a mandatory term, but, as argued above, an implied term of the contract. It may be that a fiduciary contract is subject to mandatory rules,[50] but then this is true of many contractual relationships.[51]

Similarly, it is said that the distinctive feature of a fiduciary duty is that it imposes on the fiduciary a higher standard of behaviour than the common law courts impose through the law of contract or tort, and that it requires the fiduciary to act selflessly or altruistically, whereas the common law permits people to act principally in their own interests. Thus it was said in a famous dictum that:

> [u]ncompromising rigidity has been the attitude of courts of equity when petitioned to undermine the rule of undivided loyalty ... Only thus has the level of conduct for fiduciaries been kept at a level higher than that trodden by the crowd.[52]

But the fiduciary duty does not represent an elevated moral standard; it is merely a duty that arises from an agreement whose nature is such that a duty is necessary in order to protect the other party's interest under the contract. In the ordinary contract case, by contrast, where there is no duty to act, this is not because a lower moral standard is expected, but because (by reference to the same moral principles) a duty is not necessary to protect the other party's rights under the agreement. Furthermore, although the agreement may have been entered into by the fiduciary altruistically, more commonly it will have been entered into for commercial reasons, for remuneration; and conversely it is possible for non-fiduciary agreements to be entered into altruistically in the sense that there is no remuneration, as where there is a gratuitous agreement to assume responsibility for reliance.[53] It may appear that the fiduciary duty is altruistic because it involves conferring a benefit, rather than refraining from causing harm by a positive act, as in general is required by a duty in tort. But this just follows from the nature of the usual agreement, which will be for the exchange of benefits.

Lack of consideration

Another objection might be that a fiduciary relationship cannot be contractual because, even if it involves a duty that arises from an agreement, there is no

---

[50] e.g. s.310, considered above. In fact this relates to the no-conflict rule rather than the fiduciary duty itself. In so far as the performance of the fiduciary is precisely specified the fiduciary duty will be anticipated or pre-empted rather than excluded; it is difficult to see how a contract could both imply a general duty to act for the other party and exclude such a duty. Often the fiduciary relationship is confused with the relationship of undue influence. A contract affected by undue influence is clearly subject to a mandatory rule that makes it void or voidable. Although a relationship of undue influence may be associated with a fiduciary relationship, the two are distinct in principle: see Chap. 5 at 197–8.

[51] e.g. as under the Sale of Goods Act 1979, or the Unfair Contract Terms Act 1977.

[52] *Meinhard v Solomon* 249 NY 456 at 464, 164 NE 545 at 546 (1928) per Cardozo CJ.

[53] e.g. in a case of proprietary estoppel based on a unilateral agreement.

requirement of consideration (in the sense of an exchange) in the law of fiduciaries—a fiduciary who is not paid and receives no other benefit from the principal will still be subject to a fiduciary duty. It is true that if it is part of the
definition of the law of contract that it concerns agreements that satisfy the
exchange doctrine of consideration then some fiduciary relationships will fall
outside the law of contract, although others will not. But contract law should
surely be understood to be the law concerned with enforceable agreements, and
it follows that the exchange doctrine of consideration is not part of the definition of contract, but a rule that is supposed to determine which agreements are
legally enforceable; and if it is accepted that there are agreements that are legally
enforceable but do not satisfy the exchange doctrine, then the exchange doctrine
should be recognised as an incomplete statement of the law.[54] The doctrine of
consideration cannot in itself present an objection to the contractual analysis of
fiduciary relationships.

CONTROVERSIAL CASES OF FIDUCIARY RELATIONSHIPS

Borderline cases

It is often crucial to determine whether a relationship is fiduciary, because of the
importance of establishing whether disgorgement and the no-conflict rule apply.
Certain types of relationship are always fiduciary: these are the traditional
categories of fiduciary relationship, like trustees, partners and directors.
Relationships falling within these categories are by their nature fiduciary[55]; they
are said to be fiduciary per se or as a matter of law. At the other extreme, there
are agreements that are clearly not fiduciary because performance can be satisfactorily specified and measured. In between, there are categories of relationship
that may or may not be fiduciary, depending on the particular facts of the case.
These are the so-called "fact-based" fiduciary relationships.[56] The court has to
decide whether under the parties' agreement the supposed fiduciary's performance or some aspect of it consists in generally promoting the other party's
interests, rather than merely performing a well-specified task.

In recent years there has been some controversy over the extent to which fiduciary relationships arise in commercial relationships.[57] In a sense it is true by

---

[54] Cf Chap. 3 at 128. Clearly the relationship between a trustee and the beneficiary is not based
on an agreement between them, and the trust requires special treatment. Historically, the trust
surely developed out of the agreement between the trustee and the settlor, the beneficiary being in
effect a third party beneficiary of the contract.

[55] There also seem to be relationships that would invariably satisfy the definition, but where it is
often not relevant whether the relationship is fiduciary because the fiduciary would not be likely to
be in a position of conflict of interest and so the no-conflict rule would not usually be of any application. This might be the case with a doctor or a garage mechanic.

[56] Hayton (1996), 333.

[57] e.g. Meagher, Gummow & Lehane (1992), 504.

definition that fiduciary and commercial relationships are mutually exclusive. A commercial relationship might reasonably be defined as a relationship in which the parties are each entitled to pursue their own interests, subject only to a responsibility for reliance incurred under the contract between them and possibly specific well-defined obligations of performance arising from the contract.[58] This is the position in ordinary contractual relationships. By contrast, in a fiduciary relationship the fiduciary has a general obligation to promote the principal's interests with respect to the subject matter of the relationship. However, it is perfectly possible for business people to come together to form a fiduciary relationship with a view to mutual profit. In fact, this is the ordinary form of fiduciary relationship, as in the case of commercial agencies, company directorships, partnerships and investment trusts. In forming the fiduciary relationship, the parties will generally negotiate at arm's length to promote their respective interests, but on the formation of the relationship the fiduciary will incur a general fiduciary obligation instead of merely a responsibility for reliance and specific constraints on his freedom to pursue his own interests. These relationships can be said to be commercial as well as fiduciary. However, ordinarily one would expect parties who deal with each other for mutual profit to avoid incurring fiduciary obligations, in order to promote certainty and to preserve their freedom of action, and therefore to spell out the terms of the contract in reasonable detail so far as possible. Furthermore, one would expect a term requiring one party to promote the interests of the other in some unspecified way to be stated explicitly, as the *Hospital Products* case mentioned above illustrates, at least outside the well-established and understood categories of relationship mentioned above, and that such a term would not be readily implied.[59]

Consider, for example, exclusive and non-exclusive distributors.[60] The issue is whether the contract implicitly imposes a duty on the distributor generally to promote the interests of the supplier, which would mean that the distributor is a fiduciary. This would mean also that the distributor would have a duty not to sell his own or rival products, and that he would be subject to the no-conflict rule and might be subject to disgorgement. In the case of an exclusive distributor, the supplier is dependent on the distributor, in the sense that if the distributor does not maximise the number of products sold in his designated area the supplier can do nothing to exploit the market in that area. Thus, to make commercial sense of the contract, it is natural to interpret the contract as fiduciary. On the other hand, if the distributor is non-exclusive, the understanding may well be that the supplier is to benefit just to the extent that the distributor decides, on the basis of his own interests, in the light of his profit on the supplier's products and any other considerations relevant to his business, to sell the supplier's products, since if the distributor is not fully exploiting the market in the best interests of the supplier, the supplier can appoint other distributors.

---

[58] This formulation of course reflects the reliance theory.

[59] As observed by Millett (1998), 217–8.

[60] Exclusivity refers to the distributor's exclusive right to sell the product in the designated area.

Then it would be inconsistent with the parties' understanding to imply a fiduciary duty. Of course this simple contrast is merely illustrative and is not intended to do justice to the complexity of distribution agreements or commercial agreements generally.

Fictional fiduciary relationships

The argument above seeks to show why disgorgement and the no-conflict rule are available in relation to fiduciary relationships. According to conventional law, both disgorgement and the no-conflict rule are confined to fiduciary relationships and do not apply to non-fiduciary contracts. But, although the no-conflict rule is by definition limited to fiduciary relationships, because it is associated with the difficulty of specifying performance, disgorgement should not be confined to breach of fiduciary duty. As argued in the previous chapter, disgorgement for breach of contract should in principle be available wherever, in the light of the circumstances, the defendant's assumption of responsibility generates a duty to perform the contract.[61] In order to impose disgorgement in some such cases, the courts have deemed relationships to be fiduciary that are really not fiduciary at all: "[c]ourts have resorted to fiduciary language because of the view that certain remedies, deemed appropriate in the circumstances, would not be available unless a fiduciary relationship was present. In this sense, the label fiduciary . . . is . . . merely instrumental".[62] This device has been allowed by the lack of agreement over the nature of a fiduciary relationship, and over the proper criteria for disgorgement, and by a fallacious understanding of the relationship between law and equity.

For example, as discussed in the last chapter, it is clear that a contractual restriction on the publication or use of information acquired through employment should generate a contractual duty, and so the threat of disgorgement.[63] Such a contractual restriction would not apply only to a fiduciary; a quite junior person without any responsibility might do work that exposes him to information that might be covered by such a restriction. And, even in the case of a genuine fiduciary, it will not necessarily be the case that the restriction is an aspect of the fiduciary duty; it is more likely to be a specific and clearly defined part of his contract, not an aspect of a general duty to promote the interests of the principal. But if the breach of the restriction is understood to be an ordinary breach of contract,[64] disgorgement is unavailable under the traditional rule, and so

---

[61] Chap. 12 at 390–94.

[62] *LAC Minerals v International Corona Resources* (1989) 61 DLR (4th) 14, 30 per La Forest J. See also now *A-G v Blake* [1998] 2 WLR 805, 814; Birks (1996*b*), 56.

[63] Chap. 12 at 392–3.

[64] As discussed in Chap. 12, a true breach of confidence, whether arising out of contract or otherwise, will attract disgorgement in equity in the form of an account or constructive trust.

there is a temptation to treat the relationship as fiduciary in order to take advantage of the equitable jurisdiction to award disgorgement.[65]

Recently in *Attorney-General v Blake*,[66] which concerned an ex-agent of the secret services who had a contractual duty not to publish information about his work, the court recognised that there should be disgorgement for breach of contract in an appropriate case whether or not the relationship was fiduciary, and the court deprecated the device of contriving a fictional fiduciary relationship for the purpose of imposing disgorgement. Unfortunately, in accordance with the parallel relationship fallacy, the court failed to recognise that fiduciary relationships are merely a type of contractual relationship, and therefore that disgorgement for breach of fiduciary duty is merely an example of a wider principle of disgorgement for breach of contractual duty. Thus the court in *Blake* discussed as separate issues whether there could be disgorgement for breach of contract and whether there had been a breach of fiduciary duty justifying disgorgement.

In *Reading v Attorney-General*[67] the defendant, a sergeant in the British Army in Egypt, took bribes in return for accompanying lorries smuggling alcohol, wearing his uniform so that they would not be searched, and was held liable to disgorge the bribes to the Crown, his employer.[68] One ground was said to be that the defendant was a fiduciary.[69] But the defendant was not a fiduciary in any real sense; he was not exercising a discretion as part of a task conducted on behalf of the Crown, in circumstances in which the no-conflict rule might have applied.[70] There were, however, good grounds in principle for disgorgement for the defendant's breach of contract, as discussed in the last chapter, and the characterisation of the defendant as a fiduciary provided a plausible basis given the traditional rule against disgorgement for an ordinary breach of contract.

IS THE NO-CONFLICT RULE JUSTIFIED?

The function of the no-conflict rule is to make up for the difficulty in proving a breach of fiduciary duty by creating a presumption of a breach in the principal's favour where there was a reasonable possibility of a conflict of interest. The presumption enables the principal to acquire the fiduciary's receipts, which, given the presumption, are subject to disgorgement.

---

[65] e.g. *Snepp v United States* 100 S.Ct. 763 (1980); cf *A-G v Blake* [1998] 2 WLR 805, 814.

[66] [1998] 2 WLR 805; Jaffey (1998d).

[67] [1951] AC 507.

[68] The parties are reversed; in fact the Crown had seized the profits, and the sergeant sought to recover them.

[69] The main ground was waiver of tort, but this also seems misconceived, as discussed in Chap. 11.

[70] There have also been flagrant examples of fictional fiduciary relationships, again found in order to invoke the equitable jurisdiction, in connection with a claim for priority in insolvency for a restitutionary claim for a vitiated transfer, as considered in Chap. 10 at 336.

It might be objected that the no-conflict rule is unfair because it treats the fiduciary as if he had committed a wrong when this has not been proved against him, even where it is reasonably clear that he has not committed a wrong. Thus he is sometimes forced to surrender profits that were not made through any breach of duty to the principal, still less any deliberate breach.[71] But the rule can be defended on the basis that when someone accepts a fiduciary position he knows the legal position that goes with it, and if he knows that he will not be able to make profits in the specified circumstances, and does not therefore expend time or resources under any misapprehension in this respect, the rule cannot operate unfairly against him. Furthermore, as discussed above, a fiduciary can negotiate for an exclusion of the no-conflict rule to preserve his freedom to exploit opportunities coming to him through his position (to the extent that he can do so without acting against the principal's interests). From the principal's point of view the issue with respect to such an exclusion is whether it is better to have the extra protection against breach of fiduciary duty provided by the no-conflict rule or to pay the fiduciary less, or get some other quid pro quo from him, in return for waiving or curtailing it.[72]

Another argument concerns the strictness or range of the no-conflict rule. On one view, the rule should apply whenever the fiduciary has made a profit through his position, in the sense that he would not have encountered the opportunity if he had not been in the fiduciary position. On another view the rule should apply only if there was actually a reasonable possibility of a conflict of interest in the circumstances; on this view, in some circumstances a profit made through the fiduciary position would not attract the operation of the rule. These appear to be different competing versions of the same rule, one stricter than the other, but both based on the rationale discussed above.[73]

The stricter version of the rule is the traditional version,[74] and it appears that this version was adopted in the leading case of *Boardman v Phipps*.[75] Here the defendant was a solicitor acting as a fiduciary for a trust who discovered that the trust's investment in a company could be greatly increased in value if the company was managed differently. This could be done by increasing the investment and taking over the company. The trust was not prepared to take the risk of investing any more trust money in the company, so the defendant invested his own. As a result of a great deal of work by the defendant, his plan succeeded and the trust's and the defendant's investments increased in value. The defendant's profit had clearly come to him through his position, and the majority decision was that it had to be surrendered to the trust. But although the investment opportunity arose from the defendant's fiduciary position, it may be that there was no reasonable possibility of a conflict of interest in the defendant investing

---

[71] See above at 405.

[72] See the discussion in Prentice & Bishop (1983).

[73] Although it has been asserted that there are two distinct rules: see e.g. *Chan v Zacharia* (1984) 154 CLR 178.

[74] The strict version is often traced back to *Keech v Sandford* (1726) Sel.Cas.Ch 61, 25 ER 223.

[75] [1967] 2 AC 46; see also *Regal (Hastings) v Gulliver* [1967] 2 AC 134.

his own money once the trust had declined to invest its own, because there was then no issue whether trust money rather than the fiduciary's should be used to exploit the opportunity and to reap the reward. Thus the minority in the case, who preferred the more relaxed version of the rule,[76] considered that there should have been no liability. The more relaxed version has also been preferred by some commentators.[77] Presumably, one might go further and argue that even the "reasonable possibility of conflict" rule is too strict, and that the rule should apply only if the principal can show an actual conflict of interest, in the sense that the fiduciary was actually in a position where he had to weigh up his own interest against the principal's, not merely that there was a possibility that this was the case; or even that the rule should take the still weaker form of a rebuttable presumption of a breach of duty.

The strict rule provides greater protection for the principal. It has a wider range, and so in theory covers more cases of possible (but unproved) breaches of fiduciary duty, and it is a more certain rule that leaves less room for dispute and is therefore easier to enforce than the more relaxed rule based on the reasonable possibility of conflict of interest. The main argument against the strict rule seems to be that it is more likely to be unfair to the fiduciary than the relaxed rule.[78] However, as argued above, provided that the fiduciary can be taken to know of his legal position the strict rule is not unfair to him.[79] This suggests that the traditional wide rule should be preserved in the usual case, subject to contrary agreement between the parties.[80]

Where the fiduciary does not appreciate that he is subject to a no-conflict rule, or where, as in *Boardman v Phipps*, he is under the impression that he has secured a release from it, the rule can operate unfairly, at least in the sense that the fiduciary may invest his time and money in pursuing an opportunity without realising that he will be forced to surrender his profit. The question then is whether it is unfair to the fiduciary to expect him to know that the rule applies. It may be that a more relaxed rule provides comparable protection to the principal with less risk of this sort of prejudice to the fiduciary, because its scope is narrower and because the fiduciary is more likely to appreciate that something in the nature of the no-conflict rule may apply where there is a possibility of conflict. However, this was not the issue in *Boardman v Phipps*; the possibility that, as in that case, the fiduciary will do work mistakenly thinking that he has been released from the operation of the rule cannot be avoided without abandoning the no-conflict rule altogether.[81]

[76] [1967] 2 AC 46, 124 per Lord Upjohn, referring to a "real sensible possibility of conflict".

[77] e.g. Jones (1968), 486, 501; Meagher, Gummow & Lehane (1992), para. 513. For a recent discussion see Lowry & Edmunds (1998).

[78] Jones (1968), 486, 501.

[79] Or where he can be held responsible for not knowing that he is bound by the rule.

[80] See the comments of Norris JA, dissenting, in *Peso-Silver Mines v Cropper* (1965) 56 DLR (2d) 117 at 139.

[81] Assuming the rule is not abandoned, in such a case it seems that the only feasible protection that the fiduciary can have is the right to extra payment for his work, in a measure determined by the court, as held in *Boardman v Phipps*.

Arguably it would be fairer to apply a more relaxed rule in cases of fact-based fiduciary relationships,[82] where the relationship may not be recognised as having the special nature of a trusteeship or partnership or directorship, and the fiduciary may be more easily forgiven for failing to know of the no-conflict rule and assuming that he is free to profit from his own activities so long as he does not actually act in way that is liable to damage the principal's interests. Possibly here the no-conflict rule should apply only where an actual conflict is proved; in these circumstances at least the fiduciary should appreciate that he is liable to be suspected of breaking his fiduciary duty.

It might be argued that the no-conflict rule can operate to suppress the initiative of the fiduciary not only with respect to opportunities to benefit himself, but also, as in *Boardman v Phipps*, with respect to opportunities for common benefit.[83] Thus one might argue that, although the no-conflict rule is designed to protect the principal, it may also sometimes work against his interests. For example, in *Boardman v Phipps*, the fiduciary would certainly not have invested his own time and money in a project that greatly benefited the trust as well as himself if he had realised that he would have to surrender all his profits. However, it is always open to the principal to waive the rule for the common benefit, and if an opportunity arises for common benefit generally one would think that the parties would be able to reach an appropriate agreement. Unless there are obstacles to negotiation, the requirement to obtain consent will not suppress the exploitation of opportunities.[84]

---

[82] Above at 411.
[83] See, e.g. Lowry & Edmunds (1998).
[84] Possibly there will be such obstacles in some cases, e.g. in finding someone to act for the principal in negotiations, or because of "hold out" in negotiation, but then it will usually be possible for the parties to exclude the rule at the start. Cf the efficient breach hypothesis discussed in Chap. 12.

Appendix 1: A Note on Right–Liability Primary Relations

WITH RESPECT TO contract and tort, a distinction is usually drawn between the primary relation and the remedial relation.[1] The primary relation consists of the duty of the defendant and the corresponding right of the plaintiff that subsist before a claim arises—i.e. the defendant's duty of care and the correlative right of the plaintiff, or the contractual duty of performance and the correlative right to performance of the contract. The remedial or secondary relation arises on the commission of the breach of duty by the defendant, and consists of the remedial right or claim of the plaintiff and the corresponding liability of the defendant, typically a pecuniary right to and liability for compensation. When the matter reaches court, the court's order will crystallise and implement the remedial relation, typically by way of an order for the payment of a specified sum of money. The law of contract or tort encompasses both the primary and remedial relations, together with the court orders or remedies that implement the remedial relation.

A legal relation can also take the form of a correlative right and liability.[2] "Liability" is used in this sense: a person is subject to a liability if his legal position is subject to alteration by some event, which might be called a "causative event"[3] or a "liability generating event",[4] and which does not necessarily constitute a breach of duty by him.[5] Many parts of the law involve not primary right–duty relations, but primary right–liability relations. For example, under a strict liability regime in tort, the defendant's liability arises merely from the infliction of harm or damage on the plaintiff by the defendant. Similarly, although contractual liability is often expressed as arising from a breach of duty, it is clear that there are some contractual cases where this is not so: for example, in an insurance contract the claim arises when the event insured against occurs, but the insurer does not have a duty to ensure that it does not occur. In fact, under the reliance theory of contract in the form set out in Chapter 2, it is the usual position in contract that a

---

[1] The distinction was discussed by Lord Diplock in *Photo Production Ltd v Securicor Transport Ltd* [1980] AC 827, 848ff.

[2] The distinction between a right–duty relation and a right–liability relation corresponds to the distinction between a property rule and a liability rule, as explained in Calebresi & Melamed (1972). A property rule is one enforced by an injunction or by punishment for breach, whereas a liability rule is one enforced only through a pecuniary award of compensation. Thus a property rule generates a right–duty relation and a liability rule a right–liability relation. Law and economics usage generally equates a right correlating to a duty with a property right. This is at odds with the traditional usage of "property". Furthermore, the distinction between the two types of relation is a formal distinction that is quite independent of the rationale for the rule in question, e.g. whether it is based on efficiency or fairness.

[3] This expression is used in Birks (1989a).

[4] This expression is used by Cane (1996).

[5] Hohfeld used the concept of a liability only as the correlate of a power, not a right: Hohfeld (1946). If a person has a power, he can, by exercising the power, alter the legal relations of the person subject to it. Where there is a right–liability relation, the causative event is not the exercise of a power by the plaintiff nor a breach of duty by the defendant, except incidentally.

contractual claim does not arise from a breach of duty. On this approach, as reflected in Chapter 2, the availability of specific performance is a matter of whether there is a primary duty, not whether the court should exercise a discretion to enforce a primary duty. Also, on this approach, the failure to recognise the quantum meruit as a contractual claim, where it arises as an alternative to the expectation measure, is due partly to the failure to recognise that a remedial contractual liability can arise without a breach of duty, for example in a case of frustration, where it is clear, on any account, that there has been no breach of duty. Certain types of contract characteristically generate right–duty relations, however, and one important category consists of fiduciary relationships, as discussed in Chapter 13.[6]

The restitutionary claim for payment arising from an imputed contract and the restitutionary claim arising from a vitiated transfer both arise from primary right–liability relations, not right–duty relations.[7] A defendant who receives a benefit in circumstances in which he incurs a liability to pay for it has not committed a breach of duty: the causative event is the receipt of the benefit, and it would be quite fictional to say that the receipt was itself a breach of duty. As discussed in Chapter 4, the use claim also arises from a primary right–liability relation, and does not depend on the commission of a breach of duty, whereas the claim for disgorgement with which it is usually confused does necessarily arise as a response to a breach of duty. Similarly, a defendant who receives a vitiated transfer does not thereby breach a duty.[8] The causative event is the receipt of the vitiated transfer, which again is not a breach of duty, and again it would be fictional to say that the defendant had a duty not to receive the transfer. On the other hand, a defendant can incur a duty to preserve surviving value or return it, and this is the duty of preservation.[9] As discussed in Chapter 10, the distinction between the restitutionary liability, which arises from a primary right liability relation, and the remedial liability for breach of the duty of preservation, is behind the distinction between liability for knowing receipt and the equitable in rem claim, and the old distinction between conversion and detinue. Possibly the fact that claims in restitution are based on primary right–liability relations is part of the reason they have come to be referred to in terms of the nature of the remedy—"restitution"—rather than the nature of the ground for the claim, because the primary relation and the causative event arising from it tend to be disregarded if they cannot be characterised as a right–duty relation and a breach of duty.[10]

[6] One might argue that a right–liability relation can always be expressed as a right–duty relation: e.g. L.D. Smith (1992), 674, n.8. One could simply say, for example, that there is a duty not to receive a vitiated transfer. But this is to distort the concept of a duty. A duty stipulates what the person subject to the duty is required to do. It must specify some action that the person subject to the duty is capable of carrying out, not merely an event that will have legal consequences for him. To use "duty" merely as an instrumental term to specify the legal consequences of an event involves a fiction, and, like other fictions, causes confusion and unnecessary complexity and should be avoided.

[7] The same is true of a restitutionary claim under the theory of unjust enrichment, excluding the case of disgorgement.

[8] For a similar view, see Barker (1998), 321.

[9] The "duty of inquiry" is not strictly a duty; it merely represents a condition that determines when the duty of preservation arises.

[10] Curiously, although also saying that restitution is a response, Birks takes the view that a restitutionary claim is primary, not remedial or secondary, apparently because there is no antecedent relation out of which the claim arises: Birks (1989*a*), 43. See also Barker (1998), 320.

Appendix 2: A Note on Law, Equity and Fusion

THE FRAUGHT ISSUE of the relationship between the common law and equity arises at many points in the law of restitution, and for this reason it is worth considering here at some length. The fusionist approach adopted in this book, that in determining what the law is the courts should not regard it as material whether a line of authority is derived from the common law or equity (although reference to its origin may be necessary for the purposes of exposition) seemed at one time to be on the way to general acceptance.[1] Unfortunately there has been some confusion over what this view entails, which has arisen from a failure to appreciate the nature of the original relationship between law and equity.

In the early stages of the development of equity, one might truly have said that there were two legal systems operating as rivals and giving different outcomes over which enforcing officers were in dispute, just as might happen in a country divided by civil war or under partial occupation. But as a result of the priority that came to be given to the Court of Chancery, the position was reached that in reality, if not in form, there was one body of law (comprising all the various legal relations recognised and enforced by the legal system as a whole), but certain rights and remedies were recognised and dispensed only through the Chancery courts and others only through the common law courts. In other words, the division between common law and equity was procedural. To say that a right or remedy was legal or equitable in reality meant only that it was a right or remedy that was enforceable through the common law courts or the Chancery courts respectively. Thus the law of equity did not form a substantive field of law like contract or tort, and its content was a matter of historical accident, resulting only from the particular failings of the common law that from time to time prompted the intervention of the Chancery courts.[2]

The main objection to this state of affairs was the further expense and inconvenience involved in having to take proceedings in two different sets of courts, or the risk of wasting time and money taking proceedings in one set of courts when the proceedings ought to have been taken in the other courts.[3] The purpose of the Judicature Acts 1873–5 was to fuse the administration of law and equity to remove these procedural problems. It was not understood to be concerned with the substance of the law at all. Fusion in itself would not alter the sum of the rights and remedies that were recognised and enforced, merely the procedure for securing them.[4] This position might be described as

---

[1] *United Scientific Holdings Ltd v Burnley BC* [1978] AC 904, at 925–6 per Lord Diplock; see also *Baltic Shipping Company v Dillon* (1992) 176 CLR 344, 376, per Deane and Dawson JJ.

[2] Cf Meagher, Gummow & Lehane (1992), para. 155. The definition of equity as "the body of law developed by the Court of Chancery in England before 1873" (ibid., at para. 101) is a procedural definition: it makes no reference to the content of the law. To the same effect is the statement that "[e]quity can be described but not defined": Meagher, Gummow & Lehane (1992), para. 101.

[3] Meagher, Gummow & Lehane (1992), para. 144ff.

[4] Meagher, Gummow & Lehane (1992), paras. 202, 205, 221; *Salt v Cooper* (1880) 16 Ch D 544, 549 per Sir George Jessel MR; *Bank of Boston Connecticut v European Grain and Shipping* [1989]

"procedural fusion". Indeed it seems that fusion could only ever have been a matter of procedure, because the original division of law and equity was only a matter of procedure. However, if this analysis is correct, the effect of procedural fusion was to reach the position where the origin of an authority in equity or the common law was immaterial. Although by force of practice a right or remedy might continue to be referred to as equitable or legal, with reference to the courts through which it was originally enforceable, this could have no continuing significance, because it could refer only to the procedure that originally applied with respect to it, which had now been abandoned. Thus it seems that the use of the expressions "legal" or "equitable" to refer to a right or remedy should in due course have been abandoned. However, it is commonly asserted that this latter position—that to treat the common law or equitable origins of an authority as immaterial, and to abandon the use of "legal" and "equitable" to describe particular rules or lines of authority—goes beyond the procedural fusion authorised by the Judicature Acts, and amounts to "substantive fusion", which has received vitriolic criticism in some quarters.[5]

The confusion arises as follows. In many situations, equity and the common law dealt with what were the same types of rights using different terminologies. For example, although the term "contract" (which was a common law term) was used in equity in a case where specific performance was sought of an agreement that was recognised at common law, in cases where equity enforced an agreement that was not recognised as a contract at common law it was never referred to as a contract; instead it was said that the defendant by going back on his agreement was committing an equitable fraud, or that he was subject to an estoppel, or that he had committed a breach of fiduciary duty.[6] It seems that these types of agreement did not receive the attention of the common law because the common law remedy of damages was inadequate. Furthermore, there were cases where the courts of law and equity adopted different rules to deal with what was in reality the same issue. For example, at common law an agreement was said to be unenforceable without consideration in the sense of an exchange, whereas in equity agreements could be enforced, not under the rubric of "contract", but in another form, as mentioned above, without any requirement for consideration in this sense. Another example might be that the common law set down certain conditions for an agreement to be unenforceable for mistake (where the issue might arise in connection with a claim for damages) whilst equity set down different conditions for an agreement to be unenforceable for mistake (where the issue might arise on a claim for an injunction or to recover property transferred). These differences would not strictly be a matter of inconsistency, because law and equity originally dealt with different situations. But they made the law incoherent, in the sense that, ostensibly at least, they reflected different judgments of when it was just to enforce an agreement; and they also made the law obscure because of the different terminologies.

1 All ER 545, 557 per Lord Brandon. A minor qualification might be made. Although there was no conflict in reality because of the established precedence of equity, from the standpoint of a common law judge it might be said that a certain right existed in the law when this was not in fact the case because equity provided to the contrary. On the fusion of the courts it might be thought necessary to provide that equity was to prevail because now the same judge would be applying law and equity, as opposed to making a decision at common law that was subject to being externally overridden, as it were.

[5] This is described as the "fusion fallacy": Meagher, Gummow & Lehane (1992), para. 220ff.
[6] The examples used may be thought tendentious, but they serve nevertheless to demonstrate the possibility of incoherence in the law.

A number of cases of this sort of incoherence have been discussed in this book. The restitutionary claim to reverse a vitiated transfer arises in different contexts at common law and in equity, in the form of the claim for money had and received and the equitable in rem claim, which have quite different characteristics. What is in substance the same claim for payment or reimbursement for a benefit conferred is sometimes considered in parallel in law and equity, the equivalence being disguised because the equitable claim is expressed in terms of subrogation. In equity the courts were ready to use the account of profits as a means of effecting disgorgement, whereas the common law courts were resistant to using damages for the same purpose. Similarly, where a breach of contract was fiduciary, disgorgement was available in equity, but where disgorgement was equally appropriate for a breach of contract but the contract was not fiduciary, no disgorgement was available at common law. In this case the incoherence is the parallel relationship fallacy discussed in Chapter 13, which mistakenly fails to recognise the fiduciary relationship as a type of contractual relationship.

If one accepts the validity of theoretical arguments or arguments for coherence in the sense of Chapter 1, one might have expected the judges to become aware of this type of incoherence and obscurity after fusion, and to take steps to eliminate it.[7] Strictly speaking, such a development would not be due to the Judicature Acts, whose effect was only procedural, but to the application of theoretical argument to eliminate the incoherence and obscurity that became apparent as a result of the procedural changes brought about by the Judicature Acts.[8] This development is really what is deprecated as substantive fusion. Thus the real argument over substantive fusion is not over the effect of the Judicature Acts but over the validity and significance of theoretical argument; or, as one might say, over whether it is justified to adopt the "unstated but implicit assumption . . . that principles of law and equity are fused in the sense that rules from one field may be used to indicate what should be the position in the other".[9] There is no doubt that there has been some progress towards substantive fusion in this sense. The main obstacle appears to have been the misconception that the division between law and equity is a substantive division, like that between contract and tort, which tends to be preserved by differences of terminology and by the perpetuation of a separate body of lawyers specialising in equity.

One objection that has been made to substantive fusion in the sense explained above is that it would mean the abolition of the trust. This argument, although apparently widely accepted,[10] is quite mistaken. It is worth considering this point in some detail, because, as has been seen in Chapters 9 and 10, the trust has a close connection with the law of restitution. When (many centuries ago) property owners who saw the advantage of separation of management and benefit (i.e. the trust) transferred their land to one

---

[7] These are not strictly cases of inconsistency, where the Supreme Court of Judicature Acts 1873–75 provided that equity was to prevail.

[8] The same objectives of coherence and clarity should operate in the development of a field of law that is exclusively derived from equity or the common law; and conversely, even whilst the procedural division of law and equity was in place, the judges ought in principle to have sought to build a single coherent body of law by consulting the decisions of the parallel system.

[9] Meagher, Gummow & Lehane (1992), para. 229, where it is thought that the assumption is mistaken.

[10] "It may be asked . . . why not abolish at once the distinction between law and equity? I can best answer that by asking another question—Do you wish to abolish trusts?": per Lord Selborne LC in debate on the Judicature Act 1873, quoted and adopted in Meagher, Gummow & Lehane (1992), para. 218. See also Pearce & Stevens (1998), 15; Pettit (1997), 10.

person to act as manager on the understanding that he would manage the land in the interest of another person specified by the transferor as the beneficiary, the arrangement was not recognised by the common law as creating any rights in the beneficiary: the transferee was regarded as the absolute owner of the land. In other words, the common law rejected the possibility of the separation of management and benefit. However, equity recognised the arrangement, so that the beneficiary could enforce his interest in the property in equity.

It is generally said that the basis of the trust is that equity and the law have different rules on the ownership of the property, the common law regarding the trustee as owner and equity the beneficiary.[11] This seems to imply that on substantive fusion it would be necessary for the law to take either the position of the common law or the position in equity: under the common law position, the trustee would be recognised as the absolute owner, but under the position in equity the beneficiary would be recognised as the absolute owner. Whichever position prevailed, there would be no trust because the separation of title would have been eliminated. But actually the position of equity was to recognise the separation of management and benefit, not to assert that the beneficiary was the absolute owner as if there were no such separation; it recognised a separation of function between the trustee, who could exercise the rights of the owner of the property as against third parties in the common law courts, and the beneficiary, who had the right, enforceable in equity, to benefit from the property as against the person in control of it. With the recognition of the precedence of equity, the trust was recognised in law, although before fusion action by the beneficiary against the trustee and by the trustee against third parties had to be through separate courts. It was then only a fiction, or at least a procedural point before fusion, to say that the common law regarded the trustee as the owner for all purposes. After fusion it was merely a fiction. In other words, the expressions "legal title" and "equitable interest" were used before fusion to signify both the content of the right in question, i.e. whether it was a matter of management or benefit, and also the procedure for enforcing it, i.e. whether the right was to be enforced through common law or equity. Now, after fusion, the expressions signify only the first of these. Substantive fusion, as described above, or in other words the argument for coherence, which requires rights and remedies to be distinguished and classified according to their nature and rationale and not their historical origin or the procedure that was applicable to them before fusion, in no way undermines the trust. To the contrary, it requires the distinction between the right to benefit and the rights and powers of the manager to be strictly maintained. It does suggest, however, that in order to emphasise the function of separation of title, rather than its origin in the jurisdictional divide and in obsolete procedural requirements, it might be desirable to abandon the expression "equitable title" in favour of "beneficial interest" and "legal title" in favour of "management title", or "dispositive title", which was the expression used in Chapters 9 and 10.[12]

---

[11] See, e.g. Pearce & Stevens (1998), 94.

[12] Cf above Chap. 9 at 289–91. The trust can be contrasted with the lease. Common law and equity adopted different rules for the enforceability of a lease so that a lease might arise in equity though not at law; in other words law and equity recognised different and rival conceptions of the same legal concept, viz. the lease. By contrast there were no rival conception of the trust, but a single concept, part of whose incidents were enforceable only in equity. With respect to the lease, substantive fusion requires the court to recognise that there is a single legal concept and a single relation between the parties, viz. the lease. This seems to have been the position taken in *Walsh v Lonsdale* (1882) 21 Ch D 9, criticised by Meagher, Gummow & Lehane (1992), para. 236.

Bibliography

AMERICAN LAW INSTITUTE (1937), *Restatement of the Law of Restitution*

ANDREWS, N. (1989), "Mistaken Settlements of Disputable Claims" [1989] *LMCLQ* 431.

ASHWORTH, A. (1995), *Sentencing and Criminal Justice* (2nd edn., Butterworths, London).

ARROWSMITH, S. (1991), "Mistake and the Role of the 'Submission to an Honest Claim'" in A. Burrows (ed.), *Essays on the Law of Restitution* (Clarendon Press, Oxford), 17.

ATIYAH, P.S. (1976), "When is an Enforceable Agreement Not a Contract?" [1976] *LQR* 174.

—— (1979), *The Rise and Fall of Freedom of Contract* (Clarendon Press, Oxford).

—— (1981), *Promises, Morals, and Law* (Clarendon Press, Oxford).

—— (1982), "Economic Duress and the 'Overborne Will'" [1982] *LQR* 197.

—— (1985), *An Introduction to the Law of Contract* (5th edn., OUP, Oxford), 154.

—— (1986), *Essays on Contract* (Clarendon Press, Oxford).

BANT, E. (1997), "The Development of Tracing Rules in Commercial Cases" [1997] *LMCLQ* 65.

—— (1998), "Ignorance as a Ground of Restitution—Can it Survive?" [1998] *LMCLQ* 18.

BARKER, K. (1994), "Restitution and Third Parties" [1994] *LMCLQ* 305.

—— (1995a), "Unjust Enrichment: Containing the Beast" [1995] *OJLS* 457.

—— (1995b), "After Change of Position: Good Faith Exchange in the Modern Law of Restitution" in P.B.H. Birks (ed.), *Laundering and Tracing* (Clarendon Press, Oxford), 191.

—— (1998a), "Rescuing Remedialism in Unjust Enrichment Law: Why Remedies are Right" [1998] *CLJ* 301.

—— (1998b), "O'Brien, Notice and the Onus of Proof" in F.D. Rose (ed.), *Restitution and Banking Law* (Mansfield Press, Oxford).

BATTERSBY, G. (1995), "Equitable Fraud Committed by Third Parties" [1995] *LS* 35.

BEATSON, J. (1991), *The Use and Abuse of Unjust Enrichment* (Clarendon Press, Oxford).

—— and BISHOP, W. (1991), "Mistaken Payments in the Law of Restitution" in J. Beatson (ed.), *The Use and Abuse of Unjust Enrichment* (Clarendon Press, Oxford), 137.

—— and FRIEDMANN, D. (eds.), (1995), *Good Faith and Fault in Contract Law* (Clarendon Press, Oxford).

BIGWOOD R., "Undue Influence: 'Impaired Consent' or 'Wicked Exploitation'?" [1996] *OJLS* 503.

BIRKS, P.B.H. (1974), "Restitution for Services" [1974] *CLP* 13.

—— (1983), "Restitution and the Freedom of Contract" [1983] *CLP* 141.

—— (1985), "Unjust Enrichment—a Reply to Mr Hedley" [1985] *LS* 67.

—— (1987), "Restitutionary Damages for Breach of Contract: *Snepp* and the Fusion of Law and Equity" [1987] *LMCLQ* 421.

—— (1989a), *An Introduction to the Law of Restitution* (rev edn., Clarendon Press, Oxford).

BIRKS, P.B.H. (1989*b*), "Misdirected Funds: Restitution from the Recipient" [1989] *LMCLQ* 296.

—— (1990), "The Travails of Duress" [1990] *LMCLQ* 342.

—— (1991*a*), "The English Recognition of Unjust Enrichment" [1991] *LMCLQ* 330.

—— (1991*b*), "In Defence of Free Acceptance", in A. Burrows (ed.), *Essays on the Law of Restitution* (Clarendon Press, Oxford), 109.

—— (1992*a*), *Restitution—The Future* (Federation Press, Annandale).

—— (1992*b*), "Civil Wrongs: A New World" in *Butterworths Lectures 1990–1* (Butterworths, London).

—— (1992*c*), "Trusts in the Recovery of Misapplied Assets; Tracing, Trusts and Restitution" in E. McKendrick (ed.), *Commercial Aspects of Trusts and Fiduciary Obligations* (Clarendon Press, Oxford), 149.

—— (1992*d*), "'When Money is Paid in Pursuance of a Void Authority . . .'—a Duty to Repay?" [1992] *Public Law* 580.

—— (1992*e*), "Restitution and Resulting Trusts" in S.R. Goldstein (ed.), *Equity: Contemporary Legal Developments* (Faculty of Law Hebrew University of Jerusalem), 335.

—— (1992*f*), "Mixing and Tracing: Property and Restitution" [1992] *CLP* 69.

—— (1993), "No Consideration: Restitution after Void Contracts" (1993) 23 *Univ. WALR* 195.

—— (ed.) (1994*a*), *The Frontiers of Liability*, (OUP, Oxford), i.

—— (ed.) (1994*b*), *The Frontiers of Liability*, (OUP, Oxford), ii.

—— (1994*c*), "Gifts of Other People's Money" in P.B.H. Birks (ed.), *The Frontiers of Liability* (OUP, Oxford), i, 31.

—— (1994*d*), "Proprietary Rights as Remedies", in P.B.H. Birks (ed.), *The Frontiers of Liability* (OUP, Oxford), ii, 214.

—— (ed.) (1995*a*), *Laundering and Tracing* (Clarendon Press, Oxford).

—— (1995*b*), "Overview: Tracing, Claiming and Defences" in P.B.H. Birks (ed.), *Laundering and Tracing* (Clarendon Press, Oxford), 289.

—— (1996*a*), Change of Position: The Nature of the Defence and its Relationship to Other Restitutionary Defences", in M.P. McInnes (ed.), *Restitution: Developments in Unjust Enrichment* (LBC Information Services).

—— (1996*b*), "Equity in the Modern Law: An Exercise in Taxonomy" (1996) 26 *Univ. WALR* 1.

—— (ed.) (1996*c*), *Wrongs and Remedies in the Twenty-First Century* (Clarendon Press, Oxford).

—— (1997*a*), "Property and Unjust Enrichment: Categorical Truths" [1997] *New Zealand LR* 623.

—— (1997*b*), "Change of Position and Surviving Enrichment" in W.J. Swadling (ed.), *The Limits of Restitutionary Claims: A Comparative Analysis* (UKNCCL), 36.

—— (ed.) (1997*c*), *The Classification of Obligations* (Clarendon Press, Oxford).

—— (1998*a*), "Misnomer" in W.R. Cornish, R. Nolan, J. O'Sullivan and G. Virgo (eds.), *Restitution Past, Present and Future* (Hart Publishing, Oxford).

—— (1998*b*), "Notice and Onus in O'Brien" [1998] *TLI* 2.

—— and BEATSON, J. (1991), "Unrequested Payment of Another's Debt" in J. Beatson (ed.), *The Use and Abuse of Unjust Enrichment* (Clarendon Press, Oxford), 177.

—— and CHAMBERS, R. (1997), *The Restitution Research Resource* (2nd edn., Mansfield Press, Oxford).

—— and CHIN, N.Y. (1995), "On the Nature of Undue Influence" in J. Beatson and D. Friedmann (eds.), *Good Faith and Fault in Contract Law* (Clarendon Press, Oxford), 57.

BRIDGE, M. (1996), *Personal Property Law* (2nd edn., Blackstone Press).

—— (1998), "Failed Contracts, Subrogation and Unjust Enrichment" [1998] *JBL* 323.

BRYAN, M. (1996), "Change of Position: Commentary" in M.P. McInnes (ed.), *Restitution: Developments in Unjust Enrichment* (LBC Information Services), 49.

—— (1998), "Recovering Misdirected Money from Banks: Ministerial Receipt at Law and in Equity" in F.D. Rose (ed.), *Restitution and Banking Law* (Mansfield Press, Oxford).

BURROWS, A. (1984), "Law Commission Report on Pecuniary Restitution on Breach of Contract" [1984] *MLR* 76.

—— (1988), "Free Acceptance and the Law of Restitution" [1988] *LQR* 576.

—— (ed.) (1991*a*), *Essays on the Law of Restitution* (Clarendon Press, Oxford).

—— (1991*b*)"Public Authorities, Ultra Vires, and Restitution" in A. Burrows, *Essays on the Law of Restitution* (Clarendon Press, Oxford).

—— (1993), *The Law of Restitution* (Butterworths, London).

—— (1994), "Restitution from Assignees" [1994] *RLR* 52.

—— (1995)"Swaps and the Friction between Law and Equity" [1995] *RLR* 15.

—— and McKENDRICK, E. (1997), *Cases and Materials on the Law of Restitution* (OUP, Oxford).

BUTLER, P.A. (1990), "Mistaken Payments, Change of Position and Restitution", in P.D. Finn (ed.), *Essays on Restitution* (Law Book Company, Sydney).

—— (1997), "Where do We Go from Here?" [1997] *CLP* 95.

CALEBRESI, G., and MELAMED, A.D. (1972), "Property Rules, Liability Rules, and Inalienability: One View of the Cathedral", 85 *Harv. LR* 45.

CANE, P. (1996), "Exceptional Measures of Damages: A Search for Principles" in P.B.H. Birks (ed.), *Wrongs and Remedies in the Twenty-First Century* (Clarendon Press, Oxford), 301.

CAPPER, D. (1998), "Undue Influence and Unconscionability: A Rationalisation" [1998] *LQR* 479.

CARTWRIGHT J. (1991), *Unequal Bargaining* (Clarendon Press, Oxford).

CHAMBERS, R. (1997), *Resulting Trusts* (Clarendon Press, Oxford).

CHUTORIAN, S. (1986), "Tort Remedies for Breach of Contract", 86 *Columbia LR* 377.

CLARK, P. (1996), "Frustration, Restitution and the Law Reform (Frustrated Contracts) Act 1943" [1996] *LMCLQ* 170.

COLLINS, H. (1997), *The Law of Contract* (3rd edn., Butterworths, London).

COOTE, B. (1972), "Another Look at *Bowmakers v Barnet Instruments*" [1972] *MLR* 38.

COOTER, R., and ULEN, T. (1997), *Law and Economics* (2nd edn., Addison-Wesley, Harlow).

—— and FREEDMAN, B.J. (1991), "The Fiduciary Relationship: Its Economic Character and Legal Consequences", 66 NYU Law Rev 1045.

CORNISH, W.R. (1996), *Intellectual Property* (4th edn., Sweet & Maxwell, London).

—— NOLAN, R., O'SULLIVAN, J., and VIRGO, G. (eds.) (1998), *Restitution: Past, Present and Future* (Hart Publishing, Oxford).

CRILLEY, D. (1994), "A Case of Proprietary Overkill" [1994] *RLR* 57.

DAVIES, P.L. (1997), *Gower's Principles of Modern Company Law* (6th edn., Sweet & Maxwell, London).

DENNING, A.T. (1925), "*Quantum Meruit* and the Statute of Frauds" [1925] *LQR* 79.

DIECKMANN, J.A., and EVANS-JONES, R. (1995), "The Dark Side of *Connelly v Simpson*" [1995] *JR* 90.

DIETRICH, J. (1998), *Restitution A New Perspective* (Federation Press, Annandale).

DWORKIN, R. (1986), *Law's Empire* (Fontana Press, London).

EASTERBROOK, F.H., and FISCHEL, D.R. (1993), "Contract and Fiduciary Duty" (1993) 36 *Journal of Law and Economics* 425.

ELIAS, G. (1990), *Explaining Constructive Trusts* (Clarendon Press, Oxford).

ENONCHONG, N. (1998), *Illegal Transactions* (LLP, London).

FARNSWORTH, F.A. (1985), "Your Loss or my Gain? The Dilemma of the Disgorgement Principle in Breach of Contract", 94 *Yale LJ* 1339.

FENNELL, S. (1994), "Misdirected Funds: Problems of Uncertainty and Inconsistency" [1994] *MLR* 38.

FINN, P.D. (1992), "Fiduciary Law in the Modern Commercial World" in E. McKendrick (ed.), *Commercial Aspects of Trusts and Fiduciary Obligations* (Clarendon Press, Oxford), 7.

—— (ed.) (1990), *Essays on Restitution* (Law Book Company, Sydney).

FINNIS, J. (1995), "Intention in Tort Law" in D. Owen (ed.), *Philosophical Foundations of Tort Law* (Clarendon Press, Oxford), 229.

—— (1999), "The Fairy Tale's Moral" [1999] *LQR* 170.

FOX, D. (1996), "The Transfer of Legal Title to Money" [1996] *RLR* 60.

—— (2000), "Legal Title as a Ground of Restitutionary Liability" [2000] *RLR* (Dec).

FRIED, C. (1981), *Contract as Promise* (Harvard University Press, Cambridge, Mass.).

FRIEDMANN, D. (1980), "Restitution of Benefits Obtained Through the Appropriation of Property or the Commission of a Wrong", 80 *Colum LR* 504.

—— (1983), "Payment of Another's Debt" [1983] *LQR* 534.

—— (1989), "The Efficient Breach Fallacy" (1989) 18 *JLS* 1.

—— (1991), "Valid, Voidable, Qualified, and Non-existing Obligations: An Alternative Perspective on the Law of Restitution" in A. Burrows (ed.), *Essays on the Law of Restitution* (Clarendon Press, Oxford), 247.

—— (1995), "The Performance Interest in Contract Damages" [1995] *LQR* 628.

—— (1999), "Payment under Mistake—Tracing and Subrogation" [1999] *LQR* 195.

FULLER, L.L., and PERDUE, W.R. (1936), "The Reliance Interest in Contract Damages", 46 *Yale LJ* 52 and 373.

FURMSTEN, M.P. (1996), *Cheshire, Fifoot & Furmsten's Law of Contract* (13th edn., Butterworths, London).

GARDNER, S. (1994), "Remedial Constructive Trusts: The Element of Discretion" in P.B.H. Birks (ed.), *The Frontiers of Liability* (OUP, Oxford), ii, 186.

GARNER, M. (1990), "The Role of Subjective Benefit in the Law of Unjust Enrichment" [1990] *OJLS* 42.

GILMORE, G. (1974), *The Death of Contract* (Ohio State University Press, Ohio).

GOFF., R., and JONES, G.H. (1998), *The Law of Restitution* (5th edn., Sweet & Maxwell, London).

GOODE, R. (1976), "The Right to Trace and its Impact in Commercial Transactions" [1976] *LQR* 360 and 528.

—— (1981), "The Bank's Right to Recover Money on a Stopped Cheque" [1981] *LQR* 254.

—— (1987), "Ownership and Obligation in Commercial Transactions" [1987] *LQR* 433.

—— (1991), "Property and Unjust Enrichment" in A. Burrows (ed.), *Essays on the Law of Restitution* (Clarendon Press, Oxford), 215.

—— (1992), "The Recovery of a Director's Improper Gains etc" in E. McKendrick (ed.), *Commercial Aspects of Trusts and Fiduciary Obligations* (Clarendon Press, Oxford), 141.

—— (1998), "Proprietary Restitutionary Claims" in W.R. Cornish, R. Nolan, J. O'Sullivan, G. Virgo (eds.), *Restitution: Past, Present and Future* (Hart Publishers, Oxford), 65.

GORDON, W.J. (1992), "Of Harms and Benefits: Torts, Restitution and Intellectual Property" (1992) 21 *JLS* 449.

GRANTHAM, R.B., and RICKETT, C.E.F. (1997), "Property and Unjust Enrichment: Categorical Truths or Unnecessary Complexity?" [1997] *NZLR* 668.

—— (1999), "Towards a More Constructive Classification of Trusts" [1999] *LMCLQ* 111.

—— (2000), "Resulting Trusts—a Rather Limited Doctrine" in F.D. Rose (ed.), *Restitution and Insolvency* (Mansfield Press, Oxford).

GUMMOW, W.M.C. (1990), "Unjust Enrichment, Restitution and Proprietary Remedies" in Finn (ed.), (1990).

HACKNEY, J. (1987), "Understanding Equity and Trusts" (Fontana, London).

HARPUM, C. (1987), "The Stranger as a Constructive Trustee" [1986] *LQR* 114 and 267.

—— (1994), "Knowing Receipt and Knowing Assistance: The Basis of Equitable Liability" in P.B.H. Birks (ed.), *The Frontiers of Liability* (OUP, Oxford), i, 9.

HARRIS, J.W. (ed.) (1997), *Property Problems: From Genes to Pension Funds* (Kluwer, Dordrecht).

HAYCROFT, A.M., and WAKSMAN, D.M. (1984), "Frustration and Restitution" [1984] *JBL* 207.

HAYTON, D.J. (1995), "Equity's Identification Rules" in P.B.H. Birks (ed.), *Laundering and Tracing* (Clarendon Press, Oxford), 1.

—— (1996), *The Law of Trusts and Equitable Remedies* (10th edn., Sweet & Maxwell, London).

HEDLEY, S. (1984), "The Myth of 'Waiver of Tort'" [1984] *LQR* 653.

—— (1985), "Unjust Enrichment as the Basis of Restitution—an Overworked Concept" [1985] *LS* 56.

—— (1997), "Ten Questions for Unjust Enrichment Theorists" [1997] *Web JCL* 1.

—— (1998), "Work Done in Anticipation of a Contract which does Not Materialise: A Response" in W.R. Cornish, R. Nolan, J. O'Sullivan and G. Virgo (eds.), *Restitution: Past, Present and Future* (Hart Publishing, Oxford), 195.

HETTINGER, E.C. (1989), "Justifying Intellectual Property" [1989] *Philosophy and Public Affairs* 31.

HODGSON, D. (Report of the committee chaired by Sir Derek Hodgson) (1984), *Profits of Crime and their Recovery* (Heinemann, London).

HOHFELD, W.N. (1946), *Fundamental Legal Conceptions as Applied in Judicial Reasoning* (Yale University Press, Princeton, NJ, 1946).

HOLDSWORTH, W.S. (1939), "Unjustifiable Enrichment" [1939] *LQR* 37.

IBBETSON, D. (1988), "Implied Contracts and Restitution: History in the High Court of Australia" [1988] *OJLS* 312.

—— (1999), *A Historical Introduction to the Law of Obligations* (OUP, Oxford).

JACKMAN, I.M. (1989), " Restitution for Wrongs" [1989] *CLJ* 302.

JACKSON, R.M. (1936), *The History of Quasi-Contract in English Law* (CUP, Cambridge).

JAFFEY, P. (1994), "Restraining the Exercise of Statutory Corporate Powers" [1994] *Denning LJ* 67.

—— (1995a), "Restitutionary Damages and Disgorgement" [1995] *RLR* 30.

—— (1995b), "Accounting for Wrongful Profits" [1995] *LMCLQ* 462.

—— (1996a), "Disgorgement and Confiscation" [1996] *RLR* 92.

—— (1996b), "Contractual Obligations of the Company in General Meeting" [1996] *LS* 27.

—— (1997), "Restitution and Trespass to Land" [1997] *RLR* 79.

—— (1998a), "The Restitutionary Conditional Transfer Analysis and the Death of Contract" [1998] *Edinburgh LR* 23.

—— (1998b), "The Law Commission Report on Aggravated, Exemplary and Restitutionary Damages" [1998] *MLR* 860.

—— (1998c), "A New Version of the Reliance Theory" [1998] *NILQ* 107.

—— (1998d), "Disgorgement for Breach of Contract and for a Criminal Offence" [1998] *LMCLQ* 469.

—— (1998e), "Merchandising and the Law of Trade Marks" [1998] *IPQ* 240.

JONES, G. (1968), "Unjust Enrichment and the Fiduciary's Duty of Loyalty" [1968] *LQR* 472.

—— (1983), "The Recovery of Benefits Gained from a Breach of Contract" [1983] *LQR* 443.

KAMPERMAN SANDERS, A. (1997), *Unfair Competition Law: The Protection of Industrial and Intellectual Creativity* (OUP, Oxford).

KEY, P. (1994), "Bona Fide Purchase as a Defence in the Law of Restitution" [1994] *LMCLQ* 421.

—— (1995), "Excising Estoppel by Representation as a Defence to Restitution" [1995] *CLJ* 525.

KREBS, T. (1999), "A German Contribution to English Enrichment Law" [1999] *RLR* 271.

KULL, A. (1994), "Restitution as a Remedy for Breach of Contract", 67 *Southern California LR* 1465.

—— (1995), "Rationalising Restitution", 83 *California LR* 1191.

KURSHID, S., and MATTHEWS, P. (1979), "Tracing Confusion" [1979] *LQR* 78.

LAMOND, G. (1996), "Coercion, Threats, and the Puzzle of Blackmail" in A.P. Simester and A.T.H. Smith (eds.), *Harm and Culpability* (Clarendon Press, Oxford).

LAW COMMISSION (1981), *Pecuniary Restitution on Breach of Contract* (Law Com 110, HMSO, London).

—— (1993), *Aggravated, Exemplary and Restitutionary Damages* (Consultation Paper 132, HMSO, London).

—— (1994), *Restitution: Mistakes of Law and Ultra Vires Public Authority Receipts and Payments* (Law Com 227, HMSO, London).

—— (1997), *Aggravated, Exemplary and Restitutionary Damages* (Law Com 247, HMSO, London).

—— (1999), *Illegal Transactions: the Effect of Illegality on Contracts and Trusts* (Law Com 154, HMSO, London).

LEVMORE, S. (1985), "Explaining Restitution", 71 *Virginia Law Review* 65.

LIBLING, D.F. (1978), "The Concept of Property: Property in Intangibles" [1978] *LQR* 103.

LINZER, P. (1981), "On the Amorality of Contract Remedies—Efficiency, Equity, and the Second Restatement", 81 *Columbia LR* 111.

LOWRY, J., and EDMUNDS, R. (1998), "The Corporate Opportunity Doctrine: The Shifting Boundaries of the Duty and its Remedies" [1998] *MLR* 515.

MACCORMICK, N. (1982*a*), "The Obligation of Reparation" in N. MacCormick (ed.), *Legal Right and Social Democracy* (Clarendon Press, Oxford), 212.

—— (1982*b*), "Voluntary Obligations" in N. MacCormick (ed.), *Legal Right and Social Democracy* (Clarendon Press, Oxford), 190.

MACNEIL, I.R. (1982), "Efficient Breach of Contract: Circles in the Sky", 68 *Vir. LR* 947.

MARSHALL, S.E., and DUFF, R.A. (1998), "Criminalisation and Sharing Wrongs", XI *Canadian Journal of Law and Jurisprudence* 7.

MATTHEWS, P. (1980), "Money Paid under a Mistake of Fact" (1980) 130 *NLJ* 587.

—— (1982), "Stopped Cheques and Restitution" [1982] *JBL* 281.

MCBRIDE, N.J. (1995), "A Case for Awarding Punitive Damages in Response to Deliberate Breaches of Contract" [1995] *Anglo-American LR* 369.

MCINNES, M.P. (ed.) (1996), *Restitution: Developments in Unjust Enrichment* (LBC Information Services).

MCKENDRICK, E., (1991), "Frustration, Restitution and Loss Apportionment" in A. Burrows (ed.), *Essays on the Law of Restitution* (Clarendon Press, Oxford), 147.

—— (ed.) (1992), *Commercial Aspects of Trusts and Fiduciary Obligations* (Clarendon Press, Oxford).

—— (1995), "Total Failure of Consideration and Counter-restitution: Two Issues or One?" in P.B.H. Birks , *Laundering and Tracing* (Clarendon Press, Oxford), 217.

—— (1996), "No Place for O'Brien in Scots Law" [1996] *RLR* 100.

—— (1998), "Work Done in Anticipation of a Contract which Does Not Materialise" in W.R. Cornish, R. Nolan, J. O'Sullivan, and G. Virgo (eds.), *Restitution: Past, Present and Future* (Hart Publishing, Oxford), 163.

MEAD, G. (1989), "Free Acceptance: Some Further Considerations" [1989] *LQR* 460.

MEAGHER, R.P., GUMMOW, W.M.C., and LEHANE, J.R.F. (1992), *Equity—Doctrines and Remedies* (3rd edn., Butterworths (Australia), Sydney).

MILLET, P. (1991), "Tracing the Proceeds of Fraud" [1991] *LQR* 71

—— (1995), "Equity—the Road Ahead" [1995] *KCLJ* 1.

—— (1998), "Equity's Place in the Law of Commerce" [1998] *LQR* 214.

MILSOM, S.F.C. (1981), *Historical Foundations of the Common Law* (2nd edn, Butterworths, London).

MITCHELL, C. (1994), *The Law of Subrogation* (Clarendon Press, Oxford).

MORIARTY, S. (1995), "Tracing, Mixing and Laundering" in P.B.H. Birks (ed.), *Laundering and Tracing* (Clarendon Press, Oxford), 73.

MUIR, G.A. (1990), "Unjust Sacrifice and the Officious Intervener" in P.O. Finn (ed.), *Essays on Restitution* (Law Book Company, Sydney), 297.

NICHOLLS, LORD (1998), "Knowing Receipt: the Need for a New Landmark" in W.R. Cornish, R. Nolan, J. O'Sullivan and G. Virgo (eds.), *Restitution: Past, Present and Future* (Hart Publishing, Oxford).

NOLAN, R.C. (1995), "Change of Position", in P.B.H. Birks (ed.), *Laundering and Tracing* (Clarendon Press, Oxford), 135.

NOZICK, R. (1972), "Coercion" in P. Laslett, W.G. Runciman, and Q. Skinner (eds.), *Philosophy , Politics and Society* (4th Series, Blackwell, Oxford).

O'DAIR, R. (1993), "Restitutionary Damages for Breach of Contract and the Theory of Efficient Breach: Some Reflections" [1993] *CLP* 113.

O'DELL, E.(1997), "Restitution, Coercion by a Third Party and the Proper Role of Notice" [1997] *CLJ* 71.

OESTERLE, D.A. (1983), "Deficiencies of the Restitutionary Right to Trace Misappropriated Property in Equity and in UCCC § 9–306", 68 *Cornell LR* 172.

OKUNDA, S. (1985), "Criminal Anti-Profit Laws: Some Thoughts in Favour of their Constitutionality", 76 *Cal LR* 1353.

PEARCE, R., and STEVENS, J. (1998), *The Law of Trusts and Equitable Obligations* (2nd edn., Butterworths, London).

PENNER, J.E. (1997), "Basic Obligations" in P.B.H. Birks (ed.), *The Classification of Obligations* (Clarendon Press, Oxford).

—— (1998), *The Law of Trusts* (Butterworths, London).

PERILLO, J. (1973), "Restitution in a Contractual Context", 73 *Columbia LR* 1208.

PETTIT, P.H. (1997), *Equity and the Law of Trusts* (8th edn., Butterworths, London).

POSNER, R.A. (1992), *Economic Analysis of Law* (4th edn., Little Brown, Boston, Mass.).

PRENTICE, D.D., and BISHOP, W. (1983), "Some Legal and Economic Aspects of Fiduciary Remuneration" [1983] *MLR* 289.

PROKSCH, L. (1996), "Rescission on Terms" [1996] *RLR* 71.

RAZ, J. (1977), "Promises and obligations" in P.M.S. Hacker and J. Raz (eds.), *Law, Morality and Society* (Clarendon Press, Oxford), 228.

—— (1982), "Promises in Morality and Law", 95 *Harvard LR* 916.

—— (1986), *The Morality of Freedom* (Clarendon Press, Oxford).

ROGERS, J.S. (1990), "Negotiability, Property, and Identity", 12 *Cardozo LR* 471.

ROSE, F.D. (1989), "Restitution for the Rescuer" [1989] *OJLS* 167.

—— (ed.) (1998), *Restitution and Banking Law* (Mansfield Press, Oxford).

—— (ed.) (2000), *Restitution and Insolvency* (Mansfield Press, Oxford).

RUDDEN, B. (1997), "Things as Things and Things as Wealth" in J.W. Harris (ed.), *Property Problems: From Genes to Pension Funds* (Kluwer, Dordrecht), 146.

SEALY, L. (1962), "Fiduciary Relationships" [1962] *CLJ* 69.

SEBERT, J.A. (1986), "Punitive and Non-pecuniary Damages in Actions Based upon Contract; Towards Achieving the Objective of Full Compensation", 33 *UCLA Law Rev.* 1565.

SEGAL, N. (1998), "Cross-border Security Enforcement, Restitution and Priorities" in F.D. Rose (ed.), *Restitution and Banking Law* (Mansfield Press, Oxford).

SHARPE, R.S., and WADDAMS, S.M. (1982), "Damages for Lost Opportunity to Bargain" [1982] *OJLS* 290.

SHERWIN, E.L. (1989), "Constructive Trusts in Bankruptcy" [1989] *University of Illinois LR* 297.

SIMESTER, A. (1997), "Unjust Free Acceptance" [1997] *LMCLQ* 103.

SKELTON, A. (1998), *Restitution and Contract* (Mansfield Press, Oxford).

SMITH, L.D. (1991), "Three-party Restitution: A Critique of Birks's Theory of Interceptive Subtraction" [1991] *OJLS* 290.

—— (1992), "The Province of the Law of Restitution", 71 *Can. Bar. Rev.* 672.

—— (1994), "Disgorgement of the Profits of Breach of Contract: Property, Contract and 'Efficient Breach'", 24 *Can Bus LJ* 21.

—— (1995a), "Tracing in *Taylor v Plumer*: Equity in the Court of King's Bench" [1995] *LMCLQ* 240.

—— (1995b), "Tracing into the Payment of a Debt" (1995) 54 *CLJ* 290.

—— (1997), *The Law of Tracing* (Clarendon Press, Oxford).

—— (1998), "W(h)ither Knowing Receipt" [1998] *LQR* 394.

SMITH, S.A. (1997a), "Contracting under Pressure: A Theory of Duress" [1997] *CLJ* 343.

—— (1997b), "Performance, Punishment and the Nature of Contractual Obligation" [1997] *MLR* 360.

—— (1999), "Concurrent Liability in Contract and Unjust Enrichment: The Fundamental Breach Requirement" [1999] *LQR* 245.

SPECTOR, H. (1992), "Negative Liberalism" in H. Spector, *Autonomy & Rights* (Clarendon Press, Oxford), Chapter 1.

STEINER, H. (1974), "Individual Liberty" in *Proceedings of the Aristotelian Society* NS 75 (1974–75) 36.

STOLJAR, S. (1956), "The Great Case of *Cutter v Powell*", *Can. Bar. Rev.* 288.

—— (1959), "The Doctrine of Failure of Consideration" [1959] *LQR* 53.

—— (1987), "Unjust Enrichment and Unjust Sacrifice" (1987) 50 *MLR* 603.

—— (1989), *The Law of Quasi-Contract* (2nd edn., The Law Book Co, Sydney).

SUTTON, R.J. (1990), "What Should be Done for Mistaken Improvers?" in P.O. Finn (ed.), *Essays on Restitution* (Law Book Company, Sydney), 241.

—— (1991), "Payments of Debts Charged upon Property" in A. Burrows (ed.), *Essays on the Law of Restitution* (Clarendon Press, Oxford), 71.

SWADLING, W.J. (1994a), "Restitution for no Consideration" [1994] *RLR* 73.

—— (1994b), "Some Lessons from the Law of Torts" in P.B.H. Birks (ed.), *The Frontiers of Liability* (OUP, Oxford), i, 41.

—— (1995), "The Nature of Ministerial Receipt" in P.B.H. Birks (ed.), *Laundering and Tracing* (Clarendon Press, Oxford), 243.

—— (1996a), "A Claim in Restitution?" [1996] *LMCLQ* 63.

—— (1996b), "A New Role for Resulting Trusts?" [1996] *LS* 110.

—— (1997a), "Property and Unjust Enrichment" in J.W. Harris (ed.), *Property Problems: From Genes to Pension Funds* (Kluwer, Dordrecht), 130.

—— (ed.) (1997b), *The Limits of Restitutionary Claims: A Comparative Analysis* (UKNCCL).

—— (1997c), "Restitution and Bona Fide Purchase" in Swadling (ed.), *The Limits of Restitutionary Claims: A Comparative Analysis* (UKNCCL).

—— (1998), "Property and Conscience" [1998] *TLI* 228.

TAFT, K.A. (1939), "A Defence of a Limited Use of the Swollen Assets Theory where Money has been Wrongfully Mingled with other Money", 39 *Columbia LR* 172.

TERRY, A. (1988), "Unfair Competition and the Misappropriation of a Competitor's Trade Values" [1988] *MLR* 296.

TETTENBORN, A. (1996), *Law of Restitution* (2nd edn., Cavendish Press, London).

—— (1997), "Lawful Receipt—a Justifying Factor?" [1997] *RLR* 1.

TREBILCOCK, M.J. (1993), *The Limits of Freedom of Contract* (Harvard UP, Cambridge, Mass.).

TREITEL, G.H. (1999), *The Law of Contract* (10th edn., Sweet & Maxwell, London).

VERSE, D.A. (1998), "Improvements and Enrichments: A Comparative Analysis" [1998] *RLR* 85.

VIRGO, G. (1998a), "What is the Law of Restitution About?" in W.R. Cornish, R. Nolan, J. O'Sullivan and G. Virgo (eds.), *Restitution: Past, Present and Future* (Hart Publishing, Oxford), 305.

VIRGO, G. (1998*b*), "The Law of Restitution and the Proceeds of Crime—a Survey of English Law" [1998] *RLR* 34.

—— (1999), *The Principles of the Law of Restitution* (OUP, Oxford).

WADDAMS, S.M. (1991), "Restitution as Part of Contract Law" in A. Burrows (ed.), *Essays on the Law of Restitution* (Clarendon Press, Oxford).

WALT, S., and SHERWIN, E.L. (1993), "Contribution Arguments in Commercial Law", 42 *Emory LJ* 897.

WASIK, M. (1984), "The Hodgson Committee Report on the Profits of Crime and their Recovery" [1984] *Crim LR* 708.

WATERS, D.W.M. (1964), *The Constructive Trust* (Athlone Press, London).

—— (1994), "The Nature of the Remedial Constructive Trust" in P.B.H. Birks (ed.), *The Frontiers of Liability* (OUP, Oxford), ii.

WATTS, P. (1987), "Some Aspects of the Operation of the Conflict of Interest Principle in Company Law" [1987] *Canterbury LR* 239.

—— (1995), "Restitution—a Property Principle and a Services Principle" [1995] *RLR* 49.

—— (1998*a*), "Subrogation—A Step too Far" [1998] *LQR* 341.

—— (1998*b*), "Property and 'Unjust Enrichment': Cognate Conservators" [1998] *NZLR* 151.

WEIR, T. (1996), *A Casebook on Tort* (8th edn., Sweet & Maxwell, London).

—— (1997), *Economic Torts* (Clarendon Press, Oxford).

WINFIELD, P.H. (1931), *The Province of the Law of Tort* (CUP, Cambridge).

WORTHINGTON, S. (1996), *Proprietary Interests in Commercial Transactions* (Clarendon Press, Oxford).

WRIGHT, D., "The Rise of Non-Consensual Subrogation" [1999] *Conv.* 113.

WRIGHT, LORD (1939), *Legal Essays and Addresses* (CUP, Cambridge).

Index